International Marketing

The Marketing Series is one of the most comprehensive collections of books in marketing and sales available from the UK today.

Published by Butterworth-Heinemann on behalf of The Chartered Institute of Marketing, the series is divided into three distinct groups: *Student* (fulfilling the needs of those taking the Institute's certificate and diploma qualifications); *Professional Development* (for those on formal or self-study vocational training programmes); and *Practitioner* (presented in a more informal, motivating and highly practical manner for the busy marketer).

Formed in 1911, The Chartered Institute of Marketing is now the largest professional marketing management body in Europe with over 60,000 members located worldwide. Its primary objectives are focused on the development of awareness and understanding of marketing throughout UK industry and commerce and in the raising of standards of professionalism in the education, training and practice of this key business discipline.

Books in the series

International Marketing

Second edition

Stanley J. Paliwoda

BA, MSc., PhD,

MBIM, MCIM, MIEx

Published on behalf of
The Chartered Institute of Marketing

BUTTERWORTH
HEINEMANN

Butterworth-Heinemann
Linacre House, Jordan Hill, Oxford OX2 8DP

A division of Reed Educational and Professional Publishing Ltd

ℛ   A member of the Reed Elsevier plc group

OXFORD   BOSTON   JOHANNESBURG
NEW DELHI   SINGAPORE   MELBOURNE

First published 1986
Reprinted 1988, 1989, 1990, 1991
Second edition 1993
Reprinted 1993, 1994, 1995, 1997

British Library Cataloguing in Publication Data
A catalogue record for this book is available from the
British Library

ISBN 0 7506 0424 7

Typeset by MS Filmsetting Ltd, Frome, Somerset
Printed and Bound in Great Britain by
Martins the Printers Ltd, Berwick-upon-Tweed

To

Professors Roy W. Hill and Peter J. Buckley who created
an enduring interest in this subject area; and
Professor Michael J. Thomas who provided much insight and
direction to the original work

'I should not like my writing to spare other people the trouble of thinking. But, if possible to stimulate someone to thoughts of his own.'

Ludwig Wittgenstein

Contents

Foreword

Once, and not really too long ago, markets were simply places in towns where people from the region would gather on specific days to sell and buy produce and goods.

Today, when business people talk of 'markets', they are generally speaking in worldwide terms, about anybody in virtually any country who might be a potential purchaser of their products or services.

This dramatic evolution has been brought about by the past century's revolution in communications, in particular in transport systems, especially airlines.

Whereas, a hundred years ago, it might have taken a smallholder half a day to take his vegetables to market, his only outlet, in his nearest town, today, in supermarkets in most Western nations, you can buy sugar, peas, courgettes and virtually any exotic fruit you care to name, picked the previous day in a field the other side of the world, and flown fresh in a matter of hours to their eventual consumer.

What has happened in farming is reflected in virtually any sphere of industry or commerce you care to name.

The world increasingly is becoming a global village, with its marketplace stretching across every continent.

To successful businesses, this opens a huge door of opportunity, enabling them to sell their products and services to people thousands of miles away from their base, in places their grandfathers might never have heard of.

To the inefficient, it spells danger in the form of increased competition. For, sure enough, it will not be long before a rival, perhaps from another hemisphere, woos away their clients with a better product, a more effective service or simply by offering higher value for money.

Which brings me to a side note. The next phase of the communications revolution has already begun. Information technology is transforming the way we do business. Those who ignore the advantages it brings do so at their peril.

Against this background, I share with you the principal marketing goals for British Airways:

- To secure a leading share of air travel business worldwide, with a significant presence in all major geographical markets.
- To provide overall superior service and good value for money in every market segment in which we compete.
- To excel in anticipating and quickly responding to customer needs and competitor activity.

We believe airlines are developing now to reflect the overall marketplace — with global operators able to satisfy the needs of the world at large, and smaller specialists, serving specific niches. Our aim is to remain a leading, international player, and that means finding ways of satisfying all the main geographical areas of the world, not necessarily by ourselves, but in partnership, where appropriate, with like-minded counterparts.

We can only thrive if we are providing our customers with services which they feel are more value than those of our rivals, and, as our rivals never stand still, and customer expectations shift as a result, this means being fast on our feet and introducing any changes required.

That is why we place such great emphasis on listening to what our customers have to say, with a continual programme of extensive market research in all our key markets.

This has been the basis for our efforts in recent years to 'brand' each category of our service, creating and constantly up-dating products tailor-made to meet the needs of specific groups of our customers and which stand out from anything offered by our competitors.

In any market, there are winners and losers. In the international marketplace, where the stakes are that much higher, there are bigger winners and bigger losers.

But the biggest winners of all will be the consumers, served with products and services which better meet their ever more demanding requirements and offering constantly improving value for money. And they are, of course, the sole reason for our existence as companies, a point international marketeers should never forget.

Sir Colin Marshall
Deputy Chairman and Chief
Executive, British Airways Plc

Preface to the second edition

In the preface to the first edition, I commented on the use that I had made on the cover of a new world map produced by Arno Peters. This map, unlike the traditional Mercator map which everyone had learned at school reproduced countries according to their correct size but unlike previous earlier attempts at so doing, the Peters map also worked for navigational purposes. This took away the rationale for the old map which for navigational accuracy misrepresented the size of countries such as the former Soviet Union.

To be presented with a new map of this kind presents a challenge, particularly where one's country or even continent is not as large as before or, in the case of Europe, where it has traditionally been thought of by Europeans as being at the centre of the globe.

Since then, the events of 1989 which swept through Eastern Europe created democracies where previously there was communist one-party rule. These new democracies, together with the unification of Germany as we approach another new challenge in the Single European Market of 1993, require yet further mental leaps to be made in order to comprehend the urgency and the fundamental changes which these events will in turn demand.

In this new global environment a new market for privatization skills has been awakened. Skills acquired during the Thatcher years have created a new international competitive advantage for Britain's management consultancies.

Elsewhere, strategic business alliances — an outgrowth of industrial cooperation — have become a fact of life for business in all countries. An international, even global, perspective is not an academic luxury but an economic necessity for companies seeking to survive into 2000 AD. Ever-spiralling costs of research and market development have created conditions whereby arch-rivals can collaborate together on joint product development but in all other respects continue to compete vigorously with each other.

It is important to point out, though, that in this new edition the perspective has not changed except that there is less emphasis on exporting and more on international marketing which implies more international commitment of resources over a longer period of time than does exporting. Again the focus is on the microeconomic unit of the company rather than the trading nation except where it helps to lend some background understanding to the nature of trade flows and investment.

This edition is larger in size and breadth of coverage than the first edition but this is warranted by the changes taking place in this global marketplace in which we are all live and are active as consumers.

My thanks again to the Chartered Institute of Marketing and to Butterworth-Heinemann for the invitation to write a second edition. The reader will find this to be almost a total rework of the earlier edition rather than a revision. Lecturers and teachers please take note in preparing your course outlines — not only the chapter numbers but also the substance of these chapters has changed to incorporate changes taking place and to present the reader with a realistic contemporary representation of the opportunities and the pitfalls to be found in international marketing.

To the individual reader I ask you once again to accept my assurance that I have sought to present an interesting contemporary text on international marketing. Inevitably there will be mistakes occurring as a result of transcription, perhaps even of my handwriting! We have sought to eliminate these as far as possible. However, I would welcome your correspondence as to any errors that have been found or to suggested improvements. My very best wishes to you whether studying or practising the art of international marketing.

There has not been a book published to date which has not acknowledged the very necessary cooperation and collaboration of others who have made the book happen. There are those who have granted me the right to reproduce copyright material, and there are many in this category as the reader will see in the pages following. To all of these authors and publishers I extend my thanks. Next, there are those who have helped by commenting on the text itself. This, too, has involved more individuals than the first edition when I noted in particular the help that I had been given by Dr Owen Adikibi with the chapter on Nigeria. This time I wish to acknowledge the constructive criticism that I have received from Professor Mark Kawai and Yoko Reilly with the chapter on Japan, and from Professor Huang Dingmo with the chapter on China.

Finally, and all too obviously, it would not have been possible to have completed this second edition without the help that I have received from the Faculty of Management at the University of Calgary. My thanks to the Dean, Dr P. Michael Maher, and a very special thank you also to Sheila Mikulak and all the staff of the Management Resource Centre (which is aptly named) for their unflinching patience and professionalism over a protracted period of time, dealing with questions that ranged over a very wide area. Let me tell you, I appreciated it!

Stanley J. Paliwoda
University of Calgary

1
International marketing in a global economy

The concept of advantage

The starting point begins with international trade, something which has been known to many civilizations over thousands of years. A visit to the British Museum, or any museum, will reveal some of the artefacts of daily life which were traded across vast distances, as with the Roman treasures still being found in Britain today. These goods represent what today we might call standardized products. The urns, bowls, vases and pottery ware, which are all identified as indisputably Roman, conformed to a certain specification of manufacture and were then transported.

With the Roman garrisons in Britain, there were the captive markets for products known to the Romans. Their situation was similar to that of the US army divisions in the Second World War which by taking overseas with them certain products or more importantly brands, which US soldiers regarded as being from 'home', such as Coca-Cola, a multinational product and presence was thereby created several times over.

In times of ancient Greece, there were many important stone masons and many not so important. The spread of stone carvings for example was stylized Greek but standardized. Distribution was much different then, education was not as high as today, incomes were low, and such items were low down the scale of needs that most contemporaries of the time might volunteer to an enquirer, not that there is any evidence of market research agencies having existed in either ancient Greece or the Roman Empire!

What has changed is that, then the Empire held a monopoly over supply. It owned everything, including the factors of production and the channels of distribution. Today, we have moved one step even further from Ricardo's Theory of Comparative Advantage to the point where in some sections of industrial activity, the competition which exists is global rather than national, as in computers or automobiles where the sourcing of components and assemblies is another multinational activity. Size and the well-understood principle of economics of scale have given rise to highly dynamic competition in certain sectors. The critical mass that a company requires to achieve to cover breakeven costs is also forever rising, partly because of technological push, partly also because of market-driven forces which create demand for new or improved products arising from an awareness of what is happening for example to the environment. The so-called 'Green Revolution', which has swept Europe and North America, has given rise to new car specifications able to burn unleaded fuel; and to soaps, detergents and products generally that are biodegradable and will not pollute the environment. These products in turn create costs and are passed on to the consumer.

As times change, it is noticeable how these changes sweep through different countries and, provided these countries are all at approximately the same level of economic advancement, then consumers may be expected to be aware and to be able to do something about caring for the environment, changing their behaviour, changing their product purchases, even if it does mean finding an extra few pence outlay on a shopping bill. This differential can be labelled 'conscience money', and the psychological benefit of doing something positive for the environment will easily compensate those consumers for this additional outlay. It does create marketing segmentation opportunities for companies to explore across nations, so spreading the costs of product development further, across more than one market. The Green Revolution is a good example of social change that has led to segmentation strategies for specially created environmentally friendly products.

Where is the nation state?

Absolute advantage, which is traced back to Adam Smith, stated that trade would take place between two nations, each having something the other wanted to buy, and could not produce for itself. The instances of absolute advantage were few and so the Ricardo Theory of Comparative Advantage then took hold. This said that it made sense still to trade when

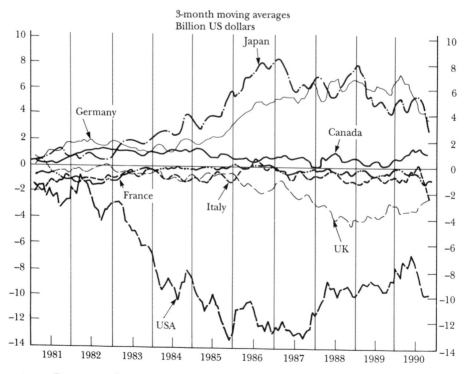

Figure 1.1   *Foreign trade*
Source   OECD (1991) *Main Economic Indicators*, Paris

Table 1.1

EXPORTS *less* IMPORTS – EXPORTATIONS *moins* IMPORTATIONS
(f.o.b. – c.i.f.) – (f.o.b. – c.a.f.)

Million US dollars, monthly averages – Millions de dollars É-U, moyennes mensuelles

				1991		1992		1991			1992					
	1989	1990	1991	Q.3	Q.4	Q.1	Q.2	OCT	NOV	DEC	JAN	FEB	MAR	APR	MAY	JUN
Canada	255	898	763	658	475	906		251	43	1133	558	1182	976	1244	1319	
United States – États-Unis	−9117	−8419	−5401	−6241	−5202	−4892		−5870	−4113	−5622	−5799	−3294	−5584	−7063	−7380	
Japan – Japon	5375	4329	6504	6827	7134	9139	8134	6563	7475	7364	9223	10108	8088	7351	9338	7712
Australia – Australie	−316	75	278	275	181	297		213	173	158	401	133	355	137	610	
New Zealand – Nouvelle-Zélande	5	6	109	130	184	12	116	241	236	75	21	−199	215	177	100	71
Austria – Autriche	−538	−661	−806	−739	−842	−691		−473	−658	−1396	−566	−562	−946	−722	−511	
Belgium – Belgique-Luxembourg	125	−170	−233	−293	−429	−392		−239	−166	−883	171	−784	−562	−663		
Denmark – Danemark	116	278	299	292	326	376		217	348	414	503	425	199	209	430	
Finland – Finlande	−105	−31	94	219	180	68		219	249	71	—	12	190	21	345	
France	−574	−759	−444	−501	103	356	644	813	−9	−495	666	130	270	1360	753	−179
Germany – Allemagne	5965	5431	1100	938	2434	1106		1833	2338	3132	−571	1420	2468	3155	309	
Greece – Grèce	−717	−985	−1071	−763	−1565			−1155	−2026	−1516						
Iceland – Islande	2	−5	−14	−15	−3	−14		−13	5	—	−24	−3	−16			
Ireland – Irlande	273	259	292	296	417	472		437	390	424	563	467	385	371	647	
Italy – Italie	−1026	−961	−1101	−1576	−807	−556		−1569	−1459	606	34	−1574	−127	−1604	−1380	
Netherlands – Pays-Bas	299	464	621	559	724	533		983	847	341	885	809	−95	1380	985	
Norway – Norvège	295	557	732	769	689	689		395	418	1253	831	534	702	709		
Portugal	−510	−711	−822	−793	−848	−854		−789	−781	−973	−573	−849	−1141	−825	−986	
Spain – Espagne	−2297	−2674	−2765	−2771	−2861	−3227	−2965	−2858	−2973	−2752	−3673	−2510	−3499	−3006	−2791	−3098
Sweden – Suède	207	230	441	387	535	576	299	542	479	584	646	638	444	270	558	70
Switzerland – Suisse	−565	−497	−426	−309	−303	−103	−101	−58	−398	−453	154	−200	−263	−38	−178	−86
Turkey – Turquie	−353	−782	−618	−621	−636	−588		−527	−588	−794	−536	−667	−561			
UK – Royaume-Uni	−3724	−3301	−2069	−1848	−2111	−2390		−2086	−2329	−1919	−2619	−2398	−2151	−3005	−2112	
OECD-Total – OCDE-Total	−6924	−7428	−4539	−5119	−2226	−307		−2932	−2500	−1247	−584	1420	−1756	−1990	−462 (e)	
Major seven – Sept grands	−2845	−2783	−648	−1743	2027	3669		−65	1945	4200	1493	5574	3940	1438	846	
OECD-Europe – OCDE-Europe	−3127	−4317	−6792	−6768	−4999	−5768		−4330	−6314	−4354	−4989	−6510	−5806	−3837	−4448 (e)	
EEC – CEE	−2089	−3105	−6081	−6459	−4618	−5705		−4414	−5820	−3619	−5495	−6262	−5357	−3506	−4911 (e)	

Source OECD (1992) *Main Economic Indicators*, Paris, August.

there was no absolute advantage. Prices may be similar to those at which you could produce yourself. What the Theory of Comparative Advantage then went on to say was that this offered the nation the opportunity for specialization in a certain sphere of activity. Depending on a nation's factor endowment, it could choose to focus and specialize in a particular area in which it then could create an advantage.

Yet to Porter, the key to whether a nation is competitive in an industry is not whether it trades, but whether it has a combination of trade and investment that reflects advantages and skills that have been created at home. Porter (1990) sees classical economic theory to be deficient in explaining trade and investment in advanced nations for three reasons:

1   Globalization which Porter says decouples the firm from the factor endowment of its home nation.
2   Factor pools of many nations have reached a certain comparability. Comparative advantage in terms of factor costs is only temporary.
3   Technology. Where labour content is too high, automation can become introduced. Similarly with raw materials, if these prove to be scarce, new synthetic ones can be created.

Porter (1990) argues for the sources of advantage to be 'relentlessly broadened and upgraded.'

Where home customers are demanding, and seek quality and sophistication, this in turn forces the firm to improve; but, where home customers are merely accepting of variable quality offerings, this then can place the firm at a disadvantage in international markets. Demanding customers and strong competition move companies away from dependence on basic factors.

In the same way, going back to what Porter had said earlier of broadening and upgrading advantages, many new products today have arisen from technologies related to mature industries. Examples of internationally competitive-related industries include Denmark in dairy products and brewing giving rise to industrial enzymes; Switzerland with its strength in pharmaceuticals giving rise to flavourings; and the UK with a strength in engines giving rise to a related industry in lubricants and 'anti-knock' preparations.

Governments are eager to help national companies but Porter does not find this governmental help to have been an advantage. It is better where the firms are self-sustaining and competing independently.

The UK share of world trade has decreased from around 25 per cent at the end of the nineteenth century to approximately 5 per cent of global exports and imports today. Nevertheless, the UK earns a greater, although declining, percentage of its GDP from exports than many other of the major industrial countries. The need to import at the same time raw materials plus half its food needs, underlines Britain's dependency on foreign trade. Table 1.3 shows that if we focus particularly on the export sector, we find that exports indexed over 1980 levels, have been stagnating in volume but increasing in value overall.

It is interesting to note, from Table 1.3, the crossover in terms of unit value where imports are now down and overtaken by exports. This would, of course, be reflected in the final column (terms of trade) but is depicted visually in Figure 1.2.

Britain has had a balance of trade deficit on manufactured goods since 1983. It is worth bearing this point in mind also when we come to discuss the product life cycle and its applications to international marketing.

Table 1.2

	Gross public debt per cent of normal GNP/GDP							Percentage of world imports				Percentage of world exports				Percentage of GDP 1989
	1985	1986	1987	1988	1989	1990	1991	1985	1986	1987	1988	1985	1986	1987	1988	
Australia	26.3	26.5	23.5	20.1	16.5	13.3	9.9	1.3	1.2	1.2	1.2	1.3	1.2	1.1	1.2	12.3
Canada	64.6	68.6	68.8	68.5	69.2	70.0	70.1	4.8	4.3	4.0	4.0	3.7	3.4	3.7	3.7	23.9
Denmark	65.7	59.3	55.7	55.7	54.9	54.4	53.3	0.9	1.0	1.0	0.9	0.96	1.0	1.0	0.95	32.3*
France	45.4	45.4	47.3	47.5	47.3	46.9	46.7	5.3	5.9	6.0	6.0	5.9	6.2	6.5	6.4	13.9
Germany	42.2	42.4	43.7	44.4	42.7	42.1	41.5	9.6	11.5	11.9	11.4	7.9	8.8	8.9	8.6	28.7
Italy	84.0	88.5	92.7	95.0	97.0	99.3	101.3	4.1	4.7	4.8	4.6	4.3	4.4	4.8	4.7	9.7
Japan	69.1	72.8	75.5	71.8	68.0	63.8	59.9	10.1	10.8	10.2	9.9	6.3	5.6	5.7	6.1	16.4
UK	53.3	51.9	49.5	44.0	39.6	37.0	34.6	5.3	5.2	5.2	4.9	5.5	5.8	6.0	6.3	23.2
USA	48.3	51.1	51.6	51.4	51.4	50.9	49.9	12.1	11.4	11.3	11.8	18.0	17.7	17.2	16.2	11.5

* 1988 Figure

Sources The International Yearbook and Statesman's Who's Who 1990, Reed Information Services, East Grinstead, West Sussex
Europa World Yearbook 1990, **1**, Europa Publications, London
OECD Economic Outlook (1990), 17 June
IMF (1989) Direction of Trade Statistics Yearbook

Table 1.3   UK visible trade (on a balance of payments basis)   1985 = 100

| | Volume indices | | Unit value indices (NSA) | | |
	Exports	Imports	Exports	Imports	Terms of trade[1]
1982	85.6	80.4	81.4	79.9	101.9
1983	87.6	87.0	88.0	87.4	100.7
1984	94.7	96.9	95.0	95.3	99.7
1985	100.0	100.0	100.0	100.0	100.0
1986	104.2	107.4	90.2	95.3	94.6
1987	109.7	115.3	93.8	97.8	95.6
1988	111.8	131.0	93.9	96.7	97.1
1989	117.3	140.9	101.2	103.4	97.9
1990 (est)	125.7	145.5	106.7	107.3	99.48

[1] Unit value index for exports expressed as a percentage of unit value index for imports.
Source   CSO *Economic Trends* (1990), HMSO, London (446), December.

Analysing national competitiveness

An analysis of international competitiveness is the annual World Competitiveness Report which uses a questionnaire survey assessing 326 criteria divided into ten categories and mailed to 10,000 selected executives in the thirty-four countries covered by the report. The ten major categories are:

1 dynamics of the economy;
2 individual efficiency;
3 market orientation;
4 financial dynamism;
5 human resources;
6 impact of the state;

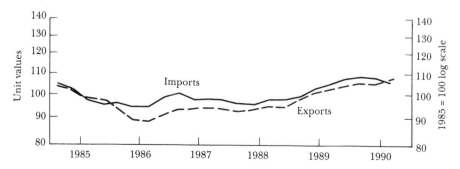

Figure 1.2   *UK visible trade: unit values of exports and imports*
Source   CSO *Economic Trends* (1990), HMSO, London

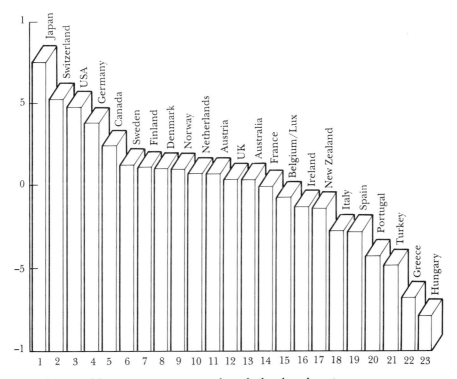

Figure 1.3   *The world competitiveness scoreboard: developed nations*
Source   *The World Competitiveness Report* (1990) IMD/World Economic Forum, Lausanne,
Switzerland

7 natural endowment utilization;
8 international orientation;
9 future orientation;
10 socio-political stability.

The report ranks twenty-four developed countries (all members of OECD) in Group I and ten
newly industrialized countries in Group II, which have been selected on the basis of their
impact on world trade. A survey of this kind is able to draw comparisons within each group,
whereas otherwise there may be too much statistical data missing and qualifications
necessary for differences in economic development. Rankings are according to standard
deviation values which means a country's position reflects its competitiveness relative to
other countries (see Figure 1.3). However, the rankings for competitiveness are not the same
as for business confidence, in which case Japan would fall into second place behind Germany.
Political stability is a factor in business confidence rankings (see Figure 1.4). The countries fall
broadly into four clusters (see Figure 1.5), and the report shows that more countries are
moving up the scale as their economies develop. The report acknowledges that although
nations may take different paths to economic success, this will nevertheless materially affect
the business climate.

Governments and national comparative advantage

Government intervention may include monopoly or antitrust control: in terms of public procurement, it can have a decisive effect in stimulating industry; taxation and regional incentives for green field investment; and policies designed to cater for the society of tomorrow, including health, education and the environment. These may help create or upgrade an advantage, but so too does the role of chance itself. Porter points out, too, that across nations, it is those industries in which government has been most heavily involved that have for the most part been unsuccessful in international terms.

In Figure 1.6 the four determinants are clearly stated: factor conditions; demand conditions; related and supporting industries; and firm strategy, structure and rivalry. Governments can influence, and be influenced by, each of these four determinants, either positively or negatively. Porter's research shows that the perception of buyer needs is most often strongly defined by the home customer. Although foreign demand may give rise to product modifications, the essential core product is designed according to home market perceptions.

This process or cycle which Porter depicts in Figure 1.7, is one of a need to move as quickly as possible from factor-driven to an investment-driven economy, where nations compete in the price sensitive or standardized segments of more advanced industries. The next stage is innovation-driven, where firms are able to attain the state of the art in technology. Finally, in the last stage in the wealth-driven economy, which is one of decline, companies exhibit different signs of complacency, which is one of unrest, and industrial decay continues while income per head still continues to rise.

Porter (1990) states clearly that while it is a significant role which government policy plays with regard to national advantage, it is only partial, and that government policy should take heed of the following:

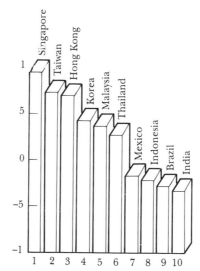

Figure 1.4 *The world competitiveness report: newly industrialized countries*
Source *The World Competitiveness Report* (1990) IMD/World Economic Forum, Lausanne, Switzerland

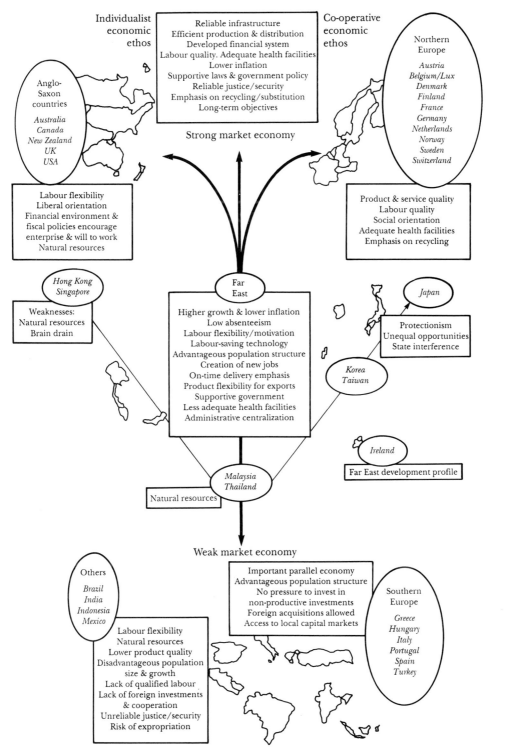

Individualist economic ethos

Co-operative economic ethos

Reliable infrastructure
Efficient production & distribution
Developed financial system
Labour quality. Adequate health facilities
Lower inflation
Supportive laws & government policy
Reliable justice/security
Emphasis on recycling/substitution
Long-term objectives

Strong market economy

Anglo-Saxon countries

Australia
Canada
New Zealand
UK
USA

Northern Europe

Austria
Belgium/Lux
Denmark
Finland
France
Germany
Netherlands
Norway
Sweden
Switzerland

Labour flexibility
Liberal orientation
Financial environment &
fiscal policies encourage
enterprise & will to work
Natural resources

Product & service quality
Labour quality
Social orientation
Adequate health facilities
Emphasis on recycling

Hong Kong
Singapore

Weaknesses:
Natural resources
Brain drain

Far East

Higher growth & lower inflation
Low absenteeism
Labour flexibility/motivation
Labour-saving technology
Advantageous population structure
Creation of new jobs
On-time delivery emphasis
Product flexibility for exports
Supportive government
Less adequate health facilities
Administrative centralization

Japan

Protectionism
Unequal opportunities
State interference

Korea
Taiwan

Ireland

Far East development profile

Malaysia
Thailand

Natural resources

Weak market economy

Others

Brazil
India
Indonesia
Mexico

Labour flexibility
Natural resources
Lower product quality
Disadvantageous population
size & growth
Lack of qualified labour
Lack of foreign investments
& cooperation
Unreliable justice/security
Risk of expropriation

Important parallel economy
Advantageous population structure
No pressure to invest in
non-productive investments
Foreign acquisitions allowed
Access to local capital markets

Southern Europe

Greece
Hungary
Italy
Portugal
Spain
Turkey

Figure 1.5 *World competitiveness report, 1990: country clusters*
Source   *The World Competitiveness Report* (1990) IMD/World Economic Forum, Lausanne,
Switzerland

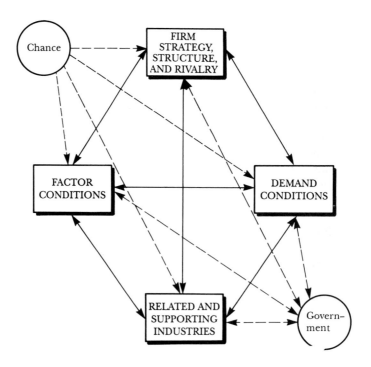

Figure 1.6   *The Porter Diamond: determinants of national advance*
Source   Porter, M. E. (1990) *The Competitive Advantages of Nations*, Macmillan, London

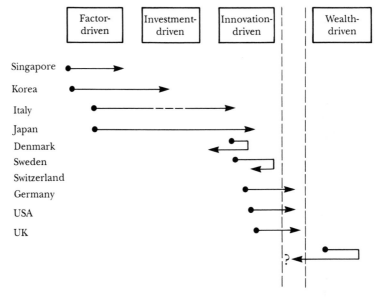

Figure 1.7   *Porter's estimated evolution of national competitive development during the postwar period*
Source   Porter, M. E. (1990) *The Competitive Advantages of Nations*, Macmillan, London

1 Firms compete in industries, not nations.
2 A nation's competitive advantage in industry is relative. With generally rising standards, some companies may not be improving fast enough to keep up with their buying public.
3 Dynamism leads to competitive advantage, not short-term cash advantages.
4 National economic prosperity demands that industries upgrade.
5 A nation's competitive advantage in industries is often geographically concentrated.
6 Competitive advantage in a nation's industries is created over a decade or more, not over three- or four-year business cycles.
7 Nations gain advantage because of differences, not similarities.
8 Many categorizations used to distinguish or prioritize industries have little relevance, e.g. labels such as 'sunrise' and 'sunset' industries.
9 The process of sustaining advantage may be intensely uncomfortable for firms and those who work in them because of the never-ending pressures for improvements, which requires also new investment.

Governments, then, cannot create advantage, but can influence the four determinants in the diamond. Education and skills training are seen as a nationally important area in which it is the responsibility of government to act, but government intervenes also in other areas, including national currency markets; industrial research and development; safety and product standards; deregulation and privatization; and foreign investment.

Supranational organizations and extraterritorial reach

The European Commission is the major force in global trade today, accounting for approximately 39 per cent of world exports and imports. The EC, and the metamorphosis that it is presently undergoing in preparation for the Single European Market of 1993, is the subject of Chapter 17.

No new members of the EC will therefore be admitted before 1993, but already Turkey is waiting to join, and so, too, are the CSFR (still better known as Czechoslovakia), Poland and Hungary.

This means also the final demise of yet another supranational body, the CMEA, or COMECON, also known as the Council for Mutual Economic Assistance and comprising the nations of the Soviet bloc. As of 1 January 1990, the basis of trading within COMECON is no longer the transferable rouble, but full convertibility. CMEA markets have opened, three have elected to pursue EC membership, and the CMEA itself is no longer, changing its name, structure and mission to become first an OIEC then an EECT.

Further changes on the world scene are likely with the North American Free Trade Agreement comprising Canada, the USA and Mexico, which if it goes ahead will effectively transform the nature of trading within the North American sub-continent as well as have major implications for traders outside.

As one bloc becomes successful, a 'demonstration' effect creates pressures in other parts of the world to develop similar structures. It transforms the stability of the particular trading bloc. The only impartial arbiter of free trade is still the GATT, the United Nations organization formed around the General Agreement on Tariffs and Trade of 1948. GATT takes it on itself to investigate the trade restrictive implications of these new international trading alliances and customs unions. GATT is discussed more fully in Chapter 3.

Table 1.4

Organization	Members	Population (000,000)	GNP (US$000,000,000)	GNP/capita (US$000)
EC	Belgium	10.02	154.69	15.44
(European	Luxembourg	0.38	100.88	28.77
Community)	Denmark	5.14	113.52	22.09
	France	56.45	1099.75	19.48
	Germany	77.31	1411.35	22.73
	Ireland	3.50	33.47	9.55
	Italy	57.59	970.62	16.85
	UK	57.48	923.96	16.07
	Netherlands	14.93	258.80	17.33
	Greece	10.05	60.25	6.00
	Turkey (Assoc)	56.28	91.74	1.63
Total		349.13	5219.83	175.94

Note   The CSFR (Czechoslovakia), Hungary and Poland have applied for membership of the EC.

Organization	Members	Population (000,000)	GNP (US$000,000,000)	GNP/capita (US$000)
EFTA	Austria	7.64	147.02	19.24
(European	Iceland	0.26	5.46	21.15
Free Trade	Norway	4.24	98.08	23.12
Association)	Portugal	10.37	50.69	4.89
	Sweden	8.55	202.50	23.68
	Switzerland	6.69	219.34	32.79
	Finland	4.98	129.82	26.07
Total		42.73	852.91	150.94

Organization	Members	Population (000,000)	GNP (US$000,000,000)	GNP/capita (US$000)
EECT** (East	Cuba	10.63	–	–
European	*Czechoslovakia (CSFR)	15.68	49.23	3.14
Cooperation	*Hungary	10.55	30.05	2.78
and Trade)	*Poland	37.97	64.48	1.70
	Rumania	23.25	38.03	1.64
	CIS	288.73	–	–
	Bulgaria	8.99	19.88	2.21
Total		395.80	201.67	11.47

* Have applied for membership to the EC.
** Previously OIEC (Organization for International Economic Cooperation) and before that CMEA (Council for Mutual Economic Assistance).

Table 1.4 continued

Organization	Members	Population (000,000)	GNP (US$000,000,000)	GNP/capita (US$000)
Arab Common	Iraq	18.91	–	–
Market	Kuwait	2.14	33.09	16.16
	Jordan	3.15	3.92	1.24
	Syria	12.53	12.40	0.99
	Egypt	52.06	31.38	0.60
Total		88.79	80.79	18.99
ASEAN	Indonesia	181.58	101.15	0.56
(Association	Malaysia	17.75	41.52	2.34
of SE Asian	Singapore	2.72	33.51	12.31
Nations)	Philippines	61.36	43.95	0.73
	Thailand	55.80	79.04	1.42
Total		319.21	299.17	17.36
NAFTA	Australia	17.00	290.52	17.08
	New Zealand	3.41	43.19	12.68
Total		20.41	333.71	29.76
ECOWAS	Benin	4.74	1.72	0.36
(The Economic	Guinea	5.72	2.76	0.48
Community of	Cote d'Ivoire	12.23	8.92	0.73
West African	Mali Republic	8.46	2.29	0.27
States)	Mauritania	1.97	0.99	0.50
	Niger	7.66	2.37	0.31
	Senegal	7.43	5.26	0.71
	Togo	3.64	1.47	0.41
	Burkina Faso	9.02	2.96	0.33
	Gambia	0.88	0.23	0.26
	Ghana	14.87	5.82	0.39
	Nigeria	117.51	31.29	0.27
	Sierra Leone	4.14	0.98	0.24
	Liberia	2.56	–	–
	Guinea-Bissau	0.98	0.18	0.18
Total		201.81	59.40	5.44

Table 1.4 continued

Organization	Members	Population (000,000)	GNP (US$000,000,000)	GNP/capita (US$000)
CACM	Guatemala	9.20	8.31	0.90
(Central	El Salvador	5.26	5.77	1.10
American	Costa Rica	2.80	5.34	1.91
Common	Nicaragua	3.85	—	—
Market)	Honduras	5.12	3.02	0.59
Total		26.23	22.44	5.04
LAIA	Argentina	32.92	76.49	2.37
(Latin American	Brazil	150.20	402.79	2.68
Integration	Colombia	32.84	40.81	1.24
Association)	Paraguay	4.31	4.80	1.11
	Uruguay	3.09	7.93	2.56
	Chile	13.18	25.50	1.94
	Ecuador	10.56	10.11	0.96
	Mexico	86.16	214.50	2.49
	Peru	21.66	25.15	1.16
	Venezuela	19.74	50.57	2.56
	Bolivia	7.31	4.53	0.62
Total		381.97	863.18	19.69
ANDEAN	Bolivia	7.31	4.53	0.62
Common Market	Colombia	32.84	40.81	1.24
	Ecuador	10.56	10.11	0.96
	Peru	21.66	25.15	1.16
	Venezuela	19.74	50.57	2.56
Total		92.11	131.17	6.54
CARICOM	Barbados	0.26	1.68	6.54
	Guyana	0.80	0.29	0.37
	Jamaica	2.39	3.61	1.51
	Trinidad-Tobago	1.28	4.46	3.47
Total		4.73	10.04	11.89
North America	Canada	26.54	542.77	20.45
Free Trade	USA	250.94	5445.83	21.70
Agreement	Mexico	86.16	214.50	2.49
Total		363.64	6203.10	44.64

Source   *The World Bank Atlas 1991*, The World Bank, Washington DC, USA.

Table 1.5 Government and business relations

	Corporate headquarters	Corporate subsidiary	Intermediary	Home government	Host government	Supranational authority	International organization
Dumping	✓	✓	✓		✓	✓✓	GATT
Parallel exports	✓		✓		✓	✓✓	–
Parallel imports	✓	✓	✓	✓		✓✓	
Counter trade	✓	✓	✓		✓		IMF World Bank
Transfer pricing	✓	✓	✓	✓	✓	✓	–
Pricing within a joint venture	✓	✓	✓		✓		UNECE
Duties and tariffs	✓			✓	✓	✓✓	GATT
Non-tariff barriers	✓			✓	✓	✓✓	GATT
Questionable payments related to orders received	✓		✓	✓		✓	OECD; UN Centre for research on Transnational
Counterfeiting	✓		✓	✓			International Chamber of Commerce IACC; ACG

Note Where a supranational authority is involved, eg EC, it has signatory powers rather than its individual members. This is emphasized by a double √√. Elsewhere, the Commissioner will take an interest in activities 'in restraint of trade.'

The question of extraterritoriality of legislation

Government everywhere has generally failed to keep pace with the demands of the business world. A fine example of this is that multinational corporations are incorporated under articles of association in a particular sovereign country (most commonly Britain after the USA) or federal state in the case of the USA (most commonly Delaware). There is no international body as yet equipped to standardize international articles of association for multinational corporations. There is no such thing either as international law, only the application of domestic law to international disputes. For joint ventures, which are increasing worldwide, the question of legal jurisdiction and of arbitration in the event of a dispute is very important. Very often a neutral third country may be chosen but whereas neutrality reassures us on impartiality of judgement, there is as yet no national code or constitution sufficiently comprehensive to easily embrace all the problems of international trading, although UNCITRAL has gone some way to solving this particular problem (see Chapter 8).

Increasingly, the EC is projecting itself as a legislator on regulations for trading within its boundaries, but although the EC accounts for the home base of very many large multinationals (British, German, French and Italian), this does not solve a global problem of accountability and control. Meanwhile, the USA is increasingly acting in the eyes of its NATO allies as *ultra-vires*, or 'beyond its legal power', in its desire to control not only US multinational corporations at home but their subsidiaries and technology licensees abroad.

For example, at the time when the Soviet gas pipeline was being constructed to bring Soviet gas into Western Europe, diplomatic difficulties arose over the US ban on General Electric rotor blade technology in the British export of turbines for the pipeline. Attempts were made by the US Administration to influence the British firm of John Brown to stop the shipment or else face reprisals against its subsidiaries in the USA. At the same time, the British Government took the line of threatening reprisals directly at the British company if it did not proceed with the export order immediately. The company found itself placed between two governments in dispute and both of which refused to back down.

Extraterritorial reach is becoming an even more important issue as these trading blocs, such as the EC, take on the rights of a legal person, able to conduct negotiations and sign treaties in their own name as well as impose duties, quotas and tariffs. Extraterritorial reach goes beyond these organizations, though, to certain national legislatures, which take it on themselves to regulate national enterprises wherever they may be located in the world, and so, in effect world business. The US Administration has passed legislation, such as the Foreign Corrupt Practices Act, which affects not only US companies but companies from other countries as well which have a stock market listing in the USA. This is discussed more fully in Chapter 13.

From economic advantage to marketing advantage

The first difficulty is in defining 'international marketing.' Too often, attention is devoted only to those activities conducted by companies which constitute in their aggregated total a foreign trade balance for individual countries. Here we are studying not just trade between nations. We are studying instead the companies at home and abroad who are the buyers and sellers, and in so doing, international marketing as a network of relationships between firms engaged in buying and selling through to the final consumer. We examine separately the variables with which they have to deal, and again later in the context of certain geographic

Exhibit 1.1

Marketing milestones of four decades reviewed

0 + A HALF-CENTURY Of pioneering efforts has laid the foundation for the new marketing concepts that are sure to emerge in what was called the "Uncertain '90s" by Philip Kotler at the AMA's World Marketing Conference in Montreal.

Before looking into the future, Kotler reviewed milestone marketing concepts from the 1950s to the 1980s that have helped to shape the discipline.

In the 1950s, six milestone concepts surfaced as marketing started to move out of economics departments and into business schools and developed into a system of thought to aid businesspeople in building and defending markets:

● The marketing mix. proposed by Neil H. Borden in 1950. "He identified 12 elements and, in doing so, was saying that marketers go further than economists (who focus mainly on price), salespeople (who focus mainly on selling), and advertisers (who see demand creation as primarily a function of advertising)."

● Product life cycle. defined by Joel Deal in 1950. "Later Theodore Levitt gave the concept additional prominence, and since then, it has undergone many refinements, although it has retained its delightful controversial character."

● Brand image, introduced by Sidney J. Levy in 1955 and given greater visibility by David Ogilvy. "It's an idea especially beloved by advertisers and public relations people because it creates reserach opportunities and employment, and justifies high advertising expenditures."

● Market segmentation, promoted in 1956 by Wendell R. Levy, who "saw segmentation as a strategy, although today we think of it more as a deft partitioning of the market into meaningful parts, after which the company decides which segments to pursue and how."

● The marketing concept outlined by John D. McKitterick in 1957. "The emphasis shifted from 'selling what we make' to 'making what we sell.' as defined by the customer."

● The marketing audit, proposed by Abe Shuchman in 1959. "Many companies are dead or dying and don't know it. Wise ones commission periodic marketing audits to check whether their strategy, structure, and systems are attuned to their best market opportunities."

In the "Soaring '60s," five milestone concepts surfaced:

● The four Ps classification of the marketing mix product, price, place, and promotion introduced by Jerome McCarthy in 1960 and expanded on by others. "Even I joined the P-naming game by proposing politics and public relations." Kotler said. "Lately I've been distinguishing the strategic marketing mix from the tactical by saying that the four strategic marketing mix elements that you do before product, price, place, and promotion, are probing (research), partioning (segmentation), prioritizing (targeting), and positioning."

● Marketing myopia, put forth in 1961, by Levitt, who "showed that certain industries fall on hard times because they focus on the product, not the customer need."

● Lifestyles, adapted from a sociological concept by William Lazer in 1963. "Increasingly we design our goods for lifestyle groups. Picture a 'yuppie dink couple,' and we can almost predict what they will eat, drink, and wear."

● The theory of buyer behavior, introduced by John Howard and Jagdish Sheth in 1967.

● The broadened concept of marketing, advanced by Levy and Kotler in 1969. "We argued that marketing can be applied not only to products and services but also to organizations, persons, places, and ideas. Furthermore, all organizations do marketing, whether or not money changes hands and whether or not they do it well or poorly."

"The 'Turbulent '70s,' a time of rapid and wrenching econo-mic and social change." gave birth to seven milestone concepts:

● Social marketing, introduced by Gerald Zaltman and Kotler in 1971, "to call attention to the role that marketing could play in diffusing worthwhile social causes such as environmental protection, family planning, improved nutrition, car pooling, etc."

● Demarketing, introduction by Levy and Kotler in 1971. "Marketing managers, under some circumstances, must be as skilled in reducing the level of demand, totally or selectively, as they are in expanding it."

● Positioning, identified by Al Ries and Jack Trout in 1972. "They argued that products are positioned in customers' minds, even if they're not carefully positioned by the company in its ads."

● Strategic marketing, an offshoot of the strategic planning concept proposed by the Boston Consulting Group in the early '70s. "The business portfolio approach mean that the marketing mission is not always to build sales. Strategic marketing is now being sharply distinguished from tactical."

● Societal marketing, a socially responsible way of doing business, mirrored a general trend toward humanism. "It called upon business to factor into its decisions the long-run interests of consumers and society."

● Macromarketing, spawned in response to increasing social problems such as consumerism and environmentalism. "Macromarketing research keeps us honest by examining the aggregate effects of our business activity on consumer welfare and values."

● Services marketing, brought to prominence by Lynn Shostack in 1977. "She argued that services marketing needed to be freed from the shackles of product marketing thinking."

In the "SLuggish '80s." marketers created seven concepts to describe how to cope with the lackluster economy:

● Marketing warfare, investigated by Ravi Singh and Kotler in 1981 and publicized a few years later by Ries and Trout in their book.

● Internal marketing, introduced by Christian Gronroos in 1981. "Having a strong marketing department doesn't mean the company itself is marketing oriented." Kotler said. "The art of creating a marketing culture in a company is something I have referred to as the problem of 'marketization,' that is, marketizing the company."

● Global marketing, proposed by Levitt in 1983. "He called upon multinationals to develop a more uniform product and communications offering around the world. He saw too much adaptation to local markets, resulting in a loss of economies of scale and, therefore, higher costs."

● Local marketing, revitalized by Campbell Soup Co., Nabisco, General Foods, and other large companies. "Since both local marketing and global marketing will be going on, we well face and decade of 'bifurcated' or 'schizophrenic' marketing."

● Direct marketing, expanded beyond door-to-door selling and direct mail to include party selling, telemarketing. TV home shopping, computer shopping, and more. "Some say the essence of direct marketing is 'data-based marketing,' made possible by the great advances in information and telecommunications technology."

● Relationship marketing, highlighted by Barbara Bund Jackson in 1985. "Relationship marketing captures the spirit of the marketing concept better than does transaction marketing."

● Megamarketing, introduced by Kotler in 1986 "to address the problem of breaking into a protected or blocked market. Today's marketers increasingly need to command political and PR skills and understandings to work effectively in the global marketplace."

Source American Marketing Association (1987) *Marketing News*, 31 July.

regions, so as to arrive at a proper understanding of international marketing as a truly dynamic force.

International marketing is seen as a relatively new adjunct to marketing itself. Even so, the meaning of the word 'marketing' has come to be devalued during the relatively short post-war period that it has been among us. It has come increasingly to be used, quite wrongly, as a synonym, or more upmarket word, for 'selling' rather than as in the words of the Chartered Institute of Marketing 'the management process which seeks to identify, anticipate and satisfy customer requirements profitably.' Or, turning to the American Marketing Association: 'the process of planning and executing the conception, pricing, promotion and distribution of ideas, goods and services to create exchanges that satisfy individual and organizational objectives.' Either or both of these definitions will serve our purpose as there is much in common between them.

Implementing the four Ps of marketing (for the six Ps, including the two new Ps of marketing, see below) – product, place, promotion and price – involves interactions with variables which will be different for the domestic and international markets. In domestic marketing, one is familiar with the extent of political risk; the nature and extent of government policy towards business; with the quality of skilled human resources and of natural resources; and with the ramifications of existing and likely legislation on such areas as safety, hygiene, employment, and ownership of capital. International marketing, on the other hand, involves dealing with societies where politics, beliefs and values may be very different from those held in the home market and, yet, legislation abroad will have important ramifications for international marketing – there may, for example, be legislation requiring the majority employment of local nationals, or of majority equity ownership by local nationals in joint ventures, restrictions on sourcing, labelling and on the use of certain product ingredients, including flavourings, preservatives and sweeteners, to name but a few.

In this context, it is useful to consider alternative views of the marketing function. Some, such as Baker (1987), see marketing as somewhere between an art and a science. Bartels (1968), however, viewed international marketing quite differently from domestic marketing, seeing marketing as having two facets: technical and social. The technical facet or the 'science' consists of the application of principles, rules or knowledge relating to the non-human elements of marketing. It is these concepts and generalizations which are held to have a universality transcending national boundaries and culture differences.

On the technical level, we are dealing with universals without regard to time and space. We are dealing with concepts which have applications across natural boundaries and language barriers, such as economies of scale, distribution channels, etc. On the social level we deal with interactions among individuals acting in role positions in the various systems involved in the distribution of goods and services. This facet emphasizes the human element, the individual acting under the full range of influences both economic and non-economic which affiliation with the social institutions of his society imposes on him.

As a social process, marketing in two nations may differ quite markedly. While the roles in which individuals interact may be identical, their expectations and behavioral patterns within two societies may be quite different. Interactions affect the societal environment, and in turn, shape marketing policies within that environment. Greater environmental differences may be found within a country than between countries, if, for example, we were to compare two cities. Yet, this is not to forget either that foreign companies by virtue of their foreign ownership will often be constrained by governments from engaging in free trade across their borders. Arguments, such as protecting national interests, are frequently raised on such occasions. This is one of the differences which Bartels points to as an 'international difference'

INDUSTRY	Denmark	Germany	Italy	Japan	Korea	Singapore	Sweden	Switzerland	U.K.	U.S.
FOOD										
Fast food										XX
Food service/vending										
RETAILING										
Convenience stores										X
Speciality stores										
EDUCATION AND TRAINING										
Secondary and university education		X						X	X	XX
Graduate education										XX
Corporate training										XX
LEISURE										
Entertainment									X	XX
Auctioneering										
MEDICAL										
Health care services								X	X	XX
Hospital management										
TRAVEL RELATED										
Hotels				X				X		XX
Car rentals										
Airlines		X				X		X	X	X
GENERAL BUSINESS										
Accounting									X	XX
Legal services										
Advertising									XX	XX
Public relations										
Mgt. consulting		X						X	X	XX
Engineering/architectural[2]										
Construction				X		X		X	X	XX
Contract research										
Design services			XX							
Temporary help										
Industrial laundry/apparel supply	X							X		XX
Industrial cleaning (facilities, tools, equipment)										
Security services							X	X	X	X
Building maintenance services										
Equipment maintenance and repair							X			
Waste disposal & management										
TRADING				X				XX	XX	XX
FINANCIAL										
Credit card										XX
Consumer finance										
Credit reporting										XX
Merchant/investment banking										
Commercial banking				X				XX	X	XX
Leasing										
Money management		XX						XX	XX	XX
Reinsurance										
INFORMATION										
Information processing										XX
Custom software[2]										
Information/data									X	XX
TRANSPORT										
Air cargo		X								X
Airport terminal										
Shipping	X			X			X			
Port services										
Ship repair						X				
Logistics management										
Service stations									X	X

XX = leading position
X = position
[1] Excludes tourism attracted to a nation.
[2] National positions in engineering tend to be in different types of projects.
[3] France also had a significant position in custom software.
Source: Author's estimates based on field interviews, case studies, and a composite of published sources.

Figure 1.8   *Estimated patterns of national competitive advantage in international service industries*
Source   Porter, M. E. (1990) *The Competitive Advantage of Nations*, Macmillan, London

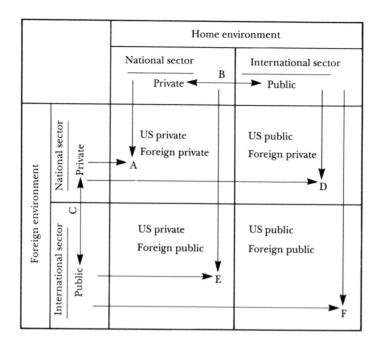

Figure 1.9   *Bartels: relations of private and public sectors in the international environment*
Source   Bartels, R. (1968) Are domestic and international marketing similar? *Journal of Marketing*, **32**, (July), 55–61

between what may otherwise have been two identical market structures with similar levels of demand. Bartels depicts this influence in Figure 1.9 by the interactions: B, C, D, E and F.

Governments relate to their own citizens (B and C), and may give encouragement to export and invest abroad through research, assistance, trade fairs, export credit insurance and investment guarantees. Equally, it may choose to discourage foreign companies through export and investment restrictions, and monopoly or antitrust legislation. In the same way each national government may affect the way in which foreign nationals trade with their own citizens (interactions D and E). Then there are, too, the interactions of government (F) which affect international marketing as through the creation of common markets and free trade areas, consummation of commercial treaties, agreements or tariffs, or the inspection of antitrust and monopoly laws (Bartels, 1968).

Kotler (1984), recognizing the political nature of the marketing environment, introduced a further two Ps to the existing four Ps of marketing, coining the term 'megamarketing'. This was now to include political power and public opinion formation. This meant that the environment had to be managed as well as the traditional marketing mix. To cite Kotler:

> Marketers are always looking at economic factors and national factors, but they fail to study political science. They should examine the conflicts, the special interest and pressure groups, the vested interests, the political realities and create appeals in those arenas. Marketers can no longer sit back and adopt a defensive posture when power is being used against them.

The implications to be drawn from megamarketing (Kotler, 1968) are then:

1   Enlarging the multiparty marketing concept. Marketers spend much time analysing how to create preferences and satisfaction in target buyers. Because other parties — governments, labour unions, banks, reform groups — can block the path to the target buyers, marketers must closely study the obstacles these parties create and develop strategies for attracting their support or at least neutralizing their opposition.

2   Blurring the distinction between environmental and controllable variables. Marketers have traditionally defined the environment as those outside forces that cannot be controlled by the business. But megamarketing argues that some environmental forces can be changed through lobbying, legal action, negotiation, issue advertising, public relations and strategic partnering.

3   Broadening the understanding of how markets work. Most market thinkers assume that demand creates its own supply. Ideally, companies discover a market need and rush to satisfy that need. But real markets are often blocked, and the best marketer doesn't always win. We have seen that foreign competitors with offers comparable or superior to those of local companies cannot always enter the market. The result is a lower level of consumer satisfaction and producer innovation than would otherwise result.

How companies think international

1   *Product maturity.* The product life cycle stage at home may be one of maturity, whereas there may be a new embryonic market abroad enabling the product to start a new life cycle from introduction where quantities available are low but the price commanded is high. The Intermediate Technology Development Group (ITDG) is a lobby based in Coventry, who are championing for mature technology product exports to the LDCs rather than the sophisticated Western products demanded of Western markets, which in turn require Western levels of maintenance and after-sales care. Increasingly, however, this argument is becoming less and less convincing. Many of Western society's more advanced products are made in Pacific Basin companies with economies least able to afford them. A further paradox is contained in the fact that these production countries are capital intensive rather than perhaps relying solely on cheaper factor costs such as labour or raw materials.

2   *Competition.* Competition may be less intense abroad than at home. This area has been the subject of study for many international economists, but suffice it to say that there may be significant differences in factor costs between the home country and other countries. Other countries may, for example, have cheaper raw material or labour costs, or they may have gained 'experience curve' cost advantages through experience of volume productivity, so that it becomes advantageous to operate abroad. Also, the market structure of other countries may reveal advantages like centralized buying, and perhaps state-buying, where market access may be assured in return for guarantees on investment, employment, etc.

3   *Excess capacity utilization.* This concept is drawn also from economics, whereon a given manufactured item which has been on sale in the domestic market for sufficiently long to have recouped its original research and development costs, may find new profitable export markets, costed only at its actual production costs, plus overhead; its original research development costs being regarded now as 'sunk' costs. However, this in effect means that the export item will be sold abroad for less than its recommended price in the domestic market of its country of origin and this leaves the company open to charges of 'dumping'. Western industrialized markets may react swiftly to what they see as the destructive effects of 'dumping' while less developed countries may actually welcome the importation of

Table 1.6

Environmental management strategies to control conditions previously thought uncontrollable

1 *Competitive aggression.* The company exploits a distinctive competence or improves internal efficiency of resources for competitive advantage. Examples: product differentiation, aggressive pricing, comparative advertising.

2 *Competitive pacification.* Company takes independent actions to improve relations with competitors. Examples: helping competitors find raw materials, advertising campaigns which promote entire industry, price umbrellas.

3 *Public relations.* Establish and maintain favorable images in the minds of those making up the environment. Example: corporate ad campaign.

4 *Voluntary action.* Company tries to manage and becomes committed to various special-interest groups, causes, and social problems. Examples: McGraw-Hill's efforts to prevent sexist stereotypes and 3M's energy-conservation program.

5 *Dependence development.* Create or modify relationships with external groups so they become dependent on the company. Examples: raising switching costs for suppliers, production of critical defense-related commodities, providing vital information to regulators.

6 *Legal action.* Company engages in private legal battle with competitor on antitrust, deceptive advertising, or other grounds.

7 *Political action.* Company tries to influence elected representatives to create a more favorable business environment or limit competition. Examples: corporate constituency programs, issue advertising, direct lobbying.

8 *Smoothing.* Company attempts to resolve irregular demand. Examples: telephone company lowers weekend rates, airline offers inexpensive fares during off-peak times.

9 *Demarketing.* Firm attempts to discourage customers in general or a certain class of customers in particular, on either a temporary or permanent basis. Example: petrol filling stations adopt shorter hours of operation.

10 *Implicit cooperation.* Firm adopts patterned, predictable, and coordinated behaviors. Example: price leadership.

11 *Contracting.* Company negotiates an agreement with another group to exchange goods, services, information, patents, etc. Example: contractual vertical and horizontal marketing systems.

12 *Co-optation.* Firm absorbs new elements into its leadership or policy-making structure as a means of averting threats to its stability or existence. Example: consumer representatives, women, and bankers on boards of directors.

13 *Coalition.* Two or more groups coalesce and act jointly with respect so some set of issues for some period of time. Examples: industry associations, political initiatives of the Business Roundtable and the U.S. Chamber of Commerce.

14 *Domain selection.* Firm enters industries or markets with limited competition or regulation and ample suppliers and customers, or enters high-growth markets. Examples: IBM's entry into the personal-computer market and Miller Brewing Co.'s entry into the light-beer market.

15 *Diversification.* Company invests in different types of businesses, manufactures different types of products, integrates vertically, or expands geographically to reduce dependence on a single product, service, market, or technology.

16 *Merger and acquisition.* Two or more firms form a single enterprise or one company gains possession of another. Examples: merger between Pan American and National Airlines, Phillip Morris' acquisition of Miller Brewing Co.

Source Zeithaml, C. P. and Zeithaml, V. A. (1984), Environmental management: strategic options, examples. *Marketing News*, American Marketing Association, 14 September.

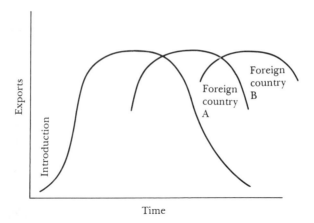

Figure 1.10 *Product life cycle*
Note The product life cycle explanation here would require an infinite number of markets accepting of mature technologies to be viable. It assumes that technology is held only by a few countries and that other markets are undemanding. Neither assumption is accurate. Chapter 2 will deal with further implications of the product life cycle and international trade

Western goods at low cost, particularly where they do not have production of their own. For domestic producers, 'dumping' may have several advantages. Since 'dumping' is seen as a short-term strategy, it may solve an immediate excess supply problem for a company unable to reduce its prices to a correspondingly low figure for domestic clients without creating embarrassing precedents for future price negotiations.

4 *Geographical diversification.* Geographical diversification may be preferable to product-line diversification. It is commonsense for a company to stick to producing what it is good at. This is one of the main themes of Peters and Waterman (1982) in their *In Search of Excellence.* Finding new markets for existing products or modified products does not expose the company to the attendant risks of expanding the product range simultaneously with foreign market entry. In terms of corporate strategy, it makes sense to focus on the strengths of the company and not to depart too greatly from these strengths whether in product innovation, adaptation or service. Recent US corporate case histories, which have seen companies, such as Gulf and Western, moving away from the conglomerate pattern to specialization in their mainstream business activity, have emphasized this point. Elsewhere, rival companies seem to be uniting together in sharing research and development on parts, components, subassemblies and product range extension as will be seen later, when we discuss strategic business alliances.

5 Potential of a population and purchasing power. Markets may be local, regional, national, international or even global. Generally, the more specialized the end-use application of any product or process, the larger the geographical market that needs then to be found. Depending on a company's technology, its place in domestic industry and resources, a company 'footprint' in foreign markets may be found which is either long and narrow (spread over many markets) or short and wide (concentrated in only a few markets). Generally, where there is a need; a willingness to find a solution to that need; plus an ability to pay for it, a market will be created. Assessing market potential requires data. Not

all countries produce data with the frequency or detail of the British Central Statistical Office. Very often, and particularly with developing countries, there will be significantly large gaps between the publications of national economic data. Even when data exist they may be of questionable value, they may be collected for different reasons on a quite different statistical base, and, therefore, may not be directly comparable to the exporter's known domestic situation. For these reasons, more is said in Chapter 4 of the techniques of foreign country selection where economic indicators are poor or non-existent.

The Porter corporate policy prescription for competitiveness

1 Create the climate for upgrading advantage.
2 Sell to the most demanding customers.
3 Find the right location at the centre of the greatest concentration of forces making for competitiveness.
4 Do not overdo globalization. The home base counts most when it comes to creation of competitive advantage.
5 Get involved in factor creation, including training.
6 Consider a base move.
7 Competition and alliances assure growth and manage competition, but do not overdo it.
8 Role of leaders is important.

The dilemma of the multinational – a force for good or evil?

The case of the multinational is frequently stated in strong terms both for and against it. Livingstone (1989) stated some of the accusations against as including:
1 That they interfere politically in the affairs of the host nation.
2 That they destroy local jobs.
3 That by exporting its knowhow and national technology, multinationals destroy its home country's technical leadership.
4 That they destroy local culture.

Yet, all in all, Livingstone states that the multinational can be seen as 'the modern metamorphosis of free trade.' It is simply resorting to a vast oversimplification to try to resort to a single element in a very complex trade equation. Singling out the multinational for undue attention in this way avoids looking at the real and highly complex world (Livingstone, 1989). The love–hate relationship with the multinational continues, however, and was well summarized by the *Economist*:

> It fiddles with its accounts. It avoids or evades its taxes. It rigs its intra-company transfer prices. It is run by foreigners, from decision centres thousands of miles away. It imports foreign labour practices. It overpays. It underpays. It competes unfairly with local firms. It is in cahoots with local firms. It exports jobs from rich countries. It is an instrument of rich countries' imperialism. The technologies it brings to the third world are old fashioned. No, they are too modern. It meddles. It bribes. Nobody can control it. It wrecks balances of payments. It overturns economic

policies. It plays off governments against each other to get the biggest investment incentives. Won't it please come and invest? Let it bloody well go home.

The arguments for and against the multinational are shown in Table 1.7, where Kinsey (1988) has listed the positive and negative impacts of the multinational against seven criteria.

Globally, competition is dynamic and forever changing. It is no longer possible to compete solely with the competitive tools that rightly belonged to the past, but to innovate. In the past, it was enough for former colonial powers to offer aid to former dependencies that was in some way 'tied' to certain goods. However, in the search for trade, other countries have willingly stepped in, offering loans and credits not as restrictive as those offered by the former European colonial powers. This has been one of the major changes to world trade, together with the new forms of financing, including countertrade (CT), which have emerged postwar and have introduced new institutions, including the World Bank, IMF, Bank for International Settlements, European Bank for Reconstruction and Development, and Euromoney markets.

Meanwhile, other newer, industrial, countries have been aggressively establishing themselves on the international scene, and it was also seen to be politically important for them to develop trade, and, through trade, a relationship and understanding with the developing countries which also enhanced their own power and prestige. At the same time, the international trading companies of colonial times were no longer recognizable as regional trading companies but were now seen as 'multinationals'.

The multinational phenomenon of the twenty-first century trades more within itself and its subsidiaries and affiliates than just between nations. With more than a third of world trade taking place between multinationals, the multinationals have created in effect their own internal markets. This internalization theory contained within Dunning's Eclectic Approach (advanced in Chapter 2) is one explanation of the growth of the multinational. The multinational corporation escapes an internationally agreed definition, being referred to as an international corporation by some, as a transnational by the United Nations, and a multinational enterprise or 'megacorp' by yet others. While it is impossible to agree on a definition, the multinational may be said to meet two important criteria, with the emphasis being laid particularly on the second:

1 Foreign direct investments either in manufacturing or service industries in more than two countries.
2 Corporate planning which employs a worldwide perspective and impartially allocates resources such as management, other personnel, company-specific technology, business expertise and funds on a global basis.

The working definition of a multinational offered here states that:

A multinational enterprise is a corporation which owns (in whole or in part), controls and manages income-generating assets in more than one country. In so doing, it engages in international production, sales and distribution of goods and services across national boundaries financed by foreign direct investment.

The multinationals have been active in dismantling psychological as well as geographical frontiers. Yet, here we touch on another very important point. The multinationals as such, in terms often of ownership as well as management style, own allegiance to no one particular

Table 1.7

Positive impact of the multinational in relation to:	Negative impact of the multinational in relation to:
1 *Technology* Industrialization initiated and promoted. Knowledge and skills transferred.	1 *Technology* Inappropriate technology brought. Key sector domination. R & D remains in home country. Knowledge and skills not transferred on a large scale.
2 *Jobs* Directly created in the multinational. Indirectly created by stimulating entrepreneurship and efficiency.	2 *Jobs* Wrong type of jobs provided. Economic and social inequalities promoted. Jobs destroyed through local competition being killed.
3 *Competition and complementary activity* Competition stimulated to improve. Entrepreneurship in complementary activity promoted. Overall efficiency improved.	3 *Competition and complementary activity* Local competition eliminated. Oligopolistic industrial structure promoted.
4 *Management* Effective management promoted.	4 *Management* Inappropriate management techniques introduced. Destruction of local culture.
5 *Foreign exchange* Earned or saved by host nation.	5 *Foreign exchange* Lost through transfer pricing and other means.
6 *Attitudes* 'Modernizing' attitudes promoted.	6 *Attitudes* Materialistic attitudes stimulated and local culture destroyed.
7 *Demand* Increased consumer and industrial demand.	7 *Demand* Demand distorted. Social inequalities promoted.
	8 *Politics* Interference by the multinational in the host nation's politics.

Source　Kinsey, J. (1988) *Marketing in Developing Countries*, Macmillan, London.

country. Consequently, the term 'national' should not appear in their title. More correctly, the largest of these are truly global companies and so the term 'global company' will be found used in this text more frequently than the term 'multinational'. An increasing number of truly global brands, such as Pepsi-Cola or Coca-Cola, underline this point. Language may change with the country concerned, there may be quite different environmental conditions of use, but still perhaps the bottle, the logo and all that is normally associated with the product, including taste, flavour, fragrance and lifestyle association, will usually remain intact and instantly recognizable worldwide. For others, such as IBM who produce and sell what are essentially industrial products worldwide, this requires a different form of co-ordination, integrating multinational sourcing of components and division of labour. With IBM's degree of integration, 'foreignness' is relatively meaningless as the company needs to know as much about its operations in say, Britain, and its market situation there as it does of its home base, the USA. With business becoming more international in a search for markets, new competitive pressures are created which result in a greater dynamism. Technological change; societal change; increasing protectionism internationally (despite the existence of a General Agreement on Tariffs and Trade), and creeping nationalism on a regional, as opposed to national, scale in purchasing, as still practised within the EC, are only a few of the challenges placed before business corporations seeking to do business in world markets today.

References

Baker, M. J. (1989) One more time — what is marketing? In *The Marketing Book* (ed. M. J. Baker), Heinemann, Oxford.

Brookes, R. W. (1988) *The New Marketing*, Gower, Aldershot, Hants.

Financial Times (1989) Dogma and reality about exports. 26 June.

Kay, J. (1990) Who needs a global strategy? *Accountancy*, July, 100–102.

Kotler, P. (1986) Megamarketing. *Harvard Business Review*, March-April, 117–125.

Kotler, P. Fahey, L., and Jatusripitak, S. (1985) *The New Competition: What Theory Z Didn't Tell You About Marketing*, Prentice-Hall, Englewood Cliffs, N.J.

Levitt, T. (1983) *The Marketing Imagination*, Macmillan—The Free Press, New York.

Letwin, O. (1988) *Privatising the World*, Cassell, London.

Livingstone, J. M. (1989) *The Internationalisation of Business*, Macmillan, London.

Marketing News (1987) Marketing milestones of four decades reviewed, July 31.

Marketing News (1984) Kotler: rethink the marketing concept — there are 6 Ps' not 4. September 13.

Peters, T.J., and Waterman, R.H. (1982) *In Search of Excellence*, Harper and Row, London.

Porter, M. E. (1986) Competition in global industries: A conceptual framework. In *Competition in Global Industries*, Harvard Business School Press.

Porter, M. E. (1990) *The Competitive Advantage of Nations*, Macmillan, London.

Stopford, J. M., and Turner, L. (1985) *Britain and the Multinationals*, John Wiley and Sons, Chichester.

Toffler, A. (1990) *Powershift: Knowledge, Wealth and Violence at the Edge of the 21st Century*, Bantam Books, New York.

Townley, P. (1990) Global business in the next decade. *Across the Board*, January/February, pp 13–18.

Turnbull, P. W., and Paliwoda, S. J. (1986) *Research in International Marketing*, Croom-Helm, London.

Young, S. Hood, N., and Hamill, J. (1988) *Foreign Multinationals and the British Economy*, Croom-Helm, London.

Key reading

Baker, M. J. (1991) One more time – What is marketing? In *The Marketing Book*, 2nd edn (ed. M. J. Baker) Heinemann, Oxford.
Brookes, R. W. (1988) *The New Marketing*, Gower, Aldershot, Hants.
Financial Times (1989) Dogma and reality about exports. 26 June.
Kay, J. (1990) Who needs a global strategy? *Accountancy*, July, 100–102.
Kotler, P. (1986) Megamarketing. *Harvard Business Review*, March-April, 117–125.
Marketing News (1987) Marketing milestones of four decades reviewed. July 31.
Marketing News (1984) Kotler: Rethink the marketing concept – there are 6 Ps' not 4. September 13.
Porter, M. E. (1986) Competition in global industries: A conceptual framework. In *Competition in Global Industries*, Harvard Business School Press.
Porter, M. E. (1990) *The Competitive Advantage of Nations*, Macmillan, London.

2
Export behaviour theories and internationalization processes for goods and services

Exporting versus international marketing

The exchange process which is the basis of international marketing is different from that found in domestic markets and more than just exporting. Active exporting would require the use of only four Ps whereas international marketing requires the six Ps of megamarketing. (see chapter 1.) To export means simply to send or carry abroad, especially for trade or sale. Marketing goes beyond that, introducing the concept of the end-user, moving the orientation away from finding sales for a company's existing products to analysing the market and assessing whether the company is able to produce a product or service for which there is either current or potential demand, given that other factors can be controlled, such as price, promotion and distribution (Paliwoda, 1991). International marketing requires greater commitment, and that may mean executive time and resource, much more than does exporting.

Exporting may be simply a short-term solution to an immediate problem of under-capacity of production or over-capacity of stocks. Marketing identifies market needs, either current, potential or latent. Marketing helps to bridge the information gap between the company and the final consumer of its product. Exporting, on the other hand, is deemed to be successful whenever a sale is concluded. That sale will usually be with a trade intermediary. The company doing the exporting has achieved a profitable sale, but knows little or nothing about the final market for his product, nor will he receive any ongoing communication about how his product is received and what customers think of it, unless, perhaps, it is either very bad, or it is simply not selling through the distribution system to the final consumer, but just gathering dust.

Root (1987) lists out the following characteristics between what we may term an export sales approach and an international marketing approach. The objectives and the criteria by which they are measured are incredibly far apart (see Table 2.2).

Four export behaviour theories

There have been a number of attempts to research the export decision process since the study undertaken by Johanson and Wiedersheim-Paul (1975). Based on empirical research of four actual exporters, their findings pointed to a 'gradual process occurring in stages', rather than large spectacular investments. They found that some expansion, immediately outside of the national market but within the immediate geographical region preceded internationalization and so they were able to state that it was reasonable to assume that the same held true for many firms in other countries with small internal domestic markets. By expanding first out of the nation state into, for example, the immediate neighbouring markets of Scandinavia, a Swedish firm could reduce its perceived risk and the overall uncertainty of exporting. It was exporting, but within a region where language and cultural values were consistent with one's own. What was interesting to note from their research was that the nature of pre-export activity influences the likelihood of a firm becoming an exporter. The firm will have a natural preference for operations in the nearby geographic areas. Again, the question of regional expansion is affected by the personal perception, individual characteristics and experience of the decision maker. Within the context of the firm, this involvement in international marketing could be viewed as an innovation, but this would be to deny the economic necessity that often prevails on companies to export or else face extinction or stagnation. In the final analysis it would move ahead with much rational analysis or deliberate planning.

The Uppsala school 'model', as devised by Weidersheim-Paul, influenced subsequent writings on the subject and identified four stages. A further study by Bilkey and Tesar (1977) (see Table 2.5) among Wisconsin exporters identified six stages:

1 Management is not interested and would not even fill an unsolicited order.

Table 2.1

Twelve most common mistakes of potential exporters

1 Failure to obtain qualified export counselling and to develop a master international marketing plan before starting an export business.
2 Insufficient commitment by top management to overcome the initial difficulties and financial requirements of exporting.
3 Insufficient care in selecting overseas distributors.
4 Chasing orders from around the world instead of establishing a basis for profitable operations and orderly growth.
5 Neglecting export business when the US market booms.
6 Failure to treat international distributors on an equal basis with domestic counterparts.
7 Assuming that a given market technique and product will automatically be successsful in all countries.
8 Unwillingness to modify products to meet regulations or cultural preferences of other countries.
9 Failure to print service, sale and warranty messages in locally understood languages.
10 Failure to consider use of an export-management company.
11 Failure to consider licensing or joint-venture agreements.
12 Failure to provide readily available servicing for the product.

Source   US Department of Commerce (1990) *A Basic Guide to Exporting*, NTC Business Books, Lincolnwood, Illinois, USA

2 Management is willing to fill solicited orders but makes no effort to explore the feasibility of active exporting.
3 Management actively explores the feasibility of exporting.
4 The firm exports experimentally to some psychologically close country.
5 The firm is an experienced exporter to that country.
6 Management explores the feasibility of exporting to additional countries, psychologically more distant.

The concept of psychological closeness of one market to another was to prove an important and useful finding. This model was subsequently refined by Cavusgil and Nevin who went on to identify yet further characteristics, finding that the internal company factors explaining export marketing behaviour fell into four groups as in Figure 2.1:

Table 2.2   Export sales approach versus international marketing approach

	Export sales	*International marketing*
Time horizons	Short-run	Long run (say three to five years)
Target markets	No systematic selection	Selection based on analysis of market/sales potential
Dominant objective	Immediate sales	Build permanent market position
Resource commitment	Only enough to get immediate sales	What is necessary to gain permanent market position
Entry mode	No systematic choice	Systematic choice of most appropriate mode
New-product development	Exclusively for home market	For both home and foreign markets
Product adaptation	Only mandatory adaptations (to meet legal/technical requirements) of domestic products	Adaptation of domestic products to foreign buyers' preferences, incomes and use conditions
Channels	No effort to control	Effort to control in support of market objectives/goals
Price	Determined by domestic full cost with some ad hoc adjustments to specific sales situations	Determined by demand, competition, objectives and other marketing policies, as well as cost
Promotion	Mainly confined to personal selling or left to middlemen	Advertising, sales promotion and personal selling mix to achieve market objectives goals

Source   Root, F. R. (1987) *Entry Strategies for International Markets*, Lexington Books, Lexington, MA, p. 5.

Table 2.3   The export decision – management issues

I Experience

  1 With what countries has business already been conducted (or from what countries have inquiries already been received)?
  2 Which product lines are mentioned most often?
  3 List the sale inquiry of each buyer by product, by country.
  4 Is the trend of sales/inquiries up or down?
  5 Who are the main domestic and foreign competitors?
  6 What general and specific lessons have been learned from past export experiences?

II Management and personnel

  1 Who will be responsible for the export department's organization and staff?
  2 How much senior management time:
     should be allocated?
     could be allocated?
  3 What are management's expectations for the effort?
  4 What organization structure is required to ensure that export sales are adequately serviced? (Note the political implications, if any.)
  5 Who will follow through after the planning is accomplished?

III Production capacity

  1 How is the present capacity being used?
  2 Will filling export orders hurt domestic sales?
  3 What will be the cost of additional production?
  4 Are there fluctuations in the annual workload? When? Why?
  5 What minimum order quantity is required?
  6 What would be required to design and package products specifically for export?

IV Financial capacity

  1 What amount of capital can be tied up in exports?
  2 What level of export department operating costs can be supported?
  3 How are the initial expenses of export efforts to be allocated?
  4 What other new development plans are in the works that may compete with export plans?
  5 By what date must an export effort pay for itself?

Source   US Department of Commerce (1990) *A Basic Guide to Exporting*, NTC Business Books, Lincolnwood, Illinois, p. 3.

Table 2.4   Outline for an export plan

Table of contents

Executive summary (one or two pages maximum)

Introduction: Why a company should export

Part I – An export policy commitment statement

Part II – The situation/background analysis

- product
- operations
- personnel and export organization
- resources of the firm
- industry structure, competition and demand

Part III – The marketing component

- identification, evaluation and selection of target markets
- product selection and pricing
- distribution method
- terms and conditions
- internal organization and procedures
- sales goals: profit (loss) forecasts

Part IV – Tactics: action steps

- countries where firm has special advantages (e.g., family ties)
- primary target countries
- secondary target countries
- indirect marketing efforts

Part V – An export budget

- pro forma financial statements

Part VI – An implementation schedule

- followup
- periodic operational/management review (measuring results against plan)

Addenda – background data on target countries and market

- basic market statistics: historical and projected
- background facts
- competitive environment

Source   US Department of Commerce (1990) *A Basic Guide to Exporting*, NTC Business Books, Lincolnwood, Illinois, p. 4.

Table 2.5 Comparison of the four export development models

Johanson and Wiedersheim-Paul (1975)	Bilkey and Tesar (1977)	Cavusgil (1980)	Czinkota (1982)
Stage 1 No regular export activities	*Stage 1* Management is not interested in exporting	*Stage 1* Domestic marketing: the firm sells only to the home market	*Stage 1* The completely uninterested firm
	Stage 2 Management is willing to fill unsolicited orders, but makes no effort to explore the feasibility of active exporting	*Stage 2* Pre-export stage: the firm searches for information and evaluates the feasibility of undertaking exporting	*Stage 2* The partially interested firm
Stage 2 Export via overseas agents	*Stage 3* Management actively explores feasibility of active exporting		*Stage 3* The exploring firm
	Stage 4 The firm exports on an experimental basis to some psychologically close country	*Stage 3* Experimental involvement: the firm starts exporting on a limited basis to some psychologically close countries	*Stage 4* The experimental exporter
Stage 3 Establishment of an overseas sales subsidiary	*Stage 5* The firm is an experienced exporter	*Stage 4* Active involvement: exporting to more new countries – direct exporting – increase in export volume	*Stage 5* The experienced small exporter
Stage 4 Overseas production manufacturing	*Stage 6* Management explores the feasibility of exporting to other more psychologically distant country	*Stage 5* Committed involvement: management constantly makes choices in allocating limited resources between domestic and foreign markets	*Stage 6* The experienced large exporter

Internationalization process

Source Ford, D., Leonidou, L. (1991) Research developments in international marketing: A European perspective. In Stanley J. Paliwoda *New Perspectives on International Marketing*. Routledge, London.

1 expectations of management, as a result of the impact of exports on growth
2 level of commitment
3 differential advantages to the firm
4 managerial aspirations, often related to security.

This incremental model identified three states of internationalization:

1 *Stimuli for experimental international involvement.* Non-exporters need stimuli to enter exporting. Cavusgil and Nevin identified external and internal stimuli. External stimuli often take the form of unsolicited orders from buyers or distributors abroad or domestic export agents. Banks, trade associations, and middlemen also serve as change agents. External stimuli clearly exceed the number of internal stimuli received. In eight separate studies, external stimuli (Cavusgil, 1976) accounted for 54–84 per cent of all stimuli. Firms which start exporting as a result of external inquiries exemplify a passive approach in international marketing, with an involvement which was fortuitous, marginal and intermittent, with short-run profits being likely to be the motivating force, rather than clearly formulated long-term objectives.
2 *Active international involvement.* This involves a systematic exploration of marketing opportunities imposing demands on the resources of the firm – physical, financial, and managerial which will test the willingness of management to allocate these resources. Smaller firms face an obvious disadvantage in not being able to commit resources, financial incentives do not immediately change matters. Another major determinant of active involvement in international marketing is management's experience-based expectations of the attractiveness of exporting for the firm.
3 *Committed international involvement.* The firm moves into the position of committed participants in international marketing. Now managers are constantly making choices in the allocation of resources between foreign and domestic markets.

Taken all in all, the internationalization approach does not appear to be a sequence of

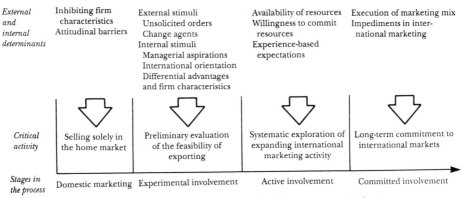

Figure 2.1 *A model of the incremental internationalization process of the firm*
Source Cavusgil, S. T., and Nevin, J. R. (1980) Conceptualisations of the initial involvement in international marketing. In *Theoretical Developments in Marketing* (eds Lamb, C. W., and Dunne, P. M.) American Marketing Association, Phoenix, April.

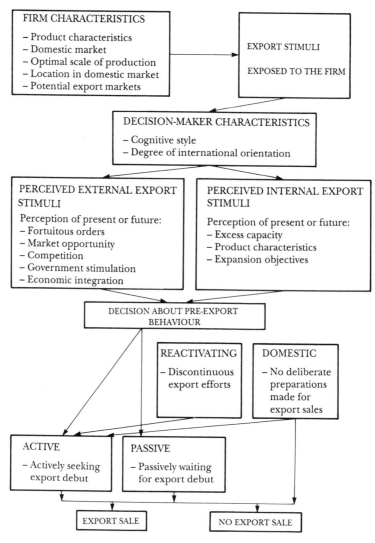

Figure 2.2   *Model of export propensity*
Source   Olson, H.C., and Widersheim-Paul, F. (1978) Factors affecting the pre-export behaviour of non-exporting firms. In *European Research in International Business* (eds Ghertman, M., and Leontiades, J.), North-Holland Publishing Co., New York, p. 285

deliberate planned steps beginning with a clearly defined problem and proceeding through a rational analysis of behaviourial alternatives. Personal characteristics of the decision makers; lack of information; perception of risk and presence of uncertainty seem to be especially valuable in understanding a firm's involvement in international marketing.

There are aspects of the internationalization process as having both a learning sequence as well as export stages. Czinkota's six-stage model overlaps with the previous models discussed, but emphasizes the experimentation aspect and the differences that may be induced by company size, small as opposed to large.

Figure 2.3 *Entry into foreign markets: the internationalization process*
Source Rugman, A. R., Lecraw, D. J., and Booth, L. D. (1986) *International Business — Firm and Environment*, McGraw-Hill, New York

Arguments against the 'stages' theory of internationalization

The sequential process of internationalization is similar then to the process of an adolescent growing up. It implies that there is only one way to go and that is to proceed further along the continuum. Rugman depicts this graphically in Figure 2.3.

Although depicting what is said to be a 'typical' process by which a firm producing a standardized product will seek to involve itself in a foreign market, it emphasizes the learning aspect of internationalization and the acquisition of market knowledge which reduces both risk and perceived risk. It does show that companies will change over time their form of market representation, but it shows that this can happen only in one direction and that the ultimate aim is foreign direct investment. In terms of knowledge and experience, the company will be in a much better placed situation than is the case at either the licensing stage or the stage which still uses agents or distributors. This is a useful and helpful contribution.

The stages model

Stopford and Wells (1972) suggested that multinational companies manage their international operations through an international division at the early stage of foreign expansion, when both foreign sales and the diversity of products sold abroad are limited. Different organizational structures are adopted at different stages of international expansion. Foreign product diversity is measured by the number of products sold internationally, while the importance of international sales to the company is implicit on the axis 'foreign sales as a percentage of total sales'. Stopford and Wells, therefore, saw the international division as an intermediate phase, as seen in Figure 2.4.

The international division is outlined in more detail below in Figure 2.4. This division is characterized by a staff group duplicating most of the functions of the corporate staff, which

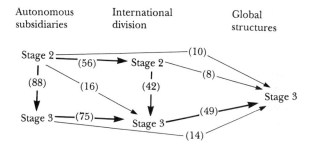

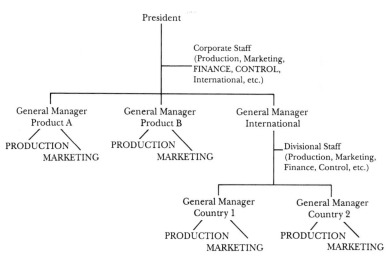

Figure 2.4.   *Sequences of structural change*
Note   The numbers in the arrows indicate the number of firms out of 170 that had undertaken the structural change by the end of 1968. Six cases of structural change by the end of 1968. Six cases of structural change in directions opposite to those shown are excluded. The term 'global structures' includes all the area division, worldwide product division, mixed and grid forms.
Source   Stopford, J. M., and Wells, L. T., Jr (1972) *Managing the Multinational Enterprise: Organisation of the Firm and Ownership of the Subsidiaries*, Basic Books, New York

Figure 2.5   *Internal structure of the international division*
Note   The functions in capital letters indicate operating responsibility; those in lower case indicate advisory and co-ordinating roles.
Source   Stopford J. M., and Wells, L. T., Jr (1972) *Managing the Multinational Enterprise*, Basic Books, New York

assists the general manager of the division. Later this duplication is lessened with the divisional staff group concerned primarily with the control of the foreign subsidiaries. It provides an illustration of how management procedures change as experience of international business is gained.

However, in other respects, this is not a working model. Companies, irrespective of size, will not actively follow this continuum. Instead, there will be within each company a portfolio of overseas opportunities being exploited simultaneously by a number of different modes of market entry across different markets. There is no one 'right' or 'best' strategy other than the one which achieves the highest degree of situational fit at that given moment in time. This means then that international modes of operation, once selected, have to be constantly monitored for effectiveness rather than instantly forgotten or, worse still, institutionally accepted. Some multinationals use the full range of market entry modes and representation across their different markets in Europe. A Single European Market creates further opportunities for rationalization of production and distribution (see Chapter 17). Thus, political and economic facts tend to diminish the effectiveness of the 'stages' theory as a viable policy option.

Internationalization processes for goods and services

To begin with, we shall start with some of the basic explanations traditionally put forward:

1 Product life cycle for international trade (Wells, 1968).
2 Product life cycle for international trade and direct investment (Vernon, 1966 and 1979).
3 Eclectic approach (Dunning, 1966 and 1988).

Taking these in order, we commence with the work of Louis T. Wells, which has held an important place in the international marketing literature for many years.

The product life cycle for international trade (Wells)

Essentially, the trade cycle identified four stages:

1 US export strength,
2 Foreign production starts,
3 Foreign production becomes competitive in US export markets,
4 Import competition begins.

Table 2.6   Preparing for the global market

> Changes expected in the next few years:
>
> - A unified Europe will emerge as a global economic power.
> - Other new trading blocs will form.
> - Japan's economic might will continue to grow, particularly in services and innovative products.
> - Investors will be seeking more opportunities throughout the world rather than concentrating on their respective domestic markets.
> - Competition among companies for new markets in developing countries and Eastern Europe will intensify.

Source   Anon (1990) Prepare for a global market, *Nation's Business*, September, pp. 29–30.

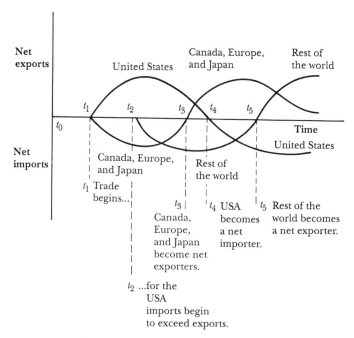

Figure 2.6   *Trade flows over the product cycle*
Source   Rugman, A. M., Lecraw, D. J., and Booth, L. D. (1986) *International Business: Firms and the Environment*, McGraw-Hill, New York

The trade cycle model was built uniquely around the US market, not that US entrepreneurs have ever had any monopoly over scientific knowhow or technical expertise, nor indeed has the US ever been the sole source of important technological breakthroughs and product innovations. The US market, however, is important in terms both of size and affluence. Wells made a statement that Porter would agree with, though, when he says:

It is also likely that the final product development leading to commercial production will be achieved by an entrepreneur responding to his own national demand.

There is consensus in the argument that a manufacturer ought to be close to his market, to be attuned to it and design for it. This means here a US base. When the product is in the early stage of the PLC, and it is not of major importance, quality is more important. Any foreign demand in the form of unsolicited orders (arising from the demonstration effect) is met by exports from the USA. As the demonstration effect continues, product familiarity abroad increases and foreign production starts. The foreign producer will have to cover factor costs, e.g., labour, which is expensive in the USA, but little or no product development costs. Imports from the USA give some guidance as to the market potential in the country concerned. The foreign producer may even be a US subsidiary realizing that if it does not start production abroad, someone else will. There are problems of scale economies, freight and tariffs. So, although foreign production has started, US exports still supply most of world demand.

In phase 3, the foreign manufacturer becomes larger and more experienced, so these costs should fall. With a different cost structure, they may be competitive with US-made goods in their markets. US exports must soon start to decline as foreign production becomes more and more competitive. The cost savings may be sufficient to enable him to pay ocean freight and US duty, and still compete with US producers on their own market. For the US producer in this situation, the only strategy is exit and future sourcing from abroad. This points to the phenomenon of 'runaway industry', whereby multinationals manufacturing products which are mature and, therefore, more price-sensitive, may continually move their bases of production around the world in a never-ending search for lower operational costs.

In phase 4, the foreign manufacturer reaches mass production and may have lower costs than his US counterpart, enabling him to pay freight and duty, and still compete favourably on the US market. A marginal pricing policy will bring forward the confrontation with US producers. US exports meanwhile have been slowed down to supplying only special customers abroad, while import competition is making inroads into the domestic market. Early foreign producers were seen to be most probably the West Europeans, who would then face a similar cycle. Manufacturers would then move down to lower income countries in a pecking order from country to country.

The cycle was not standard for all products of importance but were seen to share three common characteristics:

1 appeal of the product to the US market,
2 reduction in unit costs as the scale of production increases,
3 the cost of tariffs and freight,

Yet another factor was the product itself, of course, and so Wells classified the product again in terms of the US consumer. The US market reflected a particularly unique demand for products that fell into the following categories:

1 luxury function,
2 expensive to buy,
3 expensive to own,
4 labour saving.

Wells did say, however, that not all products could be expected to follow the cycle as they may be tied to a certain local national resource as with American cigarettes. The model did open the way, though, for market segmentation to play a role both in increasing exports and protecting against imports. Product differentiation can be advanced through a number of means, including price and design changes. Product appeal may be changed with a design change, and reflecting the needs of the home market, new product versions may be brought out for the wealthy consumer at home.

Product life cycle for international trade and direct investment (Vernon)

Vernon (1966)

Vernon starts with the premise that enterprises in any one of the advanced countries are not distinguishably different from those in any other advanced country, in terms of their access to scientific knowledge and their capacity to comprehend scientific principles. The ability to turn inventions into commercially successful innovations is not, however, equal among nations. Vernon moves away from the notion that knowledge is a universal free good, and introduces it as an independent variable in the decisions to trade or invest.

Attention is then turned towards the US market which, because of high individual disparate incomes, is an excellent market in which to introduce innovations aimed at high-level income earners. The US has high unit labour costs but relatively unrationed capital relative to other countries. This, too, conditions demand. Logically, then, goods which conserve labour would find a ready market in the USA. Because of the market potential, US manufacturers will invest more heavily in new product development than their counterparts in other countries, particularly with regard to products which substitute capital for labour, and are associated with high levels of income. In a similar way, Vernon argues that Germany's comparative disadvantage, in her lack of a raw materials base, led Germany to develop a world position in plastics.

Vernon's hypothesis is that US producers are closer to their market than producers elsewhere, and so they will be the first to identify an opportunity for high-income or labour-saving sources, and, consequently, the first production facilities for these products will be in the USA. The attractiveness of a US location can only be explained by forces that are stronger than relative factor-cost and transport considerations.

- In the early stages, the product may be quite unstandardized for a time and thus, this carries with it a number of locational implications.
- Price elasticity of demand for the output of individual forms is comparatively low. This follows from the high degree of production differentiation, or the existence of monopoly in the early stages.
- Need for swift effective communication, on the part of the producer with customers, suppliers and even competitors, is especially high at this stage. A considerable amount of uncertainty still remains regarding the market, its ultimate dimensions, competition, specifications of inputs needed for production, and the specifications of products likely to be most successful.

As demand expands, a certain degree of standardization usually takes place. Variety may appear as a result of specialization. While this product differentiation increases, a growing acceptance of certain general standards becomes established. This, too, has locational implications. The need for flexibility declines. Economies of scale, through mass production, become more important and this leads to long term commitments to some given process and fixed set of facilities.

Concern about production cost replaces concern about product characteristics, even if increased price competition is not yet present. Although the first plant may be in the USA, demand also begins to appear elsewhere. If the product has a high income elasticity of demand or it is a satisfactory substitute for high-cost labour, demand in turn will begin to grow in Western Europe. As the market expands, the question arises as to whether the time has come to establish a local production facility. While the marginal cost of production, together with the freight costs of exporting from the USA, is lower than the average cost of prospective producers in the market of import, US producers will delay investment. If economies of scale are being fully exploited, the principal differences between any two locations are likely to be factor costs. Thus, the servicing of third markets may take place from the new location, and if labour costs offset the cost of freight, the servicing of the US market as well. Vernon does not find rationality in the decision-making relating to lower cost locations abroad, but generally finds threat to be more of a stimulus to action than opportunity. Investment may, therefore, be a defensive measure. US manufacturers fear losing global market share while unaware of the production cost structure of their foreign competitors.

The Vernon Hypothesis would have the USA exporting high-income labour-saving products in the early stages of their existence; and importing them later on. Labour cost, which is high in the early stage, is high because the product is still as yet relatively unstandardized, and so with standardization comes a shift from labour intensive to capital intensive production.

With standardized products, the LDCs may offer competitive advantages as production locations, yet as Vernon points out, this leaves marketing considerations out of the reckoning. Information is not free but comes at a cost. If these products are selling on price, then the sources of market information become much less important. Significant inputs of labour, high price elasticity of demand for the output, are necessary characteristics as is production of standardized specifications for inventory without fear of obsolescence and the high value of items capable of absorbing freight costs. Vernon finds little evidence of corroboration apart from Taiwan's foreign-owned electronics plants. Japanese exports then (in 1966) were more capital intensive than the Japanese productions displaced by imports.

A reason for the lack of corroborative evidence may be that the process has not advanced far enough: due to export constraints and over-valued exchange rates. Capital costs are not a barrier to production in the LDCs.

1 Investments will occur in industries which require significant labour inputs in production.
2 Production will be concentrated in sectors capable of producing highly standardized products in self-contained production centres.

Capital costs have to be weighed against the opportunity costs, and so, this ability to compare rates internationally will not present any problems for multinational companies. The kind of investor here is not vulnerable to the limitations of only domestic capital in the LDCs themselves. Their access to capital becomes a direct function of their capacity to propose plausible projects to public international lenders. Vernon is aware of the imperfections, but is not afraid to challenge existing thought and literature.

Vernon (1979(a))

The world has changed since 1966. Firstly, in the geographical reach of many of the enterprises involved in the introduction of new products, they are now being found to have a network of overseas subsidiaries. Secondly, the differences between the markets of the advanced industrailized countries have much diminished. Consequently, Vernon now states that the product cycle concept 'can no longer be relied on to provide as powerful an explanation of the behaviour of US firms as in decades past'.

Nevertheless, some interesting points emerge. The assumption that the stimulus to innovation is provided by some threat or promise in the market is still there. The home market is still seen as the source of stimulus for the innovating firm and as the preferred location for the actual development of the innovation. Innovations reflect the characteristics of their market: USA with products responding to labour-saving or high-income wants;

continental Europe with products and processes that were material saving and capital saving; and Japan with products that conserve not only material and capital but also space.

The home market is still likely to be the first production site as the movement from research to development to production follows imperceptible stages. There will be minimal transportation costs. The specifications and manufacturing procedures are still undetermined; and there is, too, the characteristic inelasticity in the demand of the earliest users of many new products. Foreign demand is met from the home production plant although now Vernon is saying that the firm may consider other alternatives, such as licensing a foreign producer or establishing a subsidiary, balancing the delivered cost of exports against the costs of overseas production.

The decision to create a foreign producing facility is usually triggered by a threatened loss of market monopoly position due to foreign producers now ready to manufacture the product at lower costs.

Vernon points to the spread of the multinational's network of subsidiaries and affiliates, stating that innovating firms that are limited to their own home markets are no longer very common. In a study of 180 US firms, Vernon found that they typically set up their subsidiaries' product lines and new products, in a sequence that began with the geographical area with which they were most familiar, such as Canada and the UK and eventually spread to those that had originally been least familiar, such as Asia and Africa. With time, the unfamiliar became less so and the disposition to move first into the traditional areas visibly declined (Vernon, 1979(b)). Experience was another important variable. Firms that had experienced a number of prior transfers to their foreign producing subsidiaries, were consistently quicker off the mark with any new product, than were firms with fewer prior transfers. This change appears to be unaffected by changes in exchange rates or in price-adjusted exchange rates, so Vernon concludes that we are dealing with a basic change in the institutional structure of the multinationals concerned.

The descriptive power of the product cycle model was enhanced by the special post-war characteristics of the US market, then not only the largest single market in the world but by far the most affluent. Convergence has since taken place with many other countries approaching US income levels, and developing similar market needs and wants. This development weakened a critical assumption of the product cycle, namely, that the entrepreneurs of large enterprises confronted markedly different conditions in their respective house markets. The rise of the EC has been an important factor in creating new standard conditions within Europe. Other assumptions of the product cycle are therefore now questioned:

- it cannot be assumed that innovating firms are uninformed about conditions in foreign markets,
- it cannot be claimed that US firms are exposed to a very different home environment than their European or Japanese counterparts,

and

- differences among the advanced industrialized countries are reduced to trivial dimensions.

Vernon then classifies multinationals into three types to explore their likely behaviour as regards innovation:

1 The global scanner – the MNC with a powerful capacity for global scanning. Communication is virtually costless between any two points in the world; information storage and

retrieval on a worldwide scale is used to diminish risk and properly evaluate market opportunity. Innovations in response to market promise or threat can still be expected. Once the product was developed, all markets that had been identified by global scanning could then be served. As incomes rise, new markets emerge in a largely predictable pattern. New global producers might, over time, perceive an opportunity to expand, but lack now the size and the information resources of the multinationals. Whatever the original source of the exports might be, the hold of the exporting country would be tenuous, as the global scanner continuously recalculates the parameters that determine the optimal production location.

2 Producers of standardized products for homogeneous world demand, e.g. oil and chemicals. They are hoping for two benefits: to reduce or avoid the costs of processing and interpreting the information relative to the distinctive needs of individual markets; and to capture the scale economies of production and marketing on a global scale. Such firms are likely to perform consistently with the product cycle pattern. With ease of communication and transportation, the more routine aspects of product development can be directed to more distant locations. They may be able to respond to local host government demands in this manner, but they need to be integrated. The cross-hauling of components between various plants in advanced industrialized and developing countries is at odds with the product cycle. Not all companies will commit themselves to the development of standard global products even if they have the resources to do so. Different firms will make different decisions on strategies for products that are essentially seen as closely competing products.

3 Myopic innovation and home-oriented production remain while all analyses of foreign markets are left to individual foreign producing subsidiaries. The foreign subsidiaries may be allowed to select which home-based innovations they wish to transfer for production in their plant abroad. As long as this does not conflict with the activities of subsidiaries in other countries, local managers are given their independence. Explanations are seen in that the costs of processing the necessary information for a centralized policy of production and marketing as exceeding the likely benefits. Alternatively, the firm may not have the means to absorb, interpret and act on information from the subsidiaries. The product cycle is still valid here, but the role of the parent in serving foreign markets is foreshortened.

The global scanning explanation is limited and is not costless, as gathering information from the network of subsidiaries may not prove worthwhile. Flexibility is endangered. The conditions necessary for the product cycle are gone as regards the multinationals, but as regards smaller companies that have not as yet developed the resources for a global scanning activity, the assumptions of the product cycle may still apply. Even multinationals with global scanning are unlikely to make use of this facility in the siting of their first production facility, but as US home conditions are now found to be replicated abroad, only a 'shadow' of the hypothesized behaviour may well remain. Examples such as the utilization of national market characteristics in creating advantage, e.g., European and Japanese small car technology, fit within the product cycle, but would not be expected to remain with it for long.

Another aspect of this product cycle would be to expect that the industrializing countries, e.g., Brazil, Mexico, India, would start to initiate their own cycle of exportation and eventual direct investment in other developing countries. This, though, has only been reported among multinational subsidiaries. As Vernon states, the product cycle model, while it can no longer be relied on to provide as powerful an explanation of the behaviour of US firms as before, will continue to provide a guide to the motivations and responses of some enterprises in all

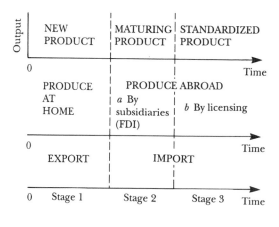

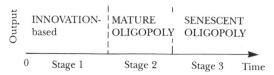

NEW MODEL (Vernon, 1977)

Figure 2.7   *Product cycle model – Vernon 1966*
Note   In stage 1 of Vernon's product cycle model the new product is produced and
consumed in the home nation. Exports take place. In stage 2 the maturing product can be
produced abroad, perhaps in subsidiaries of the MNE. Some of the good may start to be
imported by the home nation. In stage 3 the now standardized product is entirely
produced abroad, even by licensing. The home nation imports all of the good that it
needs. In Vernon's later model the stages are the same; only the terminology changes.
Source   Rugman A. H., Lecraw, D. J., and Booth, L. D. (1986) *International Business: Firms
and the Environment*, McGraw-Hill, New York

countries of the world. The link with the USA, or just the industrialized countries, has now
been totally broken.

Dunning's eclectic approach (1976 to 1980)

The word 'eclectic' was deliberately chosen to convey the idea that a full explanation of the
transnational activities of enterprises needs to draw on several strands of economic theory:
foreign direct investment, being only one of several possible channels of international
economic involvement, yet the one most closely identified with the eclectic approach.

The eclectic theory brings together three strands of economic theory: internalization
advantages; ownership advantages; and locational advantages. The propensity of a firm to
engage in international production depends on three conditions being satisfied:

1 Ownership advantages relative to firms of other nationalities in the same foreign market.
 These may comprise of intangible assets.

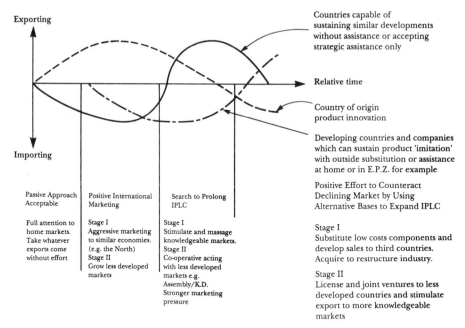

Exporting

Importing

Relative time

Countries capable of
sustaining similar developments
without assistance or accepting
strategic assistance only

Country of origin
product innovation

Developing countries and companies
which can sustain product 'imitation'
with outside substitution or assistance
at home or in E.P.Z. for example

Passive Approach Acceptable	Positive International Marketing	Search to Prolong IPLC	Positive Effort to Counteract Declining Market by Using Alternative Bases to Expand IPLC
Full attention to home markets. Take whatever exports come without effort	Stage I Aggressive marketing to similar economies. (e.g. the North) Stage II Grow less developed markets	Stage I Stimulate and massage knowledgeable markets. Stage II Co-operative acting with less developed markets e.g. Assembly/K.D. Stronger marketing pressure	Stage I Substitute low costs components and develop sales to third countries. Acquire to restructure industry. Stage II License and joint ventures to less developed countries and stimulate export to more knowledgeable markets

Figure 2.8 *Positive relationships between international product life cycle (IPLC) and inter-national commitment*
Source   Walmsley, J. (1989) *The Development of International Markets*, Graham and Trotman, London

2 It must be profitable for the firm to continue these assets with factor endowments located in the foreign markets, otherwise, the foreign markets would be served by exports (location).
3 It must be more beneficial to the enterprise possessing these advantages to use them itself rather than sell them, or the right to use them, to a foreign firm (internalization).

The eclectic approach suggests that all forms of international production by all countries can be explained with reference to the conditions in Table 2.7. These advantages are not static, but will change over time. A firm possessing an advantage can either use the advantage itself, or can sell or lease the advantage to other firms. Dunning points to the existence of multinationals as proof that some ownership advantages are transferable across national boundaries. An illustration of the eclectic approach as applied to the international hotel industry is provided by Dunning and McQueen in Rugman (1982).

Dunning's eclectic approach (post 1980)

Dunning concedes that the eclectic approach has only limited power to explain or predict particular kinds of international production or the behaviour of individual enterprises.

A country's propensity to engage in outward direct investment, or else receive foreign direct investment, will vary according to:

Table 2.7 The eclectic theory of international production*

---

1 *Ownership-specific advantages* (of enterprises of one nationality, or affiliates of same, over those of another).
   (a) Which need not arise due to multinationality.
       Those due mainly to size and established position, product or process diversification, ability to take advantage of division of labour and specialisation; monopoly power, better resource capacity and usage.
       Proprietary technology, trade marks (protected by patent, etc., legislation).
       Production management, organizational, marketing systems; R & D capacity; 'bank' of human capital and experience.
       Exclusive or favoured access to inputs, e.g. labour, natural resources, finance, information.
       Ability to obtain inputs on favoured terms (due e.g. to size or monopsonistic influence).
       Exclusive or favoured access to product markets.
       Government protection (e.g. control on market entry).
   (b) Which those branch plants of established enterprises may enjoy over *de novo* firms.
       Access to capacity (administrative, managerial, R & D, marketing, etc.) of parent company at favoured prices.
       Economies of joint supply (not only in production, but in purchasing, marketing, finance, etc., arrangements).
   (c) Which specifically arise because of multinationality.
       Multinationality enhances above advantages by offering wider opportunities.
       More favoured access to and/or better knowledge about information, inputs, markets.
       Ability to take advantage of international differences in factor endowments, markets. Ability to diversify risks, e.g. in different currency areas, and to exploit differences in capitalisation ratios.

2 *Internalization incentive advantages* (i.e. to protect against or exploit market failure).
   Reduction of costs (e.g. search, negotiation, monitoring) associated with market transactions.
   To avoid costs of enforcing property rights.
   Buyer uncertainty (about nature and value of inputs, e.g. technology, being sold).
   Where market does not permit price discrimination.
   Need of seller to protect quality of products.
   To capture economies of externalities and interdependent activities (see 1(b) above).
   To compensate for absence of futures markets.
   To avoid or exploit government intervention (e.g. quotas, tariffs, price controls, tax differences, etc.)
   To control supplies and conditions of sale of inputs (including technology).
   To control market outlets (including those which might be used by competitors).
   To be able to engage in practices, e.g. cross-subsidization, predatory pricing, etc., as a competitive (or anti-competitive) strategy.

3 *Location-specific advantages*
   Spatial distribution of inputs and markets.
   Input prices, quality and productivity, e.g. labour, energy, materials, components, semi-finished goods.
   Transport and communications costs.
   Government intervention.
   Control on imports (including tariff barriers), tax rates, incentives, climate for investment, political stability, etc.)
   Infrastructure [commercial, legal, transportation].
   Psychic distance (language, cultural, business, customs, etc. differences)
   Economies of R & D production and marketing (e.g. extent to which scale economies make for centralization of production).

   *These advantages are not independent of each other. For example, those listed in (2) may be partially dependent on how MNEs exploit those listed in (1).

Source Dunning, J. H. (1988) The eclectic paradigm of international production: A restatement and some possible extensions, *Journal of International Business Studies*, **XIX,** (1), 1–32.

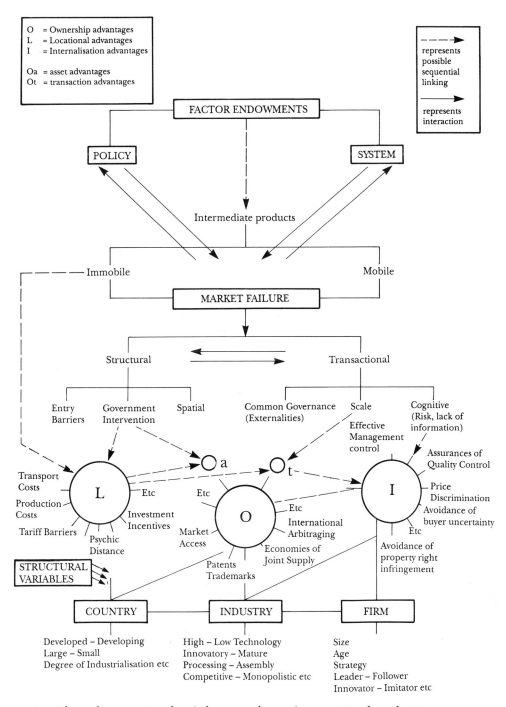

Figure 2.9   *The endowment/market failure paradigm of international production*
Source   Dunning, J. H. (1988) The eclectic paradigm of international production: a restatement and some possible extensions. *Journal of International Business Studies*, **19**, (1), 1–32

1 its stage of economic development,
2 the structure of its factor endowments and markets,
3 its political and economic systems;
and
4 the nature and extent of market failure in the transaction of intermediate products across national boundaries.

Dunning also draws the distinction between structural and transactional market imperfections. Market failure results from:

1 risk and uncertainty,
2 ability of firms to exploit the economies of large-scale production, but only in an imperfect market situation,
3 where the transaction of a good or service yields costs and benefits external to that transaction, but that are not reflected in the terms agreed to by the transacting parties.

The greater the perceived costs of transactional market failure, the more MNEs are likely to exploit their competitive advantages through international production rather than by contractual agreements with foreign firms.

In the restatement, Dunning makes two qualifications to the earlier version of the eclectic approach. Firstly, he is now drawing on the neoclassical theory of factor endowments to include intermediate products and the transferability of these endowments across national boundaries. Secondly, Dunning draws on the theory of market failure to explain, not only the location of some kinds of economic activity across national boundaries, but also the division of activity between multinational and uninational firms.

The more multinational a firm becomes, the more it is inclined to engage in internalized trade. Dunning, however, holds that internalization is only one of the three parts of the eclectic approach. It is one part not the sum of the parts, although it appears increasingly to be taken for the whole.

Looking to the future, Dunning sees the increasing complexity of foreign direct investment, and this modelling of transactional market failure requiring the fusion of a number of disparate approaches, pointing for example to the network approach developed by the Swedish researchers, Johansson and Mattson. Collaborative ventures between multinationals, their buyers and suppliers internationally will have important implications for all. (The Swedish work on the interaction approach to marketing is discussed in Chapter 8.)

References

Bartels, R. (1968) Are domestic and international marketing dissimilar? *Journal of Marketing,* Vol **32,** 56–61.

Bartlett, C. A. Ghostral S. (1989) *Managing Across Borders: The Transnational Solution,* Hutchinson Business Books, London.

Bilkey, W. J., and Tesar, G. (1977) The export behaviour of smaller sized Wisconsin manufacturing firms. *Journal of International Business Studies,* Spring, 93–98.

Bradley, Frank (1979) National and corporate images and attitudes in international marketing. *Working Paper Series No. 5,* Centre for International Marketing Studies, Faculty of Commerce, University College, Dublin.

Buckley, P. J., Casson, M. (1976) *The Future of the Multinational Enterprise*, Macmillan, London.

Casson, M. (ed.) (1983) *The Growth of International Business*, George Allen and Unwin, London.

Cavusgil, S. T., and Nevin, J. R. (1980) Conceptualisations of the initial involvement in international marketing. In *Theoretical Developments in Marketing*, (eds C. W. Lamb and P. M. Dunne), American Marketing Association, Theory Conference, Phoenix, April.

Clark, T. (1990) International marketing and national character: A review and proposal for an integrative theory. *Journal of Marketing*, October, 66–79.

Dunning, J. H. (1988) The eclectic paradigm of international production: A restatement and some possible extensions. *Journal of International Business Studies*, **XIX**, (1), 1–32.

Dunning, J. H. (1981) *International Production and the Multinational Enterprise*, George Allen and Unwin, London.

Dunning, J. H., and McQueen, M. (1982) The eclectic theory of the multinational enterprise and the international hotel industry. In *New Theories of the Multinational Enterprise*, (A. M. Rugman) St. Martin's Press, New York.

The Economist (1976) Business Brief, p. 68.

Forgren, M. (1989) *Managing the Internationalisation Process: The Swedish Case*, Routledge, London.

Gillespie, K. Arden, D. (1989) Consumer product export opportunities to liberalising LDCs: A life cycle approach, *Journal of International Business Studies*, Spring, 93–112.

Hood, N., and Young, S. (1979) *The Economics of Multinational Enterprise*, Longmans, London.

Ishikawa, K. (1990) *Japan and the Challenge of Europe 1992*, Pinter Publishers for Royal Institute of International Affairs, London.

Johanson, J., and Wiedersheim-Paul, P. (1975) The internationalisation of the firm: Four Swedish cases. *Journal of Management Studies*, **12**(3), 305–322.

Ohmae, K. (1985) *Triad Power: The Coming Shape of Global Competition*, Macmillan – The Free Press, New York.

Paliwoda, S. J. (1991) *New Perspectives in International Marketing*, Routledge, London.

Paliwoda, S. J. (1991) International marketing – Getting started. In *The Marketing Book*, (Baker M. J.) 2nd ed, Heinemann, Oxford.

Perlemutter H. V. (1969) Some management problems on spaceship Earth: The megafirm in the global industrial estate. *Academy of Management Proceedings*, New York, August.

Radice, H. K. (1984) The multinational companies and the disintegration of the UK industrial economy. Discussion Paper Series No. 138, School of Economic Studies, University of Leeds, England.

Root, F. R. (1987) *Entry Strategies for International Markets*, Lexington Books, Lexington, MA.

Rugman, A. M. (1982) *New Theories of the Multinational Enterprise*, Croom Helm, London and St. Martin's Press, New York.

Rugman, A. M., Lecraw, D. J., and Booth, L. D. (1986) *International Business: Firms and the Environment*, McGraw-Hill, New York.

Stopford, J. M. (1980) *Growth and Organizational Change in the Multinational Firm*, Arno Press, New York.

Stopford, J. M., and Louis, L. T. Wells (1972) *Managing the Multinational Enterprise*, Basic Books Inc., New York.

Turnbull, P. W. (1987) A challenge to the stages theory of the internationalisation process. In *Managing Export Entry and Expansion*, (Rosson, P. J., and Reid, S. D.) Praeger, New York.

Vernon, R. (1979(a)) *Product cycle hypothesis in a new international environment.* Oxford Statistical and Economic Papers, November, pp. 255–267.

Vernon, R., and Davidson, W. H. (1979(b)) *Foreign production of technology-intensive products by US-based multinational enterprises.* Working Paper 79–5, Harvard Business School, Cambridge, MA.

Vernon, R. (1966) International investment and international trade in the product cycle, *Quarterly Journal of Economics*, May, 190–207.

Wells, L. T. Jr. (1968) A product life cycle for international trade? *Journal of Marketing*, **32**, 1–6.

Walmsley, J. (1989) *The Development of International Markets*, Graham and Trotman, London.

3
Assessing the market infrastructure

In attempting to analyse the component parts of the international marketer's environment and the variables influencing his or her decision-making process, we have first to consider the question of exactly what constitutes a market before looking at ways in which we may come to properly assess them. In this chapter we will be studying the international environment from social, cultural and economic perspectives.

The social environment

The factors which drive international competition: costs of research, product development, market launch and the necessary market size to recover costs has meant that products need to be international and thus, so is the competition. International marketing has therefore moved from being a marginal activity to the centre of the company's operations. In so doing, brands have become international rather than national, but, as we shall see in Chapter 9, we have still a long way to go before reaching global branding. What is still happening is that the promotion for the brand can often be standardized more easily than the brand itself. Certainly, some brands have become universally recognized 'family' brands, e.g. Kellogg's and Ford Motor Co. always have their name prominently displayed before the branded product in question whether Kellogg's Corn Flakes or Ford Escort. In some instances, and this happens more on a country-by-country basis, brand names may have taken the place of the product class as is the case in Britain with Sellotape, Formica, Hoover, Thermos.

In some ways this may be seen to be unfortunate for the company in question because its branded product is now so taken for granted that it has lost any individuality and market attention. As regards global products, they are perhaps few in number but they are increasing (see also Chapter 12). Global products are classless; they are products without frontiers which benefit from international exposure whether it is an American Express card or Visa or Mastercard; McDonalds or Burger King; Coca-Cola or Pepsi-Cola.

The social environment shapes the collective attitude of the buying public to foreign companies, their product line and management orientation. A strong home country or ethnocentric approach by the company is likely to produce the most extreme reaction. It must be said that products which capitalize on their home origins may fall from favour quickly whenever political climates change. In the past this has happened to US multinationals such as Coca-Cola and American Express and to a lesser degree British Airways. A high degree of visibility as a foreign company may channel negative as well as positive feelings in society towards the home country in question. In this way, some companies suffer more than others as a result of a political backlash against the home country in question. Conspicuous links with the parent home country are to blame. To some observers it is simply the law of colonial ingratitude in that countries given independence, for example, retain only what may be called a 'love–hate' relationship with their former colonial master due to a grudging acknowledgement of political independence but not of total self-sufficiency. It will be interesting to see whether the Russians ever suffer a similar backlash in the future with their highly conspicuous Lada cars, as a consumer retaliation against Russian foreign policy in any part of the globe.

It must be said that the product or service has to be acceptable to the society in the foreign market for which it is intended. There are three levels as Terpstra (1983) has pointed out, at which the marketing mix operates as a possible agent of change within society:

1 *Folkways or conventions,* where social behaviour is learned and accepted, and followed habitually and do not require rationalizing. If someone, for example, devises a better way of doing things, the new method may very well be adopted, otherwise things will very likely stay as they are, and the status quo will remain. Calculators in Britain are very different today compared with perhaps fifteen years ago when they were relatively scarce and quite expensive; nowadays, they are used everywhere and their functions have also increased to include additional features such as an alarm, a stopwatch, or a musical instrument. It is a form of differentiation none of which is central to the main purpose for which it is bought. Persuading people to buy requires first selling them the product concept and making them aware, and then moving towards an understanding not only of the product class, but also of the particular advantages and benefits of the brand in question. Having arrived at this stage, it is relatively easy then to move consumers to a trial stage. Electronic cash registers are to be found everywhere in Britain today not just because they are more dependable than their electric forerunners but because they also incorporate a stock control and sales tax function as well and may also include an electronic funds transfer at point of sale (EFTPOS) terminal which with one simple pass of the customer's personal bank card will automatically debit his or her bank account with the sum in question. To succeed, though, an innovation such as an EFTPOS terminal requires acceptance both by retailers and by their customers.

2 *Morals* are the more strongly held and less easily assailable customs of a nation or sub-culture within the nation. A country may be composed of many nations, many peoples, many languages. It is unwise to give offence in the promotion of a product, particularly where it may offend the religion of people in the target market in question. An example in recent years was the arrival in Britain of 'Jesus Jeans' which featured a rear view of a girl's bottom in tight fitting torn denim shorts. This would have been acceptable but for the slogan underneath: 'If you love me, you'll follow me.' This company had to face the wrath not only of indignant church organizations but of many who, although they did not attend church regularly, nevertheless felt outraged. Their sensibilities were shocked by this form of blatant commercialization of the words of a man whom one half of the world regard as the son of God, and most others as a prophet. The moral here is that it is neither easy nor particularly wise to try to change the *mores* of a country; it is much easier and wiser perhaps, not to try.

3 *Laws* are the embodiment of the *mores* or the social norms of a country, but laws are always subject to review and pressure can be brought to bear by lobbying the legislature to make them aware of a given situation and to try and motivate them towards changing it. Laws are seldom more than a 'freeze frame' of society's views or wishes on a specific topic at a

specific moment in time. In a dynamic world, the relevance of laws must be steadily monitored for effectiveness. It is a rearguard action faced with technological change and changing social attitudes of a society that has itself changed, becoming more affluent and less religious than its predecessors. Laws quickly age. Financial penalties stated in an Act on the Statute Book may quickly be eroded by inflation; new technological developments such as video cassette recorders and personal computers give rise to arguments over the question of copyright over software and film; social trends such as a rise in illegitimate births create problems over the inheritance of property on the death of a parent; social change motivates pressure for that which was previously taboo, e.g. Sunday opening of shops. In other respects far from being anachronistic, the law may exhibit certain curious anomalies. For example, in England it is possible for video cassette shops to be raided by police and to be served a summons for offering for rental videos deemed to be pornographic yet which have been approved for nationwide general release in cinemas throughout Britain.

Increasingly, the interpretation of national laws has a great bearing on the activities of the international marketer. Polaroid started proceedings against Kodak when the Kodak instant film camera was launched in Britain. Although the argument is sufficiently complex for a whole battery of solicitors, barristers and technical experts to mull over for perhaps nine years, Kodak were permitted in the interim to manufacture and sell the camera in the UK. Although the decision will not have any direct bearing on its activities elsewhere, a judgement of the High Court of England will affect Kodak activities worldwide for better or for worse. Kodak, acting on their own, subsequently decided to withdraw sale of the instant film camera and film fearing perhaps a worst scenario situation of having to make restitution to Polaroid for worldwide sales. In a slightly different way, a decision by the FDA in the USA that a specific drug is found in certain circumstances to produce carcinogenic reactions will usually ensure a blanket ban in the UK as well, not because of jurisdiction, since the USA has no jurisdiction over the UK but as a precaution for the public well-being. In the same way the British Committee on the Public Safety of Drugs and Medicines may produce a similar effect in the USA.

Perhaps one of the great weaknesses of the age in which we live is that there is no international law for commercial disputes, only domestic law travelling imperfectly abroad. For example, in the creation of joint ventures with overseas partners, the terms of jurisdiction in the event of a breakdown have to be decided at the outset of the agreement. Very often a neutral country such as Switzerland proves useful, although its legal code may later be found to be lacking and so industry-wide international agencies may then be asked to arbitrate in case of dispute. No nation state has yet enacted laws within its national legal code or constitution which will allow it to deal effectively with all international trade disputes. Consequently in 1965 the Washington Convention established the International Centre for the Settlement of Investment Disputes (ICSID) which provides a conciliation service between a government and an investor. Where both parties are private persons or trading companies they can go to conciliation under the rules of the United Nations' Commission for International Trade Law (UNCITRAL) which lays down a procedure. Under conciliation it is the responsibility of the parties themselves to reach an agreement. The decisions of industrial arbitration councils or international bodies such as the International Chamber of Commerce in Paris are always considered carefully in the event of a subsequent court hearing. As more countries become signatories to the New York Convention more national case law will arise and the position of arbitration will become clearer.

At present, because of advantages such as cost and privacy, arbitration has moved from a second-best alternative position to the preferred choice (Minty, Chowdhury, Rao, 1990) of parties in dispute, as against litigation which brings with it unwanted public exposure to confidential areas of disagreement as well as the costs of professional legal representation to present argument and the costs of time measured over the duration of a court decision, balanced by the ability to enforce any subsequent damages awarded. The situation overall is unsatisfactory. Joint ventures which fail are allowed to lapse rather than be subject to divorce proceedings. Companies realize that once a venture fails it is probably too late for litigation, it being seen that litigation in the local national courts may produce only an unfavourable outcome anyway. Litigation then is only really for rather conspicuous cases where large sums of money have been lost through a failure of one partner to comply with his contractual responsibilities.

Arbitration is the next step and preferred to litigation on grounds of cost and privacy. Generally arbitration is regulated by the UN New York Convention 1986 and by the Model Law on International Commercial Arbitration of 21 June, 1985, devised by UNCITRAL. Normally there are three arbitrators who have been selected and approved by the two parties in dispute.

In other respects, the law and practice relating to commerce and industry can lead to changes in the social fabric. Product distribution in developed markets provides an example of various channels of distribution existing alongside each other: direct selling, retailing, wholesaling, 'cash-and-carry', factory-direct, door-to-door selling and house party selling. Mail-order and the 'house party' is US in origin but the concept has travelled well to other countries, including Japan. Nevertheless, it is possible for a country to make a quantum leap from developmental to advanced forms of retailing as France did in the 1960s with the introduction of hypermarkets (characterized by approximately 200,000 sq ft of sales floor space, usually like a very large warehouse conveniently sited close to a main highway with good parking and loss-leader petrol [gasoline] sales in the forecourt) without first experiencing a switch towards the US-style supermarket. Legal flexibility allowed this to happen in France but has constrained its development in the UK as local councils feared for the continuation of high-street shopping in the main city centres now being faced with this challenge to their continued existence by the out-of-town hypermarkets and their lower cost buildings.

The cultural environment

Culture is an extrapolation of the past. It is learned behaviour rather than innate, a characteristic emphasized in the *Oxford English Dictionary* definition which defines culture as the: 'Improvement or refinement of mind, tastes and manners; the condition of being thus trained and refined: the intellectual side of civilisation'.

It is ironic therefore to consider how the Nazi general Hermann Goering was once quoted as saying, 'When I hear anyone talk of culture, I reach for my revolver.' Culture is popularly used as a loose term to embody what is in effect a syndrome, as when we refer to the whole set of social norms and responses which condition society's behaviour. More than that, we tend to measure other cultures by our own. A self-reference criterion always comes into play in the assessment of a foreign culture, and this shapes expectations. When visiting foreign countries, a British salesman may find it unusual that the standard working day in Eastern Europe starts at 6.30–7.30 a.m. and continues without a lunch break until approximately

3.00 p.m. Unless prepared to expect it, he may find it difficult to adjust to a working pattern so different from 'normal' British pattern of one meeting in the morning and one in the afternoon. There may well be no-one around when he wants to do business! The same occurs with the length of the working week in the Middle East where Friday is not a working day but Sunday is. Again we could introduce, too, the further difficulty encountered with the multiplicity of local holidays worldwide as in trying to find a week in May when France does not have at least one public holiday. The obvious we can prepare for, e.g. local time differences are published and easily quantifiable but local resistance to change and innovation and the degree of psychological distance between two countries is many times more difficult to quantify and can only be experienced.

Maslow's Hierarchy of Needs (1954) depicting a pyramid hierarchy of needs would imply that lower-order needs must first be satisfied before higher order needs can initiate or influence behaviour (see Figure 3.1). As each important need is satisfied, the next most important need will come into play. It is interesting to note how many of our so-called global products, e.g. Kellogg's Corn Flakes, Coca-Cola, Pepsi-Cola, are intrinsically US products with global acceptance and so global demand creates availability. Their corporate approach is definitely ethnocentric, but on this Hierarchy of Needs is it a physiological or a higher need – e.g., esteem and social acceptance – which they satisfy? In many less developed countries, including the CIS, Coca-Cola and Pepsi are available at a premium. Other local products would suffice to quench the physiological need of thirst. Perhaps then there is more to these US products in terms of benefits brought to the consumer, of which some kudos, a taste perhaps of luxury, of merely being able to afford and have ready access to a Western product, are often the main motivations themselves. Actualization may arise from being able to have access to Western goods or goods that are otherwise scarce.

Again, what people say they drink at home, what they in fact drink at home, and what they will drink in company, are subject to a number of peer-group influences. This is society at work. The marketer's task is to try to understand the persona or personae, achieved by an understanding of the culture or cultures prevailing. According to Freud (1955) the real motives guiding behaviour were shaped in early childhood, where gratification was not always satisfied; and this led to frustration, which led to the development of more subtle means of gratification. Frustration and denial of need gratification led to repression, and feelings of guilt and shame with regard to that particular need.

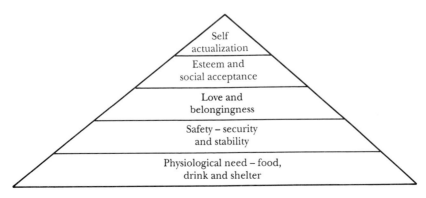

Figure 3.1 *The Maslow hierarchy of needs*

According to Herzberg (1966) human motivation is more readily understood when studied in terms of what he called 'hygiene' and 'motivator' factors. Firstly, there were those factors which did not in themselves create satisfaction but whose very absence may well cause dissatisfaction. Expectations of a particular product may be such that although a first-time purchaser, we nevertheless expect this product to be equipped or to perform to a certain specification. Cars, for example, are supplied with wheels and an engine as standard, although a stereo radio, digital clock and air conditioning may be included as 'extras', depending on the sophistication of the market segment at which it is aimed. Now, these features which are supplied as standard, are not motivators. Motivator factors are the second category according to Herzberg. These are the factors which do influence behaviour. To identify these factors precisely involves researching each individual situation, but the potential rewards from doing so are great. When the Japanese first started shipping cars to Britain around 1972 they met with instant success because their cars contained many features traditionally only found as 'extras' on other makes of car, and so would otherwise involve paying extra.

Definitional consensus on the meaning of culture

Alternative definitions from the one cited earlier in the *Oxford English Dictionary* add certain insights. Each of the following definitions seems to highlight a slightly different aspect of what may be understood by the term culture.

Culture consists in patterned ways of thinking, feeling and reacting, acquired and transmitted mainly by symbols, constituting the distinctive achievements of human groups, including their embodiments in artefacts; the essential core of culture consists of traditional (i.e. historically derived and selected) ideas and especially their attached values.
(Kluckhohn, C. The Study of Culture. In *The Policy Sciences* (eds Lerner, D., Cesswell, H. D.)
Stanford University Press, California 1951)

1. Artistic and other activity of the mind and the works produced by this. 2. A state of high development in art and thought existing in a society and represented at various levels in its members. 3. The particular system of art, thought and customs of a society; the arts, customs, beliefs and all the other products of human thought made by a people at a particular time. 4. Development and improvement of the mind or body by education or training. 5. The practice of raising animals and growing plants or crops. 6. The practice of growing bacteria for scientific use or use in medicine.

The Longman Dictionary of Contemporary English

Cultivation: the state of being cultivated; refinement; the result of cultivation; a type of civilisation; a crop of experimentally grown bacteria or the like.

Chamber's 20th Century Dictionary (1983)

1. The art or practice of cultivating; the manner or method of cultivating. 2. The act of developing by education, discipline, social experience: the training or refining of the moral and intellectual faculties. 3a. The cultivation or rearing of a particular product or crop or stock for supply. 3b. Steady endeavour of improvement of, or in, a special line. 3c. Professional or expert care and training. 4a. The state of being cultivated especially the enlightenment and excellence of taste acquired by intellectual and aesthetic training: the intellectual and artistic content of civilisation: refinement in manners, taste, thought. 4b. Acquaintance with and taste in fine arts, humanities, and broad aspects of science as distinguished from vocational, technical, or

professional skill or knowledge. 5a. The total pattern of human behaviour and its products embodied in thought, speech, action and artifacts and dependent on man's capacity for learning and transmitting knowledge to succeeding generations through the use of tools, language, and systems of abstract thought. 5b. The body of customary beliefs, social forms and material traits constituting a distinct complex of tradition of a racial, religious or social group. 5c. A complex of typical behaviour or standardised social characteristics peculiar to a specific group, occupation or profession, sex, age grade or social class. 5d. A recurring assemblage of artifacts that differentiates a group of archaeological sites. 6a. Cultivation of living material (as bacteria or tissues) in prepared nutrient media. 6b. Any inoculated nutrient medium whether or not it contains living organisms.

Webster's Third New International Dictionary

Matthew Arnold also had much to say on the issue of culture, viz:

Culture, the acquainting ourselves with the best that has been known and said in the world, and thus with the history of the human spirit.

Literature and Dogma, Preface to the 1873 edition

Not all countries are linguistically or culturally homogeneous but may, to take the example of India or Nigeria, comprise a few hundred subcultures each proud of their tribal or caste allegiance and each with their own language or dialect but communicating at a national level only by means of English. This reduction of population demographics into homogeneous units has been termed as 'clans', whereby members share a common set of values or objectives plus beliefs about how to coordinate efforts in order to reach common objectives. This is a basis for marketing segmentation, which is discussed more fully in the next chapter.

Cultural sensitivity is vitally important in international business. It is essential for the manager to be as aware of the similarities as the dissimilarities between the foreign market and his own. Too often, attention is paid solely to that which is different rather than that which unites. The Americans in the 1960s provoked a political response from the French when they profited from seeing Europe as one market while the Europeans still continued to see it as more of a patchwork quilt with too many languages and local differences to allow for uniformity. There is where part of the difference lies. It is possible to have a uniform product with a localized approach. The Japanese are no more culturally sensitive than other world traders but with good, well-researched products and locally adopted promotion have been able to make inroads into Europe despite tariff and non-tariff barriers including voluntary export restraint agreements.

When communication necessitates translation, a message becomes vulnerable to distortion by means of various idioms used that are peculiar to that foreign language. Ruthstrom and Matejka (1990) pointed to four different meanings of 'yes' in the Far East due partly to culture, and partly to a weak understanding of the language, viz:

1 *Recognition.* The first level acknowledges that you are talking to me, but I don't necessarily understand what you are saying. In many societies politeness demands that we recognize the words of the speaker either through a nodding of the head or uttering the word 'yes' more out of instinct and focusing on the conversation than any real affirmation.
2 *Understanding.* The second level acknowledges that you are talking to me and adds that I understand you perfectly, but I may have no intention of doing what you propose. This is similar to 'tacit agreement' in our US culture. The 'yes' means that your words and

meaning are clear to me. Whether I agree with what you are saying cannot be determined unless it is specifically asked.

3 *Responsibility.* The next level of 'yes' conveys that I understand your proposal, but I must consult with others and secure their agreement before your proposal can be accepted.

4 *Agreement.* The final level of 'yes' means that I understand, we are in total agreement, and your proposal is accepted.

Similarily, McCall and Warrington (1989) point to the use of language in compliance-gaining strategies as may be seen in Table 3.1. A standardized global advertising campaign is therefore most vulnerable to distortion, as a result not only of language but local slang, or regional dialect or 'patois' where this exists. Differences will be found also (Hall 1960) relative to other aspects of culture, e.g.:

- Material culture, e.g. attitudes towards acquisition of goods and services.
- Aesthetics, e.g. attitudes towards colour, brand names, design, music.
- Education, degree of national literacy, opportunities for university education, and employment of graduates.
- Mores – religion, beliefs and attitudes.
- Social organization whether hierarchical or not; role of women in society; etc.
- Political life – period of time it has been a sovereign independent nation; characteristics of its political life, whether democratic, one party state; etc.

On a comparative basis, attitudes may be expected to differ towards work and achievement; towards management; towards the concept of profit. Indeed the role of the consumer is clearly seen to be much more influential in the developed countries where he or she is deemed to be sovereign than the developing countries where some Western companies continue to sell products which have already been banned or voluntarily removed from their home market for some years. This applies to pharmaceuticals as well as high tar cigarettes to take two examples. General lack of education, low levels of literacy, poor communication and low levels of general awareness, together with political opposition, prevent consumerism from becoming a popular movement in the developing countries.

Assessing the cultural environment

Many attempts have been made over the years to devise a means of testing for cultural significance across countries. The all-pervasive effect of culture to be found in all aspects of life is reflected in the fact that Murdock (1945) composed a list of seventy-two cultural 'universals' (see list below). These could be found in all societies and encompassed amongst them courtship, dancing, incest, taboos, and sexual restrictions, although not necessarily in that order. These cultural 'universals' were to be found in every society known to man, and formed the essential social infrastructure.

Basis of comparisons would be drawn more easily now by identifying differences in attitudes with regard to any of these seventy-two universals. Hall (1960) went further with his *Map of Culture* which listed ten aspects of human activity which he referred to as primary message systems. Some things such as different languages could be compensated for by translation and interpretation but not so with differences relating to the language of time; space; things; friendship; and agreements. If we were interested in attitudes to learning we

Table 3.1 Language and compliance gaining strategies

Message strategy	*What the strategy implies*	*Persuasive message strategies*	
		Manufacturer	*Agent*
1 Promise	If you comply, I will reward you	If you agree to reduce your rate of commission, we will revoke the annual renewal of the agreement and replace it with one for five years	
2 Threat	If you do not comply, I will punish you	If you feel you can't reduce your rate of commission, we feel the market demand will be negligible and perhaps we should discontinue our relationship with immediate effect	
3 Positive expertise	If you comply, you will be rewarded because of the order of things	If you reduce your rate of commission, the stimulation of demand will result in a greater aggregate commission	
4 Negative expertise	If you do not comply, you will be punished because of the nature of things	If you don't reduce your rate of commission, our market share will fall even further and so will your annual commission	
5 Pre-giving	You reward target before requesting compliance		
6 Aversive stimulation	You continuously punish target to obtain compliance by making cessation contingent on compliance	We would certainly consider some way of speeding up commission payments on extended credit contracts if you were to reduce your rate of commission	
7 Debt	You owe me compliance because of past favours I have done you	We have regularly reduced our price under pressure from you, but have paid you full commission. We would hope that you will now reduce your rate of commission to ...	We have built up your business here as a result of our hard work and expertise. Surely you're not going to punish us for ...
8 Liking	You are friendly and helpful to get target in good frame of mind so that compliance will be achieved		

Table 3.1 continued   Language and compliance gaining strategies

Message strategy	Persuasive message strategies		
	What the strategy implies	*Manufacturer*	*Agent*
9 Moral appeal	A moral person would comply		You must agree a principle is a principle and not for negotiation
10 Positive self-feeling	You will feel better about yourself if you comply		If you accede to our request, you will live in the realization you have acted in an honourable way
11 Negative self-feeling	You will feel worse about yourself if you do not comply		If you were to insist on going back on your word, do you think you could live with yourself?
12 Positive altercasting	A person with 'good' qualities would comply	You are experienced and professional businessmen who, I'm sure will agree to the proposal in our mutual interest	
13 Negative altercasting	Only a person with 'bad' qualities would not comply	We know that when the chips are down your commercial judgement wouldn't let you make an ill-advised decision	
14 Altruism	I need your compliance very badly, so do it for me	It's important for you *and* us that we get the price down. I need your help and I'm asking for …	It's important for you and us that our relationship is maintained. I need your help and I'm asking for …
15 Positive esteem	People will think highly of you if you comply	If you agree to this reduction in commission, your associates will respect your judgement in the light of subsequent events	
16 Negative esteem	People you value will think worse of you if you don't comply	If you don't agree to this reduction events may well lose you the professional respect of your associates	

Compliance-gaining message strategies: The examples are drawn from a situation in which a manufacturer, because of appreciation of his country's currency in relation to that of the agent's country, is seeking to become more price competitive there. He is asking the agent to accept a reduced commission in line with his own reduction in margin in the belief that his business will be increased and that the agent will obtain a greater aggregate commission than under the previously agreed rate. The agent feels that there is a matter of principle involved and that his rate of commission should remain inviolate. Adapted from Marwell and Schmitt (1967) by McCall and Cousins (1989)
Source   McCall, J. B. and Warrington, M. B., (1989), *Marketing by Agreement: A Cross-Cultural Approach to Business Negotiations*, 2nd edn, John Wiley and Sons, Chichester.

Cultural Universals

Age grading
Athletic sports
Bodily adornment
Calendar
Cleanliness training
Community organization
Cooking
Cooperative labour
Cosmology
Courtship
Dancing
Decorative art
Divination
Division of labour
Dream interpretation
Education
Eschatology
Ethics
Ethnobotany
Etiquette
Faith healing
Family
Feasting
Fire making
Folklore

Food taboos
Funeral rites
Games
Gestures
Gift giving
Government
Greetings
Hairstyles
Hospitality
Housing hygiene
Incest taboos
Inheritance rules
Joking
Kingroups
Kinship nomenclature
Language
Law
Luck superstitions
Magic
Marriage
Mealtimes
Medicine
Modesty concerning
   natural functions
Mourning

Music
Mythology
Numerals
Obstetrics
Penal sanctions
Personal names
Population policy
Postnatal care
Pregnancy usages
Property rights
Propitiation of supernatural
   beings
Puberty customs
Religious rituals
Residence rules
Sexual restrictions
Soul concepts
Status differentiation
Surgery
Tool making
Trade
Visiting
Weaning
Weather control

Source   Murdock G. P. (1945), The common denominator of cultures. In *The Science of Man in the World Crisis*, (ed. Linton, R., Columbia University Press, pp. 123–42.

could not only examine responses to each of these ten variables separately but cross-refer also, to check what kind of interaction was at work between play and association or play or subsistence.

Eighteen possibilities would provide us with a more structured view of that particular culture. Looking then to each of his ten primary message systems, we have:

- Interaction, i.e. interaction with the environment through language or any of the five human senses.
- Association, i.e. grouping and structuring of society.
- Subsistence, i.e. feeding, working, making a living.
- Bisexuality, i.e. differentiation of roles along the lines of sex.
- Territoriality, i.e. possession, use and defence of space and territory.
- Temporality, i.e. use, allocation, and division of time.
- Learning, i.e. adoptive process of learning and instruction.
- Play, i.e. relaxation, leisure.
- Defence, i.e. protection to include medicine, welfare, and law.

- Exploitation, i.e. turning the environment to man's use through technology, construction and extraction of minerals.

An understanding of any civilization could therefore be attained through a study of the interaction of any single variable on this list with any other.

This attempt at using matrices to explain culture was developed further by Farmer and Richman (1971) who expanded the number of variables examined to seventy-seven. As a firm moved abroad, factors which were previously held constant – e.g. labour law or contract law – became variable as the firm found itself working within an individual framework in each country in which it was represented. Such differences could have an important effect on relative costs, influencing sourcing of inputs; forcing changes in production, marketing or financial processes; or by restricting price changes of outputs.

These variables could be identified as falling within four categories:

- economic
- political-legal
- sociological-cultural
- educational.

Farmer and Richman define an environmental constraint as

> some factor which prevents a firm from performing in a given way. The term 'constraint' implies some limitation of action, usually in the negative sense ... In one sense, every environmental factor is a constraint. One cannot have everything, and the limiting factors are the constraints referred to here.

Some of these variables have a direct effect as when there is a law relating to the employment of women or children. The second kind of impact which these variables have is in relation to the decisions and activities of managers. Managers are a product of their own culture, they argue, and their attitudes and perceptions are based on prior experience which, in turn, is in large part determined by the educational and sociological setting in which they have lived. This is the self-reference criterion, or set of criteria, we mentioned earlier. These research findings help us to understand and appreciate differences and to put parameters on culture, but culture still does not help us understand the functioning of markets and whether it is possible to differentiate between markets as between cultures. To some extent, this has been answered by Kay (1990) – whose work on identifying the strategic market we shall review in the next section – and by Barnhill and Lawson (1980) who developed a theory of modern markets characterizing markets as follows:

1 *Markets are purposive.* Exchange transactions are entered into and consummated primarily because participants to the exchange are seeking to achieve some purpose or self-interest. Exchanges are made to gain value whether in the form of personal, family or tribal sustenance; individual or corporate wealth; sales; market share; profits or some other purpose or desired condition.
2 *Markets are allocative.* Markets are initiated by the desire of bodies to reallocate their value, e.g., goods for other goods, goods for services, goods for money, etc. Markets provide means and stimulate activities that distribute goods, services, money, and other media of exchange.

3 *Markets are active.* While market potential and other latent conditions are ascribed to markets, interactive exchanges involving co-operation, competition, and conflict provide the overt characteristics of markets. These overt characteristics are necessary for classifying, organizing systematically, expressing quantitatively, and for predicting and controlling marketing (the interaction approach to marketing is discussed in Chapter 8).

4 *Markets involve operative activities or functions.* While an extensive list of functions characteristic of exchange transactions can be developed, four fundamental functions are production, finance, distribution and promotion.

5 *Markets tend to function in the form of exchange flows* at various levels of complexity, e.g. dyads, processes,and systems. In a single dyadic transaction there is a two-way flow of value, typically manifested by the movement of goods, services, money or other items of value between the two participants. Except where ultimate consumption occurs, exchanges seldom are limited to a single dyadic transaction. The flows inherent in market transactions continue as an on-going process that, in total or in aggregate, take on the attributes of more complex systems. Again, this ties in well with the IMP Group's Interaction Model which identifies the long-term nature of relationships between buyer and sellers in an industrial context, and the institutionalization and adaptations which will take place between them over time. See Chapter 8.

6 *Markets are dynamic.* Markets reflect the dynamics and complexity of exchange transactions and the conditions surrounding those transactions. The source of these dynamics can be identified as: (a) environmental, i.e. those forces and conditions that influence market participants but are outside their control; (b) transactional, i.e. those influences resulting from the exchange between and/or among the participants or a mega-body to the transaction; and (c) participant, i.e. those influences emanating, from time to time, from the parties involved in exchange transactions. Each of these sources may have a direct or indirect dynamic influence on exchange transaction(s) or the market(s) functions.

7 *Markets are constrained or inhibited.* Markets are not free or unfettered. They are constrained or inhibited by various forces and influences — among them being the ecology; resources; socio-cultural conditions; technology; economy; competition; and political, governmental, legal, and participant influences.

A set of ten inhibitors have been identified:

- ecology
- resources
- economy
- technology
- competition
- socio-cultural forces
- political influences
- legal influences
- governmental influences
- organizational influences

These ten are related to three stages of market activity — viz. entry, performance, and exit — in addition to four market functions — viz. production, finance, distribution, and promotion.

Rokeach value survey

There are five basic assumptions behind the Rokeach Value System:

1 The total number of values that a person possesses is relatively small.
2 All men everywhere possess the same values to different degrees.

3 Values are organized into value systems.
4 The antecedents of human values can be traced to culture, society and into institutions, and personality.

Table 3.2   Test-retest reliabilities of eighteen terminal and eighteen instrumental values, form D (N = 250)

Terminal value	r	Instrumental value	r
A comfortable life (a prosperous life)	.70	Ambitious (hard-working, aspiring)	.70
An exciting life (a stimulating, active life)	.73	Broadminded (open-minded)	.57
A sense of accomplishment (lasting contribution)	.51	Capable (competent, effective)	.51
A world at peace (free of war and conflict)	.67	Cheerful (lighthearted, joyful)	.65
A world of beauty (beauty of nature and the arts)	.66	Clean (neat, tidy)	.66
Equality (brotherhood, equal opportunity for all)	.71	Courageous (standing up for your beliefs)	.52
Family security (taking care of loved ones)	.64	Forgiving (willing to pardon others)	.62
Freedom (independence, free choice)	.61	Helpful (working for the welfare of others)	.66
Happiness (contentedness)	.62	Honest (sincere, truthful)	.62
Inner harmony (freedom from inner conflict)	.65	Imaginative (daring, creative)	.69
Mature love (sexual and spiritual intimacy)	.68	Independent (self-reliant, self-sufficient)	.60
National security (protection from attack)	.67	Intellectual (intelligent, reflective)	.67
Pleasure (an enjoyable, leisurely life)	.57	Logical (consistent, rational)	.57
Salvation (saved, eternal life)	.88	Loving (affectionate, tender)	.65
Self-respect (self-esteem)	.58	Obedient (dutiful, respectful)	.53
Social recognition (respect, admiration)	.65	Polite (courteous, well-mannered)	.53
True friendship (close companionship)	.59	Responsible (dependable, reliable)	.45
Wisdom (a mature understanding of life)	.60	Self-controlled (restrained, self-disciplined)	.52

5 The consequences of human values will be manifested in virtually all phenomena that social scientists might consider worth investigating and understanding.

Rokeach then goes onto define 'value' and 'value system' in the following terms:

- A value is an enduring belief that a specific mode of conduct or end-state of existence is personally or socially preferable to an opposite or converse mode of conduct or end-state of existence.
- A value system is an enduring organization of beliefs concerning preferable modes of conduct or end-states of existence along a continuum of relative importance.

Rokeach recognizes that values cannot be completely stable or else change would be impossible, nor, on the other hand, can they be unstable or else there would be no continuity. Thus, any model has to be able to incorporate both change and continuity. Citing Allport (1961) 'A value is a belief upon which a man acts by preference.' Rokeach then goes on to differentiate further in that an individual may have beliefs concerning desirable modes of conduct (which he refers to as instrumental values which may be either moral values or competence values) or desirable end-states of existence (which he refers to as terminal values, which may be self-centred or society-centred). Moral values relate to modes of behaviour which may give rise to feelings of conscience. Competence values relate to feelings of personal adequacy. Rokeach points out that an individual may experience conflict between two moral values (e.g., behaving honestly and lovingly), between two competence values (e.g., imaginatively and logically) or between a moral and a competence value (e.g., to act politely and to offer intellectual criticism). The more widely shared a value, the greater the societal demands placed on us. Nevertheless, Rokeach points out that man possesses far fewer terminal than instrumental values perhaps eighteen as against sixty or seventy. Yet values and attitudes differ:

> An attitude differs from a value in that an attitude refers to an organization of several beliefs around a specific object or situation. A value on the other hand, refers to a single belief of a very specific kind. It concerns a desirable mode of behaviour or end-state that has a transcendental quality to it, guarding actions, attitudes, judgements, and comparisons across specific objects and situations and beyond immediate goods to more ultimate goals.

Values, it is argued, occupy a more central position and are determinants of attitudes as well as of behaviour.

The Rokeach Value Survey (RVS) comprises two lists of eighteen alphabetically arranged instrumental and terminal values, each with a brief definition. The respondent is asked to rank them for importance. The value which is least important is then number eighteen. There are no prompted answers with this survey, the respondent has to fall back on his own internalized system of values to help him rank order the thirty-six values which Rokeach has distilled from a literature review and empirical research. Various tests have been conducted with different national samples as to reliability and validity measures. It has also been claimed by Brown (1976) that the RVS is the best values instrument available for management and organizational research given its design simplicity, administration convenience, reasonable measures of reliability and validity, ease of understanding by literate respondents and its self-involving, thought-provoking challenge of completion.

Payne (1988) points to a few of the criticisms of the RVS as being:

1 The ranking procedure used, normative or rating evaluations for each value may be more appropriate when investigating value perception.
2 Respondents are constrained to a standard set of values that may not effectively describe values that they recognize and view as important.
3 Values are suggested to respondents which may not actually be part of their cognitive worlds.
4 There can be questions involving respondent agreement concerning definitions, connotations or meanings of terms used in the RVS.
5 Interpretations of high- and low-value rankings must be made carefully. Rokeach poses several explanations for high and low values. A value may be ranked high either due to wanting something strongly that has been missing before or valuing something that has proved rewarding. Weakly held values may be the result of either not being mature enough to appreciate their importance or having a characteristic and over time taking it for granted.

Semiotics and the science of meaning of signs

The notion that all the seemingly disparate products of society work together to create a cultural framework has given rise to a new area of interdisciplinary research which business is turning to, and has been termed semiotics.

Semiotics as a sub-discipline in philosophy has been in existence since at least the early Middle Ages (Clarke, 1987). The term semiotics can be traced back to John Locke (1690) and is from the Greek *semeiotikos*, meaning an observer of signs, one who interprets or derives their meaning. Smoke as a sign of fire; clouds as a sign of an impending storm for the sailor at sea. One natural object or event which can be directly observed in the present standing for another which cannot. For example, as Hamlet picks up Yorick's skull it is a sign and a symbol of physiological development. Language is enhanced by the addition of signs making the one-dimensional, three-dimensional. Similarly the medical symptom as a means of diagnosing a patient's condition. Associative signs are signs as smoke/fire which stand for what is observable and for which there is a correlation in past experience between the sign and what it signifies. The stoics used certain signs such as a torch signifying an approaching enemy or a bell signifying the selling of meat. St. Augustine is on record as stating 'A sign is something which is itself sensed and which indicates to the mind something beyond the sign itself.' Later developments linked conventional signs with linguistic expressions and looked at the relation between them and the thoughts or conceptions they express. Lange-Seidl (1977) recommended that signs should be easy to represent, free from secondary notions and clearly distinguishable. This sign may be linguistic or non-linguistic, e.g. the causal effect of the object it is found to represent — bullet hole as sign of a bullet.

Locke's notion of semiotics as put forward in 1690 divided knowledge into speculative and practical (see Figure 3.2).

From this arose the concept of the semiotic triangle where there is an imputed relation between the symbol and referent. Symbolism arose from the need to give perceptible form to the imperceptible (see Figure 3.3). Yet further dimensions could be added with the mix of words and signs although in Figure 3.4 the word 'sphere' has many possible connotations and so has not been as fully or as clearly understood as might a graphical depiction. Language and experience are important in the interpretation of signs and symbols. Man is a thinking being

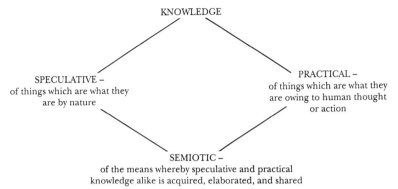

Figure 3.2
Source Deely, J. (1982) *Introducing Semiotic: Its History and Doctrine*, Indiana University Press, Bloomington, Indiana

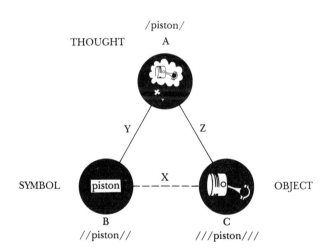

Figure 3.3 *A semiotic triangle*
Source Bunn, J. H. (1981) *The Dimensionality of Signs, Tools and Models*, Indiana University Press, Bloomington, Indiana

but in terms of trying to make sense of what he sees around himself he will fall back on himself and his own thoughts and experience to help determine exactly what he perceives.

Through language, experiences and perceptions may be shared. In Figure 3.5 language passes through different layers or groups of the social structure as a unifying process. The languages and signs of each of these groups or segments will differ. There is recognition here of society at work, of a mass public but of important differential groups or segments.

Semiotics is said to have come to prominence following the English translation of Roland Barthes' *Mythologies*. In essence, every positive trend will eventually give rise to a negative trend and so to take one example, the problems of inner-city living will create an interest in

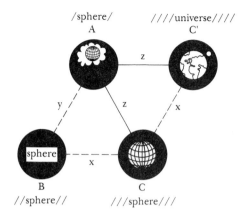

Figure 3.4
Source   Bunn, J. H. (1987) *The Dimensionality of Signs, Tools and Models*, Indiana University Press, Bloomington, Indiana

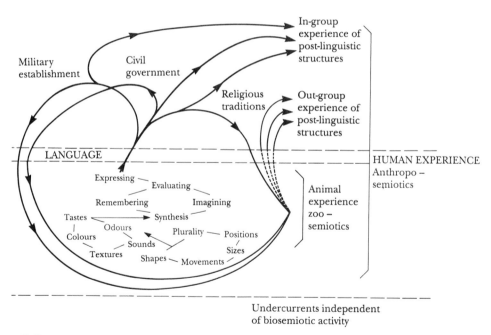

Figure 3.5

small-town and rural life. Pursuing this line of thought further, according to semiotics there can be no creativity in advertising as we are simply borrowing themes from our everyday experience, e.g., nostalgia and togetherness, and so we are not creating them. The semiotician (the practitioner of semiotics) and the advertising executive differ in that the semiotician believes that one must relate to more than one cultural sign. It is indeed likely that in future years, more will be heard about semiotics in international business activity. For the moment, much empirical and intellectual work has still to be done to develop this area as Lange-Seidl (1977) pointed out that methods which had proved useful heuristically were still not established theories.

Economic environment

A macro-environment is created when trade and transactions take place across, rather than within, national frontiers; but it is important to note that there may well be greater similarity in comparing market segments across countries than within the same country. Within any one country there are often large gaps between disposable incomes and prices in one area relative to another part of the country. This is a marketing problem and yet these differences pose both problems and opportunities for foreign firms. Selecting market segments and comparing size, measurability access and substantiality of market segments across markets often reveals greater similarity across countries than within, lending support therefore to the concept of market segmentation.

Uncompetitiveness leads to protectionism despite the best efforts of GATT to dismantle obstacles to trade; and so the constraints which are imposed on foreign firms are less in the form of tariff barriers than 'non-tariff' or 'invisible' barriers such as health and safety standards, or hygiene standards. The rationale behind these measures is simply to stem the flow of imports into the country, sometimes also to protect an infant indigenous industry from the pressures of overseas competition flooding into the home market.

Defining the market

Having examined the functions of a market it is important now to assess this in terms of the firm. Kay (1990) defines the strategic market as 'the smallest area within which it is possible to

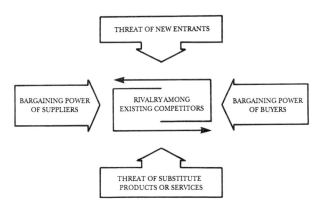

Figure 3.6 *Porter: five competitive forces that determine industry competition*
Source Porter, M. E. (1990) *The Competitive Advantage of Nations*, Macmillan, The Free Press, New York

```
┌─────────────────────────────────────────────────────────────────┐
│                         The car market                           │
│                                                                   │
│                                  The product dimension            │
│                                                                   │
│                          Small    Volume    Large    Luxury       │
│                Country                                            │
│   The                          ┌──────────────────────┐          │
│   geographic   Continental     │        Peugeot       │  ┌──────┐ │
│   dimension                    │                      │  │      │ │
│                                └──────────────────────┘  │ BMW  │ │
│                                                          │      │ │
│                Global                                    └──────┘ │
│                                                                   │
└─────────────────────────────────────────────────────────────────┘
```

Figure   3.7   *The car market*
Source   Kay, J. A. (1990) Identifying the strategic market. *Business Strategy Review,*
Spring, 2–24

be a viable competitor.' In terms of competition, Porter identifies five main forces (as shown in Figure 3.6).

Kay separates the dimensions of the market from those of the industry whether product or geographically based. Taking the car market as an example (see Figure 3.7). Porter argues that the type and scope of advantage can be used to develop a typology of strategies clearly emphasizing that there is no one type of strategy appropriate for every industry but that different strategies can and do coexist successfully in many industries (see Figure 3.8).

Kay shows how it is possible to compete either by differentiating across product classes or focusing within a product segment as does BMW for example in luxury cars. This ties in with Porter (1990) who uses similar examples in talking of competitive scope and different paths to globalization. The drug Zantac, is adapted for local markets and so is a multidomestic brand rather than a global brand. Yet in assessing markets it is sometimes difficult to arrive at the necessary level of disaggregation to obtain the information necessary for planning and control. Standard industrial classifications lack specificity. Kay cites the example of refrigera-

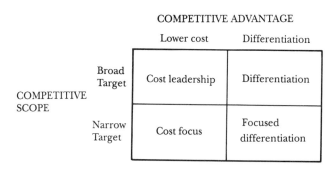

Figure   3.8   *Porter's generic strategies*
Source   Porter, M. E. (1990) *The Competitive Advantage of Nations,* Macmillan, The Free Press, New York

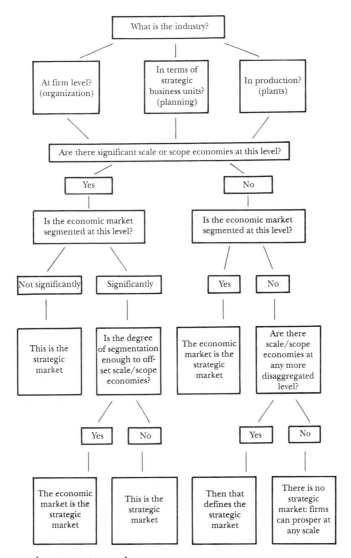

Figure 3.9   *Deriving the strategic market*
Source   Kay J. A. (1990) Identifying the strategic market. *Business Strategy Review*, **Spring**, 2–24

tors and washing machines being grouped together because they are often made by the same firms and use some interchangeable technology and componentry.

As marketers know, it is not necessary to serve the whole of a single market but to identify those segments which the firm is best equipped to serve. It is important to identify the market correctly, neither too narrowly nor too widely (see Figure 3.9).

Over time, new possibilities for competing will arise typically either through discontinuity or a change in the industry structure. These, again, according to Porter (1990) will arise out of:

1 new technologies,
2 new or shifting buyer needs,

3 emergence of a new industry segment,
4 shifting input costs or availability,
5 changes in government regulations.

Porter's generic strategies differentiate in terms of cost and differentiation. Focused differentiations have concentrated on specialized areas of production which command higher prices. The error that companies make according to Porter is to try to pursue simultaneously all of the strategies.

General Agreement on Tariffs and Trade (GATT)

The General Agreement on Tariffs and Trade (GATT) is not just one treaty but a large cluster of around 180 which have shaped the constitution and thus direction of GATT, its membership and mission. Since its inception in 1948 to reduce tariff barriers each of its seven negotiating 'rounds' has lasted an average of nine years which illustrates clearly the difficulties involved in freeing trade. The most recent, the Uruguay round, was the most difficult because negotiations were already taking place in a changed world trading situation moving further into recession and towards protectionism of areas in which the developed countries are strong and the developing countries weak, as is the case in services. Examples of protectionism abound in the practices of industrial countries *vis-à-vis* the less developed nations of the world.

There are now ninety-seven member countries of GATT which account for more than four-fifths of world trade. The basis of GATT is that trade should not be discriminatory and that preference should be given to the developing countries which account for two-thirds of the membership. Under the terms of GATT membership, nations agree to apply their most favourable or lowest tariff rate to fellow GATT signatories, but within GATT it is possible still to have preferential tariff rates. There is a basic GATT signatory tariff rate but also a preferential rate which the UK, for example, may wish to use to encourage trade with Commonwealth countries, particularly the less developed countries. Much Favoured Nation (MFN) status is the highest degree of preferential treatment that may be accorded to a fellow GATT signatory and is accorded on a bilateral basis. The Soviet Union failed some years ago to receive MFN status from the USA when the Carter Administration was unable to get the measure through Congress, where it ran aground over criticism of human rights within the Soviet Union. Subsequently, the Reagan Administration withdrew MFN status from East European countries. When martial law was imposed in Poland although political changes in that region of the world have since been quite dramatic and have led to a rethinking of all the political and defence alliances created since the war. MFN status may be seen then to have become a political means of rewarding or punishing countries.

With regard to farm subsidies, the EC, now accounting in itself for 38 per cent of world trade, is divided among its members. The EC has its own famous surpluses of agricultural produce and so is unable to make concessions in the way of trade for developing countries which are crop dependent. The situation for both industrial and less developed countries has been exacerbated by the world trade recession, in which agriculture looks likely to tear down the structure of GATT itself. The GATT Council, meanwhile, appears impotent, lacking consensus among its members to take any firm action that cannot be easily circumvented. Exhibit 3.1 sets out the issues facing GATT which in the current Uruguay round focuses on trade in services, trade-related aspects of intellectual property rights and trade-related investment measures.

The previous Tokyo round 1973–9 had been successful in addressing a number of the increasing non-tariff barriers to international trade. Yet there was a price to be paid for GATT was unable to rewrite its own constitution and so as regards the results relating to the non-tariff measures of the Tokyo round, these have been incorporated into 'side' codes which bind only those nations which separately accept them. Amending GATT rules requires a two-thirds acceptance of its members. Nevertheless, the Tokyo round produced nine special agreements, four 'understandings' on special issues describing procedures which were arguably already followed and protocols on tariff reduction.

Tariff barriers

Tariff barriers include:

- taxes, duties comprise the following:

1 *Ad valorem.* This is a percentage of the value of the goods, calculated on the landed CIF cost at port of entry.
2 *Specific duty.* This is a specific amount of currency per weight, volume, length, or number of units of measurement. It is expressed in the currency of the importing country.
3 *Alternative duty.* Applicable rate is that which yields the higher amount of duty.
4 *Component or mixed duties.*
5 *Temporary import surcharges.* Under GATT rules these must only be temporary. This device has been used in the past by Britain and the USA.
6 *Compensatory import taxes.* Manufacturers in VAT countries do not pay VAT on exports to non-VAT countries but all US manufacturers still pay and have no tax relief from the tax equivalent in the USA.
7 Anti-dumping duties.

- Customs union or common market such as EC which maintains an external tariff.
- 'Countervailing' duty is designed to raise the price of the cheapest import to the price of the nearest domestic competitor by adding the necessary additional tax to the import.
- 'Drawback' duty repaid if imported goods re-exported
- Tariff schedule
    single column (same tariff regardless of origin)
    multi-column (discriminated with regard to origin).
- 'MFN' or 'much favoured nation' status which is accorded between trading nations, is permissible under GATT regulations, and allows for bilateral trade or preferential rates of tariff duty.

Non-tariff barriers (NTBs)

These are becoming increasingly more common. As GATT continues to fight for the reduction of tariffs worldwide, sovereign states apply their ingenuity to the creation of 'invisible tariffs'. These may take many forms but their ultimate aim is to exclude or at least

Exhibit 3.1 *A simple summary of the 15 issues being thrashed out in the current round of trade talks*

What all the fuss is about

The Globe and Mail

OTTAWA – The current rules governing international trade are as complicated as the jargon being used to describe them. What the GATT round is all about is establishing a simple set of rules to which everyone can agree.

The negotiations are being conducted in 15 groups – 14 dealing with trade in goods and one dealing with services. Below is a list of the groups, some of which overlap:

Tariffs: Countries commonly levy an import tax or duty on imported goods to protect domestic manufacturers. This makes the imported good more expensive for consumers to buy. For example, the purchase price of an imported Japanese car such as the Mazda MX-6 includes a 9.2 per cent import duty.

Non-Tariff Measures: NTMs restrict imports, making them more expensive for consumers to buy without actually imposing a tariff. The orderly marketing arrangement fits in this category. In the early 1980s, Japan had such an agreement with Canada. Japan agreed to export only a certain number of its popular and cheap cars and Canada agreed to accept them. The Canadian consumer paid a higher price because of the limited supply.

Natural Resource-Based Products: Talks are aimed at reducing tariffs and non-tariff barriers on natural resource products. This would help such Canadian industries as lumber and mining (which account for some of the three million jobs that depend on exports) penetrate other markets.

Textiles and Clothing Ever wonder why a cotton blouse made in Bangladesh for pennies, costs dollars when it reaches a Canadian store? Part of the reason is that Canada has signed a number of agreements with countries that produce textiles and clothing limiting the amount they can export to Canada. As in the case of Japanese cars, squeezing the supply available to Canadian consumers increases the price and makes foreign clothing less competitive with Canadian-manufactured textiles and apparel.

Agriculture: Among other things, negotiators are arguing about government subsidies paid to farmers to produce goods for the domestic market and to export abroad. Canadian wheat farmers say subsidies paid to their competitors by the U.S. government and the EC have led to massive international surpluses and driven down the world price, thus making it difficult for Canadian farmers to make a living.

Tropical Products; These talks focus on goods produced mainly in tropical countries such as coffee, tea, sugar, exotic fruits and rubber, all of which could become more expensive for Canadians if the talks collapse.

GATT Articles: The original GATT agreement dates back to 1947. World trade has changed considerably since then. Members want to clarify and strengthen some language and add other articles to cover new trade developments. Canada would like the wording of Article 11 changed so there is no doubt that GATT sanctions Canada's system of supply management under which dairy products, poultry and eggs are produced. Under supply management, domestic production of these commodities is matched to domestic consumption and imports are restricted in order to maintain that balance.

Multilateral Trade Negotiations Agreements and Arrangements: In previous GATT rounds, members reached a number of agreements that also need to be updated and clarified. One such agreement covers technical barriers to trade. When the EC refused, for what it said were health reasons, to allow imports of U.S. beef that contained a certain hormone, it erected a technical barrier to trade.

Safeguards: If there is a sudden flood of imports into a country, the government is allowed to protect domestic manufacturers from the surge temporarily by setting quotas, imposing tariffs and signing voluntary agreements with the exporting countries. For years, Canada had so-called temporary protection for footwear, which made imported shoes more expensive.

Subsidies and Countervailing Measures: If it can be proven that a government has subsidized certain exports and this is causing injury to a domestic industry, the importing country can impose a countervailing duty equal to the government subsidy. Canada imposed a hefty countervailing duty on U.S. corn imports for a while. It was reduced when Canadian farmers said the countervailing duty was hurting them.

Trade-Related Aspects of Intellectual Property Rights (TRIPs), including Trade in Counterfeit Goods: Those fake Rolexes would become a thing of the past if all countries agreed to crack down on anyone who infringed patent, copyright or trademark protection. In the short-term con-sumers would pay the higher prices for originals. But there are long-term benefits if companies spend money on research to produce software, new fashion designs, pharmaceuticals and anything else requiring innovation.

Trade-Related Investment Measures: If Country A will not buy fighter airplanes from Country B unless Country B agrees to set up a plant in Country A to produce the engines for the planes, that is called a trade-related investment measure, or TRIM. Sometimes known as industrial offsets, these measures have been used extensively by Canada, particularly on defence contracts.

Dispute Settlement: Once negotiators agree on a set of rules, GATT members still need an efficient method of dealing with disputes. The current system requires unanimous consent at important stages of the dispute settlement process, so a country found in breach of GATT can still block the adoption of a censuring report.

Functioning of the GATT System: This negotiating group, also known as FOGS, is examining how the GATT secretariat might be more effective in monitoring its members and reporting on their conduct.

Services: Services cover a broad area, including civil aviation, shipping, telecommunications and financial services. One touchy issue heading into the Brussels meeting is whether the bilateral agreements that allow certain airlines landing rights at certain airports should be changed to multilateral arrangements so that once one country can land at an airport, all GATT countries can land.

Source   Globe and Mail (1990), Toronto, 3 December.

stem the flow of, foreign imports of any given good or politically sensitive item. NTBs may take the following forms:

1 Specific limitations including quotas and import restraints (VER = Voluntary Export Restraints). Once the quota is filled, the price mechanism is not allowed to operate. With VERs there is a 'voluntary' agreement which demands compliance.
2 Discriminatory governmental and private procurement policies, e.g. 'buying national'. One of the major barriers to fall within the EC after 1992 is public procurement previously closed to all but national suppliers. Also state trading and subsidies.
3 Restrictive customs procedures on validation, classification, documentation, health and safety and hygiene.
4 Selective monetary controls and discriminatory exchange rate, controls, e.g. the requirement for an advance deposit equal to the value of the imported goods.
5 Restrictive administrative and technical regulation including standards for products, packaging, labelling and marketing.

Government procurement and corporate 'buy-national' policies

It is a common enough phenomenon to find companies pursuing an implicit or explicit 'buy national' policy. Governments do likewise as they have to consider the employment effects of sourcing. They also have to consider the national interest in the placing of any orders for defence equipment or for products resulting from a research programme that has been heavily funded by government finance. Local government authorities often also choose to exercise their political right to choose suppliers of equipment on such bases as these. What has changed is that some of the largest international companies are moving towards single sourcing of components. This makes open-tender contracts more lucrative and the loss of such contracts can have a serious impact on the firms involved. EC regulations are now being used to challenge the status quo and open up competitive bidding to outsiders.

The Single European Market is discussed in more detail in Chapter 17, but this issue of

Table 3.3 GATT negotiating rounds

Round	Dates	Number of countries	Value of trade covered
Geneva	1947	23	$10 billion
Annecy	1949	33	Unavailable
Torquay	1950	34	Unavailable
Geneva	1956	22	$2.5 billion
Dillon	1961	45	$4.9 billion
Kennedy	1962–7	48	$40 billion
Tokyo	1973–9	99	$155 billion

Source Jackson, J. H. (1989) *Restructuring the GATT System*, Pinter Publications for Royal Institute of International Affairs, London.

public procurement is an important one as it has traditionally been a market closed to all but national suppliers and yet is estimated as being worth 15 per cent of GDP within the European Community. Good reason has now to be provided for any member state of the European Community going outside of what is now established Community policy. Defence is an area which is more integrated than before on a European-wide scale but in which national government discretion may be used in the choice of suppliers.

Accusations still continue unabated of 'dirty' business regarding government grants to companies who buy national, etc. In 1982, Burroughs, for example brought a court action against the Oxford Regional Health Authority which awarded a contract to ICL Computers Ltd for a pilot 0.5 million pound deal leading to an eventual 16 million pound deal. The British Government is then said to have stepped in and recommended ICL for the contract. Unsubstantiated evidence which had come the way of Burroughs had indicated that they had

Table 3.4 Tariff averages* on industrial products (excluding petroleum†) for ten developed markets before and after the implementation of the Tokyo round agreements

Market	Pre-Tokyo round	Simple average post-Tokyo round	Per cent reduced	Pre-Tokyo round	Weighted average‡ post-Tokyo round	Per cent reduced
USA	12.1	7.0	42	6.2	4.4	30
European Community	8.1	5.6	31	6.6	4.8	27
Japan**	10.2	6.0	41	5.2	2.6	49
Canada	12.4	7.2	42	12.7	7.9	38
Sweden	5.9	4.8	19	5.2	4.3	23
Norway	8.5	6.5	23	4.2	3.2	23
Switzerland	3.8	2.8	26	3.2	2.5	23
New Zealand	26.2	20.0	24	22.4	17.6	21
Austria	11.6	8.1	30	9.0	7.8	13
Finland	13.0	11.2	14	6.0	4.8	20
Total	10.6§	6.5§	38	7.2§	4.9§	33

*The comparability of tariff levels, and of their practical incidence, is affected by differences in methods of valuation for customs purposes. The tariff averages set out in the table cover duty-free items.

†Items CCN 2709 and 2710 are excluded.

‡Here the simple average on each tariff line is weighed by each market's MFN imports on that line. In due course the GATT Secretariat will no doubt calculate weighted averages on the basis of total world trade in each tariff item.

**After implementing the Kennedy round agreement Japan reduced her tariffs unilaterally by 20 per cent across-the-board.

§Weighted by the trade of each country.

Source *Euro–Asia Business Review*, February 1985, p. 41.

Table 3.5 The evolving economy

Old economy	New economy
(a) Standardized output Assembly lines	(a) Customized goods and services Increased variety and bundling of goods and services
(b) In-house production services	(b) Externalization of services, networking, interlinkages
(c) Local, national markets	(c) Internationalization of production and competition
(d) Vertical integration Large corporations	(d) Vertical disintegration Small firms, large transnational conglomerates
(e) Rigid embodiment of technology	(e) Flexible production modes
(f) Material inputs, outputs	(f) Non-material investments, human resource and knowledge-based inputs
(g) Factory, blue-collar employment	(g) Office, white-collar employment
(h) Sectoral regulation	(h) New forms of regulation

Source   Nicolaides, P. (1989) *Liberalising Service Trade*, Routledge, London.

won the contract on both price and performance and that ICL had come last of the bidders for the contract. The fact was that ICL were now being awarded the contract. Burroughs then took the matter to the High Court and to the Appeal Court but lost their action on each occasion, the courts refusing to award an injunction to halt the contract as they believed that it would be impossible to police '... as it would involve tracing the thought processes of the Authority's members, were they to meet again and confirm the ICL contract.'

Another similar case arose over the award of a 14 million pound contract by the Severn Trent Water Authority to ICL. This time it was over the heads of IBM who then sought in the High Court an order to require the Authority to review its decision, alleging that the Authority had violated its own rules and criteria. The Severn Trent Water Authority did decide to meet and review the decision but only ratified the contract that had already been awarded to ICL. Being a semi-autonomous body, it was also outside the EC regulations on competitive bidding. While accepting this, IBM, then left with no shots to fire, pointed out that it was a ratepayer in the Water Authority area and that it was protecting ratepayers' interests.

Dumping

Anti-dumping regulations are aimed at preventing the sale of products in one country at prices lower than those fixed in the country of origin. The EC follows the ruling of the USA in this matter, namely that for 'dumping' to be established two criteria need to be met: firstly that these are not cheap imports but goods sold for less than in their country of origin; and, secondly, that these imports are injurious to domestic industry. The difficulty is the time that it takes to substantiate allegations of dumping by which time permanent market disruption may have taken place with the closure through bankruptcy of domestic suppliers. Dumping may be of three types:

1 *Sporadic* – where it makes better commercial sense to unload surplus abroad at advantageous prices rather than on the home market where discounts once offered would create a precedent for future behaviour.
2 *Predatory* – when foreign producers use low prices to weaken indigenous competition abroad. Accusations of hidden governmental subsidies have been levelled against Italian producers of refrigerators and washing machines. These subsidies support a low price structure and allow the company to buy market share abroad. The EC outlaws such activity in restraint of trade but too often the damage is done and once done, cannot be corrected.
3 *Persistent* – the continued sales of products at prices lower than those of its country of origin. The case of Polish exports of electric golf-carts to the USA which arose in early 1970s and lasted for many years, illustrates the difficulty in implementing these regulations. Firstly, Poland did not have any golf courses nor need for electric golf-carts so there was no comparable domestic price which in any event would be distorted, because in a communist country all prices are politically set and need not bear any relation to their material or labour costs. This situation was later corrected but only through political pressure from the USA. Since 1990, Poland has moved to a full market economy model and so this situation is highly unlikely to be repeated.

While developing countries particularly those without an indigenous industry of their own are likely to welcome what will be seen as 'cheap imports', it is generally the case that the most contentious imports for any nation to receive are steel, textiles and agricultural produce together with basic industrial chemicals such as ethylene or soda ash, which would also come under similarly close political scrutiny.

The US International Trade Commission (ITC) imposed a 40 per cent duty on some EC steel producers; while the EC joined together to block imports of steel from Eastern Europe. Britain goes a little further and reserves the right to impound any ship found to be discharging steel products within its territorial waters. Sanctions when applied are designed to be punitive, and so it is interesting in this regard to note the role of the EC which acts on behalf of all members of the community. The EC imposed dumping duties of up to 33 per cent on Japanese makers of hydraulic excavators on models from 6 to 35 tonnes, following complaints from eighteen European manufacturers. Japan's market share in the UK excavator market had risen from negligible in the late 1970s to 40 per cent in 1984, during which time the British company Ruston Bucyrus left the market and Hymac and Priestman went into liquidation. The judgement delivered in March 1985 imposed 33 per cent on Kobelco-Kobe Steel; 27 per cent on Komatsu; 22 per cent on Mitsubishi Heavy Industries; 12 per cent on Hitachi and 3 per cent on Japan Steel Works.

In 1990 the US ITC was asked to investigate the flat panel display screen used in the assembly of lap-top computers. US display makers claim the Japanese imports are injuring their industry but the US computer makers disagree. US display makers are small and independent and faced with a Japanese product which is high technology but also requires the volume production of which the Japanese are well capable. The US industry is not in good shape to be able to enjoy a very long economic life and points to Toshiba meanwhile as being the embodiment of all their woes. The main result will be that the tariff decision will be political. Yet the argument is an economic one. Longer term, the end effect will be that only the consumers will suffer, paying a higher price than is necessary while US manufacturers disappear (*Economist*, 1990).

With textiles, the problem has been that the industrial countries have been successful in selling textile machinery to less developed countries who then quickly start to produce textiles at lower cost and in higher volumes than indigenous Western textiles industry, and so in a very short space of time, direct competition ensues over the end product. When it became apparent that an industry response was required in Western Europe to meet this damaging threat, a body known as CIRFS emerged. This body, known by its French acronym, is a European man-made fibre producers' association, and has acted to reduce West European production capacity.

It is often alleged that dumping incorporates hidden subsidies from the home government, whether in manufacturing location, selective employment assistance, favourable taxation treatment, etc. As these subsidies reduce factor costs, they may also reduce final price, hence the accusation of dumping. Dumping only occurs, though, if goods are sold at one price in the home market, and at another in a foreign market, or at least that is one of the main criteria. While the EC will institute anti-dumping measures on behalf of its member states, it will nevertheless 'dump' butter and other surplus dairy products in the Soviet Union because (a) agricultural prices have to be protected within the Community and (b) storage costs for butter and beef mountains and milk and wine lakes are high and the costs of selling off this produce cheaply is lower than the costs of keeping it in refrigerated storage. To the Soviet Union, with its centralized inefficient agricultural system, these sales constitute a windfall. For the EC it is only a temporary respite as the agricultural system is designed to over produce.

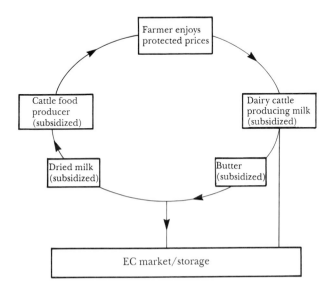

Figure 3.10 *EC milk: a model of EC efficiency?*
Note After a number of revolutions of this cycle, deposits begin to build up and surpluses accrue, which usually have to be off-loaded onto the world market at a loss.

Only in the last few years have measures been implemented to halt the growth of EC agricultural produce yet rather than just be halted, it needs instead to be cut back.

The EC concluded new agreements in 1982 with twenty five leading Third World textile exporters. It took two years of negotiation to conclude the new Multi-Fibre Agreement, to stay in force until mid-1986. The only country not to have initialled an agreement with the EC is Argentina, but there will now be unilateral controls on Argentinian exports. The British Textile Confederation was particularly concerned at exports from the Mediterranean countries in general and from Turkey and China in particular. In the case of three dominant suppliers – Hong Kong, South Korea, and Macao – the regulations provide for a 7–8 per cent cut from 1982 levels on the import of T-shirts, jeans, and certain other clothing products.

Agriculture is a contentious topic within the EC as overproduction means that surpluses have either to be stored, destroyed, or exported by means of subsidies. GATT is facing pressure over this question but it is being argued that the disciplines of industrial trade cannot be applied to agriculture as the products and technology are different. While demands then are made for some new international committee or forum to examine the question, those countries enjoying surpluses in agricultural production are able to benefit from the market disarray and to exploit their particular commercial advantage. Organization may lead to unpalatable changes for the developed countries with regard to prices, competition and perhaps the ending of export subsidies on agricultural produce. In the EC, the farming community is too powerful, and overprotected by a Common Agricultural Policy which ensures that farming is the only industry in the free world to be assured guaranteed prices for output. The USA and Canada have important grain interests but they may well find that their own self-interest is not best served by 'free trade' and so are likely to abstain from anything other than merely talking about it, preferably not too often, nor for too long.

Does anyone still practise 'free trade'?

While professing belief in a free and open exchange of goods and services many nations in effect practise something quite different. Britain, throughout the 1980s, while professing 'free trade', has been actively trying to discourage French exports of milk and has been using hygiene standards to block importation at the docks. The French, too, pursued an effective 'invisible tariff' against Japanese exports of video cassette recorders (VCRs) into France by channelling all Japanese-sourced exports of VCRs through Poitiers a small town known not to have the resources to deal with this traffic. Of course, being undermanned, this caused interminable delays which were the designed aim of this policy. Known as the Second Battle of Poitiers for its parallel with the French repulsing the Arab advance outside this town in 728 AD, this policy was effective in persuading the Japanese manufacturers that they had to come to some form of accommodation with the French.

In theory, neither France nor Britain, as members of the EC, have the unilateral right to impose tariffs as these are decided now by the EC in Brussels. The system works in the following way. Each member state has an anti-dumping unit which collects information and sends it to Brussels, which then decides on official action for the Community as a whole. In some rather sensitive areas, such as steel, agreement is easily reached; in others, where one member may be benefiting at the expense perhaps of another, agreement on action is delayed. In practice then unilateral action continues to exist. Britain has a voluntary restraint agreement with the Japanese car manufacturers restricting them to 11 per cent of the market; France has a similar understanding whereby they revealed that their market research showed that the Japanese could not hope for more than 3 per cent of the French market while Italy has continually blocked them almost entirely. The case indeed of 'an iron hand in a velvet glove', but these are illustrations only of a much greater and more general *malaise*.

Moving to finance, another important facet of trade (discussed more fully in Chapter 10), twenty-six countries including all the Western industrialized nations established in 1934 the regulatory framework of the Berne Union to try to prevent a disastrous 1930s-style price war taking place between rival government-backed export credit guarantee departments and their lines of credit. In theory, this meant that Hermes, the export-credit guarantee body in West Germany, could not offer lower terms than say the Export Credit Guarantee Department (ECGD) of Britain but they could match ECGD terms where these may be lower. Here was the danger. Proof was not always required. Hearsay may be enough to panic a government export insurance department into lower terms and allowing a higher percentage of foreign sourcing in a contract than may otherwise be normal practice. ECGD insists on British content to qualify for the lines of credit which they insure, Hermes and others are much less strict. Where the companies involved are multinationals, the bidding situation develops where one country is set against another for the prize of winning perhaps a large export order. Precedents once established cannot be easily dismissed. Multinationals may exercise choice as regards which subsidiary in which country should deal with which markets, and obviously will choose to base their business in the more accommodating countries.

To restore order to what was becoming a 'merry-go-round' with each Western partner bidding one against the other, the Western nations met in summit in 1977. As this was in breach of existing conventions, the meeting was therefore under the aegis of OECD, but due to the pressures of finding profitable trade in a recession, these meetings have been taking place rather regularly and as they have been successful in finding agreement between themselves over export finance, this grouping of the Western industrialized states has become known as the 'Consensus'. The Consensus sets minimum interest rates and maximum lengths of credit for a wide range of capital goods sold on officially supported credit terms of two years or more.

The framework of the 'Consensus' (discussed at more length in Chapter 10) has since evolved to the point where it was asked by the US Administration to implement higher interest rate charges for the Soviet Union and its East European allies as a political retaliation over the invasion of Afghanistan. Politics can never be far removed when trade is taking place across two quite different social, political and economic blocs which throughout the postwar years have traditionally viewed the other as the 'enemy'.

Article 80 of the Treaty of Rome is supposed to prohibit any measures in defiance of free trade within the EC area. In the case of the USA which ironically, earns less than 10 per cent of GDP from foreign trade, domestic legislation while national in character has always had international ramifications. The Foreign Corrupt Practices Act, for example (see Chapter 13), applies to companies with an American Stock Exchange listing; therefore many multinationals from different countries of origin will find themselves under the jurisdiction of this legislation which relates to acts of bribery and corruption, in fact anywhere the company may operate. It can and does mean that a company will be pilloried for activities viewed as 'unseemly' from a US domestic economy viewpoint even where such an activity may otherwise be totally in keeping with the commercial practice of the country concerned. Bribery and corruption, are emotive words, the question is whether local nationals will recognize this in their dealings. There may be questions of scale relating to the frequency of such events or the size of sums or other inducements offered but it has also to be said that even in countries where it may be seen to be normal to have to agree to 'facilitating' payments, bribery and corruption is still something which will not be tolerated by the local populace.

Yet another development which has arisen in the economic environment of the last ten years has been increased government activity in enticing foreign investment into its boundaries by means of tax holidays, low-cost factory buildings, low-interest loans or grants, and employment subsidies. Governments are becoming more involved and, as they become more proactive in enticing foreign companies to invest, they are demanding a say in the running of operations which are based within their jurisdiction. This has meant a sharp increase in the number of countries now seeking joint ventures with local partners rather than 100 per cent direct foreign investment. Countertrade is another area of operations in which national governments are becoming involved. It is now a major worldwide phenomenon practised by developed and developing countries alike. More will be said of countertrade and the many variants of goods-related payment terms and conditions in Chapter 10. Whereas previously Japan was the only country actively pursuing the benefits of foreign equity and participation but with some degree of local control, there are now a number of developed countries eager for this form of investment.

The Triad of Europe, USA and Japan

While Ohmae sees the triad in the above terms, other observers including futurists such as Toffler point to the focus of future attention being Germany, USA and Japan which may well prove to be the case, as Germany before unification was the largest and economically most powerful member of the European Community. However, confining ourselves to the three regions previously stated we notice that the rationale for this triad is that the bulk of global trade and economic power rests within these three regions. The global economic size of these three: Europe, USA and Japan is disproportionate to their actual number or physical size. Ohmae cites Japan and the USA alone as accounting for 30 per cent of the Free World Total and that with the addition of UK, West Germany, France and Italy, this increases to 45 per cent. Aside from economic wealth, these countries share other similarities as well: mature stagnant economies, ageing populations, unemployment among skilled trades while dynamic technological developments are taking place, costs of research and development are constantly escalating as are production facilities. This is all part of the new reality as Ohmae sees it.

This triad creates a market of 600 million with marked demographic similarities and levels of purchasing power as a result of:

- growth of capital intensive manufacturing,
- accelerated tempo of new technology,
- concentrated pattern of consumption.

A reaction to any of those forces above is protectionism. Ohmae shows that industries critical to wealth generation in the 1980s were all concentrated in Japan, USA and Europe, constituting more than 80 per cent of global production and consumption. Ohmae argues that these 600 million share the same desires for the same goods: Gucci bags; Sony Walkmans; McDonald's hamburgers, etc. While there is an international youth market for denims, CDs and tapes, tastes are not the same nor is purchasing power equal either. Psychographic segmentation based on values and attitudes which may be shared also across

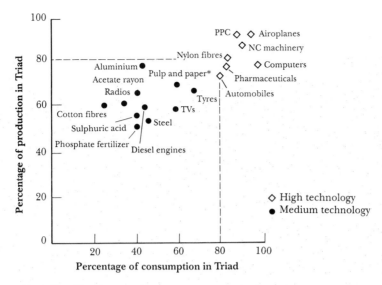

*Including Canada.

Figure 3.11
Source Ohmae, K. (1985) *Triad Power, The Coming Shape of Global Competition*, Macmillan. The Free Press, New York

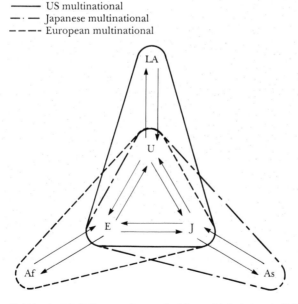

Note. Af, Africa; As, Asia; E, European Community; J, Japan; LA, Latin Ameria; U, USA

Figure 3.12 *Becoming a triad power*
Source Ohmae, K. (1985) *Triad Power, The Coming Shape of Global Competition*, Macmillan, The Free Press, New York

national boundaries is what is important. However, Ohmae's triad does not stop there. Each high technology player is in the three triad regions plus one developing region making four: Japan in Asia; Europe in Africa and Middle East; USA in Latin America.

The shape that therefore emerges is that of a tetrahedron as shown in Figure 3.12. The answer to market presence in each of the triad regions comes through consortia and joint ventures which pose a new challenge for the corporation as Ohmae points out, of learning how to communicate institutionally with the very different corporate cultures and languages of other companies. This ties in with the networking approach of the IMP research group.

References

Allport, G. W. (1961) *Pattern and Growth in Personality*, Holt Rinehart and Winston, New York.

Barnhill, J. A., and Lawson, W. M. (1980) Toward a theory of modern markets. *European Journal of Marketing*, **14**, (1) 50–60.

Brown, M. A. (1976) Values: A necessary but neglected ingredient of motivation on the job. *Academy of Management Review*, **1**, 22.

Bunn, J. H. (1981) *The Dimensionality of Signs, Tools and Models*, Indiana University Press, Bloomington, Indiana.

Clarke, Jr., D. S. (1987) *The Principles of Semiotics*, Routledge, London.

Deely, J. (1982) *Introducing Semiotic: Its History and Doctrine*, Indiana University Press, Bloomington, Indiana.

Farmer, R. N., and Richman, B. M. (1971) *International Business – An Operational Theory*, Cederwood Press, Bloomington, Indiana.

Freud, S. (1955) *Interpretation of Dreams*, translated by Strachey, A., Allen and Unwin, London.

GATT: What all the Fuss is About, (1990). *Globe and Mail*, Toronto, 3 December.

Hall, E. T. (1960) The silent language in overseas business. *Harvard Business Review*, May/June, 87–96.

Herzberg, F. (1966) *Work and the Nature of Man*, William Collins, Glasgow.

Jackson, J. H. (1990) *Restructuring the GATT System*, Royal Institute for International Affairs, London.

Kay, J. A. (1990) Identifying the Strategic Market. *Business Strategy Review*, Spring, 2–24

Lange-Seidl, A. M. (1977) *Approaches to Theories for Nonverbal Signs*, Peter de Ridder Press, Lisse, Netherlands.

Livingstone, J. M. (1989) *The Internationalisation of Business*, Macmillan, London.

Maslow, A. H. (1954) *Motivation and Personality*, Harper and Row, London, pp. 80–106.

McCall, J. B., and Warrington, M. B. (1989) *Marketing by Agreement: A Cross-Cultural Approach to Business Negotiations*, John Wiley and Sons, Chichester.

Minty, A., Chowdhury, S. R., and Rao, R. (1990) Joint Venture Divorce and the Arbitration Alternative. Unpublished MBA project paper, Faculty of Management, University of Calgary, December.

Murdock, G. P. (1945) The Common Denominator of Culture. In *The Science of Man in the World Crisis*, (ed. Linton, R.), Columbia University Press, New York.

Nicolaides, P. (1989) *Liberalising Service Trade: Strategies for Success*, Routledge, London.

Ponzio, A. (1990) *Man as a sign: Essays on the Philosophy of Language*, Monton de Gruyter, Berlin.

Priorolos, G. V. (1991) US Exporters Suffer from Failure of GATT Talks. *Marketing News*, 4 March. p. 2.

Ohmae, K. (1985) *Triad Power: The Coming Shape of Global Competition*, Macmillan — The Free Press, New York.

Ouchi, W. (1981) *Theory Z — How American Business can Meet the Japanese Challenge*, Addison-Wesley.

Rokeach, M. (1973) *The Nature of Human Values*, Macmillan — The Free Press, New York.

Ruthstrom, C. R., and Matejka K. (1990) The Meanings of 'Yes' in the Far East. *Industrial Marketing Management*, **19**, 191–192.

Terpstra, V. (1983) *International Marketing*, 3rd edn, Dryden Press — Holt, Rinehart and Winston, Chicago and New York.

Thompson, H. (1982) Caught in the Tender Trap. *Marketing*, 12 August, pp. 27–8.

Whalen, B. (1983) Semiotics: An Art or Powerful Marketing Research Tool? *Marketing News*, 13 May, pp. 8–9.

Key reading

Hall, E. T. (1960), The Silent Language in Overseas Business. *Harvard Business Review*, May/June, 87–96.

Jackson, J. H. (1990) *Restructuring the GATT System*, Royal Institute for International Affairs.

Kay, J. A. (1990) Identifying the Strategic Market. *Business Strategy Review*, Spring, 2–24.

Livingstone, J. M. (1989) *The Internationalisation of Business*, Macmillan, London.

McCall, J. B., and Warrington, M. B. *Marketing by Agreement: A Cross-Cultural Approach to Business Negotiations*, John Wiley and Sons, Chichester.

Ohmae, K. (1985) *Triad Power: The Coming Shape of Global Competition*, Macmillan — The Free Press, New York.

Rokeach, M. (1973) *The Nature of Human Values*, Macmillan — The Free Press, New York.

4

Identifying international marketing opportunities

The title may infer a short-term approach be taken to identify simply an opportunity for a 'quick kill', perhaps the off-loading on a once-only basis of overproduction of home goods or a windfall shortage of goods in a foreign market that are in over supply at home or again, a low-labour cost production advantage abroad. This though, is not the intention. The difference between what may be called a 'sales' approach and an 'entry strategy' approach has been outlined by Root (1987). The approach is quite different in a number of important respects including objectives: time horizon; resource commitment; product adaptation and innovation; price; promotion and distribution.

The same point was made equally forcibly by Virgil Dewey Collins (1935) in *World Marketing* published by the JP Lippincott Company, London:

> Throughout this practise, I propose to use the term 'world trade' rather than that of exporter in common usage at present, not because world trade is a catch phrase but because it more aptly implies the broader responsibilities of one who engages in the Science of World Trade as distinguished from the more common or garden variety of exporter making less than the sustained and intelligent effort required in this field of endeavour to insure the fullest measure of success. Exporting, in itself, is confined merely to that technical procedure and the mechanical processes by means of which an order from a foreign customer is embarked to its destination.

Market research of foreign countries is open to all companies and the governmental assistance available will be discussed later in this chapter and in Chapter 5. Further practical help may also be found in Paliwoda (1991). Before proceeding further, though, it must be recognized that a marketer contemplating a foreign market cannot possibly be as knowledge-able about all aspects of that market as he is about his own domestic market. The greatest mistakes are made by marketers who think they know a foreign market 'like the back of their hand' often to find after an ill-fated product launch that they do not. Product usage, shopping patterns and the unfortunate meanings which some brand names can have in colloquial everyday slang are merely some of the pitfalls which will be discussed in Chapter 9. The areas in which a marketer cannot hope to be fully appraised prior to market entry without actually visiting the country itself include:

1 political risk,
2 economic risk,
3 commercial risk,
4 taxes and legislation relating to company incorporation.

These risks may be properly assessed through an acquaintanceship with the facts. This will involve both secondary data, i.e., published sources of information and primary data analysis, i.e. interviews, surveys and different types of field work conducted in the target market itself.

Political and economic risk appreciation

In a world which appears to be becoming a 'global village' with ever-increasing interdependencies between nations, going international has become a necessity for companies rather than a luxury. Speed has therefore become a critical element in an international strategy which dictates that all important markets must be approached simultaneously.

The opportunities for internationalization offered by the expansion in information technology (IT) are great but so too are the risks. Companies are controlled and managed by people and people may often prefer to operate within their region or within their political and economic bloc. This often clouds their thinking in that political risk is to be found only in

Market research expenditure – worldwide

Region	1977	1979	1983
North America	1421	1766	2862
Europe	1141	1314	1912
Asia/Oceania	355	353	491
Central/South America	84	88	96
Africa	42	53	70
Middle East	21	28	48
Total world market	3063	3602	5483

Note. Figures are in millions of Swiss Francs, used because of the stability of the currency.

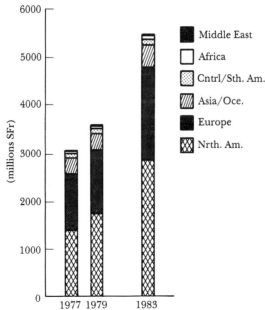

Figure 4.1
Source   Oostveen, J. C. J. (1986) Industry study: the state of marketing research in Europe. *European Research*, **14**, (3), 102

certain geographic regions of the world. The uncertainty may be higher in the Middle East or Africa but political risks are to be found everywhere including otherwise stable regions such as Europe. For example, in the early 1970s a French government under Mitterand imposed a nationalization policy. In Britain in the 1980s a privatization policy was rigorously pursued which may be partly reversed if a socialist government comes to power in the 1990s.

Another type of political risk arises with the extraterritorial reach of US legislation. In December 1981, martial law was imposed in Poland and so the USA imposed an embargo on the export of all US-origin on-land gas transmission equipment, services and technology to the Soviet Union. The political boycott of the Soviet oil pipeline by the USA created difficulties for Western countries determined to meet their obligations and yet thwarted by the US refusal to deliver any parts or supplies for this project. This posed a significant problem for the British company John Brown Engineering which had bought a licence to produce turbine blades from General Electric of the USA. As this formed a major functioning part of their turbines ordered by the USSR they then found themselves in the impossible predicament of being threatened with repercussions likely to affect their US operations by the US Administration if they did go ahead with their delivery of turbines to the Soviet Union, and being threatened with repercussions also by the British Government if they did not deliver to the Soviet Union.

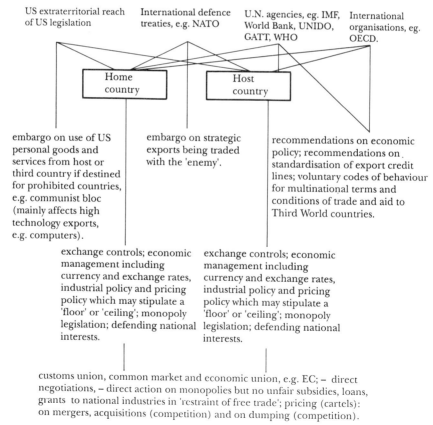

Figure 4.2 *Political intervention in business*

Table 4.1

		Perceived investment quality climate		
		High	*Medium*	*Low*
	High	Wholly owned sales and production venture	Screwdriver assembly	Franchising
Actual cost of entry	Medium	Joint equity venture	Strategic alliances contractual joint venture	Licensing: know-how agreement
	Low	Sales subsidiary	Management contract	Agent; Distributor; exporting only

Political risk may be

1 Obvious, where a new government comes into power with fixed and (to business) unfavourable ideas on the role of foreign companies in the economy.
2 Latent, where, like a slowly burning fuse there is the danger of suddenly and unexpectedly losing one's assets in a possible action of expropriation or nationalization.
3 Partial, in that it may refer particularly to certain sectors of industry and commerce and not others with regard to investment, local national pricing, local content laws, and taxation.

Instead of conducting a proper evaluation of the facts, a 'Go-No-Go' study as to whether or not to enter a market will be accepted or rejected on the basis of a subjective, cursory examination of one or two characteristics, often made by a junior company employee visiting the foreign market for less than a week and not fully conversant with the local language or business practice customs.

It may be appropriate therefore to look first at a few more realistic methods for assessing the environment of a target market (see Table 4.1).

Another way of looking at this has been provided by Ishikawa (1990) looking particularly at the EC Single Market as in Figure 4.3.

The company looks at international markets

This review of international market potential has to be undertaken by means first of an internal diagnosis of the firm: establishing strengths and weaknesses with regard to production; finance; human resources; and the current standing and client base of the firm. Against this, the opportunities and threats of the foreign market may be viewed with regard to legal; ethical; market; competition; and technology variables.

Information
↓
Analysis→Objectives ← of the company?
↓   ↙
Setting commercial targets

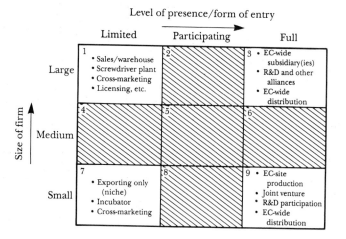

Figure 4.3

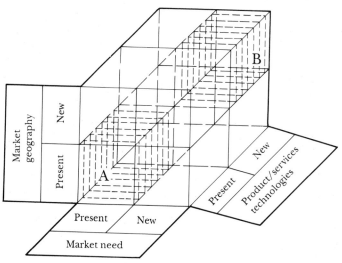

Figure 4.4
Source   Ansoff, I. (1987) *Corporate Strategy*, revised edn, Penguin Harmondsworth, Middlesex

Each firm has its own needs and these influence its strategic thinking. A useful addition to this growing literature on business strategy has been Ansoff's 1987 revision of his previous matrix. Instead of the two dimensions of the original matrix (product and mission) Ansoff now uses a three dimensional cube to define the thrust and ultimate future scope of the business as in Figure 4.4. Market need is defined in broad rather than product terms, e.g. need for personal transportation or need for amplification of weak electrical signals; product/

service technology whether it is present technology or new technology; and market geography which defines the regions or nation states in which the firm intends to do business. The extreme choices possible are to continue serving traditional needs and traditional markets with traditional technology or move to offer new product technology to serve new product needs in new markets. In between, there are also several possible permutations on the three dimensions.

We need to measure overall market size and competitive market conditions. Given that many of the 146 countries with a population in excess of one million have very limited market data, particularly among the less developed countries, to undertake this market study and fulfil these information requirements, an eight-point plan is proposed (see Table 4.2) which systematically evaluates prospects and therefore helps make recommendations for definite action.

Target market-selection decisions

It is a regrettable fact that the existing literature on the subject points to market selection as being only an informal decision on which little research has been conducted. Often it is the result of a competitive move; or a chance sighting of a product from that particular market; the result of a business conversation or a chamber of commerce seminar; or a market is chosen simply because the target market is a pleasant location, the people are 'nice' and the managing director's spouse enjoys going there on holiday! Curiously, more attention appears to be paid to 'industry talk' than to the reports and publications produced by different trade and governmental bodies. This behaviour has been reported in the UK and in the USA as well, although it must be remembered that since the USA does not have the same degree of dependence on trade as we have in the UK, this only serves to make the finding more incomprehensible.

Market selection means choosing the markets to which to devote your resources. The British Overseas Trade Board (BOTB) commissioned the British Export Trade Research Organization (BETRO) in 1976 to undertake a study on this subject of key market concentration and it found from taking a representative sample of a quarter of British companies that companies were spreading their resources too thinly over too many markets. Assuming a Pareto relationship where approximately 20 per cent of a company's markets could be found to account for perhaps 80 per cent of its exports, BETRO exhorted exporters to concentrate their resources on their 'best' markets. Newcomers to exporting, the report suggested, could build a prosperous export trade by dealing with five or six countries only. Concentration would also bring:

- less administration,
- better market knowledge,
- more opportunity to compete on non-price factors,
- less distraction,
- higher market share.

The BETRO report concluded that British companies exported to too many markets, and this was a finding that was substantiated by the Barclays Bank report on export competitiveness in the UK, France and West Germany of 1979. Piercy (1982) qualified this theory of 'market concentration' by viewing this, not in terms of limiting the company as to

Table 4.2   Requirements for a foreign market study

1 *Background information*
This is derived from published secondary sources of information and would include:
- rates of growth of the population, workforce, and GNP (but, as mentioned earlier, GNP per capita has its limitations as a credible measure of anything)
- balance of payments (although this has not stopped anyone exporting to the USA!)
- composition of exports and imports
- consumer expenditures
- formation of fixed capital in construction and equipment.

2 *Analysis of supply*
- *External competition* can be ascertained by analysing import statistics, via
UN World Trade Annual
UN Commodity Indexes for the Standard Industrial Trade Classification, 2 vols.
OECD Trade by Commodities (Foreign Trade Statistics, Series 'C', Paris, half-yearly).
- *Import analyses* usually show:
import flows over past five years, by major supplying countries, by quantity, and by value
percentage growth of imports over the years studied.
- *Apparent domestic consumption* may therefore be computed as
Total supply = (local production − exports) + imports.

3 *Demand and end-use analysis*
The aim is to study the various kinds of principal users of a product to discover where the growth points may be. The following need to be studied:
- economic sectors that use the product
- each sector's share of total consumption
- growth pattern of each of these sectors
- plans and forecasts of future growth for each major sector and the related sectors (future secondary demand).

4 *Demand forecasts*
It is best to concentrate on five- to ten-year prospects. The following points should be noted:
- Examine long-term trends, remembering cyclical pattern associated with industrial development.
- Examine substitutability of the goods in question.
- Ignore short-term economic forecasts as current events can bias thinking.
- Examine national plans.
- Listen and interpret intelligently, e.g., ask a manufacturer about his competitors.

5 *Information of prices*
- Extrapolation of unit prices over a five-year period may indicate the way in which prices are moving.
- Field enquiries at home can yield manufacturer and fob prices.
- Field enquiries in target country can yield cif prices and distribution costs.

6 *Access to the market*
Conditions of access to the market may be influenced by the following:
- customs tariffs
- import charges
- non-tariff barriers
- import regulations.

7 *Trading practices*
- sizes and grade of goods most often in demand
- preferred types of packaging or product presentation
- most popular qualities/assortments of goods
- standardization at national/international level
- usual channels of trade
- condition of payment
- problems of transport
- insurance terms.

8 *Sales promotion*
- evaluate target audience and coherent theme of message
- when, where, how should this sales message be delivered?
- media availability
- publications readership profile
- costs of advertising per prospective customer, by various media
- strengths and weaknesses of present and prospective customers
- what marketing approaches have been effective there in the past?
- trade fairs — which groups attend them and what are the conditions for participating?

Note   An initial feasibility study may be conducted by means of secondary data but before market entry much better, more timely information will be required which can only be gained from visiting the target market itself such as prices; potential new entrants to the market; potential substitute products for outside the industry and the prevailing degree of buyer — supplier dependency in the target market itself.

the market where it may sell, but to markets where it may market itself. By selling wherever demand arises but maintaining a certain selectivity over the use of marketing resources, Piercy then, and only then, confesses to a certain benefit in market concentration. Other commentators have pointed to the BETRO report and the advice on key market concentration as being responsible for the bankruptcy of many British exporters since the date of its publication. Concentration being little different from 'placing all your eggs in one basket'. When disaster strikes, everything may be lost.

International market segmentation

Market segmentation follows the rationale of concentrating resources on the best prospects. In the pursuit of market segmentation, one is adopting a 'rifle' strategy at a given target segment as opposed to the general market at large, which would constitute a 'shotgun' approach. Sometimes firing far and wide, the latter will strike a target segment but at a cost and over time, and so the 'rifle' strategy is probably the more effective of the two as there are likely to be greater similarities across similar market segments than between two country markets. For example, BMW has effectively tapped into the international segment which is attracted by sporty family cars.

Three overall possibilities exist:

● market differentiation, whereby competitors make different offerings across the entire market and with the flexible manufacturing systems made possible by computerization this has become a feasible strategy much less costly than ever before;
● market segmentation, whereby specific target markets are identified and offerings are designed especially for these segments;
● market positioning whereby competitors position their offerings differently for each market segment.

There are degrees of segmentation, but certain criteria have to be fulfilled to make segmentation a feasible strategy:

1 *Measurability.* The target segment must be capable of some form of measurement, or at least, a 'best guess'.
2 *Size.* The target segment has to be large enough to make the marketing effort financially worthwhile.
3 *Accessibility.* Targeting is useless unless this group can be accessed by promotion and distribution.
4 *Responsiveness.* The target group should react to any change in the marketing mix elements. Failure to do so indicates that this is not a proper segment that has been drawn.

If a company chooses to ignore the differences between consumers, it will be practising undifferentiated marketing. If, on the other hand, it segments the market on the basis of consumer differences, it can choose to practise either differentiated marketing – in which a marketing mix is used for each segment – or concentrated marketing - in which all or most marketing efforts are focused on one or a few segments.

Wind and Douglas (1972) tie in market segmentation with their recommendations on international market research as may be seen in Figure 4.5 which separates enduring characteristics such as the topography of the country which will affect distribution networks and situation-specific characteristics which are unique to an industry or perhaps sub-culture and should not be seen as either lasting or universal outside of that particular segment.

Mandell and Rosenberg (1981) mention also 'market integration' and 'market orchestration'. Market integration unites certain market segments, finds a basic characteristic that several otherwise different groups share in common, and designs a product that appeals to all of them. One example offered is in the area of snack foods. Market integration arose as a response to oversegmentation. Market orchestration arises where different market segments are to be included in the target range and lack compatibility. The price factor is therefore the most common means of orchestration since high and low prices will encourage some segments and discourage others.

Selecting a strategy then is by means of a review of five factors:

- *Company resources,* whether limited in terms of capital and/or marketing.
- *Product homogeneity,* degree of similarity within a product class.
- *Product age* (PLC theory of product phase and corporate response).
- *Market homogeneity,* depending on where consensus needs are like/unlike.
- *Competition,* moving into several segments or a mass market will influence corporate response.

Primary sources of information for gauging the climate for trade and investment

Excellent, but expensive is the problem. First determine what the company has to offer, undertake some research of secondary sources of information on that country and that industry. When the focus of the research has been narrowed down to perhaps one market and the trail of secondary information has petered out then this is the time for primary information gathering, provided enthusiasm for going into this market is still riding high.

There comes a time when only primary data collection can be conducted. Secondary sources are secondary because they are always collected for another and are presented for a specific purpose, e.g. governmental demographic data. Although cheap they lack specificity and timeliness. This is what primary data can offer. They can offer a custom built survey of attitudes and perspectives on a new product to that market but it takes money and time and

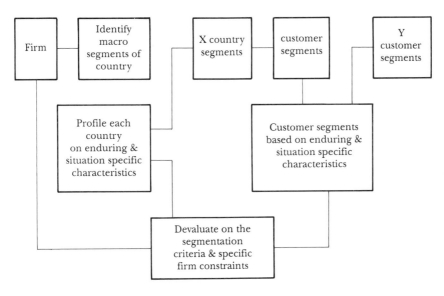

Figure 4.5
Source Wind and Douglas (1972) International market segmentation. *European Journal of Marketing,* **6**, (1)

needs to be handled by local nationals so as to eliminate much of the confusion and nonsense that often creeps in when questionnaires are transferred over from a head office at home and translated roughly into the foreign language of the country concerned.

Also under the heading of primary data comes the internal examination of the company; the suppliers; channels of distribution; and industry in the target foreign market. This then involves an examination of what Porter (1985) calls the 'value chain' for each of the company; suppliers; climate and industries. The all-important linkages within these value chains and the determination of what is value itself as perceived within the target foreign market cannot be gauged from a review of secondary published sources of information.

The value chain is composed of nine generic categories of activities which are linked together. The activities in a firm's value chain are linked to each other and to the activities of its suppliers, channels and buyers. These linkages affect competitive advantage. The firm's value chain is determined by its history, strategy, its approach to implementing strategy and the underlying economies of the activities themselves. The firm is a series of functions and the value chain is a system of interdependent activities. Simply stated value is the amount buyers are willing to pay for what a firm provides them. Creating value for buyers that exceeds the cost of so doing is a common strategic goal and so value rather than cost is used to explain how companies which offer value are able to charge a premium for this and differentiate themselves also from the competition at the same time. This means, though, that the value has to be clearly seen and appreciated by the buyer. Value activities are the physically and technologically distinct activities a firm performs. These value activities are the building blocks of competitive advantage by which a firm creates a product valuable to its buyers. The value chain displays total value and consists of value activities and margin which is the difference between total value and the collective cost of performing the value activities.

Value activities can be divided into primary and support activities. Primary activities are further divided into five categories but are the activities involved in the physical creation of the product and its sale and transfer to the buyer as well as after-sales service. Support activities provide backup for primary activities and for each other by providing purchased inputs, technology, human resources and various other functions within the firm.

The economies of each activity as well as its performance determine whether a firm is high or low cost relative to competition. How each value activity is performed will also determine its contribution to buyer needs and hence differentiation. Comparing the value chains of competitors exposes differences that determine competitive advantage.

The value chain rather than value added is the appropriate way to examine competitive advantage. Porter (1985) maintains that while value added (selling price minus cost of purchased raw materials) has been taken as the base for cost analysis in the belief that it is an area in which the firms can control costs, it is in fact a misconception. Value added simply isolates raw materials from the many purchased inputs used in a firm's activities. The value chain, on the other hand, is not an accounting classification but examines the costs of all the inputs and looks also at the linkages which a firm may have with its suppliers to reduce cost or enhance differentiation. Supplier and channel value chains also relate back to the firm as they form vertical linkages and part of the total cost that will be borne by the buyer. To fully explore these linkages requires information systems so as to achieve the necessary optimal coordination. There are also tradeoffs in the system which increase the complexity of managing and controlling the entire system, e.g. higher costs in one area may result in lower costs in another. Another factor to be considered is the degree of vertical integration and the extent to which the firm divides its activities with its suppliers, channels and buyers. Differentiation may come through offering a range of buyer activities either internally or through supplier cooperation or coalitions and strategic business alliances with independent firms.

Secondary sources of information in gauging the climate for trade and investment

Secondary sources, i.e., published sources of information are a good inexpensive place to start. There are more than 146 countries with populations greater than one million but available market data particularly from the less developed countries will be very limited. For governments in unstable economies a census can have a destabilizing effect particularly if it shows demographic shifts that indicate electoral underrepresentation of any significant part of the community and if that community displays no likelihood of supporting the government in power, the census will only have served to underline and give statistical credibility to a societal wrong. Not surprisingly, then, there are countries where only estimates are available as to how large the population may be. Examples are to be found in the Middle East and Africa. This, despite the fact that population censuses have been taking place all over the world since before the birth of Jesus Christ.

Secondary sources of information vary greatly. The greatest publisher of information is government and where international agreements on exchange of information are in place, then it will be possible to consult locally, foreign governments' statistical publications as is the case in Britain with US statistics and vice versa. Supranational bodies such as the EC and the various UN agencies publish their own statistics as do other international organizations such as EFTA, OECD and other customs unions. At a local level it will usually be possible to find reports published by export trade associations, trade unions, employer's confederations and consultancies such as Business International SA or Booz, Allen and Hamilton.

Interpretation problems in dealing with secondary sources

Marketing research problems in foreign markets

Conducting market research in one's own country, one enjoys the benefit of a certain degree of familiarity with the nature of the society, its values and laws. Foreign market research is like a great leap into the dark where many variables are unknown unless it is conducted by local nationals in the country concerned. The scope of error is vast, particularly so where a foreign company may be enquiring about the local acceptability of a product, concept, service, or slogan currently in use in other parts of the world. The problem of the self-reference criterion comes into play here. An individual looks at a foreign market and evaluates it against experience and understanding of his own market. False perceptions, misunderstandings and unfulfilled expectations lead to costly mistakes. Even where the common language may be English there are many possible instances where the same word will not be used in popular conversation or advertising in Britain and in Canada, Australia or New Zealand. It is possible to create a totally negative effect through this inability to communicate across two English-speaking communities although the comic occasions usually arise with translations, eg. 'Come alive with Pepsi' may be a familiar slogan in the English-speaking world but how would the English-speaking manager react on hearing that his product slogan has been translated in China (PRC): 'Pepsi reawakens your dead relatives'? On a more positive note, it is likely that the product would have high brand-name recall among consumers. Careful checking and preparation cannot be over-emphasized. Generally, the problems revolve around language because language is a living thing and while the world of commerce is constantly innovating products and language to communicate new product concepts, their understanding is neither total nor universal.

Time is required for good market research and familiarity with the market and the product concerned. However, this may be a stated ideal and the pressures on executive time and finances may force a decision to be made on data which is often incomplete in many respects. One of the most serious problems is the lack of a common statistical base in data collected worldwide. Keegan (1989) illustrates how a confusing array of units of measurement for Pepsi consumption nationally – whether in can, bottle or glass; and in terms of frequency: whether daily, weekly or number of times daily – can lead to the lack of a coherent standardization of data within the Pepsico organization as a whole. The lack of complementarity between statistical bases is one of the single greatest problems of foreign market research. It means statistics cannot be directly compared and contrasted and severely limits any statistical analysis on a time series, demographic, socio-economic or regional basis. It is interesting to note how the OECD and EC are making moves towards international standardization of statistical reporting. Elsewhere, a consortium of international publishers have produced a second Pan–European survey of readership habits and profiles (Ryan 1981).

Demographic, economic, and social statistics are thus not comparable since they are compiled by different agencies for different purposes. To pursue a few of these distortions along the lines laid down pursued by Barnes (1980):

- *Degree of concentration of population.* Figures may be distorted because not all of the land mass is actually habitable, as for example with Japan or Switzerland. Urban concentration will therefore be greater than the average mean which is 'smoothed' and will inevitably include lakes and mountain ranges in the number per square kilometre of land. Urban concentration in Britain or Japan will therefore be much higher than may be inferred from statistics drawn on this basis.
- *The extent of car ownership.* This may be distorted, firstly, by leasing and, secondly, by the fact that in a country such as Britain, approximately 70 per cent of the car market is accounted for by company cars as this is in turn influenced by the taxation system. Attempts to assess car ownership as against cars per household will yield quite different results, particularly if it is a study of usage. Language and the correct choice of words is important. GIGO or 'garbage in, garbage out' is the perennial problem with questionnaires where semantic nuances affect understanding and respondent evaluations.
- *Level of individual prosperity.* Beware again of per capita GNP and also of self-reference criteria that suggest that foreign market X will, with increasing personal incomes, display the same consumer wants and desires as your own domestic market. This is the self-reference criteria at work. Even if consumers are willing to divulge personal information about household incomes either in actual numbers or by agreeing to being within a predetermined income band, there are the added problems of fluctuating exchange rates and differences in direct income taxes and benefits which go to make it all the harder to approximate equivalent purchasing parities.
- *Infrastructural level to be considered* – for example, whether there is adequate electricity power supply or simply, maintenance, and repair facilities. A fax machine will require a telephone line but the telephone system may still be in another age. Photocopies require abundant supplies of paper. Computers require paper and floppy disks, etc.

- *Level of female emancipation.* The role of women in society differs greatly between Europe and North America and, for example, the Middle East. The UK, Sri Lanka, Israel and India have had women as Prime Ministers, while in the Middle East women have still to walk cloaked totally in black, behind their husbands. Again educational opportunities, career opportunities and equality of treatment between the sexes varies greatly between and sometimes within countries. In the extreme, 'the role of a woman is in the kitchen and the birthing-bed'. Opportunities to target executive toys or magazines at these women are limited. Statistics on numbers in higher education, entry to professions give some indication as to sexual equality, as does the time and the range of publications generally available in that market. Are there any specifically targeted at women in any profession or of any age?
- *Labour supply.* The shortage of labour and/or the cost of labour may not always be apparent. West Germany in the early 1970s had to import labour mainly from Turkey but when industrial conditions changed and labour unions began to complain about the societal consequences of importing perhaps three million workers, this method was dropped in favour of contractual joint ventures in Eastern Europe whereby production was secured with none of the attendant problems of immigrant labour, although new problems would soon have their place.
- *Level of industrialization related to the infrastructure.* It is costly to transfer a general technology; it is simpler and less expensive to transfer industry-specific or company-specific technology, i.e., a product or process. Markets must also be recognized as being at different economic stages of industrialization, some undergoing de-industrialization, some actually industrializing, others remaining essentially raw-material supplying countries.
- *Level of retail integration.* This gives some indication as to available channels of distribution, discussed more fully later. Enormous variances exist — from the longest channels worldwide in Japan to short retail channels in France where the hypermarket concept was first developed. Note, too, that quantum leaps are possible in development and that France made a quantum leap in retailing, bypassing the supermarket stage and moving directly to hypermarkets. Again, this was aided and abetted by a commercially favourable legal system which did not seek to obstruct this change as has happened in Britain where planning controls have been used to limit out-of-town hypermarkets and 'protect' urban shopping centres.
- Countries tend to 'adjust' published figures and learn to live with and discount statistics known to be imperfect. Figure 4.6 shows the discrepancies in the annual bilateral trade balance as reported separately by Canada and by the USA.

To take another example, for many years the UN Economic Commission for Europe has published a *Consolidated Inventory of Obstacles to Trade in the ECE Region* and this rather hefty publication has traditionally drawn attention to the poor statistical reporting emanating from the East European countries particularly in the pre-perestroika era. This paucity of data was intentional to avoid direct comparisons being made with Western economies and also to deprive Westerners of meaningful market information on the demand, production and prices of goods. Information would never be found together on units produced, events told and selling price per unit.

Also, on national statistical reporting, Kenichi Ohmae argues the case for Japan in saying that no common industrial classification system exists between the USA and Japan which would allow statistical and economic figures between the two countries to be compared. The USA for its part has argued that Japan treats it as a developing country in terms of the

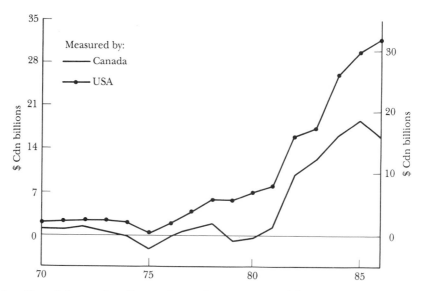

Figure 4.6 *Canada's merchandise trade surplus as measured by Canada and the US*
Source United Nations Economic Commission for Europe, *Harmonisation of International Trade Statistics*. TRADE/AC.25/R.2, 18 July 1990

commodity structure of its foreign trade with Japan. The same has also to be said of UK–Japanese trade. Ohmae argues the contrary that these classifications do not allow valid comparisons to be made and maintains that Japan is the USA's number one foreign purchaser of commercial aircraft, organic and inorganic chemicals, pharmaceuticals and photographic supplies; and the second largest foreign purchaser of medical and scientific supplies, measuring and testing devices, pulp and wood products, and semiconductors. Ohmae further argues that the net flows balance in that Japanese investment in the USA has now reached significant levels, topping $20 billion in 1983 (Ohmae, 1985). The USA then will be constrained in terms of possible actions in its trade war with Japan, if Japan owns it!

Certainly, trade studies have numerous built-in distortions. Another convention of trade figure reporting is that exports are always quoted FOB and imports CIF. Regardless of changes taking place in the INCOTERMS used for export trade quotations, this convention has been maintained. An export order FOB or 'free on board' will represent a lower value than an import quoted as CIF (cost, insurance, freight) as the FOB price may in its simplest form be the factory gate price with no overheads added for transportation, insurance, etc. as is a FOB quotation. This is the responsibility of the buyer or importer. This means then that exports FOB will have a lower price than imports CIF so comparing, say, British exports to France with French imports from Britain will not state the same values because of the FOB/CIF discrepancy as well as currency fluctuation. The added problem of different national statistical codes for products and services is a very difficult one. Technology soon renders obsolete any attempt at classifying industrial products but without a common industrial code we cannot really compare what one country imports under the heading of 'machine tools' with what another exports to it also understood to be 'machine tools'. The most recent industrial product classification has been TARIC introduced into the European Community in 1988. It is a genuine attempt to coordinate and standardize industrial classifications across the community. It has also been adopted by a number of countries outside the EC.

Yet the problem does not just lie with industrial products continually being updated and transformed with new technology into new products for new applications. The problem also lies in the human knowledge element embodied in software that makes technology function. This has traditionally been difficult to classify but, as may be seen from the table below other statistical definition problems arise as well. For example, not only do different statistical sources conflict on the issue of the number of women in the labour force but there is a fundamental split as to how to define a woman. In most countries, it will be fifteen but in the USA it is sixteen, in Italy fourteen, in Mexico, twelve and Brazil, ten. (Bartos, 1989). (See Table 4.3).

Language creates difficulties particularly with regard to multicultural multilingual question-naires. A researcher has to be quite certain that data gathered in English will bed*-$,$,directly comparable with the same gathered in French. Aside from the problems of defining a similar

Table 4.3   What percent of women are in the labour force?

	Census	OECD	International Demographics	Statistical Abstract of Latin America	Statistics Canada	Annual Abstract of Statistics UK
USA	55 (1985)	63	54	—	—	—
Canada	52 (1981)	62	61	—	46	—
Japan	49 (1985)	57	57	—	—	—
Great Britain/ UK	47 46 (1981)	59 (UK)	57(UK)	—	—	49
Australia	46 (1981)	53	52	—	—	—
Fed. Rep. of Germany	39 (1980)	49	49	—	—	—
Italy	33 (1981)	41	41	—	—	—
Venezuela	31 (1984)	—	24	21	—	—
Mexico	28 (1980)	—	—	17	—	—
Brazil	27 (1980)	—	39	20	—	—

Source   Bartos, R. (1989), International dempgraphic data? Incomparable! *Marketing and Research Today*, vol **17**, no. 4, p. 207.

sample frame across two countries and ensuring adequate representation of the sample among respondents, it also involves a great deal of cross-checking, testing and translation back into the original language once complete and so extends the time required for completion, the cost of final completion, and the credibility of the final effort to management.

Where contemporary data does not exist nor is specific to the problem in hand, then primary data collection – i.e., fieldwork – has to be undertaken. The costs and time involved cannot be exaggerated.

Where data exists to some degree but there is difficulty in establishing fieldwork, then certain approximation measures have to be turned to and this we shall deal with shortly. There are other sources – the political and economic press of the country concerned; possibly, too, discussions with importers and end-users; and reports of either government departments or trade associations. The dynamism of the market place means that competitors can often quickly find a lucrative market in an otherwise altogether undesirable market, politically, financially, and touristically. This then creates a pressure for competitors to follow into that market but without the prior knowledge and information of the leader. A 'bandwagon' effect is then created. Companies then find themselves in markets, not entirely of their own choosing, simply by following the market leader or other close rivals, and assuming also that the leader has perfect knowledge of where he is and the market in general is going, because they have not. Managing a business without a knowledge of the market that one is in has been compared to driving a car blindfolded in reverse. A lot of bruising will take place before some essential lessons are learned.

The section which follows exceeds the requirements of the Institute of Marketing Diploma syllabus. However, it may lead to a better understanding of identifying market opportunities if this section is read rather than omitted.

Commercial services such as BERI which follow do not identify export opportunities at the firm level nor are they meant to provide criteria for foreign market selection. Instead, they are offered to help develop a decision-making framework in which the criteria important to the firm may be gauged against the opportunities offered. The pages which follow are designed to shrink the psychological distance between the marketer and his envisioned target market and lead hopefully to more objective and better decision-making based on better information.

Business Environment Risk Index (BERI)

Launched in 1972, the Business Environment Risk Index was developed by Frederich Haner, of the University of Delaware, USA. It has since expanded into country-specific forecasts and country risk forecasts for international lenders but its basic service is the Global Subscription Service. BERI's Global Subscription Service assesses forty-eight countries four times a year on fifteen economic, political, and financial factors on a scale from zero to four. Zero indicates unacceptable conditions for investment in a country; one equates with poor conditions; two with acceptable or average conditions; three with above average conditions; and four with superior conditions. The key factors are individually weighted according to their assessed importance as with ingredients. Thus, if the panellists score a country's political stability at an average of 1.7, this is multiplied by the top weighting of 2.5 and becomes 4.2. Since the total weighting adds up to twenty-five and the top of the rating scale is four, 100 are the maximum points any one country can score.

At present more than 500 companies use the BERI service which also includes detailed in-depth reports on countries personally visited and assessed by its founder; each quarter ninety-eight unpaid panellists sit down to assess up to twelve countries each.

There are two points worth mentioning here: firstly, BERI tries to get nationals of each country examined as panel members as they tend generally to be more objective; secondly, to eliminate a bias within the panel the original panel of thirty-four was increased to ninety-eight by asking each panellist to find two other panellists. The panellists, however, remain anonymous and unpaid. More recently, the panel has been increased to 170 business, banking and political specialists. The users of the service are seen to be varied. It may, for example, allow a company to determine more fairly how their managers around the world are performing other than on a profit and loss basis; for example, a manager may be able to hold sales even when the economy is on a downturn, or to evaluate expansion projects and new investment possibilities, to decide whether and where to conclude licensing and trade agreements.

It is also worth pointing out that not every country in the West has the same number of people reporting on it, so Haner has started a computer programme which tests each statistic and sends out an alarm if there are inadequate statistics for any country. Since major investment decisions require three or four months deliberation, panellists try to predict nine months or a year ahead. Panellists receive their sheet back every quarter and if they wish to change their assessment of any country they simply mark over the old ratings with a red pencil. Total points are a possible one hundred but a country that rates eighty or more has a very advanced economy plus an environment favourable to foreign investors. A score of over seventy would also imply an advanced economy, but not so favourable an investment climate. The range between fifty-five and seventy embraces developing countries with investment potential, but also includes '... a few mature economies having mentalities not fully compatible with modern business.' The next level, forty to fifty-five, includes high risk countries which sometimes offer profits in relation to the risks. But even when potential earnings are in proportion to the risk, the quality of management 'has to be superior to realise potential.'

With a score below forty it would take a very unusual situation to justify the commitment of capital. Generally, ratings do not change very much nor very quickly, although Chile and Venezuela have proved to be exceptions. Political upheavals will always occur as have taken place following the Tiananmen Square massacre in Beijing, and its subsequent effects on Chinese trade and diplomatic links with the rest of the world. Equally, the dramatic quantum leaps made by the East European nations since the political convulsions of 1989 have been unparalleled. The subsequent unification of Germany in October 1990 created a new global awareness of the speed with which events were taking place in Europe. The Single Market of 1993 is now being treated more seriously as a result. Prior to this, some observers had not anticipated 1993 to take place before 2005!

The country environmental temperature gradient

In a study ostensibly of the marketing middleman – the agent – in international business, two Canadian researchers, Litvak and Banting (1968) prepared a classification system of country environmental factors on a temperature gradient whereby when the temperature was 'too hot' the agent would find himself pushed towards new institutional structures in order to survive. The variables which Litvak and Banting identified were: the nature of the product; concentration of customers; intensity of competition; resources of the middleman; market

Table 4.4 Business Environment Risk Index

Rate up to 12 countries Identify any 6 for weight	Political stability	Attitudes Foreign Investor & Profiles	National-ization	Monetary Inflation	Balance of payments	Bureaucratic delays	Economic growth	Currency convertibilities	Enforce-ability of contracts	Labour cost-productivity	Profes-sional services & contracts	Communi-cations – tele, mail, air, telex	Local mgt.	Short-term credits	Long-term loans/venture capital	MAIL To: P. T. Hamer P. O. Box 4697 Newark. Del. 1971 USA. Negative Adjustment: *Worker Co-determination Im-pact on Profits
weight	3	1?	1?	1?	1?	1	2?	2?	1?	2	?	1	1	2	2	
	1	2	3	4	5	6	7	8	9	10	11	12	13	14	15	0 1 2 3 4
AMERICAS: 9																
1 Canada																
2 Mexico																
3 United States																
4 Argentina																
5 Brazil																
6 Chile																
7 Colombia																
8 Peru																
9 Venezuela																
ASIA/AUSTRALASIA: 14																0 1 2 3 4
10 Australia																
11 China (Taiwan)																
12 Indonesia																
13 Japan																
14 Korea																
15 Malaysia																
16 Philippines																
17 Singapore																
18 India																
19 Iran																
20 Israel																
21 Lebanon																
22 Pakistan																
23 Turkey																

EUROPE/AFRICA: 20

	0	1	2	3	4
24 Belgium					
25 Denmark					
26 France					
27 Ireland					
28 Italy					
29 Germany (West)					
30 Greece					
31 Netherlands					
32 Norway					
33 Portugal					
34 Spain					
35 Sweden					
36 Switzerland					
37 United Kingdom					
38 Kenya					
39 Libya					
40 Morocco					
41 Nigeria					
42 South Africa					
43 Egypt					

	0	1	2	3	4
New Countries:					
44 Equador					
45 Saudi Arabia					

Ratings: 0 - Unacceptable conditions
1 - Poor conditions
2 - Acceptable or average conditions
3 - Above average conditions
4 - Superior conditions

*Give a number on the 1–4 scale for your impression of worker co-determinator's impact on profits from operations in the country being rated.

potential; degree of industrialization; cultural, linguistic, and geographical distance; legislation; and degree of political stability.

It was found to be the case that agents will be used: the greater the degree of political volatility; the greater the degree of cultural, linguistic and geographic, distance; and the greater the degree of legislation relating to foreign investment.

Countries were defined as being 'hot' where the market was dynamic and the agent was forced to adapt to meet the needs of the market. A market was 'cold' where there was less competition, and the agent is allowed complete freedom of movement. The variables of classification as to whether a country is 'hot', 'moderate' or 'cold' are as follows: political stability; market opportunity; economic development and performance; cultural unity; legal barriers; physiographic barriers (obstacles created by the physical landscape); geo-cultural distance. (See Table 4.5)

Taking an example of an agent in Canada, a score may emerge of five 'hot' and two 'moderate' variables which would place Canada as relatively 'hot'. An example of an agent in South Africa may reveal four 'cold' and three 'moderate' variables which would place South Africa as relatively 'cold'. It is emphasized, however, that all such ratings will of course change over time. The positioning on the gradient scale is approximate but finer calibration is possible with the introduction of further subjective weights. The gradient scale shows the susceptibility of agents to change, and also predicts how the institutional structure is most likely to evolve. A firm operating with heavily committed investments in a 'hot' country may be guided by this gradient to relinquish control if the environment becomes 'cooler'.

The gradient depends on continual auditing. However, it does suggest the favourability of new markets and the ease with which their opportunities may be realized; the degree of control other foreign principals can exercise; and the degree of local control in the planning and development of operations in the foreign country.

This threefold classification (hot–moderate–cold) of countries using seven environmental factors on a hot–cold scale has since been further developed. Firstly, as a guide to long-range planning, it presents a method of allocating scarce resources selectively. Secondly, it

Table 4.5 Litvak and Banting: country environmental temperature gradient

Degree of environmental characteristics	*Hot country*	*Moderate country*	*Cold country*
Political stability	High	Medium	Low
Market opportunity	High	Medium	Low
Economic development and performance	High	Medium	Low
Cultural unity	High	Medium	Low
Legal barriers	Low	Medium	High
Physiographic barriers	Low	Medium	High
Geo-cultural barriers	Low	Medium	High

Source Litvak, I. A., and Banting, P. M. (1968) A conceptual framework for international business arrangements. In *Marketing and the New Science of Planning, American Marketing Association Conference Proceedings*, (ed King, R. L.) (Chicago, Fall) pp. 460–67.

specifies both the magnitude and type of foreign investment involvement depending on the 'temperature' of a country. Thirdly, the conceptual framework suggests how a large body of secondary data or environmental factors can be effectively utilized to undertake long-range planning.

The following shortcomings of the Litvak–Banting model were identified by Sheth and Lutz (1973) before proceeding to describe their own multivariate model within the Litvak–Banting framework.

- No analytical framework is developed to transform values into the gradient of 'hotness'.
- The operational indicators from secondary databanks are not described.
- TThe threefold classification is judgmental and arbitrary rather than empirically derived.
- There is no weighting attached to the individual environmental factors.
- Market opportunity, being specific to an industry or product, is different from the other six variables. This factor requires primary data whereas the other six can use secondary sources of information.

The Sheth–Lutz model classifies countries on six factors and then investigates the market potential in those countries which appear to be most promising for foreign investment. To do this, Sheth and Lutz used three data sources related to 1961–2 which gave profiles of eighty-two countries including China and the USSR, this left eighty countries which were then examined from the point of view of US corporate foreign investment. Fifteen variables were finally selected which related to the six environmental factors. Political stability is indicated by governmental stability, freedom from group opposition and political incultivation. Cultural unity is represented by religious, racial, and linguistic homogeneity, each on a three-point scale. Economic development and performance are reflected by economic development on a four-point scale; and energy consumption in megawatt hours. Legal barriers are indicated by two indirect variables. The first is the level of imports and exports measured in millions of US dollars. It is argued that a greater degree of international trade will be present in a country characterized by fewer legal barriers, and vice versa. Similarly, the second variable is the level of tariff on imports as a percentage of the total value of imports. Again, the greater the number of legal barriers, the more likely it is to find a higher levy of tariffs, and vice versa. Physiographic barriers are also included, although indirectly, by the three models of transportation. It is assumed that the greater the physiographic barriers present in a country due to mountains, deserts, and rivers the less will be the density of air, road, and railroad transports. By simultaneously taking into account all the three major surface and aerial methods of transportation, we presume that substitution effects among them, if any, are included. Finally, geo-cultural distance is measured in two ways, both of which are related primarily to the distance of a country from the USA — the first measure is an index of Westernization on a six-point scale; the second is the air distance from the USA.

The multivariate method which follows, resembles factor analysis except that:

- In factor analysis, typically the interest is in the correlational structure among variables (R-type factor analysis) whereas here the interest is in the structure among countries (Q-type factor analysis).
- Typically factor analysis is performed as a correlation matrix. This model obtains the rank of the data matrix X through its cross-products matrix.
- The emphasis in factor analysis is on the overall parsimony of the data matrix. In this

Table 4.6   The 'hot–cold' gradient from a historical US viewpoint

Country	Value	Country	Value
USA	13.22	Venezuela	−0.40
UK	4.60	Panama	−0.41
W Germany	3.44	Costa Rica	−0.47
France	2.64	Turkey	−0.47
Netherlands	2.12	Bulgaria	−0.47
Canada	2.01	Ecuador	−0.52
Belgium	2.00	Libya	−0.60
Denmark	1.44	Bolivia	−0.61
Italy	1.32	Philippines	−0.64
Taiwan	1.16	Egypt	−0.72
Japan	1.13	Peru	−0.73
Sweden	1.13	Lebanon	−0.80
Poland	0.93	Haiti	−0.88
Switzerland	0.86	Guatemala	−0.93
Ireland	0.83	Liberia	−0.94
Argentina	0.81	Ceylon	−0.97
Australia	0.76	Albania	−0.99
Norway	0.73	Thailand	−1.00
Austria	0.73	Mongolia	−1.07
E Germany	0.72	Paraguay	−1.13
Mexico	0.58	N Korea	−1.16
Finland	0.47	Iran	−1.23
Brazil	0.46	Indonesia	−1.23
New Zealand	0.40	S Korea	−1.24
Czechoslovakia	0.33	Ethiopia	−1.25
Spain	0.23	Cambodia	−1.28
Colombia	0.22	Saudi Arabia	−1.31
Greece	0.16	Syria	−1.32
Hungary	0.05	S Africa	−1.33
Portugal	−0.00	S Vietnam	−1.37
Uruguay	−0.13	Jordan	−1.42
Yugoslavia	−0.16	Iraq	−1.44
Honduras	−0.16	Pakistan	−1.52
El Salvador	−0.17	Burma	−1.55
Chile	−0.18	Israel	−1.57
India	−0.19	N Vietnam	−1.62
Nicaragua	−0.23	Nepal	−1.68
Cuba	−0.26	Afghanistan	−1.86
Dominican Rep	−0.29	Laos	−1.89
Romania	−0.29	Yemen	−1.99

Source   Sheth, J. N., and Lutz, R. J. (1973) A multivariate model of multinational business expansion. In *Multinational Business Operations*, (eds Sethi, S. P., and Sheth, J. N.) **3**, *Marketing Management*, Goodyear Publ., California.

Table 4.7   Goodnow, Hansz: correlations of corporate behaviour with environmental indicators

Strategy	GNP per capita		Environmental index		
	Variation r^2 explained		Variation r^2 explained		% increase in variance explained
Ranking of countries by % of US companies entering market	.63	40%	.75	56%	40%
Ranking of countries by % of US companies going via direct channels given market entry*	.49	24%	.63	40%	67%

* Direct market entry channels include: wholly or partly-owned subsidiaries and branches, licensing agreements and direct export through overseas company owned channels or company sales forces overseas.
Source   Goodnow, H. D., and Hansz, J. E. (1972) Environmental determinants of overseas market entry strategies. *Journal of International Business Studies*, **3,** (Spring) 45.

model, parsimony is directly related to the specific viewpoints the researcher is interested in. Accordingly the rotational procedures may vary between the two methods.

The relative positive values of countries reflect the degree of 'hotness' and the relative negative values of countries reflect the degree of 'coldness' from the viewpoint of US corporate foreign investment.

Generally, advanced countries were found to have the highest 'hot' values. Although Canada and Mexico are closer in geographical proximity, other countries were found to be better candidates for investment purposes. Relative to other countries, Portugal was found to have a zero value from an investment viewpoint. The East European and other Communist countries in Latin America, Africa, and Asia do not systematically cluster together in the cold spectrum of the continuum. For example, Poland (rated twelve), Czechoslovakia (rated twenty-four), and Hungary (rated twenty-eight) have positive values. It is somewhat surprising to find that even the 'hottest' country, the UK, is considerably separated on the continuum from the USA. This implies that overseas investment in general is more problematic than domestic investment.

Goodnow and Hansz (1972) have further refined the Litvak–Banting model with stepwise multiple discriminant analysis. The fifty-nine variables used in a cluster analysis of one hundred 'free-world' countries were gathered from published sources and expert opinion. The aim was to determine:

- how many unique groups of countries would best portray the one hundred countries,
- in which group a country belonged,
- a statistical profile of the environmental characteristics of each group.

Variables were selected as which best predicted group membership: seven economic and market-opportunity variables, six political and legal variables, three cultural variables, and one physiographic variable. The discriminant model was tested to determine its ability to reproduce the original country groupings. Ninety-eight out of one hundred countries were classified correctly by the seventeen variable discriminant factors. This was a result, firstly, of the country groupings being statistically determined by a fifty-nine-variable hierarchical cluster analysis, and, secondly, the model being tested on the same data that was used to construct it. Overall, the seventeen-variable discriminant model was found to fare far better than the traditional univariate method of GNP per capita.

References

Ansoff, I (1987) *Corporate Strategy*, revised ed, Penguin, London.
Barclays Bank Report on Export Development in France, Germany and the UK (1979), London, Barclays Bank.
Barnes, W. N. (1980) International marketing indicators. *European Journal of Marketing*, **14** (2), 90–136.
Bartos, R. (1989), International demographic data? Incomparable! *Marketing and Research Today*, **17** (4).
BETRO Trust Committee (1976) *Concentration on Key Markets*, British Overseas Trade Board (BOTB), London.
Business Environment Risk Index (BERI), Newark, Delaware USA.
Collins, V. D. (1935) *World Marketing*, JP Lippincott Company, London reprinted 1978 by Arno Press Inc., New York.
Goodnow, J. D. and Hansz, J. E. (1972) Environmental determinants of overseas market entry strategies, *Journal of International Business Studies*, **3** (Spring), 45.
Keegan, W. (1989) *Global Marketing Management*, Prentice-Hall, Englewood Cliffs, N. J. Chapter 8.
Litvak, Isaiah A. and Banting, Peter M. (1968), 'A conceptual framework for international business arrangements', in King, Robt. L. (ed), *Marketing and the New Science of Planning*, American Marketing Association Conference Proceedings, Chicago, Fall, 460–67.
Mandell, M. I. and Rosenberg, L. H. (1981), *Marketing*, 2nd ed, Prentice-Hall, Englewood Cliffs, N. J.
Montgomery, D. B. and Urban, G. L. (1969), *Management Science in Marketing*, Prentice-Hall, Englewood Cliffs, N. J., 4–6.
Ohmae, K. (1985), *Triad Power*, MacMillan-The Free Press, New York.
Oostveen, J. C. J. (1986), Industry study: the state of marketing research in Europe, *European Research*, **14** (3).
Paliwoda, S. J. (1991), International marketing – getting started. In *The Marketing Book* (ed. M. J. Baker), 2nd Edition, Heinemann, Oxford.
Piercy, N. (1982) *Export Strategy: Markets and Competition*, George Allen and Unwin, London.
Porter, M. E. (1985) *Competitive Advantage*, Macmillan Publishers, New York.
Root, F. R. (1987) *Entry Strategies for International Markets*, Lexington Books, Lexington, MA.
Ryan M. (1981) 'The pan-european survey comes of age', *Admap*, October, pp. 533–36.
Sheth, J. N., and Lutz, R. J. (1973) A multivariate model of multinational business expansion, In *Multinational Business Operations* (eds Sethi, S. P., and Sheth, J. N.), **3**, *Marketing Management*, Goodyear Pub., California.

(UNECE) United Nations Economic Commission for Europe (1990), Harmonisation of international trade statistics, TRADE/AC.25/R.2, 18 July.

Wind, J., and Douglas, S. (1972), International market segmentation, *European Journal of Marketing*, **6**, (1).

Key reading on foreign market research

Basic information

Advertiser's Annual, Thomas Skinner Directories, East Grinstead, Sussex RH19 1HE.

ASLIB Directory of Information Sources in the UK (ed. Codlin, E. M.), 3 Belgrave Square, London SW1X 8PL.

Benn's Press Directory. Tunbridge Wells, Kent.

British Institute of Management, 'Where to find it', Management House, Cottingham Road, Corby, Northants, NN17 1TT, 1986.

British Institute of Management, information sheets provided on a key-word basis.

BSI Buyers' Guide 1988/89 – listing of all British Standards Institute Kitemark and safety mark licenses, registered forms and registered stockists, BSI Quarterly Assurance, PO Box, 375, Milton Keynes, MK14 6LL.

Companies Registration Office, Crown Way, Maindy, Cardiff, CF4 3UZ and London Search Rooms, 55 City Road, London EC1Y 1RB. Company records on microfilm. Microfilm index all live companies. Annual report published by HMSO.

Croner's Reference Book for Exporters, Croner Publications, Croner House, London Road, Kingston upon Thames, Surrey, KTZ 6SR, loose-leaf book with monthly supplements.

Croner's Reference Book for Importers. Commonwealth Secretariat, *Commonwealth Organizations: a handbook of official and unofficial organisations active in the Commonwealth*, 2nd edn, 1979.

Department of Trade and Industry, *Register of Quarterly Assessed United Kingdom Companies*, 3rd edn, London 1986.

Directory of British Associations, CBD Research, Beckenham, Kent.

Directory of Directors (pub. T. Skinner), Windsor Court, East Grinstead House, East Grinstead, West Sussex RH18 1XE.

European Directory of Non-official Statistical Sources, 1988, Euromonitor Publications Limited, 87–88 Turnmill Street, London EC1M 5QU.

Europa Yearbook, detailed information on every country in the world and international organizations, Europe Publications Ltd, 12 Bedford Square, London WC1B 3JN.

The Europe 1992 Directory: A research and information guide, ITCU/Coventry Polytechnic, 1989.

Hollis Press and Public Relations Annual, Hollis Directories, Lower Hampton Road, Sunbury-on-Thames, Middlesex TW16 5HG.

Key Business Enterprises, The Top 20,000 British Companies, Dun and Bradstreet, 26–32 Clifton Street, London EC2P 2LY.

Kompass Register of British Industry & Commerce, 4 volumes. Windsor Court, East Grinstead House, East Grinstead, West Sussex RH19 1XD.

OECD Economic Surveys, for all member countries, HMSO London.

Sell's Directory of Products & Services, Sell's Publications, Epsom, Surrey KT17 1BQ.

London Chamber of Commerce and Industry. *Chambers of Commerce Worldwide – a selected list: 1989*, 68 Cannon Street, London EC49 5AB.

Statesman's Yearbook, Macmillan Press, London.

Stock Exchange Official Yearbook, London (pub. T. Skinner), Windsor Court, East Grinstead House, East Grinstead, West Sussex RH19 1XE.

Telephone Directories Inc. *Yellow Pages*.

Trade Associations and Professional Bodies of the UK, ed. P. Millard, Pergamon Press, Oxford.

UN Statistical Yearbook, New York. Also IMF, UNIDO, GATT, UNECE, FAO and other UN organizations publish their own statistics.

Whitaker's Almanac, published by J. Whittaker & Sons, 12 Dyott Street, London WC1A 1DF.

Who Owns Whom, Dun and Bradstreet, London EC2A 4BU.

Willings Press Guide, Thomas Skinner Directories, East Grinstead, Sussex RH19 1HE.

Europages, European Business Directory (annual) 7th edition, Thomson Directories, 296 Farnborough Road, Farnborough, Hampshire, GU14 7NU.

Europe's 15,000 largest companies: 1989, ELC International, Sinclair House, The Avenue, London, W13 8NT.

Major Companies of Europe, 1989–90 Graham and Trotman, Sterling House, 66 Wilton Road, London SW1V 1DE.

Bank publications

Lloyds Bank personally judged to be the best overseas series of the main banks but banks with a strong regional or national base should also be included.

Financial data

ICC Directory of UK Stockbroker Reports.

Extel Cards showing balance sheets, profit and loss accounts, dividends and activities, 37–45 Paul Street, London EC2A 4PB.

Annual Company Reports.

Stock Exchange Official Yearbook (as above).

FT (Financial Times) Publications.

EIU (Economist Intelligence Unit) *Publications*, various country, industry and product reports. 25 St James' Street, London SW1A 1HG.

Times 1000, Times Books, 16 Golden Square, London W1R 4BV, annually.

World Banking Abstracts World Banking Intelligence, Professional Publishing Ltd, 7 Swallow Place, London W1R 8AB.

Guides to British statistics

Central Statistical Office, *Guide to Official Statistics*, HMSO, London.

Central Statistical Office, *Government Statistics, a brief guide to sources*. HMSO, London.

Mort D. and Siddall S., *Sources of Unofficial UK Statistics*, Gower, 1986.

Indexes and abstracts

Anbar. Published in collaboration with the Chartered Institute of Marketing. Five abstracting journals containing one paragraph abstract of articles surveyed. Anbar is a division of MCB University Press, 62 Toller Lane, Bradford, West Yorks.

Business Periodicials Index. H. W. Wilson Ltd., 950 University Avenue, Bronx NY 10452, USA. Chiefly US publications, somewhat difficult to locate in the UK.

Contents Pages in Management. Monthly publication by Manchester Business School.

Predicasts Inc, *F & S Index*, monthly reports on business, economics and industry. 11001 Cedar Avenue, Cleveland, Ohio, 44106 USA.

SCIMP European Index of Management Periodicals. European Business School Librarians Group, Helsinki School of Economics and Business Administration, Runebarginkaty 22–24, 00100 Helsinki, Finland.

Marketing Surveys Index (pub. in association with the Chartered Institute of Marketing), Marketing Strategies for Industry (UK) Ltd, Heathcourt House, Parsons Green, London SW6 4TJ.

International reports

Business International Corporation produces several regional business newsletters, e.g. *Business Asia.*

Directory of US and Canadian Marketing Surveys and Services, pub. Kline, Fairfield, New Jersey, USA.

European Company Information: EEC Countries, 3rd edn, London Business School Information Services, 1989.

Euromonitor, Market Research Europe. Industrial Marketing Research Assoc. *European Guide to Industrial Market Research*, 11 Bird Street, Lichfield, Staffs.

Industrial Marketing Research Association, *European Sources of Industrial Market Research.*

Price Waterhouse – 2 series: *'Tax in . . .'* and *'Doing business in . . .'*

Published Data on Middle and Far East, Industrial Aids Ltd, 14 Buckingham Palace Road, London SW1.

US Dept of Commerce, *Overseas Business Reports* (thanks to an Exchange of Information Act with the USA. American foreign market research reports are to be found in the Dept. of Trade and Industry's EMIC (Export Market Information Centre), Victoria Street, London SW1 (see Chapter 5).

Market research survey reports

British Library. *British Reports, Translations and Theses*, monthly, Boston Spa, Wetherby, West Yorkshire.

Business International Corporation (International), 1 Dag Hammarskjold Plaza, New York, NY 10017, USA.

Euromonitor. *Market Research Great Britain.* JICNARS, *National Readership Survey of UK Top Companies* (by local region) Jordan Information Services Ltd, Jordan House, 47 Brunswick Place, London N1 6EE.

Keynote Reports, a range of 220 industry sector reports monthly, UK, some European, Keynote Publications Ltd., Field House, 72 Oldfield Road, Hampton, Middlesex TW12 1BR.

Marketsearch (formerly International Directory of Published Market Research).

MEAL, Media Expenditure Analysis Ltd., 110 St Martin's Lane, London WC2N 4BH.

Mintel: *Market Intelligence*, monthly reports of consumer goods in Britain, Mintel Ltd, Bromley, Kent.

National Economic Development Office, occasional specific industry reports, Millbank, London.

Market sector reports

Business Monitor (aggregated sales, production, exports, etc. for specific industrial sectors). Dept. of Trade and Industry, London.
Predicasts *Overview of Markets and Technology (PROMPT)* quarterly abstracts, PREDICASTS Inc., 11001 Cedar Avenue, Cleveland, Ohio, USA.
Worldcasts, abstracts of published international forecasts, for all countries, Predicast Inc., 200 University Circle Research Center, 11001 Cedar Avenue, Cleveland, Ohio, USA.

Newspapers indexes

Financial Times, Research Publishers Ltd PO Box 45, Reading RG1 8HF. Monthly index.
Times Index, Newspaper Archive Developments Ltd, Reading RG1 8HF
Wall Street Journal Index, Dow Jones & Company Inc., 200 Liberty Street, New York, NY 10281, USA.
Research Index. pub. Business Surveys Ltd, PO Box 21, Dorking, Surrey RH4 2YU. Fortnightly index of newspapers and products by keyword – also publish *Reports Index*.
McCarthy *Information Services*. Manor House, Ash Walk, Warminster, Wilts. BA12 8PY. Company as well as subject indexes.

On-line information retrieval databases

A full listing is available in Angela Hodden, *Management and Marketing Databases, 1988*. Aslib, London. Also, *On-line Business Information*. Monthly. *On-line Business Sourcebook*, from Headland Press Publications, 1 Henry Smith's Terrace, Headland, Cleveland, TS24 OPD, Tel. 0429 231902. (Twice a year.)
Popular on-line services include:
Financial Times, *Profile*. Tel: 0932 761444. Offers McCarthy Information services as well as *Financial Times*.
Pergamon Financial Data Services. Tel. 071 992 3456. Offers Dun and Bradstreet, European Marketing On-Line, Infomat, ICC.
Various on-line services offer on-line PROMT: ICC Business Information. Frost and Sullivan market Research Reports including: *Datastar*. Tel. 071-930-5503: *Dialog..* Tel. 0101-415-858-3810; *ABI-Inform*. Tel. 0833-844123.

5
Exporting and the small business

General background

Defining a small business is a difficult task and defining what is meant by a small business across various countries is even more difficult. The *Bolton Report* (1971), which drew attention to the decline of small business in the UK, defined a small firm in the manufacturing sector as one employing 200 or less people but this is but one feature of the small firm in the UK. To arrive at a more general definition, we will have to look elsewhere to pinpoint the essential characteristics which may have a bearing on the firm's ability to export. For example, owner-management and the fact that 'the people who run it are those that bear the risks of the enterprise' is another characteristic, but it is not necessarily limited to small business either as it is to be found among Ford Motor Co.; J. Sainsbury; Getty Oil, and others, which continue to be wholly-owned and controlled by the individuals who manage them. The importance of the small firm then has to be assessed in the light of other criteria which assess its absolute and relative size in the market place and so we offer the following definition:
The small firm:

- has only a small share of its market,
- is managed in a personalized way by its owners or part-owners and does not have an elaborate management structure,
- is not sufficiently large to have access to the capital market for the public issue or placing of securities.

Once a firm has outgrown any of these three thresholds it ceases to be a small firm. Therefore to qualify as a small firm under this definition, the firm will have to simultaneously qualify under all three criteria. Naturally, it depends on the country; for Poland, a small business would mean fewer than twenty employees and any bigger would mean medium-sized, particularly in the private sector (Paradiso, 1990).

Having defined the small business we have to then acknowledge what the *Bolton Report* (1971) had to say of the UK, viz. that it '... showed the smallest proportion of total manufacturing employment in small establishments in any comparable civilized country.' Burns and Dewhurst (1986) point to Denmark which they say is, and has always been, dominated by small businesses employing less than fifty people. These small businesses have problems in exporting due to lack of scale, inexperience and inability to finance new investments in new markets. Yet in a small country like Denmark it is necessary to have to turn to the international market in order to grow. To take another example, France is the second most important economic power in Europe, behind Germany. It is the most bureaucratic and centralized of the Western industrial nations and yet has a thriving small business sector. The French definition of small business is based on employment but generally excludes the owner-manager and his immediate family members so it covers companies with between ten and 500 employees.

Small firms in France (up to 500 employees) account for about 60 per cent of all business activity, as measured by employment or by turnover. Exports account for about 13 per cent of their turnover. Above the 200 employee threshold usually all small and medium-size companies are involved in international trade. Some 2,500 of the 33,000 exceeded two million FF in exports in 1980, corresponding to about one-third of their turnover, 1500 had foreign sales subsidiaries and over 700 had foreign production facilities.

It is intriguing to note from Table 5.1 to see how even very small companies realize the importance of a global market and how at the other end of the spectrum among the 200–499 employee companies, more than half viewed their market as being global.

As to the UK, Burns and Dewhurst point to a reversal of the process of decline pointed out by the *Bolton Report* in 1971, and an annual increase of 0.2 per cent, i.e., of firms increasing their numbers of employees while larger companies were divesting. However, the risks of setting up a small business are great and data from the Business Statistics Office suggests that 60 per cent fail in the first three years of existence. On average, 9 per cent of companies fail each year. Lack of fixed capital is a problem for small companies as is collecting debts from larger companies.

On a comparative basis, the UK has been overshadowed by Italy in terms of economic importance in recent years. In Italy, as elsewhere, the principal source of extended financing is credit from suppliers, representing 40 per cent of their overall financial liabilities. The lending banks provide 25 per cent. The use of facilitated funds, which means loans with more favourable conditions or rates than those offered by banks, is not very important to small Italian businesses. Complexity of the procedures involved and the request always for security constraining many possible companies from applying. (See Table 5.2).

The UK situation where small business accounts for only 8 per cent of exports as against the Japanese situation where the figure is 60 per cent, reveals not only a great disparity but a potential opportunity for small business in Britain to grow via exports, providing they are willing to accept the challenge. Yet in the USA, only 10 per cent of total US exports are conducted by small business, for whom this activity would account for 6–7 per cent of their total sales. Japan remains an anomaly with its 46,000 enterprise cooperatives where 99 per cent of business are small and contribute more than 80 per cent of the total employment.

In 1981, the last year for which official British statistics were reported (*British Business*, 1983), half UK exports were accounted for by seventy-two firms. Excluding oil and

Table 5.1   French attitudes to international trade (1980)

Size employees	Proportion exporting	Is your market			
		Regional	National	European	Worldwide
10 to 49	48 per cent	38 per cent	38 per cent	12 per cent	12 per cent
50 to 199	70 per cent	17 per cent	40 per cent	19 per cent	24 per cent
200 to 499	90 per cent	3 per cent	28 per cent	15 per cent	54 per cent

Source   Burns, P., and Dewhurst, J. (1986) *Small Business in Europe*, Macmillan, London.

diamonds, 120 enterprises accounted for half of UK exports in 1981. Two-thirds of UK exports excluding oil and diamonds were made by 415 companies, and 688 concerns reported exports of over £5m and they were responsible for 70 per cent of UK exports. There were a further 1,153 concerns with exports under £5m which accounted for under 5 per cent of exports, although it was recognized that there were many small exporters not covered by the inquiry. Around four-fifths of UK exports, excluding diamonds, are by enterprises with related concerns overseas and in 1981 these related concerns purchased 30 per cent of UK exports. UK enterprises controlled by or associates of overseas companies continued to account for almost a third of UK exports in 1981. Just under half of the exports of these enterprises went to the controlling companies and other related concerns overseas. The share of exports accounted for by UK-owned UK companies which control overseas concerns or have associates overseas rose to 51 per cent. Nearly a third of these exports were to their overseas affiliates.

British exporting is now dominated by large firms. In the UK, 20 per cent of the visible exports derive from the activities of a mere ten firms. Although small firms account for 20 per cent of the GNP, an examination of six key industries showed that small firms accounted for 5 per cent of the exports of these industries. Small firms in the north-west of England studied in the *Bolton Report* (1971) contributed only 10 per cent of the total exports of all the firms in the sample. The report states: 'The belief that small size is an insuperable disadvantage overseas has no doubt inhibited many small firms from entering export markets.'

Martin Rumbelow, Secretary of the British Overseas Trade Board (BOTB) captured the essential difficulty of persuading small companies to think big when he was quoted as saying: 'the encouragement of small businesses to export is always an uphill battle, one that you can never win, but one that you must always fight so as not to lose'. (*Financial Times,* 24 October 1985).

In Japan, the small company sector provides about 60 per cent of direct exports. In the UK, the figure is 8 per cent. The presence of the Japanese trading house makes it possible for small and medium-sized Japanese companies to regard their export markets as being just as accessible as their home markets, whereas some of their UK counterparts are unable to penetrate international markets at all. Japan may now be on the threshold of a new era in its relations with Europe, based on on-the-spot manufacturing and assembly, rather than direct

Table 5.2   Italian exporting financial numbers using facilitated funds, 1978

Size of firms by number of employees	Number of exporting firms (a)	Number of exporting firms using facilitated funds (b)	$\frac{a}{b} \times 100$
11–50 (micro)	7840	52	0.7
51–100 (small)	3181	24	0.8
101–500 (medium)	3027	74	2.4
>501	527	61	11.6
Total	14,575	211	1.4

Source   Burns, P., and Dewhurst, J. (1986) *Small Business in Europe,* Macmillan, London.

exports, and on large-scale involvement in the economy of Europe rather than arms-length trading relations. There is the well publicized joint venture between Honda and Rover cars in manufacturing, but more importantly there is the direct investment in the manufacture of cars by Nissan and domestic electrical equipment by Sony, Hitachi, and Toshiba. The UK accounts for the majority of Japanese investment within the EC.

For small business in the UK, the main outlet appears to be Europe. The EC take 45 per cent while other European countries take a further 20 per cent according to a study conducted by Market Research Enterprises on behalf of British Telecom Europages.

The main characteristics of the exporting activities of small firms include:

1 Export market research used by minority — the norm is for overseas orders to arise by chance and to be met, but that market is not then pursued further. Unexpected export orders do not generally give rise to market research.
2 Fairly low expenditure commitment in terms of total market research budgets and specifically export market research.
3 Prime selling techniques are personal visits, use of fairs and exhibitions, and employment of agents.
4 General ignorance of government support — little use made of BOTB services, with even less use made of management consultants, chambers of commerce and embassies overseas.
5 Limited resources lead to use of export houses and selling via UK buying offices of overseas department stores.

Problems for small exporters

Specific problem areas for small exporters include:

- A relatively large domestic market and lack of exposure to other cultures, making the selection of markets and identification of customers abroad difficult.
- The lack of management time and general resources.
- Reaching the foreign markets; selecting and motivating 'arm's length' commission agents. Finding the good agents and distributors and being able to keep them motivated.
- Controlling the foreign operation, channel policy, and physical distribution. The interest of principal and agent may often differ and small businesses because of their size may be more exposed to the varying degrees of political, economic and financial risk made uncertain by the indifferent attitude of a foreign agent.
- Paperwork and management of export operations.
- Cost of supervisory flying salesmen is often very high when costed per man year of effort in the field, even more so when costed separately on a per visit basis.
- Which language is the sales staff to learn if visiting many territories? Targeting key markets rather than spreading resources thinly over a number of territories has been a message of the *BETRO Report* (1979), and *Barclays Bank Report* (1979).
- Cost of overseas offices may not be justified by the sales potential of particular territorial markets. Going it alone retains independence of action but may be financially ruinous having the same effect as 'placing all your eggs in one basket.'
- Different safety and quality standards overseas may involve a small company in expensive modifications to achieve compatibility. This adds to the 'up-front' costs before a single product may be sold.

- A long-term perspective has to be taken of many markets which may require a long company presence before achieving any payback. This is particularly true where the product concept is new, existing distribution channels are unreliable and the manufacturer wants to assure himself that the customer receives quality and service. In these cases, vertically integrated distribution networks are the answer.

The magnitude of these problems was investigated in the USA (Rabino, 1980) by asking respondents to rank order by relative importance, and this produced the following 'rank order' or 'league table' of difficulty:

1 *Paperwork.*
2 *Selecting a reliable distributor.* Lists available from embassies and trade councils do not offer a qualitative assessment, which is what may be required. Increasingly the British clearing banks are offering their services in this area previously dominated by the merchant banks.
3 Comparative disadvantages due to *non-tariff barriers,* e.g., health and safety standards used to exclude imports. Small companies do not always have the resources to modify products and fight back.
4 *Honouring letters of credit,* although not where this has been endorsed by the local bank thus creating an irrevocable confirmed letter of credit (LC) where the funds are guaranteed by a bank in the seller's country. LCs are still the most common form of payment.
5 *Communication with foreign customers.* Not only language is involved here but distance which may be both psychological as well as geographical. It may be comforting to visit a country where you feel people think, act and feel as you do, the reverse is also true.

Perceptions of non-exporting small firms

Very often perceptions are judgemental and purely subjective and so not based on fact, thus creating psychological barriers to exporting. It is not necessary to have knowledge of a subject to have opinions about it! There may be an expectation of profit maximization within

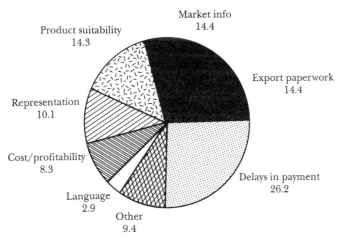

Figure 5.1 *Greatest difficulties in exporting*

a specific period, and although this expectation may be based on domestic market experience, international business does take longer to develop.

If a decision to sell or produce overseas is based on 'hunch', rather than substantiated by fact e.g. independent market research, self-imposed market limitation factors may come into play.

Companies may consider an export effort to be too much trouble or they may believe that they could not cope with the resources required for overseas selling, assembly, manufacture, construction, engineering, consulting or licensing, in which case, they are probably right for without commitment, failure becomes more certain.

The geographical scope of overseas operations may discourage some firms, yet freight costs may not be the largest component in the foreign export price as can be seen in the degree to which the Pacific Basic countries have become the World's workshop. Telephone, fax and telex and air travel can further minimize distance as can the commonality of language.

Yet, there may be structural constraints emanating from company policy as devised by owner-managers or the board of directors. For example, there may be a policy limiting the company to certain types of trading relationships, such as wholly owned subsidiaries. Or there may be financial self-imposed constraints, e.g., refusal to seek external debt or equity capital. Or there may be other corporate policies against trading with certain countries because of the political regime in power, e.g., communism or a system in force, e.g., apartheid.

Identifying the exporter

Instead of simply using the terms 'passive' and 'active' as applied to exporting, Cannon and Willis (1986) see it in terms of a four cell matrix where the two axes are 'experience' and 'commitment'. The non-exporter is a fairly small group too concerned with survival in the immediate local domestic market to get involved in exports, and too young to gain the interest of overseas buyers (see Figure 5.2).

The start-up exporter has no export experience but a commitment by top management to investigate export opportunities and invest some management time and effort.

The size of the cell containing passive exporters is by far the largest. For the UK, the Department of Trade report, *Into Active Exporting*, clearly described the economic significance

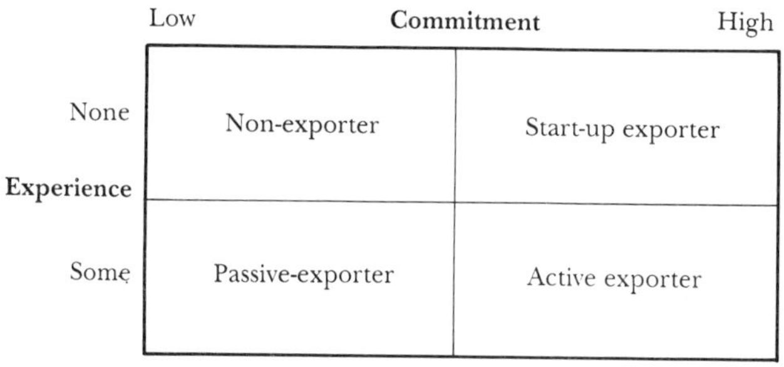

	Low Commitment High	
None	Non-exporter	Start-up exporter
Experience		
Some	Passive-exporter	Active exporter

Figure 5.2   *Export experience base*
Source   Cannon, T., and Willis, M. (1986) *How to Buy and Sell Overseas*, Business Books/ Hutchinson London.

of converting passive exporters into active exporters. If we take then the upper limit scenario where the average ratio of all passive exporters could be raised to equal that of active exporters, then UK exports of manufacturers would increase by £5.2 billion at 1985 prices, an increase of 117 per cent equal to half of the total non-oil deficit on the 1985 current account.

In this particular study for the Department of Trade, active exporters were defined as exporting more than 15 per cent of their turnover in one of the past three years; non-exporters were the firms with export ratios of 1 per cent or less and passive exporters were the residual of these two categories.

The significance of size is important. *Into Active Exporting* identified a situation in Britain where the hundred largest exporters in 1985 accounted for 85 per cent of UK exports of fuels, basic materials and manufacturers. The top fifty accounted for 47 per cent alone and the share of the hundred largest in total net output in manufacturing was 41 per cent. Against this difficult background, *Into Active Exporting* addressed three important questions:

1 To establish the extent of untapped export potential among small and medium sized UK companies.
2 To ascertain the barriers and obstacles to exporting and their significance.
3 To establish what would encourage companies with export potential, but not exporting actively, to become active exporters.

The British Institute of Export (1987) is in no doubt about this failing:

> Too many companies, too many directors and managers still think that selling their products and services outside the United Kingdom is something for someone else. Undoubtedly, the reason for this attitude is the failure of our education and training system, which in many instances does not include automatically, the international dimension in the teaching of each management subject in business studies and management courses.

Peter Williamson (1990) in a comparative study of British, Japanese and West German exporters' strategies towards the US market commented on the very significant difference which affects both the types of products exported and degree of success in US market penetration.

The British strategy was seen to be ruled by domestic supply and demand consolidation. Pricing was volatile as it was tied to sterling, availability was affected by the attitude of British suppliers who regarded exports as a 'filler' for production capacity. Consequently, British involvement in distribution, sales and marketing was limited. Where competition was intense, British exporters did not fare at all well, with the exception of certain identifiable market niches which insulated from price fluctuation, erratic product availability and competition. The Japanese were at the other end of the spectrum working to build market penetration over an extended period. Whereas British exporters saw exports as an adjunct to their core business and as products sold from the UK, the Japanese positioned their products in the US marketplace with regard to local domestic competition in factors such as pricing and dedicated long-term support, distribution and sales as investment in a target market. The difference could hardly be more telling whereas British companies were still thinking of actual exports abroad, the Japanese were treating these foreign sales as local market sales of Japanese products. Yet the British are not alone. Taking a measure such as per capita volume of foreign trade, the 1987 figures amounted to $5,343 in the EC, $4,314 in Japan and $2,599 in the USA, approximately half of the EC average. Two further points about US trade:

- approximately 85 per cent of US exports can be traced to only 250 firms (Stoffel, 1985).
- of the estimated 250,000 manufacturing exporters less than 19 per cent account for more than 80 per cent of the total export volume (Kaikati, 1984).

Dichtl, Koeglmayr and Mueller (1990) focusing on the foreign market orientation of managers established that it was possible to empirically differentiate between export-experienced and inexperienced decision-makers by using a measuring device based on managers who

- experience a greater than average psychic distance to foreign markets or countries,
- are older, have a more limited education level, are less proficient in foreign languages and travel less to foreign countries than their colleagues,
- are risk averse, rigid and unwilling to change, and expect lengthy, job-related stays abroad to have a negative effect on their careers and families,
- display a principally negative attitude toward exporting as a possible company strategy.
- are not foreign market oriented, and will, under comparable conditions be less likely to participate in export activities than foreign market oriented colleagues.

The resultant firm typology in Figure 5.3 comprises five classes that are homogeneous and can be arranged into a matrix with the dimensions 'foreign market domestic market orientation' and objective conditions.

Factors in the exporting success of small firms

Conventional wisdom states that the following factors may be important for a firm to achieve success in exporting, by exploiting an advantage in foreign markets whether in:

- high technology
- substantial research and development (R&D)
- sophisticated marketing
- advanced form of organizational design

Monk (1989) points out that there is no across-the-board success or failure rate for any industry; that no country has exclusively the knowhow that puts all its industries one step ahead of the competition; and that success – and lesser success – occurs in all industries and across all markets. Nevertheless, Monk cites the following as criteria for success:

1 geographic expansion of operations
2 degree of identification with the local market/country
3 sales growth per market
4 profit growth:
   - per market
   - intentional as a percentage of total profits
5 quality' of corporate identity/reputation in local markets
6 corporate 'will' - staying power – long-term commitment.

A study of successful small exporters in North America by Cavusgil, Bilkey and Tesar

Firms' conditions for exporting / Decision-makers	Conducive	Non-conducive
Foreign oriented	(Small firms) ① / ② Exporters / (Large firms)	③ Occasional exporters (weakness in firm conditions)
Domestically oriented	④ Occasional exporters (weakness in management)	⑤ Domestically oriented firms

Figure 5.3. *Classification of exporters and non-exporters based on personality factors and firm's conditions*
Source   Dichtl, E., Koeglmayr, H.-G., and Mueller, S. (1990) International orientation as a precondition for export success. *Journal of International Business Studies*, **21**, (1). 23–40.

(1979) showed many of these points in the recipe for success. The successful firms were seen to:

1 hold patents and/or have a technological orientation
2 have a price advantage in the market
3 have already established fairly broad market coverage
4 have sales volume in excess of $1 million per year (a measure too quickly eroded by inflation unfortunately)
5 hold high profit aspirations.

But another study by Kirpalani and Mackintosh (1980) took a different view, pointing out that the inputs which determine market effectiveness for the small firm could be different from those that apply to the large multinational corporation (MNC). Stating then the factors which may contribute towards success, but including also a few rather general thoughts, we note that:

- Government assistance does not act as a motivator although its absence would be regretted.
- Top management effort and backing are required.
- Pricing and promotion are most important.
- Firms with one or two products are more successful.
- Mature products, if modified for export, can compete successfully.
- Sophistication of a firm's manufacturing process is not a prerequisite for exporting success.

- Information for control reporting is vital – quality of information, frequency of reporting, closeness of monitoring of foreign operations.

This has been conceptualized into a model of small firm export sales (Brasch, 1979) whereby export sales are a function of *Effort Opportunity Resistance*, i.e.

$$S = f(E \times O \times R)$$

where *R* is represented by ability to compete outside home market; cultural uniqueness; logistical barriers; and government regulations. It is imperative that an exporter obtain whatever information he can about these three sales variables before entering the export field. The exporter not only needs to evaluate the opportunity that presents itself in the marketplace: he also needs to identify the resistance factors which may make it more difficult to take advantage of this opportunity and could even prevent him from capitalizing on what might otherwise appear to be a lucrative market. Finally, the manufacturer must look at the *Effort* variable, objectively assessing the quantity and quality of inputs that he is capable of providing and willing to commit. After each variable has been analysed individually, some overall evaluation should be made.

Table 5.3 depicts twenty-three different activities which executives were asked by Howard and Herremans (1988) to evaluate in terms of overall importance to their exporting operations. Many of these relate to planning and if this is performed well, the likelihood of success is much greater.

Using networks

An 'intangible', it is often a very neglected resource stored out of sight and needing only to be unlocked. Cannon and Willis (1986) emphasize the importance of this unstructured in-house resource which includes:

- Previous business and business inquiries. This may involve searching memories as well as files for requests for product information as well as requests for tender. Comparison may be usefully made with what the competition is doing.
- Contacts, acquaintances formal and informal. Links with the parent group and the extended information resource of the grapevine. Cannon and Willis point out though the common mistake of using a parent group's agency without examining whether it can handle all of the group's business or has the marketing expertise to succeed.
- External relationships. Many customers may be part of multinational firms whose annual reports will often highlight overseas activities, prospects, locations and details of senior personnel.
- Export organizations such as the Department of Trade and Industry's 'Export Initiative'; chambers of commerce; banks; buying houses; export clubs; export councils for specific trading areas e.g. East European Trade Council and professional organizations such as the Institute of Export.

Small firms concentrate their activities on neighbouring countries to keep their problems within bounds (Verhoeven, 1988). Networking can work to the advantage of the company and its parent group exposing it to the opportunities of a global market place and possible partners if unwilling to go it alone either in terms of research, product development or market expansion.

The exporting consortium alternative

Assuming size is an important variable in the exporting success of small firms, we wish now to consider the possibilities for small exporters to form themselves into export clubs or industry-wide export trade associations.

This is known as 'consortium marketing', 'federated marketing' or 'grouping' depending on which country you are in. Basically, the concept is simply one of strength in unity. Good

Table 5.3   Importance of business activities ranked by successful small exporting firms

Activity	Importance (mean*)
N = 101	
1 Selecting agents/distributors	1.902
2 Maintaining agency/distributor relations	1.880
3 Completing exporting documentation	1.774
4 Pricing decisions	1.641
5 Providing technical advice	1.626
6 Understanding local business practices	1.587
7 Collecting foreign accounts	1.578
8 Developing export sales leads	1.570
9 Sales promotion activities	1.565
10 Providing parts availability	1.448
11 Sales force management	1.429
12 Researching foreign markets	1.418
13 Obtaining credit information	1.385
14 Providing repair service	1.376
15 Understanding cultural differences	1.348
16 Physical distribution activities	1.242
17 Adapting advertising messages	1.225
18 Advertising media selection	1.178
19 Physical product adaptation	1.146
20 Analyzing political risks	1.022
21 Managing political risks	0.989
22 Packaging adaptations	0.967
23 Managing foreign exchange	0.956

Source   Howard, D. G., and Herremans, I. M. (1988). Sources of assistance for small business exporters: advice from successful firms. *Journal of Small Business Management*, July, 48–54.

Table 5.4   Main reasons for failure

1 Incorrect analysis of true market potential (often over-enthusiastic and underestimating the problems).
2 Inappropriate company structure for the host country based on country-of-origin model. Keep financial controls and reporting systems constant or you will make the venture fail.
3 Start-up cost control: including office location, quality of accommodation; level of manning, and hotel resource required.
4 Job titles have an effect on employees and clients but it makes 'promoted' employees more expensive to discuss.
5 Too rapid staff changes. Exporters may look for quick short-term results whereas local nationals may take a longer view. The corporation is what is important and continuity of policy is as important as continuity of personnel.
6 Too fast tie-ups with rural party distributors and representatives. The seduction of fast market entry may lead to market dependency and a constraint on further market development.
7 Lack of an international career track within the organization. Successful companies have done this creating executives that are broader in outlook not parochial or xenophobic. Businesses will need executives like these to survive into the next century.

Source   Adapted from Monk, K. (1989) *Go International: Your guide to marketing and business development*, McGraw-Hill, Maidenhead.

agents need a great deal of backup and supporting effort from home, which means frequent expensive visits are necessary, with management effort at a premium. Depending on the number of participants, and the degree of government financial support, costs for a company acting in consortium have been estimated at about one-tenth of those which the company would otherwise have had to meet for its own exclusive local presence, and about the same fraction for the equivalent cost of employing 'flying salesmen' to supervise agents.

Most importantly each member of the consortium keeps his own identity and sovereignty, while sharing in the combined strength; and small companies who constitute the growth sector of the economy and provide the new job opportunities, can in theory begin to sell into overseas markets as easily as they sell into the home market.

A union of three or four companies, offering complementary and non-competing products and services, collaborating through a joint organization in an overseas sales facility provides the advantages of cost-sharing and risk-sharing for the individual companies.

Other advantages may include:

- The group can deploy resources beyond the budget limits of the individual companies, and with a joint turnover which will justify the expenditure.
- On-the-spot professional top calibre sales staff arrange feedback, after-sales service, local distribution, and provide permanent sales presence.
- Concentrating on specific markets minimizes the language problem.

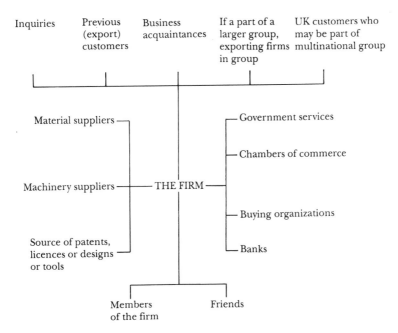

Figure 5.4 A firm's network of possible points of contact with export markets
Source Cannon, T., and Willis M. (1986) *How to Buy and Sell Overseas*, Business Books/ Hutchinson, London

Forming an exporting consortium

Exporting consortiums usually develop along the following lines:

1 A target overseas geographical market is identified, in market and not product terms.
2 A group of two or three companies with complementary products/services agree to co-operate in their export efforts. A group of companies thus formed can between them supply and design a service or package system, and in addition provide financial credits and working capital.
3 A jointly owned overseas marketing consortium is created and registered as a public company with limited liability.
4 The consortium is managed by a board of directors with one director appointed by each company. The consortium appoints its own general manager and overseas marketing staff.
5 Communications are established between the overseas offices or marketing staff, and the member companies. The role of the overseas posts is very important in agreeing and implementing plans, in collaborating, negotiating, and providing technical presence.
6 Local images may be all important. Equally a maintenance facility may be a prerequisite for sales, and the maintenance operation may in itself be very profitable.
7 The consortium will develop its own rules concerning managers and participants and third-party supplier's selling prices, stocks, publicity, and sales policies. All members are expected to quote fair prices to the consortium and not take unfair advantage of individual key inputs, e.g., raw materials.
8 A countertrade member would supply financial credits for credit sales and provide working capital for contract operations.

9 The consortium appoints, if required, a consulting engineer as technical advisor so that it can take advantage of a strong consulting system.

Attracting more small firms into exporting

More small firms could be attracted into exporting by improving the trading environment and simplifying trading operations.

Christensen, de Rocha and Gertner (1987) examined 152 Brazilian companies exporting in 1978 and interviewed them again six years later to determine the factors that were correlated with continuation to export. Firm characteristics, export management practices and manager perceptions were each found to be correlated with exporting success thus supporting the basic contention that it is possible to predict export performance. Firms that discontinued exporting relied more on the Brazilian government export incentives, possibly to be competitive in international markets without making the necessary structural changes, thereby raising important questions about the long-run impact of the Brazilian export programmes and of government export subsidies generally.

Improving the trading environment

This could be achieved by:

- Eliminating the distrust among small businessmen of government departments by making the latter more responsive to the needs of small business.
- Correcting the mistaken perception of non-exporters who view the cost factors – executive time, packaging and insurance costs, clerical time, shipping costs – to be higher than do exporters.
- Encouraging exporters to be proactive rather than reactive in their approach to international marketing, focusing on the profit advantage of international marketing activities over domestic sales, and moving away from the idea of a market of last resort.
- Encouraging trade associations to participate in exporting on behalf of their members, also to develop export market research databanks.
- Encouraging the development of voluntary export consortia which can provide the financial strength and marketing resources so many small firms lack.

Simplifying trading operations

The key to this question is in simplifying and reducing paperwork. Arranging export credit and documentation may be a small task for the large company but for the small company taking perhaps its first large export order, the export preparations can be intimidating. In Britain, too, there is a polarization of all financial services towards the south. This means that, firstly, in the north of England the general level of awareness of services will be lower, and that secondly, the expertise is mainly to be found only by travelling to London and the south since most bank branches feel quite out of their depth in trying to handle export credit assistance and prefer to have such specialist questions answered by their head office and that is based in London. The situation is changing, however, and the main clearing banks are beginning to move their financial services further north. Still, the banks impose a floor limit on the export credit facilities which they offer which they do not generally seek to go below. This may be of the order of £50,000. As this may well constitute a large order for the small company, it may feel, quite rightly, that its needs are not being served. Into this breach have stepped confirming houses such as the English Export Finance Association based in Rochdale. A licensed deposit taker by the Bank of England, it is not only physically present in its area but able and willing to handle a smaller scale of business.

With regard to paperwork particularly, much has been done by SITPRO (Simplification of International Trade Procedures), London to facilitate the processing of export documentation, also by providing task-specific pre-printed stationery, as well as occasional country reports. The Confederation of British Industry (CBI) helps with world regional area trade specialists as does the Export Credit Guarantee Department (ECGD) although it often encounters the criticism that its lines of credit are designed for large companies and not the smaller size orders which would probably still constitute very large export orders for small businesses. With regard to the ECGD, too, a Matthews inquiry into its efficiency in March 1984 found a widely held feeling that the ECGD's service and premium charges to large exporters were adversely affected by the proportionately greater amount of time devoted by the department to servicing the small exporter. In the five years to 1983, all but the largest of the ECGD's comprehensive short-term guarantees failed to contribute enough to cover the cost of administration and claim payments. About 40 per cent of the smallest policies produced less than 3 per cent of premium income and accounted for nearly 20 per cent of administration costs. Matthews recommended that the ECGD should not have to meet the costs of services to small exporters beyond its obligation as an insurer.

The Department of Trade has centralized its services to exporters under the umbrella organization of the Export Initiative and these include:

- Export Marketing Research Scheme (EMRS) which provides free professional advice to help you decide whether specific market surveys are needed, advice on how to get them underway and offers financial support often in the form of grants for market research studies undertaken overseas. This can cover:
  using professional consultants
  using your own staff
  purchasing published marketing research
  research commissioned by your trade association
- Export Market Information Centre (EMIC) brings together the former Statistics and Market Intelligence Library (SMIL); the microfilm database of product information of the former Product Data Store (PDS) and so consult:
  statistics: worldwide statistics are available
  market research reports: a selection of overseas market reports supplements the statistics collection
  directories: overseas trade and telephone directories
  mail order catalogues: deal for checking consumer goods preferences
  development plans: economic plans for selected countries are available on loan to exporters
  Other online databases: a search service is available to selected commercial online databases.

EMIC is located at:

Export Market Information Centre (EMIC)
Department of Trade and Industry
1–19 Victoria Street
London SW1H 0ET

Tel: 071–215 5444/5
Tlx: 8811074/5 (DTHQG)
Fax: 071–222 2629

Open 9:30–17:30, Monday to Friday. Last admissions at 17:00. Closed on public holidays.
Entrance on corner of Victoria Street and Abbey Orchard Street.

- British Overseas Trade Information System (BOTIS) is the Department of Trade's own electronic database of export information and deserves special mention. Visitors to EMIC can now access BOTIS through terminals in the Centre. BOTIS includes:
    The Product Data Store (PDS): DTI's computerized microfilm database of product and industry information showing market size, market structure and market share.
    The Overseas Contacts Service (OCS) which provides names and addresses of organizations, companies and individuals overseas: manufacturers, importers, distributors, agents and retailers.
    The Export Intelligence Service (EIS), a subscription service which offers tailored notification of specific export opportunities: enquiries from overseas about products or services, calls for tender, agents seeking UK principals, early notification of projects overseas. While the EIS subscription service will continue to be the main form of delivery of this service, visitors to EMIC will now be able to see examples of the types of information available.
    Promotional Events (PEV) provides information about forthcoming fairs and exhibitions. A large number of specialist trade fairs take place on the continent, especially in West Germany and France.
    EMIC Publications: the Centre's own catalogue of statistics and directories, mail order catalogues and development plans is now also available as part of BOTIS.

- PEP and major projects. Our Projects and Export Policy Division (PEP) co-ordinates all government interests and support services for large overseas projects. PEP collaborates closely with the entire range of appropriate government departments at home and with the Diplomatic Service Posts overseas. When appropriate PEP can bring the full weight of government support to bear. This can include ministerial and diplomatic initiatives, together with the involvement of other government departments such as ECGD and the Overseas Development Administration.
    It is also benefits from the advice and support of the Overseas Projects Board (OPB), a body of senior businessmen with practical experience of overseas projects appointed by the Minister for Trade. The Board advises on both policy issues and on government financial support for specific projects.
    In addition, the World Aid Section of PEP provides a single source of advance

information for UK exporters on the work of the multilateral development agencies, which help to finance projects and programmes worth billions every year.

Further information:

Large Project Support
Projects and Export Policy Division
1 Victoria Street
London SW1H 0ET

Branch 1
Airports and equipment, canals, bridges, tunnels, roads: 071–215 4911
Railways, trucks, urban transport systems, shipyards, ports: 071–215 4864

Branch 2
Hydroelectric projects worldwide except India and Pakistan, (
    cement plant: 071–215 4024
    metallurgical: 071–215 4299
Chemical, petro-chemical (except primary processing and refining), non-ferrous metallurgical and other process plant: 071–215 4905
Open-cast and under-ground mining, all power projects in India and hydro projects in Pakistan: 071–215 4909

Branch 3
Telecommunications, postal services, electronics and educational equipment projects: 071–215 5360
Water and sewerage projects, agro-industrial and urban development projects, construction projects (e.g., health and leisure facilities), forestry and fisheries: 071–215 4838
Oil and gas (including exploration, production, primary processing, refining, distribution, pipelines), industrial projects not covered elsewhere: 071–215 4838
Power generation, transmission and distribution projects, excluding all power projects in India and large projects worldwide (Engineering Markets Division): 071–215 6751/6754

World Aid Section, Room 042
1 Victoria Street
London SW1H 0ET

World Bank Group: 071–215 5369/4372
Asian Development Bank, African Development Bank, Inter-American Development Bank, Caribbean Development Bank and United Nations Agencies:
071–215 4256/5053
European Development Funds: 071–215 4255/5616
European Structural Funds: 071–215 4279/5615

● Technical help to exporters. Removing technical barriers to trade is a vital element of the Community's Single Market Programme to ensure that member states recognize each other's terms and certification arrangements. As the Single Market is completed, the effect will be that any product which can be sold in the member state in which it is produced, will be freely marketable in all other member states of the community.

Meanwhile, firms will still need to get to grips with differences in national rules and practice. Technical Help to Exporters (THE) is a service operated by the British Standards Institution (BSI) at Linford Wood, Milton Keynes. The BSI has been advising British manufacturers on foreign regulations and standards since 1966.

THE is a service operated by the British Standards Institution and its staff of engineers and information specialists. It provides advice on foreign requirements including:

National laws, particularly in relation to safety and environmental protection
Technical standards
Certification processes in relation to customer needs.

It also has a further range of services which include:

A technical enquiry service to answer day-to-day problems
A consultancy service
Technical research
Major updating services for particular industrial sectors
A library of over 500,000 standards and regulations for over 160 countries, together with 10,000 English translations. The library also offers a related technical translation service for firms. A charge is made for this service.

The THE enquiry service can answer by telephone or telex questions on the day-to-day problems faced by exporters such as the identification of foreign standards, technical requirements and approval procedures in Community member states as well as those of non-EC countries. A more detailed study is sometimes needed of products affected by a wider range of requirements, and THE can research any combination of technical standards for a specific product in a foreign market. THE engineers can visit manufacturers' works to examine products intended for export and suggest technical modifications which may be needed. THE also arranges presentations and seminars for designers and production staff.

THE produces a wide range of publications and surveys covering mainly the electrical, mechanical and building industries, and a classified list of publications is available free of charge. A special updating service is available in some product fields where companies require a consolidated manual of up-to-date technical information. The full text in English of all current requirements overseas for the product is supplied, and regular updating sheets are produced.

Further information:
THE can be contacted by
  telephone (0908) 220022
  telex 825777 BSIMK G
  fax Gr 2/3 0908: 320856
  letter c/o BSI Linford Wood, Milton Keynes MK14 6LE.

References

British Business (1983) Company analysis of direct exporters in 1981, 27 May, pp. 366–369.

Brown, R., and Cook, D. (1990), Strategy and performance in British exporters, *Quarterly Review of Marketing*, **15** (3), 42–61.

Browning, J. M., and Adams, R. J. (1988) Trade shows: an effective promotional tool for the small industrial business. *Journal of Small Business Management*, October, 30–37.

Wong Kwei Cheong, Kwan Woi Chong (1988) Export behaviour of small firms in Singapore. *International Small Business Journal*, **6** (2), pp. 42–61.

Christensen, C. H., de Rocha, A., and Gertner, R. K. (1987) An empirical investigation of the factors influencing exporting success of Brazilian Firms. *Journal of International Business Studies*, **18** (3), 61–78.

de Noble, A. F., Armann, R. J., and Moliver, D. (1988) Export Trading Company Act: structural and attitudinal barriers to implementation. *International Small Business Journal*, **6** (2), 10–19.

Dichtl, E., Koeglmayr, H. G., and Mueller, S. (1990) International orientation as a precondition for export success. *Journal of International Business Studies*, **21** (1), 23–40.

Howard, D. C., and Herremans, I. M. (1988) Sources of assistance for small business exporters: advice from successful firms, *Journal of Small Business Management*, July, 48–63.

Institute of Export (1987) *Export*, April, p. 1.

Kaikati, G. J. (1984) The Export Trading Company Act: a viable international marketing tool. *California Management Review*, **27**, 59–70.

Kathewala, Y., Judd, R., Monipallil, M., and Weinnch, M. (1989) Exporting practices of Illinois firms. *Journal of Small Business Management*, January, 53–59.

Kirpalani, V. H., and Mackintosh, B. N (1980) International marketing effectiveness of technology-oriented small firms. *Journal of International Business Studies*, Winter, 81–90.

Motoko Yesnde Lee, and Mulford, C. L. (1990) Reasons why Japanese small businesses form cooperatives: an exploratory study of three successful cases. *Journal of Small Business Management*, July, 62–71.

Nobuaki Namiki (1988) Export strategy for small business. *Journal of Small Business Management*, April, 32–37.

Paradiso, J. (1990) An interview with Dr. Roman Golar: the impact of deregulation on small business in Poland. *Journal of Small Business Management*, July, 81–85.

Rabino, S. (1980) Examination of barriers to exporting encountered by small manufacturing companies. *Management International Review*, **20**, (1), 67–73.

Stoffel, J. (1985) Why the Export Trading Act failed. *Business Marketing*, **70**, 54–55.

Verhoeven, W. (1988) The export performance of small and medium sized enterprises in the Netherlands. *International Small Business Journal*, **6** (2), 20–33.

Key reading

Ayal, I, Peer, A., and Zif, J. (1987) Selecting industries for export growth: a directional policy matrix approach. *Journal of Macromarketing*, Spring, 22–33.

Blackwell, N. (1990) Way around Europe. *Management Today*, August, 86–88.

Burns, P., and Dewhurst, J. (1986) *Small Business in Europe*, Macmillan, London.

Butler, J. (1988) *The Importer's Handbook*, Woodhead-Faulkner, Cambridge, England.

Cannon, T., and Willis, M. (1986) *How to Buy and Sell Overseas*, Hutchinson Books, London.

Daily Telegraph (1988), *How to export*, Telegraph Publications, London.

Department of Trade and Industry (1987), *Into Active Exporting*, DTI London.

How to win exports: five small firms show the way. *Management News*, October, British Institute of Management, Corby, Northamptonshire, England.

Miesenbock, K. J. (1988) Small business and exporting: a literature review. *International Small Business Journal*, **6** (2), 42–61.

Monk, K. (1989) *Go International: your guide to marketing and business development*, McGraw-Hill, Maidenhead.

Turnbull, P. W., and Valla, Jean-Paul (1986), *Strategies for International Industrial Marketing*, Croom-Helm, London.

Williamson, P. J. (1990) Winning the export war: British, Japanese and West German exporters' strategy compared. *British Journal of Management*, **1**, 215–230.

Wright, M. (1989) *Build up your exports*, Tate Publishing, Milton Keynes, England.

6
Market entry strategy decisions 1: direct vs indirect involvement

Assessing company resources and intended export involvement

Once again, it is worth repeating that there is no one, single universal 'best' foreign market entry strategy. The firm should consider all alternative channel strategies when entering each market. The 'best' strategy will be the one which is situationally best, optimal in that it is often a satisficing strategy which takes into consideration market competition, perceived risk, and established corporate policy with regard to forms of market entry. Yet it will not last for ever.

It may be useful to think in terms of a company having to deploy a broad portfolio of international investments to deal with a diversity of market conditions worldwide. While the five basic characteristics of a market must still to be found, viz: group of people, ability to buy, willingness to buy, product or service offering, and consumption; conceptually, the forms of market entry, which we describe below, do not follow a sequential order or classification. It should not be assumed then that there is an incremental internationalization process moving from export sales being part of domestic sales through to wholly-owned foreign subsidiaries. In fact, research which the author undertook within one major British multinational established that managerial thinking was moving towards the need to justify the existence of a wholly owned foreign sales subsidiary in preference to a free agent. Again, ownership has traditionally been thought to be necessary to have control, but control has a price, too, and so the optimal market entry choice can only be situation-specific.

Corporate objectives vary but may include:

- growth
- profitability and economies of scale
- new markets for existing products
- foreign earnings from existing products
- reduced vulnerability to domestic economic downturns
- access to foreign production inputs
- increased total potential market size over which to spread R&D costs.

Selection of market entry method has an important bearing on strategy, and can later prove to be a severe constraint on future intended international expansion unless due care and attention is exercised in terms of any contractual arrangement.

Selecting a strategy

The factors to be considered in selection are:

1 *Speed of market entry desired.* If speed is required, building up a wholly owned subsidiary will probably be by acquisition and licensing or use of an agent/distributor will be the likely ways to ensure access to distribution in the foreign market.
2 *Costs to include direct and indirect costs.* Subjectivity which is ever present may force a wrong decision. Savings may be outweighed by indirect costs such as freight, strikes, or disruptions to output, lack of continuity with the power supply, or irregularity in the supply of raw materials. Against this, the cost of doing nothing has to be considered; this may be higher than the attendant risks of moving forward from the domestic market.
3 *Flexibility required.* The laws of a country exist to protect that country's nationals. There is as yet no such thing as international law (although it is important to recognize the extraterritoriality of US law, and also within the EC, Articles 36, 85, and 86, as they affect trade within the European Community), and in disputes between two countries the domestic law of a third country is often called on, so that domestic law then becomes used for a purpose for which it was never designed: international disputes. Agents are appointed or distributors given exclusive sales territory rights, usually only where it is deemed unlikely that there will be very much future expansion by the company directly into that market.
4 *Risk factors* – including political risk as well as competitive risk. In a dynamic market, time is of the essence. No product remains 'new' forever. Getting the product to market is important but so, too, is avoiding the creation of a competitor, an accusation often levelled against licensing. Risk may be obviously diminished by minimizing the investment stake in the company by, for example, accepting a local joint-venture partner. Equally, investment activity in one market may lead to reprisals for the company elsewhere as has often been seen in the past with companies trading with Israel and then finding themselves subject to an Arab boycott.
5 *Investment payback period.* Shorter-term payback may be recovered from licensing and franchising deals, whereas collaborative joint ventures or joint equity ventures may tie up capital for a number of years.
6 *Long-term profit objectives* – the growth foreseen for that market in the years ahead. Here, the question of distribution channel policy is important for the future. A wholly owned foreign subsidiary may build up its own technical service department alongside a small but growing sales team. Agents who have been hired but are no longer consistent with longer-term profit objectives will then have to be given *ex gratia* payments to dispense with their services and the contract which legally binds them to the company. Otherwise it will mean litigation which may well go against the company if heard in a local court, plus, of course, there are the added costs of local legal representation.

The alternative forms of foreign market entry may, therefore, be summarized before we begin to consider them in terms of being direct or indirect (see Table 6.1). A company, perceived as being closely related to its country of origin, is termed ethnocentric; if based in a few countries with no visibly home country image, but instead a local market image in each market, it may be said to be polycentric; whereas, in the final category, those very few companies, such as IBM, Coca-Cola, or Pepsi – viewed as being globally coordinated with

Table 6.1   Essential characteristics of market entry methods

Market entry method	*Characteristics*
Freight forwarder	Acting on behalf of producer. Documentation and delivery service to foreign destination.
Export houses	Approx. 700–800 of these in UK, accounting for 20 per cent of UK exports. Export House represents a buyer abroad. Trading Company may be buying and selling on own account, or acting for a foreign principal.
Agents	Most common form of market entry worldwide. Paid on commission, usually handling more than one company and/or product line. Low cost but very difficult to get rid of a bad agent other than with a 'golden handshake'.
Distributors	Differ from agents in that they take title to the goods. For the producer, this lessens risk and improves cash flow, but weakens control as less is known about the final end-user or price charged. Distributors will seek exclusivity of sales territory.
Piggybacking	An entry method much favoured by US multinationals. Now a feature of strategic business alliances (SBAs). Uses the distribution channel of another company, and in this respect, overlap with agents but complementarity sought of distribution outlets and products carried. Size is a factor. Returns achieved by means of commission or outright sale of goods.
Consortium exporting	Used by small companies and companies with narrow specific skills to combine their skills and resources, and bid for contracts and projects as a group of independents.
Licensing	Often regarded as second-best to exporting. It confers a right to utilize a company-specific process in manufacturing a proprietary product, and may also include a know-how agreement incorporating training and the licensor's learned experience of producing according to this process, and continuing exports of components embodying advanced technology
Know-how agreement	Usually incorporated now into licensing sales, the know-how agreement is the sale of learned experience using the particular process in question and of training the licensee's operatives. A know-how agreement reduces the time required before a plant is otherwise fully operational.
Franchising	High growth in UK and Western Europe. Introduces small independents with no prior business experience to a proven business concept. Transfers the right to use the company's name, logo and all that may be identifiable with the company. Examples abound in the fast-food industry. May also include a management contract.
Management contracts	Transfer company-specific and know-how management control systems, and are widely evidenced in the services sector, e.g. hotel industry, private hospital management.
Joint ventures	Two distinct types: contractual, as in strategic business alliances (SBAs) and joint-equity. Contractual is of fixed duration; with responsibilities and duties well defined. Joint-equity involves investment, no fixed duration, and is continually evolving.

their own complex global sourcing, management reporting systems etc. – are labelled geocentric and for these very few companies, planning on a world scale is a daily reality.

These terms, ethnocentric, polycentric and geocentric, are labels to describe outward manifestations of the company; they do not relate to corporate structure, but their effects on corporate planning and policy are dealt with in Chapter 14.

Knowledge is a valuable asset and, in an age of information technology, is constantly being repackaged. Knowledge is central to licensing, to franchising, to management contracts and to joint ventures, and particularly, strategic business alliances. Although licensing and franchising are sometimes used interchangeably, licensing confers a right to produce, using a patented manufacturing process, while franchising involves the right more often to sell a service under a brand name and within strict guidelines relating to all aspects of its merchandising. Licensing, franchising and management contracts (sometimes also called technical assistance agreements) are but three ways in which knowledge, rather than a product, is transferred from seller to buyer. Brooke (1986) classifies the different modes of foreign market entry into three categories: exporting, knowledge sales, and investment in that order, see his piano keyboard in Figure 6.2.

In this chapter, we will be dealing with exporting and knowledge sales, and in Chapter 7 with those strategies related to investment. Regarding exporting, it must be said that the

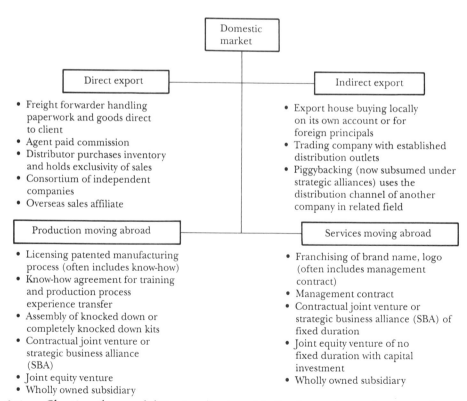

Figure 6.1.   *Charting the possibilities for direct and indirect exports, production and services*
Source   Adapted from Terpstra (1983) *International Marketing*, Holt, Reinhart and Winston, 3rd edn.

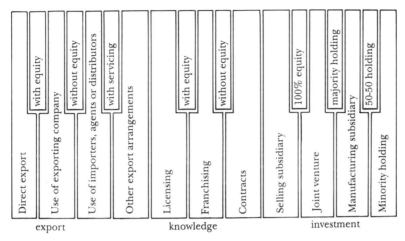

Figure 6.2   *Brooke's keyboard analogy of international strategies*
Source   Brooke, M. Z. (1986) *International Management*, Century Hutchinson, London.

popular media is responsible for creating a distorted image of exporting as a pioneering activity which is fraught with danger, but somehow noble in itself, and also patriotic. Consequently, media focus undue attention on currency exchange rates as having an unequal weighting in winning export orders. A significant fall over the day in one currency will often be seen as heralding new export opportunities, ignoring the fact that exports often have a three, six or nine month time lag before a sales contract actually is fulfilled. Daily fluctuations in exchange rates are, therefore, no more than just simply fluctuations which can be dealt with by banks. As Chapter 10 emphasizes, the serious buyer will in any event buy forward, i.e., take out an option to purchase a fixed amount of foreign currency at a set date in the future and, so, guarantee himself a fixed exchange rate which will be unaffected by any subsequent currency revision. At the same time, it is difficult also to introduce some realism into popular conceptions that exporting is noble and patriotic. Exporting is not a luxury nor is it an activity that requires bravado as much as research, skill and luck. It often requires a great deal of patience and also resource before bearing fruit, but to an increasing number of companies of different sizes across the world, exporting has become the activity on which the very survival of the company often depends.

Companies do, however, find themselves being pushed into exporting and it is in this connection that we should first consider 'indirect' market entry strategies, remembering all the while that the rather grandiose term 'strategy' may commonly apply to a strategy by default, where a company, faced with a certain market situation, chooses to do nothing. Over time, corporate attitude and strategy become more clearly visible. Those strategies termed 'indirect' are chiefly those whereby a domestic manufacturer is able to engage in the fortuitous sale of his products abroad with minimal outlay or use of his own company resources. Also in this category is the situation which is freqently encountered where a company may often be unaware that its products are even being exported. Foreign buying offices of department store chains are represented in the Export Buying Offices Association, London, which represents stores and fashion houses worldwide. This provides a prime example of an 'export-pull' effect, whereby goods are exported to a new market without the active participation of the producer himself. This may then create a demonstration effect within that foreign market which may lead to further export sales. Then, as envisaged by the product life cycle for international trade, foreign production increases imports, displacing domestic products chiefly on price. Foreign production strength leads to eventual foreign production penetration and saturation of the domestic market which first launched the product.

As indirect market entry methods involve the use of intermediaries who handle all documentation, physical movement of goods, and channels of distribution for sale, indirect exports may take place either with or without the knowledge of the manufacturer himself. Indirect market entry may occur in a number of ways.

An *export house*, of which there are many in the City of London, will buy directly from you on behalf of a foreign principal in which case the sale will be a purely domestic one with the export house arranging the export of the goods.

The *trading company* is in a quite different category. Britain owed its strength in international trading to these trading companies such as the East India Company, Hudson Bay Company and others firmly established in what were then British colonies. Today, the United Africa Company (UAC), which is part of Unilever, remains the largest trader in Africa, but Paterson Zochonis is another example of a very large trading company with well established roots. These trading companies have well connected distribution outlets in the countries in which they operate and are able to handle a diverse product range, in the case of UAC in Nigeria, from galvanized metal pails to motor car dealerships. The Japanese trading houses, the Soga Shosha (discussed in Chapter 15) offer an integrated range of financial and insurance services in addition, as they frequently incorporate their own bank into their organizational structure. The dominance of Japanese banks in world banking may be seen in Chapter 15. Offering then a range of integrated services, all the way through to the end-user, gives the Soga Shosha a competitive advantage.

Piggybacking is a quite different phenomenon and is increasingly being subsumed under strategic business alliances, of which more later. Piggybacking remains primarily a US phenomenon occurring between consenting US multinationals, and practised like sex between elephants: at a high level, with a great deal of roaring, and a long period to produce results! One-third of US companies were seen to be involved in piggybacking and so it is worth considering some of the reasons why this should be so:

1 Extending the product depth – the exporter may be seeking additional products in order to be able to offer a fuller product range, or else extend the associated benefits or services currently available.
2 Foreign customers may have asked the exporter for specific merchandise that is not currently available in the market. Here, the exporter is simply making available his distribution outlets to the manufacturer. Where the exporter is also a manufacturer or distributor of allied products, there may even be a synergistic effect in that where the goods are truly complementary to each other and non-competing, then they may lift total sales.
3 Some US exporters look for additional products to sell in foreign markets to increase their total sales. The exporters or piggybackers will ask a manufacturer to produce a product line under their own brand name.

Piggybacking seems to attract large companies rather than small, but it enables a non-exporter to exploit the distribution channels of an exporting company with a complementary, non-competing product. For the exporter, piggybacking offers the advantage of

Table 6.2 Market entry mode profiles

	Agent	Distributor	Licensing	Franchising	Joint-equity venture	Strategic business alliance	Wholly-owned subsidiary
Speed of market entry	High	High	Slower	Slower	Slow	Slow	Slowest
Costs direct and indirect	Low	Low	Higher	Higher	High	High	Highest
Degrees of freedom	Low	Low	Contractual	Contractual	Limited	Limited	Total
Total exposure to risk	Low	Low	Moderate/high	Moderate	Moderate/high	Moderate	High
Investment payback period	Short	Short	Short/medium	Short/medium	Medium	Short/medium	Long-term
Perceived long-term profitability	Moderate/low	Moderate/low	Low	High/moderate	High/moderate	High	High
Foreign market competition							
low	Less likely	Less likely	Limited	✓	Less likely	Less likely	✓
high	✓	✓	✓	✓	✓	✓	Less likely
Ability to expand within mode	✓	✓	Limited	✓	Limited	Limited	✓
Stable mature product	✓	Limited	Limited	✓	Limited	Limited	Less frequent
Excess capacity utilization	✓	Limited	N/A	N/A	N/A	N/A	N/A
New product launch	✓	✓	With caution	✓	Limited	Limited	✓
Achieving market coverage	✓	✓	✓	✓	✓	✓	✓
Receiving feedback	Limited	Limited	Very limited	Moderate	Moderate	Moderate	High
Method of recovery income for sales	Commission	Outright sale	Royalty	Royalty + fees + ongoing sales of inputs	Shared	Shared according to agreed formula	Total profits
Control over market mode by principal	Limited	Limited	Contractual and limited	High	Moderate/high	Moderate/high	Total

* May also be other barriers as well.

Table 6.3   External and internal factors influencing the entry mode decision

	Generally favours:				
	Indirect and agent/ distributor exporting	Licensing	Branch subsidiary exporting	Equity investment/ production	Service contracts
External factors (foreign country)					
Low sales potential	×	×			
High sales potential			×	×	
Atomistic competition	×		×		
Oligopolistic competition				×	
Poor marketing infrastructure			×		
Good marketing infrastructure	×				
Low production cost				×	
High production cost	×		×		
Restrictive import policies		×		×	×
Liberal import policies	×		×		
Restrictive investment policies	×	×	×		×
Liberal investment policies				×	
Small geographical distance	×		×		
Great geographical distance		×		×	×
Dynamic economy				×	
Stagnant economy	×	×			×
Restrictive exchange controls	×	×			×
Liberal exchange controls				×	
Exchange rate depreciation				×	
Exchange rate appreciation	×		×		
Small cultural difference			×	×	
Great cultural difference	×	×			×
Low political risk			×	×	
High political risk	×	×			×
External factors (home country)					
Large market				×	
Small market	×		×		
Atomistic competition	×		×		
Oligopolistic competition				×	
Low production cost	×		×		
High production cost		×		×	×
Strong export promotion	×		×		
Restrictions on investment abroad	×	×			×
Internal factors					
Differentiated products	×		×		
Standard products				×	
Service-intensive products			×	×	
Service products		×		×	×
Technology intensive products		×			
Low product adaptation	×				
High product adaptation		×	×	×	
Limited resources	×	×			
Substantial resources			×	×	
Low commitment	×	×			×
High commitment			×	×	

Source   Root, F. R. (1987) *Entry Strategies for International Markets*, Lexington Books, Lexington, MA.

Table 6.4   Agents – how many to appoint?

Some variables to consider:

- market size and accessibility
- agent's own resource base – agent's network of contacts
- number of languages/dialects spoken in the target market
- important regional differences that require regional representation
- location of the agent

---

widening the product range carried, using the sales force to the full, and earning additional revenue from carrying products into distribution channels which would have to be served anyway. For the domestic company, there is the obvious advantage of a ready made overseas market with an experienced international exporting firm at the ready. There is less risk than going it alone and there is direct access to the market, as the channels of distribution already exist. With piggybacking there are two possible forms of payment: either outright full payment or an ongoing commission basis on volume sold.

This relationship may, therefore, vary from an order-to-order basis to one of established permanence. Finding a piggybacker may prove difficult and once established there is also the problem of the nature of the relationship, the product selling price, and the potential disadvantage that since the products are subordinated to the other company's lines they may not be promoted as aggressively. The exporting manufacturer may feel greater loyalty to his own wares and he may be under greater pressure from his management to sell his own wares. Profitable business can, however, emanate from this kind of relationship, although this relationship may mean either that A is purchasing from B to resell in foreign markets under his control, or else A is the agent of B and in return for providing suitable outlets for products complementary to his own, he receives a commission on sales. However, there is the added advantage also, though much less quantifiable, of increased sales resulting from augmented product range. The points to particularly note of a potential piggybacker are:

Table 6.5   Assessing the potential agent

- date of incorporation and business experience of the principals
- resource base of the agent, including:
  human resource strength, e.g. technical skills
  financial strength
  goodwill associated to agency
- degree of motivation to accept your product line = high/low
- annual turnover of the agency
- number of foreign principals represented
- contact patterns established with the client base
- how does the agent perceive your product in terms of strengths and weaknesses?

- the products the firm presently exports,
- how your product will be promoted – in particular, who will handle your product, how often he travels abroad, etc.,
- type of distribution used in major foreign markets,
- exporting pricing policies,
- identification of others being 'piggybacked' (check with these firms to find out if they are happy with the arrangement),
- estimated amount of export sales for your product; and
- countries covered by the exporting manufacturer.

The difficulty remains, however, of being stuck with an arrangement which could in the long term hinder your ability to expand your product range or establish your own export effort, or could not be changed if dissatisfied with the piggybacker's performance.

Direct exporting activities

These begin where the company may be actively involved in foreign sales, but perhaps due to inexperience, arranges for all documentation and physical distribution to be handled on its behalf by a freight forwarder.

Beyond this stage, the most popular form of direct entry is the agent or distributor and here, the reader is recommended to turn to the twenty-seven different types identified by McMillan and Paulden (1974) in Table 6.6.

Agents

Agents are the most common form of low-cost direct involvement in foreign markets. However, there are a number of disadvantages. Firstly, although foreign embassies and national trade associations are able to supply fairly complete lists of agents, it is often difficult for them to give any qualitative assessment or evaluation, or to recommend specific agents, perhaps out of a need for impartiality rather than a fear of libel. Service quality offered can prove extremely variable and, as an agent is paid commission only on sales, his loyalty may be further questioned if it is seen to rest purely on the company currently providing him with the greatest earnings. As agents may represent a number of separate companies and product lines, this may be a problem. Meanwhile, the company holds responsibility for whatever unsold inventory is held by the agent, while at the same time being virtually deprived of market information.

No agent will willingly expose himself to the risk of being supplanted by a branch of the company's own sales organization. In market situations where there is (in Boston Consulting Group terminology) a 'problem child' syndrome evident – i.e., slow growth for the company's product in an otherwise high growth market – it may be difficult to determine exactly why this has arisen. On the other hand, where there is high market growth, this creates pressures within the company to take over the foreign market from the agent. This may often require compensating the agent handsomely, especially where local legislation exists to protect his position. Elsewhere, the situation may arise where the company wishes to expand its product line or else diversify into a quite different product, and the local agent finds himself unable to meet this new expansion but still holds a company agreement to exclusivity of sales territory.

Table 6.6   McMillan and Paulden's classification of agents and distributors

---

Agent acting for exporter as principal
1 Agent on commission.
2 Commission/fee and commission/stockist agencies.
3 Salaried salesman (i.e. own company man).
4 Independent salesman (Jack-of-all-trades).
5 Agent/distributor.
6 Agent/warehousing.
7 Agent/servicing company.
8 Agent/design office (prefab buildings, central heating, etc.).
9 Agent/customer.
10 Agent/manager (e.g., French or British in Africa).
11 Factory representative/Agent controller (for agent supervision.)
12 Export management agency (acts as an export dept.).

Agent purchasing for himself as principal
13 Export merchant.
14 Distributor.
15 Stockist.
16 Wholesaler.
17 Trading company (esp. Japanese).
18 Agents who assemble (using percentage of local parts).
19 Sales agent who buys.

Agent acting for other buyers as principals
20 Buying offices, esp. American Dept. Stores, Australia (Myers).
21 Buying houses (serve a particular territory, cf 17).
22 Buying Agents located abroad.

Agents understanding specialized aspect of export cycle other than selling
23 Confirming houses (guarantees payment on due date, intermediary).
 24 Factors, operating for exporters, financial service
    – bills are discounted with or without recourse to money.
25 Shipping and forwarding agents.
26 Technical partnership.
27 Depot distribution agents.

Source   McMillan, C., and Paulden, S. (1974) *Export Agents: A Complete Guide to their Selection and Control*, 2nd edn, Gower. Aldershot, Hampshire.

Distributors

Distributors usually seek exclusive rights to specific sales territories, but constitute yet another method of low-cost foreign market entry. The difference between the distributor and the agent is that the distributor will, like the foreign buying office, be placing an order similar to any other domestic purchase order in that the responsibility for the condition and sale of goods will end at some point to be agreed in the distribution channel between producer and distributor. The distributor actually takes title — i.e., owns the inventory which he carries — and represents the manufacturer in the sales and service of the products which he carries. Thus, in return for his capital investment, he will usually seek exclusivity of supply and sales territory plus a reasonable turnover rate of the products handled.

Similarities between agents and distributors

McMillan and Paulden (1974) identified twenty seven different types of agents/distributors, as in Table 6.6 which shows many similarities beyond the essential differences described briefly above. Both agents and distributors are intermediaries in the distribution channel between the producer and his final customer, and as intermediaries, share a number of similar characteristics. Many authors, therefore, use the term agent or distributor interchangeably, whereas, in fact, they are more correctly referring to the role of intermediaries. The distinction between agents and distributors has always to be maintained. So, assuming that we have discovered that the company has an exportable product and we have been able to identify a target market, we have then to decide on the best form of representation, finding an intermediary whose profile most clearly meets our needs, and then negotiate a working arrangement with that intermediary.

A great deal of risk and pure guesswork has been removed from the selection procedure in that the clearing banks will now offer a financial appraisal of a foreign client, and that further help is also available from the London Chamber of Commerce and the Department of Trade and Industry in terms of qualitatively evaluating those intermediaries which appear on lists circulated by foreign embassies and consulates. The advantage of using a Chamber of Commerce is that the names put forward on either side can generally be assumed to be reliable firms.

In terms of selection, Beeth (1973) offers some very concrete advice:

1 Go personally to the country, allowing ample time. Talk to the ultimate users of the equipment to find out from which distributors they prefer to buy and why. Two or three names will keep popping up in the replies you receive.
2 Then go to those two or three distributors and see which one or ones you would be able to sign up.
3 But, before making the final choice, look for the distributor who has the key man for your line.

Beeth (1973) describes how in a company which he worked for, they had a scaling system of one to ten by which to evaluate intermediaries on twenty-four different activities and abilities. These ratings were then verified against their individual importance to the company and a final assessment produced. However, the final rating figure showed no correlation at all to their actual performance. Consequently they abandoned the twenty-four criteria and started to look more closely for any commonality that existed among the excellent intermediaries. This emerged as being able to identify one capable person within the intermediary who would be committed to the company and to the product and, in Beeth's own words, 'take the new line of equipment to his heart and make it his personal objective to make the sale of that product line a success in his country.' If unable to identify a suitable local intermediary, or else persuade an intermediary to switch from handling a competitor's product line to yours, it is better not to enter that market than to enter it with a mediocre intermediary.

Retaining and motivating good intermediaries are important. Usually this means financial rewards for volume sold, but it means also providing regular stimulus to the intermediary to maintain interest in your product line. Training may be paid for and warranty obligations must be met in full as these help create goodwill. The contract is the basis on which the relationship is to be defined, so it must define the setting of targets as well as penalties.

Similarly, there have to be awards for achievement. Mediocre intermediaries can only be improved at a cost and for most companies the price will be too high. There is a need, therefore, to be able to be ruthless and extricate yourself quickly from an arrangement that appears to be going nowhere. Cancellation clauses usually involve rights under local legislation, and it is best that a contract is scrutinized by a local lawyer before signature, rather than after a relationship has ended and a compensation case is being fought in the courts.

Management contracts

Management contracts are quite different again in that they often subsume some other form of relationship in addition, such as licensing, franchising, strategic business alliance or joint-equity venture. Management contracts emphasize the increasing importance of services and

Table 6.7   Profile desired of intermediaries

- Trading areas covered.
- Lines handled.
- Size of firm.
- Experience with manufacturer's or similar product line.
- Sales organization and quality of sales force.
- Physical facilities.
- Willingness to carry inventories.
- After-sales servicing capability.
- Knowledge/use of promotion.
- Reputation with suppliers, customers and banks.
- Record of sales performance.
- Cost of operations.
- Financial strength/credit rating.
- Overall experience.
- Relations with local government.
- Knowledge of English or other relevant languages.
- Knowledge of business methods in manufacturer's country.
- Willingness to cooperate with manufacturer.

Source   Root, F. R. (1987) *Entry Strategies for International Markets*, Lexington Books, Lexington, MA.

Table 6.8   What intermediaries seek

- Differentiated, well-known, prestige product with good sales potential.
- Functional discounts that allow high markups.
- Exclusive distribution rights protected by the manufacturer.
- Contractual obligations assumed by the manufacturer for a lengthy period, with indemnities paid for any cancellation by the manufacturer.
- Right of the distributor to terminate the agreement without indemnities.
- Right to design and implement the marketing plan without interference or control by the manufacturer.
- Generous credit terms.
- Full support by the manufacturer – inventory backup, quick order servicing, technical and sales training, advertising allowances, special discounts, and so on.
- Product warranties.
- Freedom to handle other lines, whether competitive or complementary to the manufacturer's line.
- Paid visits to the manufacturer's headquarters or to regional meetings.
- Obligation to provide only minimum information to the manufacturer.

Source   Root, F. R. (1987) *Entry Strategies for International Markets*, Lexington Books, Lexington, MA.

know-how as a saleable asset in international trade. Based on a contractual form, it will concern the transferral of management control systems and know-how involving personnel training. The demand arises mainly from those countries where there exists a 'managerial gap'. Essentially, it is a 'software' package incorporating management and control systems, and frequently found in those industries where there is an expectation of quality, service, and attention. Hotels and hospitals are just two areas in which management contracts have been usefully explored. Management contracts do constitute big business, however. When the International Hospital Group of the UK won a twelve-year management contract for the 500-bed King Khaled National Guard Hospital in Jeddah, Saudi Arabia, this contract was valued at £150 million.

Franchising

Franchising is a marketing-oriented method of selling a business service, often to small independent investors with working capital but little or no prior business experience. Yet, it is almost like an umbrella term which is used to mean anything from the right to use a name to the total business concept. Franchising's origins go back two centuries to when brewers in Britain created the tied-house system to guarantee outlets for their beer. In the US the concept was developed by the Singer Sewing Machine Company. Three growing markets account for two-thirds of all franchises in the UK — home improvements and home maintenance (31 per cent), food and drink (18 per cent), and business services (17 per cent).

Franchising transfers the legal right to a third party to use a company's registered trade name, trademarks and logo, products, packaging, and business system. For example,

Table 6.9 Contracts with intermediaries

1 *General provisions*
  Identification of parties to the contract.
  Duration of the contract.
  Definition of covered goods.
  Definition of territory or territories.
  ** Sole and exclusive rights.
  Arbitration of disputes.

2 *Rights and obligations of manufacturer*
  Conditions of termination.
  Protection of sole and exclusive rights.
  Sales and technical support.
  Tax liabilities.
  Conditions of sale.
  Delivery of goods.
  Prices.
  Order refusal.
  Inspection of distributor's books.
  Trademarks/patents.
  Information to be supplied to the distributor.
  Advertising/promotion.
  Responsibility for claims/warranties.
  Inventory requirements.
  **Termination and cancellation.

3 *Rights and obligations of distributor*
  Safeguarding manufacturer's interests.
  Payments arrangements.
  Contract assignment.
  ** Competitive lines.
  Customs clearance.
  Observance of conditions of sale.
  After-sales service.
  Information to be supplied to the manufacturer.

** Most important and contentious issues.

Source Root, F. R. (1987) *Entry Strategies for International Markets*, Lexington Books, Lexington, MA.

Kentucky Fried Chicken (part of Pepsico Foods International) have a standardized red and white corporate colour, a distinctive trademark, logo and carton packaging for food. Kentucky Fried stipulate the sources from which the raw materials must be obtained, the recipes for the preparation of the food, again to be strictly controlled, and the quantity to be served in each portion. The particular benefit which franchising confers is that it allows small independents with investment capital (average £26,000 in UK in 1985), but no industry or management experience, to enjoy the benefits of belonging to a large organization while remaining owner-managers. Sixty per cent of all franchisees are women. Usually the franchisee is under forty, married with a couple of children, but the franchise can cost between £5,000 and £250,000. Drain clearing is relatively low cost while fast food operations are considerably more expensive, perhaps because of training and support. The failure rate is low, about 2 per cent per annum in the UK, whereas 75 per cent of all small businesses fail in the first five years. This is partly due to the personal motivation of the franchisee as well as guidance from the franchisor. The British Franchising Association states that 98 per cent of franchisees are working with established franchises, but the emphasis should be on the word 'established'.

Nevertheless, the proven business idea behind a franchise appeals to banks, all of whom have now established franchising departments. The *Good Franchise Guide* emphasizes that many franchises are little more than untested business ideas. Franchisees can get burned by paying high sums of money for a franchise, receiving little in return other than perhaps help with the preparation of company records, and having to pay highly also for supplies from a source to which they are contractually committed for the next ten years. Not all franchisors

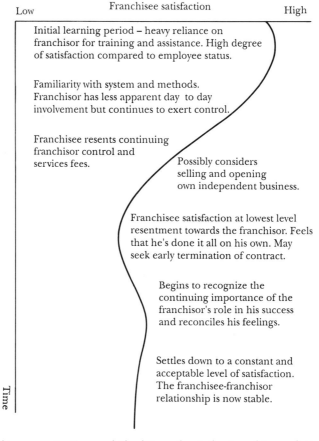

Figure 6.3   *Franchisee satisfaction and the life cycle of the franchisee relationship*
Source   Hall, P., and Dixon, R. (1989) *Franchising*, Natwest Small Business Bookshelf, Pitman Publishing, London.

Table 6.10   Franchising

- 10% of UK retail market 1988 (2% in 1983)
- 10% of retail sales in EC
- 33-1/3% of retail sales in USA

Western Europe

- Value $26 billion, 1989
- Est. $50 billion, 1990s
- 1983 –   9,000 franchisees
- 1988 –   90,000 franchisees
- 1990 – 155,000 franchisees

- 1988 –   2,200 franchisors
- 1990 –   3,500 franchisors

point out the needs for planning permission to operate a business from home. Again, some franchises operate a chain of stocking-up that comes very close to pyramid selling, which is illegal. The *Good Franchise Guide* points to a disturbing number of franchises set up without first running pilot operations, also of poor prospectuses and poor PR. The *Good Franchise Guide* gives an honest portrayal of a form of business that contains a great many questionable operators. The return on initial capital invested may be recovered on average in just under two years, the return on the full cost in just over three years, but this depends on a number of variables, including the size of the franchised territory. A large fast-food restaurant may take four to five years for the investment to be recovered.

Franchising is rapidly increasing, as are the companies actively promoting it, e.g. Sheraton Intercontinental, Holiday Inns (hotels); Coca-Cola, Pepsi-Cola (soft drinks); Budget (car rental) and many of the fast-food companies; as well as others in drain clearing (Dyno-Rod), printing, and photocopying (Prontaprint). Retail spending in franchised operations is expected to exceed 6 billion in 1991. Coca-Cola is held to provide the classic example of a franchise strategy, with its independent bottlers around the world preparing soft drinks from concentrate according to specifications supplied by Coca-Cola, which retains control over its trademark, recipe, and advertising. Franchising can often subsume a management contract and, thus, lead to profits from both royalties and management fees. It is still a relatively new concept in the international area and the tax treatment for this form of trading has yet to be standardized. Cadbury—Schweppes, who concluded a franchising deal with Asahi Breweries, part of the Sumitomo Group, to sell soft drinks in Japan, benefits also from the continuing export of essences and concentrates from the UK.

Mendelsohn (1988) points to the need for a contract stipulating the following:

1 There must be a contract containing all the terms agreed on.
2 The franchisor must initiate and train the franchisee in all aspects of the business prior to the opening of the business and assist in the opening.
3 After the business is opened, the franchisor must maintain a continuing interest in providing the franchisee with support in all aspects of the operation of the business.

Table 6.11 Advantages of franchising as a mode of market entry

A To the franchisor:
   1 fast entry and withdrawal, so lower risk
   2 moderate investment
   3 limited overheads
   4 avoid import duties and taxes as import/export content minimal
   5 access to ready-made market
   6 control.

B To the franchisee:
   1 flexible business structure
   2 shared financial responsibility
   3 legal independence
   4 tried and tested idea
   5 economies of scale in distribution
   6 motivation.

C To the consumer:
   1 standardized product
   2 fixed price
   3 new technology fast
   4 motivated/interested manager.

D To the host country:
   1 technology transfer
   2 creates employment and business opportunities
   3 royalties often remain.

4 The franchisee is permitted under the control of the franchisor to operate under a trade name, format and/or procedure, and with the benefit of goodwill owned by the franchisor.
5 The franchisee must make a substantial capital investment from his own resources.
6 The franchisee must own his business.
7 The franchisee will pay the franchisor in one way or other for the rights which he acquires and for the continuing services with which he will be provided.
8 The franchisee will be given some territory within which to operate.

An illustration of what can go wrong with a franchising deal is provided by the experience of McDonalds, the US fast-food chain, in France. McDonalds have 7,000 restaurants worldwide, but have been buying in franchises in the USA. (All of the first 126 British outlets were company owned.) McDonalds franchised a certain individual in the early 1970s to open a number of restaurants in Paris. The relationship soured when the US company charged him with not maintaining his restaurants to McDonalds' standards. There followed a long-winded lawsuit which was finally resolved in a Chicago court in 1982 in favour of the US company. McDonalds removed all names and references to the company from the franchised operation

Table 6.12   A selection of international franchisors

France:

Quelle (Photos)
Carrefour (Hypermarkets)
Pronuptia (Wedding Dresses)
Phildar (Wool)
Yoplait (Yoghurt)
Yves Rocher (Cosmetics)

USA:

Avis
Practical Rent-A-Wreck
Computerland
Holiday Inn
McDonalds
Singer Consumer Products

UK:

Wimpy
Clarks Shoes
Tie Rack
Dyno-Rod
Exchange Travel
Spud-U-Like
Prontaprint
Sketchley
Skirmish

in Paris and set to work to catch up on the time lost to its rivals, including the US Burger King chain, on the flourishing Parisian fast-food market. The franchisee renamed his restaurants O'Kitch. Meanwhile McDonalds selected for their re-entry to Paris an unusually stylish two-storey establishment which seeks to be very French, with granite bistro tables, art deco lights and lush plastic plants, plus the innovation of loose chairs for the first time in a McDonalds restaurant.

The maintenance of standards and the need also for standardization are two of the problems facing an international franchising operation. Meanwhile, it is interesting to note that the first 126 McDonalds' operations in the UK were wholly owned by McDonalds and not a franchise operation as found elsewhere among their 7,000 outlets worldwide. A legacy perhaps of their French experience, to ensure that they first got the quality right before expanding further, this has since changed and a few McDonalds franchises are now operational in the UK. Kentucky Fried Chicken called a temporary freeze on franchise recruiting and bought back thirteen restaurants. Kentucky Fried Chicken own sixty stores out of 360 in the UK. Burger King, again in the UK, are negotiating to buy in the last of their UK franchises.

Table 6.13   The top 100 franchises

The 100 franchise operations scoring the highest number of points (weighted rating) in the Franchise 500 in rank order, together with their business activity. Last year's rankings are also included, but NR = Not ranked in 1990.

1 Subway/*Submarine Sandwiches*/1
2 McDonald's/*Hamburgers*/3
3 Jani-King/*Commercial Cleaning*/23
4 Little Caesars Pizza/*Pizza*/4
5 Hardee's/*Misc. Fast Foods*/9
6 Chem-Dry/*Carpet, Upholstery & Drapery Clng./Dyeing*/8
7 Arby's Inc./*Misc. Fast Foods*/7
8 Electronic Realty Associates/*Real Estate Services*/13
9 Kentucky Fried Chicken/*Chicken*/14
10 Jazzercise Inc./*Fitness Centers*/12
11 Service Master/*Commercial Cleaning*/16
12 Intelligent Electronics Inc./*Computer-Related Products & Services*/NR
13 Domino's Pizza Inc./*Pizza*/2
14 Budget Rent A Car/*Auto Rentals & Leasing*/26
15 Dairy Queen/*Soft-Serve Ice Cream*/6
16 Midas Int'l./*Brakes, Front-End, Mufflers & Shocks*/38
17 Burger King Corp./*Hamburgers*/5
18 H & R Block/*Income Tax Services*/17
19 Coverall North America Inc./*Commercial Cleaning*/86
20 Choice Hotels & Motels Int'l./*Hotels & Motels*/34
21 Nutri System/*Diet & Weight-Control Centers*/NR
22 Century 21 Real Estate Corp./*Real Estate Services*/10
23 Big Boy Restaurants/*Family-Style Restaurants*/77
24 Mail Boxes Etc. USA/*Packing, Mailing & Shipping Services*/32
25 Re/Max Int'l. Inc./*Real Estate Services*/21
26 Wendy's Int'l. Inc./*Hamburgers*/19
27 Baskin-Robbins USA Co./*Ice Cream*/20
28 Rainbow Int'l. Carpet Dyeing & Cleaning Co./*Carpet, Upholstery & Drapery Clng./Dyeing*/27
29 Dunkin' Donuts/*Donuts*/15
30 Days Inns of America/*Hotels & Motels*/33
31 Realty World/*Real Estate Services*/22
32 Holiday Inn/*Hotels & Motels*/31

33 Packy The Shipper/*Business Add-On Services*/29
34 Decorating Den/*Misc. Decorative Products & Services*/36
35 Fantastic Sam's/*Hair Care*/30
36 Minuteman Press/*Printing, Copying & Typesetting Services*/37
37 American Int'l. Rent A Car Corp./*Auto Rentals & Leasing*/35
38 Goodyear Tire Centers/*Tires*/43
39 Sonic Drive In Restaurants/*Misc. Fast Foods*/49
40 Uniglobe Travel/*Travel Services*/47
41 Pip Printing/*Printing, Copying & Typesetting Services*/39
42 Church's Fried Chicken Inc./*Chicken*/62
43 Sir Speedy Printing/*Printing, Copying & Typesetting Services*/53
44 Meineke Discount Mufflers/*Brakes, Front-End, Mufflers & Shocks*/42
45 Servpro/*Carpet, Upholstery & Drapery Clng./Dyeing*/51
46 Kwik-Kopy/*Printing, Copying & Typesetting Services*/64
47 Help U-Sell Real Estate/*Real Estate Services*/64
48 The Medicine Shoppe/*Misc. Retail Products*/45
49 One Hour Martinizing Dry Cleaning/*Dry Cleaning*/63
50 Jiffy Lube/*Oil Change & Lubrication-Specialty Services*/25
51 Ziebart-Tidy Car/*Auto Appearance Services*/NR
52 Ben Franklin Stores/*Ben Franklin Crafts/ Misc. Retail Products*/41
53 American Speedy Printing Centers/*Printing, Copying & Typesetting Services*/52
54 Super 8 Motels Inc./*Hotels & Motels*/44
55 Denny's Inc./*Family-Style Restaurants*/48
56 Econo Lodges of America/*Hotels & Motels*/55
57 ABC Seamless Inc./*Siding*/78
58 Thrifty Rent-A-Car System/*Rentals and Leasing*/

59 Miracle Ear/*Medical/Dental Products & Services/96*

60 Heel/Sew Quik/*Shoe Repair/280*

61 Better Homes & Gardens Real Estate Service/*Real Estate Services/59*

62 Pearle Vision Center/Pearle Express/*Optical Products & Services/71*

63 Jack In The Box/*Hamburgers/54*

64 Popeyes Famous Fried Chicken & Biscuits/*Chicken/69*

65 Culligan Water Conditioning/*Misc. Maintenance Products & Services/58*

66 ComputerLand/*Computer-Related Products & Services/68*

67 General Nutrition Franchising Inc./*Misc. Specialty Foods/83*

68 Handle With Care Packaging Store/*Packing, Mailing & Shipping Services/118*

69 Novus Windshield Repair/*Auto Glass Services/87*

70 I Can't Belive It's Yogurt/*Frozen Yogurt/117*

71 Precision Tune/*Tune-Up, Lubes & Other Services/60*

72 Shoney's Restaurants/*Family-Style Restaurants/67*

73 Supercuts/*Hair Care/76*

74 Duraclean/*Carpet, Upholstery & Drapery Clng./Dyeing/65*

75 Management Recruiters/Sales Consultants/*Executive-Search Firms/66*

76 Worldwide Refinishing Systems Inc. *Porcelain/Marble Restoration/161*

77 Roto-Rooter Corp./*Misc. Maintenance Products & Services/61*

78 Sport It/*Sports Equipment/205*

79 Round Table Franchise Crop./*Pizza/79*

80 AAMCO Transmissions Inc./*Transmission Repair/72*

81 Colortyme/*Misc. Retail Products/NR*

82 Merry Maids/*Residential Cleaning/89*

83 Ponderosa Steakhouses/*Steakhouses/70*

84 Orange Julius of America/*Misc. Fast Foods/84*

85 HairCrafters/Great Expectations/*Hair Care/NR*

86 Sylvan Learning Corp./*Misc. Educ.-Related Services/97*

87 Cost Cutters Family Hair Care Shops/*Hair Care/93*

88 Sizzler Buffet Court & Grill/*Family-Style Restaurants/74*

89 Kampgrounds of America Inc./*Misc. Recreational Activities & Facilities/75*

90 International Tours/*Travel Services/82*

91 Captain D's Seafood/*Fast Food, Fish/98*

92 Homes & Land Magazine/*Publishing Businesses/172*

93 Professional Carpet Systems/*Carpet, Upholstery & Drapery Clng./Dyeing/57*

94 O.P.E.N. Cleaning Systems/*Commercial Cleaning/146*

95 Rent A Wreck/*Used-Auto Rentals/149*

96 Tom's Foods/*Food Services/NR*

97 General Business Services/*Accounting, Consulting & Tax Services/121*

98 Blimpie Co./*Submarine Sandwiches/116*

99 White Hen Pantry/*Convenience Stores/108*

100 U-Save Auto Rental of America Inc. *Auto Rentals & Leasing/100*

Source Entrepreneur (1991) 12th Annual Franchise 500, January, pp. 113–210.

Licensing

Licensing confers only a right to use a company-specific and patent-protected process in manufacturing. This right is conveyed in the transferral of original blueprints and designs. Operational experience in production of the licensed technology is usually a separately negotiable item, as will be any subsequent modifications to the product transferred, unless this has specifically been contracted and does not constitute 'new' technology. In its simplest form, then, it may involve the transmittal of original designs. Increasingly, though, use is being made of additional 'know-how' agreements which will include on-site training of supervisory staff plus an experience transferral in the operations of handling the licensed technology. Know-how, also referred to as technical cooperation or assistance, agreements

Table 6.14 Problems of franchising as a mode of market entry

A To the franchisor:
  1 bureaucracy of host government regulations
  2 high import duties and taxes
  3 monetary uncertainties and royalty
  4 share royalties not profits
  5 logistical problems
  6 selection of franchisee
  7 control of a franchisee network
  8 quality of product and service must be standardized.

B To the consumer:
  1 standardization of product with both good and negative aspects
  2 foreign technology directly exported
  3 high product price relative to domestic competitors.

C To the franchisee:
  1 high cost of items supplied
  2 lack of independence in decision making
  3 franchisor lacks local knowledge
  4 doesn't keep or reap profits due to effort.

D To the host country:
  1 direct import of foreign technology
  2 negative culture effects.

are defined as: '... any industrial information and techniques likely to assist in the manufacture or processing of goods and materials' (Mearn, 1987). 'Know-how' is estimated to save approximately two years on the tooling-up time for any major production plant. Where the licence does not include 'know-how', the buyer, while benefitting from a lower sales price, is hampered by the lack of available operational knowledge. The ability to cope with this situation depends on the technical levels of competence of the buyer and seller respectively.

When licensing agreements do turn out to be far from successful there may well be subsequent recriminations against the seller, perhaps even at a national level, for his refusal to update technology without further fee, particularly in the event of protracted delays in final production. Eastern Europe — which is on average slower than most to implement new technology as may have been witnessed in the case of the diffusion of the Corfam process by DuPont — is eager at the same time to reduce costs wherever possible, particularly as they are forever short of convertible currency reserves. This leads to money having to be saved on licensing which usually means buying the blueprints only, ensuring, therefore, that the technological gap between themselves and the West will always be maintained.

The competitive 'advantage' incorporated in the licensing deal will in any event have a finite life. What licensors seek to do, therefore, is to protect the most secret part of their technology by continuing to export that particular component which embodies state-of-the-art technology. By so doing, they decrease the risk of creating a potential competitor – an accusation often levelled against licensing – while ensuring for themselves a steady revenue from export sales which can also be expected to increase as foreign production climbs. Licensing royalties, on the other hand, usually decrease over time and beyond a certain threshold of sales volume. Licensing may also create a future strategic limitation as Xerox Corporation in the USA found when they granted Rank-Xerox, a British—US company, rights to all markets outside the USA.

Licensing applies also to the increasing phenomenon of syndicating film personality and cartoon character rights to manufacturers of toys, clothing, stationery, etc. Disney cartoon characters perhaps started this trend many years ago with Mickey Mouse appearing on children's watches, but the growth in this area of characterization since then has been phenomenal. There have been the Smurfs displayed on petrol filling stations, the Flintstones on vitamin pills, plus Garfield (200 licensees) and Snoopy on a range of coffee mugs and stationery, including posters and greeting cards. The stars of the US television programme *Dynasty* promoted the merchandise of thirty three different firms which paid to be associated with the series, with products ranging from 'Forever Krystle' perfume to Carrington House Carpets, plus jewellery and fashion wear bearing the Carrington family crest, including a $150 toiletry kit with a gold-plated toothbrush and razor, and a shaving brush made of Chinese badger hair. The film industry, theatre and the arts, Olympic Games organizers, all seek to make additional revenue from the forward promotion of merchandise associated with either their current or forthcoming productions. If Cabbage Patch Kids merchandise was all to be handled by one company, that firm would rank 236 on Fortune's 500 list. Retail sales under the Cabbage Patch name were estimated to be worth $1.5 billion in 1984, and the sales of 5,000 products from these 150 licensees increased it further in 1986.

Where markets are fragmented and exporting the final goods is not possible, industrial process or product licensing remains a clear possibility. Where there is no direct investment permitted by law and no access to venture capital, etc., licensing remains a viable option. Curiously enough, there are no trade statistics on licences. The only organization which seeks to collect information in this area is the UN World Intellectual Property Organization (WIPO) based in Geneva.

Although criticized as being a 'second best' strategy to exporting, product or process licensing may prove to be the only way to enter a market. This was certainly true in previous years of Japan or Eastern Europe. Again, licensing may offer the best method of entry faced with a given level of risk. For smaller companies, licensing may hold many advantages such as lower level of capital required for market entry, lower risk, shorter term payback period. For the larger company, licensing payments may prove to be an effective means of siphoning funds out of a country, where exchange control regulations are in operation, by means of transfer pricing. A low transfer price rate from a high-tax country to a subsidiary in a low-tax country would have two effects. First, the manufacturer in the high-tax country is only marginally profitable, thus, minimizing his exposure to taxation. Secondly, the subsidiary overseas benefitting from a low transfer price will be able to record large profits in a low-tax country. For the company as a whole, the strategy may make sense. What this equation leaves out, though, is the role of customs officers in exporting and importing countries, and the effect of unprofitability on the morale of the workforce.

The disadvantages of licensing include then:

- creation of a potential competitor without the designation of specific sales territories,
- difficulties of maintaining control or 'leverage' over the licensee to avoid damage to

Table 6.15

(A) Conditions for adopting licensing policies

(1) The possession of patented devices and attractive trade marks, preferably in some novel or advanced technology, or special knowhow to which no one else has access.

(2) The ability to protect patents across different legal systems.

(3) That trading conditions in the licensee country inhibit other means of conducting business.

(4) That licensing is the most profitable option.

(5) That a general appraisal of the investment required by the licensee, both in plant and in promotional activities, has been undertaken. The length of time required for establishing the facilities has also to be estimated.

(6) That the results of market research are known, suggesting at least adequate sales in the first and subsequent years, and confirming the breakeven and other calculations. The licensee's profits can then be estimated.

(7) The type of licence has to be considered – whether it will confer exclusive or non-exclusive rights in the area, whether all or limited parts of the manufacture and sale of the product are included, and whether the right to sublet will be a part of the deal and if so on what terms.

(B) Advantages of licensing

(1) To increase the income on products developed as a result of expensive research.

(2) To retain a market to which export is no longer possible or which is likely to become unprofitable due to: import prohibitions, quotas or duties, transport costs, lack of production facilities at home or other related factors.

(3) To protect patents, especially in countries which afford weak protection for products not produced locally.

(4) To make local manufacture possible where this is favoured, for other reasons than those listed above. Examples are the need to adapt the product, the opportunity to cash in on local nationalism, the lack of use for the particular patent in the domestic market. This last advantage may well apply to low-technology products for which there is still a market in developing countries.

(5) To make possible the rapid exploitation of new ideas on world markets before competitors get into the act.

(6) The penetration of new markets. Licensing agreements may open up parts of the world previously closed to a company, either in the licensee's own country or through exports from that country to others.

(7) There may be a valuable spin-off if the licensor can sell other products or components to the licensee. If these are parts for products being manufactured locally or machinery, there may also be some tariff concessions on their import.

(8) A means of entering a market where the nature of the competition — a few dominant and highly competitive firms for example — makes any form of entry apart from licensing too expensive to be contemplated.

(9) A means of entering markets that are less competitive than the domestic. This provides funds for extra Research and Development which then, in its turn, improves the chances of licensing where the competition is stronger.

(10) One considerable advantage for the small firm with an appropriate product is that licensing can be a much more plausible means of expanding abroad than exporting. It is easier to handle a number of markets this way.

(11) Licensing is a viable option where manufacture near to the customer's base is required.

(C) Disadvantages of licensing

(1) The danger of fostering a competitor. This is strongly maintained when technical information is being provided; and there is no substitute for a satisfactory working arrangement to minimize the danger. The use of internationally promoted trademarks and brand names may also deter the licensee from setting up in opposition. To this end it is advisable that the parent company registers the trademarks in its own name.

(2) The danger of a reducing award.

(3) The fact that there is often a ceiling to licensing income per product, sometimes about 5% on the selling price. Innovating products, at least, could rate higher rewards if marketed in other ways.

(4) The danger of the licensee running short of funds, especially if considerable plant expansion is involved or an injection of capital is required to sustain the project. This danger can be turned to advantage if the licensor has funds available by a general expansion of the business through a partnership.

(5) The licensee may prove less competent than expected at marketing or other management activities; hence the licensor may find his commitment is greater than expected. He may even find costs grow faster than income.

(6) Opposition is encountered in some less developed countries to royalty payments on the grounds that too high a price is being charged for the knowledge provided.

(7) Negotiations with the licensee, and sometimes with the local government, are costly and often protracted.

Source   Brooke, M. Z. (1986) *International Management*, Century Hutchinson, London.

trademarks or brand names as a result of the licensee's inferior quality control, after-sales service, etc.,

- increasing production by the licensee may result in lower royalties where there is a sliding scale in operation.
- the licensor is ceding certain sales territories to the licensee for the duration of the contract — should he fail to live up to expectations, renegotiation may be expensive,
- problems involved in the transferral of funds, e.g. exchange control restrictions, exchange parities, plus of course, the refusal to pay!

For some processes particularly — and one may think back to DuPont's Corfam or Pilkington's float glass technique — exporting is not a practicable affair. Market entry and market expansion for the product or process can only be effected by a presence within the market. Territorial sales boundaries can also be agreed so as to defuse the criticism of the potential threat in licensing a potential competitor. This is the greatest single accusation levelled against licensing, together with performance requirements and procedures for the settlement of disputes (Root, 1987), yet masks the simple fact that much profitable business can be obtained via licensing. For a company which is small but technologically efficient, licensing has much to commend it, particularly as the royalties received on overseas production may well go to finance further expansion or fuel the research and development effort which created this invention, thereby maintaining the technological lead.

Also, consider cross-licensing, where two companies will exchange rights to access patents or know-how. There will be no money exchanged, simply technology or know-how transfer. This adds a further layer of complexity, when it is found that one party has a patent which he cannot employ without the cooperation of another patentee so as to avoid infringing another's industrial property rights. Patents are discussed in Chapter 9.

References

Attwood, T., and Hough, L. (1988) *The Good Franchise Guide*, Kogan Page, London.

Ayling, D. (1988) The universe of franchising. *Management Today*, April, 117–121.

Bain, J. S. (1965) *Barriers to New Competition: Their Character and Consequences in Manufacturing Industries*, Harvard University Press, Cambridge, Ma.

Baillieu, D. (1989) Franchising. In *Marketing Handbook*, (M. J. Thomas) 3rd edn, Gower, Aldershot, Hampshire.

Beeth, G. (1973) Distributors – finding and keeping the good ones. In *International Marketing Strategy* (H. Thorelli, and Becker, H. 1980), revised edn, Pergamon Press, Oxford.

Brooke, M. Z. (1985) *Selling Management Services Contracts in International Business*, Holt, Reinhart and Winston, Eastbourne, East Sussex.

Brooke, M. Z. (1986) *International Management*, Century Hutchinson Ltd., London.

Entrepreneur (1991) 12th Annual Franchise 500, January, 113–210.

Financial Times (1982) The risks and rewards of plunging into collaboration ventures. 15 November;

   (1984) McDonalds returns to the Paris Boulevards, January 24;

   (1981) After BL and Honda: Who's linked up with whom, November 18.

Hall, P., and Dixon, R. (1989) *Franchising*, Natwest Small Business Bookshelf, Pitman Publishing, London.

Hearn, P. (1986) *The Business of Industrial Licensing*, Gower, Aldershot, Hants.

Katz, B. (1989) Agents. In *Marketing Handbook* M. J. Thomas, 3rd edn, Gower, Aldershot, Hants.

McCall, M. B., and Warrington, M. B. (1989) *Marketing by Agreement*, 2nd edn, John Wiley & Sons, Chichester.

McMillan, C., and Paulden, S. (1974) *Export Agents: A Complete Guide to their Selection and Control*, 2nd edn, Gower, Aldershot Hants.

Mendelsohn, M. (1985) *The Guide to Franchising*, 4th edn, Pergamon Press, Oxford.

Root, F. R. (1987) *Entry Strategies for International Markets*, Lexington Books, Lexington, Ma.

Streetwise Business, Newsletter of the Franchisee Advice and Consultancy Trade Organization (FACTO), Birmingham.

Wright, M. (1989) *Build Up Your Exports*, Tate Publishing Company, Milton Keynes, England.

Key reading

British Franchise Association, 75A Bell Street, Henley on Thames, Oxon RG9 2BD, publish several directories, books and pamphlets on franchising.

Baker, N C. (1990) Franchising into the '90s. *Nation's Business*, March, 61–69.

Beeth, G. (1973) Distributors – finding and keeping the good ones. In *International Marketing Strategy* (H. Thorelli, and H. Becker 1980), revised edn, Pergamon Press, Oxford.

Brooke, M. Z. (1985) *Selling Management Services Contracts in International Business*, Holt, Reinhart and Winston, Eastbourne, East Sussex.

Cleaver, J. Y. (1987) Going it alone – often a noble option. *Advertising Age*, June 1, 56, 58.

McCall, M. B., and Warrington, M. B. (1989) *Marketing by Agreement*, 2nd edn, John Wiley & Sons, Chichester.

McMillan C., and Paulden S. (1974) *Export Agents: A Complete Guide to their Selection and Control*, 2nd edn, Gower, Aldershot, Hants.

Mendelsohn, M. (1988) *The Guide to Franchising*, 4th edn, Pergamon Press, Oxford.

Root, F. R. (1987) *Entry Strategies for International Markets*, Lexington Books, Lexington, Ma.

Whittemore, M. (1990) Changes ahead for franchising. *Nation's Business*, June, 49–53.

Zantinga, J. (1989) *Countertrade Arrangements: The Country and the Firm – An Overview*, IESE Research Paper No. 164, April. Available from the Research Division, IESE Graduate School of Business, Universidad de Navarra, Av. Pearson 21, 08034 Barcelona, Spain.

7
Market entry strategy decisions 2: investments

Use of screwdriver assembly operations

Assembly as a form of market entry is usually found where there is insufficient market size and the host government is seeking some form of production base. As such, assembly is a compromise and, as it usually also involves small-scale operations, its assembled products are usually destined only for the home market. The label 'screwdriver', as applied to assembly operations, was introduced by the EC in July 1987 in scrutinizing Japanese assembly operations within the Community and elsewhere. The new rule, Council Regulation 1761/87, resulted from more than one year's lobbying by industrial organizations throughout the Community and was an amendment to the Community's anti-dumping rule.

Few products exist today which are manufactured from start to finish within one country. Instead, the components, sub-assembly, and finishing may well originate in several different countries, and yet the 'made in' label will be applied to the finished article on the last stage of its production cycle. The 'made in' label is important. Whereas few countries will ask for a label or plate to be affixed to the product in question indicating exactly where an individual product was made, the importation of final goods en masse to third markets is very often likely to arouse political action, particularly where it competes with local industry. Country of origin rules allow products preferential tariff treatment when sourced from one country as opposed to any other. The rules allow for the last 'substantial stage of manufacture' howsoever defined as to be sufficient to meet the criteria for a certificate of origin from the final producer. However, with Japanese investment in Europe being centred mainly in the UK, there is the accusation that Britain is inviting in a Trojan Horse which will then attack European industry from within the Community. The technical argument of what is a British car extends to British assembled Japanese Nissans now being exported to Community markets. If deemed to be Japanese, they would be excluded from the French and Italian markets, but if deemed to be British, would be allowed tariff-free entry to all Community markets. This then raises the question as to how to evaluate country of origin. The usual criteria is by means of measuring local content, but the French, for example, will not allow marketing costs to be included in this sum. Again, there are two means by which to gauge local content: by volume or by value.

If by volume, it would be possible to show that only a small percentage of the final car is still dependent on imports from abroad. However, these continuing imports may contain the real added-value in that they encapsulate proprietary technology, and so, import costs may still be high. With cars, it may be possible to have an ongoing trade in engines which would fit our example of accounting for only a small import percentage of the total volume of the car, but a substantial part of the value. Politicians will choose whichever measure best suits their needs.

Within the Community, the rules are laid down in Regulation 802/68 and Article 13(7) of Regulation 2423/88 on protection against dumped or subsidized imports from third countries. The debate over the determination of rules of origin has moved to GATT and the Uruguay round of talks. The EC is a signatory to the Kyoto Convention of 1975 on the simplification and harmonization of customs procedures negotiated by the Customs Cooperation Council (CCC) in Brussels, which also says: 'When two or more countries have taken part in the production of the goods, the origin of the goods shall be determined according to the substantial transformation criterion.' While the CCC Secretariat is keen to devise a more substantive set of rules applicable to country of origin, its member countries are much less enthusiastic.

Present regulations 802/68 allow for a Committee on Origin within the EC which must record a majority role to continue an action. The Commission applies a technical test based on the change in tariff heading approach as opposed to a value-added test for the purposes of adopting product-specific origin rules. The EC, for example, determined that Ricoh's photocopiers, made in the USA, actually had Japanese origins because the operations effected in California were not sufficient to confer origin. Examples of decisions made by the Origin Committee, and actions finally taken by the EC, are detailed in Table 7.1. Subsequent European Court rulings have taken issue with the substantiality of the last stage of manufacture, whether more than 10 per cent, and whether the objective was to change tariff heading and circumvent the existing regulations. As stated above, the technical test has been applied rather than an examination of value added. If the parts/sub-assemblies as assembled had acquired European origin, the whole parts/sub-assemblies would be treated as European even though they might have contained sub-parts from other countries. If, on the other hand, the parts/sub-assemblies had not acquired European origin in the production process, the Commission adopted a case by case approach, whereby it broke down the sub-assemblies into sub-parts.

As regards production from third countries, the EC may wait for a complaint from European industry of dumping, or they may dispute the origin of such products outright. Finding Ricoh's photocopiers to be of Japanese origin meant application of a tariff appropriate to Japanese imports into the Community. With regard to dumping, the adoption by the EC of 'selective normal value' (Didier, 1990) whereby only sales to unrelated domestic distributors are used as a basis of normal values and domestic prices to other categories of customers (dealers, end-users, etc.) are omitted from calculations. For a discussion of the issues, see also Matsumoto and Finlayson (1990), who identify:

1 arbitrary and unreasonable 'minimum' amounts, and unreasonably high imported rates for selling, general and administrative expenses and/or profit applied by certain countries,
2 use of fully allocated costs,
3 use of home market costs rather than export costs, and
4 administrative burden of preparing cost data in addition to price data.

It is useful to note, though, the Japanese reaction, as in Ishikawa (1990) who sees in EC legislation something quite sinister and in restraint of free trade: 'Its aim is to offer West European manufacturers protection in the new areas where the Japanese industry based in Europe has acquired a competitive advantage.'

Returning to Porter (1990), the types of international strategy are to be seen in Figure 7.2.

A specific example for the car industry is shown then in Figure 7.3. The point that Porter is making is that coordination of dispersed production facilities, R & D laboratories and marketing is becoming increasingly important. Success will increasingly depend on seeking out competitive advantages from global configuration/coordination anywhere in the value chain, and overcoming the organizational barriers to exploiting them.

Direct investment activities

The company may decide to do any or all of the following but the first issue to consider is the question of ownership and control. Although linked, the two words are not synonymous, and each of these three strategies viz: wholly owned merger/acquisition joint venture below has to be examined in a situational context for optimal fit.

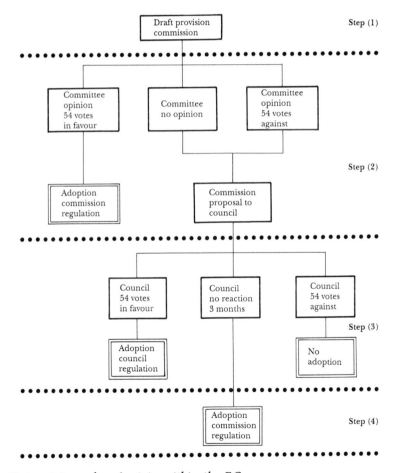

Figure 7.1   *Determining rules of origin within the EC*
Source   Vermulst, E., and Waer, P. (1990) European Community rules of origin as commercial policy instruments? *Journal of World Trade*, **24**(3), 55–90

Table 7.1   Table of product-specific origin regulations

Product	Step	Comments	Type of rule
1 Eggs	2		Technical
2 Spare parts	2		Technical
3 Radio/television receivers	2		Value added
4 Vermouth	2		Technical
5 Tape recorders	2		Value added
6 Meat/offal	4	No concurring opinion	Technical
7 Woven textiles	2		Technical
8 Ceramics	2		Technical
9 Grape juice	2		Technical
10 Knitwear	4	No opinion	Technical
11 Textiles	4	No opinion	Technical
12 Ball bearings	2		Technical
13 Integrated circuits (ICs)	2		Technical
14 Photocopiers	4	No concurring opinion	Technical

Source   Vermulst, E., and Waer, P. (1991) European Community rules of origin as commercial policy instruments? *Journal of World Trade*, June, 55–9.

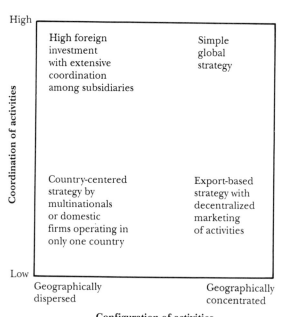

Figure 7.2   *Types of international strategy*
Source   Porter, M.E. (1990) *The Competitive Advantage*, Macmillan, New York

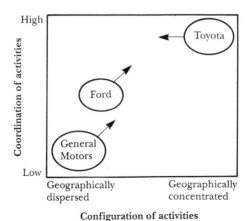

Figure 7.3   *The dimensions of international strategy*
Source   Porter, M.E. (1990) *The Competitive Advantage of Nations*, Macmillan, New York

Wholly owned subsidiaries

Build-up representation in the foreign country as a wholly owned subsidary. This is slow to achieve, expensive to maintain and slow also to yield any tangible results. If a very favourable growth rate is envisaged for the market in question, it may be the only effective mode of entry because, although costly to maintain, it does allow for flexibility in future strategic shifts.

A wholly owned sales subsidiary may provide a presence in the foreign market but a sales presence alone is unpopular particularly among those developing countries least likely to support production. Sales subsidiaries may then be perceived as only taking money out of the country and contributing nothing of value in return to the host country in which it is based. However, it does ensure company control over all aspects of the marketing mix in the foreign market, i.e. product, place (channels of distribution), promotion and price. Problems may arise in that local recruitment may be required by host government legislation; and long-term growth may be encouraged which runs counter to the establishment of an agency base. In these circumstances, establishment of a branch subsidiary may be the only real alternative preceding local manufacture in the target market with the establishment of sales, marketing, and servicing facilities.

The sales subsidiary will generally not be in existence long before demands are made for some manufacturing or production base. Often the market will not support a full scale manufacturing plant and so these developing countries have to settle for assembly operations which at least to some degree provide employment, training and import substitution effects.

Merger/acquisition

Acquire a foreign company. If speed of market entry is important then this may be more easily accomplished by acquiring or merging with a company already in the market. This effectively purchases instant market information, market share, and channels of distribution. It

Table 7.2   Some potential benefits and costs associated with inward direct investment in the UK

Impact issue	Potential benefits to the UK economy	Potential costs to the UK economy	Some criteria for evaluating impact
Technology transfer and innovation	Transfer of advanced product/process technology; local technology creation via subsidiary R & D; technology diffusion and indigenous 'spin-off'; improved competitiveness and quality of employment	Transfer of standardised technology in assembly operations and mature sectors; royalty and other technology payments; technology dependency	Sectoral distribution of inward direct investment; forms of technology transfers (packaged/unpackaged, embodied/disembodied); local R & D activity; terms of technology diffusion: technology concentration and dependence; corporate/subsidiary strategies and coordination
Market structure	Reduction in entry barriers and concentration levels; improved efficiency directly and indirectly; reallocation of resources towards growth sectors	Increase in concentration levels through market power and defensive mergers; anti-competitive practices; vulnerability to changing comparative advantage through international linkages	Market shares of MNE subsidiaries; spillover effects; sectoral distribution of inward direct investment; changing corporate strategies
Trade and balance of payments	Direct investment inflows; increased exports and improved competitiveness; import substitution effects	Repatriation of profits, royalties, etc.: imports of parts and components; transfer pricing; limitations on local sourcing; restricted export franchises	Capital inflows and remittances to parent company; export/import propensity of MNE subsidiaries; changing MNE sourcing strategies
Employment and productivity	Direct employment created through plant openings: multiplier employment effect: improved quality of employment; advanced personnel practices	Job security effects; low skill content in assembly operations; impact on union bargaining power	Employment in foreign-owned sector; plant closures/rationalisations; management and labour practices; industrial relations performance; MNE subsidiary performance *vs* domestic firms, other MNE subsidiaries in UK and abroad

Source   Stephen Young, S., Hood, N., and James Hamill, J. (1988) *Foreign Multinationals and the British Economy*, Croom-Helm, London.

is not an optimal strategy, though, as the companies generally available for acquisition are those that have made themselves so with high debt gearing, poor market performance, or lack of top management direction. Bad companies may be easily acquired while desirable acquisitions can only ever be bought at a premium.

The acquisition route was favoured for a period in the 1960s when managing was regarded as being a universal skill that was portable from one industry to another. This led successful companies to diversify by investing outside of their industry and become more of a conglomerate enterprise. Those companies, which then diversified their industrial interests, have since divested themselves of their ancillary activities and have concentrated once again on their mainstream activity.

In the same way as a tailored made-to-measure suit is preferable to a ready made one, so it is between acquisition and the steady development of a wholly owned subsidiary. In return for speedy access to the market, one has to make certain sacrifices, such as absorbing a company with suitable distribution channels but heavily laden with debt or a weak product line, or endowed for too long with an ineffective top management in which case the change of corporate culture is likely to lead to tension. There is a further problem always with a wholly owned subsidiary and that is the political risk of nationalization, expropriation or imposition of new legislation affecting their profitability and ability to perform.

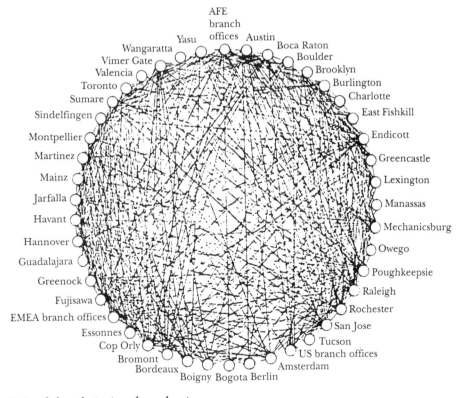

Figure 7.4   *Manufacturing dependencies*
Source   Doz, Y. (1986) *Strategic Management in Multinational Companies*, Pergamon, Oxford

Wholly **owned** subsidiaries, in which **there** is 100 per cent foreign investment stake, are becoming **fewer** in response to host government pressure worldwide. Globally, there is a desire to **both** entice and to control the multinational corporation as though it were a necessary **evil** of our age. Foreign ownership and control of assets are issues constantly under review in all countries. Once an investment is made, the company may then find itself subject to a local monopoly law or regulatory governmental body. There is also the greatest potential risk of expropriation of assets as there will be the maximum level of investment with this type of foreign market entry. There is also the highest degree of visibility, in that with no local ownership or control, the foreign subsidiary remains very foreign and highly conspicuous, and will be correspondingly identified closely with the home country of the parent company, whether it be British, US, or Japanese. Politically this may be undesirable. For globally integrated multinational corporations it may be difficult to undertake any other form of investment since it would involve not only the issues of ownership and control, but with control, the question of pricing components and sub-assemblies within the integrated multinational network, thereby upsetting a sophisticated global sourcing pattern and displacing traditional suppliers, some of whom will be internal, others external with whom long-lasting relationships may now be finally severed. Recent years have seen increasing demands and host country legislation for local content whether in equity, employment or value-added. This is true of Japan, Nigeria, and other fast expanding world markets and is likely to continue.

Joint venture

Enter into a joint venture with a local partner. Certain countries, such as Nigeria, Japan, and some Middle Eastern and Eastern European countries, still place restrictions on 100 per cent foreign ownership. A joint-equity venture under these circumstances may, therefore, be the only means of ensuring an effective market presence. Elsewhere, there is a growing trend towards the strategic business alliance (SBA), a contractual form of joint venture, which is being increasingly adopted by industry in recent years as a result of ever increasing research and development costs and the critical mass required to achieve economies of scale in sectors such as automobile and aeronautical engineering.

Issues of control and ownership continually surface in any discussion on joint ventures. Schaan (cited in Young, Hood, Hamill, 1988) concluded that there were two types of control; positive and negative. Positive control was an ongoing process of influence whereas negative control was seen more as an exercise of raw power designed to bring a recalcitrant child to heel. The joint-venture agreement, particularly from a negotiation skills perspective, is to be found in McCall and Warrington (1989).

Joint ventures (speaking generally) have been defined as 'the commitment, for more than a very short duration, of funds, facilities, and services by two or more legally separate interests, to an enterprise for their mutual benefit' (Tomlinson, 1970). This, then, goes deeper than mere trade relationships since it concentrates on the deliberate alliance of resources between two independent organizations in order to mutually improve their market growth potential (Walmsley, 1982). The anatomical structure of a joint-venture is fully delineated in Figure 7.5.

The reasons for a joint venture, leaving aside for the moment that there are essentially two types: the joint equity venture and the strategic business alliance, include:

1 Explicit pressures by the host government which may include a definite ruling.

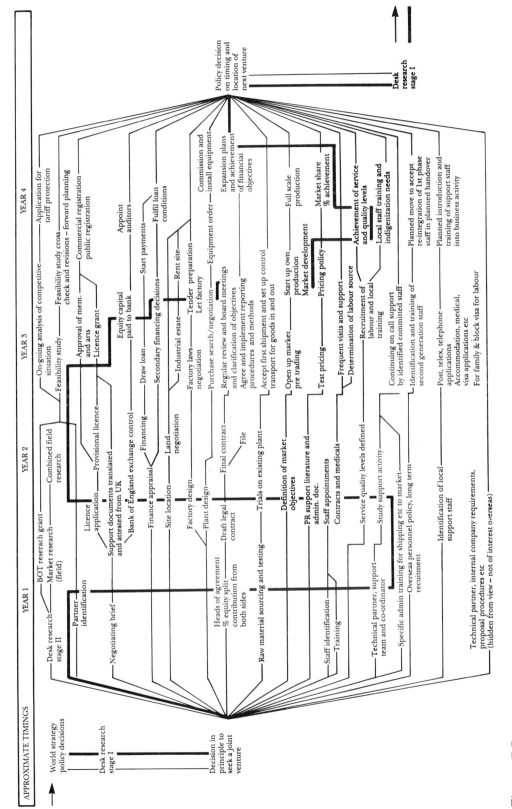

Figure 7.5
Source Walmsley. J. (1982) *Handbook of International Joint Ventures*, Graham and Trotman London

Table 7.3   Analysis of prospective partners. Examples of criteria that may be used to judge a prospective partner's effectiveness by assessing existing business ventures and commercial attitudes.

---

1 *Finance*
>   (i) Financial history and overall financial standing (all the usual ratios).
>   (ii) Possible reasons for successful business areas.
> (iii) Possible reasons for unsuccessful business areas.

2 *Organization*
>   (i) Structure of organization.
>   (ii) Quality and turnover of senior managers.
> (iii) Workforce conditions/labour relations.
>   (iv) Information and reporting systems, evidence of planning.
>   (v) Effective owner's working relationship with business.

3 *Market*
>   (i) Reputation in market place and with competitors.
>   (ii) Evidence of research/interest in service and quality.
> (iii) Sales methods, quality of sales force.
>   (iv) Evidence of handling weakening market conditions.
>   (v) Results of new business started.

4 *Production*
>   (i) Condition of existing premises/works.
>   (ii) Production efficiencies/layouts.
> (iii) Capital investment and improvements.
>   (iv) Quality control procedures.
>   (v) Evidence of research (internal/external), introduction of new technology.
>   (vi) Relationship with main suppliers.

5. *Institutional*
>   (i) Government and business contacts (influence).
>   (ii) Successful negotiations with banks, licensing authorities, etc.
> (iii) Main contacts with non-national organizations and companies.
>   (iv) Geographical influence.

6 *Possible negotiating attitudes*
>   (i) Flexible/hardline.
>   (ii) Reasonably open/close and secretive.
> (iii) Short-term or long-term orientated.
>   (iv) 'Wheeler/dealer' or objective negotiator.
>   (v) Positive quick decision taking or tentative.
>   (vi) Negotiating experience and strength of team support.

These suggestions only form an outline sketch of the type of information which can be used to grade partners and cover areas where there is a reasonable chance of forming a view by appraisal of published information and by sensible observation and questioning.
Source   Walmsley, J. (1982) *Handbook of International Joint Ventures*, Graham and Trotman Ltd., London.

2 Implicit pressure by the host government which may include suspicion or fear of discriminatory action.
3 The desire to spread risk both:
   ● normal business risks, and
   ● the risk of unpredictability of the environment, e.g. national political and economic uncertainty.
4 The need for local facilities and resources best obtained through a local interest with local influence and local knowledge of the customs and legal systems.
5 The opportunity to participate in any local project undertaken by the local partner.
6 Local identity — the benefits accruing to a locally identified operation.
7 Internal company reasons, e.g. goodwill, or the desire to spread corporate capital over a wide range of interests and markets.

Killing (1983), writing on joint ventures, foresaw the coming of ever larger joint ventures more closely attuned to the mainstream business of the joint venture parents. He also foresaw that more favourable attitudes developing towards joint ventures would change as more experience was gained in managing them. Yet, making recommendations about choosing a partner was still a little like advising your daughter on the kind of man she should marry. Nevertheless, Killing did suggest:

1 The more similar the culture of firms forming a shared management joint venture, the easier the venture will be to manage. Culture is considered to have two components, one being the culture of the country in which a company is based, the other one corporate culture of the particular firm in question.
2 The more similar in size are the parents of a shared management venture, the easier the venture will be to manage. A significant size mismatch between a venture's parents can create a lot of problems for the venture.

In any event, the advantages must be strong enough to compensate for the initial lack of knowledge about economic, social, and legal conditions, and the market must be protected relatively well from entry by competitors. A US survey asking businesses to list the advantages of joint ventures revealed the following positive features:

1 the gaining of experience
2 risk reduction
3 capital saving
4 access to lower-cost skilled labour
5 improved government relations.

Harrigan (1987) went considerably further as may be seen from Table 7.4 which clearly outlines the internal, competitive and strategic motivations for joint venture formation.
   In a study of the joint venture process in India and Pakistan, Tomlinson (1970) identified four clear stages in the investment environment:

1 *Unilateral antagonism.* The host nation fears the dangers of economic imperialism.

Table 7.4   Motivations for joint-venture formation

A. *Internal uses*
   1 Cost and risk sharing (uncertainty reduction).
   2 Obtain resources where there is no market.
   3 Obtain financing to supplement firm's debt capacity.
   4 Share outputs of large minimum efficient scale plants.
     a Avoid wasteful duplication of facilities.
     b Utilize by-products, processes.
     c Shared brands, distribution channels, wide product lines, and so forth.
   5 Intelligence: obtain window on new technologies and customers.
     a Superior information exchange.
     b Technological personnel interactions.
   6 Innovative managerial practices.
     a Superior management systems.
     b Improved communications among SBUs.
   7 Retain entrepreneurial employees.

B *Competitive uses* (strengthen current strategic positions)
   1 Influence industry structure's evolution.
     a Pioneer development of new industries.
     b Reduce competitive volatility.
     c Rationalize mature industries.
   2 Preempt competitors ('first-mover' advantages)
     a Gain rapid access to better customers.
     b Capacity expansion or vertical integration.
     c Acquisition of advantageous terms, resources.
     d Coalition with best partners.
   3 Defensive response to blurring industry boundaries and globalization
     a Ease political tensions (overcome trade barriers).
     b Gain access to global networks.
   4 Creation of more effective competitors.
     a Hybrids possessing parents' strengths.
     b Fewer, more efficient firms.
     c Buffer dissimilar partners.

C *Strategic uses* (augment strategic position)
   1 Creation and exploitation of synergies.
   2 Technology (or other skills) transfer.
   3 Diversification.
     a Toehold entry into new markets, products, or skills.
     b Rationalization (or divestiture) of investment.
       Leverage-related parents' skills for new uses.

Source   Harrigan, K. R. (1987) *Strategies for Joint Ventures*, Lexington Books, Lexington, MA.

2 *Mutual suspicion.* Both foreign investors and capital-importing governments may have considerable doubt over the mutuality of their interests. There is concern over the stimulus of economic development with scarce resources, so both foreign capital and technology are required. Imports are paid for by earning from extractive industry exports. Entry conditions for foreign capital and labour are relaxed but still constrained.

3 *Joint acceptance.* The social benefits are perceived to exceed the social costs, and as the needs of development create their own self-generating momentum, their relaxation continues.

4 *Sophisticated integration* – the logical extension of the relaxation mentioned. Foreign investors may be permitted entry in any form of operation which they desire. In so far as local collaboration and participation are felt to be desirable or even necessary, they may well be promoted through discriminatory fiscal and financial incentives, rather than through legislative prohibitions.

These are universal truths. Grouping the possible reasons for partnership, Tomlinson (1970) produced six situations:

1 *Forced partnership.* The choice is effectively forced on the foreign investor either because of explicit host government direction, or indirectly because the partner preempts an exclusive licence.

2 *Convenience to the foreign partner of local facilities under the control of the partner.* Among these would be a site or plant, marketing or distributive facilities, or a strong market position where the partner was already in the same line of business as that of the proposed joint venture.

3 *Resources.* Convenience of local sources of managerial and technical personnel, materials, components or local capital which can be contributed to the partner.

4 *Status and capability of the partner in dealing with local authorities and public relations.* This would also include status defined in terms of general financial and business soundness and standing.

5 *Favourable past association with the partner when the latter had been an agent, licensee, major customer or partner in a previous joint venture.* This category includes special cases in which there might have been strong personal contacts between individuals in the foreign and local parent companies, possibly individuals common to both.

6 *Identity.* A partner is chosen chiefly to obtain local identity, often through association with a potential sleeping partner.

It is interesting, then, to compare this with Harrigan's (1987) four cell matrix (see Figure 7.6). Nationality by itself was not enough justification in itself for entering a joint venture; a local partner would have to have something more to offer. Equally a shared management venture had to be differentiated from a dominant parent venture. As Killing (1983) bluntly put it: 'A shared management volume should not be established unless it is abundantly clear that the extra benefit of having two parents managerially involved will more than offset the extra difficulty which will result.' This is a critical question which it seems all too few firms bother to ask. As one manager put it: 'You've got to have a very large carrot to keep both parents committed during the tough periods!' Killing (1983), however, emphasized that joint ventures are more successful if one company is willing to play a passive role. Having more

than one parent led to dissension, confusion and inability to undertake clear concise and unambiguous decisions. Shared management ventures may work in theory but not in practice where uncertainty may predominate in various forms; political, economic and technical.
    Joint ventures are of two types:

1   Joint-equity venture (JEV). There is the familiar form of a *joint-equity venture* which is well known, and documented, whereby each of the respective partners contributes a sum either in equity or technological know-how in return for a given stake in the operation of a joint venture. Unlike contractual ventures, these are open-ended and not of fixed duration.
2   Strategic business alliance (SBA). This is the increasingly popular form of *contractual joint venture* to be found in the aerospace industry and various other branches of engineering. It is to be found throughout the automobile industry as may be seen from the accompanying figures and diagrams which relate to Fiat. In the now defunct Comecon bloc, these contractual joint ventures are still referred to as industrial co-operation and such agreements known as 'industrial co-operation agreements' or ICAs, a term originally coined by the United Nations. Unlike equity ventures the investment stake may be in technology on one side only. The duration of the joint venture is laid down in the contract which designates the respective tasks and responsibilities of each party over the period of the joint venture. Any change or diversion has to be the subject of negotiation between the two partners. Lewis (1990) points to how companies can build operational strength through alliances, citing the example of how Boeing, pressed by capacity shortages, averted an operational crisis by turning to its rival, Lockheed, for a loan of 600 workers. For Boeing, in civil aircraft, flying these Lockheed workers to Washington State made clear sense as these were experienced technicians. For Lockheed, where military aircraft were being built and jobs were dwindling, the deal retained a skilled workforce until new business could be developed.

    Joint-equity ventures (JEVs) suffer in that the absorption of local equity capital from the foreign market will dilute the company equity base; whereas, an SBA, ICA or contractual

	Product configurations cannot be standardized across markets	Product configurations can be standardized across markets
Customer sophistication and bargaining power is high	Multinational joint ventures: 'Spider's web' of co-operative strategies for cost reduction styling (see Fiat diagram). Many short-term cross-licensing arrangements for new product features, cost reductions.	Few joint ventures, except as required to enter. High co-ordination control by global partner to keep costs lowest.
Customer sophistication and bargaining power is low	More longer term joint ventures (depends on competitors' activities), primarily for new product features.	Few joint ventures, except as required to enter (local partner allowed some co-ordination controls).

Figure 7.6   *Single firm analysis: hypothesized effect of customer bargaining power and market standardization on joint-venture formation and use (assuming firms will co-operate)*
Source   Harrigan, K. R. (1987) *Strategies for Joint Ventures*, Lexington Books, Lexington, MA

joint venture, on the other hand, is quite different in that the respective duties of both parties are clearly designated over a fixed period of years within a legal contract and the issue of ownership does not exist while control is still maintained. Both forms of joint venture seek to answer claims for local national ownership and involvement in foreign-based firms, yet the means by which they do so vary quite widely.

Conditions which particularly favour the development of SBAs include:

- low degree of centralization in marketing and/or production,
- low research and development expenditures,
- high diversification,
- small size of firm or group, and
- need for vertical linkages.

The particular attractions of the SBA, looking at Eastern Europe (Paliwoda, 1981) include:

1 The political and psychological attraction of an association with foreign investors which does not entail any degree of physical ownership of the host nation's resources. The latter remains in full legal control of its oil or copper deposits, while the foreign investor or consortium shares the capital expenditure, development costs, risks as well as profits, and contributes needed technical skill and equipment.
2 Lack of choice. The country in question may not allow wholly owned subsidiaries and there is a desire for more control than is found in simple licensing. Again, the question of payment in resultant goods produced under licence necessitates some form of partnership and market sharing agreement. Developments in terms of both market and product development are also jointly shared and this lessens the perceived risk of entry to that particular target market.

For the Western company, the responsibilities of a contractual joint venture are much easier to bear as it provides many of the advantages of a joint-equity venture without many of its attendant risks. Taking the example of Eastern Europe again, the following advantages may be seen to include:

1 royalties from sales in Eastern Europe,
2 access to an increasing volume of low-cost output for marketing in the West,
3 no responsibility for management unless this has been specifically contracted for on a fee basis,
4 no company capital involved and so the return on investment – limited to personnel and technology – may be very high.

In cars, commercial vehicles, computers, robotics, video, telecommunications, office equipment, aerospace and all other key sectors, strategic business alliances are on the increase. This movement, forced by competitive pressures is linking archrivals such as Philips and Sony; Volvo and Clark Equipment; Fiat and Alfa Romeo; Rover and Honda; Rolls-Royce and Pratt & Whitney, to join forces to manufacture, sell, or conduct research development and yet still remain independent companies.

Fiat's grand European design

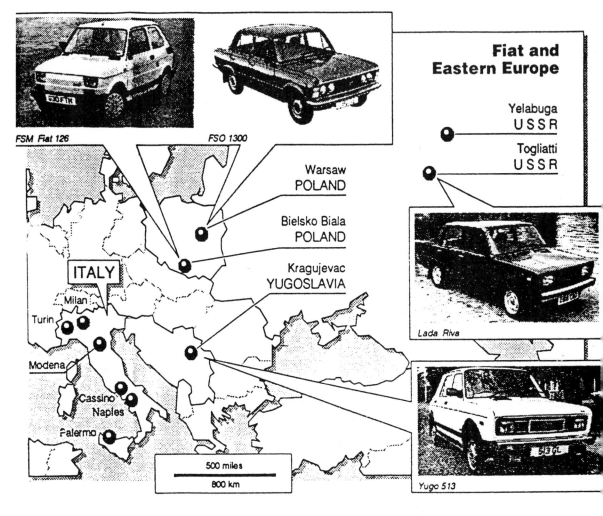

FSM Fiat 126

FSO 1300

Fiat and Eastern Europe

Yelabuga
U S S R

Togliatti
U S S R

Warsaw
POLAND

Bielsko Biala
POLAND

Kragujevac
YUGOSLAVIA

ITALY

Milan

Turin

Modena

Cassino
Naples

Palermo

500 miles

800 km

Lada Riva

Yugo 513

Exhibit 7.1
Source   Financial Times (1990) 9 July.

Table 7.5   Checklist for joint-venture entry

A Purpose of joint venture
   1 Objectives/strategy of foreign partner.
   2 Objectives/strategy of local partner.
   3 Reconciliation of objectives.

B Contributions of each partner
   1 Knowledge of local environment.
   2 Personal contacts with local suppliers, customers, and so on.
   3 Influence with host government.
   4 Local prestige.
   5 Existing facilities.
   6 Capital.
   7 Management/production/marketing skills.
   8 Technical skills and industrial property.
   9 Other.

C Role of host government
   1 Laws/regulations/policies.
   2 Administrative flexibility.
   3 Interest in this joint venture.
   4 Requirements for approval.

D Ownership shares
   1 Majority (foreign partner).
   2 Minority (foreign partner).
   3 50–50.
   4 Other arrangements.

E Capital structure
   1 Legal character of venture.
   2 Equity capital
   3 Loan capital (local and foreign).
   4 Future increase in equity capital.
   5 Limits on transfer of shares

F Management
   1 Appointment/composition of board of directors.
   2 Supply/installation of machinery and equipment.
   3 Expatriate staff.
   4 Organization.

G Production
   1 Planning/construction of facilities.
   2 Supply/installation of machinery and equipment.
   3 Operations.
   4 Quality control.
   5 R & D.
   6 Training

H Finance
  1 Accounting/control system.
  2 Working capital.
  3 Capital expenditures.
  4 Dividends.
  5 Pricing of products provided by partners.
  6 Borrowing and loan guarantees by partners.
  7 Taxation.

I Marketing
  1 Product lines, trademarks, and trade names.
  2 Target market(s) and sales potentials.
  3 Distribution channels.
  4 Promotion.
  5 Pricing.
  6 Organization.

J Agreement
  1 Company law in host country.
  2 Articles and bylaws of incorporation.
  3 Contractual arrangements (licensing, technical assistance, management, and so on).
  4 Settlement of disputes.

Source Root, F. R. (1987) *Entry Strategies for International Markets*, Lexington Books, Lexington, MA.

Research and development costs for the automobile industry together with the critical mass required to achieve economies of scale ensured that this industry would be one of the first to find ways to make savings through joint collaboration. Figure 7.7 examines existing strategic alliances within the European truck industry, where co-operation is close but clearly no-one is particularly interested in ever owning any part of any other company. Instead, various links are forged between companies seeking to combine their engineering strengths in the development of:

● cars (Rover/Honda)
● cars under licence (Rover/Standard Motors of Madras, India)
● diesel engines (BMW/Steyr-Daimler-Puch)
● cars under licence (Suzuki-Maritu, India)
● cars (VAG/Nissan) Germany
● cars (Nissan/Alfa Romeo)
● car components (Alfa Romeo/Fiat)
● cars under licence (Seat/Fiat, Spain)
● cars under licence (Lada/Fiat, USSR)
● development work (Lada/Porsche, USSR)

- cars under licence/component exchange (Zastava/Fiat, Yugoslavia)
- component exchange (Zastava/Yugoslavia, Polmot/Poland)
- cars under licence/source of Fiat 126 for Europe (Polmot/Fiat, Poland)
- light commercial vehicles (Peugeot, India)
- commercial vehicles (General Motors/Enasa, Spain)
- commercial vehicle components (General Motors/MAN, West Germany)
- joint development of automatic parts (Lancia/Saab)
- 1 million engines per year plant (Fiat/Peugeot)
- production of 130,000 new cars (Citroen/Olteit)
- diesel engines (Peugeot/Chrysler)
- V6 engine (Peugeot/Volvo/Renault)
- development work (Renault/Volvo)
- trucks 6–11 tonnes (VW/MAN, West Germany)
- medium duty transmissions (Iveco, Italy/Eaton, USA)
- truck axles (Iveco, Italy/Rockwell, USA)
- CF6–80C2 aero-engines (Rolls-Royce/General Electric, USA)
- V–2500 aero-engines (Rolls-Royce/Pratt and Whitney, USA)
- RB 211 - 535E4 series aero-engines (Rolls-Royce/General Electric, USA)
- CFM 56 aero-engines (Snecma, France/General Electric, USA)

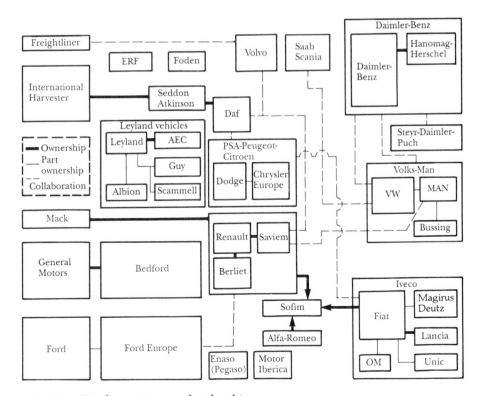

Figure 7.7 *Euro-Trucks – sisters under the skin*
Source Walmsley, J. (1982) *Handbook of International Joint Ventures*, Graham and Trotman, London

There are, of course, some pitfalls associated with joint ventures generally. These include:

- Board level disagreement between the two parents on the priorities, direction and values of the joint venture.
- Difficulty of integrating into a global strategy with cross-border trading.
- Conflict when corporate headquarters endeavour to impose limits or even guidelines.
- Unacceptable positions can develop with a local market when the self-interest of one partner conflicts with the interest of the joint venture as a whole, as in the pricing of a single-source input or raw material.
- Objectives of the respective partners may be incompatible.
- Problems of management structures and dual parent staffing of joint ventures as well as nepotism perhaps being the established norm.
- Conflict in tax interests between the partners particularly where one may represent the local government interest.

A joint venture requires sharing rewards as well as risks. Harrigan (1985) has identified the following as joint venture change forces:

1 Changes in the venture's industry (and success requirements therein).
2 Effectiveness of joint venture's competitive strategy.
3 Changes in partners' relative bargaining power *vis-à-vis* each other.
4 Changes in owners' strategic missions.
5 Changes in importance of the joint venture to owners.
6 Changes in venture's need for autonomous activities.
7 Changes in patterns of owner-venture coordination needed for competitive success.

The main disadvantage is the very significant costs of control and co-ordination associated with working with a partner. *Business Week* (21 July 1986) reported that seven in ten fall short of expectations and were disbanded. Franko (1971) revealed that more than one-third of the 1,100 joint ventures of 170 multinational corporations studied, were unstable, ending in 'divorce' or in a significant increase in the US firms power over its parent. Killing (1983) also found this 30 per cent failure rate in his study of thirty-seven joint ventures. Franko also found that joint ventures with a local government partner were more lasting. Research elsewhere has also shown that where business had the choice between joint-equity and SBA-type contractual joint ventures, they were increasingly moving towards contractual joint ventures.

As an innovative form, SBAs assume complex forms and do not readily correspond to the known established forms of commercial contracts and so the UN Economic Commission for Europe in its *Guide on Drawing up International Contracts on Industrial Co-operation*, in 1976, was forced to state:

the drafters of contracts relating to industrial co-operation are obliged to use their imagination and to resort to legal innovation while endeavouring to conform as closely as possible to the economic, financial and commercial realities of industrial co-operation transactions.

Tripartite ventures

Tripartite ventures are few in number. Originally they developed as a means of third country market exploitation by a joint company owned by two separate foreign principals, perhaps also from different politico-economic blocs.

East-West *détente* of the early 1970s facilitated the trade exchange. During this period a few joint stock companies were established such as Polibur based in Manchester, England, a joint venture in the chemical engineering consulting and services field, owned equally by Petrocarbon Developments as a subsidiary of Burmah Oil (which later sold out to the construction company, Costain) and Polimex-Cekop of Poland. The expectations for the joint venture were that the Poles would be able to access Socialist countries with Western technology; the British partners would have lower cost on Polish inputs to offer on Western markets. All profits would be shared equally. The identity and image of the company would change relative to the market which it was approaching. Unfortunately the downturn in the petrochemicals sector which has produced overcapacity has created problems for this joint venture. Its success overall has been limited.

Industrializing nations continue, however, to make demands of the developed industrial nations to form partnerships. Indian engineering companies took an unusual unprecedented step when they drew up a list of ten major contracts totalling more than 120 million where they would like to be awarded sub-contracts.

Buckley, Pass and Prescott (1990), in their empirical study on the impact of foreign market servicing strategies on the competitiveness of UK manufacturing firms in five industry sectors, point out:

1 Choice of market servicing policy is highly constrained by the nature of the product, the firm's previous involvement with the market, the actions of competitors, demand conditions in the market, financial considerations and cost conditions.
2 Firms have an approach to market servicing rather than a strategy. In many cases, the market servicing still is reactive rather than proactive.
3 Choices made do not have a universally positive impact on the competitiveness of firms. In each of the categories: performance, potential, and management process, there are examples of changes in market servicing stance which had negative impacts. Two particularly problematical areas appear to be entry via exporting through a foreign distributor and the take-over of a foreign company, which form the opposite ends of the size and involvement spectrum.
4 No definite causal relations were discerned between market servicing mode and competitive outcome.

In the *Future of the Multinational Enterprise*, Buckley and Casson (1985) acknowledge the role of the multinational corporation in the development and transferral of knowledge internationally, and, through foreign investment, the MNE's ability to bypass imperfect external markets for knowledge. While arguing for internalization as the explanation for multinational growth, Buckley and Casson foresee also a change to the multinational working environment in the lessening of competitive R & D, and through more effective marketing of knowledge. Such a change would affect competitive policy, rationalize R & D activities, and may substitute licensing for foreign direct investment. Through the advent of SBAs, relatively unknown in 1976, this rationalization of R & D has come about but without any

Table 7.6 Operational variable analysis contrasting strategic business alliances and joint equity ventures

Operation variables	Strategic business alliances		Joint equity	
	Possible advantages	Possible disadvantages	Possible advantages	Possible disadvantages
Ownership	None, no company finance involved	Lack of control	Equity stake	Weakening of company equity base
Venture control	Contractual limitations, plant, local partner responsibility	Limited control	De facto control greater than equity share	Inability to reconcile objectives
Venture capital	No capital investment by company	Entails acceptance of goods made under licence	Capital and managerial investment	Commitment of company resources
Return on investment (ROI)	Fast	Speed of project rests with local partner	Gradual ROI shows willingness to stay in market	Venture has to achieve profitability first
Risk sharing	Contractual liability only	Diminished risks diminish opportunity for spectacular profits	Half share only	Eastern partner may refuse to kill-off an unprofitable joint venture
Venture duration	Fixed duration	Renewal or extension requires separate contract	Unlimited	Termination a possible problem
Western company repayment	Hard cash and goods	Adjustment to Western business cycles	Goods made under licence and hard cash	Subject to local taxes
Manufacturing	Extra facility at cost	May flood market eventually	Extra plant at cost	Exposure to risk

Management skills	Limited, contractual obligations	Costs of this transfer may be greater than anticipated	Full access	Too great a dependence on the Western partner
Marketing	Lower cost goods made under licence	Co-ordination with Western business cycles	Lower cost goods made under licence	Investment in capital, machinery and management
Market expansion	Market access contractually limited	Ability to vary deliveries according to demand	Market access contractually limited	Sales priced only in 'hard' currency
Pricing	Lower costs	Western inability to forecast partner's expectation	Lower costs	All costs priced in 'hard' currency only
Quality control	Goods to Western quality standards	Free access but geographical distance and costs of quality control	Goods to Western quality standards	Free access but geographical distance and costs of quality control
Research and development	May be included or may develop	Dependent on mutual capabilities	Ability to capitalize on local partner	Difficulties of co-ordination
Updating of technology transferred	Contractual	Ambiguity of contract and defined limits	Closer integration	Sharing of current company specific technology

Source Paliwoda, S. J. (1981) *Joint East-West Marketing and Production Ventures*, Gower Press, Farnborough.

increase in licensing over foreign direct investment, so as an alternative to investment, licensing still appears to be commonly perceived by industry as having too many shortcomings.

References

Ansoff, I. (1982) *Strategic dimensions of internationalisation*. European Institute for Advanced Studies in Management, Brussels, Working Paper No. 82–37, October.

Bain, J. S. (1965) *Barriers to New Competition: Their Character and Consequences in Manufacturing Industries*, Harvard University Press, Cambridge, MA.

Bartlett, C. A., and Ghoshal, S. (1989) *Managing Across Borders: The Transcontinental Solution*, Hutchinson Business Books, London.

Beamish, P. (1988) *Multinational Joint Ventures in Developing Countries*, Routledge, London.

Blank, A. H. (1987) The growth of joint venture marketing. *The Banker's Magazine*, March–April, 60–63.

Buckley, P. J., and Casson, M. (1976) *The Future of the Multinational Enterprise*, Macmillan, London.

Buckley, P. J., and Casson, M. (1985) *The Economic Theory of the Multinational Enterprise*, Macmillan, London.

Casson, M. (1979) *Alternatives to the Multinational Enterprise*, Holmes and Merer Publishers Inc., New York.

Clark, T. R., and Guscott, P. F. (1986) Technology or marketing – which is master? *The Banker's Magazine*, April, 91–95.

Commission of the European Communities DG XXIII, and T.I.I. European Association for the Transfer of Technologies, Innovation and Industrial Information (1989) *Partnerships Between Small and Large Firms*, Graham and Trotman Ltd., London.

Conference Board (1983) *Matrix Organization of Complex Businesses*, Elsevier, Barking, Essex.

Curtin, T. F. (1987) Global sourcing: is it right for your company? *Management Review*, **76**(8), 47–49.

Didier, P. (1990) EEC anti-dumping: the level of trade issue after the definitive CD player regulation. *Journal of World Trade*, **24**(2), 103–110.

Doz, Y. (1986) *Strategic Management in Multinational Companies*, Pergamon Press, Oxford.

Dunning, J. H. (1985) *Multinational Enterprises, Economic Structure and International Competitiveness*, John Wiley and Sons, Chichester.

Fennema, M. (1982) *International Networks of Banks and Industry*, Mertinus Nighoff Publishers, The Hague.

Financial Times (1982) The risks and rewards of plunging into collaboration ventures, 15 November 1982.

Forsgren, M. (1989) *Managing the International Process*, Routledge, London.

Franko, L. G., (1972) *Joint Venture Survival in Multinational Corporations*, Praeger, New York

Goldberg, W. K. (1983) *Mergers: Motives, Modes, Methods*, Gower, Aldershot, Hampshire.

Goldenberg, S. (1988) *International Joint Ventures in Action: How to Establish, Manage and Profit from International Strategic Alliances*, Hutchinson Business Books, London.

Harrigan, K. R. (1987) *Strategies for Joint Ventures*, Lexington Books, Lexington, MA.

Harrigan, K. R. (1985) Why joint ventures fail. *First Boston Working Paper Series*, Columbia University Graduate School of Business, FB–86–01, September.

Ishikawa, K. (1990) *Japan and the Challenge of Europe 1992*, Pinter Publishers, London, for the Royal Institute of International Affairs, London.

Killing, J. P. (1983) *Strategies for Joint Venture Success*, Croom Helm, London.

Lewis, J. D. (1990) *Structuring and Managing Strategic Alliances*, Free Press, New York.

Matsumoto, K., and Finlayson, G. (1990) Dumping and anti-dumping: growing problems in world trade. *Journal of World Trade*, **24**(4), 5–20.

McCall, J. B., and Warrington, M. B. (1989) *Marketing by Agreement: A Cross-Cultural Approach to Business Negotiations*, 2nd edn, John Wiley and Sons, Chichester.

Paliwoda, S. J. (1981) *Joint East-West Marketing and Production Ventures*, Gower, Aldershot, Hampshire.

Perlemutter, H. V. (1969) Some management problems of spaceship Earth: the megafirm in the global industrial estate. *Academy of Management Proceedings*, New York, August.

Porter, M. E. (1990) *The Competitive Advantage of Nations*, Macmillan, New York.

Roman, D. D., and Puett, E. F. Jr. (1983) *International Business and Technological Innovation*, North Holland.

Root, F. D. (1987) *Entry Strategies for International Markets*, Lexington Books, Lexington, MA.

Shepherd, J. Silberston, A., and Strange, R. (1985) *British Manufacturing Investment Overseas*, Methuen & Co., Ltd., London.

Stopford, J., and Turner, L. (1985) *Britain and the Multinationals*, John Wiley and Sons, Chichester.

Taylor, W. (1991) The logic of global business: an interview with ABB's Percy Barnenk. *Harvard Business Review*, March-April, 91–105.

Terpstra, V. (1983) *International Marketing*, 3rd edn, Holt Rinehart Winston, Montana, USA.

Tomlinson, J. W. C. (1970) *Joint Ventures in India and Pakistan*, Praeger, New York.

UN Economic Commission for Europe (1976), *Guide in Drawing up International Contracts on Industrial Co-operation*, Geneva, ECD/TRADE/124.

Vermulst, E., and Waer, P (1991) European Community rules of origin as commercial policy instruments? *Journal of World Trade*, June, 55–59.

Walmsley, J. (1982) *Handbook of International Joint Ventures*, Graham and Trotman Ltd., London.

Young, S. Hood, N., and Hamill, J. (1988) *Foreign Multinationals and the British Economy*, Croom Helm, London.

Key reading

Bartlett, C. A., and Ghoshal, S. (1989) *Managing Across Borders: The Transcontinental Solution*, Hutchinson Business Books, London.

Buckley, P. J., and Casson, M. (1976) *The Future of the Multinational Enterprise*, Macmillan, London.

Buckley, P. J., and Casson, M. (1985) *The Economic Theory of the Multinational Enterprise*, Macmillan, London.

Commission of the European Communities DG XXIII, and T.I.I. European Association for the Transfer of Technologies, Innovation and Industrial Information (1989) *Partnerships Between Small and Large Firms*, Graham and Trotman Ltd., London.

Forsgren, M. (1989) *Managing the International Process*, Routledge, London.

Harrigan, K. R. (1987) *Strategies for Joint Ventures*, Lexington Books, Lexington, MA.

Harrigan, K. R. (1985) Why joint ventures fail. *First Boston Working Paper Series*, Columbia University Graduate School of Business, FB–86–01, September.

Ishikawa, K. (1990) *Japan and the Challenge of Europe 1992*, Pinter Publishers, London, for the Royal Institute of International Affairs, London.

Killing, J. P. (1983) *Strategies for Joint Venture Success*, Croom Helm, London.

Lewis, J. D. (1990) *Structuring and Managing Strategic Alliances*, Free Press, New York.

McCall, J. B., and Warrington, M. B. (1987) *Marketing by Agreement: A Cross-Cultural Approach to Business Negotiations*, 2nd edn, John Wiley and Sons, Chichester.

Root, F. D. (1987) *Entry Strategies for International Markets*, Lexington Books, Lexington, MA.

Stopford, J., and Turner, L. (1985) *Britain and the Multinationals*, John Wiley and Sons, Chichester.

Walmsley, J. (1982) *Handbook of International Joint Ventures*, Graham and Trotman Ltd., London.

Young, S. Hood, N., and Hamill, J. (1988) *Foreign Multinationals and the British Economy*, Croom Helm, London.

8
Monitoring the effectiveness of market entry strategies

There is no one single mode of market entry that may be termed 'best'. Market entry modes have to be assessed within their context. The expectations of head office management and the resources which they are willing to commit are important factors. Also a factor is the fact that at certain points in business history various forms of market entry have been fashionable. Over the years licensing gave way to franchising which is still buoyant in Europe but the greatest single trend has been towards strategic alliances. No one market entry mode is fault free or able to compensate for the deficiencies of alternative forms. For this reason, the mode must be assessed within the context within which it will be placed.

However, selection of a market entry mode is not the end of the process but the beginning. Evaluation starts as soon as the market entry mode is operational. Naturally, a reasonable period of time will usually be allowed against which to properly assess performance but a particularly poor or unimpressive performance may hasten withdrawal or replacement by another form of market entry. Seeing this process then as iterative it is useful now to consider the framework offered by Bartlett and Ghoshal (1989).

Bartlett and Ghoshal see the national environments as important to the firm's global strategy. A national subsidiary is placed in one of the four categories in Figure 8.1 depending on its strengths in technology, production, marketing or any other area that may lend competitive advantage. Strategic leaders develop organizational responses in certain areas. This is similar to the world product market advocated by Rugman and others (see Chapter 9). A certain area of competence may be developed to become the company's international specialist division or production or research base. Contributors are national subsidiaries who may have strong technological capability but a limited market. These subsidiaries feed into the worldwide network. Implementers are those who maintain operations in a non-strategic market but cannot contribute much to the strategic knowledge of the firm. They do not control resources or have access to critical information so they are limited in their operations but in pursuing what they do efficiently they can contribute greatly to the firm in pursuing their quest for ever greater efficiency in economies of scale perhaps and so competitive advantage. Most subsidiaries fall into the implementer category.

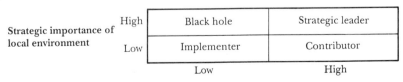

Figure 8.1 *Generic roles of national organizations*

Source   Bartlett, C. A. and Ghoshal, S., *Managing Across Borders: The Transnational Solution*, Hutchinson Business Books, London

Finally, the 'black hole'. This exists where companies have only taken positions in the markets in which they are based. It has minimal capability and is not held to be an acceptable strategic position. A strategy of a small monitoring unit to exploit the potential of the market does not work. 'One needs to be aware of developments as they emerge, and for that one must be a player, not a spectator' (Bartlett, Ghoshal, 1989). A strategic alliance is possible in these circumstances but it depends as much on the organizational capability of the parties as the motivating force of the potential to be tapped.

Relationship management and interaction theory

Unlike economists who still busy themselves with concepts such as pure competition which do not exist, businessmen take a different view of the market place. Academic theory is leagues behind practice in the area of international marketing. Various studies have been made on locational decision-making, on assumptions that companies move towards lower cost factor endowments. Less has been written on the organizational abilities of global corporations to exploit profitable sales rather than production or even to consider market entry as being a move that will later have strategic importance, as is evidenced in much investment being made in the EC prior to 1992.

When the importance of market concentration is considered and how with the ever increasing costs of research and development, the critical mass of production necessary to achieve economies of scale is forever being pushed upwards, it is not hard to imagine how hard the competition must be. Industries are not national but global and so, therefore, is the competition.

Interaction theory was developed by the Swedes but spread into France, Britain, Italy and Germany when a group of like-minded researchers formed what became known as the IMP Group, basing their research on the Interaction Model.

The interaction model recognizes the customer as important and puts at the very centre of its research the nature of this relationship between buyer and seller. Relationship management is crucial when one considers that for every customer complaint received, there are twenty-seven who feel the same way but who would not otherwise complain. These, too, could be lost customers and when one considers that it takes five times as much to replace a customer than it does to retain one, the importance of relationship management becomes self-evident (*Marketing News*, 1991). This however requires market 'presence', see Table 8.1.

The differences which the interaction model brings to a study of market dynamics include:

- Recognition of an active dynamic market rather than a passive market, and its implications of simply manipulating marketing mix variables to achieve a response from a generalized, passive market.
- Questioning an atomistic structure to understand markets which assumes a large number of buyers and sellers with easy and costless change between suppliers and customers.
- Investigation of the characteristics of different organizations as they relate to other organizations.
- Analysis of the links between the units in terms of formalization, intensity and standardization.
- Relationships between buyers and sellers in the industrial context are frequently long-term, close, and involve a complex pattern of interaction between and within each company.

Table 8.1 Market control and modes of entry

		Control over market strategy	Product policy	Pricing policy	Promotional policy	After-sales service
Exporting without presence	Agent	Weak to none	Standardization	Uncontrolled	Uncontrolled	Uncontrolled
	Exclusive agent Concession	Weak to good Contractual	Standardization	Better control	Good control	Good control
	Sale of patent or licence	None	Adaptation	No control	No control	No control
	Franchise	Rather good	Adaptation	Weak control	Weak control	Weak control
	Management contract	Good	Adaptation	Weak control	Weak control	Weak control
Small presence	Joint venture	Moderate	Standardization	Better control	Better control	Better control
	Wholly owned subsidiary	Excellent	Standardization	Well controlled	Well controlled	Well controlled
	Sub-contracting	Moderate	Adaptation Problem of quality control	Badly controlled	—	—
	Joint venture assembly production integration	Moderate	Partial adaptation Well controlled Adapted Badly controlled	Moderate control	Moderate control	Moderate control
Heavy presence	Wholly owned subsidiary assembly production integration	Good	Partially adapted Adapted	Well controlled	Well controlled	Well controlled

Source: Translated and adapted from: de Leersnyder, J.-M. (1982), *Marketing International*, Dalloz, Paris, p. 106.

- Tasks of marketers and buyers often have more to do with maintaining a relationship than with a straightforward sale or purchase.
- Links between buyer and seller often become institutionalized into a set of roles that each party expects the other to perform. This extends into product development, test procedures and the carrying of inventory.
- Importance of experiences of previous purchases, mutual evaluation and the relationship established during the course of that single transaction.

Figure 8.2 displays the interaction model with four groups of variables:

- parties involved both as organizations and individuals
- environment in which the interaction takes place
- elements of and the process of interaction
- unique atmosphere affecting and affected by the interaction.

Transactions are different from relationships which are frequently long term. To distinguish between them, the simple transaction is called an 'episode' which may or may not be

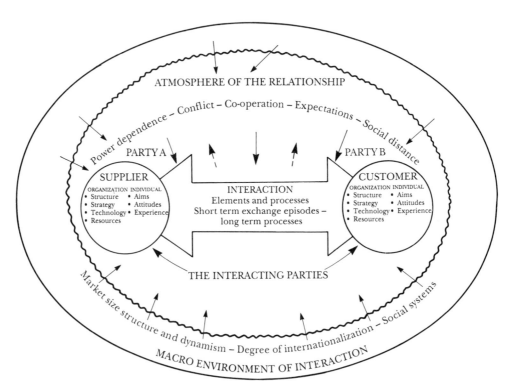

Figure 8.2   *The interaction model*
Source   Turnbull, P. W., and Paliwoda, S. J. (1986) *Research in International Marketing*, Croom Helm, London

repeated. It may evolve, if repeated over time, into a relationship. Episodes have four elements:

1 Product or service exchange which is at the very core of the exchange.
2 Information exchange which may be personal or impersonal.
3 Financial exchange.
4 Social exchange which helps also to further reduce uncertainty in a relationship based on market trust.

Relationships arise out of the routinization of these exchange episodes over time and so to a clear expectation on the part of either party with regard to roles and responsibilities. Again, over time, these expectations become institutionalized. Also, contact patterns become established between the two parties in terms of either individuals or groups seeking to transmit communications across the two organizations. Another important factor of relationships is the adaptations which one party may make either to the elements exchanged or the process of exchange. The structure of each organization and the extent of centralization, specialization and formalization will influence the interaction process. Individuals are also part of this process, usually several will be involved exchanging information, developing relationships, and perhaps building up the kinds of social bonds which may influence further future stages of their business relationship. Experience gained from individual 'episodes' becomes part of the total corporate memory of a relationship.

Market structure depends on the concentration of buyers and sellers and the degree of stability or change prevalent in that market. Markets are not just regional or national but may be international. This influences the interaction environment as the degree of dynamism is very central to interaction. Internationalism of the market as it affects buyers and sellers is another central issue shaping attitudes towards nationalism and so protection and perceptions about the ability of either parties to perform as is the position of either party in the distribution channel.

The unique atmosphere created between the companies is that of power and dependence; of conflict and cooperation; and of mutual expectations. The atmosphere affects, and is affected by, the other variables already mentioned. The parties can give each other valuable technical and commercial information but the ability to control the relationship is related to the perceived power of either party which may be low, or poorly understood, in the critical stages of the relationship but which will in any event, change over time. A close relationship may be technologically advantageous but will in turn have opportunity costs.

International studies related to interaction theory

The first and major study of the IMP Group was the five country study of France, Germany, Sweden, UK and Italy whereby the perceptions of national suppliers were investigated by each of the national teams with the exception applying that national research teams were excluded from asking foreign buyers their perceptions of suppliers from their particular country. In this way, a certain bias that would otherwise have been introduced was completely eliminated at the outset. This study clearly showed supplier-customer relationship management to be an important issue. (See Table 8.2.)

A further IMP study was Hakansson, 1982 which was more industrial case study than international-marketing oriented. Then Turnbull and Valla, 1986 provided a country-by-country perspective of international industrial marketing strategies and the nature of

Table 8.2 Supplier/customer relationship: summary profiles of each country market

France	Germany	Italy	Sweden	United Kingdom
Highest average age	Highest average age among export markets	Lowest customer adaptations score	Highest customer adaptations among export markets	Lowest average age
Highest sourcing average	Lowest degree of reciprocal adaptations	Lowest supplier adaptations score	Highest combined volume of adaptations among export markets	Highest sourcing average among export markets
Highest customer adaptations score	Lowest human investment by customer	Lowest combined volume of adaptations	Highest degree of reciprocal adaptations	Highest supplier adaptations score
Highest combined volume of adaptations		Lowest human investment by supplier	Highest human investment by customers among export markets	Lowest degree of reciprocal adaptations
Highest human investment by suppliers		Highest stability of turnover		Highest human investment by supplier among export markets
Highest human investment by customers				
Lowest stability of turnover				

Source: Turnbull, P. W., and Valla, J.-P. (1986) *Strategies for International Industrial Marketing*, Croom-Helm, London.

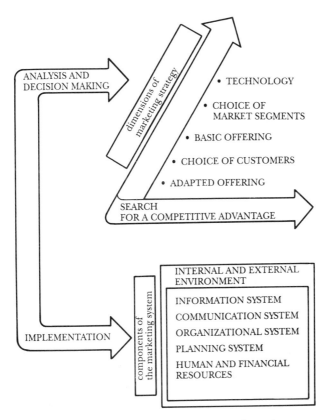

Figure 8.3   *The multistrat model: a framework for industrial marketing strategies*
Source   Turnbull, P.W., and Valla, J.-P. (1986) *Strategies for International Industrial Marketing*, Croom-Helm, London

relationships between national suppliers and their customers. Moving away from the industrial marketing mix concept, Valla proposed the multistrat model which introduces the five main marketing dimensions firms have to make: technology; choice of segments; basic offering; choice of customers; adapted offering. A sixth dimension is that the firm will normally look for one or more competitive advantage so as to be able to compete successfully. Against these six dimensions, there are five components of the marketing system: the information system; the communication system; the organizational system; the planning system and the human and financial resources. The IMP Group view industrial marketing as an investment process over time in which the interaction model provides a useful framework for understanding and presenting marketing strategy. Suppliers who have successfully entered into a relationship with a customer have an initial advantage over potential competitors, but this may be eroded if not maintained through continued investment activity. Figure 8.3 provides a framework for testing strategic alternatives although it should be emphasized that the nature of the business activity is an important factor in terms of value perceived or otherwise i.e. commodity or stable or growing non-commodity may be simply one means of differentiation. The more the business activity resembles a commodity, the fewer are the strategic alternatives.

A portfolio of market entry strategies

Market concentration and spreading have been dealt with earlier. Piercy (1983) points to a portfolio approach which assesses market attractiveness against the company's competitive strengths by means of weighting a number of indicators representing several variables. This would allow a selection of the most appropriate markets which match the exporter's profile of needs. It blends hard data on export markets with a substantial examination of criteria appropriate for the individual exporter. A portfolio approach will also pinpoint change within

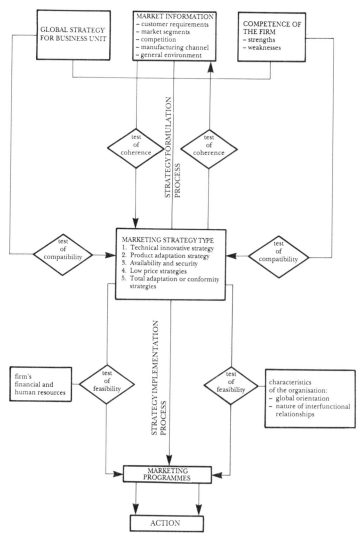

Figure 8.4   *A framework for testing marketing strategies for coherence, compatibility and feasibility*
Source   Turnbull, P. W., and Valla, J.-P. (1986) *Strategies for International Industrial Marketing*, Croom-Helm, London

market clusters and identify the appropriate strategy whether growth, hold, rebuild, harvest, or divestment. Designing an export market strategy requires information not just on growth and profitability but also risk and stability and to be meaningful, in a situational context (see Figure 8.5).

Conclusions

This chapter has sought to confront the measures against which relative degrees of success may be determined. Expectations are important as are resources, but what can be expected out of any investment is determined by what is actually put in, in way of investment. In order that the 'sharp-end' of the business, the actual contact with the foreign customer was not overlooked, a summary of interaction theory focusing on relationship management and the need to invest in customers to maintain relationships was provided.

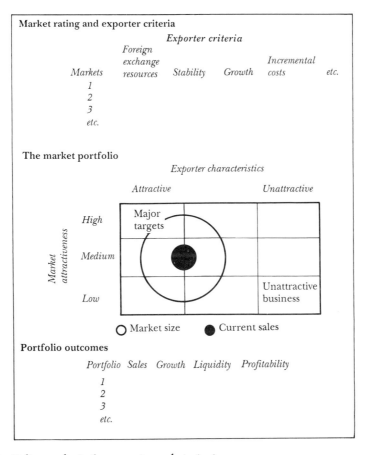

Figure 8.5   *Portfolio analysis for export market strategy*
Source   Piercy, N. (1983) Export strategy – the market portfolio. *European Research*, **11**, 168–176

References

Bartlett, C. A., and Ghoshal, S. (1989) *Managing Across Borders: The Transnational Solution*, Hutchinson Business Books, London.
Hakansson, H. (ed.) (1982) *International Marketing and Purchasing of Industrial Goods - An Interaction Approach*, John Wiley and Sons, New York.
Marketing News (1991), American Marketing Association, Chicago, 4 February, p. 4.
Piercy, N. (1983), Export strategy – the market portfolio. *European Research*, **11**(4), 168–176.
Turnbull, P. W., and Cunningham, M. T. (1981) *International Marketing and Purchasing: A Survey Among Executives in Five European Countries*, Macmillan, London.
Turnbull, P. W. (1985), Image and reputation of British suppliers in Western Europe. *European Journal of Marketing*, **19**(6), 39–52.
Turnbull, P. W., and Paliwoda, S. J. (1986) *Research in International Marketing*, Croom Helm, London.
Turnbull, P. W., and Valla, J.-P. (1986) *Strategies for International Industrial Marketing*, Croom Helm, London.

Key reading

Ford, D., and Leonidou, L. (1991) Research developments in international marketing: a European perspective. In *New Perspectives on International Marketing*, (S. J. Paliwoda), Routledge, London.
Fraser, C., and Hite, R. E. (1990) Impact of international marketing strategies on performance in diverse global markets. *Journal of Business Research*, **20**, 249–262.
Gemunden, H. G. (1991) Success factors of export marketing: a meta-analytic critique of the empirical studies. In *New Perspectives on International Marketing*, (S. J. Paliwoda), Routledge, London.

9
Product policy decisions

A useful starting point may be in examining the definition of a 'product'. The definition used here is that offered by Philip Kotler (1984). Although Kotler was later to change his definition for his sixth and seventh editions, in the opinion of this author, at least, it remains the most suitable for our purposes in that it is concise, measurable and comprehensive.

> A product is anything that can be offered to a market for attention, acquisition, use or consumption; it includes physical objects, services, personalities, places, organizations and ideas.

A product may, therefore, be seen to embrace more than a branded, packaged good offered for sale. The definition has been widened to include services which include tourism, as well as the benefits and services that products bring with them. Black and Decker is an example of one company which has for many years had a marketing orientation which is evident in the way in which they perceive their customers. Asked about what business they are in, the company's response is that it is to sell solutions to clients who purchase their products with a particular problem in mind. Black and Decker do not see their mission as being particularly to sell electrical drills, but to make and sell equipment to meet client needs. So, if clients wish to bore holes in wood, steel or plaster, Black and Decker will seek to meet that need with the best product formulation, incorporating the most up-to-date technology available. Looking at the business in these broad terms, it becomes clear that with 'technology push', the tools used to drill holes will change substantially over the years. By taking a broad view, Black and Decker are, therefore, prepared to consider alternative technologies, perhaps thermal lances or laser technology, as they become available. The problem of drilling holes leaves itself open to a number of possible future solutions.

Competition is changing globally and important writers, such as Levitt, Kotler and Drucker (1985), have signalled this change in writing of the 'new competition'. Kotler (1984) has stated for example, that:

> The new competition is not between what companies produce in their factories but between what they add to their factory output in the form of packaging, services, advertising, customer service, financing, delivery arrangements, warehousing and other things that people value.

This emphasis on the attendant benefits and services that people value is what essentially separates the companies who practise the marketing concept from those who do not. If this is not presently being provided by a local competitor, the chances are that it will be provided by a foreign one. The internationalization of competition is apparent everywhere with the established multinational companies chasing each other around the world in a never-ending search for global market share. The multinationals have had to adopt a suitable 'positioning' strategy with regard to their products alongside local competitors, but derive instant benefit from the fact that their name and product are often already known, ahead of their actual arrival in that target market, as a result of the effects of the media: newspapers, magazines, cinema, radio and television. For multinational companies, the aim then is to seek to transfer that same level of product satisfaction across national boundaries.

Another important element of the 'new' competition is the arrival on world markets of the Japanese as a formidable trading nation. Using what has been termed as a 'cascading' strategy (Lorenz, 1981), they will initially seek penetration of well-defined segments, then move to volume stimulation and segment domination, before cascading into other areas and moving across.

This raises the question, why do products fail? There are the problems of tariff barriers, of non-tariff barriers or 'invisible' barriers which seek to exclude products or services from a given market (see Table 9.4). Where access is granted, tariffs or subsidies to a local competitor may mean inability to compete or even match on price. Related to this also is the question of 'dumping', which may upset a market sufficiently to persuade existing local suppliers that there is no long-term future for them.

Other reasons for failure would include cultural insensitivity; poor planning such that there is limited availability of the product in question; poor timing so that the regularity of supply or even first appearance on the market is ill-timed; misguided enthusiasm of top management concerned; product deficiencies with regard to the target market; and, finally, lack of Unique Selling Proposition (USP) generally, indicating that neither in the product, its accompanying benefits, nor its advertising, is there any criterion to differentiate this particular product from any of its competitors.

With regard to product suitability for foreign markets, this depends on the product itself;

Table 9.1   The ten countries with the most telephones

	Country	Telephones per 1,000 population
1	Monaco	733
2	Sweden	642
3	Switzerland	520
4	Denmark	513
5	Canada	512
6	USA	506
7	Finland	462
8 =	Norway	439
8 =	Liechtenstein	439
10	West Germany	438
	UK	*382*

There are many countries in the world with fewer than ten telephones per 1,000 population, including China (6.2 phones per 1,000), Pakistan (5.2), India (4.6), Indonesia (3.9) and most of Africa-Niger, for example, has only 1.4 telephones per 1,000.

Source   Ash, R. (1989) *The Top 10 of Everything*. Queen Anne Press, London.

its stage in the product life cycle — whether introductory or not; and the intended host country and its economic life cycle stage — whether mature industrial, or one of the types of less developed country; as well as situation-specific characteristics, such as the country's current product offering. Product life cycles have already been discussed, but it is important to remember also that this is only one part of the equation, and one must take cognizance of the state of development of transferor country and transferee. As Livingstone (1989) has pointed out, there are three important elements to consider in terms of production: the size of the market, the level of local technology, and the local distribution of the factors of production. The example of McDonalds, the US hamburger chain, serves to illustrate this point with their entry to the UK. When this took place, the McDonalds mode of counter service and of production line hamburger preparation was new to Britain, so it meant that not only were McDonalds' US recipes being introduced, but also the specifications for the fast-food catering equipment as well as McDonalds' distinctive style of merchandising. Once British suppliers were found, it made it easier for competitors to enter on the scene: profit-seeking suppliers now sought other potential clients for the fast-food equipment which they had imported or developed. (see Exhibit 9.1)

Suitability is not, however, the same as acceptability and it is worth noting at this point the work done on international market segmentation by Wind and Douglas (1972). They pointed out that segmentation could usefully be performed after first conducting a study of the enduring characteristics, such as target market geography, topography and demography. Little could be expected to change among these variables except over time. The second set of variables were the situation-specific characteristics and here they included factors such as buying patterns and consumption. Figure 9.1 is a flowchart of their basis for segmentation.

Table 9.2   The top ten television-owning countries

	Country	TV sets per 1,000 population
1	USA	813
2	Monaco	741
3	Oman	734
4	Guam	709
5 =	St. Pierre and Miquelon	617
5 =	Bermuda	617
7	Japan	585
8	US Virgin Islands	566
9	Canada	546
10	UK	534

These very high densities in the most affluent countries contrast sharply with the position in most parts of the Third World. In Ethopia, for example, there is the equivalent of 1.7 television sets per 1,000 population, and in Mali, where there are only 1,000 television sets in the entire country, the figure is close to 0.1 per 1,000

Source   Ash, R. (1989) *The Top 10 of Everything*. Queen Anne Press, London.

Table 9.3   The top ten radio-owning countries

Country	Radio sets per 1,000 population
1 USA	2,030
2 Australia	1,300
3 American Samoa	1,260
4 Bermuda	1,218
5 Guam	1,200
6 Gibraltar	1,170
7 Christmas Island	1,100
8 UK	993
9 Finland	987
10 Norfolk Island	900

Source   Ash, R. (1989) *The Top 10 of Everything*. Queen Anne Press, London.

At the same time, it should not be forgotten that prevailing local attitudes towards a particular product or product type should be monitored. Marketing can play an important role in influencing behaviour where stereotyped attitudes exist.

Where the source of origin is deemed to have a positive effect – which is only one of three possible outcomes – this may even allow a foreign product to remain competitive when not actually price competitive. The other two possible outcomes in relation to product recall are the 'inept set' and the 'inert set'. Only the 'evoked set', i.e. those products which consumers are able to recall and react to favourably, is a really acceptable outcome. (See Figure 9.2).

Communicating with your customers

In 1979 the Plain English Campaign was founded in Britain. Politicians, including Margaret Thatcher who opened the first Plain English Exhibition, have given strong endorsement to this campaign. British Government statistics indicate 16,000 forms have since been abolished and 21,000 forms clarified, including an indemnity payment form which until 1985 had a 55 per cent error rate.

The campaign cites a study in 1986 by pharmacists Reynor and Sillito which found that 40 per cent of patients questioned misunderstood 'complete the prescribed course', 31 per cent misunderstood 'to be instilled', and 33 per cent misunderstood 'use sparingly'. This failure to provide clear information has led to unnecessary deaths and injuries. Would patients readily understand this example?:

> A non-greasy, water-miscible cream with a marked anti-pruritic and analgesic action. The special base achieves intimate contact with moist surfaces, thus having a drying effect on exudative skin conditions, and is particularly suitable for application to exposed surfaces.

Readers of plain English prescription labels made 15 per cent fewer incorrect statements than those reading the traditional labels. They also gave 5 per cent more correct statements.

Table 9.4

Actual problems ...

The problem: different markets — different rules.

Gaining access to markets is often difficult because:

- every Community country, including the UK, has its own laws, for example on product safety;
- in many cases these national laws differ widely;
- many authorities will not accept the results of checks on a product conducted elsewhere.

So products have to be adapted to meet the different laws in each market and have to be rechecked — all of which takes time, costs money and restricts the free movement of goods.

> A toy maker in Leicestershire produces 250 toys in about 2,000 variants because of different laws on safety around the world.
>
> A Lancashire manufacturer of respiratory protective equipment and hearing protectors had to wait over six months for a product to be tested and approved for sale (at a cost of £30,000), but these tests and this approval are not necessarily accepted in other countries — so the tests have to be repeated in order to obtain approval for the sale of the product throughout the Community.
>
> A manufacturer of PVC profiles for windows, trading in many European Community countries, spends 2 per cent of EC turnover on getting approvals for its products in the different countries.
>
> A manufacturer of woodworking and metal-sawing equipment for the professional market at present has to produce up to eight different models of each machine to meet differing national standards.
>
> A maker of wall, ceiling and window duct fans for ventilation purposes has a current range of 65 products. Each product has an average of two variants.

With real solutions ...

The solution: a single market — a single set of rules.

The Community is agreeing a single, shared set of rules, through what are called 'New Approach' Directives, to replace those national laws.

These shared rules include:

- a statement of the broad requirements that all products must meet;
- the use of European standards, to fill in the detail and to provide the main way for businesses to satisfy those requirements;
- the tests and other checks that the manufacturer must have carried out.

Products may then carry the CE mark and be put on sale in the UK — or anywhere else in the Community — without adaptation or rechecking.

> With common requirements in all Member States, the toy maker can plan to halve the variants from 2,000 to 1,000.
>
> Under the Personal Protective Equipment rules one set of commonly recognized test and approval will suffice to give this manufacturer access to the whole Community market.
>
> The introduction of relevant common European standards under the Construction Products rules will greatly reduce these costs.
>
> When the relevant European standards are in place under the Machinery Safety rules it plans to produce a single type of each machine, making significant cost savings in manufacturing and stock holding.
>
> Once the relevant standards are in place under the Electromagnetic Compatibility rules the number of variants should be halved.

Source   DTI (1991) *The Single Market: Keeping Your Product on the Market*, Dept. of Trade and Industry, London.

These modest improvements represent a reduction of approximately one error per twenty prescription items. With 400 million prescription items dispensed annually in Britain, the use of plain English labels could do much to improve the health of our nation. (See Table 9.5).

Examples of bad translation, such as the Zanussi cooker hood, are just incomprehensible: 'Please care that the superior border of the calibre is on the inferior border of the incorporated board.' I certainly could not answer questions on that, but too often professional people sound as though they are reading from an economics or legal textbook. Have you ever understood a statement on the economy from any political party or been led to believe that they understood it either? The same is true of courtrooms where, legal jargon aside, we hear of the Head of our Civil Service in Australia being 'economical with the truth' or Lieutenant-Colonel Oliver North admitting that he used 'additional input that was radically different from the truth.'

The campaign present awards for examples of English that are extremely good or hideously bad. Nominations are received until mid-November each year. In 1986, the award winners were those shown in Figure 9.3.

Rather than just campaigning, the Campaign for Plain English operates a language and

Exhibit 9.1

'McCastro's' Cuba's answer to Big Macs

McDonald's won't be going to Havana

By Pascal Fletcher
Reuter News Agency

HAVANA — Forget McDonald's in Havana. Cuba has "McCastro's."

Although McDonald's Corp. has recently opened outlets in the Soviet Union and China, Cuba remains one corner of the world unreached by the Oak Brook, Ill.-based fast food chain.

One reason is that a 29-year-old U.S. economic embargo against the island prevents trade with U.S. companies.

Another is that Cuba now has its own version of Big Macs.

The state-run Food Industry Research Centre has produced a new line of pork burgers, which are drawing big crowds at snack bars in Havana where they were recently introduced.

President Fidel Castro is the biggest fan and promoter of the new Cuban product.

"Our hamburgers are better than the McDonald's," Mr. Castro said. "They're nutritious and delicious."

Some young Cubans have started calling the Cuban burgers "McCastro's."

Long lines outside the 14 snack bars and cafés in Havana currently selling the new burgers are a sign that most Cubans share their President's enthusiasm.

"I like them, I like the taste," said Yolanda, a woman in her 30s in a line outside the La Cocinita café near Havana's Malecon seafront. "It's something new," said office worker Juan Perez, 40.

The Cuban burger consists of a centimetre-thick slice of pork

placed inside a sesame seed bun and lightly — very lightly — smeared on either side with mustard and ketchup. Price: two pesos ($3).

No French fries, no onions, no cheese, no relish. The only drink served is a sweet, flat Cuban cola.

Cuban authorities are planning to open snack bars all over the country selling the burgers, which are made of 60 per cent minced pork topped up with animal plasma and blood, soya flour and spices.

By Western standards, one thing the Cuban hamburger could not be described as is "fast food." Customers wait at least half an hour before they can find a free table and 20 minutes more to be served.

Source   Globe and Mail (1990), Toronto, 10 October.

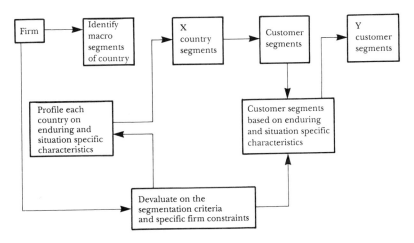

Figure 9.1 *International market segmentation*
Source   Wind, J., and Douglas, S. (1972) International market segmentation. *European Journal of Marketing*, **6**, (1)

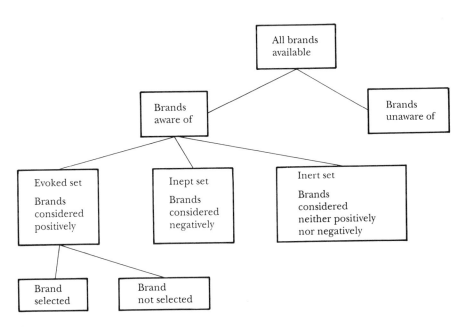

Figure 9.2

layout service which offers specialist practical help on forms, leaflets, booklets, instructions, posters, standard letters and consumer contracts. Complex legal documents are often also revised into more everyday English. (Contact Plain English Campaign, Outram House, Whaley Bridge, Stockport SK12 7LS England, UK.)

Product modification or standardization

The importance of the Triad of Japan, USA and Europe has been underlined by Ohmae (1985) in pointing to a market of over 600 million consumers with shared demand patterns because of a high standard of living. Indeed, the rich industrial countries, which make up the membership of the Organization for Economic Cooperation and Development (OECD), account for 15 per cent of the countries in the world, but 55 per cent of the global GNP. Jain (1989) points to a few reasons as to why this then should lead to standardization.

1 The purchasing power of OECD residents as expressed in discretionary per capita income is eight to fifteen times that of residents of the LDCs or NICs.

Table 9.5

Traditional style	Plain English style
The Eye Drops	The Eye Drops
One–two drops to be instilled into both eyes every six hours for four days.	Drop one or two drops into both eyes four times a day.
Not to be taken.	Do this at regular intervals for four days.
Discard 28 days after opening.	Don't swallow this.
	Throw this away one month after opening.
The Cream	The Cream
To be applied sparingly to the affected area twice a day.	Spread thinly on the affected skin twice a day.
For external use only.	Use on the skin only.
Discard 28 days after opening.	Throw this away one month after opening it.
The Tablets	The Tablets
One to be taken three times a day. Avoid exposure of the skin to direct sunlight or sunlamps. Do not stop taking this medicine except on your Doctor's advice.	One to be taken three times a day. Protect your skin from direct sunlight. Don't use sunlamps. Keep taking this medicine until your Doctor tells you to stop.
The Tablets	The Tablets
One to be taken every eight hours, with or after food.	One to be taken three times a day, with food.
Take at regular intervals.	Space the doses evenly through the day.
Complete the prescribed course unless otherwise directed.	Keep taking this medicine until it is finished.
Warning. Avoid alcoholic drink.	Don't drink any alcohol.

Source   S. Paliwoda (1988) "Plain English Campaign", *MBA Review*, December.

Winners of the Plain English Awards 1987

Taking someone on?

Department of Employment: Series of fact sheets and accompanying leaflet on employment law.
Campaign verdict: The fact sheets are clearly written and made more inviting by using full colour and detailed illustrations.
Inland Revenue: 'An Employer's Guide to Pay As You Earn.
Campaign verdict: This is a complicated subject which the Inland Revenue has worked hard to clarify.

Manic depression

MIND, the National Association for Mental Health: Set of four fact sheets on various aspects of mental health.
Campaign verdict: Information about mental distress is often clouded by medical jargon. These fact sheets give honest and clear explanations of different types of mental distress and how to cope with them.

A·I·D·S AND YOU

An illustrated guide

British Medical Association

British Medical Association: 'AIDS and You.'
Campaign verdict: This booklet states the facts about AIDS and uses pictograms to help people with reading difficulties understand the disease.

Provincial Insurance plc: 'The Little Blue Book.'
Campaign verdict: Liability

insurance is a complicated subject but this lively guide helps the reader to understand the different types of liability insurance available.

Advisory, Conciliation and Arbitration Service: 'Employing People.'
Campaign verdict: Small firms need all the help and advice they can get and this well written handbook will

NatWest at your Service
YOUR ACCOUNT GUIDE

☆ NatWest

be invaluable.

National Westminster Bank plc: 'NatWest at Your Service — Your Account Guide.'
Campaign verdict: Clearly written and well illustrated — a great aid to new account holders.

London Borough of Hackney: Three housing benefit guides.

Figure 9.3
Source   Paliwoda, S. (1988) Plain English campaign. *MBA Review*, December, 9–10

2 Television penetration within OECD countries exceeds 75 per cent, whereas in NICs it is 25 per cent and less than 10 per cent in LDCs.
3 More than one-third of OECD consumers graduate from high school or higher educational institutions.

According to Jain (1989), this standardization among OECD countries is feasible because of their educational level (what they read and see), their television watching (their level of awareness), and their purchasing power, and makes OECD residents similar to each other in behaviour and distinguishes them from the rest of the world.

However, global branding does not automatically include global advertising. Ritchie (1986) emphasized how a global perspective must not override local market requirements. Thus, according to Ritchie (1986), whatever cost benefits there may be in standardizing production, and even if there are financial advantages in standardizing the advertising process (which may in practice prove to be less than anticipated), the local dimension has to be maintained to withstand local segmentation and local commodity brands.

The chairman of a US multinational corporation was once quoted as having said that, all things being equal, given that his company had completely standardized global products and given the potential economies of scale in production, he would ideally have only one worldwide production centre in the USA from which he would then source worldwide. However, this is an imperfect world and so there proved to be numerous obstacles in the way of what was for the company perhaps an ideal cost-efficient sourcing solution. Apart from a few companies fortunate enough to enjoy global products such as Coca-Cola and Pepsi, the question for the remainder is not single sourcing of a global standardized product, but, instead, the degree to which they will be able to standardize or have to bow to local modification. Economies come from standardization, but the local pressures, which may arise from consumers as well as governments, may be in favour of some degree of local modification. We shall now examine these factors under the separate headings of standardization and modification.

Before doing so, however, it is worthwhile to consider what Livingstone (1989) says on product orientation which he sees as taking three policy forms among the larger international companies:

1 A policy of designing a 'universal' product, universal in the sense only that the design takes account of conditions in economies similar to the major market.
2 A policy of introducing the product into markets for which it is not very obviously designed if this is going to be cheaper than giving the market what it would prefer.
3 A policy of phasing out the product as and when it becomes obsolescent in the major market, and only then manufacturing in the less important market, satisfying any remaining demand for that product by exporting.

A life cycle profile of the product in relation to the market offers some insights into the strategic alternatives available.

Product modification

Mandatory product modifications arise as a result of the following:

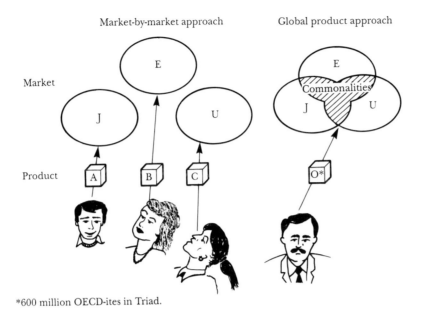

Figure 9.4   *Strategies should be developed to capitalize on similarities and potential for shared resources*
Source   Ishikawa, K. (1990) *Japan and the Challenge of Europe 1992*, Pinter Publishing for the Royal Institute of International Affairs, London

1 *Legal requirements.*
2 *Tariffs; 'invisible' tariffs.*
3 *Nationalism* as a response to lack of company presence on the market other than just in sales; unfortunate brand name; high perceived degree of 'foreignness' in the product offered.
4 *Technical requirements* are another means of excluding a product from a market until the technical specifications have been met. Regulations for such things as foodstuffs, drugs, electrical equipment are a few examples.
5 *Taxation* has to be considered. For example, with regard to cars, Britain has a system whereby the 'road tax' is levied as a flat rate on all users. Whereas in France it is dependent on engine size and the age of the car. Indeed, it is a much more equitable system, but it is likely to add significantly to the running costs of luxury cars in France.
6 *Climate* plays a part, too, in that special modifications need to be made often with regard to higher and lower working temperatures for machinery, and with special packaging for consumer goods to ensure freshness in actual use. North America contains all these possible climatic extremes, from the snowy wastes of Northern Canada to the sunshine of Florida.

Other factors influencing modification include:

1 *Consumer tastes.* Traditionally, food has been held to be society's most culture-bound product, but perhaps it is time to rethink this, in view of the fact that Kentucky Fried Chicken is now sold in Japan and that McDonalds and others are now to be found in

France, the gastronomic capital of the world. Consumer tastes will have an important bearing on the name used; product features, labelling, packaging and materials; pricing and sales and advertising promotion.

2 *Low personal disposable income* in the target market will affect frequency of purchase as well as product sizes offered.

3 *Illiteracy and low levels of education* will necessitate product simplification with the use of symbols instead of words. Within the EC, it has been the case for many years that all the instrumentation in the dashboard of the car is now labelled with symbols rather than words. It is presumably no reflection on the prevailing standards of education and general

Table 9.6 Product profile and strategic implications

Product profile Strategy	Yesterday's products	Today's products	Tomorrow's products
Critical function	Marketing	Product development	New product assessment
Nature of turnover with time	Sharp decline	Limited life	Growth potential maximum
Penalties for mistakes	Very high	High	Can be compensated
Advertising and sales promotion	To push the demand to the maximum	To maintain the demand at an increasing rate	To pull the potential demand to the highest possible value
Customer education and training	Limited efforts	Increased efforts	Vigorous efforts
Service function and spares policy	Very important	Important	Increased importance
Competition monitoring	Not very critical	Keep a watch	An alert lookout
Scope for exporting	Minimum	To other developing countries	Joint ventures with developed countries
Integration of marketing with other functions	Active interaction with production	Interaction with production, finance, and sales	Active interaction with R & D

Source Pal, S. K., and Bowander, B. (1979) Marketing challenges of technical industries in developing countries. *Industrial Marketing Management*, **8**, 69–74.

5 *Technological content* is standard internationally for the industry.
6 *Consumer mobility* as a result of increasing travel opportunities which leads to familiarity with international products, such as perhaps Gillette or Bic razors; Coca-Cola; Pepsi; and a wide range of clothing, toiletries and other articles. The brand name, rather than the country of origin, is what sells the product.
7 *Market homogeneity* is increasing with the market concentration effects of the EC for example. Concentration has taken place in many areas, leading to European industries rather than national industries. As the costs of research and development increase, and as the needs of critical mass become apparent, then companies begin to treat neighbouring country markets as an extended regional market rather than as a number of separate foreign markets.

The benefits of standardization are:

1 Cost savings through experience-curve effects and economies of scale.
2 Consistency, with customers acknowledging consumer mobility and cross-border flows of television, radio, newspaper and periodical advertising.
3 The remaining barriers are common to all markets, such barriers as social conventions regarding product use and purchasing patterns.

Keagan, Still and Hill (1987) undertook a study of the transferability and adaptability of products and promotion themes in marketing by multinationals in the LDCs. They set out with three questions:

1 To what extent are products transplanted from one market into another? Products have to be transferred between nations before any standardizing or adapting occurs.
2 What is an adapted product? Products have multiple components, e.g., packaging and labelling. A change in any component is an adaptation, and 'degree of adaptation' better describes product change than does the dichotomous 'adaptation-standardization'.
3 When products are transferred, what proportion of their promotion themes undergo substantial change?

A conceptualization of the process of product and promotion transfer and adaptation by Keegan, Still and Hill (1987) is to be found in Figure 9.5. Overall, nineteen MNCs responded to their survey (eighteen US; one UK) from both international headquarters and from the LDCs. Finally, sixty-one responses were computer analysed. In all, the 174 products sold in LDCs had 718 adaptations, an average of 4.13 changes out of a possible nine. (See Table 9.8.)

Firms changing three or fewer components believe they reap many of the advantages of standardization for one of three reasons:

1 Their products have universal appeal, e.g., Coca-Cola or Pepsi.
2 They are moving toward greater standardization, e.g., Kodak or Gillette.
3 Consumers prefer some products with strong modern images, e.g., Max Factor cosmetics.

Three important findings emerged from this study:

1 Economic and cultural gaps between modern markets, e.g., US or UK, and LDCs do not deter MNCs from transferring modern consumer products between them.

Table 9.7   Obstacles to standardization in international marketing strategies

Factors limiting standardization	Product design	Pricing	Distribution	Sales force	Advertising and promotion, branding and packaging
Market characteristics					
Physical environment	Climate / Product use conditions		Customer mobility / Consumer shopping patterns	Dispersion of customers / Wage levels, availability of manpower	Access to media / Climate / Needs for convenience rather than economy
Stage of economic and industrial development	Income levels / Labour costs in relation to capital costs	Income levels			Purchase quantities
Cultural factors	Custom and tradition / Attitudes toward foreign goods	Attitudes toward bargaining	Consumer shopping patterns	Attitudes toward selling	Language, literacy / Symbolism
Industry conditions					
Stage of product life cycle in each market	Extent of product differentiation	Elasticity of demand	Availability of outlets / Desirability of private brands	Need for missionary sales efforts	Awareness, experience with products
Competition	Quality levels	Local costs / Prices of substitutes	Competitors' control outlets	Competitors' sales force	Competitive expenditure messages
Marketing institutions					
Distributive system	Availability of outlets	Prevailing margins	Number and variety outlets available / Ability to 'force' distribution	Number, size, dispersion of outlets / Effectiveness of advertising, need for substitutes	Extent of self-service
Advertising media and agencies					Media availability, costs, overlaps
Legal restrictions	Product standards / Patent laws / Tariffs and taxes	Tariffs and taxes / Antitrust laws / Resale price maintenance	Restrictions on lines / Resale price maintenance	General employment restrictions / Specific restrictions on selling	Specific restrictions on messages, costs / Trademark laws

Source Buzzell, R. D. Can you standardise multinational marketing? *Harvard Business Review*, November–December, 102–13.

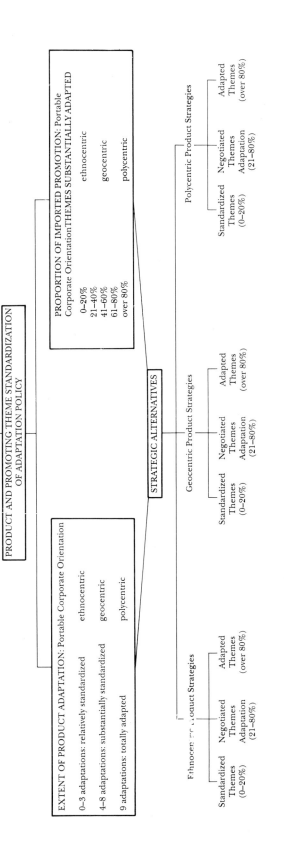

Figure 9.5 *Transfer and adaptation process of consumer non-durable products – a conceptual framework*
Source Keegan, W. J., Still, R. R. and Hill, J. S. (1987) Transferability and adaptability of products and promotion themes in multinational marketing in MNCs and LDCs. *Journal of Global Marketing*, **1**, (1/2), 85–103

2 The MNCs sampled substantially adapt most modern products before marketing them in LDCs, suggesting that universal products, e.g., Coca-Cola and Colgate toothpaste, are the exceptions rather than the rule. However, this finding may not hold for less culturally sensitive products, such as consumer durable and industrial products.
3 Although many modern themes are transferred into LDCs without substantial change, the extent of theme adaptations parallels the degree of product adaptation, suggesting interdependence between marketing adaptations and standardization decisions.

Whitelock (1987), in her study, *Global Marketing and the Case for International Product Standardisation*, acknowledged this gap of consumer durables and incorporated it into her framework (see Figure 9.6).

Product standardization and world product mandates

The world product mandate is to be found chiefly in the Canadian literature deriving from the internalization aspect of Dunning's Eclectic Theory. A world product mandate (WPM) is defined as the full development and production of a new product line in a subsidiary of a multinational company, thereby changing the nature of the subsidiary—parent multinational relationship to that of a strategic business unit or division. It is rapidly becoming a major topic of public policy discussion, although there still remain many unresolved technical and conceptual issues.

Table 9.8   Extent of adaptation of US/UK products in LDC markets

Number of adaptations	Number of products	Per cent total	Corporate orientation
0	15	8.6	
1	17	15.5	
2	15	8.6	Ethnocentric
3	9	5.2	
4	18	10.3	
5	21	12.1	
6	39	22.4	Geocentric
7	22	12.6	
8	3	1.7	
9	5	2.9	Polycentric
Totals	174	100.0	

Source   Keegan, W. J., Still, R. R. and Hill, J. S. (1987) Transferability and adaptability of products and promotion themes in multinational marketing in MNCs and LDCs. *Journal of Global Marketing*, **1**(1/2), 85–103.

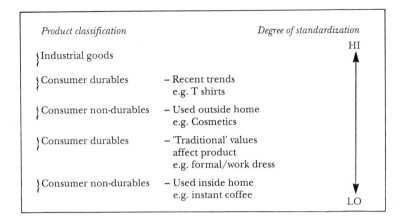

Figure 9.6   *A standardization/modification decision framework*
Source   Whitelock, J. M. (1987) Global marketing and the case for international product standardisation. *European Journal of Marketing*, **21**, (9), 32–44

A world product mandate permits the subsidiary to be responsible for the development and worldwide marketing of a specific innovation. The subsidiary needs to bargain with its parent to secure a potentially profitable mandate, but once it has it, the subsidiary can use the internal market of the multinational organization to distribute and control the new process. It is necessary, therefore, to examine the cost benefits from the viewpoint of the three parties involved: host country, subsidiary company, and parent multinational.

Host countries seek employment, growth, and development technology and expertise from companies located within their boundaries. As was pointed out earlier, host countries do complain about the perceived quality of investment made by multinationals within their boundaries. Such complaints may include:

- absence of, or insufficient, R & D at the subsidiary level, especially when the market size is small,
- insufficient transfer or diffusion of technology,
- employment of obsolete technology,
- inefficient subsidiary operation/no economies of scale,
- high transfer pricing for goods imported from other sister subsidiaries,
- downward pressure on the host's currency and drain on foreign exchange,
- low local content ratio,
- low or no exports,
- negative or neutral effect on economic growth and development; and,
- low, or no, adherence to host country's national goals.

For the most part, host countries have refused to bear a proportionate share of the cost or risk of developing technology, a product, or a market. Furthermore, they have been the primary source of environmental, sovereign, and political risk.

The WPM is an arrangement whereby the MNC allows the subsidiary to transcend the restrictions of miniature or truncated operations by enlarging the subsidiary's mandate, and hence its associated responsibilities, above and beyond the geographical or political boundaries of the host country. The sphere of the new mandate's activity and coverage depends on the interactions between the costs and benefits of the mandate in terms of economies of scale and learning, transportation charges, added cost of logistics, cost of tariffs, non-tariff barriers, etc. For example, when economies of scale are reached at relatively low volumes or economies of learning are realized in comparatively short periods of time, the mandate is expected to be more united in geographical scope than the global coverage implied in WPM.

It is possible to have regional product mandates (RPMs), especially when the demand of the contiguous region is larger than, or as large as, the optimal plant size. In that case, instead of a real WPM, a more limited mandate in terms of authority and responsibility with respect to at least one product is given to the subsidiary, but this is awarded on a competitive basis and a mandate must be earned.

From the host country viewpoint, there are the advantages of having relatively autonomous and internally directed institutions which are operating on a worldwide basis

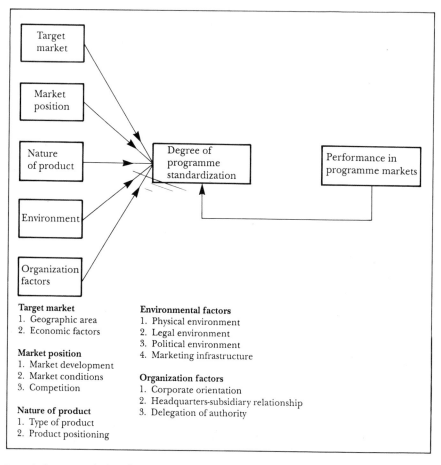

Figure 9.7   *A framework for determining marketing programme stadardization*
Source   Jain, S. C. (1989) Standardisation of international marketing strategy: Some research hypotheses, *Journal of Marketing*, **53**, (1), 70–79

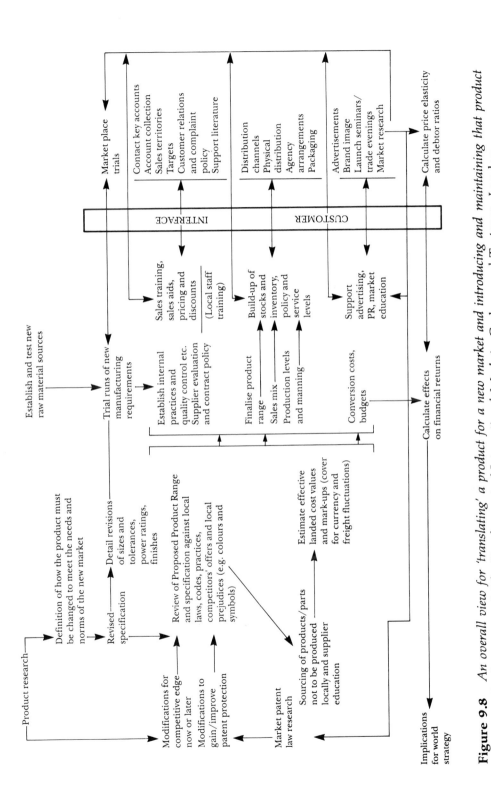

Figure 9.8 *An overall view for 'translating' a product for a new market and introducing and maintaining that product*

Source Walmsley, J. (1989) *The Development of International Markets*, Graham and Trotman, London

Table 9.9 World product mandates from the points of view of the respective parties

Host country	Subsidiary	Multinational corporation
1 Economies of scale and expertise	1 Reduced dependence on local market	1 Decentralization of power in R&D
2 More efficient, higher value-added production, lower unit costs	2 Increased stability with market diversification	2 Loss of some control
3 Relative independence from local market	3 Market research information now required	3 Restricted to source of supply
4 Local content ratio up to 100 per cent	4 Staff product support to sister subsidiaries	4 Need to protect the mandate and avoid duplication
5 Creation of local suppliers	5 International marketing skills required even if using parent network	5 Mandate must ensure continued competitiveness
6 Local purchasing eliminates transfer pricing disputes	6 Interact with host government	6 Safeguards to ensure product compatibility worldwide
7 High exports with low imports	7 Illustrate benefits clearly to host government	7 Subsidiary needs now to be kept informed of product changes/ legislation and research
8 Ongoing R&D at subsidiary level	8 Stronger management team required	8 MNC has to ask all subsidiaries to cooperate with the mandated subsidiary
9 Possible future exporter of technology	9 Subsidiary becomes a centre for that product's R&D	9 Mandated subsidiary must be fully integrated and accepted within the MNC organization
10 Access to world markets	10 Convince parent MNC that benefits outweigh costs	10 Smooth communications between sister subsidiaries
11 Pressure to remain competitive supplier for a world market		11 More intense planning and coordination necessary as options now reduced and dependence increased
12 Improved relations with subsidiary		12 MNC has to act as an adjudicator in the event of dispute
13 Improved relations with MNC		

Source Adapted from Etemad, H. (1983) World product mandates in perspective. In *Multinationals and Technology Transfer: The Canadian Experience*, (ed. Rugman, A.) Praeger, New York.

without much of the actual costs associated with developing such institutions. Young, Hood and Hamill (1988) state that whereas multinationals such as NEC and Philips have been quoted as examples of firms which have made considerable strides in these directions, it is doubtful whether many others exist.

The parent MNC has very little incentive to grant a WPM to any subsidiary. Doing so defeats the very basic feature of MNCs – flexibility and freedom of choice with regard to source and location of supplies. In so far as worldwide procurement of the mandated product is concerned, a fully developed or natural WPM implies that the parent enterprise gives up this privilege and commits itself to the mandated subsidiary as the sole source in control of supplies for its worldwide markets.

In order to receive a mandate, a subsidiary must become highly competitive or find other sources of support. As a result of a mandate, the host country receives substantial benefits. Indeed, there is such a great deal at sake for the host country that it cannot remain indifferent. It finds itself obliged to lend active support to the subsidiary to bid for and finally secure a mandate. Given the profound future benefits to the subsidiary (due to the mandate), a subsidiary finds it difficult not to accept the help and support from an old adversary in fighting for the mandate. In this process, a new coalition (i.e., subsidiary—host country) is formed and the old coalition (i.e., subsidiary—parent) is weakened. As a result, in order to receive, operate, and continue with the mandate successfully, the subsidiary will need the host government's continued active and substantial support.

A WPM restores a sense of power and accomplishment to the newly formed subsidiary; it can produce a new coalition between the subsidiary and the host country; while it increases their interdependence with the rest of the MNC's system simultaneously.

In summary, WPM cultivates an environment which is highly conducive to efficient, complete, and co-operative operation for all the participants – the host country, the subsidiary, and its parent company.

Branding

Branding is important as a means of distinguishing a company offering, and differentiating one particular product from its competitors. To the company with a product with any commercial life left in it, branding is able to offer an advantage. Given all the other factors already mentioned – pricing, distribution, and promotion – branding is a means whereby the consumer can identify a particular product, and, if satisfied with it, ask for it by name. For the company concerned, there are clear advantages to branding in that branding enables the company to differentiate its product more clearly, but also to fetch a higher return than could be expected from generic products. Shalofsky (1987) points to 'producer quality' and 'consumer quality'; the former determined in the manufacturer's laboratories, R&D department, and takes into account product characteristics.

'Consumer quality' is what in the store may move it off the shelf. The 'consumer quality' of an international brand entering a new market may well be poor. Something then will have to be found to increase consumer acceptance and this may be in the area of brand image. When Interbrand arranged for Rank Havis McDougall's brand names to be listed as assets, the balance sheet rose by £678 million (Birkin, 1989).

Table 9.10 Products for markets

Corporate perspective of the market

	Market stage	Government attitudes and business policy	Supranational control	Brand product protection	Target product market
Short term	Mature/declining	Weak	Expensive bureaucratic control build-up or acquire	Weak	Standardized brand or generic
Medium term	Mature	Indeterminate	Build-up	Strong	Standardized brand or generic
Long term	Innovative	Strong	Standardization potential of a homogeneous market with similar requirements	Strong	Non-standardized brand/niche market servicing

Exhibit 9.3   *World truck nears launch*

Ford's 'world' truck will go on sale this year. It will have a European cab, a North American chassis, and a diesel engine developed from one used by the group's agricultural tractor division. The components will be assembled in Brazil.

The first 'family' of designs for the new medium-to-heavy range is aimed primarily at the Brazilian and North American markets, where the first products will go on sale in the autumn.

Mr. Edson Williams, Ford vice-president and general manager of the group's truck operations, says: 'The Brazilian world truck takes the best we have within Ford and puts it together'.

The company has the capacity to build about 40,000 a year.

The cab will be adapted from the one used for the Ford Cargo range in Europe. Cab panels will be sent from the UK to Brazil for the new vehicle.

But the heavy cost of transport to Europe and the 14 percent tariff barrier it would face before entering the EEC makes it unlikely that built-up trucks will find their way from Brazil to Europe, Mr. William says.

However, Mr. Williams reveals that other export markets are being considered and there seems to be potential in Asia.

Ford has invested about $100m in a new diesel engine plant in Brazil which will come into operation shortly, providing power units mainly for the domestic market. The engine is a six-cylinder, direct-injection 7.8 litre unit. There will also be an option of the existing Ford 6.6 litre turbo engine, but in a South American version. Output of 55,000 engines a year is envisaged.

The company will start by building what are known in North America as Class 6 and 7 trucks (medium-weight). Eventually heavyweight (Class 8) versions will be introduced – but using bought-in engines, because Ford has no intention of developing a 10-litre diesel engine of its own, Mr. Williams points out.

The Brazilian project is part of Ford's response to the substantial over-capacity for heavy truck manufacturing worldwide.

Ford can simplify its heavy truck designs worldwide and establish those parts of the truck which could be made common to Ford vehicles the world over.

He looks ahead at the time when 'components for our heavy trucks will be of a single, world-class design and will be built in a number of countries. We will buy from those international suppliers who can supply in the countries where we assemble trucks and need the components'.

A locally-produced ZF gearbox will be used in the Brazilian-built 'world' truck for instance.

Ford began working its world truck programme in 1982. It will take another eight years to complete, says Mr. Williams.

'We must prove it can work and that we can make money on heavy trucks'.

The company will spend about £1bn on truck development and production over the four or five years from 1983 out its worldwide budget of £4bn. Britain will receive about 80 percent of the £1bn for trucks.

This is because, although the group has truck plants in Australia and Brazil, the two big design centres are in the US and Britain.

Ford makes a profit on its total commercial vehicle operations, but its strength is at the light end – with the Transit van and car-derived vans in Europe, and with pick-up trucks and vans in the US.

However, the launch of the Cargo range in March 1991 at the cost of £125m was proof that Ford wants to win a much larger share of the European market for medium and heavy trucks.

The Cargo got off to an inauspicious start with many niggling problems and recalls by the company to put them right. Ford's share of the West European market for trucks of more than 3.5 tonnes, which stood at 7 percent in 1980, has shrunk to just over 6 percent.

With the full Cargo range in place and the initial technical problems behind it, Ford will concentrate on building sales, particularly in the UK, and getting some return on its investment.

Source   *Financial Times* (1985) 16 January.

Exhibit 9.4   *An IBM view of worldwide product standardization*

The trend in recent years has been for many companies to view the world as one massive market and achieve low cost through preeminent economies of scale in R&D and manufacturing, while simultaneously gaining market share through highly efficient and effective worldwide distribution channels. For many global exporters, this strategy has proven successful, however, our research suggests that these organizations are now required to have the capability to customize or localize 'prime' products. We learned from a major European manufacturer of domestic appliances that the design of core product specifications based on universal components must be complemented with the ease of local tailoring through a production process of interchangeable, soft tools. This approach enables the introduction of products on a global basis much faster than before and is necessary to meet the needs of consumers whose lifestyles transcend national borders.

On the other end of the spectrum, companies who are closely attuned to local markets are facing requirements from their global customers to provide local or country specific applications on a worldwide basis. In our own case, we recognized the need to develop Kanji work stations for the Japanese market some time ago, but did not anticipate the demand for these products in Detroit, Michigan, where our customers were developing applications for their operations in Japan.

Throughout the research study, similar examples of market forces were cited, suggesting that as companies deliberate a global strategy for their products and services, they are being confronted with an equally strong requirement for a business delivery system highly sensitive to local tastes and specifications. This ability to balance 'global' versus 'local', coincident with attaining the highest levels of customer satisfaction, is perhaps the pivotal challenge strategists face during the next decade.

The approach at IBM has been to develop a worldwide product line which is adaptable to local country markets. Serving these markets requires recognition of many variables. In Canada, for example, I believe that banking systems are more advanced than in other parts of North America. Language requirements are such that systems need the additional flexibility of Canadian French software or the capability to operate in two languages at the same time. These demands, coupled with the existence of unique distribution channels, are illustrations of the challenges global suppliers face in serving both local and global markets with excellence.

The importance of branding and of language in exports to Third World countries is seen from the following example:

Ashton Chemicals is a Manchester company (whose name has been changed for the sake of this example) who specialize in manufacturing solely for export the kinds of pharmaceutical preparations which were common in Victorian Britain. A few of these have a brand name but many are generic, and a few are packaged and presented to closely resemble the market leader in their particular field. Ashton's advantage in the export trade is that it is a long established company and it is based in Britain. Clients abroad still buy from Ashton although there may well be even a local competitor for these unexciting grandmother's recipes, and their explanation of this is simply that where health is concerned, people are less exacting about price. Quality is much more important and here the fact that they are a long established company, able to boast a 'Made in England' on their labels, enhances their standing in the market place of many of the less developed countries. An attempt to actually package and label one of their more popular products for a specific African market proved counter-productive when consumers then began to consider it as a local product and, therefore, of inferior quality to equivalent imported products.

Branding is perceived as a means of guarantee of quality offered by the manufacturer to the consumer. There is the expectation of standardization, that each and every product will meet these same specifications. Where there is a high degree of standardization accompanied by a high degree of customer satisfaction, the brand is likely to become, if it has not already done so, the market leader. Brand names, according to Interbrand (Fisher, 1989), can be seen to fall into three categories:

1 *descriptive*, like Corn Flakes and British Rail
2 *associative*, like Fruit Bursts and InterCity
3 *stand-alone*, like Hob-Nobs or Casey Jones.

Occasionally, though, brands suffer the fate of being too successful in that they pass into the language and lose the distinctiveness which they once had. Sometimes, this is due to market dominance because of patent protection, sometimes implying just market leadership. Where a brand becomes the name for all products of that type, it has become a generic. The German firm Bayer once had the rights to Aspirin, which was a protected brand name until after the war. Indeed, the only country still to recognize protected rights to the name Aspirin as a registered brand name is Argentina.

Pharmaceutical products are likely to be standardized, but as reflected in Keegan's *Five Strategies for Multinational Marketing*, brand names often meant that although the name is the same, the ingredients may be quite different from the product sold in the home country. *The Economist* in 1982 carried a report on how Bangladesh imposed a ban on 2,000 drugs. The aim was to both save foreign exchange and save also on drugs that did not work. For nearly three-quarters of these prohibited drugs had been listed by the World Health Organization or by US or British drug authorities as useless, harmless, or both. Madawar and Freese (1981) raised this issue of branded pharmaceuticals as well as adequate instructions and directions for use. Their reservations include:

Table 9.11   Product quality variables

Performance:	Effectiveness of product primary operating characteristics.
Features:	Make-up, shape, proportions and attributes.
Reliability:	Measured over a specific period of time under stated conditions of use.
Conformance:	Degree to which physical and performance characteristics of a product match pre-established standards.
Durability:	Period of time a product is in use before suffering deterioration.
Serviceability:	Speed, courtesy and competence of repair.
Aesthetics:	How a product looks, feels, sounds, tastes or smells.
Perceived quality:	Subjective assessment resulting from image, advertising, or brand name.

Source   Garvin, David A. (1987) Competing on the Eight Dimensions of Quality, *Harvard Business Review*, Nov–Dec, p. 101.

Table 9.12   Branding perspective (from manufacturer's viewpoint)

Advantages	*Disadvantages*
No Brand	
Lower production cost	Severe price competition
Lower marketing cost	Lack of market identity
Lower legal cost	
Flexible quality control	
Branding	
Better identification and awareness	Higher production cost
Better chance for production differentiation	Higher marketing cost
Possible brand loyalty	Higher legal cost
Possible premium pricing	
Private brand	
Better margins for dealers	Severe price competition
Possibility of larger market share	Lack of market identity
No promotional problems	
Manufacturer's brand	
Better price due to more price inelasticity	Difficult for small manufacturer with
Retention of brand loyalty	unknown brand of identity
Better bargaining power	Requiring brand promotion
Better control of distribution	
Multiple brands (in one market)	
Market segmented for varying needs	Higher marketing cost
Creating competitive spirits	Higher inventory cost
Avoiding negative connotation of existing brand	Loss of economies of scale
Gaining more retail shelf space	
Not hurting existing brand's image	
Single brand (in one market)	
Marketing efficiency	Assuming market homogeneity
Permitting more focused marketing	Existing brand's image hurt when trading up/down
Elimination of brand confusion	
Good for product with good reputation (halo effect)	Limited shelf space
Local brands	
Meaningful names	Higher marketing cost
Local identification	Higher inventory cost
Avoidance of taxation on international brand	Loss of economies of scale
Allowing variations of quantity and quality across markets	Diffused image
Worldwide brand	
Maximum marketing efficiency	Assuming market homogeneity
Reduction of advertising costs	Problems with black and grey markets
Elimination of brand confusion	Possibility of negative connotation
Good for culture-free product	Requiring quality and quantity consistency
Good for prestigious product	LDC's opposition and resentment
Easy identification/recognition for international travellers	Legal complications
Uniform worldwide image	

Source   Onkvisit, S. and Shaw, J. J. The international dimension of branding: strategic considerations and decisions. *International Marketing Review*, **6**, (3).

1 Drugs which are simply dangerous. Clioquinol and Aminopyrine, both banned in some countries, yet actively being promoted in others, are two particularly horrifying examples.
2 Products which are more or less undesirable as 'bad medicine'. An example of these would be a mad combination of antibiotics and other drugs. Combination drugs are bad because if a patient suffers from more than one complaint, each complaint should be treated with the appropriate dose of the appropriate medicine. The reason combinations are commercially preferred is, of course, that they allow the manufacturer to promote something 'unique'.
3 Products which do no harm, but which are not needed and which account at best for serious economic waste. Tonics and vitamin pills are obvious cases in point.
4 In addition to this, the instructions and precautions for use supplied with such products may be wholly inadequate, if not dangerously wrong. Two recent examples include: a migraine treatment where the maximum dose recommended in developing countries was twice the maximum recommended elsewhere; and an anti-nauseant, contra-indicated for use in pregnant women in the USA but specifically recommended for the control of 'morning sickness' elsewhere.

Ethical questions arise equally over products sold in the Western hemisphere. Citing one example which arose in the USA, a Dallas federal district judge denied an injunction to end a ban on a cereal which was promoted as a drug to reduce cholesterol levels (*Marketing News*, 1991, 13 May).

A quite separate example entirely is that of cigarettes where high tar level cigarettes are freely available in some of the less-developed countries, although now withdrawn from sale in the West. Branding may be international but the assurance of branding varies with national frontiers.

Yet branding lies behind the success of franchising. Franchising conveys the right to use a name, logo, plus access to company-specific know-how, including management systems. The

Table 9.13   The ten most recognized brands

	The World	USA	Europe	Japan
1	Coca-Cola	Coca-Cola	Coca-Cola	Sony
2	Sony	Campbell's	Sony	National
3	Mercedes-Benz	Disney	Mercedes-Benz	Mercedes-Benz
4	Kodak	Pepsi-Cola	BMW	Toyota
5	Disney	Kodak	Philips	Takashimaya
6	Nestlé	NBC	Volkswagen	Rolls Royce
7	Toyota	Black & Decker	Adidas	Seiko
8	McDonald's	Kellogg's	Kodak	Matsushita
9	IBM	McDonald's	Nivea	Hitachi
10	Pepsi-Cola	Hershey's	Porsche	Suntory

Source   Strauss, M. (1991) Cashing in on the clear Canadian image. *Globe and Mail*, Toronto, 13 March.

Table 9.14   The ten bestselling prescription drugs in the world

	Brand name	Manufacturer	Prescribed for	Revenue $	Revenue £*
1	Zantac	Glaxo/Sankyo	Ulcers	1,479,000,000	875,000,000
2	Tagamet	Smith Kline	Ulcers	1,132,000,000	670,000,000
3	Tenormin	ICI	High blood pressure	867,000,000	513,000,000
4	Capoten	Squibb	High blood pressure heart failure	779,000,000	461,000,000
5	Vasotec	Merck & Co	High blood pressure heart failure	635,000,000	376,000,000
6	Adalat	Bayer/Takeda	Angina: furring of arteries	587,000,000	347,000,000
7	Naprosyn	Syntex	Arthritis	555,700,000	328,000,000
8	Voltaren	Ciba-Geigy	Arthritis	544,100,000	322,000,000
9	Feldene	Pfizer	Arthritis	524,000,000	310,000,000
10	Ceclor	Eli Lilly	Infections	515,000,000	305,000,000

*calculated at rate prevailing in April 1989

The revenues of the international drug industry are among the world's largest. In 1987 the total income from the top fifty branded pharmaceutical products was $19,242,900,000,000 — more than the Gross Domestic Product of many large countries.

Source   Ash, R. (1989) *The Top 10 of Everything*, Queen Anne Press, London.

key to this form of market representation is the importance attached to an established brand name, many of which are quite international: McDonalds hamburger chain, Budget Rent-a-Car; Kentucky Fried Chicken. All derive their income from the use of their names.

Marks and Spencer, the British firm with a quality image chain of department stores (Cheeseright, 1982), has no manufacturing capacity of its own, but, nevertheless, exports amounted to £58 million in 1982. Marks and Spencer have three strategies. The first is to grant the St. Michael brand name franchise to freestanding sales outlets. The second is to establish shops within shops that sell the St. Michael marque exclusively, as in Finland and Japan where Marks' goods are sold within the Daiei department store chain. The last is to sell directly to selected retailers or to market through a wholesaler. The company policy is not to export to countries where they already have stores, i.e., France, Ireland, Canada and Holland.

To take another example, International Harvester (IH) acquired two small, but well-respected Lancashire lorry builders in Seddon and Atkinson, in 1974. The Atkinson was a cult vehicle and dubbed the 'knight of the road', being quite identifiable with its trademark of the letter 'A' in a circle mounted on an old-style grille. IH merged the two companies and discarded the old imagery, but the old imagery is now returning. In Spain, IH have bought into Enasa, which makes the Pegaso which dominates the Spanish market, and the Spanish are very proud of their product. The dilemma for IH, therefore, arises with the next expected generation of trucks, for not having a visible image in Europe in trucks themselves, they will be forced into a few decisions, as to which name to carry into Europe — British or Spanish? Or

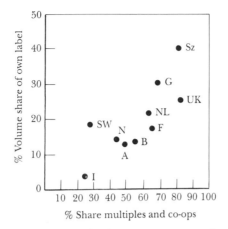

Figure 9.9 *Own-label penetration and multiple-co-operative market share in European grocery retailing*
Source Davies, G, (1990) Marketing to retailers: a battle for distribution? *Long Range Planning*, **23**, (6), 101–108.

will it be US? What degree of commonality can we expect to see from these truck producers across their separate brand names? These are questions for the not too distant future.

Coca-Cola and Pepsi-Cola have licensed bottlers around the world who pay for the right to use the name. Pepsi is now based in 145 countries but they never patented their recipe as they feared they might lose it after the traditional fifteen to sixteen year period of first registration. Coca-Cola dates back to 1893 as originally a cure for peptic ulcers. Although both Coke and Pepsi are seen as virtually interchangeable today to the majority of the buying public, forty years ago the situation was quite different. Pepsi then was identified with the working classes and perceived as being better value than Coke. Pepsi first began to receive television advertising in the USA from 1939, but the development of the two giants is fascinating.

Coca-Cola benefited from the Second World War when the US army took it with them overseas, but Coke was still being sold in war-time Germany. There was a Coca-Cola manager, Max Keith, who was head of soft drinks for all occupied Europe. Fanta was developed at this time because sugar was short in Hitler's Germany. Elsewhere, the US Defence Department was paying for bottling plants to be sent to the frontline.

Banking provides other quite different illustrations of the importance of branding, as with travellers' cheques and plastic bank cards which are now universal. In travellers' cheques, Thomas Cook was in at the very beginning, followed by American Express, and the travel and entertainment cards of Diners Club and American Express which were the first truly global cards, followed belatedly by the various banking consortia such as Visa International – who now issue travellers' cheques as well as credit cards – and Master Charge. These last two are consortia which allow local member banks to append their name to an internationally recognized and standardized card format. Obviously, a local bank will gain more respect from its clients when its travellers' cheques are readily accepted abroad at a wide variety of outlets instead of just correspondent banks. Here the power lying behind the name of the consortium constitutes the differential advantage. Interestingly, British television advertisements for travel and entertainment cards emphasize the freedom of international movement and purchasing power, while for the bank credit cards, the high number of outlets which will accept their cards. The approach in either case is quite different, but here is an example of banks now being able to offer a highly standardized globally branded product.

Selection of a brand name

Textbooks and management checklists often state that a good brand name should be able to meet a number of criteria, such as being short, unique, memorable and able to connote an important quality or image. Above all, it has to be available to use, registrable and protectable. The name should describe the product, be distinctive, be pronounceable, lend itself to graphic display, be acceptable, be legal (i.e., not an already registered name), be suggestive of the product that it represents, and be easy to remember.

In the international marketing arena, many products fail to meet these criteria once transferred to the foreign market. An unfortunate branding example is GEC-Osram, a long and well-established lighting division of the British General Electric Corporation (GEC). Now, although both GEC and Osram are well respected quality brand names in Britain, the name Osram in Polish is very close to the word for excrement.

Products sometimes travel better than do brand names, although brand names are often well-known before even the product arrives. 'Coke' and 'Pepsi' are known worldwide, even in markets where there is general scarcity. General Motors sell a small hatchback car throughout

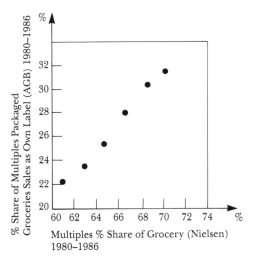

AGB Data Quoted in *Food Retailing* (1987)
Institute of Grocery Distribution

Nielsen Grocery Trade Report Data
Quoted in 'Shifting Power Patterns
in Groceries' Carter D. *Retail Marketing
and Management*, Vol. 14 No.8 Feb (1989)

Figure 9.10   *Own-label penetration and the rise in multiple powers in UK grocery retailing*
Source   Davies, G. (1990) Marketing to retailers: a battle for distribution? *Long Range Planning*, **23**, (6), 101–108

Europe known as the Opel Corsa, using the German subsidiary name although the car is actually manufactured in Spain. In Britain, again with the same car, General Motors decided to use instead the name Vauxhall Nova as Vauxhall is the GM British subsidiary. Curious to relate then that 'Nova', in Spain, where this car is after all made, means 'doesn't work'!

Types of branding

1 *Individual brand names.* This was a policy pursued by Rowntree-Mackintosh who, only in the last few years (before being bought over by Nestle), introduced a corporate logo onto their packs. Products were stand-alone brands, such as 'Smarties', or 'Kit-Kat', or 'After-Eight', with little mention of who the manufacturer was. It mattered little as they are all quality products, but there was no association with the parent manufacturer. This has always been the case, too, with the promotion and sale of soaps and detergent washing powders with Unilever and Proctor & Gamble fighting an international battle for market share with competing brands in each sector, few identifiable with their parent company.

2 *Blanket family name for all products* is what is practised by Heinz who used to emphasize 'Heinz 57 Varieties', although the total product range must extend now into hundreds. The phrase '57 Varieties' is attributed to the French philosopher Voltaire who, on a visit to England, commented favourably on the freedom of speech and the fifty-seven varieties of religion.

3 *Separate family names for all products.* This is practised by department stores who may have different in-house brand names for different types of merchandise. Woolworth's and Littlewoods practise this.

4 *Company name and individual product name* is the strategy adopted by Kellogg's who emphasize their name strongly alongside all of their brands. Similarly, Ford Motors do likewise with each of their cars.

5 *'No-name', unbranded merchandise.* In grocery stores, this has been adopted by Carrefour hypermarkets in France and Britain, and by International Stores in Britain. Woolworths have introduced a range of generic 'no-name' products at discontinued prices. Germany has experienced this effect quite markedly with cigarettes, particularly where the 'no-name'

Table 9.15 Brand names from the totally abstract to the completely descriptive

Completely freestanding arbitrary or coined	Associative or suggestive	Completely descriptive
Kodak	Slalom	Sweet 'N' Low
Exxon	Visa	Supa-Save
Schweppes	Coca-Cola	Bitter Lemon
Formica	Sunsilk	
Replay		

Source Blackett, T. (1989) Brand-name research – getting it right? *Marketing and Research Today*, May, pp. 89–93.

cigarette packs made abroad now account for 40 per cent of the supermarket trade, and has led to the market leader Reemstra having to slash its prices. The market had been rocked also by a rise of 39 per cent in the German tax on tobacco which influenced smokers to trade down. The problem then for the established brands, such as Peter Stuyvesant, Ernte, Marlboro, HB, etc., was to re-establish themselves as being value for money brands offering premium quality at a premium price.

Brand names take account of good commercial sense – making use wherever possible of a

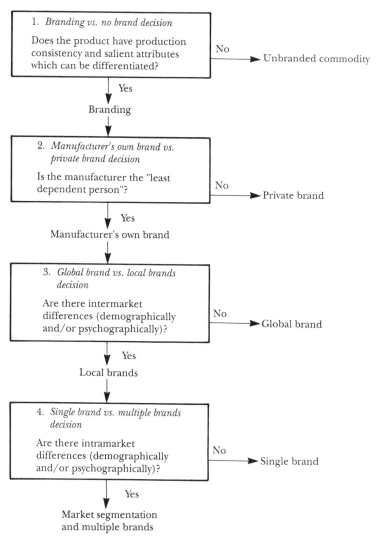

Figure 9.11   *The international dimension of branding*
Source   Onkvisit, S., and Shaw, J.J. (1989) The international dimension of branding; strategic considerations and decisions. *International Marketing Review*, **6**, (3)

Table 9.16 Before conceptualizing your next new product

---

 1 Be aware of trends, use them and respect them.
 2 Do not discount demographic trends.
 3 North America and Europe show the same trends of the bulk of the population moving into middle-age.
 4 Acknowledge the post-war baby boomers as now a greying set.
 5 Appreciate the home as a comfort zone.
 6 Acknowledge the increased value society puts on time.
 7 Do not adulterate the environment.
 8 Participate in the electronic revolution.
 9 Acknowledge that the marketing environment of the 1990s is different from that of years before.
10 Do not steal market share.

Source Adapted from Clark, A., and Femina, D. (1989) Ten most important trends that will impact your next new product. Paper to the American Marketing Association New Product Conference, February 16th. Reproduced in the AMA Worth Repeating Series as a separate paper.

local subsidiary name, culture, and language. There is no good reason to explain why a Fiat Ritmo which sold well in Europe could not sell well in Britain, or why it should sell better as a Fiat Strada in Britain when Strada means only 'Street'? The Japanese did have a car called the Cedric and a small truck in Japan which was not exported but known locally as the 'Little Bugger'. Sales of Tide in Denmark were low until it was deduced that it was the Danish word for menstrual flow. However, the Danes do sell successfully a hair product called Blackhead which obviously must have a different meaning over there. (See Table 9.17.)

The folklore of brand names is very rich – some companies use agencies to help them. Some will make a computer search, but the difficulty always with a brand name is that unfavourable associations are usually because it is connected with a slang or colloquial usage, and dictionaries do not usually provide any help whatsoever in this regard. The Japanese registered 3,000 names in 1983 which they thought would help them sell cars. One thousand were names of Italian towns, rivers or regions.

Taking an established legend in international advertising folklore, Esso's 'Tiger in your tank' was undoubtedly a successful standardized campaign, but it did undergo modification. To the French, the concept of putting a tiger in the tank was bizarre and so it had to be translated as putting a tiger in your engine. Shell used to have a slogan 'I love Shell' and they benefited greatly from French colloquial usage when they used their slogan in France 'C'est celle que j'aime', a phrase used to point out an attractive lady more often than a motor oil, but the closeness of 'celle' and 'Shell' made it effective. The point is that it is not just translation that is necessary, but the transposition of a concept into another culture. Without checking back on the original, disasters do arise.

The problem with names is that more and more are being registered, making the search for a suitable name more difficult and creating a market for professional name search companies, such as the US company, Namestormers, or the British company, Interbrand, which earned £5 million in 1988 for creating names. Namestormers follow a six-step approach:

1 *Information gathering* using one or more in-depth telephone interviews with key members of the organization. During these conversations, a fairly lengthy series of questions are asked about what it is you are naming, what you want the name to communicate, your target market, your competitors' names, how your name will be used, the positioning and brand strategy for the product or company, and other related issues.

2 *Old-fashioned brainstorming.* After reviewing notes with the entire naming project team (typically five people) and calling back with a few more questions, Namestormers conduct a series of informal brainstorming sessions. Often held over breakfast or lunch, these sessions are designed to encourage a very creative, non-defensive interplay between team members. At this point, there is no such thing as a stupid name or bad idea (having discovered that some of the worst initial ideas often ultimately yield some of the best name candidates).

These sessions focus on identifying naming 'dimensions' or avenues of thought to pursue for developing the names themselves, rather than immediately trying to develop specific name alternatives. For example, 'textures' and 'shapes' may be identified as two dimensions to pursue when naming a new kind of donut, and specific name candidates (like *RingLeaders* or *Softballs*) will be arrived at after reviewing a long list of existing texture and shape words, roots and names. Or, if the object is a company name, the question may

Table 9.17   Names: avoid the ten great blunders

---

1 *The newly minted mystery.* People respond most positively to names they can immediately understand, and are least enthusiastic about abstract and meaningless names.

2 *The rational dud.* Names that simply explain products lack imagination, memorability and emotional appeal.

3 *Alphabet stew.* Replacing corporate names with a string of letters works only for highly visible and established companies with large advertising budgets.

4 *The nearsighted name.* Too specific a name may threaten future expansion if tied too closely to a single market, product or service.

5 *The equity exterminator.* Names build up equity and imagery which can easily be lost with a name change. Retaining the old name with a fresh visual image may be equally effective.

6 *The dirty word.* Names need to be checked for vulgar meanings in popular slang.

7 *The ugly duckling.* The look of its name, its graphic potential and sound are important to be able to pronounce and memorize.

8 *Names without a market.* Names communicate to an already defined market, they do not create markets.

9 *The absentee veto.* Market testing may suggest popular associations with names that may have escaped management's attention.

10 *The legal quick kill.* Avoid lawyers for names as they will offer legally safe names without marketing value.

Source   O'Neill, T. (1986) Avoid the 10 great naming blunders. *Marketing News,* 12 September, p. 72.

be, 'If this new company were an automobile, what kind fits the company's objectives and desired image the best — would it be a Mercedes, a Honda, or . . .?' Once the type of car is identified, related naming dimensions can then be pursued.

3 *Individual name development.* Independent of the brainstorming sessions, individual team members start exploring different naming dimensions and building their own list of favourite name candidates. Some members will make extensive use of computer naming programs, name-part dictionaries, synonym finders, and databases of words and roots categorized by connotation and industry group. Others will go on 'field trips' to look at competitive products on the grocery store shelf, take a long drive out in the country, or hibernate in a restaurant for a few hours scribbling ideas. The individual approaches vary as greatly as the resulting names do.

4 *Feedback and evaluation.* As the individual name development proceeds, team members submit their name candidates for inclusion on the master list. This list is then sorted and distributed back to the entire team. A group session is held to discuss, critique and rank everyone's name ideas. This step involves team members identifying the worst and best names, defending their favourites and lambasting many others. After what often becomes a fairly heated and lengthy debate, each members' scores and comments are combined together and turned over to the team leader.

5 *Limited trademark search and profanity check.* The team leader takes the top name candidates and has preliminary trademark and profanity checks performed on each name. The preliminary trademark check compares each of the top name candidates to a directory of US registered trademarks. The comparison is based on exact spelling matches from the relevant International Classes. If a match is found, the name is flagged as potentially unavailable. While this preliminary check often catches many of the obvious problems and, saves considerable time and money (from having to perform the more exhaustive search on a lengthy list of name candidates), it is not a substitute for the comprehensive computer search. Since the trademark database Namestormers use is typically six to twelve months out-of-date, and includes no state or common-law information, a patent and trademark counsel is still needed to conduct a comprehensive trademark search (for similar as well as exact spellings) using the most current data available.

The preliminary profanity check uses a database of obvious vulgarities and obscenities in five languages: English, Spanish, German, Italian and French. Other languages are not checked and Namestormers do not reference an exhaustive listing of all the contemporary negative or obscene words in a language (e.g., in English, you might not want to name a product *Valdez* given the tie with the Exxon oil spill, even though it wouldn't be flagged during the profanity check). This check does give you an early warning of many possible vulgar or obscene meanings connected with a name.

6 *Report preparation.* Namestormers then print an eight section report which includes the three lists of name candidates, sample results from some of the computer runs, and results of the limited trademark search and preliminary profanity check. The top forty name candidates are ranked on the criteria jointly established during the initial interview and displayed in a format shown in Table 9.18 (these categories and rankings are fictitious).

Packaging

The example above of the movement on Western markets into plain, unbranded generic products is providing satisfaction for the consumerist lobby, long anxious about the size of advertising budgets and questionable promotional costs being added to overheads and, hence, final selling price. However, in Britain already, the packaging industry and the printing trades federation have made representation to trade and industry bodies about the effects that this is having on their industries.

Branded products fetch a premium over generic products. Aside from actual product qualities, there is the expectation of a 'no-nonsense' package which is purely functional rather than aesthetically or intrinsically appealing. Branded products offer the highest value-added to the packaging industry. Quality is implicit in the presentation of the product and that presentation is usually the package itself. Materials used are often laminated rather than single thickness. Lacquering of the printing inks gives an impressive sheen and means there is no smell or tainting from the inks. On generic products, this does not matter, it may even be expected as a result of lower price. Packaging, then, is no longer a promotional tool, but simply a barrier medium with generic products to protect the product as best it can and as cheaply as possible until final sale. Generic products display high-volume, low-value unit sale characteristics, so specifications change quite dramatically over the branded products. There is need only for an identification label of the contents only, and as the lower priced product has a higher turnover rate, the degree of protection may be reduced for a projected shorter shelf life. This will lower packaging costs further.

Packaging is often seen merely as a barrier property, but for many products it is the product that you see on the shelf. Dehydrated soups, for example, are sold in sachets, or pouches as the Americans call them, but this container represents the product visibly to the buying public, whereas actual sight of the dried powder itself may not appear quite so appetizing.

Packaging sizes change with personal disposable income, but also with the available channels of distribution. There may be a clear split also in the infrastructure available to urban and rural dwellers. There may be special characteristics of the distribution channels, such as a proliferation of wholesalers, or alternatively the large supermarket chains may effectively control distribution. These factors, in addition to the nation's topography, influence shelf life, and that in turn is affected by climate: again, a packaging problem. Packaging, therefore, has not only to act as a barrier, but to come in what the end-user perceives as being the 'right'

Table 9.18

Name	Memorable	Clarity	Descriptive	Value	Total
Pandora's Secrets	5	4	3	5	17
Orbitoes	5	3	4	3	16
Double Think	3	4	5	4	14
BioStar	4	4	3	5	16
Yieldflex	4	4	4	3	15
Vision Quest	4	4	4	2	14
Accucheck	3	4	4	3	14
Power House	5	4	3	2	14

Source   The Namestormers, Tel: (214) 692-9091

sizes; and to be easily identifiable in terms of contents and labelling. It is possible, therefore, to pursue a dual-brand strategy whereby the same product, or a very similar product, is sold through two quite different channels of distribution as they are intended to be targeted at two or more quite different market segments. This is quite separate from the argument over 'own-label' manufacturing where the large supermarket chains in Britain now have manufacturers producing under their own label. Tesco and Safeway now both offer an 'own-label' whisky so their range is quite extensive. It is sometimes assumed that the contents are identical with the brand leader. This is a false assumption argument. Indeed, it may be quite wrong to assume so, for both Nestle, with their Nescafe, and Kelloggs, with their Corn Flakes brand, have been advertising that they do not manufacture for anyone other than themselves, nor under any other name than their own registered brand names. British supermarket chains, such as Tesco, Sainsbury, etc., have become both irritating to manufacturers over this issue,

Table 9.19 New names that have been created (1986–1991)

Names	Description	Client
Rate Wise	A new CD account	Citibank
The Sensible Chef	Line of frozen meals	Conagra
Cold Rush	New beverage	Soft drink bottler
Vision Gate	On-line computer service	Computer services company
Techelm	New engineering consulting firm	Cape systems
Visual Edge	Computer board for improving the quality of laser printing	INTEL
IMPAC – Idea Management & Patent Assistance Corporation	Company that had to change their name	AIM – American Idea Management
Cleansweep	Line of brooms	Broom and mop manufacturer
Spider's Silk	New line of lingerie	Lingerie retailer
Talent Pulse	Headhunter	Executive search firm
Pandora's Secrets	Adult chocolate candy	Canadian liquor manufacturer
Step Savers	Alternative to the post office	New company
Cushion Tip	New line of bedding	Pillow and mattress manufacturer
Permagized	Treated lumber	Large timber company
Dawn Harvest	Bread	Bakery
Satisfaxtion	Fax machine	INTEL

Source *The Namestormers*, Tel: (214) 692-9091

but at the same time, attractive because of the size of their market dominance. For manufacturers it may not be their first choice entering into 'own-label', but the volume considerations must surely make this a proposition worthy of consideration.

Two other categories of names are the arbitrary name, such as Guess ? Jeans, and the suggestive name. The arbitrary name has no real meaning relative to the product, service or company. It describes whatever meaning becomes attached to the name as the result of a company's marketing efforts and thus enjoys excellent protection under the law. As Unikel (1987) points out, arbitrary names are a lawyer's first choice, but frequently undesirable from a marketing point of view. Unless a company is able to invest sizeable marketing dollars to give meaning to an arbitrary name, it has little intrinsic value.

Suggestive names are a compromise between legal and marketing requirements, e.g., 'Suave' shampoo and 'Accent' flavourings. However, where a manufacturer chooses a descriptive name, e.g., 'chocolate fudge drink', then this cannot be protected, whereas had this come to be expected of a brand name drink, then it would be protectable (Unikel, 1987).

Brand name and trademark protection

Brand names operate under two separate conventions internationally – either prior use elsewhere of the brand name; or first registration, which would allow a private citizen to record all rights for one country to what were protected brand names elsewhere. A certain individual was reputed to have registered over 300 brand names in the early 1960s and to have bartered furiously with multinationals subsequently seeking entry to that particular market.

Brand name protection, therefore, means registration in each country likely to be a market for the product concerned. It all depends on the market potential of the product concerned and the resources of the company. Nevertheless, these costs of brand name protection are expensive, amounting to 10–20 per cent of the development costs of certain new products. Du Pont had heavy registration costs with Corfam, the synthetic leather material for shoes, and only made break even on its development costs when selling the process to the Soviet Union. Registration and protection, therefore, add to total costs, while protecting the commercial advantage embodied in the product concerned from external competitions. This means, though, that either the product or the process itself has to be offered to a wider market in order to recover the costs of development. Ironically, this emphasizes both the need to go abroad as well as the need for international protection.

Trademarks is a separate area from brand names, yet although the name is what you would probably ask for or look for in a shop, the trademark is what would probably help you recognize the product even though a pack may be redesigned.A trademark can be any word, symbol, or device, or any combination of these which identifies goods or services. Registration at the Patent Office confers on the proprietor a statutory right to exclusive use of the mark. For example, the style of a typeface can be registered. Consider the distinctiveness of the typefaces used in the Kellogg's logo or the IBM logo or the Wrangler logo on shirts and denim jeans. Trademarks are the manufacturer's way of assuring the consumer that he is purchasing an authentic product at a time when brand piracy is certainly on the computers from the Far East. A standard pack of Kellogg's Corn Flakes, therefore, has protected rights to the Kellogg's logo: the cockerel graphic; the slogan in 'the sunshine breakfast'; and the slogan underneath the brand name, 'the best to you'. Loss of control over any or all of these could invite product imitation, which Kelloggs have been able to avoid completely in the UK until the advent of generic products.

It is interesting, therefore, to note how the Coca-Cola bottle was found not to be registrable as a trademark in a reapplication by the Coca-Cola company to the Court of Appeal, January 23, 1985. From the early 1920s, the company had been selling Coca-Cola in unusually shaped bottles in the UK, and there was ample evidence to show that the public in the USA, and in the UK, associated the shape with Coca-Cola. The verdict was that a line drawing of a bottle may be registrable as the trademark of a beverage if the bottle depicted is unusual and distinctive; but the bottle itself or its shape are not registrable in that they are not 'marks' capable of being applied to or incorporated in the beverage.

Goods are classified under different sections at the Patent Office, so a name in use under one category would not prevent registration of the same name by a different company in a different product category. Examples of names used by different companies for different products include Colt, which can be a gun, a car, a lager, or ventilating equipment; Titan and Jaguar, both of which can be aircraft or motor vehicles; and Lloyds Bank and Lloyds, the insurance market.

Trademarks are protected by the Paris Union, known formally as the International Convention for the Protection of Industrial Property, established in 1882, which allows a company registering in one country six months grace to register in any other he chooses. The former Soviet Union is a member. The Paris Union allows for:

1 Mutual recognition and reciprocity in that each signatory nation has to provide the same degree of protection to nationals of other members states as to its own nationals.
2 Filing a claim in any other member state within twelve months of first registration and have the original date of application recognized.
3 Common rules and regulations applicable to all member states.

Note though that this is a convention and does not form part of English law. The UK Copyright Act stems from the Berne Convention and the current Patents Act from the European Patents Treaty.

The second agreement is the Madrid Arrangement, known formally as the Madrid Arrangement for International Registration of Trademarks of 1891. This is mostly European, has only twenty-five members, and does not include the USA or Britain, but allows for registration in one country to be effective for all member countries.

Trademarks licensed to the sole distributors of pharmaceuticals, and protected under national trademark laws, were in the past often used as a barrier against imports of identically branded goods sold by the manufacturer on another national market at a lower price. The EC Commission has been waging a long and successful war against such trademark-assisted compartmentalization of the Common Market, and has received powerful support from the European Court. The European Court ruled, in the *American Home Products Case*, that two different trademarks must not be used for the same or similar product with the sole purpose of separating the national markets, or at least they must not be used to stop the parallel importer. The EC Commission's proposals would go much further. It would lead to an automatic invalidation of trademarks if the protected goods were marketed in another member state under another trademark. The EC has still to decide whether to have examination preceding registration, as in Britain and Ireland, or simply registration as elsewhere. If Britain and Ireland do give up the examination system, this will bring them in line with the rest of the Common Market who are all members of the Madrid Arrangement whereby one registration is effective for all member countries.

The Trademark Registration Treaty (TRT) of August 1980 opened up the possibility of having simply one application for registration, channelled through the UN World Intellectual Property Organization (WIPO), and valid for all countries. However, to date this has attracted only five signatories, including the USSR and four developing countries: Burkina Faso, Congo, Gabon, and Togo. The main obstacle is that Britain and the USA presently enjoy strong trademark registration and, while aware of the advantages which a common international system would bring, they view this as meaningless if the degree of protection conferred is to be in any way reduced. WIPO continues to act as the prime mover, but is seen to have a bias towards the less developed countries seeking easier access to Western technology. In 1985, talks were held on what is called a Third Variant, i.e., a third variant of the Madrid Arrangement, the TRT being the second, the intention being to supersede the Madrid Arrangement, and yet incorporate more flexibility to try to entice US and British participation.

Industrial property rights

Licensing confers the right to produce under a company-specific technology in return for a fee or royalty. It allows access to an outsider to technology that has been protected by patents. In the past, industrial property rights which concerned technology have been the easiest to protect, but in today's world markets there is a great deal to be gained from product imitation or closely related brand names, sometimes even instituting a brand name that looks quite different but is phonetically identical in the local market abroad. Another large loophole at the moment is the question of computer software, for the regulations have to be rewritten in order to encompass rights of authorship over computer software programs where development costs are high and duplication may be carried out with ease.

At the moment, there are three international agreements on patent protection in addition to the Paris Union and Madrid Arrangement which cover trademarks as well. The European Patent Convention encompasses sixteen countries; the European Community Patent Convention, its member countries; and the Patent Co-operation Treaty has twenty signatures including all the major Western trading nations. Registration in one member country is effective for all nations signatory to the agreement.

Brand piracy

In an interview, Robert Littas of Interpol (Bresler, 1987) stated that there were thirty main categories of fraud, of which brand piracy then forms only part, although a prominent part.

Kaikati (1981) identified five different basic ways of forging famous trademarks which have been developed:

1 *Outright piracy* – false product in the same form and same trademark as the original. Records and tapes are common examples.
2 *Reverse engineering* – stripping down the original product and then copying it, underselling the original manufacturer. This is happening currently in the electronics industry.
3 *Counterfeiting* – altering the product's quality without altering the trademark. Clothing

companies, such as Levi Strauss, Lacoste and others, suffer heavily from this. The addition of an identifiable logo or trademark, such as the Lacoste crocodile, increases the perceived value of the product to the customer. Fake Cartier watches can be bought for $5 to $10 and then sold for $40 to $50, as against more than $700 for the original. In this case, the consumer believes that he is getting a good deal and that no-one is being hurt by this practice.

4 *Passing off* – modifying both the product and trademark, adapting a trademark that is similar in appearance, phonetic quality, or meaning, to the original product. All that is normally associated with the product is copied, e.g., Del Mundo for Del Monte; Coalgate for Colgate toothpaste, or Pineapple for Apple Computers. Yet, it may not be illegal to produce imitations. It raises a legal question as to whether all 'me-too' products are not imitations and whether any market follower would not then become a counterfeiter. Sony introduced the Walkman but many companies have since introduced very similar competing products.

5 *Wholesale infringement* – this involves the questionable registration of famous brand names overseas rather than the introduction of faked products. Although Kaikati (1981) cites this as a form of brand piracy, it is entirely within the law, and applies chiefly to those markets adhering to the Madrid Convention and the concept of 'first registration'.

Brand piracy or product counterfeiting is becoming much more prevalent than ever before, and entering into more and higher value-added areas such as microcomputers. A British response to this has been to establish the Anti-Counterfeiting Group (ACG) which is financed by thirty-eight major companies seriously concerned with the growth of this activity. This works in conjunction with the American IACC (International Anti-Counterfeiting Coalition), International Chamber of Commerce based in Paris, Interpol, also based in Paris, and the Comité Colbert, a French organization formed in 1954 to combat counterfeiting.

Some of the activities of product counterfeiters are comic, such as the Asian manufacturer who promised Scotch Whisky made from real Scottish grapes and matured in the cellars of Buckingham Palace! There was also the Singapore manufacturer who tried to imitate the steering wheel covers of a West German company called Arus by even having a similar name, but his choice of 'Anus' in bold in the middle of a steering wheel met with some consumer resistance!

Elsewhere, the activities of these counterfeiters are not so funny. While Levi's and Wrangler clothing have long suffered from product imitations, and few have grieved over this except when challenging the manufacturers over the poor quality of their goods to find that they were in fact counterfeit, this is now spreading to higher value-added products as well, such as heart pacemakers and to birth control pills which are look-alikes but contain only chalk. G. D. Searle now mark their pills using more than one method. The House of Courreges says that it only has 40 per cent of its 'own' market, worth $15 million a year; its image so devalued by copies that most retailers have given up hope of restoring it. Other designer houses, such as Gucci and Celine, also suffer from this trade as do Cartier watches, Apple computers and Raleigh bicycles. Much of this sourcing is based on the freeports of the Far East, such as the export hungry 'Four Dragons' of Asia: Singapore, Hong Kong, Taiwan and South Korea. The ACG estimates that there are thirty different countries involved in product counterfeiting and that their output reaches most parts of the world. There is the obvious loss of revenue to the genuine company whose brand has been stolen but there is often a serious danger associated with the use of certain of these products. While heart pacemakers and pharmaceutical prescription drugs are newer counterfeits, imported brake linings and tyres of poor quality have long been a problem. The involvement of organized crime becomes apparent with the realization that an estimated two-thirds of the video business in Britain is illicit, costing the industry £130 million in Britain alone or £700 million internationally.

Effective copying of the packaging where it is particularly distinctive helps pass off counterfeit products on an unsuspecting public. *Packaging Review* in September 1983, carried a report on how the whisky distillers Walker and Sons had been awarded £50,000 exemplary damages against a former director of the Rockware Group for breach of its trading rights. The High Court judgement followed proceedings instigated in 1977 following the discovery of cases of counterfeit Johnny Walker Red and Black Label en route to Lebanon. The whisky was found in Walker-shaped bottles with forged labels in warehouses in Holland and West Germany. Investigations led to both civil and criminal proceedings against a former Rockware director and an interim injunction was granted on 30 May 1977 to stop any further breaches of Walker's rights. Final judgement in the civil action was made in November 1978, but the damages and costs totalling £116,000 were not assessed till May 1983.

Counterfeiting is now acknowledged to be damaging to Taiwan's national image. The fear is now real that foreign firms will be wary of bringing high technology to Taiwan if people can steal it with impunity. Even local firms may become reluctant to invest in expensive know-how if it can be lifted by competitors. Already the Taiwan High Court has overturned a lower court decision which had cleared two firms selling imitations of Apple Computers. The Lower Court had argued that imitations of Apple's small computers were legitimate since Apple was not registered as a company in Taiwan. Whereas previously courts sided with local entrepreneurs, the government is keen now to introduce a new understanding. The penalty for making fake goods has been raised from two to five years' imprisonment. The High Court decision will help support this new drive. Plans are afoot also to introduce a special court to deal with cases involving infringement of trademarks, patents, and copyrights. Taiwan still remains the major base for counterfeiting but counterfeiting is increasing in South Korea and India. In 1985, US and UK vehicle-component and replacement-parts manufacturers established an independent investigation team in Taiwan to compile evidence against counterfeiters. The loss to the US car industry is estimated at $3 billion (£1.7 million) and £100 million to the UK. Note, though, that legal changes introduced into the UK in 1989 no longer make the making of spare and replacement parts for cars an offence. Nevertheless, the fear is that Taiwan, after a short period of overtly tough action against counterfeiters, may once again relapse into a laissez-faire attitude. Extensive computerized dossiers are now being exchanged and legal action is being taken where the parties are identified, while dossiers are being sent also to GATT headquarters in the hope that some internationally co-ordinated action might be taken to remove this menace. Converted to job losses, it means 6,000 jobs lost in Europe alone just in one industrial sector.

The difficulty for individual customs authorities, such as the UK Customs and Excise Department, is that they are mainly concerned with ensuring that consignments entering the country are properly labelled and that duty is paid. Action needs to be taken by the company whose product is being counterfeited. For example, British Customs and Excise are willing to hold goods pending civil action, but they are not empowered to seize. The losses, therefore, on tax revenue and lost company sales are almost impossible to estimate.

The EC has joined with the USA in pressing for firm action against counterfeiting under GATT, but has revealed a plan which will block and possibly ultimately prevent counterfeit goods crossing community frontiers. Suspected counterfeit goods would be impounded for ten days during which time the trademark holder would be allowed to prove his case. If the goods were found to be counterfeit they would then be confiscated and 'disposed of outside the normal channels of commerce.'

Interpol devised a piece of model legislation in 1985 which they then sent around the 142 member states of the organization. They also publish the *Counterfeits and Forgeries Review*.

Five corporate strategies to handle counterfeiting

Kaikati (1981), who has been one of the most important researchers in this area, has advanced the following counter-strategies from his research of counterfeiters and their victims:

1 *Compete and attempt to overcome the opposition.* A feasible strategy when the firm's stakes and power are relatively high. The objective is domination and forcing the counterfeiters out of the market. Many large companies, as well as the International Anti-Counterfeiting Associations themselves, now have a security force tracking down counterfeiters and pursuing them with legal actions wherever and whenever they are found.
2 *Avoid conflict and withdraw from the fray.* This is feasible where the firms' stakes and power are relatively low. The strategy objective is to throw in the towel or move on to 'greener pastures' at the lowest possible cost.
3 *Accommodate the opposition, where the objective is appeasement.* Customers may switch to their brand if they knew their products were being faked. The company which is the victim of such action is hoping that the problem will disappear. There is a further consideration in that pursuit of the offenders requires conclusive evidence which is a difficult and expensive proposition as it entails hiring private detectives for lengthy periods of time. Again, criminal action is speedier and more effective than civil action, but loopholes in the law are being fully exploited by very professional criminals.
2 *Collaborate.* This is likely to be best when the firm's relations with the opposition are relatively positive. Fiorucci, an Italian jeans maker with outlets in the USA, has been charged with ordering cheap Korean copies of its own luxury jeans and marketing them as though made in Italy. There have even been occasions when the quality of the counterfeit exceeds that of the original!
5 *Compromise.* In this situation, the firm's stakes are moderate and power is slight. The trademark Persil is owned by Unilever in Britain and France, and by Henkel in Germany, Belgium, Luxembourg, Holland, Italy and Denmark. Agreement had to be reached when Britain entered the EC and there were price differentials between the manufacturers, Unilever being cheaper than Henkel. Also, price differentials between countries, which gave rise to parallel exporting opportunities. The two manufacturers agreed to respect each other's trademark, and agreed that Henkel would use the name Persil on pockets in red inside a red oval whereas Unilever would use a green Persil trademark.

Distribution of counterfeit goods

Where goods are offered for sale by street traders, the public are right to be suspicious when massive discounts are being offered, although even at this level more professionalism has crept in. In the past few years there has been a problem with street traders in Britain offering supposedly French perfumes for sale at very low prices. To support their sales talk, they flaunt glossy colour advertisements allegedly from quality magazines, which refer to these perfumes. In fact, these advertisements are also fake. The appeal of some of the 'knock-off' perfumes is also hard to understand. Since 1981, a Connecticut based firm, Perfums de Coeur, has been advertising: 'If you like Opium, you'll love Ninja.' They also offer Confess (similar to Obsession), Primo (similar to Giorgio), and Turmoil (similar to Poison). They use comparative advertising copy, comparing their product with the brand leader (Sloan, 1987), but give it a different name so not actually promising the original.

However, counterfeit goods are well beyond the level of just street traders, but have entered many high street retailers and department stores in Britain and the USA. In the USA alone, it is a trade estimated at $20 billion in 1984, which is well up on the $3 billion estimate for 1978, but proposals to deal with the counterfeiters, including seizure of any goods suspected of being counterfeit, has run into opposition from US cut-price retailers. K-Mart is a large well known US chain of discount stores, who have a store in Los Angeles which was found by federal marshals to be selling 100 pairs of counterfeit Jordache designer jeans. Jordache refuses to sell to K-Mart directly because it looks for outlets which reflect the image which it wishes to portray. K-Mart, therefore, obtain their supplies from middlemen known in the trade as 'diverters', and it is these people whom Jordache are keen to pursue, although there is nothing illegal in the practice of 'diverting' or selling to outlets that the manufacturer may not approve of.

While opinions are divided as to what role government should have in this situation, eighty-five US corporations have meanwhile formed the International Anti-Counterfeiting Coalition. An international code to let trademark owners intercept and seize shipments of suspect merchandise is the next step for the Coalition. The code being considered by the General Agreement on Tariffs and Trade (GATT) is opposed by Brazil, India, Hong Kong and Singapore because it is alleged that they fear that their trade in low-cost imitations will suffer. A few developed countries, including Austria and Switzerland, are opposing the code as well. Meanwhile, the Reagan Administration passed a law in 1984 which allows for goods to be confiscated, and distributors to be fined or even sent to jail. The US software industry estimates losses due to piracy in 1989 as $1.5 billion, and for Canada at $190 million. For software, such as Wordperfect, or spreadsheets, such as Lotus 1–2–3, the ratio of pirated to legitimate copies is around 5:1. An industry action group, the Software Publishers' Association, based in Washington, DC, now has 645 members.

Technology provides another part of the answer in that companies, now more security conscious than ever before, spent $50 million in 1985 on a variety of high technology gadgetry which provides a means of unobtrusively authenticating products with hidden magnetic or microchip tags, disappearing—reappearing inks, holographic images, and digitized 'fingerprints' of labels which read the unique pattern of fibres in each label. The verifiable label was developed by Light Signatures Inc. in 1981, and has been used by Nike Inc. (running shoes), MCA Inc. (records) and Levi Strauss, whose attorney, Peter M. Phillipes, was able to boast: 'We have virtually eliminated our counterfeiting problem in the US.' Clearly, other developments are not so encouraging, for in 1986 Sue Goldstein, author of *The Underground Shopper*, along with the Irving Texas-based mail order house, IMOCO, started 'Facsimile', a catalogue offering designer look-alikes of clothes from Ralph Lauren, Calvin Klein, Adrienne Vittadini, and others. The cover caption reads: 'If you like the Ralph Lauren look, you'll love Facsimile' (Sloan, 1987).

Britain has recently changed its position quite substantially in this area. The Copyright, Designs and Patents Act 1989 extended copyright to computers and satellite broadcasts, and changed the provisions relating to industrial designs allowing ten years protection. Copying necessary to make spare parts, as with cars, is allowable. Yet, designs with 'eye appeal' are to be given twenty-five years' protection. 'Moral rights' are accorded authors, artists, and film directors, giving them the right to be identified with their work. Penalties have been introduced for making, importing or infringing copies of any kind of copyright material, allowing for an unlimited fine and up to ten years' imprisonment. Copyright ownership in relation to literary, dramatic, musical and artistic works produced by an employee is now automatically granted to the employer. The question of copyright, and of its ownership, and of obtaining payment for the use of copyright material has, therefore, been resolved to some degree.

After-sales service

There are obvious advantages where it is possible to standardize, if not globally, at least regionally, the level of service accorded to customers. From cars to electronic hi-fi stereo systems, product guarantees and warranties are common in all parts of the world. Where previously they were national, the clear trend is now international. In the past there may indeed have been valid reasons for separate warranties, country by country. With cars, for example, servicing periods were at 3,000-mile intervals, whereas in more recent years this has been extended to six months or 9,000-mile intervals. Products have improved but alongside this, there needs to be a uniformity on the dealer network internationally. Standardized servicing facilities, availability of parts, even standards of training of mechanics and maintenance personnel, are all factors to be considered before internationalizing a product warranty. It does add to company prestige and the consumer perception of product quality and reassurance in the event of breakdown. There may well, however, be instances of local market requirements, as in the case of the USA or the EC, but these needs can still be met. Production costs on the warranty booklets can be reduced by producing them in large numbers, and comprehension can be aided by having it contain warranty guidelines in several languages.

References

Ash, R. (1989) *The Top 10 of Everything*, Queen Anne Press, London.

Banks, B. (1988) Double trouble. *Canadian Business*, **61**, (5), 40–44, 97–103.

Baumwell, J. (1986) Life cycle for brands? Forget it!. *Advertising Age*, **57**, (21), 18, 22.

Blackett, T. (1989) Brand-name research — getting it right? *Marketing and Research Today*, May, 89–93.

Bouchard, W. M. (1986) Courts tend to favour trademarks. *Advertising Age*, **57**, (56), p. 48.

Bradley, M. F. (1979) National and corporate images and attitudes in international marketing. Working Paper Series No. 5, Centre for International Marketing Studies, Faculty of Commerce, University College, Dublin.

Bresler, F. (1987) The man from Interpol. *Business Life*, February/March, 30–34.

Buzzell, R. D. (1968) Can you standardize multinational marketing? *Harvard Business Review*, November–December, 102–13.

Chan, A. K. K. (1990) Localisation in international branding: A preliminary investigation on Chinese names of foreign brands in Hong Kong. *International Journal of Advertising*, **9**, (1), 81–91.

Cheeseright, P. (1982) St. Michael and the crusade for overseas sales outlets. *Financial Times*, 9 July.

Clark, T. (1990) International marketing and national character: A review and proposal for an integrative theory. *Journal of Marketing*, October, 66–79.

Clark, A., and Femina, D. (1986) Ten most important trends that will impact your next new product. Paper to the American Marketing Association New Product Conference, February 16th. Reproduced in the AMA *Worth Repeating* Series as a separate paper.

Clement, M., and Werner, H. W. (1990) The literature positioning process: An international approach from the pharmaceutical industry. *Marketing and Research Today*, **June,** 85–96.

Clements, J. (1989) Value is where you find it. *Forbes*, **143,** (6), 62–64.

Collar, L. (1990) Effective management of international research and planning in brand and advertising developments. *European Research*, June, 109–114.

Davies, G. (1990) Marketing to retailers: A battle for distribution? *Long Range Planning*, **23,** (6), 101–108.

Davies, R. (1985) Coke bottle not registrable as trade mark. *Financial Times*, 30 January.

Drugs on the run (1982) *Economist*, 11 September.

DTI (1991) *The Single Market: Keeping Your Product on the Market*, Dept. of Trade and Industry, London.

Etemad, H. (1983) World product mandates in perspective. In *Multinationals and Technology Transfer: The Canadian Experience*, (ed. Rugman, A.) Praeger, New York.

Feucht, F. N. (1989) It's symbolic. *American Demographics*, **11,** (11), 30–33.

Fisher, P. (1989) The name is the game. *Intercity*, July/August, 16–18.

Fletcher, P. (1990) McCastro's: Cuba's Answer to Big Macs. *Globe and Mail*, Toronto, 10 October.

Globerman, S. (1988) Addressing international product piracy. *Journal of International Business Studies*, Fall, 497–504.

Greguras, F. M. (1987) Intellectual property protection in the USA. *Information Age*, **9,** (4), 215–219.

Haigh, P. (1983) Brand busters. *Executive World*, April, 26–27.

Hermann, A. H. (1982) [Legal Correspondent] The perils of harmony. *Financial Times*, 24 March.

Howard, D. G., and Mayo, M. A. (1988) Developing a defensive product management philosophy for third world markets. *International Marketing Review*, Spring, 31–40.

IH buys itself a dual problem (1982) *Management Today*, February, p. 72.

Ishikawa, K. (1990) *Japan and the Challenge of Europe 1992*, Pinter Publishing for Royal Institute of International Affairs, London.

Jain, S. C. (1989) Standardisation of international marketing strategy: Some research hypotheses. *Journal of Marketing*, **53,** (1), 70–79.

Jennings, C. (1983) The trade mark maze. *Marketing*, 3 March 31–33.

Kaikati J. C. (1981) How multinational corporations cope with international trademark forgery. *Journal of International Marketing*, **1,** (2), 69–80.

Keegan, W. (1970) Five strategies for multinational marketing. *European Business*, January, 35–40.

Keegan, W. J., Still, R. R., and Hill, J. S., (1987) Transferability and adaptability of products and promotion themes in multinational marketing in MNCs and LDCs. *Journal of Global Marketing*, **1,** (1/2), 85–103.

Kern, H. Wagner, H. C., and Hassis, R. (1990) European aspects of a global brand: The BMW case. *Marketing and Research Today*, February, 47–57.

Kotler, P. (1984) Marketing Management: Analysis, Planning and Control (4th Edition), Prentice-Hall, Englewood Cliffs, NJ, p. 351.

Lipson, H. A., and Lamont, D. F. (1969) Marketing policy decisions facing international marketers in the less-developed countries. *Journal of Marketing*, **33**, 24–31.

Livingstone, J. M. (1989) *The Internationalisation of Business*, Macmillan, London.

Lorenz, C. (1981) How Japan cascades through Western markets. *Financial Times*, 9 November.

Madawar, C., and Freese, B. (1981) Drug multinationals in the Third World. *Business and Society Review*, Summer, 22–24.

Mallet, V. (1990) Seeking a wider market for a perfume of Arabia. *Financial Times*, 3 May.

Marketing News (1991) Judge rules Kellogg wrongly promoted cereal as drug. 29 April 12.

McLoughlin (1983) Japan acts to avoid car clangers. *Guardian*, 6 December.

Morello, G. (1984) The 'made-in' issue. *European Research*, **12**, (1), 4–21.

Noble, K. (1990) Alleviating guilt of disposable diapers. *Globe and Mail*, Toronto, 10 October.

O'Neill, T. (1986) Avoid the 10 great naming blunders. *Marketing News*, 12 September, 72.

Onkvisit, S., and Shaw, J. J. (1989) The international dimension of branding: Strategic considerations and decisions. *International Marketing Review*, **6**, (3).

Pal, S. K., and Bowander, B. (1979) Marketing challenges of technical industries in developing countries. *Industrial Marketing Management*, **8**, 69–74.

Paliwoda, S. (1988) Plain English Campaign. *MBA Review*, December, 9–11.

Rawstorne, P. (1990) Brand repositioning: United Distillers from whisky galore to whisky grands Crus. *Financial Times*, 14 June.

Rawstorne, P. (1989) The coming battle at the breakfast table. *Financial Times*, 21 December.

Rawstorne, P. (1988) Importance of naming names. *Financial Times*, 21 July, 12.

Rawstorne, P. (1988) Product development: The crop of the creme. *Financial Times*, 31 March, 14.

Ritchie, R. (1986) Global branding need not mean global advertising. *Admap*, January, 39–42.

Sales and Marketing Management (1989) Trademark woes: Help is coming. **140**, (1), 84.

Shalofsky, I. (1987) Research for global brands. *European Research*, May, 88–93.

Skapinker, M. (1990) Battlelines drawn on the small screen. *Financial Times*, 21 May.

Sloan, P. (1987) Knock-off deliver blows to fragrance market. *Advertising Age*, **58**, (9), 3/4.

Srikantham, S. Ward, K., and Neal, R. (1989) Brand accounting: myth or reality? *Management Accounting*, **67**, (4), 20–22.

Strauss, M. (1991) Cashing in on the clear Canadian image. *Globe and Mail*, Toronto, 13 March.

The Independent on Sunday (1990) Message in a bottle that changed Europe. London, 6 May, 27.

The Namestormers, tel: (010 1 214) 692–9091

Tuohy, M. (1987) How can we protect our ideas? *Accountancy*, **100**, (1131), 90, 92.

Ughanwa, D. O., and Baker, M. J. (1989) *The Role of Design in International Business*, Routledge, London.

Unikel, A. L. (1987) Imitation might be flattering but beware of trademark infringement. *Marketing News*, 11 September, 20–21.

Ushikubo, K. (1986) A method of structure analysis for developing product concepts and its applications. *European Research*, **14**, 174–184.

Van Slyke, P. C. (1989) Sweeping trademark revisions now in effect. *Marketing News*, 18 December, 2.

Whitelock, J. M. (1987) Global marketing and the case for international product standardisation. *European Journal of Marketing*, **21**, (9), 32–44.

Whittemore, M. (1990) The adaptable enterprise. *Nation's Business*, November, 47–56.

Wind, J., and Douglas, S. (1972) International Market Segmentation. *European Journal of Marketing*, **6**, (1).

Key reading

Blackett, T. (1989) Brand-name research − getting it right? *Marketing and Research Today,* May, 89–93.

Clark, T. (1990) International marketing and national character: A review and proposal for an integrative theory. *Journal of Marketing*, October, 66–79.

Clements, J. (1989) Value is where you find it. *Forbes*, **143**, (6), 62–64.

Collar, L. (1990) Effective management of international research and planning in brand and advertising developments. *European Research*, June, 109–114.

Feucht, F. N. (1989) It's symbolic. *American Demographics*, **11**, (11), 30–33.

Jain, S. C. (1989) Standardisation of international marketing strategy: Some research hypotheses. *Journal of Marketing*, **53**, (10) 70–79.

Kaikati, J. G. (1981) How multinational corporations cope with international trademark forgery. *Journal of International Marketing*, **1**, (2), 69–80.

Marketing News (1991) Judge rules Kellogg wrongly promoted cereal as drug. 29 April, 12.

Shalofsky, I. (1987) Research for global brands. *European Research*, May, 88–93.

Ughanwa, D. O., and Baker, M. J. (1989) *The Role of Design in International Business*, Routledge, London.

Unikel, A. L. (1987) Imitation might be flattering but beware of trademark infringement. *Marketing News*, 11 September, 20–21.

Ushikubo, K. (1986) A method of structure analysis for developing product concepts and its applications. *European Research*, 174–184.

10
Pricing, credit and terms of doing business

Pricing strategies compared with domestic pricing strategies

Pricing is a most conspicuous element of the marketing mix and has many publics to satisfy. As well as the buying public, there are other interested parties such as competitors, society, government – particularly if there is a domestic prices and incomes board, other governments if the item is exported, and possibly even supranational bodies, such as the EC, if there is any hint of the exported product being 'dumped' within the community, or enjoying any subsidy, or artificial advantage which may be in contravention of free trade within the community as laid down in the Treaty of Rome.

For management in what is often termed the 'real world' as opposed to an academic environment, there is no such thing as perfect knowledge of any market situation nor is there ever any such thing as perfect competition where all companies active in a market are equal. The major problem with price-setting is that there are few goal posts. Pricing within the domestic market, there are strategic implications as to whether one chooses to price high, low, or merely be a price-follower, and these same strategies can be pursued internationally, provided one is sure that there is a market segment to be found within several countries, and that it is of a size and ability to respond. For example, pricing high and producing in low volume, and so skimming only the cream of the market, is the strategy employed by Rolls Royce, which enjoys a niche market position in luxury cars. Following the product life cycle theory, when companies first introduce a new product and it embodies a new product concept, or where there is no clear competition in supply, there is the temptation to charge what the market will bear. In the initial stage at least, there is for a time a certain exclusivity and this helps build a product image and maintain a high product price.

At the other end of the pricing spectrum is market-penetration pricing which means a low price but requires a high volume market. This strategy was encapsulated by Sir Jack Cohen, founder of Tesco food supermarkets: 'Pile it high and sell it cheap!'. This is a valid strategy for a product that is either mature or reaching saturation, and so lowering the price may draw in further sales, exactly as economists predict with elasticity of demand. For the manufacturer, penetration pricing may also help keep out competition because of the low final price and through the perception that low final prices are the result of economies of scale, and that with mature products, the cost savings are due to the experience curve effect (which produces cost savings of approximately one-third whenever production doubles). There are many examples that may be drawn of products adopting penetration-pricing once they had moved along the product life cycle, including calculators, digital watches and personal computers.

As the product has become more established, the buying public have become more aware and knowledgeable, and the need for a branded product can now be satisfied with a generic one. The product life cycle affects all four Ps of the marketing mix simultaneously and not just price alone. With digital watches, the price lowered, the volume increased and changes took place in the promotion and distribution as well. The channel of distribution moved from specialist jeweller to 'blister packs' on supermarket shelves. The jeweller is not redundant, however, since he now chooses to specialize in higher value added goods, which means lower volume growth, but provides a higher unit return. Calculators are another interesting product which have made themselves virtually indispensable to a public who did not know them one generation before. As a mass-market product, calculators fulfil a basic function and are difficult to differentiate, thus pricing plays a major role. The PLC also provides an explanation for what has been happening with the sale of personal computers. As these have moved along the PLC to become mature products, a knowledgeable buying public was less concerned with brand name, knowing the componentry to be virtually identical across different brands. This shifted the focus away from brands and specialist retailers to pricing, and so lower cost distribution outlets. While specialist computer retailers have been trying to expand, an ever-increasing volume of sales has shifted to the traditional retailers now selling their own in-house label personal computers. This in turn has created a massive shakeout among the specialist retailers unable to differentiate their product offering in any way, as for example, offering added service warranty or after-sales care that would help justify their higher levels of pricing.

Appropriate pricing over the cycle depends on the development of three different aspects of industry, which usually move in parallel base paths:

1 *Technical maturity*, indicated by declining rate of product development, increasing standardization among brands, and increasing stability of manufacturing processes and knowledge about them.
2 *Market maturity*, indicated by consumer acceptance of the basic service idea, by widespread belief that the products of most manufacturers will perform satisfactorily, and by enough familiarity and sophistication to permit consumers to compare brands competently.
3 *Competitive maturity*, indicated by increasing stability of market shares and price structures.

Somewhere in between the two strategies of skimming and of penetration, there is the flock of sheep who diligently follow the market leader, fearful of lowering prices and meeting retaliation, or raising prices and losing sales. The danger which often passes unrecognized is that the company following the price of the market leader may not have a true knowledge of his own costs, particularly in industries where there is a critical mass that has to be produced, or of economies of scale, or of experience curve effects that may be reached beyond a certain level of production, and so there are inherent dangers always in basing sale prices on someone else's costs. Skimming, penetration, and price-following (or me-too prices) are features to be found in all markets. What often happens though, is that when a product travels abroad it will, in seeking to position itself in the foreign market, allow itself to be influenced by domestic experience, and so perhaps just extend whatever pricing strategy is used in the domestic market to this new foreign market, thus failing to optimize on pricing. At either end of the pricing continuum there are international products which may be identified with a standardized pricing strategy, e.g., disposable razors, pens, and ladies' tights, where the price is cognizant of the fact that these are disposable products and so are sold cheaply in high volume. At the other end of this continuum would be those products which ignore a mass market and essentially appeal to an international market segment (if not niche), such as Rolls Royce. Essentially, a premium price is being paid for a quality product and all the prestige that ownership of that quality marque may confer.

Consumer sensitivity to pricing

Sampson (1964) has argued that many desensitizing factors operate to diminish the impact of price changes. Insensitivity will, therefore, be greater where the following conditions prevail:

- personal selling, and, therefore, variation in point-of-sale effectiveness
- promotion is local rather than standardized nationally
- service after sale is important
- consumer loyalties are significant
- products are highly differentiated and difficult to compare
- There are multiple dimensions of product quality
- unit price is low
- the product is sophisticated.

A multi-stage approach to pricing

There are six major elements which have been identified by Oxenfeldt (1960) in a domestic pricing decision, which in sequential order are:

1 Selecting market targets.
2 Choosing a brand image.
3 Composing a marketing mix.
4 Selecting a pricing policy.
5 Determining a pricing strategy.
6 Arriving at a specific price.

However, international pricing has to take many more variables into consideration, and this is assuming that payment will be made almost immediately and in the seller's currency. Credit, payment in other currencies, barter and the new and important forms of countertrade, introduce new and urgent problems, given the levels of competition prevailing in world markets.

International price standardization

In an ideal world the same price for one's product would prevail everywhere, but this does not happen. When it does happen within a domestic market, it happens as a result of resale price maintenance (abolished in Britain in the early 1970s, but still practised in Japan). Price standardization cannot happen within international marketing because of currency fluctuations, different factor costs, different product requirements, and national standards, plus official governmental controls on pricing and discounting. It is just not possible, therefore, to find the exact same product available for sale across different markets at exactly the same price. The next best thing that happens is that this price differential may be contained within a few percentage points across markets, thus preventing the movement of this particular product across markets because of price differential alone. Nevertheless, price deviation will occur for the same product across different markets.

The *Economist* (1991), together with McDonalds of fast food fame, publishes an annual 'Big Mac' index. The index is based around McDonalds' 'Big Mac' hamburger made locally to strict standards in more than fifty countries, and so free from the distortions that international transportation and distribution costs might otherwise introduce. *The Economist* sees this index as one of purchasing power parity and so revealing to some degree whether a currency is under- or overvalued. Table 10.1 would indicate, for example, that the dollar is 61 per cent undervalued against the Soviet rouble.

One consequence of international price comparison is the ever-present danger of 'grey' or of 'parallel' exports taking place. Parallel exporting is an illicit activity undertaken by intermediaries in the distribution channel who often find unofficial export sales more lucrative than selling on the domestic market. By taking advantage of retail price maintenance and currency differentials elsewhere, these exporters – often wholesalers or retailers – are able to earn returns many times what they could have gained by selling in the domestic market.

Table 10.1   Economist 'Big Mac' index

Country	Price* in local currency	Implied PPP† of the dollar	Actual exchange rate 9.4.91	% over (+) or under (−) valuation of the dollar
Australia	A$2.45	1.09	1.27	+17
Belgium	BFr100	44.44	34.50	−22
Britain	£1.67	0.74	0.56	−24
Canada	C$2.35	1.04	1.15	+11
Denmark	DKr26.75	11.89	6.42	−46
France	FFf18.00	8.0	5.65	−29
Germany	DM4.30	1.91	1.67	−13
Holland	F15.25	2.33	1.88	−19
Hong Kong	HK$8.90	3.96	7.79	+97
Hungary	Forint115	51.11	75.12	+47
Ireland	I£1.40	0.62	0.62	—
Italy	Lire3600	1600	1239	−23
Japan	¥380	169	135	−20
Singapore	$2.80	1.24	1.77	+43
S. Korea	Won2100	933	721	−23
Soviet Union	Rouble10	4.44	1.74**	−61
Spain	Ptas350	155	103	−34
Sweden	SKr26	11.56	6.04	−48
USA†‡	$2.25	—	—	—
Yugoslavia	Dinar32	14.22	15.12	+6

*Prices may vary locally. **Commercial rate. †Purchasing-power parity in local currency; local price divided by dollar price. †‡New York, Chicago, San Francisco and Atlanta.
Source   Economist (1991) 'Big Mac currencies', 13 April, 78.

Table 10.2   Price differentials in Europe

Drug	Manufacturer	UK Price index	UK Sales ($m)	West Germany Price index	West Germany Sales ($m)	Italy Price index	Italy Sales ($m)	France Price index	Belgium Price index
Ventolin	Glaxo	1.00	95	2.09	16	0.52	—	—	0.81
Zantac	Glaxo	1.00	175	1.44	130	1.12	230	0.79	1.00
Tenormin	ICI	1.00	60	1.39	25	0.85	12	0.39	0.52
Voltarol	Ciba-Geigy	1.00	80	0.74	50	n/a	50	0.46	0.56
Adalat	Bayer	1.00	120	1.17	80	0.81	80	0.52	0.78
Zovirax	Wellcome	1.00	20	0.98	20	0.66	14	0.80	0.67

Source   Green, D. (1989) Learning to live with uncertainty. *Financial Times*, 6 November.

What they are doing is not illegal but unofficial and without the prior consent of the manufacturer or producer concerned. They undercut the manufacturer's official prices in the entry market concerned, thus affecting his profitability and his established channel of distribution, and perhaps also consequently bringing his brand into disrepute.

Electrical equipment, for example, has to be constructed to different standards across Western Europe; pharmaceutical preparations may also be slightly different for different national markets, but such differences are often glossed over in the search for large price differentials and quick profit. This is not marketing that is being practised, it is scanning for short-term market opportunity. Pharmaceutical price differences have already been signalled out by Cecchini in his report on the costs to the European Community of not having the standardization measures being adopted as 'Europe 1992'. Table 10.2, from the *Financial Times* outlines the significant differentials between markets for branded pharmaceutical products. While Portugal, Spain, France and Greece are relatively cheap, Benelux, Scandinavia, the UK and Germany are more expensive. The UK is the major consumer of re-imports of pharmaceuticals in Europe, estimates going as high as 10 per cent of UK drug sales being re-imports or in this sense 'grey'. No European country has a free market in pharmaceuticals nor is there as yet a single European approvals board. Companies still prefer to pursue multiple applications in several countries than wait to see whether in fact the concept of reciprocity works in practice. Delays can cost many months of lost sales to a rival that will never be made up. Equally, the politics of the situation, where one European Community country is expected to recognize the standards of another has not been fully put to the test as yet. Meanwhile, this practice of gray imports continues. An example of this is Zantac, produced by Glaxo of the UK and held to be the world's best selling drug. It is exported to Greece, then bought by the UK wholesalers in Greece and re-imported to the UK, where wholesalers, licensed by the UK Government, are alleged to relabel the packaging (*Financial Times*, 1989). Even more ludicrous is to consider that the sole buyer in the UK for prescription drugs is the UK Government itself.

As a strategy, parallel exporting is similar to encyclopaedia selling in that it forever requires a large pool of customers to be replenished as there are all kinds of barriers to repeat business. Those who sell in this way lack the resources of the original producer which they undermine. Product guarantees may, therefore, be suspect, and reliability of subsequent deliveries doubtful being dependent on the continuation of a price differential which in turn is subject to continued product availability on the domestic market at the same terms as before, plus the good fortune that currency devaluations do not take place to a degree that eliminates this differential.

Occasionally though, there is humour in what happens, as when a Glasgow wholesaler decided to take it on himself to export a Rowntree-Mackintosh confectionery product, 'Smarties', to the USA. To the best of his knowledge there was no registered brand on the US market of this name. Unfortunately, a very similar product was already on the US market, being produced by Hershey and known there as 'M and M's' (now in the UK). The consignment of a few hundred pounds weight of Smarties passed through New York customs and was met by the local agent, but no-one had checked the position with regard to the importation of confectionery into the USA. Clearly, the colour red could not be used, being specifically prohibited as it could conceal hard drugs. The result was that the local agent and his wife and children had to wade through this mountain of small brightly-coloured sugar coated chocolate drops to pick out all the red ones! Not knowing your market can be very expensive if you intend to stay in business.

Cavusgil and Sikora (1988) in Tables 10.3 and 10.4 chart out the proactive and reactive strategies that a company can adopt to counteract gray market channels. This is becoming now a critical management issue, since both the European Commission and the US Supreme Court (in 1988) have ruled on the legality of gray market imports.

Export market overheads

Overheads arise with the sale of goods to their final destination, the consumer. In international marketing, there are the costs of freight and of distribution if the goods are simply to be exported but remain competitive on the foreign markets; and, the problems of critical mass and economies of scale if the products are to be produced locally in that foreign market. The decision between exporting abroad and producing locally is often made more difficult by the frequent imposition by local governments of tariff and non-tariff barriers including 'countervailing duties', which seek to ensure that foreign goods will not undercut local manufacturers in price, this price differential now being replaced with the imposition of additional taxation to make its price similar to the nearest domestic competitor.

The cost of market entry and representation is an overhead, as is any required product modification or any modification to advertising and promotion, where modification is primarily for one market and cannot easily be replicated in whole or in part elsewhere. More will be said of this in later chapters. Bear in mind, though, that the exchange that is being effected between buyer and seller may often also require the use of an intermediary — whether an agent, distributor or even countertrade specialist — who has been engaged to realize cash from the manufacturer's or buyer's goods. Also, the terms agreed between buyer and seller may subsequently change the entire profitability of a contract if there is a dramatic rise or fall in currency exchange rates, world commodity prices, or imposition of any governmental action leading to 'force majeure' and the inability to complete a contract.

For the moment, then, we assume that the product being exported is one which is known to the domestic market. The company may then reduce the product price to the actual costs of production plus an overhead contribution, i.e., it is assumed that research and development originally invested in the product is now a sunk cost, which has already been recovered from

Table 10.3   Reactive strategies to combat grey market activity

Type of strategy	Implemented by	Cost of implementation	Difficulty of implementation	Does it curtail grey market activity at source?	Does it provide immediate relief to authorized dealers?	Long-term effectiveness	Legal risks to manufacturer or dealers	Company examples
Strategic confrontation	Dealer with manufacturer support	Moderate	Requires planning	No	Relief in the medium term	Effective	Low risk	Creative merchandising by Caterpillar and auto dealers
Participation	Dealer	Low	Not difficult	No	Immediate relief	Potentially damaging reputation of manufacturer	Low risk	Dealers wishing to remain anonymous
Price cutting	Jointly by manufacturer and dealer	Costly	Not difficult	No, if price cutting is temporary	Immediate relief	Effective	Moderate to high risk	Dealers and manufacturers remain anonymous
Supply interference	Either party can engage	Moderate at the wholesale level; high at the retail level	Moderately difficult	No	Immediate relief or slightly delayed	Somewhat effective if at wholesale level; not effective at retail level	Moderate risk at wholesale level; low risk at retail	IBM, Hewlett-Packard, Lotus Corp., Swatch Watch USA, Charles of the Ritz Group Ltd., Leitz, Inc., NEC Electronics
Promotion of grey market product limitations	Jointly, with manufacturer leadership	Moderate	Not difficult	No	Slightly delayed relief	Somewhat effective	Low risk	Komatsu, Seiko, Rolex, Mercedes-Benz, IBM
Collaboration	Dealer	Low	Requires careful negotiations	No	Immediate relief	Somewhat effective	Very high risk	Dealers wishing to remain anonymous
Acquisition	Dealer	Very costly	Difficult	No	Immediate relief	Effective if other gray brokers don't creep up	Moderate to high risk	No publicized cases

Note   Company strategies include, but are not limited to, those mentioned here.
Source   Cavusgil, S. T., and Sikora, E. (1988) How multinationals can counter gray market imports, *Columbia Journal of World Business*, Winter, 75.85

Table 10.4 Proactive strategies to combat gray market activity

Type of strategy	Implemented by	Cost of implementation	Difficulty of implementation	Does it curtail grey market activity at source?	Does it provide immediate relief to authorized dealers?	Long-term effectiveness	Legal risks to manufacturer or dealers	Company examples
Product/service differentiation and availability	Jointly, with manufacturer leadership	Moderate to high	Not difficult	Yes	No; impact felt in medium to long term	Very effective	Very low risk	General Motors, Ford, Porsche, Kodak
Strategic pricing	Manufacturer	Moderate to high	Complex; impact on overall profitability needs monitoring	Yes	Slightly delayed	Very effective	Low risk	Porsche
Dealer development	Jointly, with manufacturer leadership	Moderate to high	Not difficult; requires close dealer participation	No	No; impact felt in the long term	Very effective	No risk	Caterpillar, Canon
Marketing information systems	Jointly, with manufacturer leadership	Moderate to high	Not difficult; requires dealer participation	No	No; impact felt after implementation	Effective	No risk	IBM, Caterpillar, Yamaha, Hitachi, Komatsu, Lotus Development, insurance companies
Long-term image reinforcement	Jointly	Moderate	Not difficult	No	No; impact felt in the long term	Effective	No risk	Most manufacturers with strong dealer networks
Establishing legal precedence	Manufacturer	High	Difficult	Yes, if fruitful	No	Uncertain	Low risk	COPIAT, Coleco, Charles of the Ritz Group, Ltd.
Lobbying	Jointly	Moderate	Difficult	Yes, if fruitful	No	Uncertain	Low risk	COPIAT, Duracell, Porsche

Note Company strategies include, but are not limited to, those mentioned here.
Source Cavusgil, S. T., and Sikora, E. (1988) How multinationals can counter gray market imports. *Columbia Journal of World Business,* Winter, 75.85

Table 10.5   Short guide to export credit terms

Berne Union (International Union of Credit and Investment Insurers.)

This is an association of thirty-six export credit insurance agencies founded in 1934.

It works for sound principles of credit insurance and maintenance of credit insurance discipline in international trade.

Buyer credit

A financial arrangement under which a bank or export credit agency in the exporting country extends a loan directly to a foreign buyer or to a bank in the importing country.

Consensus Arrangement (The Arrangement on Guidelines for Officially Supported Export Credits)

The arrangement, which first came into force in 1978, is adhered to by twenty-two member countries on the Paris-based Organization for Economic Co-operation and Development (OECD).

It aims at limiting competitive subsidization of export financing. The arrangement sets minimum allowable interest rates and maximum repayment terms for officially financed or subsidized export credits of at least two years duration.

Mixed credits

Arrangements which cunningly bundle export credits with aid funds. The French are past masters at this art; the Americans are not amused. The Consensus Arrangement discourages their use.

Paris Club

The forum in which creditor countries meet with the debtor country to consider a request for rescheduling of payments on official debts. Terms hammered out in such meetings are embodied in an Agreed Minute, and then recommended to the governments concerned.

The club has no fixed membership and no institutional structure. It is open to all official creditors who accept its practices and procedures.

Short-term commitments

Export credit undertakings on which the credit terms do not normally exceed six months. In some cases the term may be as long as two years.

Supplier credit

A financing arrangement under which the supplier (exporter) extends credit to the buyer in the importing country.

Source   Export credit agencies seek new strategies, *Euromoney* (1989), February, 5–8.

domestic market sales. Theoretically, the seller may price lower for this product. If he does, however, he is guilty of dumping as he is no longer selling in foreign markets at a price comparable to that in his own domestic market. If existing domestic demand is sluggish, this strategy of dumping may prove beneficial. Firstly, it does not damage his share of the domestic market. Secondly, the lower prices abroad are usually acceptable on a short-term basis and are preferable to the much longer term damage which would result from offering similar product discounts on the domestic market. Once the precedent of offering domestic price discounts has been established, it is difficult to break. As a strategy, dumping may, therefore, protect the domestic price structure. Elsewhere, dumping may be predatory, as when an exporting manufacturer working with factor costs much lower than his local foreign market competitors, offers a low price in the foreign market with the intention of buying market share. Persistent dumping of this kind will lead to a restructuring of market supply as it will force many companies out of business, at which point the dumping company may then revert back to price levels closer to pre-existing market levels.

Dumping and anti-dumping measures have become issues of increasing concern to the world trading system, and the complexity of dumping within a global economy is seen from the six topics of an international symposium in Tokyo in 1989 concerning the need for reform in the GATT Anti-dumping Code (Matsumoto, Finlayson, 1990):

1 Symmetry in the comparison of normal value and export price.
2 Calculation of constructed value.
3 Sale prices below the cost of production.
4 Like products.
5 The definition and treatment of related parties.
7 Anti-circumvention measures.

The EC have outlined a new calculation formula which attempts to bring more fairness into dumping calculations. When export sales are made to distributors (whether related or not), only sales to unrelated domestic distributors should be used as a basis of normal values. Domestic prices to other categories of customers (dealers, end-users, etc.) should be omitted from calculations. In EC terminology, this new method is called 'selective normal value'. It means that export prices to distributors are now compared against domestic prices to distributors. Exclusion from the average normal value of usually high sales prices to other domestic clients, e.g., dealers, retailers, end-users, yields a lower normal value, thus, a lower dumping margin. However, where there are no, or not enough, domestic sales to unrelated distributors (e.g., when goods are sold by the manufacturer/exporter to a related distributor), the normal value is still calculated, as in the past by averaging all domestic sales prices on the open market, including those charged by a related distributor to unrelated customers. The EC imposes certain conditions for accepting to calculate normal values in a selective way. Respondents have to prove that their domestic unrelated distributors have functions clearly distinct from those of other categories of unrelated customers, such as dealers. Only if these conditions are met will selective normal values be admitted by the EC.

Export quotation terms

Trade results from the negotiations between a potential exporter and an importer. Either side will wish to maximize its return. Given an otherwise acceptable product, the first problem is currency. The exporting firm may wish to quote in its own domestic currency, particularly if it is inexperienced or it is a small firm uninterested in currency speculation and buying on forward currency markets. In any event, exporters will studiously seek to avoid inconvertible currencies and those experiencing now, or in the past, rapid depreciation and/or high inflation rates. The problem is lessened to some degree in that anticipated foreign currency earnings can often be sold on the forward market at a premium (depending on the currency).

The exporter will seek an export quotation which will lessen his responsibility or terminate it at the earliest opportunity. This can be one through a form of contract traditionally known as fob (i.e., free on board) or 'ex works'. On this contractual basis, it is the foreign client's duty to collect the goods from the manufacturer and arrange shipment himself. The exporter's responsibility is probably less here than that of a domestic sale. Importers prefer a cif (cost, insurance, freight) quotation or ex dock with a named port of importation. Either of these means that the responsibilities of the importer begin only when the goods are in his own country. Importers prefer these two means because they provide an instant price comparison between competing foreign exporters and local suppliers. (See Chapter 11 for a discussion on the new Incoterms.)

When the supplier company is faced with a cashflow crisis, money owing to them constitutes collateral and may be sold, i.e., factoring or else discounted or forfaited — not for the full value, but at a discounted value, of which more will be said later. Risk may be covered by national export credit insurance schemes which cover governmental lines of credit, plus commercial and industrial projects and exports worldwide for a fee based either on the company's global insurance business as in the case of the ECGD or on the risks inherent in the market concerned. The situation changes frequently with countries moving up and down the insurance scale, either in terms of wealth (as happened with the Eastern European bloc, the Soviet Union being reclassified among the wealthy nations). The insurance terms for a market will be influenced by perceived exposure to risk in that market; or changed economic market conditions which affect the local market's ability to repay; as well as by the export credit agency's total portfolio and exposure.

Foreign currency invoicing and financing

When a UK supplier sells abroad he can either price in sterling, in which case he will be sure of receiving the exact price requested, or else price in a foreign currency and bear an exchange risk. The exchange risk arises since national currencies continually fluctuate one against another and even when one country will devalue, this will not be uniform against all other countries. So currencies may weaken and find themselves devaluing against stronger currencies, or, they may appreciate relative to other currencies, or remain stable irrespective of currency movements elsewhere. Sterling experienced a 20 per cent devaluation against the US dollar within the first few months of 1985, and Japan had to devise a new commercial strategy when its currency was revalued by 35 per cent against the US dollar. Except in extreme cases, the more usual is for a few percentage points of difference although such

Table 10.6   OECD consensus credit guidelines

Countries of destination	Maximum repayment terms
Category I: Relatively rich	Five years; but after prior notification in accordance with paragraph 14 b) 1), eight and a half years;
Category II: Intermediate	Eight and a half years;
Category III: Relatively poor	Ten years.

Source   OECD (1990) *The Export Credit Financing Systems*, 4th Edn, Paris.

Table 10.7   Volume of business supported by official export credits[1] (SDR Millions, credit value)

Country *Volume of export credit repayment term over five years*	1982	1984	1987	1988
USA	2,008	1,542	772	548
Canada	1,489	903	455	478
France	4,465	4,321	1,544	4,131
Germany	2,035	745	789	868
Italy	630	513	233	1,359
Japan	3,112	728	669	382
UK	2,539	645	744	560
Seven Major Countries	16,278	9,397	5,206	8,326
All OECD Countries	18,792	10,783	6,304	9,414
All OECD (US $)	20,747	11,455	8,152	13,652

[1] Data reported to the OECD. SDRs were used for this table to minimize the effect of US dollar exchange-rate fluctuations.
Source: Letovsky, R. (1990) The export finance wars. *Columbia Journal of World Business*, Spring/Summer, 25–34.

differences may be crucially important in high-value industrial contracts. The solution for the foreign buyer is, therefore, to consider buying forward foreign exchange markets.

Foreign currency is sold either at the spot rate, which is the daily rate prevailing on the day of the requested exchange transaction, or 'forward' for any number of months ahead, usually three, six or nine. An exporter may wait until he receives payment for his goods and then convert it at the spot rate. However, production and delivery lags often mean a few months have elapsed since the initial order was taken and, while it is possible for an exporter to speculate on future movement of foreign currencies, he is as liable to lose as to win. Much better to stipulate a fixed sum in an agreed currency and transfer the exchange problem to the buyer. Forward rates of exchange remove further uncertainty because the bank agrees to buy the exporter's foreign currency payment and change it into sterling when it falls due in six months' time. The important point to note here is that the rate of exchange is specified and known to the exporter when the forward contract is made. Accordingly, he can assure himself of his return plus perhaps benefit from a possible upturn in the value of the foreign currency relative to his own in the intervening six-month period. The forward rate will, therefore, specify a premium or discount over the spot rate, meaning that the financial markets expect that particular currency to appreciate or devalue over that given period.

The advantages of foreign currency invoicing include the following:

- The ability to invoice in international currencies such as the US dollar which may be more attractive to buyers in the country concerned.
- The buyer is relieved of exchange risk where the price quotation is given in his own currency.
- When sterling is at a discount on the forward exchange markets, an exporter can sell his

expected foreign currency receipts forward for more sterling than he would receive at currently prevailing spot rates. This may enable him to quote a more competitive price in foreign currency or may provide him with a higher profit than would otherwise be the case.

Another point is that it is increasingly common for finance to be provided in foreign currency. One way of minimizing exchange risk is to borrow the currency in which the contract is invoiced. Provided there is no default, this means that the debt outstanding will be covered. Financing in foreign currency may also allow the exporter to obtain cheaper supplies of finance credit, depending on relative interest rates. The UK Government has actively promoted the use of foreign currency financing to ease pressure on the international role of sterling, and the ECGD has had a ceiling on prospect finance, beyond which underwriting will only take place in a foreign currency. However, interest rates may lead the unwary into thinking that foreign loans are attractive, but if, for example, sterling swings sharply against the deutschmark or French franc, repayment of loans in these currencies could prove to be particularly expensive when the buyer does not have any earnings in that currency.

Methods of payment

Many exporters still rely on overdrafts unconnected to the company's export business, but overdrafts are for short-term needs and must be repaid on demand. In the following pages we shall be discussing the use of credit and export finance with and without recourse to the exporter.

Payment in advance

Payment may be either cash with order (CWO) or cash on delivery (COD), but this has very limited application and is quite rare.

Open account

As this is based purely on trust, it offers the least security to the exporter, so should be limited to the most credit worthy customers, as well as subsidiaries and affiliates. Seventy per cent of UK exports are said to be paid for in this form, but this may be explained by the high degree of internationalization among UK firms who may, therefore, simply be transporting goods still within the company by exporting to subsidiaries and affiliates overseas on open account. It saves money and procedural difficulties, but increases risk. It is popular within the EC. Goods are sent to an overseas buyer who has agreed to pay within a certain period after the invoice date, usually not more than 180 days. Consignment Account is a variation of Open Account where the exporter retains ownership of the goods until they are sold.

Bills of exchange

A bill of exchange is defined as 'an unconditional order in writing, addressed by one person to another, signed by the person giving it, requiring the person to which it is addressed to

Table 10.8   Export credit agencies, relationship of government, and services offered

Country	Organization		Insurance	Loans
Australia	Export Finance and Insurance Corporation (EFIC)— a Division of the Australian Trade Commission	Division of a statutory authority	X	X
Austria	Oesterreichische Kontrollbank AG (OKB)	Statutory body reporting to the Ministry of Finance	X	X
Belgium	Office National du Ducroire (OND)	State guaranteed public agency	X	
	L'Association pour la Coordination du Financement a Moyen Terme des Exportations Belges (Creditexport)	Non-profit joint venture involving public and private sector institutions		X
Canada	Export Development Corporation (EDC)	Crown corporation wholly owned by the Government of Canada	X	X
Denmark	Eksportkreditradet (EKR)	Governmental council responsible to the Ministry of Industry	X	
	Dansk Eksportfinsieringsfond (DEFC)	Corporation owned jointly by the Central Bank of Denmark and various private sector banking associations		X
Finland	Export Guarantee Board (VTL)	Government agency reporting to the Ministry of Trade and Industry	X	
	Finnish Export Credit Ltd.	Joint stock company majority owned by the Republic of Finland, with minority holdings by private sector banks and firms		X
France	Compagnie Francaise d'Assurance pour le Commerce Exterieur (COFACE)	Semi-public joint stock company	X	
	Banque Francaise du Commerce Exterieur (BFCE)	Public institution		X
Germany	Hermes Kreditversicherungs AG/Treuarbiet AG	Private sector consortium operating for the account of the federal government	X	

Country	Institution	Description			
	Kreitanstalt fur Wideraufbau (KfW)	Corporation majority owned by the federal government with minority ownership by various governments		X	
Italy	Sezione Speciale per l'Assicurazione del Credito all'Esportazione (SACE)	Section of the National Insurance Institute, a statutory authority	X		
	Mediocredito Centrale	Public financial institution supervised and financed by the Ministry of the Treasury		X	
Japan	Export Insurance Division (EID) Ministry of International Trade & Industry	Division of a government ministry	X		
	Export-Import Bank of Japan	Government financial institution		X	
Netherlands	Nederlandsche Credietverzekering Maatschappij N.V. (NCM)	Privately owned consortium, reinsuring political as well as medium- and long-term risks with the Dutch government	X		1
Sweden	Exportkreditnamden (EKN)	Official agency of the Swedish Government			
	AB Svensk Exportkredit (SEK)	Joint stock company owned by the Swedish government (50 per cent) and the private sector (50 per cent)	X		
UK	Export Credit Guarantee Dept. (ECGD)	Government department responsible to the Secretary of State for Trade and Industry	X		2
USA	Export-Import Bank of the United States (Eximbank)	Independent agency of the US government	3	X	

Notes: 1 The Netherlands does not have a designated official institution for granting medium- or long-term export credits. However, the Central Bank of the Netherlands does have an arrangement with Dutch banks which permits the banks to offer such financing at below market rates.

2 The UK does not have a designated official institution for granting medium- or long-term export credits. However, ECGD does provide guarantees to commercial banks for buyer and supplier loans with terms of two or more years.

3 The Foreign Credit Insurance Association, a consortium of private insurance companies, acts as the exclusive agent of Eximbank for short- and medium-term coverage.

Source   Letovsky R., (1990) The export finance wars. *Columbia Journal of World Business*, Spring/Summer, 25–34.

pay on demand or at a fixed or determinable future time, a certain sum in money to, or to the order of, a specified person, or to bearer.' The exporter draws a bill of exchange on an overseas buyer or third party as designated in the export contract for the sum agreed. When the customer signs it, it becomes 'accepted', and this means that the customer has accepted the terms and agreed to pay by the date designated in the document.

If the amount payable falls due on delivery of the goods, this is a sight bill, i.e., payable on receipt; otherwise the variation is a time bill which allows perhaps thirty, sixty or ninety days before payment falls due. For exporters, a 'sight' bill would be preferred to a 'time' bill as it would delay payment once the goods had already been delivered.

Letter of credit

Worldwide, letters of credit are very important and very common, although less so in Britain and the rest of Europe. According to a rather dated SITPRO estimate, 20 per cent of British exports are undertaken by letters of credit. However, letters of credit do not predominate in the countries of destination of the majority of British exports. Western Europe accounts for 56 per cent of British foreign trade; North America 15 per cent, and Australia 2 per cent. Thus, 78 per cent of British exports fall outside of this means of facilitating payment. A letter of credit (or documentary credit) is a conditional undertaking by a bank regarding payment. It is a written understanding by a bank (issuing bank) given to the seller (beneficiary) at the request and in accordance with the instructions of the buyer (applicant) to effect payment (that is, by making a payment, or by accepting or negotiating bills of exchange) up to a stated sum of money, within a prescribed time limit and against stipulated documents. A letter of credit offers both parties to a transaction a degree of security combined with a possibility, for a creditworthy partner, of securing financial assistance more easily.

The letter of credit is an undertaking by a bank and so the seller can look to the bank for payment instead of relying on the ability or willingness of the buyer to pay. It has three forms: revocable, irrevocable, and confirmed irrevocable. In its simple form, it is a conditional undertaking and so the seller must meet all his obligations. Only if all his obligations are met can he then demand payment. In its simple form, this is a *revocable credit* (now rare) which gives the buyer maximum flexibility as it can be amended or cancelled without prior notice to the seller up to moment of payment by the bank at which the issuing bank has made the credit available. An *irrevocable credit* is much less flexible and can only be amended or cancelled if all parties agree. A *confirmed irrevocable credit* means that a bank in the seller's country has added its own undertaking to that of the issuing bank, confirming that the necessary sum of money is available for payment awaiting only the presentation of shipping documents. While it guarantees the seller his money, it is much more costly to the buyer. Generally, the buyer pays a fixed fee plus percentage of the value, but where the letter of credit is confirmed, the confirming bank will also charge a fee.

The different forms of a letter of credit, therefore, have the following characteristics:

- They are an arrangement by banks for settling international commercial transactions.
- They provide a form of security for the parties involved.
- They ensure payment, provided that the terms and conditions of the credit have been fulfilled.
- Payment by such means is based on documents only and not on merchandise or services involved.

However, it is worth pointing out that a Midland Bank International Division survey of 1,200 letters of credit showed that because of mistakes in documents and delays, in one in every two transactions the documents are rejected by the bank on first presentation. This means that payment is denied and that in turn may produce a cashflow crisis for the seller, having then to resort to borrowing at high interest rates to cover perhaps a short-term cash crisis. The Midland Bank report found a quarter of all transport and insurance documents to be flawed and one in seven invoices to be incorrect. The total for this loss thus created (and this is for Britain alone) was £50m per annum in 1984, and it means also that 10 per cent of business previously regarded as secure was not now so secure. Given the high levels of computerization and the standardization of exporting paperwork with the introduction of UN overlays, such statistics are really unforgivable.

Leasing

Exporters of capital equipment may use leasing in one of two ways:

1 To arrange cross-border leases directly from a bank or leasing company to the foreign buyer.
2 To obtain local leasing facilities either through overseas branches or subdivisions of UK banks or through international leasing associations.

The second is a more common arrangement. In both cases, it may also be possible to take advantage of ECGD facilities.

With leasing, the exporter receives prompt payment for goods directly from the leasing company and at the same time avoids any recourse. A leasing facility is best set up at the earliest opportunity, preferably when the exporter receives the order.

Bonding

In some countries, in the Middle East particularly, contracts are cash or short-term. Whereas this is an ideal situation for suppliers, it means that the buyer loses some of his leverage over his supplier as he cannot withhold payment as elsewhere where contracts are of a longer duration. In this situation, a bond or guarantee is a written instrument issued to an overseas buyer by an acceptable third party, either a bank or insurance company. It guarantees compliance by an exporter or contractor with his obligations, or the overseas buyer will be indemnified for a stated amount against the failure of the exporter/contractor to fulfil his obligations under the contract.

Bonds are of three types which may be either conditional or unconditional (known as 'on demand'). With a conditional bond, the onus is on the buyer to prove default by the exporter. 'On demand' bonds can be called for any reason at the sole discretion of the buyer, whether or not the exporter has fulfilled his contractual obligations. ECGD has a scheme designed to provide cover for the issue of all types of bonds for overseas contracts which are worth a quarter of a million pounds or more, and are on cash or near-cash terms. At the same time a recourse agreement is concluded with the contractor so that if he is held to be failing in his duties, ECGD may have recourse to him. The three types of bond, then, are:

1 *Tender or bid bond* which provides the buyer with an assurance that the party submitting

the tender is making a responsible bid. If the contract is awarded to the bidder, the latter will comply with the conditions of the tender and enter into the contract. If he does not, the surety is liable to pay the costs incurred by the buyer in re-awarding the contract, subject to a limit of liability set by the amount of the bond. The amount may vary but generally represents between 2 and 5 per cent of the tender value.

2   *Performance bond* guarantees that the exporter will carry out the contract in accordance with its specifications and terms. The liability of the surety is limited to the total amount of the bond, which is generally 10 per cent of the contract price but can be as low as 5 per cent or as high as 100 per cent.

3   *Advance payment or repayment bond* — A buyer often requires a bond guaranteeing that if the contract is not complete, the surety will make good any loss suffered by the buyer as a result of making the advance payment.

Discounting and factoring

The factors are mainly owned by the large banks. They offer two services — invoice discounting and factoring. Invoice discounting is a means of financing whereby the exporter sells his invoices to the factor at a discount in return for up to 80 per cent of purchase price in advance. This service is most suited to exporters selling on open account with charges normally at a margin above usual bank borrowing rates. Payments are made by the customers to the exporter and customers are usually not aware of the invoice discounting facility with the factor. Bad debt losses are taken by the exporter.

The second service is that of factoring. The types of business likely to be acceptable for invoice discounters will be the same as for export factoring. The factor investigates the creditworthiness of customers and establishes credit limits. The exporter sells within the credit limits, and delivers to and invoices customers in the usual way, but sends a copy invoice to the factor. The factor maintains the sales ledger and also produces statements and reminders. If the exporter sells above the credit limit, this may be allowable, but the factor then has recourse to the exporter in the event of non-payment by the customer. Customers are asked to pay direct to the factor.

With factoring, the exporter is able to sell his export debts and relieve himself of the task of credit checking, ledgering, some documentation, and collection as well as usually eliminating any risk of bad debt or currency loss. Factoring companies do not usually purchase trade debts on terms exceeding 120 days, but some companies will exceptionally accept debts arising from contracts which provide for terms of up to 180 days. Thus, factoring is clearly most appropriate for exports on open account terms. It is used by exporters of all sizes and is particularly appropriate for those who are expanding rapidly. The factor charges a service fee of between 0.75 and 2.5 per cent of the sales value, depending on the workload and risk carried by the factor. The factor agrees to purchase without recourse the exporter's debts as they are invoiced, on terms up to 180 days, and to pay a proportion of the invoice value to the exporter immediately.

The advantages to the exporter of factoring include:

1   Only one debtor — the factor.
2   No sales ledgering necessary.
3   No need to credit check or credit insurance.
4   Non-recourse finance available.

5 Regular cash flow.
6 No foreign currency risk.
7 Substantial savings in staff and collection systems.

The disadvantages are:

1 Factoring companies are inevitably selective in their choice of client and of the debts they will factor. The country of distribution will be a major consideration.
2 The service charge may be greater than the cost of employing own staff and systems.
3 Contact with customers is reduced or eliminated.
4 As the business grows and the factor's charge becomes unacceptable, the exporter will have developed no in-house experience.

Factoring is simply a method of exchanging book debts for cash on an agreed and regular basis. Apart from smoothing cash flow, it increases working capital. Factoring is not lending. It does not increase a company's debt so banks have found it an ideal source of new business while small businesses see in it a means of easing cashflow difficulties. Between 1971 and 1981 total UK-based sales factored by the nine members of the Association of British Factors (ABF) increased from £200 million to £2 billion, a total which comprises the sales of more than 2,600 companies. Barclays Factoring pulled out of the factoring market in 1983. As Mr Burton of Barclays Factoring put it, 'In the recession climate factoring companies have to live with the problems of their clients.' Similarly, in 1990–91, many more have withdrawn from the factoring market, again as a result of recessional pressures.

Forfaiting

This was developed in the 1950s primarily by the Swiss bank group, Credit Suisse. The word is derived from the French term 'à forfait' which is a form of non-recourse financing which is always denominated in leading Western currencies. In Switzerland, 75 per cent of special trade financing is in the form of forfaiting while leasing accounts for 20 per cent and factoring for 5 per cent. Worldwide exports of between two and three billion US dollars are forfaited each year. It is estimated also that two-thirds are claims on the socialist countries of Eastern Europe and developing countries in Latin America, Asia, and Africa.

Forfaiting is an arrangement whereby exporters of capital goods can obtain medium-term finance, usually for periods of between one and seven years. Under this arrangement, the forfaiting bank buys at a discount bills of exchange, promissory notes or other obligations arising from international trade transactions. Promissory notes are the preferred instruments of payment because it is then possible for the exporter to free himself from all recourse obligations. The purchasing bank (forfaiter) may commit itself to buying promissory notes even before the supply contract is signed. A commitment fee is then payable.

For a transaction to be eligible for forfaiting, it has to carry an internationally known banking name as guarantor.

Unless the importer is of first-class undoubted financial standing, any forfaited debt must carry a security in the form of an 'aval', or unconditional bank guarantee acceptable to the forfaiter. This condition is of the utmost importance because of the non-recourse aspect of the business: the forfaiter relies on such a bank guarantee as his only security for lending. The bill or promissory note must also be unconditional and not dependent on the exporter's performance, since the forfaiter has no right of recourse against the exporter. The forfait agreement then carries 80–90 per cent of the value of an export, as 10–20 per cent is usually paid in cash at the time an order for capital goods is placed. The forfaiter must consider risk, liquidity, and the fixing of the rate of return. To spread risk in terms of size and also geographical region, larger forfaiting transactions in excess of US$2 million are often syndicated.

When the forfaiter accepts the business, he often gives a declaration waiving right of recourse to the drawer as by law the drawer always remains responsible for the payment of the bills. For the exporter, the most important advantage is that he can sell his capital goods on credit and receive cash payment immediately from the forfaiter, who then assumes the rights and responsibility for collection of the debt. The only disadvantage is the high forfaiting rate, but this is due to the fact that the forfaiter combines the service of a bank in financing with that of an insurance company in the assumption of risk, so the forfaiting role must include not only a margin for financing but also a risk margin. Forfaiting is being seen as particularly appropriate for the export of capital goods. It is medium-term business, unlike factoring, and could range from one to seven years, although in practice a forfaiting financier will impose his own limits determined largely by market conditions and assessment of the risks involved for particular transactions.

Forfaiting is carried out by discounting in advance the interest for the whole life of the credit, and is done at a previously agreed fixed discount rate: thus, the exporter receives immediate cash and is liable only for the satisfactory delivery of the goods, all other risks being borne by the forfaiter. It is primarily this latter fact, coupled with the fixed-rate nature of the business, which makes forfaiting generally a very attractive service to the exporter, although occasionally relatively expensive on a short-term view.

Barter and other forms of countertrade (CT)

Countertrade is a genuine response to a difficult world trading environment, although much disliked by banks and international institutions such as the IMF and World Bank. It is a means of payment for countries with limited reserves of convertible currency to purchase goods from the West, and pay partially in cash and partially in goods. There have been numerous conflicting estimates of the value of countertrade (CT). The term, now commonly used as an umbrella for all the increasing variants of goods-related payment, was previously (and wrongly) referred to as simply barter. GATT estimates countertrade to account for 8 per cent of total world trade, which would value it at $2 trillion (i.e., million million), but this is held by bankers to be grossly underestimating the situation. The Organization for Economic Cooperation and Development (OECD) estimates countertrade to account for 20 per cent of world trade, while Japan's External Trade Organization believes the figure may be as high as 30 per cent. Certainly, whereas in 1975 there were perhaps only ten nations involved in countertrade, the figure now exceeds one hundred. For Britain alone, it is estimated to be equivalent to 5 per cent of British exports, but this alone will represent £3 billion.

Countertrade (CT) has arisen because of:

1 Acute shortages of both foreign exchange and international lines of credit. Many developing countries are now no longer eligible for traditional medium and long-term export finance because of indebtedness to Western banks.
2 World markets for raw materials and low technology manufacturers are weak.
3 CT can be used to fight protectionism in developed countries.

	MNC seller strong (near capacity)	MNC seller weak (has excess capacity)
Buying country's currency strong	Sale made No CT needed	Sale made CT sometimes not requested
Buying country's currency weak	No deal Cash on barrelhead or seller goes elsewhere	Perhaps a sale CT needed

Figure 10.1   *Countertrade matrix*

Source   Elderkin, K. W., and Norquist, W. E. (1987) *Creative Countertrade: A Guide to Doing Business Worldwide*, Ballinger Publishing Company, Cambridge, MA, p.11

4 Fierce competition exists between Western exporters of manufactured goods and capital equipment.
5 Philanthropic and political attraction of bilateralism.

Countertrade is a generic term for a number of variants previously all collectively known as barter. Before discussing the variants, it is as well to remember that countertrade produces its own problems. Payment in goods is always a poor substitute for cash and even where the countertrade goods may be used within the exporting firm, there is a potential threat created to existing suppliers as well as the continual danger implicit in using a new supplier with unknown reliability in quality, reliability, and continuity of supply. The value of countertrade is increasing in both the developed and developing world, where in some instances, it has become mandatory. Indonesia, for example, has used a mandatory countertrade policy to increase her non-oil exports. However, the US at an annual Inter-Governmental Group Meeting on Indonesia (IGGI), which is composed of fourteen countries and four international aid organizations, attacked the countertrade policy for the following reasons (Maynard, 1983)

1 Countertrade degrades the contract process by focusing on countertrade requirements rather than price, quality and financing.
2 Countertrade raises prices for goods the Indonesian Government buys.
3 Countertraded goods will cause prices to fall on international markets which are based on supply and demand.
4 Countertrade is not tied to world demand; the market place is more efficient.
5 Barter is an antiquated system — a very rigid way to operate.
6 Competition for contracts is reduced because source companies choose not to participate in countertrade.

Countertrade involves the participation of specialists who may be found in major clearing banks as well as merchant banks, trading houses and many multinational corporations, including Ford which have specialist trading departments which will act on behalf of third parties for a commission (disagio). Countertrade does introduce its own problems, including increasing the cost of deals by 20 to 40 per cent (Michaels, 1989), and traditional supplied long-term displacement effects, particularly with regard to offsets. Nigeria's economy might have been different if it had actively pioneered the use of countertrade on a 'maxima' strategy basis rather than being an indecisive market follower, waking up to see more of its customers committed to other countertrade suppliers and fighting back only when the oil price falls below $20 (Asiwaju, Paliwoda, 1986). Long-term compensation agreements of high value may give rise to complaints of injury to the domestic industry and so, charges of 'dumping'. As countertraded goods are most often sold at a discount, this leaves them particularly vulnerable to a countervailing duty.

Antitrust legislation is another potential obstacle as the countertrade acceptance has introduced a distortion to the practice of free trade, so excluding other competitors. Taxation treatment in the home economy is yet another issue, whether to use the nominal sales price or the actual resale value of the goods in determining whether the exporter had a gain or a loss. Use of a foreign sales corporation may be one solution to allow deferral of income on the export sale, while any losses from the discounted resale of the countertraded goods could be used immediately by the parent to offset other income and reduce its taxes (Downey, Aldonas, 1985). Having said this, the US Government is also concerned with the growth in tax evasion, bribery, dumping and unfair competition as a result of increased countertrade activities (Michaels, 1989). Countertrade deals could be used to disguise bribes.

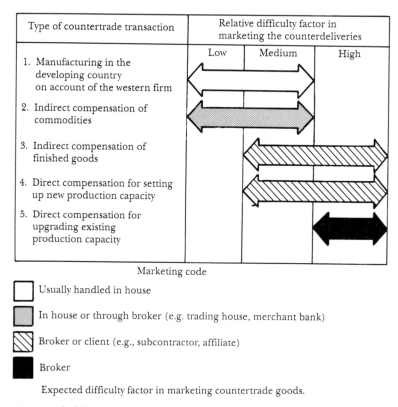

Figure 10.2   *Expected difficulty factor in marketing countertrade goods*
Source   Verzariu, P. (1985) *Countertrade, Barter and Offsets: New Strategies for Profit in International Trade*, McGraw-Hill, New York, p. 76

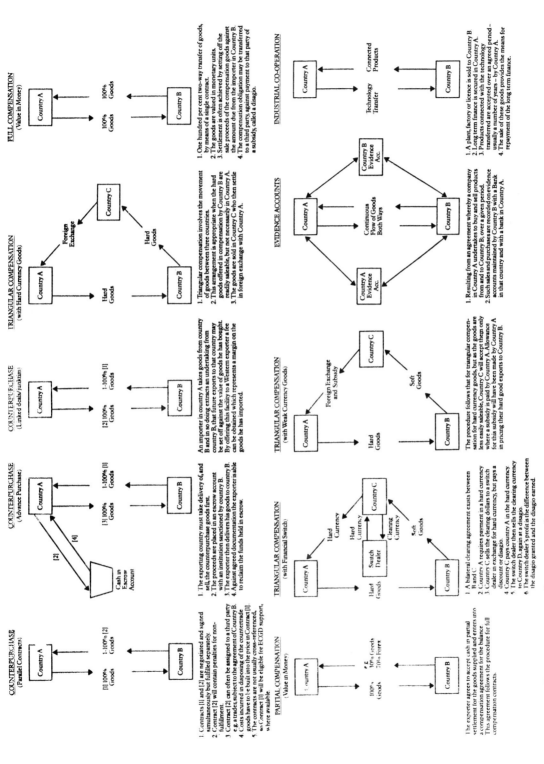

Figure 10.3 *Common types of countertrade*

Source Financial Times, 6 February 1985

In the different variants of countertrade described below, it is important to remember that the type of countertrade goods offered will depend on the nature and the economic priority to the importing nation of the product to be acquired. High technology and high priority items will be accompanied by more favourable countertrade offers than, for example, consumer goods where the capacity to trade has only been made possible through the offer of a countertrade. A proactive attitude towards countertrade can yield success because more than just acceptance of CT, it means being able to integrate CT into the customer offer, and planning ahead with how to accommodate a given value and volume of CT products, and how and where to dispose of it if it is not being used directly by the company or in the company's production processes.

Evidence accounts

Where the government of the country concerned has a mandatory countertrade policy for all foreign suppliers, companies will find it in their best interests to have all transactions duly noted by the appropriate authorities. The evidence account ensures compliance with this legislation and gives a parent group the flexibility of using one subsidiary's CT purchases to another subsidiary's possible advantage in that same country. Where subsidiaries often trade under different names from the parent holding group, the evidence account eliminates all possible confusion and may well work to the group's advantage. The evidence account operates like a revolving line of credit, where a debit is recorded for any exports to the country and a credit recorded for purchases made by the Western exporting company. An evidence account may prove to be useful for any company considering being in the market for the long term but not for a single deal.

Bilateral trading clearing account

This occurs where an exchange of goods is effected under a mutual payments agreement between two sovereign states. It also involves the central bank or centralized foreign trade organization which runs a clearing bank account in the name of the importing partner, and a designated bank that in turn pays the exporting partner in local currency. This currency is inconvertible, and so termed soft, as opposed to hard currency which is convertible. This gives rise to barter, where no surpluses and no deficits are allowable. When these deficits and surpluses exist because of an imbalance created by the economic structure of the two trading partners, an intermediary is often required to restore equilibrium, and this will then introduce 'switch trading'. It is politically expedient to have bilateral trading agreements, but they do not work in practice as developing countries are unable to find within themselves the goods and services in which they are most lacking. Bilateral trading agreements between nations are on the increase and GATT had voiced concern that this trend threatened its very structure.

Bartering

Barter stems directly from bilateral trading agreements. It is a means whereby one partner trades with another and all resultant balances are cleared by an exchange of goods and/or services. Bilateral trade agreements among the developing nations have traditionally been hailed as examples, but in case it should be thought that this is a phenomenon of trading with African and Asian countries, it exists also in trade within Europe – with Greece and Finland to take but two examples. The Swedish pop group Abba when they performed on a tour of Poland some years ago received a rapturous welcome everywhere they went, but payment for their services in potatoes! Abba undertook so much business with the communist bloc that they organized their own deals in Russian heavy machinery, Polish potatoes and Czechoslovakian glass among other things. Where the goods offered cannot be readily used for the supplier's own consumption, the next best alternative is to employ the services of a specialist trader who will off-load these unwanted goods on a third market and realize cash for them. His services will cost about 10 per cent, and the goods handled may require to be heavily discounted by up to 50 per cent in the case of machine tools, for example.

Switch trading or triangular trade

This arises where one of the two parties to a bilateral trading agreement introduces a third party who then accepts the obligation to take either surplus or unwanted goods offered under the bilateral agreement and thus, either convert them into cash or effect a further series of international exchanges before converting them into goods which are desired. An imbalance in a bilateral trading clearing agreement is simply being bought by a third party who purchases the goods at a discount of 20–50 per cent and then sells them, perhaps through a number of exchange deals, for hard currency which may then settle the trading account.

Compensation trading

Compensation trading is another variant whereby the form of contract will usually allow part payment in cash with the remainder being paid with a restricted selection of goods. The goods available are limited, and are usually restricted to those which could not readily be sold for convertible currency on Western markets. Again, the specialist services of a trading house may be necessary to realize cash from these goods. The Soviet Union commonly requests compensation trading but where the Western goods which they seek are earmarked for a national priority project and/or are of a high technology nature, then they will pay cash.

Buyback

'Buyback' is now a specialist term to denote the relationship whereby payment for a licensed product or process will partly be made by means of the resultant product. The duration of these contracts is usually in excess of three years and can extend to sixteen on occasion. Buyback has been found in Eastern Europe where Polish factories producing Fiat cars and International Harvesters crawler tractors discharge their obligations by sending back a certain volume of production to the original licensor. There are some advantages on either side. For the licensor, it ensures a new production plant coming on stream with no investment and with product price and quality control assurances. For the East European country, it means the acquisition of new or state-of-the-art technology; access to 'know-how', which is often only contained in the minds of company personnel as in production, for example; plus softer terms on which to buy technology with guarantees of exports of a fixed percentage. In order not to conflict with corporate suppliers elsewhere, the contract would have to ensure either that new markets were capable of being accessed or that transfer prices to the licensor were on a par or lower than those of corporate subsidiaries elsewhere, a margin being allowed for freight costs.

Parallel trading (or counterpurchase)

'Parallel trading' (or counterpurchase) is quite separate from parallel or grey exports. Parallel trading occurs, for example, when an East European country agrees to purchase a certain, usually much sought-after, item such as a computer for hard currency, but wishes to tie the seller down to spending some of the purchase price in his country. For desperately sought-after items, convertible currency is always available. What changes the situation slightly is that the convertible-currency contract will be dependent on the signing of a second contract, whereby the seller must agree to repurchase a certain amount of goods available from within the importing country – the goods thus purchased to be of an agreed value, say 30 per cent of the initial contract price. There is no limit on the goods that may be selected, so goods which are easily exchangeable on Western markets, including commodities, may be included. This form of contract perhaps incurs the least penalties, identifies new raw material sources of supply for the seller, but is reserved for much sought-after imports by the East European nations.

Escrow account trading

This form of trading involves a third party, usually a specialist countertrader. Exports are made only when sufficient funds have been raised from the sale of goods on behalf of the initial buyer. Payment is then made against the usual shipping documents from a blocked or trust account in convertible currency as normal. There are time lags involved in the sale of countertraded goods to release of the funds. Escrow accounts are generally used only where there is some doubt about the ability of the buyer and his countertrading specialist to complete a transaction.

Industrial offset trading

Two problems arise here. Either the exporter has undertaken a direct commitment to incorporate locally produced certain materials or components into his final products, sourced from within the importing country, or, in the second case, a sale may be tied to making 'best efforts' to assist the importing developing nation to earn hard currency and ease the cost of the sale. Through offsets, the importing nation can ensure that its domestic industries earn a percentage sale of the contract value. Important in the civil aircraft industry, offsets has, for example, ensured a place for domestic avionics companies in high technology aircraft contracts. As the value of these offsets can often exceed 100 per cent, there is a significant supplier displacement effect to be noted. This was the case with the Boeing AWACS deal concluded with the British Government, but then again, it is worth noting that perhaps 60 per cent of the final aircraft will be contracted out by the airframe manufacturer.

Swap trading

This does not affect the buyer, but is an arrangement purely between suppliers. For bulk products, such as oil, where the freight cost is heavy, it may be advantageous for one supplier to exchange an obligation to supply with another supplier closer to the market of the buyer in question. The producers save on transportation costs while the buyer has only to assure himself of the quality of goods delivered are similar to those for which he has contracted to pay. For commodities, such as oil, there are clearly defined standards which must be incorporated into the sales contract and must be complied with.

Transfer pricing

Transfer pricing essentially refers to the prices at which goods and services are transferred within the corporate family but across national frontiers, as they move globally – division to division or to a foreign subsidiary or minority joint equity venture. Generally, the clarity of the reference price for transfer becomes higher as the product concerned moves through the product life cycle (Cats-Baril, et al, 1988), but what constitutes acceptable international accounting practice has never been properly defined. Transfer pricing becomes a problem at two quite different levels – within the company and with trade with the outside world. Transfer pricing may be used to remove funds from a particular country by charging more for intra-corporate inputs. By means of low transfer prices, it could also be seen as a means to finance a foreign affiliate or to evade tax. The influences driving transfer pricing and its features are described in the Tables 10.9 and 10.10.

Where a profitable international division is an intermediary, there will be an inevitable conflict over price when goods move from the manufacturing division to the international division, and from there to the foreign subsidiary. For the manufacturing division, the price should be high enough to encourage a flow of products for export and build up export trade. Where service or follow-up is needed, the prices fetched should make the manufacturing division willing to provide it. Low prices have the effect of showing poor returns for the manufacturing division, and losses can have a very bad effect on morale. However, from the viewpoint of the international division, the transfer price should be low enough to enable it to be both competitive and profitable in the foreign market. The international division also likes to be able to register profits and successes. Given these conflicting objectives the only

Table 10.9   Transfer pricing features

- Higher transfer prices permit funds to be accumulated within the selling country.
- Tax haven affiliates have been used to drain off income from transactions between related affiliates.
- Not subject to withholding taxes.
- Creates surplus cash to pay off debt, finance new investment, or acquire securities.
- Permits purchase of foreign securities to diversify risk.

But:
- Can create difficulties in performance evaluation and with governments.

Table 10.10   Influences driving transfer pricing

- Market conditions in the foreign country.
- Competition in the foreign country.
- Reasonable profit for the foreign affiliate.
- Home country income taxes.
- Economic conditions in the foreign country.
- Import restrictions.
- Customs duties.
- Price controls.
- Taxation in the host country, e.g., withholding taxes.
- Exchange controls, e.g., repatriation of profits.

outcome can often be that of mutual antipathy and only stalemate as the company is no longer working together to a common objective.

Possible solutions for this impasse include eliminating one of these divisions as a profit centre. The manufacturing division could be judged on the basis of costs and other performance criteria instead of profit. Secondly, the international division may operate as a service centre rather than as a sales centre, but this downgrading may also have a bad effect on morale. Finally, it may be possible to use the international division as a commission agent, functioning purely on sales handled.

A second and more recent problem is that of transfer pricing to joint equity ventures. Should these ventures enjoy the same price levels as wholly-owned subsidiaries or pay a higher level of prices and, thereby, invite some political retaliation? This problem arises with the price paid for inputs from the corporation to the joint equity venture, as with supplies from the joint venture to the corporation. For the joint venture, which may well even be a minority joint venture holding for the corporation, price setting of components must be competitive with the corporation's subsidiaries elsewhere. The joint venture wishes to be profitable and to be successful in exporting. For the corporation this may occasionally present a dilemma over supplier choice. It may involve choosing among old, trusted suppliers; wholly owned suppliers, and untried, untested joint-venture partners – the corporate objective being not to upset anyone and yet act in the best way for the group overall.

To the outside world, an important feature of interest to politicians, consumerists, and trade unions alike, is the ability of multinational corporations to source globally for their components and sub-assemblies. To cite but a few examples, IBM does it in the computer industry, and so too, do multinationals in the automobile industry such as General Motors and Ford, but there are few sectors in which global products are not found, and these global products are, in turn, the final products of a very complex network of sourcing and multi-stage production.

Where this freedom exists, the possibility at least of abuse also exists. It is this that attracts the politicians. Host countries all over the world dislike losing tax revenue, yet there is the prospect here, that since the component engineering and pricing structure is company-specific knowledge, with multinational sourcing it may be possible to move funds in the transfer of goods to a foreign country. Transferring at a low price from a high-tax country would allow a subsidiary in a low-tax country to make a larger than normal profit, and would best serve the interests of the firm (see Table 10.11). Some African countries, such as Nigeria, introduced import inspection procedures as a result of repeated allegations of over-invoicing on imports. This has the effect of withdrawing money from the country.

Equally, restrictions may exist with regard to repatriation of capital or the payment of fees for consultancy, licences, etc., or there may just be the fear of losses through devaluation, high inflation, or impending tax legislation. In such circumstances, the prospect of being able to pay lower taxes in another country must seem enticing. In effect, it is difficult to establish whether these transfers are in fact taking place. For these reasons, customs authorities check values on imports more closely than exports, but it is not always possible to have a reference point on the value of exports of either parts or components. Because there is an important political issue here, many multinationals, including Exxon, IBM and Caterpillar, actually publish a code of business ethics.

The strategic choices in transfer pricing are either then to transfer at direct manufacturing cost, which may seem suspect to the local country's customs authorities; at cost plus, at a percentage to be agreed — usually of the order of 10 per cent; and finally, at arm's length.

Table 10.11 Tax effect of low versus high transfer price on net income

	Manufacturing affiliate	Distribution affiliate	Consolidated company
Low-markup policy			
Sales	$1400	(sales) $2000	$2000
Less cost of goods sold	1000	1400	1000
Gross profit	$ 400	$ 600	$1000
Less operating expenses	100	100	200
Taxable income	$ 300	$ 500	$ 800
Less income taxes			
(25 per cent/50 per cent)	75	250	325
Net income	$ 225	$ 250	$ 475
High-markup policy			
Sales	$1700	(sales) $2000	$2000
Less cost of goods sold	1000	1700	1000
Gross profit	$ 700	$ 300	$1000
Less operating expenses	100	100	200
Taxable income	$ 600	$ 200	$ 800
Less income taxes			
(25 per cent/50 per cent)	150	100	250
Net income	$ 450	$ 100	$ 550

Assumptions: Manufacturing affiliate pays income taxes at 25 per cent. Distribution affiliate pays income taxes at 50 per cent.
Source   Eitemann, D. K. and Stonehill, A. I. (1986) *Multinational Business Finance*, 4th edn, Addison-Wesley Publishing Co., Reading, MA.

Table 10.12   Tax-neutral impact of low versus high transfer price on flow of funds

	Manufacturing affiliate	Distribution affiliate	Consolidated company
Low-markup policy			
Sales	$1400	(sales) $2000	$2000
Less cost of goods sold	1000	1400	1000
Gross profit	$ 400	$ 600	$1000
Less operating expenses	100	100	200
Taxable income	$ 300	$ 500	$ 800
Less income taxes (50 per cent)	150	250	400
Net income	$ 150	$ 250	$ 400
High-markup policy			
Sales	$1700	(sales) $2000	$2000
Less cost of goods sold	1000	1700	1000
Gross profit	$ 700	$ 300	$1000
Less operating expenses	100	100	200
Taxable income	$ 600	$ 200	$ 800
Less income taxes (50 per cent)	300	100	400
Net income	$ 300	$ 100	$ 400

Assumption: Both manufacturing affiliate and distribution affiliate pay income taxes of 50 per cent.
Source   Eitemann, D. K., and Stonehill, A. I. (1986) *Multinational Business Finance*, 4th edn, Addison-Wesley Publishing Co., Reading, MA.

'Arm's length' pricing means in fact that one is charging company divisions the same amount as one would an outside client. 'Arm's length' is, therefore, the term that is most often quoted by bodies such as the International Chamber of Commerce, but it is also very difficult to narrowly define and to enforce, which probably also helps explain its popularity.

Conspiracy to fix prices

This is outlawed under anti-trust legislation in the USA and by the EC under Section 80 of the Treaty of Rome. Even so, tacit collusion is much more difficult to establish than is an actual price cartel. A US lawyer writing in the *Harvard Business Review* pointed out that even price fixers who do not get caught may not benefit by conspiring. His twenty-two rules on how to conspire to fix prices were:

1 Do not overlook the fact that the purpose of a price-fixing conspiracy is to make more money than you would have made had you not conspired in the first place.

2 Don't wink at a conspiracy unless it is a moneymaking proposition.
- Get your economists and analysts busy. Do not continue a profitless conspiracy. And, if you are not now conspiring, do not overlook this potentially profitable marketing technique.
- Price-fixing works best where no one conspirator has a substantial cost advantage over his co-conspirators.

3 Threaten a reluctant conspirator with antitrust action in order to bring him into the fold.

4 Before conspiring, be sure that follow-the-leaderism and conscious parallelism are not in the cards. They are much less dangerous and work every bit as well.
- A successful leader-follower constantly repeats the incantation: 'A like price is a competitive price, a like price is a competitive price ...'
- Conscious parallelism may be illegal but is certainly not as illegal as conspiring. Moreover, it is hard to prove.
  — Get to know your competitors.
  — Develop effective lines of inter-firm communication.
  — Get in the habit of announcing policy and price changes in the press.

5 Do not have more active conspirators than necessary; do not have working-level meetings if not absolutely necessary; and do not include personnel any further down the hierarchical ladder than is 100 per cent necessary.

6 Do not take notes; do not leave papers, work sheets, scratch pads, and the like lying around in hotel rooms and other meeting places; do not register under your real name; do not travel with your co-conspirators in public transportation to or from meetings; do not make conspiratorial telephone calls from your office (particularly if your efficient secretary keeps a log); in other words, do not keep records of any kind.

7 Do not meet in hotel rooms if you can avoid doing so.

8 Avoid complicated schemes.

9 Have some reason for meeting besides fixing prices.

10 Gripe a lot, especially about prices.

11 Develop a jargon.

12 Send up 'trial balloons'.

13 Remember that the line between overt price collusion and mere discussion of a common problem is fine indeed.

14 It is advisable to have at least one member in the conspiracy who has monopoly experience.

15 Do not be greedy.
- The share of each individual conspirator relative to the shares of any or all of his co-conspirators must be, by mutual consent, treated as irrelevant.
- If you are getting more than you would have expected, stay in; if you are not, get out.

16 Do not overlook the possibility of dividing up sales revenues at the end of a prearranged conspiracy accounting period, irrespective of who actually made the sales.

17 Have an adequate contingency fund for educating (or eliminating) mavericks.
- Avoid giving the appearance of selling below cost. It antagonizes the Federal Trade Commission.

18 Conspiracies work best on shelf items, but are least necessary. They work worst on special-order items, but are most needed in these areas.
- If you sell special-order items, do not allow your enthusiasm to conspire to get out of hand.

19 When the heat is on, get out.

20 Do not worry about being a good citizen and a respected member of the community. It will not help you.
21 Do not worry about avoiding identity of price. This will not solve your problem.
22 Get the advice of an experienced conspirator.

Cartels

In a domestic situation these are illegal but for exporting, they are permissible. This is similar to the consortium or federated approach to exporting, where several independent companies may choose to collaborate to make a concerted pitch to a target foreign market.

References

ACECO (1985) *Practical Guide to Countertrade*, Metal Bulletin Inc., Park House, Park Terrace, Worcester Park, Surrey.
Asiwaju, G. O. A., and Paliwoda, S. J. (1987) Countertrade in the North—South context: a marketing investigation. Paper to the Academy of International Business UK Region Annual Conference, Manchester, April.
Asiwaju, G. O. A., and Paliwoda, S. J. (1986) Nigeria rethinks the countertrade basics. *Countertrade and Barter Quarterly*, **10**, (3), 51–56.
Bank of England (1979) *Money for Exports*, London.
Bracher, R. N. (1984) If countertrade is inevitable make the best of it. *The Banker*, May, 69–71.
Capoglu, G. (1990) The internationalisation of financial markets and competitiveness in the world economy. *Journal of World Trade*, **24**, (2), 111–118.
Cats-Baril, W., Gatti, J. F., and Grinnell, D. J. (1988) Transfer pricing in a dynamic market. *Management Accounting*, **69**, (8), 30–33.
Cavusgil, S. T., and Sikora, E. (1988) How multinationals can counter gray market imports. *Columbia Journal of World Business*, Winter, 75–85.
Department of Trade and Industry (1985) Project Export Policy Division, *Countertrade: Some guidance for exporters*, London, July.
Didier, P. (1990) EEC anti-dumping: the level of trade issue. *Journal of World Trade*, **24**, (2), 103–110.
Dow, F. (1990) *Understanding Documentary Bills and Credits: A Practical Guide for Exporters, Importers, Forwarders and Bankers*, Croner Publications Ltd., Kingston Upon Thames, Surrey.
Downey, A. T., and Aldonas, G. D. (1985) US legal implications of countertrade deals, *International Financial Law Review*, September.
Duhan, D. F., and Sheffet, M. J. (1988) Gray markets and the legal status of parallel importation. *Journal of Marketing*, **52**, (July), 75–83.
Economist (1991) Big Mac currencies. 13 April, 78.
Edwards, H. (1980) *Export Credit*, Gower, Aldershot.
Eeckhoudt, L., and Louberge, H. (1988) Export credit insurance. *Journal of Risk and Insurance*, **55**, (4), 742–750.
Eitemann, D. K., and Stonehill, A. I. (1986) *Multinational Business Finance*, 4th edn, Addison-Wesley Publishing Co., Reading, MA.
Elderkin, K. W., and Norquist, W. E. (1987) *Creative Countertrade: A Guide to Doing Business Worldwide*, Ballinger Publishing Co., Cambridge, MA.
Euromoney (1989) Export credit agencies seek new strategies. February, 5–8.

Farley, J., Hulbert, J., and Weinstein, D. (1980) Price setting and volume planning by two European industrial companies: a study and comparison of decision processes. *Journal of Marketing*, **44**, (I), 46–54.

Feinschreiber, R. (1984) How equipment manufacturers can profit from export cartels. *Journal of Information and Image Management*, December, 62–63.

Financial Times (1983) Barclays pulls out of factoring market. 10 February.

Financial Times (1982) Factoring: a means to a cash flow end. 30 March.

Finanz, A. G. (1979) *The Forfaiting Manual*, Zurich.

Gray, F. (1988) Botswana, too, has exports. *Euromoney: Special Supplement − Forfaiting*, February, 511–515.

Green, D. (1989) Learning to live with uncertainty. *Financial Times*, 6 November

Griffin, J. C., Jr., and Rouse, W. (1986) Countertrade as a Third World strategy of development. *Third World Quarterly*, January, 177–206.

ICC (International Chamber of Commerce) (1979) *Guide to Documentary Credit Operations*, Paris.

Jones, T. (1988) Lines of credit supported by ECGD. *London Commerce*, June, 9.

Kaikati, J. G. (1976) The reincarnation of barter as a marketing tool. *Journal of Marketing*, **40**, (April), 19.

Laurie, S. (1989a) Eximbank's can of beans. *Banker*, **139**, (763), 77–78.

Laurie, S. (1989b) Export credit insurance. *Banker*, **139** (766), 44–46.

Laurie, S. (1989c) Paying a forfait. *Banker*, **139**, (766), 47–48.

Lawyer, J. Q. (1963) How to conspire to fix prices. *Harvard Business Review*, March-April.

Letovsky, R. (1990) The export finance wars. *Columbia Journal of World Business*, Spring/Summer, 25–34.

Matsumoto, K., and Finlayson, G. (1990) Dumping and anti-dumping: growing problems in world trade. *Journal of World Trade*, **24**, (4), 5–20.

Maynard, C. E. (1983) *Indonesia's Countertrade Experience*, American Indonesian Chamber of Commerce, New York City.

Michaels, P. (1989) Countertrade: a powerful global competitive strategy for US international traders. *SAM Advanced Management Journal*, Summer, 8–14.

OECD (1990) *Export Credit Financing Systems in OECD Member Countries*, Paris.

OECD (1987) *International Trade in Services: Securities*, Paris.

Okoroafo, S. C. (1988) Determinants of LDC-mandated countertrade, *International Marketing Review*, Winter, 16–24.

Oxenfeldt, A. A. (1960) Multi-stage approach to pricing. *Harvard Business Review*, July–August.

Paliwoda, S. J. (1989) Countertrading. In *Marketing Handbook*, Thomas, M. J., 3rd Edn, Gower, Aldershot.

Paliwoda. S. J. (1981) East-West countertrade arrangements: barter compensation, buyback and counterpurchase or 'parallel' trade. UMIST Discussion Paper 8105, March.

Pilcher, R. (1989) Managing exports effectively. *Accountancy*, **103**, (1148), 75–78.

Purchasing and Supply Management (1980) Will counter-purchase deals bring economic suicide? December, 25.

Rice, M. R. (1988) Four ways to finance your exports. *Journal of Business Strategy*, July–August, 30–33.

Sampson, R. T., (1964) Sense and sensitivity in pricing. *Harvard Business Review*, November–December.

SITPRO (1985) *Letter of Credit Management and Control*, London.

Strodes, J. (1989) Banana bonds: the movie. *Financial World*, 13 June, 24–26.
UN Economic Commission for Europe (1991) *International Buyback Contracts*, Geneva.
Verzariu, P. (1985) *Countertrade, Barter, Offsets: New Strategies for Profit in International Trade*, McGraw-Hill, New York.
Walmsley, J. (1989) *The Development of International Markets*, Graham and Trotman, London.
White, J., and Niffenegger P. (1980) Export pricing – an investigation into the current practices of ten companies in the South West of England. *Quarterly Review of Marketing*, **5**, (4), 16–20.

Key reading

ACECO (1985) *Practical Guide to Countertrade*, Metal Bulletin Inc., Park House, Park Terrace, Worcester Park, Surrey.
Cavusgil, S. T., and Sikora, E. (1988) How multinationals can counter gray market imports. *Columbia Journal of World Business*, Winter, 75–85.
Department of Trade and Industry (1985) Project Export Policy Division, *Countertrade: Some Guidance for Exporters*, July, London.
Didier, P. (1990) EEC anti-dumping: the level of trade issue. *Journal of World Trade*, **24**, (2), 103–110.
Dow, F. (1990) *Understanding Documentary Bills and Credits: A Practical Guide for Exporters, Importers, Forwarders and Bankers*, Croner Publications Ltd., Kingston Upon Thames, Surrey.
Duhan, D. F., Sheffet, M. J. (1988) Gray markets and the legal status of parallel importation. *Journal of Marketing*, **52**, (July), 75–83.
Elderkin, K. W., and Norquist, W. E. (1987) *Creative Countertrade: A Guide to Doing Business Worldwide*, Ballinger Publishing Co., Cambridge, MA.
Kaikati, J. G. (1976) The reincarnation of barter as a marketing tool. *Journal of Marketing*, **40**, (April), 19.
Laurie, S. (1989c) Paying a forfait. *Banker*, **139**, (766), 47–48.
Letovsky, R. (1990) The export finance wars. *Columbia Journal of World Business*, Spring/Summer, 25–34.
Matsumoto, K, and Finlayson, G. (1990) Dumping and anti-dumping: growing problems in world trade. *Journal of World Trade*, **24**, (4), 5–20.
OECD (1990) *Export Credit Financing Systems in OECD Member Countries*, Paris.
Paliwoda, S. J. (1989) Countertrading. In *Marketing Handbook*, Thomas, M. J., 3rd edn, Gower, Aldershot.
Paliwoda, S. J. (1981) East-West countertrade arrangements: barter compensation, buyback and counterpurchase or 'parallel' trade. UMIST Discussion Paper 8105, March.
UN Economic Commission for Europe (1991) *International Buyback Contracts*, Geneva.
Verzariu, P. (1985) *Countertrade, Barter, Offsets: New Strategies for Profit in International Trade*, McGraw-Hill, New York.
Zurawicki, L., and Suichmezian, L. (1991) *Global Countertrade: an annotated bibliography*, Garland Publishing Inc., New York and London.

11
Logistics and marketing channel decisions

Distribution channels and EDI

The advent of information technology (IT) has brought with it another popular acronym found in all spheres of commercial activity: EDI. This is electronic data interchange. EDI has been defined in the British International Freight Association (BIFA) Yearbook 1990 as, 'The transfer, by electronic means, of structured data from machine to machine, using agreed standards.'

Computers in this sense are being used, not just to receive and read a message, but to interpret it, notify the user of significant items, and update the user's database with the new information. BIFA estimates cost savings for EDI of anything up to 10 per cent of turnover. It affects everything now, including the movement of goods, the documentation which accompanies the goods and so, ultimately, payment as well. Later, we shall discuss the new INCOTERMS, but it is worth noting at this point that they were introduced because of a need to adapt to the use of EDI. Through an internationally agreed set of rules, such as INCOTERMS, buyer and seller can be assured of equality of treatment for EDI messages as for formal documents. As noted in Chapter 17, the Single Administrative Document has an EDI version and electronic signatures are now permissible.

EDI has had an important effect on buyer–seller relations in the international as well as national context. Payment delays used to be common and resulted from a variety of different sources. EDI has changed all that, permitting the use of plastic credit cards often as a preferred means of payment. For consumers, the ability to spend with credit cards while abroad has meant that one did not have to exchange more foreign currency than was needed. Also, some card companies offered their clients a more favourable commercial rate of exchange on their purchases abroad. It has made spending easier while allowing the banks to retain their monopoly over the exchange of foreign currency. In other areas, including defence, travel and entertainment, cards such as American Express, have been issued to air force pilots whereas once they would have had to carry an emergency cash 'float' in case of a sudden need to purchase fuel. Similarly for businesses, some credit card companies will offer a specialized detailed monthly statement of expenses. Service is generally improving, and much is due to EDI, but the ramifications of the EDI revolution have yet to be experienced in their entirety.

EDI creates a databank of clients and their spending patterns which has effectively transferred some of the traditional market power and knowledge of the manufacturers to those retailers offering store cards. Manufacturers, even with large market research expenditures, are often lacking the specificity of detail to be found in credit card databanks as controlled by major retailers. Instant processing and direct debit by means of computers being able to talk to each other across nations have made life more comfortable than before for the retailers. Direct connections with the credit card issuing company eliminate much of the fraudulent use that was prevalent before, although major differences between world time zones still mean that British credit cards stolen in Hong Kong, for example, will not be logged onto the central computer for some hours. Counterfeiting of credit cards has been especially prevalent in France, but as the companies seek continually to make their cards more secure, the costs of doing so escalate while the pressure for lowering charges to both card carrying clients and retailers continues unabated. France, meanwhile, is at the forefront of what is now called the 'smart card', a plastic card which incorporates a microchip rather than just a magnetic stripe. This allows the card itself to be updated if, for example, it carries a memory bank of transactions. It is more secure but more costly.

To the consumer, these EDI networks control individual access to credit. Information is exchanged but, provided no-one is blacklisted as a poor credit risk, there is no finite number as to the quantity of credit cards which one may apply for and receive. In the industrialized countries, 'plastic money', as it has come to be called, has changed shopping patterns. Instead of saving to buy a certain item as our parents used to do, one can buy it immediately on credit. A materialistic society is therefore being built on a foundation of credit. For the developing countries, the situation is the opposite: the more unstable the economy, the more likely the request for immediate payment in convertible currency. The disadvantaged are thus further disadvantaged because of an inequitable system where credit is most readily given to the affluent.

EDI has also had two other important effects relating to purchasing and procurement. Firstly, electronic cash register tills, and even more modern laser reading check-outs, require a computerized bar-coding system on all products. Would-be suppliers to these retailers are of necessity required to have a bar-code system in place before being considered as a supplier. This creates a further, and quite new, barrier to entry for prospective suppliers.

In a similar vein, many of the industrialized Western nations have developed a national system of quality awards, to recognize quality in manufacturing or service among the nation's industry. The need then to compete for a quality award, or to retain an existing one, places further additional barriers to entry for would-be suppliers. A company that presently has such an award will want to deal only with suppliers who either have such an award or are willing to enter for such a national quality award. This, in turn, creates a further effect, whereby Western developed nations are forced to trade with each other and cannot afford to go outside of a concentrated network of suppliers for fear of damage, real or perceived, to their quality-enhancing status.

In sum, EDI has created parallel interfaces with distribution networks, giving a new and prominent identity to certain key players internationally who were only peripheral before, such as in banks, finance and insurance, who are all now heavily involved to a degree that is quite unprecedented, busily engaged in lubricating new wheels of finance that they have created to help turn the machinery of industry.

The meaning of logistics

Logistics is frequently used as a term to describe the movement of goods and services between supplier and end-user. So, let us begin by tracing its origins. According to the *Oxford English Dictionary*, the term 'logistic' could be defined up to 1644 as 'pertaining to reason', then after 1706, 'pertaining to reckoning or calculations'. Its root meaning embraced the elementary processes of arithmetic. In its plural form, 'logistics' has become synonymous with distribution, but in this context it has strong military associations, it is 'the art of moving and quartering troops' (i.e., quartermaster's work), now especially of organizing supplies.

Military objectives, such as speed and continuity of supply, may be shared with marketers also, but the essential difference between marketing and the military is that military strategists have never considered the satisfaction of the final consumer of their product as being their main focus! Marketers also have to deal with competition, often in the shape of a much less visible target, and use weapons of persuasion which may be forceful in their own way, but are much less direct than armaments, take longer, are wasteful and so relatively more expensive when compared with military strategies.

As Davies (1987) pointed out, there are a number of differences between national and international distribution which complicate logistic matters. The documentation for an international sale:

1 costs more,
2 involves more parties,
3 involves higher financial penalties for errors, and
4 requires more data and knowledge.

The average export order size is much larger than the domestic order, requiring more rigorous credit checks and, often, the services of an intermediary. A way to deal with this is to develop a style of thinking of international logistics as a concept emphasizing the movement of the export order rather than just the movement of goods. It does, however, require close integration of export shipping and sales.

Market entry decisions have already been discussed in Chapters 6 and 7, so here, the intention is to examine the decision areas involved in moving goods from supplier to end-user when this involves crossing international frontiers; also, to compare channels of distribution within local markets for similar goods. It must be noted that worldwide the length of marketing channels as a result of increasingly necessary cost reductions, are becoming shorter between supplier and end-user, and so this entails a reduction in the number of intermediaries who require price maintenance or recommended prices, discounts and rebates. Overall, SITPRO in 1979 estimated distribution costs in the UK to account for over 20 per cent of GNP. Distribution costs are not uniform across markets, the peculiarly long and rather anachronistic distribution channels of Japan will be dealt with separately, however, in Chapter 15.

International conventions have meant that companies operating within Europe are finding that the border controls between member states have eased; regulations on packaging and labelling have been standardized throughout the European community; and the ever-increasing volume of traffic between member states has continually increased.

Cabotage remains a problem, however. Cabotage is the freedom for truckers registered in one EC country to collect and deliver loads between two points inside a second EC country. This is expected to change with the package of reforms built around the Single European Market for the end of 1992. Meanwhile, 35 per cent of trucks on EC roads travel empty. Cabotage remains a problem also for the airline industry to the same degree.

A draft resolution of the EC proposed in 1985, which would have allowed road hauliers to provide a maximum of two domestic journeys within the return journey to their own EC country of residence, was locked by road hauliers and trade unions within the EC member states. A compromise plan came into effect in 1990 to apply to the end of 1992, while a definitive scheme was being worked out. This introduced the concept of a cabotage quota of

15,000 cabotage permits for the whole community (1,107 for the UK), each being valid for a period of two months. A permit is required for each vehicle and is non-transferable between hauliers. Real problems arise over VAT accountability for the service provided; and on adherence to the laws and regulations in force in each member state which otherwise may well invalidate international insurance provided in another country.

Movement across frontiers

The speed employed in the transit of goods is an important consideration, but is cost relative to the total value-added of the item in question. Another factor is the packaging cost of the product for the export market, which will be affected by availability of materials and by local legislation relating, for example, to the recycling of containers for re-use and, therefore, requiring a system for deposits and returns into the distribution channels. Additional protective export packing is another factor, although in recent years, this has become greatly simplified by the use of low-cost polystyrene moulded to fit the shape of the product in question, and so adding very little extra weight. Packaging has also been simplified by palletization, which has moved into computer systems software available from packaging suppliers who can now design individual product packaging to maximize the number of units per pallet, and thus per container load. Palletization with shrink wrap protection, together with containerization, have served both to protect goods against damage and diminish losses through theft, otherwise referred to within the haulage industry as 'shrinkage'.

Logistics is primarily an operations research tool to contain costs and optimize efficiency in the flow of goods or services. However, within the channel between supplier and end-user, there will usually be a number of intermediaries, as with the car industry, where there may be an importer who is an agent or distributor, a national stockholding centre; then regional wholesalers; perhaps smaller wholesalers, then the retailers. The channel depends on the good or service itself, as much as local prevailing market conditions, but the exporter will be seeking the provision of accompanying services, as well as a return on his product and his general investment. The uncontrollable elements with regard to distribution are the political and legal systems of the foreign market(s); economic conditions; degree of competition prevailing in the given market(s); level of distribution technology available or accessible; the topography, i.e., the geographical relief of the country's market (i.e, whether mountainous or flat, well endowed with good highways, main rail routes and navigable rivers); and the social and cultural norms of the various target markets.

Changes in approach and practice brought about by multi-modal transportation apply equally to ordinary through-container transportation. Much of our deep sea shipping trade operates on a port-to-port basis with optional pick-up and on-carriage. There is separate liability for each stage of handling. The operations of booking and delivering goods are the same as for combined or multi-modal transportation, but when damage or loss occurs, the different system of separate liabilities creates some special problems. Export staff need to be aware of whether they are dealing with goods under a full combined transport bill of lading/waybill, or through a container bill of lading/waybill. Yet, as noted earlier, EDI is changing this documentation quite dramatically, creating internationally accepted changes towards simplification of procedures for electronic processing.

Air freight must now be seen as a form of through or combined transport. Yet, air carriers themselves employ other modes. Goods are trucked, for example, from Manchester to Heathrow under a flight number and air waybill, for onward carriage by air to their ultimate destination. Some airfreight to Western Europe is ferried over by surface, often by airlines themselves, under flight and air waybill routines. Some long-distance air-sea services are quicker than all-surface and cheaper than air alone. Any airfreight movement has by definition to be multi-modal as, unless both the exporter and importer are airport-based, a pick-up and delivery leg cannot be avoided. For all these reasons, export departments should see airfreight movement as door-to-door transport and organize their routines accordingly. For example, exporters should make sure that their air forwarders consolidate, fly, and break down consignments at destination as promptly as possible.

In rail freight, as in air or other through/combined transport movements, the export department is concerned with selecting the optimal means of delivering goods to the customer rather than the fact that part of the journey will be by a particular mode.

Marketing and logistics

Companies which practise marketing can also implement logistics. Recent studies by the Council of Logistics Management indicate that if a firm has an internal department handling

Table 11.1   Moving goods across frontiers: international transportation conventions

Sea transport:
   Hague-Visby Rules, 1968, which amended the Hague Rules, applies to all UK exports, but only to UK imports where the source country is party to Hague-Visby.

Road transport:
   CMR Convention, or the Convention on the Contract for the International Carriage of Goods by Road, devised by the UN Economic Commission for Europe, 1956.

Rail transport:
   COTIF/CIM Convention, 1985, mainly European in force. The railway authorities have quasi-common carrier status, the exporter designates the route to be followed.

Air transport:
   Warsaw Convention, 1929, and amended at the Hague in 1955, and in Guadalajara in 1961, but with fewer signatories.

Notes:
1 There is no convention relating to multi-modal transportation using a combination of the above.
2 These conventions have been incorporated into the laws of the UK.
3 The USA and Japan are not parties to the Hague-Visby Rules, and so goods from these countries imported into the UK will not be subject to the Hague-Visby rules, but the unamended Hague Rules.
4 There is no uniformity in the basis of the carrier's liability. Where multi-modal transportation has been used, there may be a contractual clause to the effect that any claims must be addressed to the carrier who had actual custody of the goods at the time of the loss (i.e., if that can be worked out!).

foreign shipments, the knowledge and experience of the personnel is often country-specific. Successful global companies face international markets as a team rather than as a group of disparate functions (Trunick, 1989). General Motors, who implemented an International Logistics Operation in 1977, differentiates between logistics and materials management (Kropfel, *et. al.*). The generic term at GM is materials management while international logistics focuses on transportation, packaging, and handling of both inbound and outbound freight. GM has forty-eight major overseas operations with plants in sixty cities. Nearly 200,000 GM employees live outside the USA, and overseas activities are responsible for the employment of an additional 60,000 within the USA. Outside of the USA, the largest market is Europe where GM own Adam Opel AG of West Germany; Vauxhall Motors of the UK; assembly and component plants in Belgium, France, Ireland, Netherlands and Portugal; and major new factories in Austria, France and Spain. At present, virtually every European car manufacturer uses some GM components.

GM are found to practise the total-cost approach, i.e., material availability is accorded first priority followed closely by cost accordance or reduction. Alterations in transportation and packaging, and the qualification of costs with possible alternatives, lead to reasoned trade-offs being made, prejudgments being made on total corporate benefit rather than divisional benefit alone.

International logistics have been introduced within GM to a divisional structure and must be held to be a good idea at local level rather than be seen as a measure of centralization, but they have not been able to accommodate and analyse the data necessary to its operations other than manually. GM is also constrained by what may be termed 'local infrastructure deficiencies', namely the state of port and local transportation and warehousing facilities – limited or no container handling at dockside, lack of weather-protected warehousing, different national groups in different regions or across political boundaries, and largely impaired highway systems. Taken together, the effect of these factors is cost multiplication due to delay, multiple handling, and damage in transit or storage. These difficulties are compounded because of the lack of internationally standardized documentation, such as with bills of lading or with invoicing (see INCOTERMS later).

On the one hand, customer service levels must always be attained or improved; on the other, the cost of GM logistical activities to support worldwide operations must constantly be reviewed. This leads then to the consideration of new institutional arrangements and modes of operation.

Cost of trade procedures and documentation

With regard to documentation, the work of SITPRO, the Committee for the Simplification of International Trade Procedures, has achieved international agreement on certain items of trade documentation, including pre-printed computer paperwork for trade procedures, which they design, print and sell, and offer systems software to complete multiple documentation tasks from one typing. The increasing availability of relatively inexpensive small business computer systems facilitates this, and avoids the need for stocks of preprinted stationery and forms which may become obsolete. SITPRO systems are designed to Universal Nations' design standards, incorporating the UN Layout Key. Computer models specifically adopted to international logistics applications are yet to be developed.

Information handling by traditional means has come under review because of questions over cost and efficiency. As to these costs, SITPRO in their 1979 report, *Costing Guidelines for Export Administration,* commented:

> In analysing the cost aspect of trade procedures and documentation, SITPRO has been able to draw on a number of assessments of the overall cost of present systems. We have, for example, the US figures following a detailed examination of procedures in that country which showed that the costs of compliance with essential documentation and procedures in typical export and import transactions were of the order of $7\frac{1}{2}$ per cent of the average consignment value – that is 15 percent for a full two-way transaction assuming that costs in other countries are not greatly different. As a very general indication of the possible orders of cost in the UK in export transaction, we would be quite ready to accept this ratio – viz one seventh of the value of the goods exported.

Since then, of course, there has been the introduction of SAD, the Single Administrative Document, within Western Europe, as a necessary precondition for the Single European Market post 1992. (This is discussed in Chapter 17.)

The use of INCOTERMS 1990

In 1936, the International Chamber of Commerce, based in Paris, established the first set of international rules for the interpretation of the most commonly used trade terms in foreign trade. These became known as 'INCOTERMS 1936', and later, additions and subsequent amendments followed to bring the rules in line with current international trade practices.

'INCOTERMS 1990' is the latest version, based on suggestions from governments, major importers, exporters and trade organizations, to adapt to the use of containerization, door-to-door intermodal transportation, roll-on/off and electronic data interchange (EDI). This revision incorporates some new terms as well as revising and dropping altogether some existing ones. The thirteen INCOTERMS can be grouped into four categories (see Table 11.3):

Table 11.2   Ten distribution myths

1 A channel of distribution is the movement of a product from the manufacturer to the ultimate consumer.
2 A channel's structure is determined by the characteristics of its products.
3 A distribution channel is managed by the manufacturer.
4 A firm should strive to maximize co-operation within its distribution channel.
5 The primary function of a warehouse is storage.
6 A firm sells to, or buys from, another firm.
7 Eliminating the middlemen will reduce distribution costs.
8 Administered channels are more efficient than non-administered channels.
9 A profitable channel is an efficient channel.
10 Planning distribution strategy is the responsibility of the distribution manager.

Source   Pearson, M. M. (1981) Ten distribution myths. *Business Horizons,* May-June, 17–23.

Table 11.3   INCOTERMS 1990

Group	Abbreviation	Explanation	Mode of transport usage
Group E: Departure	EXW	Ex works	Any
Group F: Main carriage unpaid	FCA	Free carrier	Air/rail
	FAS	Free alongside ship	Sea/waterway
	FOB	Free on board	Sea/waterway
Group C: Main carriage paid	CFR	Cost and freight	Sea/waterway
	CIF	Cost, insurance, freight	Sea/waterway
	CPT	Carriage paid to	Any
	CIP	Carriage and insurance paid to	Any
Group D: Arrival	DAF	Delivered at frontier	Any
	DES	Delivered ex ship	Sea/waterway
	DEQ	Delivered ex quay	Sea/waterway
	DDU	Delivered duty unpaid	Any
	DDP	Delivered duty paid	Any

Source   Adapted from: *INCOTERMS 1990*, ICC Publishing S.A., Paris. (Publication no. 460, © 1990 ICC)

1 E-terms, where goods are made available to the buyer at the seller's premises.
2 F-terms, where the seller is required to deliver goods to a carrier.
3 C-terms, where the seller contracts for carriage, but does not assume the risk of loss or damage after shipment.
4 D-terms, where the seller has to bear all costs and risks needed to bring the goods to the destination point.

INCOTERMS relate only to trade terms used in the contract of the sale, and are used to delegate responsibility to each party for customs clearance, packaging, inspection and destination.

The ICC, therefore, recommends that all traders wishing to use these new terms specify that new contracts will be governed by 'INCOTERMS 1990'. The ICC continues to operate an international arbitration service, and further recommends that resort to ICC arbitration be clearly and specifically stated in the contract; the incorporation of INCOTERMS alone in a sales contract does not constitute in itself an agreement to have resort to ICC arbitration.

Long-established terms, such as 'FOB', are now restricted to port-to-port maritime movement, and 'FOB airport' is among the terms now dropped. Multi-modal transportation should now use the term 'free carrier' or FCA. Similarly, CIF is also being restricted to maritime transportation. The more common term replacing CIF is 'Carriage and insurance paid' (CIP). The USA, with its own American Foreign Trade Definitions (AFTD), developed in 1919, and revised only once in 1941, has, according to BIFA (1990), agreed to accept INCOTERMS for international transactions.

Accessing foreign market channels of distribution

Distribution is an integral part of the marketing programme and so should always be considered in relation to product positioning strategy, price, and communications. On a comparative country market basis, little has been done since Bartels produced his work in 1963 on wholesaling and retailing in fifteen countries.

Direct comparisons are difficult between a home market and foreign target market because size alone is not an indicator of efficiency; competitive pressures surrounding the two markets will differ; and there may well exist a very sophisticated 'black' market or 'dual economy', where goods officially banned from entering the country may be found to be easily and openly available for either high prices or convertible currency or both. The same black market phenomenon occurs, too, where goods may be in short supply and not generally available at what may be officially determined governmentally controlled prices, but available neverthe-less to those willing to pay a little extra.

Technology also imposes change on channels of distribution as with containerization, in the use of freeports based near existing airports for the assembly and manufacture of duty-free goods for export only; and in electronic payments transfer, which allows for instantaneous transfer of funds between countries. Technology also affects the distribution channel ranging from vending machines to goods material handling, as in laser scanning of purchases at check-outs in large supermarkets or even larger hypermarkets. One example is the development of home shopping in Britain via a home computer keyboard link through the public telephone system to a specially converted television set, whereby it is possible to view data on anything from bank statements to household items, book holidays, transfer money in and out of bank accounts, and make purchases. This works through the British Telecom service, Prestel, which through a computer mainframe system gives a guide to goods on offer from the main retailing chains, and all companies including airlines, subscribing to the service.

Yet, it is still far removed from the sophistication of the French Minitel system, which opting for a penetration pricing strategy, succeeded in getting the necessary communications hardware into the majority of French households. Similar to a computer keyboard with a modem, it offers advantages over the British system in terms of speed and the total number of subscribers to it, whereas previously they would never have considered a telephone number. Most French advertisers now include a Minitel number for further information. Technology is changing also in the home, and marketers must take cognizance of this as growth in the percentage of the population with personal computers, microwaves, compact disc players, fax machines, and other consumer durables affects not only what they buy, but how they buy, in what quantities, and how frequently.

Distribution is also affected by environmental change whereby changes arise within the society itself in terms of consumer attitudes; available means of distribution; and the role that distribution is expected to fulfil. In many of the developed countries, the trend has been towards inner city decline in both industry and population, and towards the growth of suburbia. However, with near zero growth in population, this trend has been arrested, and is being reversed in some countries, Britain included.

Alternatively, environmental change may affect the profile of the channel, and the respective role to be adopted of the intermediaries who will be used, from importation or assembly, down to final sale to the consumer or end-user, and the relationships between these intermediaries and the manufacturer. The state may even decide that all importing has to be undertaken via a state trading enterprise.

Rising levels of personal disposable income in France created the postwar phenomenon of the hypermarket: an enormously large commercial shopping complex usually comprising a very large supermarket and general household departments, all located under the same roof on one ground level store located outside of town, and strategically positioned for major highway intersections. As an incentive, hypermarkets, such as the French chain Carrefour (which incidentally translates as 'crossroads'), operate petrol filling stations at their out-of-town locations which offer low-priced petrol for their customers as a draw to get them to visit their locations.

This quantum leap which France made in retailing with hypermarkets illustrates the fact that in distribution there can never be any guarantee against obsolescence. The hypermarkets in France have changed not only the buying situation for consumers, but also the selling situation for manufacturers, as the hypermarkets have become important customers for all the large manufacturing companies, and not just in food but for all the other items which they stock, such as domestic electrical equipment and clothing.

For the foreign company, the question of location will be important. There is the question of ownership and control, whether it be a matter of finished goods, inventory or assembly. Manufacturers may choose to extend into retailing, as some multinational companies, such as Singer and Philips, have done, or take part-ownership of channel intermediaries, whether wholesalers or retailers. It is also possible for a foreign company to engage in some other means of distribution, such as direct mail order involving lower costs against the fixed costs of shopfronts and retail staff. However, against this are the heavy costs of postage in some countries, together with high illiteracy rates and the fact that there may be a significant gap between dispatch of goods and receipt of payment. This lead time may create a cash flow problem for the company which is also to maintain high levels of stock, and herein lies another problem. Interest rates are not equal between nations. If borrowings are expensive and inflation is high, then, there may be no advantages whatsoever in direct mail order unless there are also important differences in local taxation. Other possibilities include exclusivity of sales for a retailer whether he is continuing with the manufacturer's name or having his 'own label' added, an area of operations that has been increasing significantly increasing over the past ten years in Western Europe.

In terms of transit of goods there is a wide variation in the possibilities on offer, not only of the mode of transportation, as already discussed, but also in terms of whether the company should decide to lease plant, equipment, vehicles, etc. – as is common in France or the USA – or buy, which would involve tying up capital. Aside from the relative advantages and disadvantages inherent in each respective method, there is always the guiding influence of competitive pressure to help shape the corporate decision as to the overall cost structure. (See Figure 11.1.)

It is accepted that to create sales it is necessary to have a communications package, but aside from the problem of devising a successful communications package that will make sense in a foreign country, there is the perennial problem of foreign market intelligence and feedback, other than in waiting for sales figures. Choice of distribution channel may inhibit or eliminate the flow of market information from the country concerned. One may expect to receive less information from an agent than from a sales subsidiary, and virtually no information to emanate from a distributor who has exclusive sales territory rights.

Questions as to packaging and the necessary barrier and promotional properties of products for export are dealt with separately in Chapter 9. For the moment, let us just bear in mind that for small retailers, the product packaging is also the promotional material he is most likely to use within his shop-wide displays. For the manufacturer, there are certain cost advantages in having a standardized product package design which is acceptable to several markets: it eliminates the need for separate designs for each market, allowing the firm to capitalize on its presentation which at the same time benefits the production area, facilitates transit and enhances corporate image and brand awareness internationally, as well as helping small retailers with regard to product recognition, storage and display.

Changing marketing perceptions of the customer

Perry (1989) interprets the market dynamic as leading to fierce competition, which will in turn force companies towards new and innovative distribution channels tailored to individual

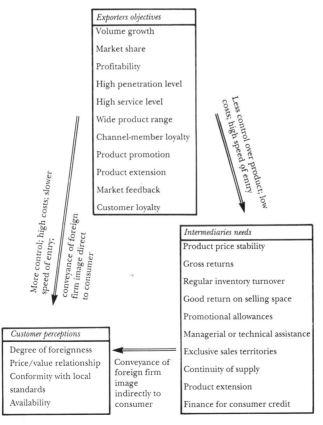

Figure 11.1 *Comparative objectives and channel member expectations*

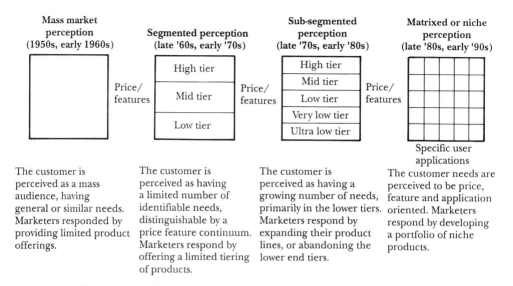

| Mass market perception (1950s, early 1960s) | Segmented perception (late '60s, early '70s) | Sub-segmented perception (late '70s, early '80s) | Matrixed or niche perception (late '80s, early '90s) |

Price/features   Price/features   Price/features

Segmented perception tiers: High tier / Mid tier / Low tier

Sub-segmented perception tiers: High tier / Mid tier / Low tier / Very low tier / Ultra low tier

Specific user applications

The customer is perceived as a mass audience, having general or similar needs. Marketers responded by providing limited product offerings.

The customer is perceived as having a limited number of identifiable needs, distinguishable by a price feature continuum. Marketers respond by offering a limited tiering of products.

The customer is perceived as having a growing number of needs, primarily in the lower tiers. Marketers respond by expanding their product lines, or abandoning the lower end tiers.

The customer needs are perceived to be price, feature and application oriented. Marketers respond by developing a portfolio of niche products.

Figure 11.2   *Changing marketing perceptions of the customer*
Source   Perry, D. (1989) How you'll manage your 1990s distribution portfolio. *Business Marketing*, **74**, (6)

market niches. This will result from a fine-tuning of the segmentation process that has been in force since the late 1970s, and is seen by Perry as being the only way for US companies to compete with foreign competitors who are all-too-often satisfied with occupying the lower end of any market. Figure 11.2 depicts on the right a matrix which pinpoints customer needs with greater accuracy, and will be serviced by a portfolio of a multiplicity of distribution channels, including non-traditional channels.

Channel intermediaries

The exporter's overall objective is to achieve some target rate of return on investment. The first point to consider is that irrespective of whether or not we use intermediaries in the channel between us and our final customers, the functions of a conventional or vertical marketing system do not change. In a vertical marketing system, the company is simply bringing 'in-house' certain activities which would be performed by others. It is still necessary to fulfil these functions, however. As we go down the channel, these functions change from design, production, branding, pricing, promoting, and selling, to a new set with a greater emphasis on functions, such as stocking, promoting, display, selling, delivery, and finance. Whenever a manufacturer looks grudgingly, therefore, at discounts offered to intermediaries, it is worthwhile remembering the importance and the cost of the functions that these intermediaries perform before deciding to bring these activities within the company. The cost savings, once the discount structure has been abolished and the activities have been brought in-house, may then only be marginal.

The benefits of using intermediaries have to be set against the disadvantages of loss of control. Primarily, where speed of market entry is important there may be instant access to a number of outlets, low selling costs, and the advantage of an experienced distribution outlet; but intermediaries, whether agents or distributors, may not give a product the attention which the manufacturer would like. Given that some of these intermediaries may be handling products for a number of companies, their motivation may lie more with the product earning them the highest returns in commission. This loss of control for the manufacturer is difficult to quantify. The manufacturer may not have any reasonable marketing objectives or sales projection figures established for the market in question, and so the intermediary may simply be a low-cost presence for an anticipated low level of sales. Control, though, is lacking. Information, too, is likely to be limited or biased in view of the fact that if the market is booming then the intermediary will only commit economic suicide by admitting it to the manufacturer, thereby inviting him to bring in his own sales organization and gear up for a future anticipated higher level of sales without intermediaries. Similarly, customer service may also be seen to be at risk. International warranties and brand awareness break down in markets where there is inadequate provision for service maintenance personnel and spare parts. Direct distribution avoids these problems but means a higher degree of investment is required, and perhaps also a greater length of time before a local sales team is recruited and trained for the task.

Avon Cosmetics maintain an approach of selling door-to-door wherever possible through a workforce of freelance agents who are also technically self-employed. Tupperware is another example of a US company that has been successful in transferring its house-party style of selling to other markets, including Japan. Elsewhere, the pattern seems to be that wherever direct control is not possible or desirable, settle for the next best alternative. In this regard, it is worth bearing in mind how Avon Cosmetics have traditionally sold their cosmetics into the CMEA countries, and how Marks and Spencer successfully export their name and branded product range into countries where they are not officially represented other than as a brand name administered by a distributor. Retailing, too, has become an international activity for many including Marks and Spencer, House of Fraser, and in franchising, Tie Rack, Benetton and Body Shop.

Identifying the intermediaries

Intermediaries may take various forms, but must also be acknowledged to be specialists of considerable experience, often with an important network of contacts in the trade in which they are based. They include importers who are wholesalers, importers who are cash-and-carry wholesalers; brokers; commission agents; exclusive distributors; sales offices; and international co-operative food and grocery distribution groups, such as the Dutch based VG and Spar purchasing associations, which have themselves undergone profound organizational change in recent years. Spar is a member of the Schuitema group, which is majority-owned by the Dutch supermarket chain, Ahold, but rival Unigro also maintains an equity stake, buying out through Sagara of Spain the Spanish wholesaler Penagrande, a supplier to independent Spanish Spar stores. In Belgium, the food distributor to Spar, Alimo, has been acquired by Unidis, a Belgian subsidiary of Unigro, which now controls two of the three Spar dealers in Belgium. In conjunction with Axel Johnson (Sweden), Spar is opening a chain of stores in Sweden. In Germany, Axel Johnson is an established supplier to Spar, having a joint equity stake in each other's organizations. Axel Johnson subsidiaries handle Spar's overseas import activities, including exotic and tropical fruits. A joint purchasing organization has now been created by the two companies, further integrating their activities.

VG, meanwhile, is actively developing its activities in Spain, but has operations also in Britain, Italy, Austria, the Netherlands and Ireland. The cash-and-carry concept proved to be short-lived and is now in decline within Europe, but the internalization of retailing is on the increase in Europe. Three leading European retailers: Argyll from the UK; Ahold from the Netherlands; and the French Group Casino have carried out a cross-shareholding deal to cement their European Retailing Alliance (ERA), and are looking at the possibilities for a European own-label family of brands. ERA is now looking at the potential for packaging, labelling and distribution across Europe.

Relating to channel strategy, consideration should be given to the number, quality and type of outlets to be used, whether it would be possible for some of the distributive tasks to be absorbed at an acceptable cost, or, if not, which form of channel intermediary has to be engaged. Retailing operators at the lower level include door-to-door hawkers and street traders. Service levels, too, are important, but these may be influenced also by the margins made available to the intermediary by the manufacturer. Where labour is cheap and plentiful, labour may be hired. Elsewhere, the move is to automate. Allied to service level is the question of inventory, and who exactly takes title to inventory and so responsibility for it as this is a cost to be borne in the foreign market. Finance and credit is another area for joint participation by both manufacturer and intermediary, as is promotional activity at the local level. Complete standardization of distribution strategy across markets is difficult to achieve because of customer expectations as to service levels, and the competitive pressures existing to ensure that one either responds to these local demands or else leaves the market. Expectations with regard to customer service levels vary as do local distribution costs. The problem for the company is one of demand management – developing a distribution mix which best serves each market in which the company is represented.

Total customer satisfaction is a good route to pursue. Figure 11.3, Perry (1989) depicts exactly how a matrix distribution may work towards the salvation of US companies threatened by foreign distributors. Short product cycles, low profit margins, changing management emphases, have led to a neglect of the customer. In aiming for value-added niche marketing, companies will not take customers for granted, but instead, seek to provide full service and need satisfaction through traditional and non-traditional channels, exploiting all opportunities for synergy along the way through perhaps even a strategic business alliance.

Parallel exporting

This arises where domestic wholesalers begin to perceive greater returns available from the illicit exports of goods intended only for the domestic market. (See Figure 11.4). It undercuts the manufacturer's official recommended price abroad, upsets his foreign distribution channel members, and does damage to its corporate image at home, even where product specification between the two countries is different and is partly reflected in the price differential. The dilemma for the manufacturer is whether or not to withdraw the product from sale in the domestic market when this foreign leakage appears excessive. Alternatively, increasing the domestic product price may have a similar effect, making these illicit exports much less profitable, but will also develop hostility among domestic customers, consumer groups and even government in the home market.

The market may be upset by illicit exporting by wholesalers or retailers, as in seen in Figure 11.4, but sometimes also by third party clients who then resell to the manufacturer's distribution outlets in another country. L'Oreal has suffered the embarrassment of cut-price outlets in France obtaining supplies from third countries and supplying French customers at levels lower than L'Oreal's officially recommended prices. In the UK, there have been many similar examples. In the 1960s, Mallory Batteries tried to raise prices in the UK to discourage parallel exports taking place from the UK and ruining its official market price and distribution structure in France and Germany, but this ran foul of a UK Government Prices Board. Johnny Walker Red Label, a product of the Distillers Company, a subsidiary of Guiness plc, was taken off the UK market while it was still brand leader, and remained off the shelves for six years

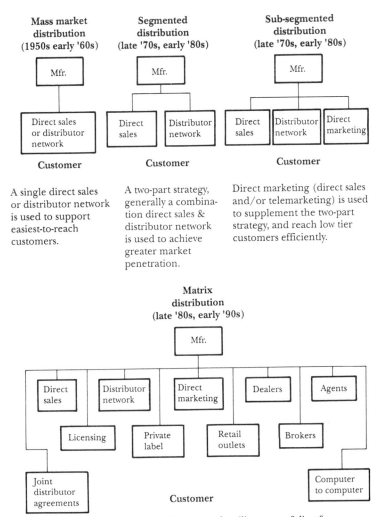

Figure 11.3 *Changing distribution strategies*
Source Perry, D. (1989) How you'll manage your 1990s distribution portfolio. *Business Marketing*, **74**, (6)

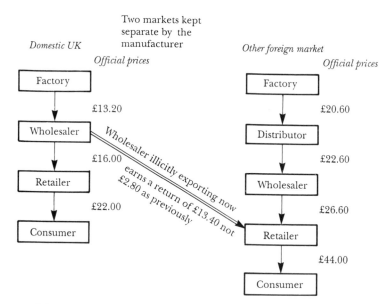

Figure 11.4 *Parallel or 'gray' exports*
Note   To understand parallel exporting, one has to remember that countries have different tax regimes and that many have recommended resale price mantainance structures — making it virtually impossible for multinational corporations to standardize price structure — and that, combined with rises and falls in foreign exchange rates, can create market opportunities for channel members

between 1977–1983, before a change of policy restored it. Red Label had had 12 per cent of the market when it was withdrawn. It was later reintroduced to a stagnant home market at the expense of Distiller's other brands (White Horse and Haig) and with no assurance that parallel exporting would not begin again.

The EC response to parallel exporting is clear from the *Hasselblad (GB) Ltd. versus Commission supported by Camera Care Ltd case*. Significantly, Hasselblad was prosecuted by the EC Commission in 1981 for infringing Article 35(1) of the EC Treaty, which relates to free trade. The Commission contended that Hasselblad acted in concert with six sole distributors to prevent, limit, or discourage exports of Hasselblad equipment between the members states, and that the sole distributorships and selective distribution system operated, constituted infringements. Hasselblad (GB) Ltd. was fined £93,642. On appeal, this was reduced to £45,218. The aim of the concerted practice had been to prevent imports into the UK of Hasselblad cameras intended for Camera Care, and as such, constituted a flagrant breach of the EC competition rules. Although corporate responses to combat parallel exporting may include withdrawing the product or raising the price in the domestic market, the probability of EC intervention has also to be considered.

Waddington, the famous British games manufacturer, won an interim injunction in the Singapore High Court, in 1984, against a local importer, which involved the seizure of 559 sets of Monopoly and 531 sets of Cluedo purchased from a British export house and intended for sale and at a discount on sets made by Waddington in Singapore. However, in January 1985, when the case for the injunction was heard before the Singapore High Court, it was ruled that the injunction could not be continued as there had been no misrepresentation. The overall situation, therefore, is far from satisfactory. Although some consumers will temporarily enjoy the parallel importers' lower prices, there are important ramifications for foreign investment generally; for the licensed distributors who have invested in goodwill; and the employment effects if a company like Waddington chooses to leave the foreign market as a response, particularly as this action will likely then be taken by other companies as well.

To turn to a more complex case of parallel exporting, that of the pharmaceutical products, here we have a case where opinions are divided about the morality of behaviour on either side. Firstly, to take the industry case, the British pharmaceutical industry believes that it is losing sales worth about £100 million a year to companies which buy British-made drugs cheaply in Europe and bring them back to the UK for re-sale. One large chemists' wholesaler, UniChem, which claims about 22 per cent of the wholesale market, said that they are losing about 10 per cent of their sales to parallel importers, costing them about £3 million per month.

Not all wholesalers have the same view, for in 1984, the Association of Pharmaceutical Wholesalers was formed by thirty-two wholesalers with the aim of establishing a code of conduct, lobbying MPs and mounting a public relations drive. Benefits obviously flow to the wholesalers and retailers making better margins on these parallel imports. The pharmaceutical companies, themselves, have been active in trying to curb the practice by conducting a campaign emphasizing the dangers to the public of being supplied with foreign language packaging or possibly slightly differently formulated products.

One such wholesaler, Malcolm Town, and his company, Maltown, were fined £6,360 in 1982 for illegally importing drugs which were then sold to health authorities and chemists for as little as half the manufacturer's list price. The defence counsel argued the case that the interests of his client were very much allied to the public interest. Nine summonses related to the import and sale of three drugs: Septrin, used for treating bronchitis, manufactured by the Wellcome Foundation in Kent; Zyloric, prescribed for gout, made by the Wellcome Foundation in Spain and imported via Malaga and Gibraltar; and, Daonil, given to sufferers of diabetes mellitus, which was a Swiss drug which arrived in Britain via Hong Kong. The drugs were all being imported on a commercial basis and sold on a commercial basis. All drugs were sent for laboratory analysis before being sold on the British market.

The pharmaceutical price structure in Britain is a national agreement between the National Health Service and the industry, and allows for a 21 per cent profit margin to include advertising, promotion, research and development. However, this margin and this style of structure is sufficient to create disparities with other neighbouring European markets. Maltown has a list of about 300 imported drugs sold at prices substantially lower than the Health Service pays chemists for prescriptions. The trade price for 500 Septrin was £52.58, while Maltown obtained the same amount for £20.53. Zyloric was £14.34 for 100 milligrams, while Maltown paid £6.34, and Daonil listed at £9.64 for 5 milligrams was only £4.37. Ventolin, an asthmatic inhaler, made in Britain by Glaxo Pharmaceuticals costs the Health Service £2.91 per prescription, but Maltown reimports the drug at £1.45 from France, Belgium and Italy.

Although corporate responses to combat parallel exporting may include withdrawing the product or raising its price in the domestic market, the UK Government refused to act in the case of these pharmaceutical products, and was actually bringing the case against Maltown. The position of the EC with regard to this phenomenon has, therefore, to be considered. Any action viewed as being in restraint of free trade will invite EC intervention, and so the EC has maintained the right for individuals to shop around for cars and bring them back into their home market as a personal import. This right extends also to companies engaged in parallel or 'gray' exporting, which is not illegal and which the EC views as being an extension of free trade within the community.

Use of freeports

Freeports are based on the concept of manufacturing or processing in bond free of all taxes, but whereas this has always been the case with the manufacture of whisky, which by law required a minimum of three years to mature before being ready for sale at home or abroad, freeports usually exist only for the export market.

The term 'freeport' may be potentially misleading as the facility does not have to be based around a seaport, but may be a transit zone, a free perimeter or free trade zone. The terminology changes from country to country and includes free trade zone (FTZ), export processing zone (EPZ), free trade area (FTA), investment promotion zone (IPZ), export promotion processing zone (EPPZ), or just freeport. The term freeport will be used here as being synonymous with all the other terms presently in use.

Although freeports have attracted a good deal of attention in recent years, the concept started with the Phoenicians 3,000 years ago, although the first in Europe was Hamburg in 1189, when Frederick I, then Holy Roman Emperor, granted a charter to the City of Hamburg, releasing it from the payment of customs duties. Others then followed. The freeport concept in the Middle Ages included Bruges, Antwerp, Amsterdam, Marseilles, London and Genoa, which were important transhipment centres, as direct routes did not generally become available until a few centuries later with the steamships and the creation of established conference lines.

In 1982, there were reputed to have been more than 350 of these freeports around the world, of which more than two-thirds were in the developing world. They are estimated to have accounted for 9 per cent of world trade in that year and to have generated six million jobs. In a global economy experiencing little growth, this particular area of operations appeared to offer some promise, and, for this reason, the British Government in 1984 announced that six freeports were to be established, each based alongside an existing port or provincial airport, as with Belfast Airport, Prestwick Airport, Liverpool Port, Southampton Port, Cardiff Port, and Birmingham Airport, none of which is an important throughput centre in its own right, there being no equivalent of a Rotterdam among them. With the sole exception of Liverpool Port whose business is now 75 per cent import, all of these UK freeports have failed. Elsewhere, other examples of thriving foreign freeports in existence include: Hong Kong, Singapore, Hamburg, Amsterdam, Stockholm, Bombay, Sri Lanka, South Korea, plus an estimated forty-plus in the USA.

The Adam Smith Institute in London estimated, in 1985, the total number of freeports at over 500, and estimated that they accounted for 10 per cent of world trade in 1981 and would account for more than 20 per cent of world trade by 1985, but it should also be noted that the Institute's publication was the proceedings of a one-day seminar aimed at the promotion of freeports in the UK (Pirie, 1983).

Manufacturers operating within a freeport are not liable to the import duties or the local or governmental taxes which manufacturers would pay immediately outside of the freeport area, but items which are assembled or produced within this area are not allowed to enter the domestic economy without payment of appropriate taxes and duties. It is on this understanding, that the goods are produced solely for export, that these tax concessions are made. Freeports outside the UK also have certain important competitive advantages, such as relief from controls on planning, health and safety regulations, and legislative controls related to the work place. Wages are generally 10–30 per cent of those in industrial nations.

Benefits of freeports

1 Better cash flow for firms located on freeports. Goods may be imported from overseas for transhipment to other markets without the bureaucratic 'red-tape' of customs entries and subsequent withdrawals. Firms located on the zones do not pay customs duties or valued added taxes (VAT) on goods brought into the zone until they are released on to the domestic market. An exception to this arrangement is that VAT is payable on transactions between firms operating on the freeport, but this can be recovered if the goods are subsequently sold to customers outside the domestic market.
2 Freeports provide firms with a degree of flexibility in adjusting to market conditions. Goods can be stored on the zone without payment of duty until market prospects improve. For commodities which experience volatile shifts in pricing, this can be important for the nation state where it is economically dependent on a single commodity crop.
3 Freeports provide firms with freedom from paperwork and bureaucratic legislation.
4 Firms located on a zone can benefit from the concentration of export facilities therein, including customs, insurance, packing and certification.
5 Firms located on a zone could benefit from savings in insurance and policing costs. Freeports are fenced-in areas policed and monitored by customs authorities and provide a safe and secure environment for firms.
6 Freeports could make a substantial contribution to employment. They could be a source of both direct and indirect employment opportunities. Increased investment from both home and foreign sources would make a direct contribution to employment. Raw materials can be processed into finished or intermediate goods which may then be re-exported. In addition, there would be indirect job creation in the form of jobs attached to storage, warehousing and servicing the zones.

The test for success of a freeport is whether it is able to create investment additional to that which already exists, and avoid merely a dispersal and relocation of firms within the domestic economy. Another point is that intra-EC trade is already exempt from duties and so, for the concept to work within the EC it would have to involve a manufacturing or assembly activity which relied on imports outside of the EC for re-export outside of the community. Because of this, and because of the geographical location of Britain which is not close to any non-EC country, British freeports would, obviously, hold little attraction for Continental European firms. As regards the VAT position, this has changed recently in the UK, whereby importers now have to pay VAT immediately on receipt of goods rather than when they are sold. As to the freeport, no tax would be paid on entry to the freeport zone, which has its own customs entry and departure points. Only if freeport goods were to enter the domestic market would payment of taxes and duties be required. Thus, should the expected strong export orientation fail to materialize, the future for the freeport is one of only becoming a bonded warehouse for imported goods awaiting entry to the domestic market.

The Malaysian port of Pasir Gudang is now operating in a freeport. Malaysian shippers are now able to store their goods at Pasir Gudang while waiting for prices of any particular commodity to pick up before exporting. It is hoped, too, that this freeport undergoing a $70 million expansion plan will take some traffic from neighbouring Singapore. It handled 3 million tonnes with a capacity of 3.5 million tonnes but has a projected capacity of 7.6 million tonnes. Taking another example, Bausch and Lomb base their European distribution at Schipol airport in the Netherlands, which allows them day-to-day delivery throughout Europe. Similarly, periodicals such as, *Time, Newsweek, Business Week,* are also distributed from this same base; getting information to the consumer on time necessitates air freight, but here, using a major hub and spoke airline distribution network, based on Schipol airport, there are the potential savings of bulk distribution.

The concept has spread so widely that there was even a suggestion in *The Times* of 5 January 1987 that the granting of freeport status to Port Stanley in the Falkland Islands might be one way to attract investment to those islands. Yet, like the UK freeports, it is difficult to see any clear locational or communications advantage for a Port Stanley freeport. (See Table 11.4).

The enabling environment for freeports

In a 1983 study of freeports, Dr. Madsen Pirie identified the following as 'defining conditions'.

Duties

There should be no duties or tariffs on goods entering the freeport.

Taxation

Taxation must be lower in the freeport than outside. Pirie cites the examples of Belgium offering remission on seven different taxes affecting business, and of Spain offering no VAT and other concessions within the freeport at Cadiz.

Regulation

A lower level of regulation within the freeport to attract foreign traders unable or unwilling to cope with domestic regulations. Different standards, including product quality and packaging standards, can apply within the freeport. In some countries, this extends to there being less or even no legislation in respect of health and safety at work, and less or even no wage and price controls.

Independence

Freeports should be free of government and be independently managed by an authority largely outside the scope of political manipulation).

Table 11.4   Freeport advantages compared

UK	Rest of the world
Concentration of exporting facilities, e.g., customs, certification, packing, forwarding	Concentration of exporting facilities, e.g., customs, certification, packing, forwarding.
Freedom from customs duty	Exemption from all forms of taxation
Politically located around declining centres of high unemployment	Located alongside thriving ports and airports
No locational advantage of freeport as entire EC is a free trade area	Exemption for wage and welfare legislation
	Generous depreciation allowances
	No trade unions (as in South Korea)

Product life cycle and distribution

Companies each have their own corporate culture and corporate ethic – a belief as to which product and geographic markets they should be in, and which channels of distribution are most suited to their needs. However, the competitive environment does not always respect this, and in a multi-modal channel situation a product may have to forge a new channel of its own or die. Some companies have remained in business through the maintenance of a highly individual channel of distribution such as Tupperware or Avon, as mentioned earlier. The product life cycle works in two ways: first, with regard to the product itself and its stage in the cycle, and secondly, with regard to its distribution. Falling unit manufacturing costs leading to lower unit selling costs are signals of a mature product reaching into the saturation and decline phases of the cycle. Distribution, therefore, has to be adjusted accordingly, to minimize costs but still ensure product availability, and this may lead to a change in the choice of channel used; perhaps, following the example of Perrier Water in the USA, from low-volume specialist health foods or delicatessen retailer to high-volume general trader such as a supermarket chain. A differential advantage that may be identified when moving into a new channel or distribution away from the mainstream competition may not only provide a breathing-space, but a clear gain in profitability if it means leadership of a small but lucrative market segment now being accessed by means of this new distribution channel. Mature goods which are now being distributed in this way through new distribution channels include in Britain: spectacles and telephone sets now available from department stores. Distribution channels, therefore, need to be reviewed periodically, and not just with regard to cost of the product, but with regard to customers as well (Combs, 1987). Even mature products, such as fruit and vegetables, can benefit as Del Monte found in Florida when they met with a five-fold increase in the sale of pineapples after providing retailers with a pineapple cutting machine. Research had shown that consumers would buy more pineapples if only they knew how to peel them. Del Monte showed them the way (Fortune, 1985).

Channel changes, according to Lele (1986), follow the product life cycle pattern, and the two factors responsible for this are value-added by the channel and the growth rate of the overall market. Firms then lose market share if they do not switch channels as the technology

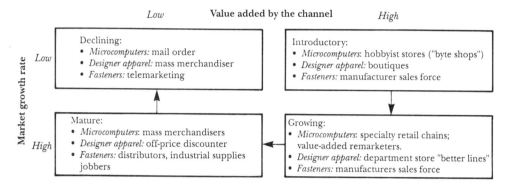

Figure 11.5   *Value-added versus market growth matrix*
Source   Lele, M. (1986) Matching your channels to your product's life cycle. *Business Marketing*, **71**, (2), 60–69

matures. In Figure 11.5, Lele (1986) shows how the two variables, 'value-added by the channel', in terms of services provided to the customer before, during and after the sale, and 'market growth rate', which measures the speed with which demand for that type of product is growing, interrelate. Each of the four cells corresponds to a stage of the PLC. The microcomputer is an example of a product that has moved very quickly from introduction to maturity, so while the dedicated vertical distributors were trying to expand, distribution was already moving to the mass marketers, the major retailing chains and mail order catalogues. Keeping pace with the PLC, marketers must shift to less costly channels that do not add as much value, or provide as much service, in order to achieve the strategic objectives of expanding the market and maintaining market share.

Lele emphasizes that no one channel will be sufficient to manage a product through all the stages of its development; that marketers ought to be responsive to market changes, and change their channels accordingly and not assume ever that channels can be controlled, even with attempts to motivate channels through volume-oriented financial incentives to intermediaries doomed to failure before they start.

Performance measures have to differ with each stage of the PLC and this, too, has to be considered in planning overall channel strategy. It should certainly lead to some further consideration before the implementation of an incentive campaign.

Returning to an Ansoff Mark I matrix of new and existing markets and new and existing products, Band (1987) offers a few recommendations:

1 Market modifications:
   ● convert non-users
   ● enter new market segments
   ● win competitor's customers
   ● encourage more frequent product use
   ● develop more usage per occasion
   ● develop new and more varied uses
2 Product modifications:
   ● quality improvement
   ● features improvement
   ● style improvement

3 Marketing-mix modifications:
- prices
- distribution − more or different channels?
- advertising
- sales promotion
- personal filling
- services

References

Bailey, R. (1983) Should you set up in a freeport? *The Accountant*, June, 18–20.

Balasubramanyam, V. N., and Rothschild, R. (1985/1984) Free zones in the United Kingdom. *Lloyds Bank Review*, October.

Band, W. (1987) Achieving success in mature markets requires careful approach. *Sales and Marketing Management in Canada*, **28**, (2), 16–17.

Barks, J. V. (1989) Logistics broadens its horizons: international survey results. *Distribution*, **88**, (10), 58–63.

Basile, A., and Germidis, D. *Investing in Free Export Processing Zones*, OECD.

British International Freight Association, *Exporter and Forwarder: The Professional Guide 1990*, Feltham, Middlesex.

Buckingham, L. (1984) What freeports could be worth. *Marketing Week*, **7**, (24), 34–35.

Combs, L. S. (1987) Fine-tuning the channels. *Journal of Business and Industrial Marketing*, **2**, (1), 61–65.

Consolidated list of goods subject to security export control. (1989), *British Business, Supplement*, March.

Cutting the costs of international trading. (1984) *British Business*, 23 March, 560–564.

Davies, G. J. (1987) The international logistics concept. *International Journal of Physical Distribution and Materials Management*, **17**, (2), 20–27.

Davies, W., and Butler, E. (1986), *The Freeport Experiment*, Adam Smith Institute, London.

Eastman Kodak streamlines its product distribution (1990), *Industrial Engineering*, **22**, (9), 42–44.

El-Ansary, A. I. (1986) How better systems could feed the world. *International Marketing Review*, **3**, (1), 39–49.

Foster, T. A. (1990) The language of foreign trade. *Distribution*, **89**, (10), 89–90.

Houlihan, J. B. (1987) International supply chain management. *International Journal of Physical Distribution and Materials Management*, **17**, (2), 57–66.

INCOTERMS 1990, ICC Publishing S.A., Paris.

Johnson-Tracy, E. (1985) Here come brand name fruit and veggies. *Fortune*, 18 February, 105.

Krapfel, R. E., Mentzer, J. T., and Williams, R. R. (1981) International logistics management at General Motors: philosophy and practice. *International Journal of Physical Distribution and Materials Management*, **11**, (5/6), 12–21.

Lele, M. (1986) Matching your channels to your product's life cycle. *Business Marketing*, **71**, (12), 60–69.

McDonnel, W. R., and Kossack, E. W. (1983) The financial benefits to users of foreign trade zones. *Columbia Journal of World Business*, **Fall**, 33–41.

Pellow, M. (1990) Physical distribution in international retailing. *International Journal of Retail and Distribution Management*, **18**, (2), 12–15.

Perry, D. (1989) How you'll manage your 1990s distribution portfolio. *Business Marketing*, **74**, (6), 52–56.

Pirie, M. (1983) *Freeports*, Adam Smith Institute, London (based on a seminar).

Rowe, M. (1987) The international sales contract – central to trade transactions. *International Trade Forum*, **23**, (3), 14–19, 31.

Rowe, M. (1986) What's in a word? A lot when it comes to trade terms. *ICC Business World*, **4**, (3), 17–19.

Shiotani, T. (1988) Outline of Japanese distribution system. *Business Japan*, August, 89–97.

SITPRO, *Costing Guidelines for Export Administration*, 1979.

Slater, A. (1980) International marketing: the role of physical distribution management. *International Journal of Physical Distribution and Materials Management*, **10**, (4), 160–184.

Stock, J. R., and Lambert, D. M. (1983) Physical distribution management in international marketing. *International Marketing Review*, Autumn, 28–41.

The Revised INCOTERMS: key features. (1990) *International Trade Forum*, **26**, (2), 4–9, 28–30.

Trunick, P. A. (1989) International distribution is in your future. *Transportation and Distribution*, **30**, (2), 12–15.

Value-added marketing (1989) *Global Trade*, **109**, (5), 26, 28.

Key reading

British International Freight Association, *Exporter and Forwarder: The Professional Guide 1990*, Feltham, Middlesex.

Davies, W., and Butler, E. (1986) *The Freeport Experiment*, Adam Smith Institute, London.

Houlihan, J. B. (1987) International supply chain management. *International Journal of Physical Distribution and Materials Management*, **17**, (2), 57–66.

INCOTERMS 1990, ICC Publishing S.A., Paris.

Lele, M. (1986) Matching your channels to your product's life cycle. *Business Marketing*, **71**, (12), 60–69.

Perry, D. (1989) How you'll manage your 1990s distribution portfolio. *Business Marketing*, **74**, (6), 52–56.

12
Promotion strategy decisions in an international context

In this chapter we deal with all the means by which marketers may communicate with their target markets. Yet the communication task facing any company goes beyond its target market, it extends to its public image; employee morale; and shareholder perceptions of corporate efficiency often based on analysts' readings of annual company reports. Marketing's publics change with the product or service offered and the task with the degree of acceptance found in the target market.

Communication has been made easier through the advent of telecommunications and information systems which has effectively eliminated geographical distance. The challenge which still remains is that of psychological or 'psychic' distance which may be felt to be greater between two neighbouring countries than two from different hemispheres. There has, for example, been a multiplicity of ties between Britain and the countries of the Commonwealth such as Australia, New Zealand and Canada and, on the other hand, France. The process of taking Britain into Europe which started in 1972 will be fully completed with the advent of the Single European Market by the end of 1992. Within a twenty-year span, political positions have changed radically. Communication helps each of us as individuals to cope with these changes.

While cultural convergence remains a distant and purely theoretical concept, communications have brought about what Marshall McLuhan called the 'global village', where everyone buys similar products that are sold with similar messages. This demand for a particular product or product class and the homogeneity of the market offering has been brought about by communications which have helped shape aspirations of ownership and expectations of usage.

The great divide still exists with the global brand. There are very few global brands beyond Coca-Cola, Pepsi-Cola, IBM and a few of the fast food franchises such as McDonalds or Kentucky Fried Chicken. The communication of a unified image of quality and service to the customer is paramount. Occasionally this may go awry because of either bad public relations; a 'whisper campaign' by competitors; the need to engage in 'corrective advertising' as a result of either advertising industry pressure or governmental pressure so as to rectify previous advertising deemed to be misleading or even practising deception; or finally just plain ill-founded rumour quite divorced from fact.

An example of how wild rumour is soon able to gather its own momentum is provided in the case of Proctor & Gamble:

The problem started in the Southern states of the USA where the word began to spread that Proctor & Gamble through the use of their trademark encourage satanism. The only supporting evidence was the Proctor & Gamble crescent moon and 13 stars, a registered trademark which no-one had probably examined too closely before, including most probably senior management of Proctor & Gamble themselves. In this particular case, Proctor & Gamble were being attacked from what is sometimes referred to as the 'bible belt' of the Southern states. The news of this scare took a while to reach Proctor & Gamble and to be taken seriously by its management but given the time lags of reporting market response even to sales, delay is inevitable, by which time considerable damage has already been done to market share. What would be their competitive response? Ignore it and continue to promote individual brands or take it seriously, and take on the Devil?

This example serves to show the difficult challenge that can sometimes be presented to those in charge of promotion. The scare started in 1980 and did not die down and by 1982, had reached a peak where Proctor & Gamble were receiving 15,000 calls per month routed through to their consumer services department. Moving to the offensive, Proctor & Gamble then enlisted the support of one of the deans of the 'moral majority', Jerry Falwell; hired two detectives agencies to trace the culprits; filed six suits against people for spreading rumours and then set up a toll-free telephone number to handle anxious customer enquiries. The rumours, however, continued and calls were still pouring in at a rate of 5,600 a month when the company decided it had spent enough and suffered enough and was therefore discontinuing the use of its corporate logo on products over the next few years though they would continue with it on letterheads and at corporate headquarters.

Promotion has many sides to it including:

- Personal selling
- Exhibitions
- Public relations
- Sales promotion
- Advertising

Too often, advertising is viewed to be promotion and vice-versa. However, we shall see as we come now to examine each of these in turn, that the differences which exist are not only between regions but within countries. There may well be a traditional way of doing things which has little bearing on how rich a particular economy may be, as is the case with the rather anachronistic distribution channels in Japan, for example.

Personal selling

The use of the salesperson particularly in selling high value-added industrial goods is unquestioned. Sound product knowledge and the ability to relate to consumers' needs is the objective. However, while it may be difficult to identify the members of a DMU or informal 'decision making unit' within one's own domestic market, the problem becomes greatly exacerbated when one starts to consider the different forms of ownership as well as outright state control which a monopoly over foreign trade may take. In that situation, the aim of identifying buyers, deciders, users, influencers and gatekeepers may well mean trying to identify individuals within different institutions and yet all having some bearing or influence on the awarding of a contract to purchase. In such situations the human element and being able to relate well to the customer are what often constitute the decisive element.

In international marketing, the use of a flying salesperson is without doubt expensive and many times that of a domestic field sales operative. Ironically, if this salesperson does move around a great deal then he or she is open to the accusation of spreading him or herself too thinly over too many markets, leading only to personal exhaustion and poor company representation. The use of a consortium whereby small companies together may be able to afford the services of an expert salesperson is one way in which to defray the high costs involved. Yet there are many industries in which this is practised without which, you could not expect to compete. Specialty markets, highly specialist industries and high-risk countries make high demands on the use of personal selling. The costs may be high but so are the potential rewards without which no company would enter.

Exhibitions and trade fairs

Perhaps not surprisingly North America predominates in this sector. It is difficult to imagine a section of industry or interest so esoteric that is not represented in an annual meeting somewhere in North America. There is even an national association of suicidology although whether this is an academic association or group of practitioners is not certain. If it is an association of practitioners there may be problems in maintaining memberships! A selection of exhibitions and trade fairs across the rest of the world includes among others the 'International Brotherhood' Old Bastards Annual Conclave in Hong Kong.

As may be seen from Table 12.2, exhibitions and fairs may be general or specialist. Details of these fairs may be obtained from the Department of Trade's Fairs and Promotions Branch. Where specialist, the global competition will be seen to gather together in that exhibition hall for the duration of the show to display their wares but also check on what everyone else is doing within the industry. Trade enquiries are more likely to be converted into sales at such exhibitions because buyers worldwide will usually congregate there. The expense of exhibiting therefore has to be set against the cost of not exhibiting. For British companies, the Department of Trade usually offers some financial assistance to encourage participation in the national pavilion. Industrially and internationally, these exhibitions provide some degree of image building for the participants, the value of which may greatly exceed the actual orders taken during the exhibition itself. In countries where one is dealing with a state buyer, this factor has to be taken into account. In Eastern Europe prior to the events of 1989, the importance of the national trade fair was inflated by having the signature of contracts postponed until the opening of the fair. This artificial mechanism inflated both the numbers attending and the volume of total business concluded during the national fair and because of this almost compulsory attendance, perhaps also the costs of individual contracts concluded.

The problem with trade fairs is that the costs are high and the rewards uncertain. Rosson and Seringhaus (1989) did a very good job of reviewing the existing literature as well as conducting their own survey. Lilien (1982) had found the most important variables to be: product complexity; sales level; purchase frequency and customer concentration. Furthermore that levels of spending were influenced by the magnitude of product sales and the stage in the life cycle.

Public relations/publicity

Public relations, also termed publicity, is of special significance. It is a form of free advertising whose value cannot be underestimated. Saatchi and Saatchi once reckoned the value of taking on the Conservative Party advertising account in 1979 to have been worth £2m to them in terms of advertising their name and promoting their agency.

Any company can benefit from a favourable unsolicited media report. Television, radio and the press often look for free news stories of this kind. To meet this demand, many large companies employ a public relations agency to handle all external relations. Press releases are then distributed to the various media and these may detail important personnel changes; foreign contracts won; technological breakthroughs that have been made which give the company a 'leading edge'; or mergers, acquisitions or strategic alliances that have been entered into to ensure that the company remains competitive in the dynamic global market that exists for high technology products today. Certain high technology and some not so high technology companies have benefited from exposure of this kind which enhances their public image at large, informs the general public including consumers of their products, and reassures shareholders and other interested bodies all at the same time.

Word-of-mouth advertising is not only cheap, it is very effective. Public relations seeks to enhance corporate image building and influence favourable media treatment. Not all companies are naturally gifted in putting the best possible face on their technological achievements or enlightened employee and customer care programmes. Public relations seeks to redress this balance as well as dealing often with fire-fighting situations which may emerge when, for example, an oil tanker has an accident and starts to lose some of its cargo of crude

Table 12.1 Trade show criteria

Categories and criteria	Rank
Audience quality	
Proportion of decision makers among visitors	1
Proportion of visitors in your target market	2
Show limited to specific types of exhibitors	8
Number of per cent of new contacts last year	9
Screening of visitors	15
Audience quantity	3
Number visiting exhibit	5
Extent of promotion by show organizers	6
The show's audience size in past years	
Display location	4
Booth position/location on floor	7
Ability to specify/negotiate size, location, etc.	13
Aisle traffic density	
Logistical aspects	10
Easy registration or pre-registration	11
Security	12
Easily available move-in/out assistance	16
Move-in/out facilities	

Source Dickinson, J. R., and Faris, A. J. (1985) Firms with large market shares, product lines, rate shows highly. *Marketing News*, 10 May, p. 14.

Table 12.2 Selective listing of international fairs outside North America in 1990

AUSTRALIA

GUNNEDAH
- AUG Australia Intl Agricultural Machinery Exh (Ag-quip)

MELBOURNE
- APR Melbourne Telecommunications Exh
- JUN Melbourne Intl Swimming Pool SPA Outdoor Living Exh
- AUG Australia Intl Plumbing Exh (IPEX)
- AUG Melbourne Intl Home Exh

SYDNEY
- MAR Sydney Intl Toy Sporting Goods Fair
- JUN Sydney Intl Catering Trade Shows (FOOD-PROX)

BAHRAIN

MANAMA
- FEB Middle East Intl Educ Materials Sports Equipment Exh (Education Arabia)
- FEB Middle East Intl Food Equip Fair (MEFEX)
- NOV Middle East Intl Building Construction Industry Exh (Arab Build)
- NOV Middle East Intl Solar Energy Exh (SOLTECH)
- DEC Middle East Intl Book Fair

BELGIUM

BRUSSELS
- FEB Brussels Intl Agricultural Fair
- FEB Europe Heating Air Condtg Exh Insulation (Euroclima)
- MAR Brussels Intl Building Exh Trade Decoration Show (Batibow)
- MAR Brussels Intl Trade Fair
- APR Brussels Intl Business Promotion Exh (SIPAB)
- APR Brussels Intl Hospital Medical Equip Exh (EXPOMED)
- MAY Brussels Intl Packaging Exh (PROPACK)

DENMARK

COPENHAGEN
- JAN Copenhagen Camping Exh
- JAN Copenhagen Intl Boat Show (Bella Centret)
- FEB Copenhagen Intl Mini Microcomputers Exh Special Software (Mikrodata)
- MAR Copenhagen Intl Travel Tourism Exh (REJS)
- MAY Scandinavia Intl Furniture Fair (SFF)
- JUN Copenhagen Intl Home Textiles Carpeting Exh (TEXPO)
- JUN European Orthodontic Soc Congress & Exh

ENGLAND

BIRMINGHAM
- FEB Birmingham Intl Spring Fair (ISF)
- FEB Birmingham Intl Elec

LONDON
- NOV London Intl Accountants Financial Services Exh
- NOV London Intl Computer Peripheral Small Computer Systems Exh (COMPEC)
- NOV London Wholesale Buyers Gift Fair
- DEC London Intl Agricultural Machinery Exh Royal Smithfield

FRANCE

BESANCON
- SEP Besancon Intl Precision Engrg Exh

BORDEAUX
- MAR Bordeaux Hotel Catering Exh (Exp'Hotel)
- MAR Bordeaux Intl Electronics Show (Electron)
- MAY Bordeaux Intl Fair
- SEP Bordeaux Intl Wood Building Exh (Batibois)
- OCT Bordeaux Intl Household Exh (Conforexpo)
- NOV Bordeaux Intl Racing Cars Exh Racing Motor Bikes

CANNES
- JAN Cannes Intl Records Exh Music Publishing Market (MIDEM)

GERMANY

BAD DURKHEIM
- SEP Bad Durkheim Intl Construction Equip Exh

BERLIN
- JAN Berlin Intl Food Agricultural Fair (Green Week)
- MAR Berlin Intl Tourism Exchange (ITB)

GREECE

ATHENS
- NOV Athens Intl Heating Refrigeration Air Condtg Exh (Interclima)

INDIA

NEW DELHI
- 90 Soc Automotive Engrs Air Cargo Forum & Expo
- SEP

INDONESIA

JAKARTA
- MAY Indonesia Intl Construction Building Municipal Public Works Exh
- SEP Indonesia Intl Mining Minerals Recovery Exh
- OCT Indonesia Forestry Woodworking Timber Processing Exh

ISRAEL

TEL AVIV
- JAN Tel Aviv Intl Elec Exh Technology Electronics (RAX)
- FEB Jerusalem Intl Cargo Exh (Transport)
- NOV Tel Aviv Office Automation Exh (FIS)

ITALY

MILAN
- FEB Milan Intl Kitchen Exh (Eurocucina)
- MAR Milan Intl Industrial Automation Robot Exh
- MAR Milan Intl Trade Fair
- MAY Italy Intl Machinery Equip Products Breadmaking Products Confectionery Exh (MIPAN)

JAPAN

OSAKA
- APR Osaka Intl Fair (Intl Trade Fair Commission)

TOKYO
- MAR Japan Intl Hotel Restaurant & Food Exh Fair (Hoteres/Foodex)
- MAR Tokyo Intl Prof Photo Fair (IPPF)
- MAR Tokyo Intl Shop Exh System Show
- SEP Tokyo Intl Optoelectronics Exh (Interopto)

NETHERLANDS

AMSTERDAM
- JAN Amsterdam Intl Agricultural Machinery Exh (Landbouw)
- JAN Amsterdam Intl Hotel Restaurant Insts Hospitals Industrial Canteens (Horecava)
- FEB Amsterdam Intl Commercial Vehicles Show (Bedrijfsauto)
- FEB Amsterdam Intl Two Wheelers Show
- MAR Amsterdam Intl Exh Oil Gas Petrotechnical Industries (Petrotech)

NEW ZEALAND

AUCKLAND
- MAY New Zealand Intl Engrs Machinery Equip Exh (Trade Industrial Exhs)
- AUG New Zealand Intl Business Exh (Infotech)
- NOV Auckland Intl Catering Trade Show (Foodtech)

WELLINGTON
- AUG New Zealand Intl Trade Fair

NORWAY

OSLO
- MAR Oslo Intl Boat Show Motor Show (Sea for All)
- May Norway Intl Electro Technical Exh (eliaden)

PERU

LIMA
- NOV Lima Intl Fair For Agricultural Industry (Agrotec)

PHILIPPINES

MANILA
- JAN Philippines Intel Trade Fair (PIITF)
- FEB Manila Intl Book Fair
- FEB Manila Office World Intl Exh (OWI)
- 90 Manila Intl Food Beverage
- SEP Equip Fair

POLAND

POZNAN
- MAY Poznan Intl Woodworking Machinery Exh (Drema)

SCOTLAND

ABERDEEN
- NOV Aberdeen Offshore Inspection Repair Maintenance Exh (Irm-Aodc)

GLASGOW
- FEB Scottish Spring Fair
- MAR Scottish Building Public Works Exh (Scotbuild)
- MAR Scottish Computer Show

SINGAPORE

SINGAPORE
- APR Asia Intl Communications Business Office Hardware Software Show (Infotech)
- APR Singapore Intl Catering Trade Show Food Drink Hotel Equip
- MAY Intl Exh Food Drink Restaurant Equip (Food Asia)
- SEP Toy Fair Intl (Toycraft)

SPAIN

BARCELONA
- JAN Barcelona Intl Boat Show and Caravaning Sector
- MAR Barcelona Intl Food Fair Exh (Alimentaria)
- APR Barcelona Intl Motor Show Transport (Expomovil)
- SEP Barcelona Intl Book Fair (Liber)
- SEP Barcelona Intl Image Sound and Electronics Show (Sonimag)
- OCT Barcelona Intl Watch Jewellery Clock Machinery Fair (Barnajoya)
- NOV Barcelona Intl Chemical Fair (Expoquimia)
- DEC Spain Intl Children Youth Fair

SWEDEN

STOCKHOLM
- MAR Stockholm Intl Building Industry Trade Fair (Nordbygg)
- AUG Intl Fed Library Assn
- OCT Stockholm Intl Technical Trade Fair

SWITZERLAND

ZURICH
- SEP Zurich Intl Trade Fair (Zuspa)
- OCT Zurich Intl Fashion Show Professional Fair (Kongress)
- OCT Zurich Intl High Precision Engrg Measurement Control Exh (Microtechnic)
- NOV Zurich Intl Christmas Fair (WIWA)
- NOV Zurich Intl Medical Hospital Equip Exh
- DEC Zurich Intl Christmas Collectors Fair (Sammlerborse)
- DEC Zurich Intl Mineral Fair (Mineralien)

TAIWAN

TAIPEI
- MAY Taipei Intl Hardware Building Materials Exh
- JUN Taipei Intl Computer Show (Computex)
- NOV Taipei Intl Machinery Equip Exh
- NOV Taiwan Intl Furniture Woodworking Machinery Fair

UNITED ARAB EMIRATES

DUBAI
- FEB Dubai Intl Air Freight Exh (Fairs & Exhibitions Ltd.)

Source   1989 tradeshows and exhibits schedule, *Successful Meetings Magazine*, New York.

oil and creates problems of ecological and environmental concern not just locally or regionally but globally.

Sales promotion

The most frequently used singly, or in combination, would include:

- point of purchase advertising including displays
- premiums: self-liquidating; direct 'on-pack' or 'in'-pack; continuity premiums; tie-in premiums; and fulfilment premiums.
- specialty advertising; gifts to consumers to build goodwill that will generate future purchases
- coupons (goes back to 1885 in the USA)
- sampling
- deals
- sweepstakes and contests
- cooperative advertising between retailer, manufacturer or trade association
- booklets and brochures
- trade shows and exhibits
- directories and yellow pages
- trade incentives, price reductions, in the form of promotional allowances.

Sales promotion relates these to so-called 'below the line' activities such as point of sale displays and demonstrations as well as leaflets, free trials, contests and premiums such as 'two for the price of one'. Unlike media advertising which is 'above the line' and earns a commission, 'below the line' sales promotion does not. To an advertising agency, 'above the line' means traditional media for which they are recognized by the media owners, entitling them to commission. When agencies are fee-based the situation no longer exists, so when the commission system operates – as it does in most countries – all those services which interfere with the earning of commission (usually 70 per cent of total income) go down below the line, that is, at the bottom of the list (Jefkins, 1976, 21).

Targeting directly at the potential buyer, the sales promotion material seeks to encourage a response to action and to actual trial of the product or service concerned. In some countries, this area of operations may be quite constrained because the market is small or sluggish because of political impediments, low personal disposable incomes and poor distribution and low product availability.

Advertising

Advertising was defined by the British Code of Advertising Practice, published in 1979 as: 'paid-for communication, addressed to the public (or some of it) with the purpose of influencing the opinion or behavior of those to whom it is addressed'. Advertising exists to inform, persuade, and remind a buying public of a particular product or service and it does so at a lower cost per head to the company than personal selling or exhibitions. Advertising as defined by Kotler (1988) is: 'Any paid form of nonpersonal presentation and promotion of ideas, goods or services by an individual sponsor'.

Not all advertising is seeking a profitable transaction in the exchange of a good or service. Instead there are organizations such as the World Health Organization which have sought to nurture ideas of personal well-being through attention to diet and shaping attitudes towards tobacco and alcohol through promotion. There is now more to advertising than the creation of a brand image for a product, or corporate image for the company.

Taking brand advertising first, attention is paid first to the segments at which to target lifestyle advertising, so selective demand stimulation through advertising is what is sought. Primary demand stimulation would be a 'shotgun' approach to total demand for the product class whereas selective demand stimulation is a 'rifling' strategy narrowing in closely on the target.

In practice, where there is an oligopoly situation, advertising can create some confusion as to the identity of the advertiser as in the Vermouth sector. There is both Cinzano and Martini. However, when one advertises, even if confusion results as to the advertiser, it will lift total sales in this sector and so this confusion is not viewed as a problem.

Brand names wear out over time and so what were once branded products become generic, almost as a result of their own success. The effect of the brand name may then be seen to be greatly diminished if not lost totally. An example to quote is aspirin which was once a branded protected name. Again through popularity and common usage, certain products have become entrenched in the common everyday language of the country and in so doing have lost their significance as brand names, eg. in Britain adhesive tape is always popularly referred to as 'Sellotape' whereas in France, Germany and elsewhere in Europe it is known as 'Scotch' because of the 3M brand name. In Britain, people refer to a vacuum cleaner as a 'hoover' and will talk of 'hoovering' carpets or a staircase. Similarly, a Thermos flask is really a vacuum flask but is not popularly called that either.

Advertising seeks to stimulate demand for branded products and may do this in one of two ways either by means of a 'pull' strategy whereby a manufacturer might succeed in moving goods into retail shops by advertising to the end-users and ensuring that they ask for this particular product from their usual retailer. A 'push' strategy is where the manufacturer works down the channel of distribution 'pushing' the goods by means of financial discounts or incentives. The car industry which has its own tied distribution network has used the push strategy. Companies manufacturing convenience goods, for example, use 'pull' strategies in their fight against competitors for space on retailers' shelves.

With regard to advertising, choice has to be exercised as to the medium to be used whether press, television, radio, cinema or outdoor advertising. Points to note here are:

- the *reach*, i.e., the total number of members of the target audience who are expected to receive this message at least once,
- *frequency*, i.e., the number of times the target audience will be exposed to the message,
- *impact* dependent on the medium used and the message, this depends on compatibility between the two. Playboy magazine continues to attract advertisers for high value-added consumer durables, e.g., cars, hi-fi equipment and clothes that are geared primarily to a high-income male segment but there must have been some shift in the readership profile over the past ten years particularly since the closure of the Playboy Clubs and the demise of the Playboy 'bunny', and
- *continuity* which relates to the length of time a campaign will run and the pattern of timing of the advertising within a campaign.

Inevitably, therefore, there has to be a trade-off between high-frequency low-reach or low-frequency high-reach. Certain products identify with one or other strategy, e.g., soap powders will appear on television during the day, occasionally during the evening. Advertisements for cars will be shown primarily in the evening. This is partly a question of value of purchase, partly a question of appealing to all the decision-makers as well as to their users. Husbands may wish to be involved in the purchase of washing machines or dishwashers even if they do not wish to be around to physically operate these machines once purchased.

The communications process

The transmission of a chosen 'message' by a manufacturer through any form of media to an identifiable target segment audience is what we mean by the communications process. In this process, it is seldom that one manufacturer will be alone in proclaiming the benefits of his products, there will usually be many. This introduces the concept of 'noise'. We cannot hear clearly what this manufacturer is trying to tell us about his product because of this 'noise' from rival manufacturers making similar and often contradictory claims about their products. Thorelli and Thorelli undertook a study a number of years ago to attempt to count the number of 'messages' that each individual received in the course of a day. From early morning, waking to radio or breakfast television, reading the morning paper that has been delivered to chatting over breakfast about perhaps a planned new acquisition or a neighbour's recent acquisition. As one walks along any street – or drives as is the practice in the USA – there are billboards, shop front displays and different advertising signs with product messages. This continues on public transport where there is also advertising, even the traditional British black taxis in Manchester now have small television advertising screens in the passenger compartments. To the office or place of work, the continual imperceptible bombardment of advertising messages continues even in conversations with colleagues who may share value judgements on good or bad experiences of products or services. This continues until returning in the evening and exchanging with one's spouse the events of the day and opening oneself up yet again perhaps to an evening newspaper, an evening of television or even if going out, to advertising in the cinema or theatre.

Thorelli and Thorelli (1977) counted the number of messages directed at US citizens as consumers as being literally in the range 100–200. That we remember few of them is another important characteristic. As consumers, we screen out claims which conflict with our own attitudes and beliefs but make ourselves more open to advertising if we are about to buy a product in that product-class and want to know more or have a favourable leaning towards that particular brand because it is one which we have perhaps bought before. Reassurance is an important element in communicating with the consumer. Equally, the effectiveness of communications may be seen in terms of sales and of the consumers' ability to recall that particular brand. Moving from unawareness to the point where the buying public are able to recall unaided the particular brand and report strongly positive perceptions of it, is indeed the ultimate objective. The 'hypodermic model' is depicted in Figure 12.1.

We have spoken of 'noise' but the other important point to consider is the degree of 'fit' between medium and message. A wordy message would be better for the press than a visual medium such as television or cinema. Alternatively, radio simulates sounds to give vent to the imagination. On television, you have to see sandy beaches or the ski slopes; on radio, you can concentrate on the noises of travel, or of being on a beach or of skiis on snow. It is a different appeal to the senses as is the press for those who may prefer a totally dispassionate

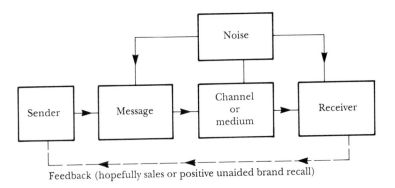

Feedback (hopefully sales or positive unaided brand recall)

Figure 12.1   *Hypodermic communications model*

unemotional and purely factual statement. Newspapers and consumer reports carry detail with comment which would be omitted from advertisements on radio or television. The weakness of the hypodermic model is that it is injecting a message into the buying public but the leads and lags of advertising make its direct effectiveness in achieving sales difficult to assess.

Another factor to consider is the degree of newness of the product to the market in question. It has been said that success is more likely if the advertiser's goal is consistent with the goals of the target audience. Word-of-mouth advertising has been found to be important where one has been able first to influence those who, in innovation studies, are called 'opinion leaders'. These people are more open to the mass media than the people they influence. They are usually better educated and knowledgeable, they are the ones to turn to when seeking advice on a purchase about which you have no present knowledge either in terms of the meaning of product specifications or even in the recognition of reliable brand names. So if new to the market or if you have not bought a new product of this type for some years, the opinion leaders are the people to turn to, because they are educated and informed people with special knowledge in this area of purchase that you are presently considering.

Actually changing attitudes is beyond the scope of most advertising, as was pointed out in the discussion on cultural variables. Nevertheless it is possible to influence behaviour where opinions are not strongly held and do not have the strength of convictions. It is possible to persuade people to switch brands of toothpaste, or to accept trial of a new product which embodies a new concept and brings new benefits such as word processing, for example. In all of this, reference groups play an important role as has been shown in various studies.

Figure 12.2 shows only a general model and it must be remembered then that the divisions may be somewhat arbitrary and may not apply to the same degree to all products. Yet Everett Rogers (1962) sees important differences in these five adopter groups as to their value orientations. The early adopters make a reasoned judgement and the early majority who follow may be seen to be adopting new ideas before the average person but they are rarely leaders like the early adopters. The late majority are composed of sceptics who will only accept an innovation as proven. Finally, the laggards and there may be many reasons here as to why they are so slow. Primarily this group consists of those without a fixed income so unable to fulfil all their desires. So students who are adventurous may be grouped together here with unadventurous senior citizens. Freddie Laker with Skytrain was pitching his product mainly at laggards, those who would most probably not fly but for his low airfares.

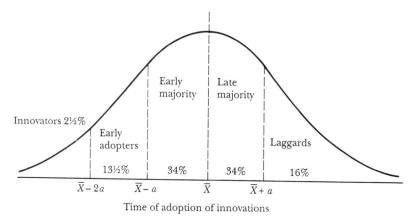

Figure 12.2 *Innovation adoption cycle*

As a segment they may be sufficiently numerous and advertising to them reduces the 'phychic' distance that much further. Yet to turn the situation around is difficult as Laker found. Once an image of a 'no-frills' service becomes fixed in the minds of the public, it was impossible to entice businessmen to use their airline despite assurances that every need was met and all comforts were produced for them.

The 'lunatic fringe', who desire to acquire all new products just introduced onto the market, account for only 2.5 per cent of those who will finally adopt the product. They do not therefore constitute a viable market segment of their own for any product. It is important then to emphasize that the early adopters are those opinion leaders whom it is crucial to have on your side. Their behaviour influences others. People are not sheep but are influenced by others particularly when nervous about the purchase of a totally new product concept or high-value item. This is where word-of-mouth communication is so important.

Perhaps one may meet a friend or colleague and discuss his new car which was a personal import from Belgium and think 'strange, I didn't think it was so easy to import cars straight into the UK from Belgium and save 25 per cent on the British list price!' Again, at the office or place of work, the same is continuing even in a lunchtime visit to the bank since banks are now all active in a wide variety of secondary activities, and literature on their range of services may be everywhere apparent. The process is then repeated on the way home from work when an evening paper will be on sale, and one goes back home to listen to the family, listen about their day, what happened to their friends and perhaps watch television, read a newspaper or weekly television guide, or listen to radio.

As a means of self-protection, each individual exercises selective exposure which means exposure to messages that fit his existing attitudes and the avoidance of messages that are incompatible with his existing beliefs or attitudes. Second, individuals are guilty of selective perception, that is they may distort or misinterpret the intended meaning of a message when it differs with their deeply-set values. The greater the gap between values held and messages presented, the greater the likelihood of message distortion. Third, being exposed to such a vast number of messages in the course of a day, we could never be expected to remember them all. Each individual has a capacity only for selective retention, remembering better those messages that reinforce their own values than those at variance. If it is of particular interest now or in the near future, it is more likely to be remembered.

Another point to note is that of cognitive dissonance whereby the individual having made a high-value purchase will experience a period of doubt immediately afterwards. During this period, he will be seeking reassurance in his purchase and may for a time read the manufacturer's advertisements more avidly for false or misleading claims. To this end, car manufacturers, to take one example, seek in their advertising both to persuade people to buy and reassure those who have just made a purchase. Flattering the client by telling him how wise he is in purchasing this particular model at this seasonal price is quite common.

Advertising seeks to promote change by moving the individual through the following successive stages:

Unawareness	
Awareness	(that this brand exists)
Comprehension	(what this brand can do)
Conviction	(that this brand is supreme)
Action	(i.e., purchase)

Creating awareness is always the first step but secondly, one has to remind customers of the availability of existing products and their relative competitive strengths. Within the distribution channel, this may have to be relayed perhaps in a different way to each member using a selection of trade press; direct mail; product demonstrations and sales force visits.

Advertising induces mental readiness often pre-selling products. The USA has failed often to realize the global importance of Hollywood in its cinema and television dominance to pre-sell products or product concepts in virgin markets. Through cinema and television, the USA has been able to soften up a global market for its brands. When those brands or concepts did finally arrive they were approached by consumers who were inquisitive but already aware. Awareness then of brand names, product concepts and favourable perceptions towards these brands with accompanying expectations of their quality was a worldwide advantage which Hollywood gave to US companies through its marketing of US lifestyles.

Yet, not all advertising is designed to produce sales as a certain percentage will be devoted simply to non-profit communication, as in the case of governmental health warnings on AIDS, alcohol abuse, tobacco or road safety which are to be found all over the world. Increasingly, in times of change, companies advertise their good corporate behaviour rather than their products. In situations where markets are already well saturated for commodity products such as petrol (gasoline) and the commodity market prices for the raw material which is oil are turbulent, there is perhaps more to be gained in terms of consumer loyalty and non-government intervention from an institutional advertising campaign showing the company indeed to be an honest broker investing in the future of the market concerned. (This campaign may be repeated over several markets.)

Advertising – the global situation

First, irrespective of how low their per capita GNP may be, all countries engage to some extent in advertising. However, it is also important to note that countries report this expenditure data in different ways as in expenditures in local currency, for example, and so there is not always consistency in reporting or comparability of the statistics provided. Moreover, the effectiveness of advertising reaches a point of diminishing returns in the more affluent countries as a result of competitive advertising already being in existence, and hence a high degree of 'noise'. Keegan (1989) expressed it thus:

$$A = f[(B)(C)(D)]$$

where:

A = sales/awareness impact of any particular advertising message
B = f(effectiveness of advertising/media combination)
C = potential market size
D = receptiveness of audience to additional advertising messages

So as personal disposable income increases, the effectiveness of advertising decreases, thus C and D move in opposite directions to each other.

As advertising expenditure in national currencies gives only a distorted view since it may both conceal inflation in an outwardly growth trend, or else, purely in terms of large numbers, give a false impression of importance or of total expenditure, we shall examine advertising expenditure as a percentage of Gross Domestic Product, and market prices (see Table 12.3). Worldwide, advertising is increasing in terms of volume and in terms of media availability. The former Soviet Union concluded an agreement in May 1989 with Saatchi and Saatchi for them to handle commercial television advertising in the Soviet Union.

It is difficult to put a definitive figure on the worldwide value of advertising but in Table 12.4 certain dollar figures are given for the European Community and for EFTA members but this omits Japan and the Japanese agency Dentsu is number one worldwide. Again, there is perhaps a definitional problem. Are we dealing with expenditures within or by these countries concerned? Could Japanese companies active within these markets have perhaps inflated the figures?

Table 12.3 expresses what Figure 12.3, shows graphically. Having listed GNP, we have had to resort to other sources of information for advertising as a percentage of GDP because this was not available for GNP. There should only be perhaps a few percentage points, however, in the differences between GNP and GDP. As Table 12.5 omits Japan, we turn to the Advertising Association again for Table 12.6 which shows advertising expenditures in Europe at current prices and exchange rates. Note that the ECU or European Currency Unit is in fact a weighted average of a basket of European currencies and is roughly approximate to the value of one dollar.

Japan is now a major player because as Japanese companies move abroad, Japanese advertising agencies follow. Not in the 'camp-follower' mode which has been found to explain the rise of certain service-industry multinationals in the West but for a different reason. Japanese companies have financial ties with each other and long histories of supplying one another. It is like when one member of the family goes abroad, the rest of the family go abroad too. These family ties help explain also the lack of movement in the Japanese agency ratings for what is multibillion dollar business.

The importance of Japan may be seen in Table 12.7 which details billings in millions of dollars. This is worth comparing in total value to Table 12.8 which looks at the role of the USA which was traditionally pre-eminent in international advertising. Japan is clearly pre-eminent as may be seen now in the table of the top fifty advertising groups worldwide in 1989 (see Table 12.9).

If, however, we look at the top ten holding companies, the names change (see Figure 12.4).

Table 12.3   Population and per capita gross national product of some countries 1989

Country	Population millions	GNP per capita $US	World Rank	Country	Population millions	GNP per capita $US	World rank
Switzerland	6.5	30.270	1	Greece	10.0	5,340	27
Japan	123.0	23.730	2	Korea, Republic	42.4	4.400	29
Finland	5.0	22.060	3	Portugal	10.6	4.260	30
Norway	4.2	21.850	4	Hungary	10.6	2.560	34
Sweden	8.5	21.710	5	Brazil	147.3	2.550	35
USA	248.2	21.100	6	Yugoslavia	23.7	2.490	36
Germany (West)	61.3	20.750	7	South Africa	34.9	2.460	37
Denmark	5.1	20.510	8	Venezuela	19.2	2.450	38
Canada	26.3	19.020	9	Bulgaria	9.0	2.320	39
United Arab Emirates	1.5	18.430	10	Argentina	31.9	2.160	41
France	56.1	17.830	11	Malaysia	17.3	2.130	42
Austria	7.6	17.360	12	Mexico	86.4	1.990	43
Belgium	9.9	16.390	13	Chile	13.0	1.770	47
Kuwait	2.0	16.380	14	Poland	38.1	1.760	48
Netherlands	14.8	16.010	15	Jordan	4.0	1.730	49
Italy	57.5	15.150	16	Turkey	54.9	1.360	50
UK	57.3	14.570	17	Colombia	32.3	1.190	53
Australia	16.8	14.440	18	Thailand	55.2	1.170	54
New Zealand	3.3	11.800	19	Philippines	61.2	700	68
Singapore	2.7	10.450	20	Egypt. Arab Republic	51.4	630	72
Hong Kong	5.7	10.320	21	Indonesia	178.2	490	75
Israel	4.5	9.750	22	Kenya	23.3	380	85
Spain	39.2	9.150	23	Pakistan	110.0	370	87
Ireland	3.5	8.500	24	China	1,105.1	360	88
Saudi Arabia	13.6	6.230	25	India	832.5	350	89
				Nigeria	113.7	250	95
				Bangladesh	111.6	180	101
				Ethiopia	48.9	120	108
				Mozambique	15.4	80	109

*GNP is calculated at market prices.

Note   The *World Bank Atlas* gives data, sometimes incomplete, for 185 countries, 109 countries have been ranked by per capita GNP. All countries with less than 1 million people and, of necessity, those countries (mostly in the Soviet bloc or at war or civil war) for which GNP data are not available have been excluded. The above table shows all industrial countries and selected other countries.

Source   *Marketing Pocket Book 1991*, Advertising Association, London.

Table 12.4   Advertising as a percentage of gross domestic product (at market prices)

Country	1984	1985	1986	1987	1988	1989
Austria	0.52	0.52	0.54	0.56	0.60	0.68
Belgium	0.40	0.41	0.42	0.47	0.49	0.53
Denmark	0.81	0.82	0.82	0.87	0.94	1.07
Finland	1.05	1.07	1.10	1.09	0.98	0.88
France	0.48	0.50	0.53	0.59	0.64	0.68
Germany	0.72	0.74	0.72	0.74	0.75	0.77
Greece	0.34	0.35	0.42	0.48	0.58	0.65
Ireland	0.50	0.53	0.62	0.70	0.72	0.77
Italy	0.41	0.43	0.47	0.52	0.54	0.53
Netherlands	0.66	0.67	0.72	0.75	0.77	0.77
Norway	0.78	0.79	0.90	0.91	0.84	0.74
Portugal	0.26	0.29	0.33	0.46	0.58	0.62
Spain	0.79	0.86	0.99	1.16	1.32	1.45
Sweden	0.54	0.56	0.58	0.61	0.65	0.67
Switzerland	0.80	0.83	0.84	0.89	0.91	0.91
UK	0.86	0.86	0.93	0.94	0.97	0.98

Note   This table has added in estimates of production costs, classified advertising and commission for those countries which exclude these factors from their advertising statistics.
Source   *European Marketing Pocket Book 1991*, NTC Publications, Henley-on-Thames, Oxon.

Campaign transferability

Few brands are marketed on a worldwide basis because of language or lack of general transferability resulting from the product being climactically or culturally unsuitable, too expensive, too large or too small. Smaller product sizes may be required for poorer nations. One is left then to standardize only on what is left in terms of the common component parts once all cultural, communicative, legislative, competitive and executional problems are resolved (Killough, 1978). The famous Esso 'Put a tiger in your tank' campaign did create an image for an unromantic non-standardized product (petrol/gasoline). Yet what is forgotten is that this particular campaign happened a few generations ago. There are junior members of staff in advertising today who were too young to remember that campaign that is much spoken of in the advertising literature. That is not to say that standardization does not work or does not exist because it does. The degree, however, to which campaigns may be transferable is, however, limited. Perhaps 30 per cent of good campaigns may give rise to some international extension which may include modifications as well as language dubbing (Killough, 1978).

In this search for product image, advertisers perceive the similarities more than the dissimilarities among global consumers (vindicating the Maslow Hierarchy of Needs) so

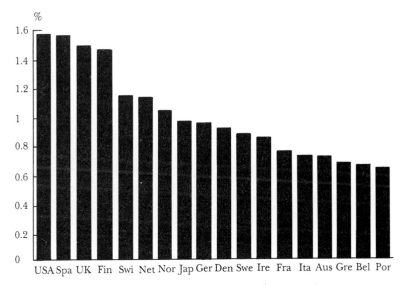

Figure 12.3   *Advertising as a percentage of GDP (at market prices)*
Source   Advertising Statistics Yearbook 1990, Advertising Association, London

potentially the same offering may be made to Malaysians or Nigerians as Americans or Europeans. This has held true for Hertz, Avis, Pepsi, Coke and McDonalds, who are not representative of all multinational companies. A quite different experience was reported by Ford of Europe when seeking to test consumer reaction to a new Ford Granada in Germany, UK, France and Sweden. Using a sample of 200–300 people in each of Germany, UK, France and Sweden to test the new Ford of Europe model against the 'next car' intended purchase on a number of variables, provided a test bed for the international marketing standardization of the product. Here there were quite important variations in the way in which consumers perceived the same product and so the advertising was accordingly changed. This then meant segmentation of promotional strategies for international markets by allowing cross-country differences in product perceptions and product attribute preferences. (See Table 12.10.)

This is the strategy employed by Coca-Cola and Pepsi. Food may generally be held to be culture-bound but both these products are global with a centrally produced advertising that incorporates local differences in language, etc. It coincides well with the production orientation because no differentiation is to be seen. This was true until Pepsico started to take market share from Coca-Cola who then changed their formulation to suit this new market change. It suited some but not others so Coca-Cola effectively split their market between the new and classic Coke.

In the second strategy, the same product can be communicated in different ways for different markets. Bicycles may either be for recreation or basic transportation; a small tractor may be a garden tractor in an affluent society or a small agricultural tractor in a less-developed country. Next, there is the third strategy where the communications remain the same but the product formulation changes. The prime example here is that of Esso with its 'Put a tiger in your tank' campaign which remained constant despite the fact that in some markets only 91 octane petrol was available, yet the advertising image employed throughout was the same as for 100 octane and the promise of performance was the same. In the fourth

Table 12.5   Trends in advertising expenditure 1982–1986

| | National currencies (million) | | | | | Total $ million | Per capita $ |
	1982	1983	1984	1985	1986	1986	1986
EC members							
Belgium	16239	18957	21077	22954	24933	558	56
Denmark	3288	3578	4175	4739	5272	652	127
France	17955	21655	23945	26890	30654	4426	80
Germany	11342	11945	12,672	12770	13462	6199	102
Greece	9029	10632	12820	15314	23322	167	17
Ireland	72	72	82	95	116	156	44
Italy	2079	2705	3270	3934	4515	3029	53
Luxembourg							
Netherlands	3322	3335	3566	3729	4198	1713	118
Portugal	4338	6544	7348	10133	14319	96	9
Spain	140400	164600	197000	239900	315000	2249	58
UK	3126	3579	4059	4441	5117	7506	132
EFTA members							
Austria	5296	5927	6574	6959	7465	489	65
Finland	2952	3555	4192	4635	5025	991	202
Iceland							
Norway	2835	2970	3520	3968	4650	629	151
Sweden	4063	4628	5378	6023	6855	962	115
Switzerland	1826	1950	2061	2286	2432	1352	208

Source   Euromonitor (1989) *European Marketing Data & Statistics, 1988/89*, 24th edn, Euromonitor Publications London.

situation, the product and the communications both change; here the examples offered are greetings cards which vary with local and national holidays and feast days, but also in their nature, too, because of different attitudes to colour and the aesthetics of design. Clothing too, Keegan held, is culture bound. (See Table 12.11.)

However, in the past twenty years there has been the upsurge of multinational clothing led by the denim manufacturers behind Levi's and Wranglers, diversifying now into a range of casual wear to a global market segment which is the youth market. Similarly, the syndicated franchises behind the 'Snoopy' and 'Garfield' cartoon characters have produced blank greetings cards for all occasions. One may well question whether the fourth case still remains applicable, as well as the actual examples offered. It includes no allowance either for the 'own label'/generic brand/acquisition or introduction of local brands. The final Keegan strategy is the market gap where no product exists but the needs exist. Here, the example offered is of Colgate who developed a hand-powered washing machine and then subsequently developed

Table 12.6   Advertising expenditure in Europe at current prices and exchange rates (million ECUs)

	1982	1983	1984	1985	1986	1987	1988
Austria	301	360	408	408	512	567	646
Belgium	404	465	516	569	633	748	813
Denmark	411	446	491	542	594	635	670
Finland	627	722	885	990	1017	1088	1279
France	2792	3198	3485	3965	4539	5163	5872
Germany	5032	5549	5992	6490	7029	7579	7976
Greece	138	136	145	152	169	194	256
Ireland	102	99	113	132	158	181	198
Italy	1571	2004	2367	2717	3351	3615	4277
Netherlands	1320	1385	1495	1599	1838	1996	2169
Norway	449	458	549	609	639	656	645
Portugal	56	66	64	78	99	147	204
Spain	1319	1309	1572	1858	2304	2904	3794
Sweden	663	678	826	924	980	1075	1264
Switerland	922	1048	1117	1236	1407	1594	1671
UK	5578	6097	6872	7540	7620	8204	10203
Europe	21684	24020	26897	29850	32888	36346	41935
EC	18722	20754	23112	25642	28334	31366	36431
Japan	8164	10008	11830	15023	16994	18235	22619
USA	44355	55864	72801	80388	66753	60499	63107

Source   *Advertising Standards Yearbook 1990.* Advertising Association, London.
Note   These figures have not been adjusted to account for different methods of compilation and are therefore not fully comparable.

a communications package to accompany it. The realization that 600 million women still washed clothes by hand provided a feasible market for a multinational who saw possibilities of increasing sales of detergent powders at the same time. However, an alternative perspective could be as shown in Table 12.12.

It does not pay, however, only to listen to the company's advertising people and the advertising agency. For one thing they all talk in jargon and for another in their search for creativity they are often quite divorced from how the customer perceives the product as Exhibit 12.1 shows.

Britt (1969) had long ago raised the question still to be answered: are so-called successful advertising companies really successful? Obviously, this was a question of setting clear objectives and if there were deficiencies in the statement of objectives, there would be problems devising criteria for assessment. Most advertising agencies he maintained then do not know whether their campaigns are successful or not and are unable to prove or demonstrate the success of the campaigns which they themselves had publicly stated were successes.

Table 12.7 Japan in international advertising

Rank		Agency	Billings 1989 ($'000)
1989	1988		
1	1	Dentsu Inc.	10,063,184
2	2	Hakuhodo Inc.	4,449,166
3	3	Tokyu Agency	1,259,398
4	4	Daiko Advertising	1,214,107
5	5	Dai-Ichi Kikaku	1,052,953
6	6	Asatsu Inc	837,272
7	7	I&S Corp	770,480
8	8	Yomiko Advertising	753,480
9		McCann-Erickson Kakuhodo Japan	618,389
10		Man-Nen-Sha Inc	550,376

Table 12.8 USA in international advertising

Rank		Agency	Billings 1989 ($'000)
1989	1988		
1	1	Young & Rubicam	3,114,800
2	3	Saatchi & Saatchi Advertising Worldwide	2,778,900
3	2	BBDO Worldwide	2,656,000
4	5	DDB Needham Worldwide	2,386,300
5	4	Backer Spielvogel Bates Worldwide	2,158,000
6	6	Ogilvy and Mather Worldwide	2,104,400
7	8	D'Arcy Masius Benton & Bowles	2,055,300
8	10	Leo Burnett Co.	1,945,300
9	7	Foote, Cone & Belding Communications	1,871,200
10	9	J. Walter Thompson Co.	1,851,000

Multinational advertising agencies

Multinational advertising agencies have been in a state of flux over the past few years. First, the Japanese arrived. Next, the British entered the USA in the shape of WPP and Saatchi and

Table 12.9   The world's top fifty advertising agency groups in 1989

Rank 1989	Rank 1988	Group	Billings Million $
1	1	Dentsu Inc	10,063
2	2	Young & Rubicam	6,251
3	3	Saatchi & Saatchi Advertising Worldwide	6,050
4	4	Backer Spielvogel Bates Worldwide	5,143
5	7	Ogilvy & Mather Worldwide	4,828
6	5	McCann-Erickson Worldwide	4,772
7	8	BBDO Worldwide	4,550
8	11	Hakuhodo Inc	4,449
9	9	J. Walter Thompson Co	4,408
10	15	DDB Needham Worldwide	4,095
11	10	Lintas: Worldwide	3,958
12	13	D'Arcy Masius Benton & Bowles	3,803
13	6	Foote, Cone & Belding Communications	3,414
14	12	Grey Advertising	3,267
15	14	Leo Burnett Co	3,246
16	-	EWDB Worldwide	2,702
17	-	Publicis-FCB Communications BV	2,405
18	21	Bozell Inc	1,400
19	20	N W Ayer	1,398
20	24	Tokyu Agency	1,259
21	18	RSCG	1,234
22	23	Daiko Advertising	1,214
23	-	Chiat/Day/Mojo	1,060
24	22	Dai-Ichi Kikaku	1,053
25	-	Lowe International	919
26	27	Ketchum Communications	916
27	25	Wells, Rich, Greene	885
28	26	Scati, McCabe, Sloves	870
29	28	Asatsu Inc	837
30	31	TBWA Advertising	827
31	29	I&S Corp	770
32	32	Yomiko Advertising	754
33	33	Ross Roy Group	651
34	50	Man-Nen-Sha	550
35	36	BDDP	528
36	35	Asahi Advertising	509
37	47	Orikomi Advertising	436
38	48	W.B. Doner	381
39	40	Chuo Senko Advertising	376
40	-	Armando Testa Group Worldwide	349
41	39	Hill, Holiday, Corners, Cosmopulos	344
42	41	Nihon Keizaisha Advertising	337
43	-	Clemenger/BBDO (46.46% BBDO)	325
44	-	Ally & Gargano	316
45	49	Jordan, McGrath, Case & Taylor	315
46	-	Earle Palmer Brown	311
47	38	FCAI Group	282
48	-	Laurence, Charles, Free & Lawson	275
49	-	Tokyu Agency International (25% DMB&B)	272
50	-	Collett Dickenson Pearce	270

Source   *Advertising Statistics Yearbook 1990*, Advertising Association, London.

Saatchi and started buying up long-established agencies. Soon it will be French advertising agencies arriving on the world advertising scene. What then was seen always to be a US industry has now changed ownership but not without turmoil. When agencies are acquired or merge there is always a movement in account business, and a possible conflict of interest situation is seen to arise. Similarly when a multinational advertising agency is offered the

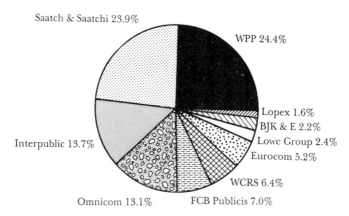

Figure 12.4 *Agency holding companies — share of top ten in 1989*
Source   Advertising Statistics Yearbook, Advertising Association, London

Table 12.10   Results of test of consumer reaction to new Ford of Europe car and 'next car'

Attributes	UK New model high awareness	'Next car'	France New model high awareness	'Next car'	Sweden New model high awareness	'Next car'
Luggage capacity	7.4	6.2	6.8	6.2	6.8	6.4
Technically advanced	7.2	6.7	6.6	6.6	7.4	6.6
Journey comfort	7.5	7.3	7.5	7.2	7.4	7.4
Styling	6.6	7.0	6.9	7.3	7.1	6.5
Prestige	6.5	6.9	7.0	7.2	6.6	6.4
Safety	6.8	6.7	6.3	6.5	5.8	6.4
Roadholding	7.0	7.4	6.7	7.7	7.0	7.5
Reliability	6.9	7.5	6.8	7.3	6.5	7.7
Purchase interest (%)	33		33		37	
Sample size	n = 286		n = 193	n = 223		

Source   Colvin, Heeler and Thorpe (1980), Developing international advertising strategy, Journal of Marketing, **44**, 73–9.

Table 12.11   Keegan's five strategies for multinational marketing

	Product strategy	Communications strategy	Product examples	Product function or need satisfied	Conditions of product use	Ability to buy product
1	Uniform	Uniform	Coca-Cola, Pepsi	Same	Same	Yes
2	Same	Different	Bicycles	Different: recreation or transportation	Same	Yes
3	Different	Same	Camay soap, Nescafé coffee, Petrol (gasoline)	Same	Different	Yes
4	Different	Different	Clothing, greeting cards	Different	Different	Yes
5	Invention	Develop new communications	Hand-powered washing machine	Same		No

Source   Keegan, W. (1970) Five strategies for multinational marketing, *European Business*, January, 35–40.

Table 12.12   International product/communications standardization

	Generic/own label	Regional brand	International brand
Communication	No responsibility	Responsive and specific	Unresponsive and generalized
Distribution	No responsibility	Standardized	Varied
Pricing	No responsibility	Flexibility	No flexibility, fluctuations give rise to parallel importing/exporting
Profitability	Only on volume	Premium	Premium
Product	No change ensures long production runs	Quality/value	Constant reviewed safeguards the marque
Development	No responsibility	Under constant review	Constant monitoring locally and by headquarters

worldwide business of a multinational company, it can often only make room by letting some accounts go.

This is what Young and Rubicam in fact did when offered Colgate business worldwide. Otherwise, in more normal times it is estimated that only 5 per cent of major accounts change hands each year.

Advertising agency usage criteria

1 Multinationals may select an international agency group with strong central control capable of imposing decisions on regional offices. Kodak and the Ford Motor Company

Exhibit 12.1

Coke's kudos

A global brand is what every company dreams of spawning, but how many are there? The biggest survey yet of brand awareness, covering some 6,000 brands and 10,000 consumers around the world, indicates that only one, Coca-Cola, has definitely made it. Another 18 brands are close all of them finishing among the top 50 in each of Europe, Japan and America.

The survey, carried out by Landor, a design consultancy, measures a brand's power in two ways: "share of mind", or familiarity, and "esteem", or how good consumers reckon the products are. Reliable and posh goods tend to do best:

Global brands

	Share of mind	Esteem
Coca-Cola	1	6
Sony	4	1
Mercedes-Benz	12	2
Kodak	5	9
Disney	8	5
Nestlé	7	14
Toyota	6	23
McDonald's	2	85
IBM	20	4
Pepsi-Cola	3	92

Rolls-Royce finished 23rd in share of mind and third in esteem, leaving it in 11th place overall.

Given that stress on esteem, polluters and drug-pushers do worst. Exxon finished 75th in share of mind and 157th in esteem, leaving it 94th overall. Marlboro, many marketers' favourite after Coca-Cola, finished 123rd, dragged down by its 328th rating in esteem; it finished 49th in familiarity.

Coca-Cola won by a landslide. The gap between Coke and its nearest rival, Sony, was enormous, but the distance between Sony and the rest was also considerable. Mr Alan Brew of Landor cites Sony as the marketing phenomenon of the past two decades. It finished top in esteem, elbowing aside brands like Mercedes-Benz and IBM. It also had a higher overall score than Coca-Cola among the under-40s.

Mr Brew says all the top ten brands, plus nine others (Rolls-Royce, Honda, Panasonic, Levi's, Kleenex, Ford, Volkswagen, Kellogg's and Porsche), can now be called "global". Some define their product categories so well that their names are used instead (eg, a Kleenex instead of a tissue). Xenophobia, however, remains a problem. All the top 20 brands in America were home-grown—as were most in Japan. Global brands still have a long way to go.

Source   Economist, 15 September 1990, reproduced with permission.

both use J. Walter Thompson in all markets. Colgate use Young and Rubicam in all their markets. Proctor and Gamble, Unilever, Mars all follow this pattern as well.

2 Foreign marketing may require the services of an international agency federation with more decentralized control giving greater local autonomy. (This would include minority interest and associate partner relationships.)

3 For local selling an agency in each territory is considered best for that territory. It may lead to fragmentation but it is the strategy adopted by ITT.

4 A home market agency devises the campaign strategy and places advertising directly into the chosen foreign target market media.

5 A company can go it alone without an advertising agency and place advertisements direct or via local correspondents.

The final choice of agency would be very much influenced by the relative strengths of agencies measured against the following criteria:

A market coverage
B quality of coverage
C market research, public relations, and other marketing services available in-house
D definition of the respective roles of company advertising department and agency
E communication and control
F international co-ordination
G size of company's international business
H image
I company organization
J level of involvement.

Multinational client/agency relationships

Historically, most of the big US advertising agencies owe their international expansion to their clients. In 1954, it was Coca-Cola which did it for McCann-Erickson. Next, it will be the French agencies in the new Single European Market and strategic business alliances with the Japanese which will ensure that the US hold on global advertising is forever broken.

The 'mirroring' effect is a feature to note. Documented by Vardar (1989) this is an extension of point (J) above. Vardar and Paliwoda (1988) identified certain preconditions for successfully transferable global campaigns by examining the relationship between the local agency, the local client, the Agency Head Office (AHO) and Client Headquarters (CHQ). The findings revealed that apart from the actual head office, there was another body called the 'lead agency' which acted as the actual head office for each specific account.

The extent of involvement agencies experienced from their Head Offices was very much determined by their clients' corporate cultures, which was best displayed by the clients' organizational structure. The way clients organized themselves and their affiliates affected the extent of HQ involvement which would be exercised both in their own affiliates and indirectly in their agencies. Figure 12.5 alongside provides a simplistic depiction of agency-client organizations.

Agency–client relationships never remain static, while clients and agencies separately undergo organizational metamorphoses at certain periods of their corporate life, remodelling

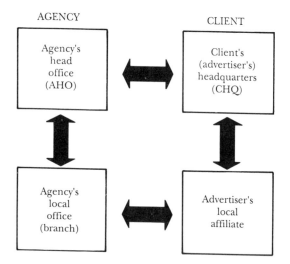

Figure 12.5   *Simplistic depiction of agency-client organizational structure*

and reorganizing themselves accordingly. The relationship formed simply evolves and in the long term transforms into a new bond.

The findings show that clients were the initiators of any change which would take place within their own organization as well as in the agency's. Invariably each restructuring inflicted certain transfigurations on the agency–client relationship.

The organizational structure adopted by agencies and clients in global campaigns

Having examined the agency–client relationship and viewing this as mainly client-led, we turn to the client agency organizational structure adopted while running global campaigns, to give a better service to international clients. Based on the research findings it was possible to visualize a more detailed version of an agency-client organizational structure being adopted for running global campaigns, than the one depicted earlier in Figure 12.5.

Yet again the starting point was the client. In order to be able to supply the best service and satisfy their clients, agencies mirrored their client's organizational structure, as seen in Figure 12.6. Following the completion of interviews and the data collection stage, it was possible to envisage a more comprehensive structure both within clients and agencies, than was possible at the beginning of the study.

Figure 12.3 provides information on how agencies literally mirror the organizational set up of their clients. Agencies tried to match their customer's organizational structure to such an extent that if clients had a regional European co-ordination body, they would also form one within their own agencies.

In some accounts, this co-ordinating function would be undertaken by the UK agency. In other cases, this would be technically within the same agency and perhaps operating even in the same building but independently – one as the UK agency and the other as the European regional co-ordinator. Which specific combination of possible organizational structures will

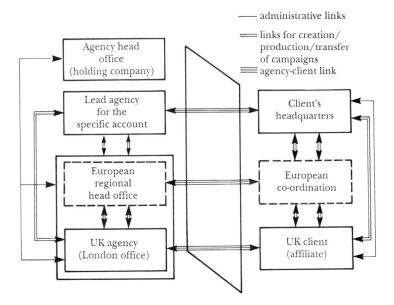

Figure 12.6 *How agencies and clients organize themselves to conduct global advertising campaigns (the mirroring effect)*
Source Vardar, N. (1992), *Global Advertising: Rhyme or Reason?*, Paul Chapman, London

be found for a particular account in an agency is determined by the client's specific organizational structure.

Links with the 'lead agency'

The nearest agency to the client's HQ would usually undertake the 'lead agency' role, which did not always coincide with the location of their official HQ. These 'lead agencies' were expected to handle the creation of campaigns, developing them from ad ideas and possibly producing or co-ordinating its production and then finally transferring the campaign to other local agencies that had the account in their own markets.

Throughout the campaign preparations there would be constant contact among the 'lead agency', 'European regional HQ' and the 'UK office'.

Furthermore, the 'lead agency' for account X might also be the local agency for account Y where client Y was based in a different country or town and the organizational structure for Y might be different from that required for client X. Thus, the agency closest to the client's HQ would be assigned the role of the 'lead agency' for that particular account.

Links with the official agency head offices

On the other hand, the agency's official HO where the holding company was based generally had administrative links with the European HO and individual agency branches.

These local offices reported to their holding company, mainly on financial issues and on meeting their annual targets. Other than that, these official AHO did not have any involvement in the creation of advertising campaigns that ran in local markets. Lead agencies were responsible and had the authority over campaign development. If the client's HQ was in the same city as the agency's HO, then the official AHOs became involved on the creative side.

The findings of this research did not yield any information as to the links formed between the official AHO and the 'lead agency' although these two roles were distinctly separated within agencies contacted.

The agency–client link

The third type of link found among agencies and clients while conducting global campaigns was the agency–client link. Again agencies restructured themselves so that their clients in each market, at each management level found their counterparts within the agency.

There were vertical lines of communication within both the client's organization and agency organization and horizontal lines of communication at the corresponding levels between the agency and the client. Each office kept in contact with its corresponding office. For example the UK agency never directly contacted the client's HQs. If it was required, they involved the lead agency or took the problem to the UK client, so that the client could handle it within its own organization.

Links within the client's organization

Finally links that were observed on the client side, with minor modifications. Three parties – HQ of the client, European co-ordination and the UK affiliate, each had administrative links and links for campaign development with each other. The client was not involved in the creation of the campaign. However, knowing their products and what is required for their brand, clients initiated the campaign. Therefore, within the client's organization, ideas were exchanged regarding a brief, product policy and all other relevant marketing mix elements.

Reasons behind the 'mirroring' effect

One of the major reasons was that these international clients were major world advertisers, devoting huge advertising budgets to their marketing activities worldwide.

One of the account executives stated that his client came within the top three or four of the agency's major worldwide accounts, with only 15 per cent of the client's total advertising expenditure. Yet this amount of advertising spending was probably a thousandth of the client's business. Therefore, the agency did not attempt to change the client's way of doing business, but rather tried to understand and work around the parameters established by the client.

Another reason for matching the client's organization within the agency was 'operational efficiency'. For example, if the client had divided itself as North and South Europe and if the agency had split Europe as Scandinavia, Central Europe and Mediterranean countries, responsibility would overlap, giving rise to further complications, e.g., 'Who would go to which meeting?' 'Who would be whose counterpart?' 'Who would communicate with whom?'

These were the major practical reasons for setting up a similar organization to that of the client.

Probably another less rational reason, although equally important was securing the smooth conduct of business between parties and showing goodwill and courtesy to the client in meeting their requirements.

We wanted to find predictor variables that would enable us to identify campaigns that could be successfully transferred from one country to another. As a result of this we came up with some preconditions for running smooth global campaigns.

One of the these requirements was to make sure that the agency exactly reflected the client's organization from senior to junior management levels, extending over HQs as well as local affiliates.

The matching of organizational structures between the agency and the client was one of the preconditions for successful global campaign transfers across borders.

Furthermore, agency and client relationships never became static and both parties experienced continuous change. However, clients were always the initiators of any reorganizational change to take place. If clients underwent organizational change, then their agencies would automatically reorganize themselves to match their client's structure.

There were three links identified in agency–client organizations while conducting global advertising, which were:

- Administrative links between the agency HO and the local UK office (such as reporting on financial issues).
- Links for creation/production transfer of campaigns between the UK agency and the agency assigned to the role of the 'lead agency' for the specific account. Lead agencies were appointed depending on the proximity of a local agency, within the international network, the client's HQ. Lead agencies had considerable flow of input to other local offices on the creative side of a global campaign. Administrative links and links for creation/production transfer of campaigns were also replicated on the client's side at each corresponding level.
- The third link was the agency—client link. Clients had their 'shadows' in their agencies at each seniority level, with matching responsibilities and titles.

Miracle (1966,87) suggests that as no two companies are alike, companies should choose an agency 'that most nearly meets its own particular requirements'. However, findings of this research indicated that in the past thirty years, international agencies have become flexible and very much client-led, most probably as a result of fierce competition faced in the international advertising arena. Therefore, agencies choose to adopt a method of adapting their own organizational structure to suit the needs of each individual client, by mirroring the client's organizational set up within their own agencies.

The findings of the Vardar-Paliwoda study may also be useful in assessing a brand's readiness for 1992 with regard to advertising activities.

Until now, it has been left to the discretion of the individual company whether or not to mount an international or global campaign. However, quite soon that freedom of choice will be regulated and shaped by the EC's efforts towards harmonizing Europe into a single market. Therefore, the findings of this research could also be applied by agencies in preparing their brands for 1992, in addition to other intra-agency controls they might have devised themselves.

Table 12.13   International advertising expenditures by media, 1987

	Print	TV	Breakdown % Radio	Cinema	Outdoor/ transit	Other including direct mail
Argentina	35.9	36.7	12.7	3.5	11.2	
Australia	47.8	34.3	9.2	1.5	7.2	
Austria	51.0	29.2	13.0	0.7	6.5	
Belgium	67.0	15.0	2.0	2.0	15.0	
Brazil	40.4	51.0	8.5			
Canada	43.0	16.2	9.0		8.4	23.4
China	34.2	14.6	4.0	4.8	42.4	
Colombia	20.6	53.8	19.2	3.0	3.3	
Denmark	96.0	0	0	1.0	3.0	
Finland	85.0	12.0	1.0	0	2.0	
France	57.0	22.0	7.0	1.0	12.0	
Germany	33.5	60.0	3.2	1.4	2.0	
Greece	39.0	48.0	5.0	1.0	6.0	
Hong Kong	36.4	57.4	2.5	1.1	2.5	
India	71.0	17.9	3.7	1.6	5.9	
Indonesia	61.1		17.8	3.3	17.8	
Ireland	33.0	37.0	11.0	0	10.0	
Israel	55.6	8.2	15.4	3.3	17.5	
Italy	55.0	47.0	3.0	0	5.0	
Japan	35.7	35.3	5.2	9.2	14.6	
Kuwait	70.0	30.0				
Malaysia	51.9	43.0	1.5	0.2	3.5	
Mexico	17.6	48.4	19.8	1.1	13.2	
Netherlands	77.0	11.0	2.0	0	10.0	
New Zealand	51.0	28.0	13.0	0	7.9	
Norway	96.0	0	1.0	1.0	2.0	
Philippines	28.0	51.7	20.0	1.0	0	
Portugal	23.0	42.0	10.0	19.0	6.0	
Singapore	59.8	32.9	3.0	0.6	3.7	
South Africa	63.5	31.8	0	1.4	3.4	
Spain	49.0	44.8	6.0	0.3	0	
Sweden	52.0	31.0	12.0	1.0	5.0	
Switzerland	96.0	0	0	1.0	4.0	
Taiwan	80.0	7.0	2.0	1.0	11.0	
Thailand	50.9	30.1	6.0	1.0	12.0	
Turkey	31.4	48.3	19.5	0.8	0	
UK	33.0	59.0	2.0	0	5.0	
USA	61.6	32.4	1.9	0.4	3.7	
Venezuela	34.0	21.9	6.7	0	1.2	
Zimbabwe	81.0	10.0	4.0	1.0	3.0	
	61.1	21.8	12.4	2.6	2.1	

Source   *International Marketing Data and Statistics*, 14th Edn, 1990. *European Market and Media Facts 1989*, Saatchi and Saatchi Advertising Worldwide, London.

Media availability

The ability to standardize a campaign internationally presupposes the availability of suitable media.

Television is by far the most important media internationally. Yet two-thirds of Western Europe may be said to be under-served in terms of programme choice, with government controlling the number of television channels, amount of broadcasting hours, and availability of advertising. No indigenous commercial television exists as yet in Sweden, although it receives commercial television from its neighbours including Norway and Denmark who have only recently started. Television reception like radio, often extends beyond its intended

Table 12.14   Commercial radio in Europe

Austria	2	Netherlands	3
Belgium	approx. 200	Norway	427
Denmark	approx. 250	Portugal	21
Finland	37	Spain	500 +
France	1,000 +	Switzerland	32
Greece	48 +	Turkey	1
Ireland	2	UK	44
Italy	approx. 1,000	West Germany	121

Source   *European Market and Media Facts.* Saatchi and Saatchi Advertising Worldwide, London.

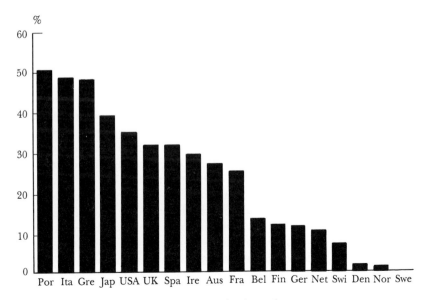

Figure 12.7   *TV adspend as a percentage of total adspend*
Source   *Advertising Statistics Yearbook 1990*, Advertising Association, London

Table 12.15 Major satellite channels

Channel	Programming Content	No of countries reached	Language	No of homes connected (millions)
Sky/Arts*	General	14	English	14.7
Super Channel*	General	14	English	13.9
TV5	Cultural	14	French	10.8
MTV	Music	11	English	6.7
Drei Sat	Cultural	3	German	5.7
Sat-Eins	General	3	German	5.2
RTL-Plus	General	4	German	4.6
BR3	General	1	German	4.6
Eins-Plus	Cultural	1	German	4.6
WDR3	General	1	German	4.6
Tele 5	General	1	German	4.6
Pro 7/Eureka*	General	1	German	4.6
RAI	General	3	Italian	3.6
TV3/Scan-Sat	General	3	Scandinavian	2.9
CNN	News	10	English	1.5
Screensport	Sport	12	English	1.2
Lifestyle	Women's	10	English	1.1
Children's Channel	Children's	4	English	0.8
NRK	General	1	Norwegian	0.4
Filmnet	Films	6	Dutch	0.2

*Channel currently undergoing major restructuring
Source *European Market and Media Facts 1989*, Saatchi and Saatchi Advertising Worldwide, London.

market coverage, which means that markets which do not allow the establishment of an indigenous or local station, but are unable to jam or block signals from a neighbouring transmitter, do in effect have a commercial station. Lastly, there are wide differences in television viewing rates where the West European daily average is between one and a half hours and five hours; the UK average of 5.79 hours and the US average of six and a half hours. Cable television varies from a penetration of 1.3 per cent in the UK to a high of 88.6 per cent in Belgium. Modern installation methods together with fibre-optic cable have significantly reduced the capital costs involved in cabling homes. However, penetration will increase slowly as it is still a slow and costly method of carrying television signals, particularly in rural areas. Cable television will remain complementary to satellite television rather than compete with it. Belgium has fifty-five licensed cable operators and for advertisers this allows a measure of targeting to a selected audience which satellite television can never hope to achieve.

However, satellite television holds the greatest promise for the future although it does present problems not only for advertisers and their clients in terms of standardization but for governments in terms of regulation. Table 12.15 lists the major satellite channels currently available in Europe. Note that the World Administrative Radio Conference (1977) assigned five satellite channels to every country in the world.

Pan-European research: readership data

There is generally no shortage of media data. The problem such as it exists is that surveys are restrictive, certainly national in character and usually sponsored by the publishers. Apart from the question of objectivity, there is a lack of verification for readership and circulation figures claimed. There is little complementarity as each uses a quite different means of sampling, and this non-standardized research methodology means that this plethora of existing national research material offers little insight into readership segments across nations. Just in Europe alone, there is for example:

Germany

'Media Analyse' covers all media.
'Frauentypologie', deals with female demographic and psychographic categories.
'Soll und Haben' analyses private capital investment patterns.

France

'CESP' (Centre d'Etudes des Supports de Publicite) covers all media.
'SECODIP', consumer market oriented research.
'SOFRES', consumer market oriented research.

Netherlands

'NOP' consumer market survey.
'NOJ' consumer market survey.
'DMS' survey of decision-makers.

Italy

'ISPI' (Indagine Stampa Periodica Italiana) is the most comprehensive.
'Lancio' is much more recent and less tried and tested.

Benelux

'CIM' (Centre of Information about the Media) all media, similar to the British Target Group Index.
'SOBEMAP' for qualitative studies of page traffic and product interest.

Spain

'EGM', the most reputable survey.

All sorts of problems arise in the study of the individual media in each of these countries. Benelux, for example, is not a country but a region incorporating Belgium, Netherlands and Luxembourg and with Flemish as well as French speakers. There are certain patterns of buying newspapers or magazines which are regional or national. There is the question too, of literacy levels and to a lesser extent of production both of which affect the demand and supply of print media.

Since 1980, various initiatives have been undertaken to arrive at surveys which examine readership segments across nations and these include:

1 *Fack Orvesto*, a Swedish publication which undertakes a postal survey of top male income earners in Sweden and some international publications.
2 German, Swiss and Dutch surveys of decision-makers which were all on an in-home personal interview basis but only the Dutch survey included women and each has a slightly different sampling framework.
3 *1980 European Businessman Readership Survey.* (A postal survey covering fifteen countries and including senior management in companies with more than 250 employees but the total universe is small, only 201,237.
4 *Pan European Survey II* (Twelve countries surveyed, not just top management). It identifies men of high status. This sample identifies a universe of 3,755,000 businessmen and a total universe of 6,258,333.

The use of international publications like these can help advertisers establish an international image. For most products, national media have had to be used to provide the range, frequency and level of coverage thought to be required for success.

Advertising standardization versus local adaptation

The technology for standardization including satellite television is now available but local tastes will still influence whether products will be successful or not. Food is often held to be the most culture-bound product. It is arguable whether this extends also to soft drinks but Coca-Cola's canned diet drinks did not have the success in Britain that was expected from US experience, not from lack of advertising but due to the British habit of drinking tea and coffee during the day and not canned drinks, as in the USA. With younger generations being weaned on Coke and Pepsi, this may well change, however, within the course of a generation. Another strategy to penetrate this market is currently being discussed between Nestle who makes Nescafe coffee and Nestea instant tea, and Coca-Cola to actually 'can' tea and coffee and offer it through vending machines.

Table 12.16 shows that although there may be an international youth segment which knows no frontiers, young people also have different national attitudes towards advertising. This does not prevent them, though from identifying with their international superstars of

Table 12.16   Attitudes of young people toward advertising; all 15–25 year olds agreeing

	Austria (%)	Greece (%)	Italy (%)	Nether-lands (%)	Spain (%)	Sweden (%)	UK (%)
1 Overall, advertising is more good than bad							
15–19	62	57	37	28	22	36	66
20–25	54	50	27	31	17	29	65
2 Advertising is mostly quite entertaining							
15–19	56	49	53	57	49	61	75
20–25	57	43	41	49	28	54	76
3 Advertisements are useful in giving me ideas about what to buy							
15–19	63	54	48	46	47	79	68
20–25	58	40	39	53	38	80	68
4 Advertising makes people buy things they do not want							
15–19	88	88	75	89	89	74	69
20–25	86	85	80	91	92	83	84
5 Advertisements have made me buy things I did not want							
15–19	31	46	44	23	51	33	38
20–25	35	46	42	29	50	33	38

Source   Rijkens, Rein and Miracle, G. E. (1986) *European Regulation of Advertising*, North-Holland, Amsterdam.

music, television and cinema nor dressing nor seeking to behave like them. Sometimes even anti-social behaviour has a favourable corporate outcome. In 1987, because of a fashion trend started by a pop group, youths started stealing manufacturer's name badges and logos from cars to wear as badges or pendants at nightclubs. Volkswagen were pleased to find their VW symbols so much in demand that they launched full page advertisements offering to give them free on demand through their dealership networks. The only problem was human nature: the excitement of stealing them would be gone and so VW owners as well as all other car owners continued to experience frustration with these thefts despite the best efforts of Volkswagen to stop it. The thefts stopped only once the fashion had died away.

There is little chance of a brand achieving a coherent international image when there is fragmentation in the market response. Secondly, as we have seen, not all media are universally available nor to the same degree. Worldwide advertising messages have to be suited to the best available media. A verbose TV commercial is unlikely to travel, on grounds of language alone. Marstellers estimate that an English language ad runs 15 per cent longer in French and 50 per cent longer in German, sometimes creating unforeseen difficulties in translating one print ad into several languages. Nevertheless, a multinational such a Kodak is now starting to regionalize its advertising in Europe.

To summarize, the media is seen then as the following.

Newspapers

Both national and international, e.g., *International Herald Tribune*, printed in Paris; the *Financial Times* now printed in London, Frankfurt and Tokyo, with proposals for printing daily also in the USA. The *Wall Street Journal* has had a European edition for a few years now but its circulation is less than a third that of the *Tribune*. Behind the *Wall Street Journal*, is the first national US newspaper, the tabloid *USA Today*. Few countries resemble Britain in this respect, however, and so it is more usual to find local or regional newspapers abroad. In France, for example, the pattern seems to be to buy a national daily in the morning and the regional paper in the evening. Of course another more recent entrant in this market was the launch of *The European* in May 1990 by the late Robert Maxwell. This has achieved a circulation of 340,000, approximately half of which are to be found in the UK. Although paraded as the first newspaper of the European Community it fails to present its readers with much of the hard news to be found in the more serious quality national dailies or periodicals such as the *Economist*. Its lower quality reporting, insufficient depth of coverage and lack of editorial policy place *The European* at a disadvantage with respect to the competition bidding for the European business person readership market.

Periodicals

These include business ad financial periodicals such as *Business Week; Economist; Euromoney; Fortune; International Management; L'Express International* and general magazines including *National Geographic; Newsweek; Time; Paris Match International;* and *Scientific American*. Many of these appeal to the same market segment across national boundaries. There are others also including certain international women's magazines, e.g, *Cosmopolitan, Elle* and various specialized interest and trade and technical publications which because of their very esoteric nature command only a small but dedicated readership. In-flight magazines may be seen as another way to target the business audience. Lufthansa has a circulation of 600,000; Swissair 500,000; Iberia 280,000; and British Airways with two magazines around 250,000 for each while Air France has one publication *Atlas* with a circulation between 250,000 and 380,000.

The cinema

A declining medium in western countries for a number of years because of home video recorders, but still very important in India, for example. Problems with this type of media are over the control of choice of cinema and the specific feature film which you wish your advertisement to accompany, and so this leads to lack of control over targeting, and quality of likely audience.

Increasingly, cinema makes use of international advertisements such as those prepared by Coca-Cola in their famous 'I'd love to teach the world to sing' advertisement. Not that this was an international advertisement as much as a blatantly US advertisement for a conspicuously US consumer product that has held a vast international market precisely on those grounds. For more than twelve years, the advertising industry has held to this advertisement as an example of global advertising. The true effectiveness of this particular advertisement could, however, only be judged by recall tests of the person in the street paired alongside the advertising executive. Both may have recall but for different reasons.

Television

There are few markets today which do not receive television. More than half the world's households have at least one. The role of advertising in television will vary more from country to country although it has elevated numerous 'rock' stars to the status of global commodities in the pursuit of the youth market. Exciting developments are taking place here which will retain television as the prime medium such as the developments of programming for certain identifiable niches, e.g., Nashville country and western music; religions, including islamic programming; ethnic and special interests including science fiction. Targeting like this makes it easier for advertisers to reach their chosen audience. Within Europe there are two broadening systems in operation. PAL and SECAM exist in 95 per cent of Europe's 125 million households and plans for more direct-broadcast satellites will cover 44 million people in France, 55 million in Germany and 22 million in Scandinavia. (See Table 12.16.)

Again national and international advertisements are being used because of origination costs. Multinationals, particularly, reap the benefits of such economies with video recorded adverts. On the negative side, the adverts are usually very US in style and fail to have as high a degree of impact on a British audience as on an US one. New developments are taking place in satellite television broadcasting which are likely to increase the number of television channels. The first Pan-European satellite television channel, SKY, is already available. Broadcasting from London, it makes use of a low-power 20 watt solar EC51 satellite. This satellite's 'footprint' covers Europe but because its signals are coded they have to be decoded at the other end. This is being done by means of linking up with existing television cable networks. One point which must be emphasized then is its precision because of this cable link. It is possible to state exactly who is receiving this signal and where.

The owners of News International, have invested heavily in a two-part strategy. The first objective is to maximize potential existing cable links. A lower-powered satellite, as at present, would otherwise require the viewer to purchase a large dish in order to receive its signal. Using existing cable networks means that the channel is able to start life with a ready-made audience. The second objective is to use a high-power satellite which will be a Direct Broadcasting Satellite (DBS) which will require only a small dish so cabling will not be necessary to receive SKY Channel. SKY merged operations in 1990 with the only other British satellite television company BSB (British Satellite Broadcasting) but as BSB use a different technology: a high power satellite and small dish converting a digital sound signal, the benefits of synergy will not be realized before the technology is standardized.

Developments in private subscriber cable television will create opportunities to target directly at selected market segments only; teletext services operated by the television companies including the new faster retrieval of Fastext provide free computer databank information on a variety of subjects including programme titles. Viewdata services such as Prestel operated by British Telecom which connects the television by telephone to a central computer and transmits pages of computer text back to the television screen at home, allows the viewer to interrogate the computer, order goods and withdraw, deposit or ask questions of his bank or building society account.

Yet the outright winner in the application of this technology has been the French PTT in their development of the Minitel system which has more than 60 per cent penetration of households in France.

Radio

Availability differs considerably. This may be regional, national or international. In Britain, commercial radio is regional; only the BBC which does not allow commercial advertising, is national, although plans exist to change this situation in the mid–1990s. Across Europe there is the mighty Radio Luxembourg, which broadcasts a strong signal across Western Europe and is a commercial station broadcasting in several languages. In general, though, fewer listen to radio except for certain hours of the day and for certain programmes. Audiences are selective.

Posters

Outdoor hoardings appear to be found everywhere apart, perhaps, from socialist countries, where they are less common. (See Table 12.18.) The former communist countries of Eastern Europe now have posters in abundance. Trams (streetcars) and buses are like painted posters.

Leaflets

These may be black and white, or colour, with or without photograph. This form of advertising is dependent on the local sophistication of the printing industry and this requires local organization.

Point-of-sale materials

These should be localized for the market concerned and are dependent on prevailing customs as well as average sales and storage area of retail outlets.

Direct mail

Again, this is a localized form of advertising. The tendency may be not to use mail but the telephone. Mail may be slow and unreliable. People may not be used to receiving mail other than official letters which are usually bad news. There may be no special commercial mailings rates which would also make this method expensive and the response slow.

Trade fairs and exhibitions

These are international in scope and seem to be expensive relative to the duration of the fair concerned, although governments usually support first-time exhibitors. It is up to the

Table 12.17 Household penetration of TV accessories and cable (%) 1987

	Colour TV	Multiset	VCR	Teletext	Remote Control	Cable TV Sets ('000)	% connected
Argentina	66.0	26.6	8.0	0	44.0	76.2	0.8
Australia	98.0	36.0	51.0	1.0			
Austria	85.2	25.6	20.5	9.4	54.2	423	15.2
Belgium	82.0	20.0	20.1	n.a	42.0	3,100	88.6
Brazil	48.0	32.0					
Canada	93.0						82.3
Colombia	50.2	27.4	18.2	0	25.4	184.0	5.0
Denmark	85.0	20.0	28.0	25.0	40.0	535.6	24.3
Finland	84.0	37.0	35.0	22.0	38.0	421	23.4
France	84.7	28.2	21.9	n.a	49.8	140	0.7
Germany	93.0	19.0	28.0	15.0	86.0	4,600.0	18.9
Greece	59.7	20.6	31.1	n.a	60.8	0	0
Hong Kong	97.0	5.0	23.0	0 0	11.0		
India	24.0	14.0	2.0				
Indonesia	25.0						
Ireland	85.0	16.0	26.0	2.0	25.0	310	32.9
Italy	75.5	32.9	9.0	14.3	68.4	0	0
Japan	99.0	46.0	45.0	0.1	0	4,586.0	12.3
Malaysia	70.0	11.0	33.0			100.0	1.0
Mexico	29.0	37.0	6.0			4,271	77.0
Netherlands	95.0	25.0	37.0	24.0	50.0	425	
New Zealand	92.0	0	46.0	6.5		2.0	27.4
Norway	96.0	n.a	50.0	30.3	n.a.	0	0.1
Philippines	8.0	0	4.0				0
Portugal	44.9	1.3	14.3	n.a	n.a		
Singapore	96.0	0	62.0	8.0			
South Korea	64.0						
Spain	81.4	21.6	24.6	0.5	12.1		0
Sweden	90.0	n.a	33.0	13.0	n.a	0	20.1
Switzerland	97.0	8.0	22.0	19.0	74.0	620.0	61.7
Taiwan	97.0	0	38.0			1,426.0	
Thailand	34.0	6.0	9.0				
Turkey	55.0	n.a	14.2	n.a	n.a		
UK	91.6	46.1	49.6	22.0	48.8	267.7	1.3
USA	97.0	63.0	62.0	1.0	72.0	49,500.0	54.8
Venezuela	60.0	0	12.0			50.0	1.5

Source *International Marketing Data and Statistics,* 14th ed, 1990 *European Market and Media Facts 1989,* Saatchi and Saatchi Advertising Worldwide, London.

Table 12.18   Poster site distribution in 1988

	Small	Medium	Large	Total
Austria	-	9,000	96,000	105,000
Belgium	-	52,000	18,200	70,200
Denmark	18,700	-	-	18,700
Finland	39,060	2,961	500	42,521
France	-	150,000	300,000	450,000
Germany	80,000	25,000	180,000	285,000
Ireland	3,153	753	2,611	6,517
Italy	60,000	8,000	3,500	51,500
Netherlands	40,000	8,000	3,500	51,500
Norway	11,000	1,000	3,500	15,500
Portugal	-	2,500	7,500	10,000
Spain	26,000	3,000	25,000	54,000
Sweden	-	8,210	2,380	10,590
Switzerland	128,500	30,000	1,000	159,500
UK	69,906	12,567	29,601	112,074

Source   *European Marketing Pocket Book 1991*, NTC Publications, Henley-on-Thames, Oxon.

company to decide the relevance, size and quality of the anticipated audience relative to his target audience. There are high costs of space, stand construction, and manning.

In addition, we could add transport advertising; outdoor advertising at sports grounds including football matches; and neon signs and local attitudes towards their use. Against this listing, a few questions have to be set such as prevailing literacy levels. This would rule out printed advertising messages and would influence advertising more towards the spoken word on radio and on television. Reception coverage of television and radio may be open to some doubt, as may the reliability of circulation figures paraded for foreign newspapers and periodicals, unless there is a counterpart for the Audit Bureau of Circulation (ABC) which conducts an independent audit of magazines sold and therefore confirms circulation figures.

As countries differ, so must the way of putting the message across. The best approach is to 'preserve some covert multinationalization in the campaign but to add a deft touch that is distinctly French or British or Italian'. A study of a select group of multinationals operating in Western Europe found that there was a high degree of standardization in over 70 per cent of these enterprises. Companies sought standardization without sacrificing the benefits of local entrepreneurship.

Pattern standardization is a more planned, flexible form of standardization. The overall theme and individual components of a campaign are designed originally for use in multiple markets, developed to provide a uniformity in direction but not in detail. A pre-planned effort is made to develop an overall corporate advertising strategy and to provide some of the benefits attributed to standardizations while permitting local flexibility in response to individual market differences.

The main objectives in standardizing include:

1 To present a worldwide corporate image through media that are becoming increasingly international.
2 To reduce production and creative costs through economies of scale.
3 To reduce message confusion where there is media overlap or country-to-country consumer mobility.
    One television film could be used in twenty-five or so markets. Also there is media overlap on the continent as, for example, among Dutch/Belgian/French/German channels. Multinationals tend to rely heavily on home-country agencies with overseas branches.
    Greater standardization is likely in the future.

Table 12.19   Issues in advertising and the countries where they are particularly sensitive

Issues	*Sensitive countries*
Advertising to children	Canada, Scandinavia, USA, Greece, West Germany, Austria, Holland (toothbrush symbol in confectionery ads)
Class action by consumer associations	EC Commission, USA.
Comparative advertising	EC Commission (encouragement), France (relaxation), Philippines (ban), USA (encouragement)
Consumer protection in general	EC Commission, Scandinavia, UN organizations, USA.
Corrective ads	USA, EC Commission.
Feminine hygiene commercials (mandatory prior screening)	Canada (British).
Food, drugs, and cosmetics commercials (mandatory prior screening)	Canada, Mexico, Austria, Netherlands, Switzerland, West Germany.
Infant formula promotion	World Health Organization/UNICEF.
Reversal of the burden of proof on the advertiser	EC Commission, Scandinavia, USA.
Sexism in advertising	Canada, Netherlands, Scandinavia, UK, USA.
Use of foreign languages in advertisements	France, Mexico, Quebec Province.
Use of foreign materials, themes and illustrations	Korea, Moslem countries, Peru, Philippines.
Wording used in food and drug ads	Belgium, EC Commission, USA.
Cigarette advertising	Luxembourg, UK, Italy, Spain, Switzerland, Canada.
Alcohol advertising	Netherlands, Portugal, Spain, Switzerland, Canada.

Source Boddewyn, J. J. (1981) The global spread of advertising regulations. *MSU Business Topics*, Spring, 5–13.

Table 12.20　Advertising regulations and response to these regulations

Key regulatory factors	Major regulatory developments	Suggested business responses
Consumer protection (for example, against untruthful, unfair, misleading ads). Protection for competitors (for example, against the misuse of comparative and co-operative advertising). Environment protection (for example, against outdoor advertising). Civil rights protection (for example, against sexist ads). Religion (for example, against the advertising of contraceptives). Standards of taste and decency (for example, against sexy ads). Nationalism (for example, against the use of foreign languages, themes, and illustrations).	Prior substantiation of advertising claims is becoming the norm. Growing product restrictions affect the advertising of them. More informative ads are in order. Advertising language is being restricted. Vulnerable groups such as children are becoming the target of advertising regulations. More groups and people can now sue advertisers. Penalties are getting stiffer.	More self-regulation by industry. Collaboration with consumer organizations. Greater self-discipline by advertisers. Expanded lobbying and public advocacy. Revised marketing and promotion policies.

Source　Boddewyn, J. J. 1981 The global spread of advertising regulations. *MSU Business Topics*, Spring, 5–13; *Marketing*, 16 August 1983, 52.

Substantiating advertising claims

Firstly, countries where false advertising claims will not be entertained and substantiations may be sought. Clearance is mandatory for all commercials in France, Australia, Finland and the UK, and for Canada in relation to advertising to children. Self-regulatory bodies exist in at least fourteen countries including Denmark, Norway, UK, Spain, Sweden, and Venezuela.

Product restrictions

If the product is considered immoral, unsafe, or unhealthy, its promotion is likely to be restricted. Thus most countries ban or severely limit the advertising of cigarettes, alcoholic beverages, lotteries and pharmaceuticals because their use, misuse or overuse is considered undesirable.

Balancing information and emotional appeal

Slogans like 'Things go better with Coke' allow people to imagine themselves in new situations. Are they being sold the sizzle or the steak? The concept or the product? The backlash over the new Coke formulation tends to show how consumers confuse the two. The advertiser seeks to move the audience from past awareness and interest to evaluation, trial and adoption. Comparative advertising is supported by the EC and the US administration because it is more informative, identifying and contrasting brands.

Table 12.21   US corrective advertising cases

Company	Product	Claim	Order Type	Disclosure features
Amstar Corp. (1973)	Domino sugar	sugar benefits	consent	25 per cent of ad costs
Beauty-Rama Carpet Center (1973)	Retailer	prices	consent	firm used 'bait & switch'
Boise Tire Co. (1973)	Uniroyal tyres	tyre ratings	consent	one ad
ITT Continental Baking (1971)	Profile bread	caloric content	consent	25 per cent of one year's ads
Lens Craft Research (1974)	Contact lenses	medical claims	consent	four weeks
Matsushita Electric of Hawaii (1971)	Panasonic TV sets	hazard ratings	consent	one ad
National Carpet (1973)	Retailer	prices	consent	firm used 'bait & switch'
Ocean Spray Cranberries (1972)	Cranberry drink	food energy claim	consent	one of every four ads
Payless Drug Co. (1973)	Motorcyle helmets	safety	consent	equal number to original ads
Rhode Island Carpets (1974)	Retailer	prices	consent	firm used 'bait & switch'
RJR Foods Inc. (1973)	Hawaiian punch	juice content	consent	every ad until effects are shown
Shangri La Industries (1972)	Swimming pools	availability and terms	consent	25 per cent of one year's ads
STP Corp. (1976)	Oil additive	effectiveness	consent	one ad, 14 media
Sugar Information (1974)	Sugar	sugar benefits	consent	one ad, seven media
Warner-Lambert (1975)	Listerine	effectiveness claim	litigated	correction in $10 million of ads
Wasems Inc. (1974)	Wasems vitamins	vitamin benefits	consent	one ad, seven insertions
Yamaha International (1974)	Yamaha motorcycle	motorcycle safety	consent	corrective letter

Table 12.22   Wilkie, McNeill, Mazis' conclusions on corrective advertising

1 The FTC is empowered to order corrective advertising as a remedy against deceptive advertising campaigns.
2 There are important legal constraints as to when and in what manner the FTC can employ this remedy form.
3 Corrective advertising holds the potential to yield beneficial effects for consumers.
4 Corrective advertising appears to hold the potential to affect the sales and/or image of the advertised brand.
5 There is little evidence of a systematic FTC program for corrective advertising: <ul><li>bursts of case activity have been followed by long periods of inactivity.</li><li>philosophical and personnel changes occurred throughout the 1970s and early 1980s at both the staff and Commissioner levels.</li><li>past orders have used a wide range of requirements for corrective advertising.</li></ul>
6 Consent negotiations between FTC staff members and company representatives have played a key role in the exact requirements in almost every case to date.
7 Consumer effectiveness of corrective advertising has not been the primary concern of the orders issued to date.
8 In communication terms, past corrective advertising orders against major advertisers appear to have been weak.
9 In terms of consumer impacts, the major corrective advertising orders appear *not* to have been successful in remedying consumer misimpressions across the marketplace.
10 If corrective advertising is to continue as an FTC remedy, some changes in the form of the orders will be required.

Source   Wilkie, W. L., McNeil, D. L., and Mazis, M .B. (1988) Marketing's scarlet letter: the theory and practice of corrective advertising In   *Promotional Management: Issues and Perspectives*, Govoni, N., Eng, R., and Golpe, M., Prentice Hall, Englewood Cliffs, NJ.

Use of language

The US and the EC are considering the legitimacy of words such as 'health', 'homemade', and 'natural', and 'organic' when applied to food. The USA does not allow 'cough remedies' but 'cough suppressants'. French xenophobia prohibits totally the use of English words which have almost successfully passed into the French language such as 'cash and carry', 'jumbo jet', 'supermarket', etc. French law now forbids the use of English in French advertising. These new products and concepts need now to be translated into French in order to find a market in France. Similarly, bilingual Canada is facing similar difficulties where most products appear with labels in French and English.

Vulnerable groups

The unwritten convention that is generally adhered to is that it is unfair to advertise to the young, old, poor, sick, recently bereaved, and ignorant and this is generally observed.

Legal action

The traditional view that only injured parties can sue is now being changed within the European Community on the grounds that everyone has an interest in having false, unfair, and misleading advertising stopped before damage can be done. A draft EC directive would allow customers and competitors as well as their legitimate associations, to start legal action against unfair or misleading advertising.

Penalties

In settling a suit brought by the US Federal Trade Commission (FTC), the STP Corporation – a company in the main producing oil additives was ordered to spend $200,000 to place notices in thirty-five newspapers and eleven magazines with an estimated readership of 78 million. The notices stated that tests conducted by STP cannot be relied on to support its claim that its product reduces oil consumption.

An EC draft directive on misleading and unfair advertising would permit courts to issue injunctions to cease and desist 'even without proof of intention or neglect or of actual prejudice.' Courts would be allowed to require publication of a corrective statement and of the court decision as well as to impose penalties taking into account the extent of the damage (this is already the case in France and the USA).

Develop self-discipline

Some companies have their own code of ethics, and in general these would suggest that perhaps there are less untruths to be found in industry and commerce than in personal classified advertisements for house and car sales, or armed services recruiting campaigns and supportive literature.

Finally, the last word on multinational standardization and regulation must go to George M. Black, Chairman of J. Walter Thompson's Frankfurt office, 'If I were to make a film for Europe-wide distribution, by the time we went through all the rules governing national advertising, we would be left with a poster.'

References

Anderson, R. D. (1982), Creativity and compromise in multinational advertising. *Industrial Marketing Digest*, **7**, (1), 37–43.

Boddewyn, J. J. (1981) The global spread of advertising regulations. *MSU Business Topics*, Spring.

Britt, S. H. (1969), Are so-called successful advertising campaigns really successful? *Journal of Advertising Research*, **9**, 3–9.

Brooke, A. S. (1983), Psychographic segmentation in Europe. *Journal of Advertiser Research*, **22**, (6), 19–27.

Jefkins, F. (1976), *Advertising Today*, International Textbook Company Ltd., London.

Keegan, W. (1974), *Multinational Marketing Management*, Prentice-Hall, Englewood Cliffs, NJ.

Keegan, W. (1989), *Global Marketing Management*, Prentice-Hall, Englewood Cliffs, NJ.

Killough, J. (1978), Improved payoffs from transnational advertising, *Harvard Business Review*, July-August, 102–110.

Lilien, G. (1982), A descriptive model of the trade show budgeting decision process. *Industrial Marketing Management*, 12 February, 25–29.

Peebles, D. M., Ryans, J. K., and Vernon, I. R. A New Perspective on Advertising Standardisation. *Journal of Marketing*, **22**, (1), 28–34.

Rogers, E. M. (1962), *Diffusion of Innovations*, New York, Free Press.

Rosson, P., and Seringhaus, R. (1989), Business Performance of International Trade Fairs. In *Dimensions of International Business no. 2*, Carlton University School of Business, International Business Study Group, IBSG Occasional Paper V, June.

Ryans Jr., J. K., and Ratz, D. G. (1987), Why standardize? *International Journal of Advertising*, **6**, 145–158.

Samiee, J. K., and Ryans, J. R., (1982) Advertising and consumerism in Europe. *Journal of International Business Studies*, Spring/Summer, 109–14.

Thorelli, H. B., and Thorelli, S. V. (1977), *Consumer Information Systems and Consumer Policy*, Ballinger Publishing Co. Ltd., Cambridge, MA.

Vardar, N. (1989), Management of international advertising: involvement of foreign headquarters in US subsidiaries and agencies. Unpublished Ph.D. thesis, Manchester School of Management, University of Manchester.

Vardar, N., and Paliwoda, S. J. (1989), International advertising agencies – organisational structure for global campaigns. Marketing Education Group (MEG), 22nd Annual Conference Proceedings, Glasgow Business School, Scotland, pp. 425–452.

Wiechmann, U. E., and Lewis, G. P. (1979), Problems that plague multinational markets. *Harvard Business Review*, July-August, 118–24.

Key reading

Govoni, N., Eng, R., and Galper, M. (1988), *Promotional Management: Issues and Perspectives*, Prentice-Hall, Englewood Cliffs, New Jersey.

Boddewyn, J. J. (1987), International advertisers face government hurdles. *Marketing News*, 8 May, 20–21, 26.

Britt S. H. (1968), Are so-called successful advertising companies really successful? *Journal of Advertising Research*, June, 3–9.

Buzzell, Roy (1968), Can you standardize multinational marketing? *Harvard Business Review*, November-December, 102–113.

Day, B. (1985), Global advertising: the facts and the fantasy. *Admap*, September, 434–437.

Douglas, S. P., and Wind, Y. (1987), The myth of globalisation. *Columbia Journal of World Business*, Winter, 19–29.

Gates, S. R., and Egelhoff W. G. (1986), Centralisation in headquarters-subsidiary relationships. *Journal of International Business Studies*, Summer, 77–92.

Gerrie, A. (l987), Ads sans frontières. *Marketing*, 2 April, 43–44.

Hawkins, S. (1983), How to understand your partner's cultural baggage. *International Management Europe*, September, 48–57.

Jain, S. C. (1989), Standardisation of international marketing strategy: some research hypotheses. *Journal of Marketing*, **53**, 70–79.

Marketing News (1987), Marketing can be global but ads must remain cultural. 31 July, 26–28.

Martenson, R. (1987), Is standardisation of marketing feasible in culture-bound industries? A European case study. *International Marketing Review*, Autumn, 7–17.

Rau, I. A., and Peeble, J. F. Standardisation of marketing strategy by multinationals. *International Marketing Review*, Autumn, 18–28.

Rosen B. N., Boddewyn, J. J., and Louis, E. A. (1989), US brands abroad: an empirical study on global boundary. *International Marketing Review*, **6**, (1), 7–19.

Ryan, J. K. Jr., and Ratz, D. G. (1987), Advertising standardisation: a re-examination. *International Journal of Advertising*, **6**, 145–148.

Schwoerer, J. (1987), Measuring advertising effectiveness: emergence of an international standard? *European Research*, **15**, (1), 40–51.

Terpstra, V., and Yu, M. C (1988), Determinants of foreign investment of US advertising agencies. *Journal of International Business Studies*, Spring, 33–46.

Note EIBIS International specializes in the preparation, translation and distribution of information to the world press. They issue technical, scientific, industrial and business information to over 25,000 publications throughout the world. They produce a number of booklets which they distribute free of charge. Their address is EIBIS International, 3 Johnson's Court, Fleet Street, London EC4A 3EA (Tel: 071 353 5151; Fax 071 583 0210).

13
International marketing planning

The international marketing plan

Planning is a process which logically we would expect to find taking place at all levels in the corporate organization. Unfortunately the evidence which exists shows that companies exercise planning more in the domestic sales organization than in the international. As an activity, planning should encompass all the factors which have been dealt with separately in this book so far, namely the marketing mix variables and the consideration of environments. So if there is lack of planning and consequent lack of control it is because top management motivation is lacking in knowledge of what to do next. A positive approach is required of international marketing planning, planning to make things happen. As John Lennon observed, 'Life is what is happening to you when you are busy making plans.'

International marketing cannot succeed without the active support and commitment of top management, yet market research, as applied to foreign markets, is still dominated by subjectivity and lacks the commitment in both the time and resources devoted to domestic market research. Consequently, international marketing planning is pursued at a much lower level and with less commitment than domestic marketing planning. With international marketing planning, the purpose, form and methodology employed differs according to company size, organization structure and length of involvement in international business activities. In its simplest form, international marketing planning as such may consist of no more than a sales budget or allocation handed to country managers by corporate management. Equally, it may also be complex, recognizing the higher-ordered interdependencies created by a global perspective of a truly multinational corporation. It has been argued in fact, that co-ordinated plans and strategies are the hallmarks of the truly global company (Hulbert, 1980).

Mike Wilson, in *The Management of Marketing* identifies the following main elements of marketing plans.

- A statement of basic assumptions with regard to long- and short-term economic, technological, social and political developments.
- A review of past sales and profit performance of the company's major products by markets and geographic areas.
- An analysis of external opportunities and threats by markets and products.
- An analysis of the company's and competitors' strengths and weaknesses in facilities, products, finance, customer acceptance, distribution, personnel, pricing, advertising, sales promotion, etc. This analysis will often include assessments of indirect competition.
- A statement of long-term objectives (marketing, financial, growth, etc.), and the strategies for achieving them.
- A statement of the objectives and strategies for the next year with a detailed breakdown in

units and revenue for each product, each market, each geographical area, and each unit of the company's marketing force.

- A programme schedule which is carefully co-ordinated with the budgets for the units involved and which shows the sequence of all marketing activities for each product in each market and geographic area so that public relations, advertising, product publicity, sales promotion, and field selling can be co-ordinated.
- Statements of objectives for each of the following years similar to the statements for the next year but less detailed.
- A summary of how the company intends to capitalize on its opportunities and correct its weaknesses; key priorities, etc.

Cain (1970) sees international marketing planning as having three levels:

1   Operational planning

Shorter range (one- and three-year) planning is the responsibility of each overseas operating unit. The format in general follows that of US divisions and is supplied by the headquarters' planning staff. Plans include sales, profit and cash-flow projections by product line, market share, capital requirements, etc. Although plans are integrated at regional levels, individual unit plans are forwarded intact to New York headquarters.

2   Strategic planning

Operating units – most of which are national in scope – are asked to plan ahead on a longer term basis for new products which might be developed from within or acquired. Headquarters deliberately provide only very general guidelines as to how far afield a local

Table 13.1   International marketing planning matrix

	Marketing planning variables					
International decisions	*Situation analysis*	*Problems – opportunity analysis*	*Objectives*	*Marketing programme*	*Marketing budgets*	*Sales vol cost/profit estimate*
A Commitment decision						
B Country selection						
C Mode of entry						
D Marketing strategy						
E Marketing organization						

Source   Becker, H., and Thorelli, H. B. (1980) Strategic planning in international marketing. In *International Marketing Strategy.* (Thorelli and Becker), Pergamon, Oxford, p. 370.

operation might explore. This is done to encourage the local managers to stretch their outlook. However, the scope normally is confided to the unit's country of operation, and plans are subject to review at headquarters.

3   Corporate planning

Worldwide plans are developed at international headquarters, tied closely to overall corporate objectives and plans. This planning takes two forms:

- protective planning
- opportunity planning

Protective planning is strategic and long-range in character, anticipating worldwide changes in markets and business conditions relating to the present scope of operation. On the other hand, 'opportunity planning' is directed toward seeking new business directions for growth and diversification.

Overall, corporate expectations of planning are that it must:

- Minimize the negative consequences of a variety of adverse exogenous and endogenous conditions.
- Balance the available corporate resources against the set of global opportunities and alternatives.
- Co-ordinate and integrate the activities of a necessarily decentralized organization.
- Create a framework for a communication system which ensures that all parts of the organization are striving towards the same set of overall objectives and in doing so are using policies which are beneficial for the corporation as a whole rather than just individual parts of it.

Shruptine and Toyne (1981) argue that multinationals should concentrate on standardizing the process of planning rather than standardizing their marketing strategies. Planning is a decentralized activity not because of the geographic dispersion of the individual company units or because their individual legal status frequency provides them with a high degree of autonomy, but because differences in local operating conditions demand a local response.

Selectivity and distortion can, however, enter into the environment surveillance process via the data-gathering behaviour of the organization. Perceptual bias can enter the process at the stage of interpreting or evaluating the data, often performed by someone other than the data gatherer. Perceptual bias also occurs at the data transmission linkage between the data gatherers and the interpreters and between interpreters and users. A lingering doubt remains as to whether data gathers tend to ignore data which is more qualitative than quantitative in nature, and so less easily verifiable.

The task facing a head office then is to ensure conformity within a set of overall objectives, performance criteria and company-wide policies to eliminate or at least minimize intra-company effects and inefficiencies. In many multinationals this situation has led to the institution of two distinctly separate long-range planning cycles which can be referred to as 'bottom-up' and 'top-down' planning. 'Top-down' planning may be a particularly appropriate approach when subsidiary managers around the world are not very familiar with the concepts and practices of long-range planning. 'Bottom-up' may be particularly relevant where local conditions are sufficiently different to necessitate a local plan. Here there is management recognition of the local subsidiary manager as an expert in the corporate planning cycle. In many cases, however, locational decisions seem to evolve from the culmination of a series of apparently unrelated events rather than a specific plan. There are three broad sets of factors to consider here.

1 Country-related variables that characterize the business conditions in a certain country or region in terms of the political, economic, legal, competitive and tax situation, the market potential, cost and availability of manpower, local capital, and required supplies.
2 Product-related characteristics such as a product's typical life cycle, the degree of technical sophistication, and economies of scale that are associated with its production, the relative importance of transportation costs, etc.
3 Company-related variables which take into account such characteristics as a firm's size and its experience in international operations and policies as an expression of the firm's management philosophy.

Managerial decision making will result in specific marketing programmes on a global basis, with differentiated marketing programmes. This differentiation is in respect of both budget

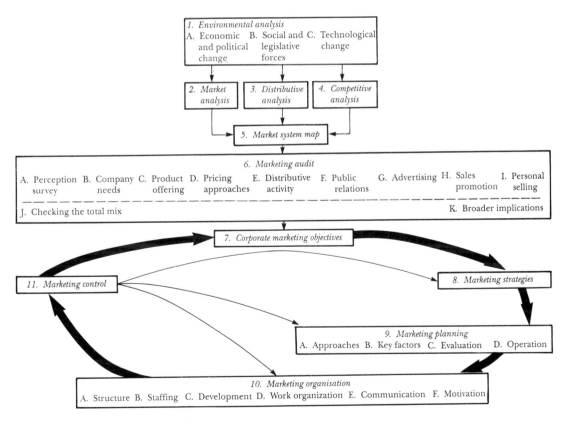

Fig 13.1   *Planning the marketing function*
Source   Wilson, M. (1980) *The Management of Marketing*, Gower, Aldershot, Hants, p. 127.

allocations and specific emphasis on marketing mix elements. The annual operating plan is the basis of planning in virtually all multinational subsidiaries. For most it is the starting point for longer term planning, typically for a five-year period. In the majority of cases, long-term planning is an exercise in extrapolation and very few companies practise strategic market planning.

Marketing programmes should be based on the concept of global segmentation. Unlike differentiating markets on a purely demographic or geographic basis, a segmentation study of urban dwellers across different countries may reveal greater similarities than a similar study conducted across the same country. The most viable and profitable segmentation basis is the examination of underlying factors which determine buyer demand. These factors can be broadly classified as *buyer expectations* and *buying climate*. The first is based on culture, social stratification, and family structure. The second refers to the specific situation in which consumers make decisions to buy and consume goods and services. It includes the economic, demographic, and physical settings in which buyers go about choosing and consuming products and services. It is based on

- financial factors (disposable personal income, asset holdings, etc.),
- geographical factors (temperature, humidity and altitude, tropical v temperate climate, etc.), and
- demographic factors (size of family, age distributions of family members, life cycle of family, etc.)

In addition to difficulties often encountered in gathering information within the host country, there can sometimes be delays in the communication of information within the multinational. If there is difficulty in communicating relevant information from one subsidiary to another, or from a domestic product division to an overseas subsidiary, the planning activity within that subsidiary can be severely disrupted. It is not unusual for a subsidiary to be given a new product to introduce without adequate information on how that same product may have fared on launch elsewhere. It is even more common to find careless requests for information which emerge from head offices. Educating home-office personnel to the realities of subsidiary life may help, but companies must also pay more attention to the planning of intra-company communication flows. Procedures often need streamlining and more careful information management should result in a communication flow better co-ordinated to subsidiary needs. Similarly, there may be excessive emphasis by head office on short-term sales and product results. In either situation, strategic planning is neglected to the longer term detriment of the company involved.

Again, culture has a role to play here. Chapter 14 deals with markets and organizations which are created and managed by people. In this regard, the work by Williamson (1975) is particularly interesting for we adopt value orientations which we have learned. The degree to which people align themselves on the following six paired variables helps identify these values:

1 Egalitarian or elitist.
2 Laying emphasis on accomplishment or inherited attributes.
3 Expecting material or non-material rewards.
4 Evaluating individuals or product in terms of objective norms or subjective standards.
5 Focusing on the distinctiveness of the parts (intensiveness) rather than the general characteristics of the whole (extensiveness).

Table 13.2 Information used for marketing planning by nationality of subsidiary

Source of information	Proportion of firms using			All firms
	American	European	Japanese	
Distributors	43%	38%	33%	40%
Sales force	75%	71%	83%	74%
Management of other subsidiaries	39%	54%	50%	47%
Marketing research dept.	57%	71%	0%	57%
Historical data	75%	79%	33%	72%
Trade sources	29%	29%	50%	31%
Commercial suppliers	36%	8%	33%	24%
Official sources	39%	58%	50%	48%
Home Office	14%	38%	17%	24%
Number of firms	(28)	(24)	(6)	(58)

Source Hulbert, J. W., Brandt, W. K. and Richers, R. (1980) Marketing planning in the multinational subsidiary: practices and problems. *Journal of Marketing*, **44**, 10.

6 Oriented towards personal or group gain.

A problem-solving orientation appears most commonly in a culture that has strong egalitarian, material, and individual value orientations. Individuals compete for, and win, status and material rewards on the basis of performance. Rewards for performance may take the form of increased status, wealth or both. In the USA, positional rewards limited to title rather than increased salary are viewed as almost no rewards at all, whereas in Britain they are highly respected. Promotional information which supports products in culturally differentiated markets must also be individualized. Cultural values will strongly influence meaningful associations. They will control the types of product claims people are predisposed to entertain or consider plausible; they will influence the basis on which claims may be rendered verifiable but to admit the relevance of cultural values is not enough; management must assess the significance of cultural attitudes and not just take into account 'comparative curiosities like polygamy and cannibalism, or merely study such consumer habits as the frequency with which people change their clothes'. Table 13.2 examines the differences in information used for marketing planning by nationality of subsidiary while Table 13.3 examines the relative importance of data sources for five environmental domains.

As to the conditions under which planning has failed, a study by Ringbakk (1976) into corporate planning failures of 300 companies in Europe and America revealed ten reasons:

- Planning is not integrated into the total management system.
- Only some levels of management are involved in the process.
- Responsibility for planning is vested solely in planning staff.
- Management expects plans to be realized exactly as planned.
- Too much detail is attempted.
- Management fails to implement the plan.

- Extrapolation and financial projections are confused with planning.
- Inadequate information inputs.
- Too much emphasis is placed on only one aspect of planning.
- The different dimensions of planning are not understood.

However, it must be remembered that this is related to corporate strategic planning rather than international marketing planning which is inherently more difficult again because of the extra variables to be considered.

Turning specifically to international marketing planning, the four most prevalent problems adjudged by Cain (1970) for planning in the international arena may be said to relate to:

1 *Failure to 'take off'*. This may be due to distance, language, management climate, diversity and other factors unique to individual companies.
2 *Lack of acceptance by management*. It has been difficult for US companies to get overseas managers – whether nationals or Americans – to accept or use planning. This is often experienced when plans have originated solely at home base and do not reflect the 'real world' of the manager. As with planning anywhere, 'textbook' plans are doomed to failure.
3 *Quality of planning*. In many companies, foreign operating units have not yet attained the same quality of planning as their domestic counterparts. One reason for this is that planning data are neither as accurate nor as reliable as companies would wish.
4 *Lack of co-operation* among international units.

One of the accepted objectives of planning on an international scale is to realize synergistic benefits among various independent operations. While international planners must, and do, think synergistically, management abroad is inclined to think parochially.

With regard to the current practice of international marketing planning in the multinational corporation, Sheth (1977) argued the following.

1 There is no systematic and continuous assessment of buyer needs and expectations in the current practice of most corporations. Most of the marketing research is after-the-event: to

Table 13.3 Relative importance of data sources for the five environmental domains (combined US and European samples)

Domains	Outside services	Outside experts	Home Office staff	Home Office top management	Business unit top management
Social	1.84	1.11	2.41	2.80	2.27
Political	1.80	1.32	2.31	2.82	1.96
Ecological	1.77	1.51	2.49	2.06	2.27
Economic	1.67	1.65	2.86	2.60	2.07
Technological	1.47	1.58	2.79	2.30	2.46

Source O'Connell, J. J., and Zimmerman, J. W. (1979) Scanning the international environment. *California Management Review, XXII*, (2), 19.

find out whether a new concept or product developed by R & D will be acceptable to the customers. A continuous research effort to systematically monitor the current and changing needs of the market place is required.

2 Present practice is to perform marketing research on a country-to-country basis. In addition, most multinational business decisions are centred around the question of whether the company should extend its strategic programmes to new countries or adjust it to suit local conditions. While such a practice was probably quite appropriate in previous times, and may continue to be useful even today for exporting or trading companies, it is myopic in the long run. It is not difficult to trace a number of failures in multinational activities directly to this practice. A systematic and continuous worldwide assessment of buyer needs and expectations is likely to point out that:

- potential markets are mostly in the metropolitan areas especially in the less developed countries,
- clustering metropolitan areas both within and between countries is more meaningful from a marketing viewpoint, and
- we shall probably find greater similarity between metropolitan areas across countries than within countries.

3 The assessment of customer needs and expectations should be based on data collected at the micro level, namely the household or business unit.

The focus on customer needs is a more enduring concept and tends to avoid the myopic tendency which a company is likely to fall into as its products become mature in their life cycle.

The limits of standardization

Quelch and Hoff (1986) consider four functions with regard to the appropriate degree of standardization or adaption:

- *Business functions* from marketing and finance to research and development.
- *Products.* Variables such as economies of scale and whether the product may be in any way regarded as culture-bound are important here.
- *Marketing mix elements.* Few companies use the same marketing programme worldwide.
- *Countries.* Small markets may more willingly accept a standard programme than large markets with strong management teams.

It is not to be seen as an either/or proposition but as an approach that may fall somewhere between the two ends of a wide spectrum. As Quelch and Hoff point out: 'The big issue today is not whether to go global but how to tailor the global marketing concept to fit each business.'

Taking the example of Coca-Cola and of Nestle, Quelch and Hoff identify five points at which headquarters can intervene with regard to three major problems: inconsistent brand identities; limited product focus; and slow new product launches. Persuasion can take the form of specialist headquarters staff visiting the subsidiaries 'not as critics but as coaches' so building trust while disseminating information about new methods and techniques. A matrix

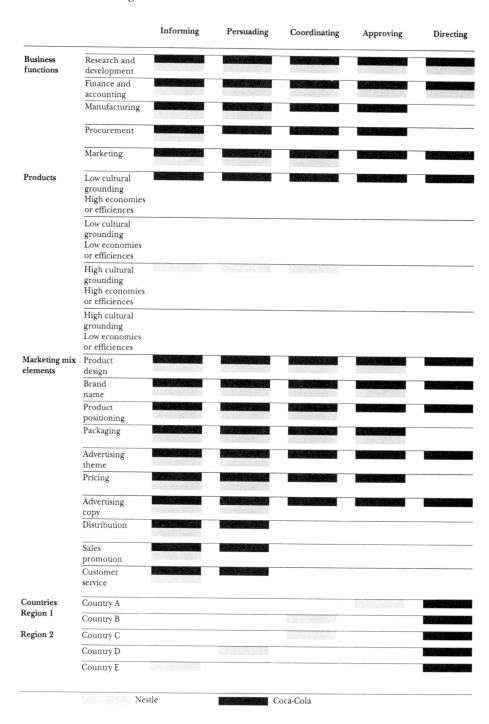

Figure 13.2   *Global marketing planning matrix: how to get there*
Source   Quelch, J. A., and Hoff, E. J. (1986) Customising global marketing. *Harvard Business Review*, May–June, 59–68.

organization will mean headquarters shares responsibility and authority for programming. Co-ordination can take place with local subsidiaries working to headquarters approval or on their own working with certain agreed guidelines. While it is relatively easy to delegate authority it is not possible to direct motivation. This stimulus and encouragement is very necessary but difficult to build into an organizational plan, other than in ensuring that local subsidiaries have a degree of autonomy in their decision making and a mix of global and local brands.

In this respect Ohmae (1990) usefully points to the difference existing between Japanese and other Western multinational companies. The Japanese multinational is much more of a 'listening post' in that foreign market. The Japanese organizational structure is designed to transfer resources to critical areas.

Ohmae (1990) also points to the function division of labour among headquarters, regional headquarters and country management emphasizing how many important functions can be effectively delegated to regional headquarters within the Triad.

Concentration on key markets

A study which had great influence for a while was *Concentration on Key Markets*, undertaken by the British Export Trade Research Organization (BETRO). It was published by the British

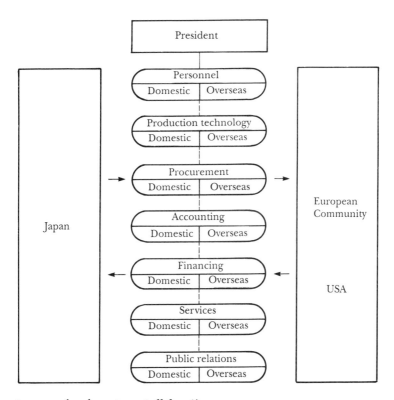

Figure 13.3 *Japanese headquarters staff functions*
Source Ohmae, K. (1990) *Triad power: The Coming Shape of Global Competition*, The Free Press, p. 199.

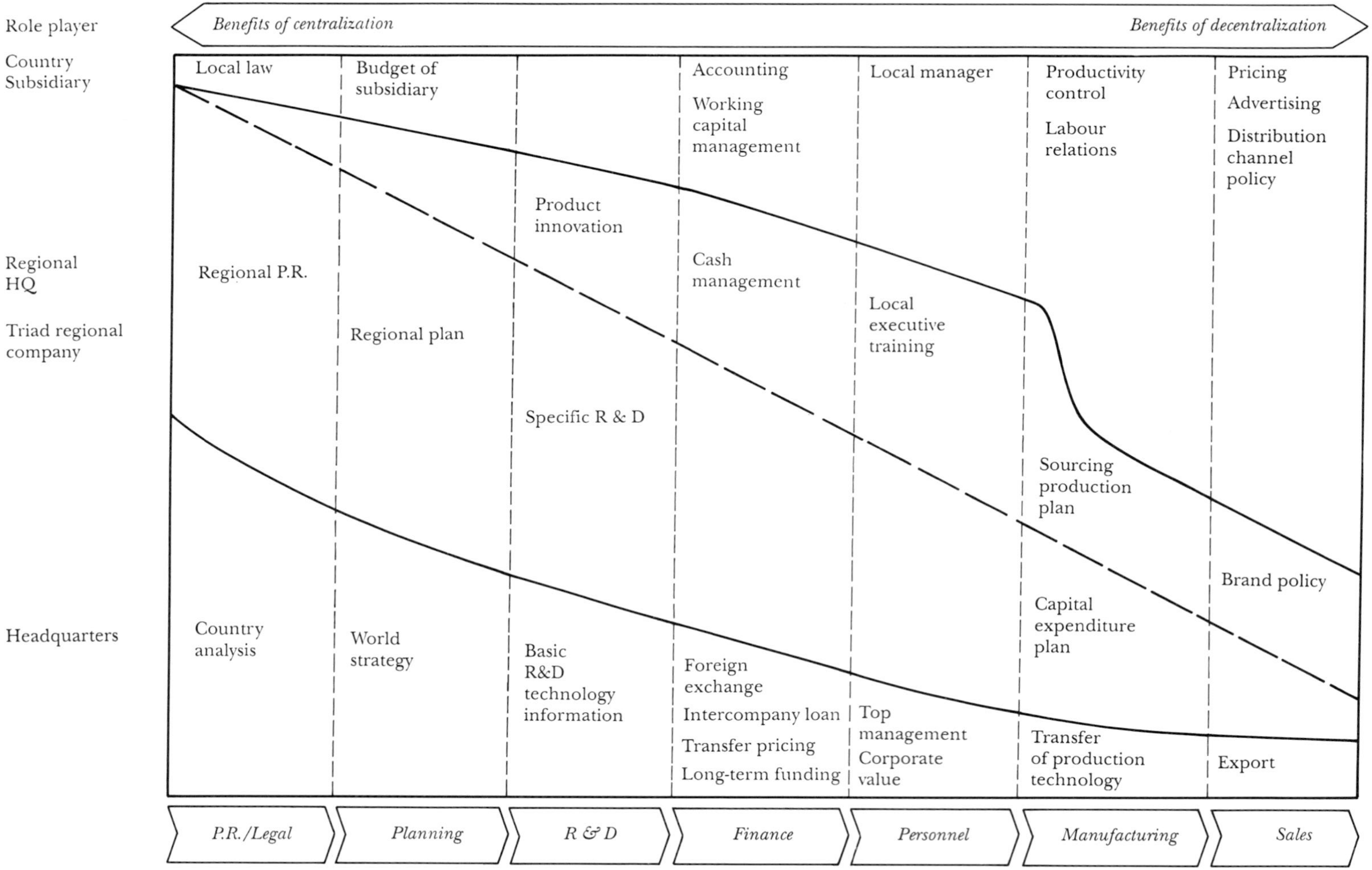

Figure 13.4

Source Ohmae, K. (1990) *Triad Power: The Coming Shape of Global Competition*, The Free Press, 186.

Overseas Trade Board (BOTB) in 1975 and in revised form in 1979. The basic objective of this study was to establish among exporting companies the markets in which they were successful out of all the export markets in which they were represented. Reviewing the allocation of company resources to these export markets, the overall recommendation was made that companies should concentrate on those markets which accounted for the bulk of their current export sales.

The BETRO study claimed a representative sample of 25 per cent of all British exporters, broken down into the following groups.

- One-third selling to less than thirty countries: exporting some 75–80 per cent of their output in the range £10 million or more, yet with a surprisingly small salesforce of some two to four men.
- A further one-third sold to between thirty and sixty countries, but here the large number of countries included some seen as an insurance policy in case existing markets elsewhere turned sour.
- The final one-third were selling to between sixty and 180 countries but were suffering from the diffusion of total effort expended over some many markets which proved a poor utilization of resources for the company concerned.

The issues which the BETRO report addressed specifically were the following:

1 Is it right to dissipate the efforts of a small selling organization over 154 countries with relatively modest returns?
2 Would it be wise to have a fresh look at the ten countries taking 90 per cent of company exports and ask 'Which are the four or five where we stand the best chance of increasing substantially our market share?' and when the answer is found, to deploy there all the marketing and technical talent that the company can muster?

Behind this was the principle of 'reinforcing success', and fighting against overextending the company resources. Nevertheless, the resources in finance and manpower required to develop a prosperous export business are surprisingly modest; they are well within the reach of the small company employing no more than 100 people. Advantages of market concentration following through this principle of 'reinforcing success' included:

- A span of control especially when conditions become tough.
- Greater market knowledge in total and to a wider spread of people within the organization.
- Ability to identify the best markets and concentrate on them solely.
- The belief shared by 80 per cent of respondents that exports will grow faster than domestic sales in the next four to five years.

Inexperience in exporting was no more a barrier to success than was size. As the BETRO report stated: as far as newcomers to exporting are concerned, it can be stated with a fair measure of certainty that they can achieve just as good or even better results by never selling to more than ten countries as other companies who sell to 160.

There were in fact particular advantages of the small operation:

1 It needs a smaller organization with fewer staff and lower overheads.

2 It can acquire more detailed knowledge and a better understanding of agents' and distributors' capabilities. The small company has a chance to get to know them personally through close contact and so it has better knowledge of their needs and market requirements. This is primary information quite different from secondary, published sources of information. Here there was the ability to know what competitors were doing and how to adapt to market conditions.

3 Products may be sold less on price than on other factors such as:

- reliability of delivery
- after-sales service including technical support and spare parts
- credit and discount terms
- brand loyalty among customers
- manufacturer's image within the trade and among customers
- ability to establish whether competition is primarily on price, quality, design, etc.

4 No potential distractions at least from various sources, as is the case with large organizations. The organization is structured instead for maximum effectiveness.

5 Concentration will lead to a rise in sales if a decision to concentrate is made during a period of boom and long delivery dates, and a company can gain a lot of goodwill by giving better delivery to its most important key markets. In periods of declining sales a 'concentrating' company will be in a better position to secure orders than those trading in a haphazard manner (even in a depression, when many companies lose market shares, some do gain a bigger share. This is more likely to be the company that knows its market and can seize the opportunity rather than others whose contacts are more superficial).

The recommendation for all companies irrespective of size is to:

- Concentrate scarce resources of talent, effort, and cash on a few markets.
- Invest manpower in export markets on a par with home markets.
- Maintain frequent personal contact with overseas customers.
- Invest in areas geared towards export growth.
- Undertake, as continuing company policy, comparative cost studies of home and export activities.

While this theory attracted interest and was meticulously followed by many, it has in fact proved disastrous for some, particularly those smaller more vulnerable exporting companies who now concentrated their effort on key markets. In many of these markets, the ability to consume was less in doubt than the ability to pay and so many companies have been brought to bankruptcy. Concentration proved to be little other than putting all your eggs in one basket. When disaster struck, everything was lost. Refer also to Chapter 8 and Piercy on export portfolios.

Planning and Third World markets

Third World markets are notably dissimilar as will be seen in Chapter 20. Basically, these fall into the following categories:

1 High-volume, low-value raw material exporters but with infrastructural base.
2 High-volume, low-value raw material exporters with little infrastructural base.
3 Low-volume, low-value traditional exporters but with infrastructural base.
4 Least developed nations.

It is not possible to segment on the basis of being single commodity exporters as this would apply to many in the first three categories. There are therefore those in category 2 above, such as Saudi Arabia, with little infrastructure but with new-found wealth and so able to make a quantum leap by buying in expertise from abroad to provide education and technical services wherever necessary.

Political risk is one of the most obvious dangers to international business. 'Political risk is the likelihood that political forces will cause drastic changes in a country's business environment that affect the profit and other goals of a particular business enterprise'. Risk of this kind may apply to an industry as a whole or to one company in particular. The most frequently encountered risk arises from political forces hostile towards foreign enterprise for philosophical reasons that diverge sharply from prevailing government policies. Other risks are social unrest and disorder; the private vested interests of local business groups; recent or impending independence; new international alliances; and armed conflicts or terrorism. Less predictable, and political only in the sense that it is a tool of politicians, is the exposure of corruption or scandal. This is often linked to a government official who might well have provided influence for a foreign firm.

Market access is another problem and investment has taken place by multinationals is in the past in order to produce goods within the protection of tariff walls. Market access may be restricted by the local government. Alternatively, for those choosing to enter there may be the attendant benefits of supplying a captive market, further protected from the entry of foreign competition. This has enticed some multinationals in the automobile industry for example to make investments which otherwise would not have appeared quite so attractive.

Market access implies not only entering the country and meeting the standard tariff and duty barriers, the various so-called 'invisible' tariff barriers relating perhaps to areas as diverse as health and safety but providing also for distribution to the final consumer. There may in fact be more similarity between city dwellers across nations than between nationals themselves. Marketing must identify this where it exists and make full use of this advantage.

Capital is not always the missing factor and this is why we began with a classification of developing countries. For oil-rich countries with new-found wealth the new problem is one of learning how to manage wealth after years of planning for poverty. Income from the oil industry may be seen too, as in the Boston Consultancy Group (BCG) product portfolio matrix, in terms of a 'cash cow' to be used and milked for cash to produce new 'stars' high in relative market share in high-growth markets. To diversify, technology and management are both required, and marketing is subsumed within these, as partly a social act, partly a technical science. To cite Drucker (1980):

> Marketing is generally the most neglected area in the economic life of developing countries. It is manufacturing or construction which occupies the greatest attention in these countries. Its effectiveness as an engine of economic development with special emphasis on its ability to develop rapidly much-needed entrepreneurial and management skills needs hardly any elaboration. Because it provides a systematic discipline in a vital area of economic activity it fills one of the greatest needs of a developing economy ... Marketing occupies a critical role in respect to underdeveloped 'growth' countries. Indeed, marketing is the most important

Table 13.4   Some of the common international terminology for small-scale irregular payments

Baksheesh	In Turkey, Egypt, India and other Eastern countries a gratuity or gift of alms.
Mordida	A Spanish word meaning 'little bite' found in Mexico.
Jeito	Found in Brazil, means a favour rather than a transfer of money.
Dash	Used in Africa; quite commonly encountered.
Grease	Also 'facilitating payments'. Refers to legal and permitted payments of modest sums to foreign officials for speedy action of their normal duties.
Kumshaw	South-East Asia term for bribe.

Source: Adapted from Axtell, R. E. (1990) *Do's and Taboos Around the World*, Benjamin Company, Inc. © Parker Pen Company 1990. Reproduced by permission.

the global size of a corporation such as IBM, nor have the immediate visibility of such a large corporation and hence the need to produce a statement on corporate ethics. Many multinationals do, however, produce a leaflet on their corporate policy and business ethics.

Ethics do enter into the question of international business. Again, the extraterritoriality of US legislation, such as the Foreign Corrupt Practices Act of 1977, is making the issue more problematic. The Act prohibits companies from engaging in 'questionable payments', with penalties ranging from a million dollars for each corporate offence to $10,000 per offender and up to five years in prison. This Act affects not only US companies but also multinational corporations with representation in the USA. Therefore it is open to the USA to pursue a British or German multinational for what may be interpreted as irregular payments or inducements to trade in perhaps let us say an African country through its US representative base. The Act requires companies with securities registered under the Securities and Exchange Act of 1934 to keep books, records and accounts that in reasonable detail accurately and fairly reflect the disposition of their assets. Yet the Act does allow for certain 'grease' payments. In practice, few actions have been brought since the Act was passed and these have been resolved through negotiated settlements. There has been little opportunity therefore to test this Act in the courts.

The practice of business is not uniform the world over, and although shareholders or members of the public in an industrialized Western country may be shocked to hear that one of their largest companies has been active in what they interpret as being bribery and corruption, these terms of trading will almost certainly not have the same emotive appeal in the host country concerned. Payments for example made as 'dash', a fairly innocuous but generally almost standard payment in Nigeria, to ensure that the bureaucracy will deal with an application, are legitimate under the US Foreign Corrupt Practices Act which therefore does not recognize this as bribery but as 'grease'. The African term is 'dash', the US term 'grease', but it is not bribery or corruption. It ensures that papers on a crowded desk will be moved from the bottom of the pile to the top of the pile for action. In bureaucratically infested countries this may be a common means of expediting business. Other non-payment forms of persuasion include nepotism which exists to varying degrees throughout the world.

There is no country in the world which openly welcomes bribery and corruption. It is seen as a social sin. Certain countries such as the CIS have heavy penalties for anyone found guilty under such a charge.

The crucial variables to consider here are the gifts, the timing of the exchange process and the relationship created. Cultural barriers are difficult to surmount and all actions have to be viewed; actions and the degree to which corporate outcomes have been influenced by inducements of one kind or another; changing what may otherwise have been the natural outcome of events. As Jain (1979) points out there are five different possible courses of action for dealing with questionable payments: regulatory; legislative; diplomatic; code of conduct; and corporate action. However, governmental attitudes to this question vary quite enormously. In the USA, aside from the Foreign Corrupt Practices Act, the SEC will seek detailed information on previously unreported legal, business and financial activities of a company which may be considered material information from an investor's point of view. The SEC does not however define which may constitute material information to an investor. Elsewhere, France, Germany, Japan, Britain and Italy do allow for 'special expenses' abroad which qualify them for tax deductions. The regulations, however, are not explicit. The tax deduction is made easier where the payments are made to foreign nationals abroad to gain export business as existing laws may prescribe such payments by home-based to individuals within the national frontiers of the home country. What may be seen to be double standards is lessened to a degree by the fact that these companies are complying with the laws of the countries in which they operate.

In 1981, Reardon (Axtell, 1990) conducted a study of international gift-giving practices on behalf of the Parker Pen Company. A telephone survey was conducted of 200 international business executives, producing ninety-seven responses. Responses indicated that gifts were typically distinctively American, useful, of conversational value, personalized or given with the recipient's personal preferences in mind, more often than not brand name items and below $26 in cost. These are intended courtesy gifts and approximately one-third of them carried a logo. There has to be separation between what is seen as a gift from what may be viewed as a bribe. Axtell (1990) quotes a Fortune 500 vice president of personnel as saying: 'If there is no compromise of business or personal interests by either party in the exchange, it is a gift.' Rarely though is giving an act of disinterested generosity. Many weary and experienced businessmen have been heard to exclaim over the years that there is no such thing as a 'free' lunch! This is at a low level but nevertheless isolates one aspect of the difficulty. Again, to cite Axtell (1990), he in turn quotes a corporate spokesman as saying: 'No business problem gets solved by simply throwing money at it and that includes what to give the client!' A lavish present can cause more lasting embarrassment than a modest one and in the mind of the recipient be a constant reminder of a duty to be performed. This then becomes unacceptable even where some local form of irregular payments is held to be the practice.

The question of corporate ethics in confronting such a practice abroad which is not in itself illegal is another matter. A three-step process by which a matter may be termed 'material' or 'misleading' and the issue of moral responsibility are outlined in Figure 13.6 which sees this issue as involving both internal and external dissent (Loeb and Cory, 1989).

'Whistleblowing' is to be seen therefore rather as a process than an event. Much thought and consultation should therefore be taken before going public to establish whether the general welfare of society is likely to be maintained or improved by public awareness.

This situation is less likely to occur when there is a system in place designed to prevent the very occurrence of such incidents but equipped to deal with such an incident, if and when it should arise. It is worth looking at an example of a corporate code of ethics. Provided for employees rather than the public, the corporate code of ethics seeks to forestall problems which may arise by instituting a code of practice to be implemented every day of the year with appropriate reporting procedures rather than as a set of emergency procedures when crises arise. Taking the example of Esso, known also as Imperial Oil in Canada, and as Exxon elsewhere, the tone is set in the opening foreword by the Chairman and Chief Executive Officer, Arden R. Haynes:

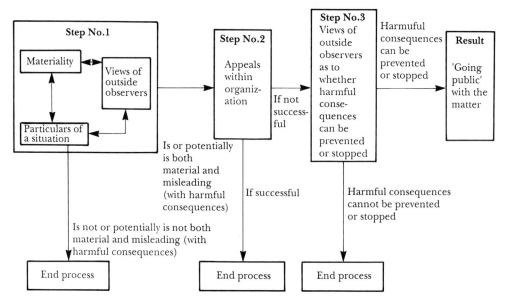

Figure 13.6
Source   Loeb, S. C., and Cary, S. N. (1989) Whistleblowing and management accounting: an approach. *Journal of Business Ethics,* **8,** 903–916.

Table 13.5   Why do irregular payments continue to exist?

Home country perspective	Host country perspective
1 Price of doing business in certain countries.	1 ' Easy money.
2 Established practice impossible to circumvent.	2 Political involvement in decision making.
3 Governmental pressure.	3 Token of appreciation.
4 Creation of favourable public relations.	4 Friendly gesture.
5 Increasing competition worldwide.	5 Commission.
6 Pressure to achieve results.	6 Pressure for vendors.
7 In final analysis, Swiss bank secrecy.	

Source   Jain, S. C. (1979) What happened to the marketing man when his international promotion payoffs became bribes? In *International Marketing: Managerial Perspectives,* (Jain, S. C., and Tucker, L. N., Jr.) CBI Publishing Company Inc., Boston, MA.

Table 13.6   Major types of bribes

1 Facilitating payments	Often termed 'grease', these are small amounts of payment in cash or kind to expedite documentation or to continue with the metaphor 'lubricate the administrative machine'.
2 Middleman commissions	Those are individuals appointed in an ad-hoc manner to formulate sales 'in a non-routine manner, and payment to them of excessive allowances and commissions which are not commensurate with the normal commercial services they perform'. Often part or all of the commission may be deposited in a bank in a third country.
3 Political contributions	Contributions which take the form of extortion since they are in violation of local law and practice. Also payments which while not illegal are specifically made with the intent of winning favours directly or indirectly.
4 Cash disbursements	Cash payments made to important people through slush funds or in a third country for a number of different reasons which will promote the company's advantage.

Source   Jain, S. C. (1979) What happened to the marketing man when his international promotion payoffs became bribes? In *International Marketing: Managerial Perspectives*, (Jain, S. C., and Tucker, L. N., Jr.) CBI Publishing Company Inc., Boston, MA.

In all its actions, Imperial Oil is dedicated to the principle of ethical leadership. This calls on all of us individually, and as a company, to adhere to the highest of ethical standards, which surpass the letter of the law and embrace open and honest dealings in all of our relationships. It means capturing the high moral ground and standing on it.

It is perhaps not ideal to just select from such a document but it does Esso no discredit to extract that part of their code which deals with gifts and entertainment.

Employees are expected to take actions and make decisions based on an impartial and objective assessment of the facts of each situation, free from the influence of gifts and similar favours that might adversely affect judgment.

   Similarly, the company must avoid both the fact and appearance of improperly influencing relationships with the organizations and individuals with whom it deals. Therefore, employees should think carefully about the implications before either accepting or giving a gift in their capacity as representatives of Imperial Oil, no matter how modest the gift or benefit may appear to be.

   It is company policy to discourage the receiving of gifts or entertainment by employees from persons outside Imperial Oil and to discourage the giving of gifts or entertainment by employees on behalf of Imperial Oil to persons outside the company. Such practices are permissible only where they involve items of moderate value and conform to the following *basic principles*:

- they are infrequent
- they legitimately serve a definite business purpose

- they are appropriate to the business responsibilities of the individuals
- they are within limits of reciprocation as a normal business expense.

These principles are also contravened if the action involves the giving or receiving of gifts or entertainment by an employee's immediate family member.

In no case are employees permitted to give or receive gifts of cash, commissions, loans, shares in profit, securities or the equivalent of any of these things.

Employees should neither give nor receive gifts of more than a nominal value without the knowledge of managers who have the authority to provide consent. The level deemed to be of nominal value for gifts is $25 or less.

Employees may give or receive entertainment (dining or an amusement, sporting or recreational event) if the circumstances conform to the requirements set out in the statement of basic principles.

If you suspect that undue favouritism is being sought from you, it should be reported to your supervisor.

If you have any doubts, about the company's policy on gifts, honoraria and other benefits, a procedural memorandum is available from division or department management.

There should be no gaps or loopholes in a corporate code of ethics which is designed to protect the individual employee as well as the institution. Nevertheless, an ethics checklist is also provided as a further safety net:

Is it legal?
Am I making or proposing a decision that breaks the law or runs contrary to a company policy?

Is it fair?
Will my decision disadvantage or perhaps even bring harm to anyone – colleagues, customers, suppliers, the community? Or is it a decision that will make those affected by it feel they have been treated fairly in the long run as well as the short term?

Can I defend it?
If I had to justify my decision to my family, the media or the directors, would I feel embarrassed and uncomfortable? Or could I explain my decision with pride, believing that in making my decision I have done the right thing?

In 1976, the OECD adopted guidelines for multinational corporation behaviour as well as host country behaviour as part of a broader understanding on various investment issues. The OECD ministers have signed a *Declaration on International Investment and Multinational Enterprises*, which includes several interrelated elements.

- A reaffirmation by OECD members that a liberal international investment climate is in the common interest of the industrial nations.
- An agreement that they should give equal treatment to foreign controlled and national enterprises.
- A decision to co-operate to avoid 'beggar thy neighbour' actions, pulling or pushing particular investments in or out of their jurisdictions.
- A set of voluntary guidelines, defining standards for good business conduct which the ministers collectively recommended to transnational enterprises operating in their territories.
- A consultative process under each of the above elements of the investment agreement.

However, it carried no sanctions for violators. Similarly, the International Chamber of Commerce (ICC) based in Paris had its report *Extortion and Bribery in Business Transactions* ratified by its Council but could only hope that it would be adopted widely on a voluntary basis by companies and countries.

The UN has had two parts of its organization working on this problem. The Commission on Transnational Corporations finalized a code on transnational corporations but socialist and Third World member states of the UN worked to ensure that this applied to privately owned multinationals and not state companies. The other UN organization involved is the Committee on International Agreement on Illicit Payments. This would involve (Kirpalani, 1984) all members states bringing under its national law criminal penalties to cover

> The soliciting, demanding, accepting or receiving, directly or indirectly, by a public official of any payment, gift or other advantage, or undue consideration for performing or refraining from the performance of his duties in connection with an international commercial transaction.

References

Axtell, R. E. (1990) *Do's and Taboos Around the World*, John Wiley & Sons, New York.

Beck, P. J., and Maher, M. W. (1989) Competition, regulation and bribery. *Managerial and Decision Economics*, **10**, (1), 1–12.

Berman, P., and Wechsler, D. (1989) The five-percenters: Moscow's pet capitalists. *Forbes*, **143**, (3), 93–97.

Cain, W. H. (1970) International planning: mission impossible? *Columbia Journal of World Business*, July-August, 53–60.

Drucker, P. F. (1980) Marketing and economic development. *International Marketing Strategy* (Thorelli, H. and Becker, H.) Pergamon, Oxford, 392.

Economist (1988) Business bribes: on the take, 19 November, 21–24.

Fadiman, J. A. (1986) A traveller's guide to gifts and bribes. *Harvard Business Review*, **64**, 122–126, 130–136.

Gillespie, K. (1987) Middle East response to the US Foreign Corrupt Practices Act. *California Management Review*, Summer, 9–30.

Goldmark, F. M. (1974) Strategy: worldwide long range market analysis. *Columbia Journal of World Business*, Winter, 50–53.

Gubernick, L. (1987) You die for sure. *Forbes*, **140**, (9), 94–96.

Haynes, A. R. (1990) *Our corporate ethics*. Esso Imperial Oil, Toronto, Ontario, March.

Hulbert, J. M., Brandt, W. K., and Richers, R. (1980) Marketing planning in the multinational subsidiary: practices and problems. *Journal of Marketing*, **44**, 7–15.

Jain, S. C. (1979) What happened to the marketing man when his international promotion payoffs became bribes? In *International Marketing: Managerial Perspectives*, (Jain, S. C., and Tucker, L. R., Jr.) CBI Publishing Company Inc., Boston, MA.

Kirpalani, V. H. (1984) *International Marketing*, Random House, New York.

Loeb, S. E., and Cory, S. N. (1989) Whistleblowing and management accounting: an approach. *Journal of Business Ethics*, **8**, 903–916.

Mayerowitz, S. A. (1987) Treading the line between 'grease' and bribery. *Business Marketing*, **72**, (1), 92–94.

McDonald, M. H. B. (1978/9) Marketing planning in an industrial and international context. *Cranfield Research Papers in Marketing and Logistics*, **5**, (23).

O'Connell, J. J., and Zimmerman, J. W. (1979) Scanning the international environment. *California Management Reviews*, **XXII**, (2).

Pisani, R. L. (1987) What is the price of security abroad? *Security Management*, **30**, (2), 44–49.

Ringbakk, K. A. (1976) Strategic planning in a turbulent international environment. *Long-Range Planning*, **9**, 2–11.

Robock, S. H., and Simmonds, K. (1983) *International Business and Multinational Enterprises*, Irwin, 3rd edn, p. 342.

Schollhammer, J. (1972) Long-range planning in multinational firms. *Columbia Journal of World Business*, September-October, 79–86.

Sheth, J. N. (1977) A market-oriented strategy of long-range planning for multinational corporations. *European Research*, January, 3–12.

Shruptine, K. F., and Toyne, B. (1981) International marketing planning: a standardised process. *Journal of International Marketing*, **1**, (1), 16–28.

Sommers, Montrose and Kernan, J. (1967) Why products flourish here, fizzle there. *Columbia Journal of World Business*, March-April, 89–97.

Key reading

Axtell, R. E. (1990) *Do's and Taboos Around the World*, John Wiley & Sons, New York.

Gillespie, K. (1987) Middle East response to the US Foreign Corrupt Practices Act. *California Management Review*, Summer, 9–30.

International Chamber of Commerce (ICC) (1977) *Extortion and Bribery in Business Transactions*, Paris.

Loeb, S. E., and Cory, S. N. (1989) Whistleblowing and management accounting: an approach. *Journal of Business Ethics*, **8**, 903–916.

Mayerowitz, S. A. (1987) Treading the line between 'grease' and bribery. *Business Marketing*, **72**, (1), 92–94.

14
International marketing control systems

Patterns of organizational development

The intention here is not to study organization *per se* but to look inquisitively at the way in which the company operating internationally modifies its organizational structure to accommodate market dynamics including competition affecting product and service offerings as well as changes in consumer tastes. This will be the path along which transactions take place between the firm and its customers. Literature on the subject of multinational organization development has in the past questioned whether structure influenced strategy and vice versa. Let us state now that it is transactional considerations, not technology nor deregulation that are typically decisive in determining which mode of organization will be optimal in a given set of circumstances. Organizational deficiencies have meant that companies were unable to respond at precisely the right time to changes in market dynamics.

Related issues are the level and quality of communication between the head office and not just the subsidiary as is often supposed, but what now amounts to an international portfolio of different investments from wholly owned to joint venture to licensing or franchising and consortium marketing. Williamson (1975) traces the chronology of these changes which have been taking place. In the beginning there were markets, and progressively more refined forms of internal organization have successively evolved. First, peer groups, then simple hierarchies, and finally the vertically integrated firm in which a compound hierarchy exists.

In the quest to optimize resources, close monitoring has to take place with regard to the level of interaction between head office and its subsidiaries and affiliates. There is no single correct solution to this problem. The choice of organizational form must be situational, i.e. that which best suits the company concerned given the characteristics of the industry, the product range, customer characteristics, and national markets in which it is trading. Each company finds its own solution. There is no 'industry' solution either, for some companies have changed their corporate structure more than once as has Massey-Ferguson, for example, from a product structure to a regional structure and back again. Another point to bear in mind is that over time no variables are held constant. Companies divest themselves of certain product lines or subsidiaries or else acquire by takeover, merger, and slow and gradual build-up of market presence.

Corporate organization has therefore to take into account a certain degree of flexibility for growth and product extension. Against this, there are often governmental barriers inhibiting foreign direct investment for example, or pressure — explicit as well as implicit - towards industrial co-operation and contractual joint ventures. There may well be variations to the trading environment peculiar to one particular trading region. Governments may impose political and philosophical strictures on the forms of organization which it will countenance within its own jurisdiction. Some designed to ensure a degree of local ownership; some designed to give a degree of local ownership of foreign subsidiaries to trusted political allies; and finally, the communist countries where foreign majority ownership has only been possible since the Gorbachev era, although still not common. The question of corporate culture – whether the firm is ethnocentric (home country orientation), polycentric (host country orientation), regiocentric (regional orientation), or geocentric (world orientation) - can also be a barrier as this will influence the degree of freedom granted to the subsidiaries and affiliates in their reporting procedures to head office. An ethnocentric-oriented company attaches little value to international sales whereas a polycentric orientation means that each country subsidiary has independence of action. It is only with a regiocentric or geocentric orientation that the company starts to think of integrated marketing strategies.

As Figure 14.1 shows, there are five main groups of international company organization.

Type A – the direct type

The most senior staff of the company have a direct relationship with the foreign subsidiary. Multinationals such as the Swedish SKF ball-bearing company have traditionally been organized along these functional lines which transcend national boundaries. This means that home-based functional managers are responsible for functional activities internationally.

Type B – the geographical type

This relationship is mediated through local managers who may have international, regional or national titles. The company sees more diversity in its markets than its products and so may choose to group area and technical specialists under this geographical grouping.

Type C – the product type

Product group managers have direct control over the subsidiaries operating in their product area. Standardization is ensured but at the cost of duplication of many head office services and a loss of coordination over subsidiary activities.

Type D – the matrix type

The matrix organization in which the subsidiary managers report along both the product group, and geographical lines, sometimes even functional lines as well. A country manager at head office is responsible for channelling all communication between head office and the subsidiary abroad. On the one hand, this creates the benefit of belongingness for the foreign subsidiary but there may be first too much communication between head office and subsidiary to make this feasible. Theoretically, a matrix organization should have created responsiveness, efficiency within the organization and the creation of direct reporting channels of communication. However, Bartlett and Ghoshal (1989) report on the companies which experimented with this form of organization and found it to have failed them. These companies include Dow Chemical and Citibank.

Type E – the project type

The application to the total organization of the project organization devised for large-scale assembly operations like aircraft building. The company is organized into a series of project groups which bring together staff drawn from any relevant functional area and are constantly changing.

Type F – the mixed structure

The mixed structure is one which is made up partly of a product division and of an international division. Lack of co-ordination can have serious effects on any firm. Here, in Figure 14.4 product A has two divisions while product B has one. If co-ordination is not achieved, the costs can be serious. International division is responsible here for communications between the two product A divisions.

In general, the B type (geographical) is more frequently decentralized; the C type (product) more usually centralized; the E type (project) almost always centralized; while A (direct) and D (matrix) may be either.

Williamson (1975) refers to the issue of vertical specialization along product lines as the unitary form of organization or the U-form enterprise. Williamson summarizes the difficulties that the large U-form enterprise experiences in terms of indecomposability, incommensurability, non-operational goal specification, and the confounding of strategic and operating decisions. Incommensurability makes it difficult to specify the goals of the functional divisions in ways which clearly contribute to higher level enterprise objectives. Indecomposability makes it necessary to attempt more extensive co-ordination among the parts; for a given span of control, this naturally results in a greater loss of control between hierarchical levels. Moreover, to the extent that efforts at co-ordination break down and the individual parts suboptimize, the strategic interconnectedness between them virtually assures that spillover costs will be substantial.

The inherent weakness in the centralized and functionally departmentalized operating company becomes critical only when the administrative load on the senior executives increases to such an extent that they are unable to handle their entrepreneurial responsibilities efficiently. Unable to identify meaningfully with, or contribute to, the realization of global goals, managers in each of the functional parts attend to what they perceive to be operational subgoals instead.

Williamson's six-way classification scheme for company organization

1 *Unitary (U-form).* This is the traditional functionally organized enterprise. Williamson makes an important contribution in acknowledging the importance of human factors when approaching the problems of economic organization. In addition, Williamson focuses also on transactions and on uncertainty. It is still the appropriate structure in most small to lower middle-sized firms organized along functional lines, e.g. sales, finance, manufacturing. Some medium-sized firms in which intercommunications are especially rich may continue to find this the appropriate structure. A variant on this structure occasionally appears if that enterprise is of U-form character but the firm has become diversified to a

Table 14.1   Key problems identified by headquarters executives

	Rank (out of 182)	Score (in per cent)		Rank (out of 182)	Score (in per cent)
Lack of qualified international personnel			There is too much bureaucracy in the organization	5	55
Getting qualified international personnel is difficult	1	73	Too much paperwork has to be sent to headquarters	6	54
It is difficult to find qualified local managers for the subsidiaries	1	73	Headquarters staff and subsidiary management differ about which problems are important	17	46
The company can't find enough capable people who are willing to move to different countries	15	60	Headquarters tries to control its subsidiaries too tightly	22	45
There isn't enough manpower at headquarters to make the necessary visits to local operations	22	57	*Excessive financial and marketing constraints*		
			The emphasis on short-term financial performance is an obstacle to the development of long-term marketing strategies for local markets	1	65
Lack of strategic thinking and long-range planning at the subsidiary level					
Subsidiary managers are preoccupied with purely operational problems and don't think enough about long-range strategy	3	71	The subsidiary must increase sales to meet corporate profit objectives even though it operates with many marketing constraints imposed by headquarters	7	50
Subsidiary managers don't do a good job of analysing and forecasting their business	5	65	Headquarters expects a profit return each year without investing more money in the local company	10	49
There is too much emphasis in the subsidiary on short-term financial performance. This is an obstacle to the development of long-term marketing strategies	13	61	*Insufficient participation of subsidiaries in product decisions*		
			The subsidiary is too dependent on headquarters for new product development	13	47
Lack of marketing expertise at the subsidiary level					
The company lacks marketing competence at the subsidiary level	4	69	Headquarters is unresponsive to the subsidiaries' request for product modifications	22	45
The subsidiaries don't give their advertising agencies proper direction	8	63	New products are developed centrally and are not geared to the specific needs of the local market	22	45
The company doesn't understand consumers in the countries where it operates	8	63	Domestic operations have priority in product and resource allocation; subsidiaries rank second	31	43
Many subsidiaries don't gather enough marketing intelligence	17	59			
The subsidiary does a poor job of defining targets for its product marketing	20	58	*Too little relevant communication between headquarters and the subsidiaries*		
			The subsidiaries don't inform headquarters about their problems until the last minute	5	65
Excessive headquarters control procedures					
Reaching a decision takes too long because we must get approval from headquarters	2	58	The subsidiaries do not get enough consulting service from headquarters	13	61

Table 14.1 *(continued)*

	Rank (out of 182)	Score (in per cent)		Rank (out of 182)	Score (in per cent)
There is a communications gap between headquarters and the subsidiaries	31	51	Headquarters makes decisions without thorough knowledge of marketing conditions in the subsidiary's country	12	48
The subsidiaries provide headquarters with too little feedback	33	50	Marketing strategies developed at headquarters don't reflect the fact that the subsidiary's position may be significantly different in its market	13	47
Insufficient utilization of multinational marketing experience			The attempt to standardize marketing programmes across borders neglects the fact that our company has different market shares and market acceptance in each country	27	44
The company is a national company with international business; there is too much focus on domestic operations	25	56			
Subsidiary managers don't benefit from marketing experience available at headquarters and vice versa	28	53	*Shortage of useful information from headquarters*		
The company does not take advantage of its experience with product introductions in one country for use in other countries	36	49	The company doesn't have a good training programme for its international managers	7	50
The company lacks central co-ordination of its marketing efforts	45	46	New product information doesn't come from headquarters often enough	22	45
			The company has an inadequate procedure for sharing information among its subsidiaries	27	44
Restricted headquarters control of the subsidiaries					
The headquarters staff is too small to exercise the proper control over the subsidiaries	8	63	There is very little cross-fertilization with respect to ideas and problem solving among functional groups within the company	27	44
Subsidiary managers resist direction from headquarters	17	59			
Subsidiaries have profit responsibility and therefore resist any restraints on their decision-making authority	36	48	*Lack of multinational orientation at headquarters*		
			Headquarters is too home-country oriented	17	46
Insensitivity of headquarters to local market differences			Headquarters managers are not truly multinational personnel	17	46
Headquarters management feels that what works in one market should also work in other markets	2	58			

Source Weichmann, U. E., and Pringle, L. T. (1979) Problems that plague multinational marketers, *Harvard Business Review*, **July–August**.

slight degree and the incidental parts are of proven semi-autonomous standing. Unless such diversification accounts for at least one-third of the firm's value-added, such a functionally organized firm will be assigned to the U-form category.

2 *Holding company (H-form).* This is the divisionalized enterprise for which the requisite internal control apparatus has not been provided. The divisions are often affiliated with the parent company through a subsidiary relationship. The divisions enjoy a high degree of autonomy under a weak executive structure.

3 *Multidivisional (M-form).* This is the divisionalized enterprise adopted by General Motors and DuPont in which a separation of operations from strategic decision-making is provided, and for which the requisite internal control apparatus has been assembled and is systematically employed. General managers are concerned with strategic decisions including resource allocation. This separation from operating duties and technical decisions is important and designed to give freedom of action. To perform the high-level planning and control functions, the general management cannot become over-involved in operating matters.

4 *Transitional multidivisional (M-form).* This is the M-form enterprise that is in the process of adjustment. Organizational learning may be involved or newly acquired parts may not yet have been brought into a regular divisionalized relationship in the parent enterprise.

5 *Corrupted multidivisional (M-form).* The M-form enterprise is a multidivisional structure for which the requisite central apparatus has been provided but in which the general management has become extensively involved in operating affairs. The appropriate distance relation is thus missing, with the result that M-form performance, in the long run, cannot reliably be expressed.

6 *Mixed (X-form).* Conceivably a divisionalized enterprise will have a mixed form in which some divisions will be essentially of the holding company variety, others will be M-form, and still others will be under the close supervision of the general management. Whether a mixed form is likely to be viable over the long run is perhaps to be doubted. Some 'exceptions' might, however, survive simply as a matter of chance. The X-form classification might thus be included for completeness purposes and as a reminder that organizational survival is jointly a function of natural and chance processes. In the long run the rational structures should thrive but deviant cases will appear and occasionally persist.

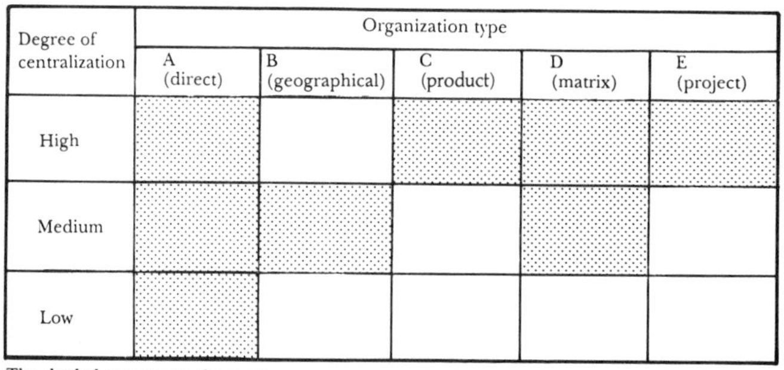

Degree of centralization	Organization type				
	A (direct)	B (geographical)	C (product)	D (matrix)	E (project)
High					
Medium					
Low					

The shaded squares are the most common

Figure 14.1   *Organization types*
Source   Brooke, M. Z. (1984) *Centralization and Autonomy: A Study in Organization Behaviour*, Holt-Rinehart-Winston

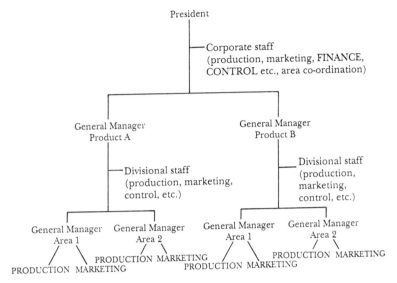

Figure 14.2
Note   The function in capital letters indicates operating responsibility. Those in lower
case indicate mainly advisory and co-ordinating roles.
Source   Stopford, M., and Wells, L. T. (1972) *Managing the Multinational Enterprise:
Organisation of the Firm and Ownership of the Subsidiaries*, Basic Books, New York

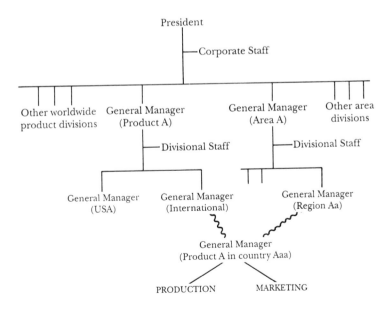

Figure 14.3
Note   A straight line indicates reporting relationships where responsibility is not shared.
A zig-zag line represents reporting relationships where responsibility is shared
Source   Stopford, M., and Wells, L. T. (1972) *Managing the Multinational Enterprise:
Organisation of the Firm and Ownership of the Subsidiaries*, Basic Books, New York

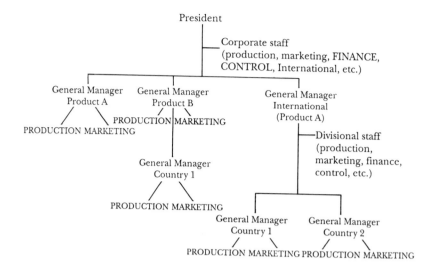

Figure 14.4

Note   The functions in capital letters indicate operating responsibility, those in lower case, mainly advisory or co-ordinating roles

Source   Stopford, M., and Wells, L. T. (1972) *Managing the Multinational Enterprise: Organisation of the Firm and Ownership of the Subsidiaries*, Basic Books, New York

The multidivision structure (M-form), requires an elite staff to assist general management in strategic decision-making responsibilities, including control. Relieved of operating duties and tactical decisions, a general executive is less likely to reflect the position of just one part of the whole. The characteristics and advantages of the M-form innovation is summarized by Williamson in the following way:

1 The responsibility for operating decisions is assigned to essentially self-contained operating divisions or quasi firms.
2 The elite staff attached to the general office performs both advisory and auditing functions. Both have the effect of securing greater control over operating decision behaviour.
3 The general office is principally concerned with strategic decisions, inviting planning, appraisal, and control, including the allocation of resources among the competing operating divisions.
4 The separation of the general office from operations provides general office executives with the psychological commitment to be concerned with the overall performance of the organization rather than become absorbed in the affairs of the functional parts.
5 The resulting structure displays both rationality and synergy: the whole is greater, more effective, more efficient, than the sum of the parts.

Divisionalization

Operating decisions are no longer taken at the top but are resolved at the divisional level, which relieves the communication load. Strategic decisions are reserved for the general office which reduces partisan political input into the resource allocation process. The internal auditing and control techniques which the parent office has access to, serve to overcome information-impactedness conditions and permit fine tuning to be exercised over the operating parts. Cash flows in the M-form firm are not automatically returned to their sources but are instead exposed to an internal competition. The usual criterion is the rate of return on invested capital. This assignment of cash flows to high-yield uses is the most fundamental attribute of the M-form enterprise.

Optimum divisionalization thus involves:

1 The identification of separable economic activities within the firm.
2 According quasi autonomous standing, usually of a profit-centre nature to each.
3 Monitoring the efficiency performance of each division.
4 Awarding incentives.
5 Allocating cash flows to high yield uses.
6 Strategic planning.

The general management of the M-form organization usually requires the support of a specialized staff to discharge these functions effectively. The performance potential in divisionalized firms frequently goes unrealized because general management 'either continue to be overly responsive to operating problems – that is, non-strategic but interventionist – or reduce the size of the corporate office to a minimum level at which no capacity exists for strategic and structural decision making.'

Hierarchy in the organizational framework

With regard to the hierarchy, which he points to as an alternative contracting mode to the market but subject to size and transactional limits, Williamson points to the affirmative ways in which hierarchy affects each of the factors in the organizational framework:

Bounded rationality

This refers to human behaviour that is 'intendedly rational but only limitedly so'. Hierarchy extends the bounds of rationality by permitting the specialization of decision making and economizing on communication expense.

Opportunism

Hierarchy permits additional incentive and control techniques to be brought to bear in a more selective manner, thereby serving to curb small-numbers opportunism.

Uncertainty

Interdependent units are allowed to adapt to unforeseen contingencies in a co-ordinated way and furthermore hierarchy serves to absorb uncertainty.

Small numbers

Small-numbers bargaining indeterminacies can be resolved by decree.

Information impactedness

This arises when true underlying circumstances relevant to a transaction or set of transactions, are known to one or more parties but cannot be costlessly discerned by or displayed for others. Hierarchy extends the constitutional powers to perform an audit, thereby narrowing, prospectively at least, the information gap between autonomous agents.

Atmosphere

As compared with market modes of exchange, hierarchy provides, for some purposes at least, a less calculative exchange atmosphere.

It is interesting next to compare Ouchi's *Theory Z* alongside Williamson's writings on hierarchy. Ouchi's *Theory Z* companies were those which had developed naturally in the USA but with many characteristics similar to firms in Japan. Theory Z organizations do have hierarchical modes of control and so do not rely entirely on the self-direction of the workforce. Nevertheless, self-direction does replace hierarchical direction to a great extent, which enhances commitment, loyalty and motivation.

Ouchi differentiates between a hierarchy or bureaucracy and type Z, in that the Z organizations have achieved a high state of consistency in their internal culture. They are, according to Ouchi, most aptly described as 'clans' in that they are intimate associations of people engaged in economic activity but tied together through a variety of bonds. Clans are distinct from hierarchies and from markets which are the other two fundamental social mechanisms through which transactions between individuals can be governed. In a market, each individual is in fact asked to pursue selfish interests. In a clan, each individual is also effectively told to do just what the other person wants. In the latter case, however, the socialization of all to a common good is so complete and the capacity of the system to measure the subtleties of contributions in the long run is so exact, that individuals will naturally seek to do that which is in the common good. Despite its remarkable properties, the clan organizational form in industry possesses a few potentially disabling weaknesses. A clan always tends to develop xenophobia, a fear of outsiders. At the extreme, Theory Z companies will express the 'not invented here' (NIH) mentality — 'We have most of the top people in the field so why should we?' The trouble comes if the company starts to slip. They will not know it since they have no external point of comparison. Building an organization, is, says Ouchi, not like building a house but more like building a marriage. An organization constantly in the process of development will degenerate without attention.

A Theory Z culture has a distinct set of values — among them long-term employment, trust, and close personal relationships. No area or facet of a Z company is untouched by that culture, from its strategies to its personnel - even its products are shaped by those values. Corporate cultures are not easily changed. Significant corporate cultural change may take between six and fifteen years according to one source, but according to Ouchi, it takes two years to persuade managers but ten to fifteen years to allow for this new work ethic to percolate through an organization at every level. Theory Z is to be distinguished from Theory X and Theory Y management approaches outlined by McGregor (1960). Nevertheless there are some clear parallels to be drawn. Theory X management assumes people are fundamentally lazy, irresponsible and need constantly to be watched. Management is centralized and authoritarian and both rewards and punishment are clearly detailed. On the other hand, Theory Y management assume people to be responsible individuals who need support and encouragement. Theory Z management, which we are discussing here, places more emphasis on a consensual participative decision-making process which makes co-workers feel part of a team. The Japanese organization emphasizing collective decision making, collective responsibility, and a concern for the whole.

In most businesses, strategic tensions are created by balancing the economic and political imperatives for the multinational managers to work with a variety of hybrid structures. Whether organized by area or product the hierarchy dominates. The hierarchy determines:

1 The nature of the information that managers collect and use, or their 'world view'. In a geographical structure this may be information that is relevant to national portfolios of diverse businesses; while in a product structure it may be information that is relevant to business portfolios consisting of diverse countries.
2 The way managers decide to compete – on a local for local basis (geographical structure) or by global rationalization (product organization).
3 The people who have the power to commit strategic resources (area managers or product managers).
4 The basis for administrative procedures, such as career progression (across businesses in a geographical organization or within a business across geographical organizations).

If one understood the hierarchy, one could understand the organization, its capabilities, and limitations. However, as global corporations are frequently complex organizations rather than 'pure' in product, functional, or geographical structure, then the following four orientations may usefully be considered, as by suitably modifying them, strategic direction can be altered.

1 *Cognitive orientation* or the perception of the 'relevant environment' by individual managers within the organization. The relevant environment of a business is constructed of an understanding of the key competitors, the competitive structure and the forces that are likely to mould the pattern of evolution of that business. We have to recognize that in a complex organization, different types of managers (area, product, or functional) and managers at different levels can have different perceptions of the relative environment. In other words, their cognitive orientations can be very different.
2 *Strategic orientation,* or the competitive posture and methods of competition that the various groups of managers are willing to adopt. If the various managers have different cognitive orientations, then they will have different perceptions of the appropriate strategic orientation to cope with the threats or to exploit the opportunities inherent in their different world views.
3 *Power orientation* or the locus of power among managers in the organization to commit resources – financial, technological, and managerial – to pursue a strategy.
4 *Administrative orientation,* or the orientation of support systems such as the accounting

system and the personnel system. Accounting data, for example, may be consolidated along product lines or along national subsidiary lines.

The mechanisms which managers in the hybrid or matrix structure can use to influence these four orientations include:

- Data management mechanisms.
- Manager management mechanisms – power to assign managers to key positions.
- Conflict resolution systems – mechanisms to resolve conflict including decision responsibility assignments are necessary.

These mechanisms can exist within four strategic control situations: fragmented, dependent, autonomous or integrated.

Alternative organizational patterns

The demise of the international division is detailed in Chapter 2 but thinking on the international division, and influences such as Stopford and Wells, have had a very profound and lasting effect long beyond the usefulness of the theory itself. Bartlett and Ghoshal (1989) point to the need for global integration and efficiency and to develop and diffuse worldwide innovations internationally. They differentiate between multinational, global and international companies before advocating the arrival of the transnational corporation. Similar to Perlemutter's classification above, the multinational as seen by Bartlett and Ghoshal has established itself through a local presence in many markets arising from a sensitivity and responsiveness to national differences. The global corporation has established cost advantages for itself through centralized global scale operations while the international company has been able to exploit parent company knowledge through worldwide diffusion and adaptation.

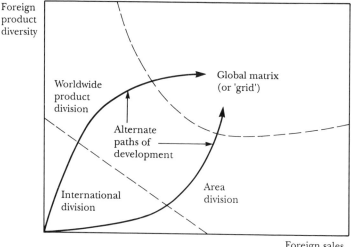

Figure 14.5   *Stopford and Wells' international structure stages model*
Source   Bartlett, C. and Ghoshal, S. (1989) *Managing Across Borders: The Transnational Solution*, Hutchinson, London.

Table 14.2   Organizational characteristics of the transnational

Organizational characteristics	Multinational	Global	International	Transnational
Configuration of assets and capabilities	Decentralized and nationally self-sufficient	Centralized and globally scaled	Sources of core competencies centralized, others decentralized	Dispersed, interdependent, and specialized
Role of overseas operations	Sensing and exploiting local opportunities	Implementing parent company strategies	Adapting and leveraging parent company competencies	Differentiated contributions by national units to integrated worldwide operations
Development and diffusion of knowledge	Knowledge developed and retained within each unit	Knowledge developed and retained at the centre	Knowledge developed at the centre and transferred to overseas units	Knowledge developed jointly and shared worldwide

Source   Bartlett, Ghoshal, 1989.

Relevant control systems

The Boston Consulting Group (BCG) product portfolio matrix

It is a commonplace to raise questions such as 'Where are we now?' 'Where do we want to go?' 'How do we get there?' It is infernally difficult, however, to answer these questions, particularly as to which business the company sees itself being in. In one particular example, it was found that substandard gas pipes could also be used as scaffolding and so this opened up a new market for an existing product. Other existing products are finding new applications with the development of North Sea oil which, as an industry, has spawned many new developments of its own in welding, pipes, drilling, and construction.

A study of the market would be expected to examine sales trends: previous forecasts in relation to performance; assessment of the general market situation and competitive environment; problems and opportunities envisaged in the marketplace; planning assumptions and constraints. A distillation of this data combines with company strengths and weaknesses and is then moulded by corporate policy and the corporate view of the direction the company should take, so as to set marketing objectives in realistic terms, e.g., sales volume in money terms and in units, and market share in percentages.

The BCG product portfolio matrix has attracted a lot of attention among managers because it seeks to compartmentalize the company's entire product range into a 2x2 matrix where the respective axes are relative market share and market growth. The theories underpinning the BCG product portfolio matrix include the product life cycle hypothesis; the experience curve effect whereby each doubling of production volume will produce attendant cost savings of 25–30 per cent; and the correlation between relative market share and profitability which BCG emphasize strongly.

BCG makes an important distinction between actual market share and relative market share. Relative market share means a particular manufacturer's product market share relative to that manufacturer's largest competitor. Two companies may have the same actual market share but BCG would argue that there was a difference in the competitive position between two companies if one had a relative market share of 5 per cent and the other 15 per cent. A general rule is that relative market share would be deemed 'high' if in excess of 10 per cent. An example of market growth is that of word processors which grew at a rate of 34 per cent in 1984.

Next, to the technology employed (see Figure 14.7). BCG recognize only 'high' and 'low' on the two axes, market growth and relative market share. Where the company has a relatively high market share and is in a high growth market, this product would be a 'star'. This is a rising product in a buoyant market. The situation where there is a low-growth market but the company has a high market share is a 'cash cow'. Note that each cell has strategic implications. Cash cows are to be 'milked' to produce the cash to finance future

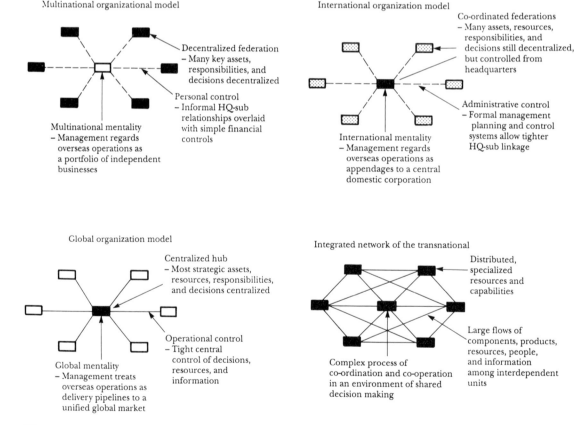

Figure 14.6
Source   Bartlett, C., and Ghoshal, S. (1989) *Managing Across Borders: The Transnational Solution*, Hutchinson, London.

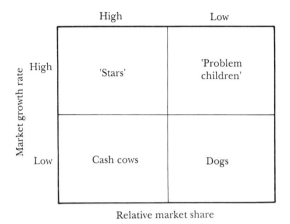

Figure 14.7   *BCG business portfolio matrix – implications for investment*

'stars'. Next, the situation where the company is enjoying relatively low market share in a buoyant growing market – this is termed a 'problem child', and is a suitable case for treatment. There is something wrong then with this present product offering in its current cost per unit, its packaging, or presentation and so a product in this category should be closely scrutinized and hopefully will, on relaunch, re-establish itself in the market place as a 'star'. On no account, should 'problem children' be allowed to continue without some form of investigation taking place first. Finally, there is the least enviable situation of all, a low growth market and a relatively low market share which is a category which the company should pull itself out of immediately. This is the 'dog'. Unfortunately, for the British, 'dogs' are to be put down, there is never any stay of execution for a 'dog'.

The ramifications for investment that are implicit in the product portfolio matrix are seen in Figure 14.7 while the possible outcomes are depicted in Figure 14.8 which shows a success sequence pattern and Figure 14.9 which shows a disaster sequence pattern. As well as watching product sales, the company should also be keeping a close watch on those products

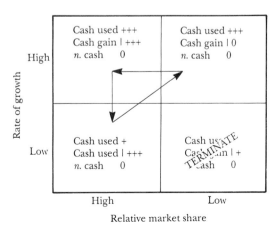

Figure 14.8   *BCG business portfolio matrix – success sequence*

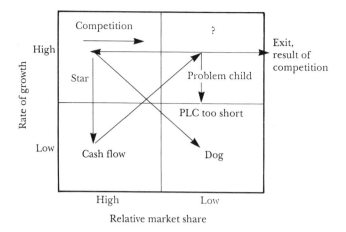

Figure 14.9   *BCG business portfolio matrix – disaster sequence*

consuming, rather than generating, funds although there are definitional problems. McNamee (1985) has pointed out how BMW of Germany would be a 'dog' company if its relative market share were relative in all motor cars produced and its marketing segment was the 'motoring public'. However, if BMW's market segment is regarded as fast, high quality, prestigious saloon cars, then its relative market share appears much higher.

The product portfolio matrix has a number of failings, however. The company's own financial resources may not be adequate to pursue market share. Also, if competitors use the same technique of market analysis, they may well follow the same strategy. Other problems arise as well in the unit of measure adopted for the matrix and so any consequent interpretation. As in the BMW example above, is the product market to be defined in broad or narrow product or need terms? Focusing on the total product market and just on the part of the market served by the company, will produce different results. So, too, will the definition of the market depending on whether it is seen as local, national or international. Narrow definitions will exclude longer term conceptual issues of a larger market. Again, focusing only on the market served may lead the company to overlook a significant opportunity or a competitive threat from the unserved portion of the market. Employing several alternative definitions varying product and market segments will help get around this problem (Day, 1977). However, there is a further problem with the matrix in that it may confuse slow growth for decline, for example, as it has only one model of the product life cycle and its stages in its formulation. The definition of market share can also be manipulated by managers who are in turn evaluated by this system. While providing a useful synthesis, it is a fallacy to treat all business as being similar. Day (1977) points also to a number of factors beyond share and market growth which may have a greater bearing on the attractiveness of a product market or business, including:

- contribution rate
- barriers to entry
- cyclicality of sales
- rate of capacity utilization

- sensitivity of sales to changes in prices, promotional activities
- extent of 'captive' business
- nature of technology (maturity, stability, and complexity)
- availability of production and process opportunities
- social, legal, governmental and union pressures and opportunities.

There is perhaps too rigid a compression into only four cells and this is what gave rise to the Shell or General Electric directional policy matrix (see Figure 14.10). This recognizes that products may actually be on the fence between 'dog' and 'cash cow' or any two categories. Besides this, there was, too, the fact that there was room in the market for the company that either could not be number one or wished only to be number two, due perhaps to size or technological capability, etc

If the market is growing it may be relatively easy to acquire market share, but in a static or declining market, market share can only be bought at the expense of competitors who are likely to retaliate perhaps with price reductions, thereby jeopardizing the market for all concerned.

The matrix is as viable in an international context as in a domestic one, the only reservation being that governments may take notice of 'cash cows' being milked in their particular country to finance some 'stars' being nurtured in an overseas freeport. In the same way as Wells and Vernon showed how the PLC theory could be used for international markets, the same is true here of the BCG matrix. It has the same roots after all in the PLC theory but the experience curve emphasizes product unit cost advantages, and relative market share serves to emphasize this commercial advantage under the BCG guidelines. Whereas the PLC offered a postmortem rationalization for US investments, the BCG offers strategic alternatives as a result of the data-gathering exercise, e.g., market segment concentration, market share holding, harvesting (taking the cash), and termination.

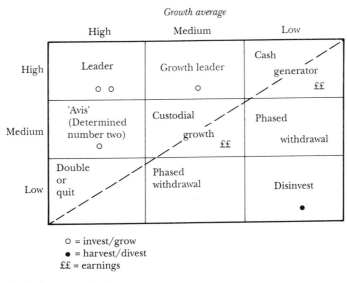

Figure 14.10 *Shell directional policy matrix*

PIMS database

PIMS is an acronym for 'profit impact on marketing strategy'. Based in the Strategic Planning Institute, Cambridge, Massachusetts, PIMS has a database of 1,800 subscribers who are mainly US though it has subsidiary branches now throughout Europe, including London. For a subscription of several thousand dollars per annum, subscribers do not receive any 'omnibus' study or industry or product report. Instead, what they receive for their money is the ability to interrogate that database with a number of 'what if' questions. The subscriber inserts some key data about his company into the computer which then searches its memory for a similar company. The computer would then be able to respond to a question about the likely effect of a 4 per cent price increase, or to reveal trends, or to explain market phenomena.

PIMS does not predict the future. It tells instead what happened in highly similar circumstances based on millions of facts submitted by member companies. PIMS is based entirely on real life not theory. Academics and researchers decry the fact that it has a long list of variables, in excess of 120, and so, in arriving at a given point there is the problem known to statisticians of multicollinearity; in other words, we cannot be sure which of the 120 plus variables was responsible for this situation. No two companies are after all identical, so this is a weakness. However, PIMS exists as a business tool for businessmen and as such it appears to be receiving wide acclaim. Even if it cannot explain all the answers it is getting sufficient of the answers right to satisfy the businessmen who are generally much less interested as to how a particular solution was arrived at, than the solution itself.

PIMS make the following generalizations based on their experience:

1 Higher profitability is accounted for by
 • lower capital intensity (investment)
 • high market share
 • high product quality.
2 High market position and high product quality:
 • are very profitable
 •can be used as substitutes for each other.
3 If market is weak
 • do not use high prices
 • do not do R & D, imitate other products instead.
4 If market position is strong increase R & D expenses.
5 If one's product is of low quality do not advertise it.
6 To be profitable
 • introduce new products at the bottom of a recession (a most difficult theory to put into practice)
 • do not spend more than 10 cents of the sales dollar for marketing.

References

Bartlett, C. A., and Ghoshal, S. (1989) *Managing Across Borders: The Transnational Solution*, Hutchinson Business Books, London.
Brooke, M. Z. (1984) *Centralisation and Autonomy: A Study in Organisation Behaviour*, Holt-Rinehart-Winston, Eastbourne.

Day, G. S. (1977) Diagnosing the product portfolio. *Journal of Marketing*, April, 29–38.

Doz, Y. L., and Prahalad, C. K. Headquarters influence and strategic control in MNCs. *Sloan Management Review*, Fall, 15–29.

McGregor, D. (1960) *The Human Side of Enterprise*, McGraw-Hill, New York.

McNamee, P. M. (1985) *Tools and Techniques for Strategic Management*, Pergamon, Oxford.

Ouchi, W. (1981) *Theory Z: How American Business Can Meet The Japanese Challenge*, Addison-Wesley, London.

Prahalad, C. K., and Doz, Y. L. (1981), An approach to strategic control in MNCs. *Sloan Management Review*, Summer, 5–13.

Stopford, J. M., and Wells, L. T. Jr (1972), *Managing the Multinational Enterprise: Organization of the Firm and Ownership of the Subsidiaries*, Basic Books Inc., New York.

Stopford, J. M. (1980) *Growth and Organizational Change in the Multinational Firm*, Arno Press, New York.'

Wiechmann, U. E., and Pringle, L. G. (1979), Problems that plague multinational marketers. *Harvard Business Review*, July-August, 118–124.

Williamson, O. E. (1975) *Markets and Hierarchies: Analysis and Antitrust Implications*, Macmillan—The Free Press, New York.

Key reading

Bowman, C. (1990), *The Essence of Strategic Management*, Prentice-Hall, Hemel Hempstead, Herts.

Doz, Y. (1986) *Strategic Management in Multinational Companies*, Pergamon Press, Oxford.

Godiwalla, Y. H. (1986), Multinational planning – developing a global approach. *Long Range Planning*, **19**, (2), 110–116.

O'Driscoll, A. (1986), The change to industry maturity: an Irish firm's experience. In Turnbull, P. W., and Paliwoda, S. J. *Research in International Marketing*, Croom-Helm, London.

Ould, J. (1986) *Controlling Subsidiary Companies: A Guide to Group Management and Financial Control*, Woodhead-Faulkner Ltd., Cambridge.

15
Marketing to Japan

Japan in the world economy

Japan is the second largest consumer market in the free world – very close in size to the now united Germany, but more than three times that of Great Britain.

The Gross National Product of Japan is the second largest in the industrialized world after the USA, and even if the former CMEA countries are included, Japan still ranks as number three. It is more than three times as large as that of the UK and is expanding at a much faster rate than that of any other advanced industrialized country. Japan is a market of 112.6 million people and has an average growth rate of 0.3 per cent with a per capita income higher than that in the UK. Imports have been increasing fast but have not kept pace with Japan's exports.

While the world economy was expanding, Japan was not unfavourable to trade liberalization, but the oil shock of 1973/74 and successive oil shocks since then have changed this. Against a backcloth then of a static world market, the law of comparative 'disadvantage' holds sway over that of comparative advantage. In Japan, it has been particularly noted that the terminology of trade has taken on military overtones in the usage of such terms as 'trade war', for example. The USA now refers to the trade talks with Japan as being under the Structural Impediment Initiative. Talks have gone on now for decades without any real tangible results. Those talks with the USA now focus on rice, the distribution system and defence spending. However, Japan's production costs still remain relatively low and its productivity is improving.

Insatiable world demand for Japanese exports, combined with limited domestic imports, low inflation rates, an embarrassingly large trade surplus, and a fairly steady rate of GNP growth, have made Japan's record appear unavoidably good compared with that of any of its partners or competitors in the West. In 1988, the Japanese trade surplus with the EC was $22.8 billion, twice what it was just three years before.

Approximately 60 per cent of Japan's imports are fuels and raw materials, with only 27 per cent accounted for by manufactures. Japan, however, claims that its strategy has been to implement a domestic demand-oriented economy. Despite Japan's trading performance the yen is not an international currency and is artificial also in that it makes imports higher than they should actually be. One of the US demands is for Japan to do more to bolster and internationalize the yen. Ninety-seven per cent of Japanese imports and 60 per cent of exports are priced in US dollars. Pressures on high inflation and interest rates do not exist in Japan to the extent known in other Western economies.

Japan's very large trade surpluses have been a political agenda item for many years, but continue still to grow while Japan's trading partners in the West, including Britain and the USA, both accuse Japan of treating them as developing countries because of the imbalance in the value of the commodity composition of their bilateral trade flows. Japan imports fuel and raw materials and some beverages, while being a world leader now in cars, computers and electronics, all high value-added export items, further worsening the trade imbalance.

The Japanese yen appreciated by 50 per cent against the pound sterling over the five-year period, 1983–1988. Previously the boast was that Japanese industry could withstand a 25 per cent worsening of the yen relative to the dollar and still be competitive, but as we have seen, Japanese industry is dependent on the small firm. The period September–November 1985 saw a 20 per cent appreciation of the yen to 203 yen to the dollar, and MITI's survey of small firms with export ratios over 20 per cent found about half either reporting foreign exchange losses or contraction of new export business.

The Japanese, despite their large investments in Europe, centred mainly in Britain, are mistrusted by both continental European industrialists and their governments, over a range of issues, including (Sasseen, 1989):

- the targeting of strategic industries,
- the low quality of investment and jobs,
- dependence on important components,
- lack of R & D facilities,
- lack of true integration into Europe, and
- the still closed Japanese market.

The Japanese respond by saying that they are investing in Europe in order to get around the high yen, and the 'dumping' charges levied by the EC. This is true of Canon and Ricoh, to take but two examples. However, to take this investment into a proper perspective, the total amount is small compared, for example, to the US investment in Europe or Japanese investment in the Pacific Basin, which is 8.3 times that invested in Europe (Bruce, 1990). Only 2 per cent of the foreign money coming into Britain is from Japan, yet this investment is strategically placed in manufacturing and the electronics industry, and Britain accounts for more than one-third of Japanese investment in Europe. Given these facts and what he calls 'a

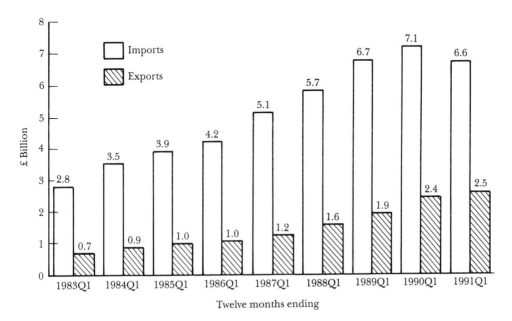

Figure 15.1   *United Kingdom trade with Japan*
Source   *Overseas Trade Statistics of the United Kingdom*

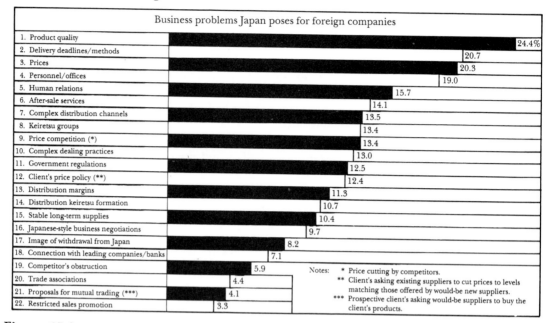

Figure 15.2

Source   Fujigane, Y., and Ennis, P. (1990) Keiretsu — what are they doing, where are they going? *Tokyo Business Today*, September, p. 29

spiral of disindustrialization', Fred Burton, of the University of Manchester, has argued for a more aggressive stance to be taken by the EC in trade with Japan, creating a European model of the Japanese MITI (Ministry of International Trade and Industry), and setting a clear policy line. Without this, Japan will emerge dominant over all of Europe. It is, perhaps, worth

Table 15.1   Britain and Japan statistical profile.

	Britain	Japan
Population (million)	57.08	122·61
Area ('000 sq. miles)	94	143
GNP ($ billion)	834	2,819
GNP per head ($)	14,585	22,901
Life expectancy (years, male/female)	72(m) 78(f)	75(m) 81(f)
Aid (Total, $ million)	2,645	9,134
Direct overseas investment outstanding ($ billion)	117	105.9
Manufacturing wages (1987 = 100)	130	115.4
Days lost in labour disputes (per 100,000 employees)	16,027	578
Higher education enrolment (%)	33·8	80.7

(Latest year, mostly 1988)

Source   *The Economist Book of Vital World Statistics* (1990). Eurostat, *Europe in Figures Deadline 1992*, London.

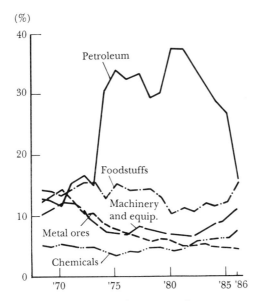

Figure 15.3   *Trends in Japan's exports share by commodity (1968–86)*
Source   Japan Tariff Association, *The Summary Report: Trade of Japan*

pointing out that a survey of Japanese citizens found their favourite words to be 'effort' and 'persistence' (Turpin, 1990).

Japan's export performance is due to:

1 *Stable prices.* First, the impact of an artificially low yen exchange rate on the price of its

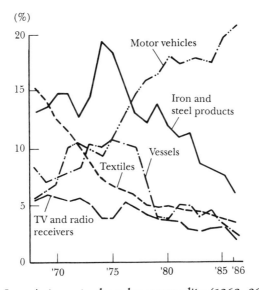

Figure 15.4   *Trends in Japan's imports share by commodity (1968–86)*
Source   Japan Tariff Association, *The Summary Report: Trade of Japan*

US stock of direct investment in EC

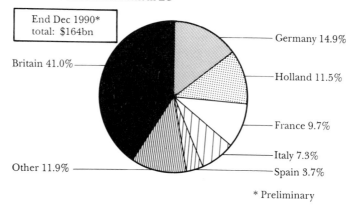

End Dec 1990* total: $164bn	Germany 14.9%
Britain 41.0%	Holland 11.5%
	France 9.7%
	Italy 7.3%
Other 11.9%	Spain 3.7%

* Preliminary

Japanese stock of direct investment in EC

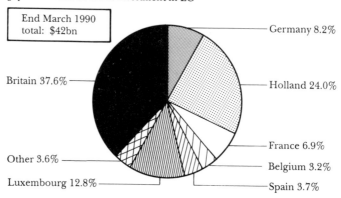

End March 1990 total: $42bn	Germany 8.2%
Britain 37.6%	Holland 24.0%
	France 6.9%
Other 3.6%	Belgium 3.2%
Luxembourg 12.8%	Spain 3.7%

Sources: US Department of Commerce: Japanese Ministry of Finance

Figure 15.5
Source   The Economist (1991) 20 April, p. 65

exports, then as the yen appreciated, the substitution of parts and components from offshore production plants in the Pacific Basin, and the growth of Japanese foreign direct investment generally.

2 *Slack domestic demand.* Holding down imports of raw materials and fuels as well as manufacturing goods, plus soft prices for imported energy.

3 *Interest rates.* The Ministry of Finance cannot lower interest rates because lowering interest rates would probably weaken the yen, thus making Japanese exports even more competitive and Japan's trade partners more unhappy. Western nations should continue to press for the internationalization of the yen, forcing yen export prices higher at least in the short term.

In the long term, Japan should continue to attract foreign direct investment (FDI). It presumably restricts FDI but the strength of the economy is to be seen in the lowest inflation rate of any major industrial country. Slowly, Japan is moving to the point where its own capital markets now play a significant role in the international financial system. The Tokyo Stock Exchange is now the largest in the world. Yet pressure continues to mount on Japan, which has taken steps since 1980 to revise its formerly very rigid exchange control laws.

Reasons for the Japanese moving into foreign markets

1 Satellite manufacture became profitable because of yen revaluation.
2 Commercial and other services, required to support satellite manufacturing, increased the outflow from Japan.
3 Strategic overseas investment in the extractive industries safeguards the supply of essential basic materials, e.g., copper, iron ore, bauxite, and coking coal.

Economic and social background

Japan consists of four main islands: Kyushu, Shikoku, the main island Honshu, and Hokkaido. Others lying to the south of Kyushu, such as Okinawa and others, were administered by the USA until May 1972.

Table 15.2   Top hosts. Stocks of direct investment in Europe, by sector, 1989

| | | US | | | Japan | |
		$bn	%		$bn	%
Manufacturing total	UK	22.1	28	UK	1.1	23
	Germany	14.4	19	Holland	0.9	19
	France	9.5	12	Spain	0.8	17
Chemicals	UK	3.5	20	Holland	0.3	43
	Belgium	2.6	15	Germany	0.1	18
	France	2.5	14	Spain	0.1	13
Metals	Germany	1.1	35	France	0.06	19
	UK	0.8	27	UK	0.06	17
	Holland	0.4	13	Spain	0.04	13
General machinery	Germany	3.6	21	UK	0.2	28
	UK	3.4	20	Holland	0.1	22
	France	3.3	20	France	0.1	19
Electrical machinery	UK	1.1	25	UK	0.4	34
	Holland	0.9	21	Holland	0.4	30
	Germany	0.5	12	Germany	0.2	13
Transport equipment	UK	4.1	44	Spain	0.6	60
	Spain	1.0	10	UK	0.2	21
	France	0.6	6	Holland	0.1	6
Commerce	France	2.5	12	Germany	1.1	29
	Holland	2.5	11	UK	0.9	24
	UK	2.5	11	Holland	0.8	22
Finance insurance	UK	20.6	53	UK	5.7	41
	Holland	3.8	10	Luxembourg	4.6	33
	Germany	2.5	6	Holland	2.5	18

Source   *The Economist* (1991). 20 April, 65.

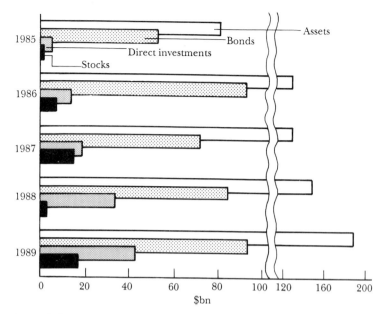

Figure 15.6   *Annual flow of Japanese assets overseas*
Financial Times (1990) 15 March

The land mass is almost double the size of the UK, comprising 145,000 square miles (94,000 square miles in the UK). The country is mountainous and volcanic, with short fast-flowing unnavigable rivers.

Table 15.3   Japanese exports to the UK
Source   *Financial Times* (1990) Special Supplement: Japan, 9 July

	1988 ($'000)	1989 ($'000)
Total exports	10,532,200	10,740,877
Raw materials and fuels	29,739	21,088
Light industry goods	1,012,411	988,943
Heavy and chemical industry products	9,421,922	9,570,258
Machinery, total including:	8,871,709	8,936,820
General machinery	2,743,396	2,683,830
Office machines	1,321,597	1,259,529
Electrical machinery	3,162,340	3,153,426
Semiconductors and other electronic parts	592,496	616,568
Transportation equipment	2,300,255	2,512,059
Passenger cars	1,515,489	1,708,054
Precision instruments	665,719	587,504

Source   JETRO (1991) *White Paper on International Trade Japan 1990*, Tokyo.

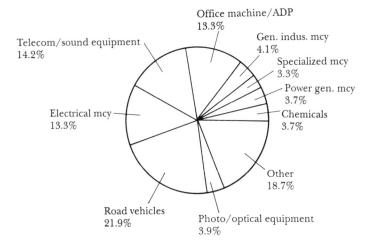

Figure 15.7 *UK imports from Japan twelve months to March 1991 – £6643 million*
Source   Overseas Trade Statistics of the United Kingdom

The country is influenced by the Chinese who introduced their script into Japan in 400 AD. From the twelfth century, political power lay with the military rulers, the Shogun. The first European contact came in the sixteenth century from the Portuguese in 1542 at Tanegashima.

Table 15.4   Japanese imports from the UK

	1988 ($'000)	1989 ($'000)
Total imports	4,193,005	4,465,984
Foodstuffs	375,469	526,558
Raw materials	101,757	106,490
Mineral fuels	9,100	11,504
Manufactured goods	3,180,829	3,411,179
Chemical goods	807,276	830,425
Machinery, total including:	1,073,125	1,256,010
Electrical machinery	375,052	377,644
Office machines	85,850	86,954
Semiconductors and other electronic parts	91,144	96,843
Transportation equipment	222,019	374,753
of which passenger cars	163,558	311,723
Precision instruments	80,895	81,833
Textile products	338,234	361,238
Metal goods	495,904	416,712
Other manufactures	466,289	546,794

Source   JETRO (1991) *White Paper on International Trade Japan 1990*, Tokyo.

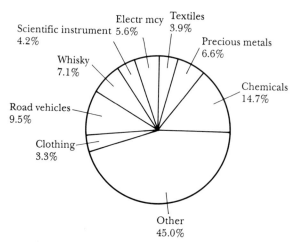

Figure 15.8   *UK exports to Japan twelve months to March 1991 — £2537 million*
Source   Overseas Trade Statistics of the United Kingdom

The Portuguese and Spanish brought Christianity which taught that God was all powerful and to be respected above all others, a philosophy which certainly did not appeal to the leading class of society at the time who saw in Christianity something that was revolutionary to their way of thinking and so could be highly disruptive. For this reason Japan lived in near isolation for some 260 years, trading only with the Dutch through one small port as the Dutch did not try to spread Christianity. In a mirror image of what is taking place in our present time the US sent out an ambassador, Townsend Harris, in 1856 to convey the message to Japan that it must open up its market. This broke Japanese isolation. The overthrow of Tokugawa Shogun and restoration of the Emperor Meiji followed. The latter moved from the traditional imperial capital of Kydo to the Tokugawan Shogun's capital at Edo, which was renamed Tokyo, which means 'Eastern capital'.

Japan annexed Taiwan in 1884–85, and acquired Korea as a colony in 1911. It joined the Allies in the First World War, and has in the past shown a desire to dominate China. In 1941, Japan attacked the USA and later there was the US bombing of Hiroshima and Nagasaki, which ended the war for Japan. The Peace Treaty, which ended the occupation, was signed at San Francisco on 8 September 1951. Japan regained its independence in April 1952. Neither the USSR nor China was a party to this treaty.

Japan has since looked to the USA for security, as her largest market and supplier of foodstuffs. Relations with the USSR have for long been cool because of the Soviet annexation of four small islands off Hokkaido at the end of the war. The USSR has also criticized the Japanese Treaty of Peace and Friendship with China as being 'anti-Soviet' in nature. Previously Japan supported Taiwan but after the Nixon visit to China, Japan moved to recognize the People's Republic of China. Article 9 of the Japanese Constitution renounces war as a sovereign right and declares that war potential will never be maintained. There is a self-defence army, navy and air force, but the country spends a total of only 1 per cent of GNP on defence.

Religions are not mutually hostile nor mutually exclusive. For example, although Buddhism is the most common religion, there is a common practice of having a Shinto priest bless a new commercial enterprise. There is respect for religions, and more overlap between religions in Japan than would be found elsewhere. The main religions are:

Shinto

An indigenous religion which worships a deity as manifested in works of nature or man, which inspire feelings of awe or respect.

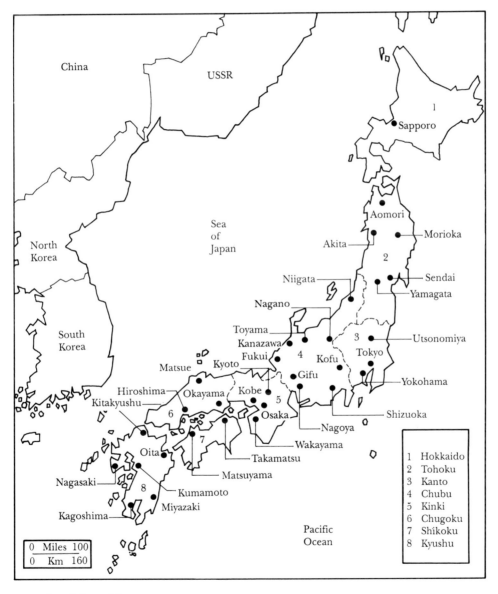

Figure 15.9 *Map of Japan*
Source *Financial Times* (1990) Special Supplement: Japan, 9 July

Buddhism

This was introduced from China in the sixth century. There are a number of different sects, but this is the most common religion now in Japan.

Christianity and new religions

Christianity is a minority religion. The Soka Gakkai or Value Adding Society combines the pursuit of material benefit with an intolerant form of Buddhism (Nicheren Shoshu Sect).

Coming to terms with Japanese growth

As perceived by Westerners, an aura of mysticism surrounds the East, and Westerners are unable to understand a religious reverence for the Japanese imperial family. The culture and value system is different in Japan from that practised in Britain. Nevertheless, there is the danger of unquestioning acceptance of Japanese invincibility, stemming perhaps from the unity of mind and body found in Japanese exports such as the martial arts, which in fact originated first in India then moved to China and then Japan.

Important societal changes are taking place. Japanese consumers are becoming accustomed to affluence and to finding, through travel, that Japanese goods are cheaper abroad than at home.

A rapidly growing proportion of Japan's population is over sixty-five, thus creating further opportunities for retirement and leisure as well as automation, roboticization, retraining and health care programmes. As a nation, Japan's strengths lie in innovation not invention, and not in labour cost either, for Japan is demanning heavily. Yet, as Martin Beresford (1981) noted in *Management Today*, October, pp. 60–66, 'much of Japan's success has resulted from just "doing things better"', i.e., applying quite unexotic technology steadily to improve product design or productivity in existing industries.'

The Japanese have an organizational system, known as 'keiretsu', which is the engine behind their growth. These we shall deal with later, but it is important to note their history, centralization, family ties, cross-holdings, debt ties and managerial exchanges, also the closeness of banks to Japanese industry. Next, it pays to examine the Japanese strategy in entering Western markets. This has been said to resemble a cascading strategy pattern (Lorenz, 1981). They enter into carefully selected small segments and then gradually move across the entire market. An examination of Japanese marketing strategies since the 1950s shows how, in numerous cases – transistor radios, televisions, cars, stereo, hi-fi – the Japanese have consistently used essentially the same strategy. The strategy is to launch a single product into the foreign market. This will be aimed at a small but well-defined market segment. Consequently, it does not arouse competitive reaction. Meanwhile, the gradual build-up of parts, maintenance, and after-sales is taking place. Once this has been done, the product range is extended, 'cascading' into the market with new lines of products.

Company size alone is not the reason for Japanese growth, as we shall see. While Japanese companies are large on a global comparison, as can be seen from Tables 15.5, 15.6 and 15.7 over 80 per cent of the country's labour force of thirty-four million work in small or medium-size companies, which are just as dynamic and competitive as their larger counterparts.

Geographical distance, but more importantly, psychic distance, appear to be creating an

Table 15.5 Japan's largest companies

	Sales		Profits	
	$ millions	Global 500 rank	$ millions	Global 500 rank
Toyota Motor	64,516.1	6	2,993.3	7
Hitachi	50,685.8	12	1,476.9	28
Matsushita Electric Industrial	43,516.1	17	1,649.1	21
Nissan Motor	40,217.1	20	808.2	64
Toshiba	30,181.3	29	922.9	54
Honda Motor	27,069.6	37	571.8	95
NEC	24,390.5	40	596.6	91
Mitsubishi Electric	21,228.2	49	537.6	105
Nippon Steel	21,155.5	50	817.8	63
Sony	20,927.9	51	719.7	71

Source *Fortune* (1991) 'Fortune 500', 29 July.

Table 15.6 The most productive worldwide, 1990

The ten highest in sales per employee			The ten highest in sales per dollar of stockholders' equity		
Showa Shell Sekiyu	139	$4,085,361	Lyondell Petrochemical	211	$171.26
Lyondell Petrochemical	211	$2,892,444	Bull	216	$67.04
Idemitsu Kosan	107	$2,315,034	Idemitsu Kosan	107	$40.36
Cosmo Oil	158	$2,016,667	Kanebo	296	$31.49
Honam Oil Refinery	387	$1,634,238	Taiyo Fishery	169	$30.09
Nippon Oil	79	$1,527,844	FMC	363	$25.10
Petrogal (Petrol de Port)	232	$1,342,946	Gillette	316	$16.56
Tonen	246	$1,337,959	Showa Shell Sekiyu	139	$16.21
Mitsubishi Oil	325	$1,281,070	Cosmo Oil	155	$15.27
Neste	97	$1,140,156	Seiko	443	$15.27

Note Japanese firms were not in the most profitable sector, nor were any in Fortune's listing of money losers. It would appear to suggest that the Japanese were selling, then, at keen prices rather than attempting to maximize their profits.

Source *Fortune* (1991) 'Fortune 500', vol. 124, no. 3, 29 July, p. 238. © 1991 Fortune Inc. Magazine Company.

Table 15.7   The Fortune 500 by country

	1–100	101–200	201–300	301–400	401–500	Total	Largest company	Sales '$ millions'	Rank
Australia	0	0	2	4	2	9	Broken Hill Pty	10,825.5	1202
Austria	1	0	0	0	0	1	Austrian Industries	13,587.4	91
Belgium	1	1	1	1	0	4	Petrofina	17,289.3	67
Brazil	1	0	0	2	0	3	Petrobras	20,473.8	52
Britain	6	8	11	7	11	43	British Petroleum	59,540.5	8
Britain/Netherlands	2	0	0	0	0	2	Royal Dutch/Shell Group	107,203.5	2
Canada	0	3	3	2	4	12	Alcan Aluminium	8,846.0	150
Chile	0	0	0	0	1	1	Codelco-Chile	3,338.8	404
Finland	1	0	2	1	4	8	Neste	12,858.7	97
France	10	2	7	6	5	30	Elf-Aquitaine	32,939.2	26
Germany	12	9	2	5	2	30	Daimler-Benz	54,259.2	11
India	0	1	1	2	2	6	Indian Oil	9,422.7	144
Italy	4	2	0	1	0	7	IRI	61,433.0	7
Japan	16	24	22	24	25	111	Toyota Motor	64,516.1	6
Luxembourg	0	0	1	0	0	1	Arbed	6,247.1	221
Malaysia	0	0	0	1	0	1	Petronas	4,279.6	322
Mexico	1	0	0	0	0	1	Pemex (Petroleos Mexicanos)	19,329.5	57
Netherlands	1	1	1	2	2	7	Philips	30,865.7	28
Netherlands Antilles	0	0	1	0	0	1	Schlumberger	5,433.6	260
New Zealand	0	1	0	0	0	1	Fletcher Challenge	7,134.4	188
Norway	0	2	0	0	0	2	Statoil	11,368.9	114
Panama	0	0	0	0	1	1	McDermott International	2,719.4	479
Portugal	0	0	1	0	0	1	Petrogal (Petroleos de Portugal)	6,043.3	232
South Africa	1	0	1	1	1	4	Barlow Rand	13,664.1	89
South Korea	2	4	2	2	1	11	Samsung	45,042.1	14
Spain	2	0	0	1	1	4	INI	18,089.1	62
Sweden	2	2	5	2	6	17	Volvo	14,688.6	78
Switzerland	3	2	0	4	2	11	Nestle	33,359.0	25
Taiwan	0	1	0	0	0	1	Chinese Petroleum	8,008.2	149
Turkey	0	1	1	1	0	3	Koc Holding	9,450.1	142
United States	33	35	35	31	30	164	General Motors	125,126.0	1
Venezuela	1	0	0	0	0	1	Petroleos de Venezuela	23,469.1	43
Zambia	0	0	1	0	0	1	Zambia Industrial & Mining	4,622.5	2975

Source   *Fortune* (1991) 'Fortune 500', vol. 124, no. 3, 29 July, p. 259. © 1991 Fortune Inc. Magazine Company.

Table 15.8   Estimated number of Japanese rivals in selected industries

Air conditioners	13	Motorcycles	4
Audio equipment	24	Musical instruments	4
Automobiles	9	Personal computers	16
Cameras	15	Semiconductors	34
Car audio	12	Sewing machines	20
Carbon fibres	7	Shipbuilding**	33
Construction equipment	15*	Steel***	5
Copiers	14	Synthetic fibres	8
Facsimile machines	10	Television sets	15
Lift trucks	8	Truck and bus tyres	5
Machine tools	112	Trucks	11
Mainframe computers	6	Typewriters	14
Microwave equipment	5	Videocassette recorders	10

* The number of firms varies by product area. The smallest number, ten, produced bulldozers. Fifteen firms produced shovel trucks, truck cranes, and asphalt paving equipment. There are twenty companies in hydraulic excavators, a product area where Japan is particularly strong.
** Six firms had annual production in excess of 10,000 tons.
*** Number of integrated companies.
Source   Porter, M. E., (1990) *The Comparative Advantage of Nations*, Macmillan, London.

advantage in favour of Japanese businessmen *vis-à-vis* UK businessmen where, by way of comparison:

> An attitude born in the British Empire and corner-store tradition seems to prevail among many [British businessmen] of best doing business with people who think the same way as they do. One effect is this failure to realize that much good business can be done with countries with different economic systems – consequently there is defensiveness where there should be aggression.

Meanwhile, the Japanese hold continues to spread from electronics and motor vehicles to computers and telecommunications to numerically controlled machine tools, tractors and construction machinery.

From 1953 to 1973, Japan invested more per unit of added value than its major Western competitors, i.e., 24.2 per cent compared with 13.3 per cent for the UK, and taking base index as 100 for Japan in 1953, the 1973 figure for the UK is 40 (Boulton, Jenney, 1981). It must also be conceded that Japan has earned an outstanding reputation for its harmonious relationship between government and industry in backing innovation.

The most significant single item in Japanese export trade is the sale of computers and telecommunications equipment, followed by automobiles. In 1960, crude oil accounted for 28.7 per cent of Japan's imports. In 1985, crude and refined oil was responsible for 28.7 per cent of imports, followed by natural gas and oil products. By way of further comparison, the USA which developed the automobile industry at the turn of the century, sells too few cars to Japan to have them recorded in official statistics, but Japanese car imports into the USA in 1990 accounted for 21.5 per cent of Japanese imports. US auto manufacturers do not make right-hand drive cars for the Japanese market but ask dealers instead to make 'conversions'.

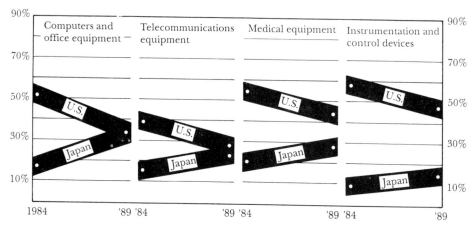

Figure 15.10   *Production structure of typical Japanese automaker as of 1981*
Source   Sako, M. (1989) Parntership between small and large firms: The case of Japan. In
Partnership Between Small and Large Firms, Directorate for Enterprise of the Commission of
the European Communities, Brussels, Graham and Trotman, London

Nevertheless, Japanese industry has demanned wherever possible. Citing the case of the
Japanese electronics industry, for example, as having multiplied its output 3.4 times between
1968 and 1978 while its exports increased 5.2 times, its production finally became 25 per cent
larger than the combined production of West Germany, France, Italy and the UK. Again,
there are colour television assembly lines nearly 70 per cent of which are now fully
automated, lowering production times from six man hours to one and one-half, and reduced
power consumption per 20-inch set from 325W in 1972 to 95W in 1977. A 1984 survey of
763 Japanese companies showed the proportion allocated to basic research to be an average
5.2 per cent of total outlay. While 117 firms replied that they spent over 20 per cent on basic
research, 291 stated only 2 per cent. This survey also showed heavy dependence on
universities and research institutes, which does not happen in the Western world.

There was little Japanese investment in the EC in the 1960s, except for relatively
insignificant areas like zips and stationery. In the 1970s this came to include ball bearings,
colour televisions, chemicals, and synthetic fabrics. In the 1980s, Nissan and Honda began car
production in Europe, and as Europe prepares for the Single Market this flow has increased.

The Sogo Shosha: Japanese international trading companies

In postwar Japan, the Sogo Shosha were divided up into many different and separate
companies. Mitsui, then the largest (now it is Mitsubishi), was divided up into over 200
companies, but by 1959 it had reassembled, and now handles approximately 10 per cent of
Japanese exports on its own. Mitsui is now the fourth largest US exporter after Boeing,
General Motors and General Electric.

The nine big Sogo Shoshas account for an estimated 50–60 per cent of Japan's external
trade. The Sogo Shosha have an impressive pedigree going back more than a hundred years.
Their strength lies in their integration of trading, manufacturing, and banking affiliates.
Mitsubishi is linked with Mitsubishi Bank; Mitsui with Mitsui Bank; Marubeni with Fuji; C.
Itoh to Dai-Ichi Kangyo Bank. These banks rank among the largest in the world in asset

terms. At the end of 1981, the nine major Sogo Shoshas had a total of approximately 57,000 personnel. Of these, about 23,900 (including 6,300 expatriate personnel) were working at a total of 1,044 overseas offices, including wholly owned affiliates and joint ventures.

It is usual to read of obituaries for the Sogo Shosha – only 20 per cent of Japan's domestic wholesale trade now goes via the top ten trading houses compared with a majority situation in early 1950. The threat derives from the increasing independence of Japanese car manufacturers and others; from Japanese banks lending directly to the small company rather than via them; and from the fact also that gross profit margins for the traditional business of Sogo Shoshas is falling, signalling stagnant turnover and rising costs. Against this, it should be noted that the Sogo Shoshas are moving increasingly into third-country trade, acting as an intermediary for other Western companies, while at home they are being seen to be active in new investments, e.g., cable television and data communications.

Imports into Japan

Japan is said to still retain an ancient complex distribution system that has evolved from agricultural produce. This poses a problem for domestic as well as foreign companies. Japan has more wholesalers and retailers per capita than any other industrial nation. It is explained by the 'Keiretsu' system in which producers, importers, distributors, and retailers are all financially linked with each other, either directly or through a bank or Sogo Shosha. This results in close ties and bonds forged by mutual obligation and service.

Technically, all imports require licences under Article 52 of the Japan Foreign Exchange Law. However, most goods enter unrestricted and with nominal formality. This can be done under the Import Declaration Scheme (IDS) or under the import quota scheme. Under the Import Declaration Scheme, the only requirement is to report to the Ministry of International Trade and Industry (MITI) through foreign exchange banks on the remittance of payment abroad. Under the import quota scheme, certain goods are subject to a specific quantitative restriction. Under Articles 21 and 22 of GATT, the Japanese Government is allowed to restrict imports for security, public health, revenue or other reasons (including heavy aircraft, aircraft engines, explosives, arms, swords, tobacco products, and narcotics). Under this system, an importer must first obtain an Import Quota Allocation Certificate from MITI which entitles him to receive an import licence on application to an authorized foreign exchange bank. The size of import quotas are decided by the Japanese authorities on a global basis, but the amounts are not made public. Allocations are made to importers on the basis of their past performance, usually twice a year.

Table 15.9   The myths of the Japanese market

1 How Japanese distribution system is impenetrable.
2 Product testing and certification requirements make it impossible for foreign companies to enter Japan.
3 The Japanese will only buy Japanese products.
4 The Japanese will not work for a foreign company.

Source   Alden, V. Z. (1987) Who says you can't crack Japanese markets? *Harvard Business Review*, **65,** (1) 52-56.

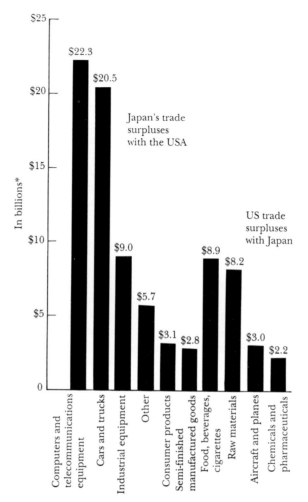

Figure 15.11   *US-Japanese trade and surpluses*
Source   *Fortune* (1991) 6 May, p. 39

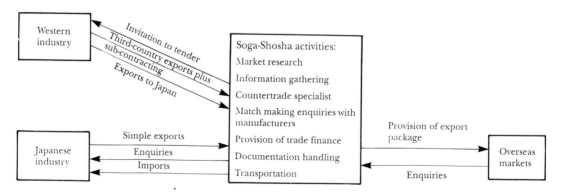

Figure 15.12   *The Zaibatsu approach to OEM/supplier relationships*
Source   Blenkhorn D.L., and Noori, A.H. (1990) What it takes to supply Japanese OEMs.
Industrial Marketing Management, **19**, 21–30

Tariffs

Except for certain raw materials, essential items of industrial equipment, antiques, and a few other manufactured goods, imports are liable to customs duties. Most are calculated as a of the value of the goods. Of the 2,576 headings in the Japanese Customs Tariff, 412 are duty free and these are mainly raw materials which represent almost 50 per cent by value of Japanese imports. The tariff rates then are:

- Basic Rate
- GATT Rate
- Temporary Rate (reviewed annually)
- Special Rate under Generalized Preferences

Japan's tariffs are on average lower than those of most industrialized countries, but 'non-tariff barriers' constitute a problem. Toyota produce a booklet to help foreign suppliers around the maze of bureaucracy which, combined with long distribution channels, can be a barrier to entry to the market. Import regulations include the following.

Duty assessment

This is on the basis of the declared CIF value. On this basis, the customs may increase the basis for assessment of duty in order to bring the CIF price up to the value which an independent buyer would have to pay, assuming he had no special relationship with the supplier. This 'arms length' concept is introduced here and is in fact a countervailing duty to ensure that imports do not gain over domestic products.

Duty is normally levied *ad valorem*. However, for wool and Scotch whisky, a specific duty may be levied solely on the basis of the quality.

Internal taxes

These operate, regardless of whether they are for domestic for foreign goods, from five per cent on cosmetics to 30 per cent on motor boats, etc., but there are also excise duties.

Import documentation.

Certificates of origin are not required for goods for which conventional or beneficial rates of duty are claimed, such as goods entitled to GATT or MFN status. A declaration of origin in the commercial invoice is sufficient.

Transit and bond

Although there are no designated free ports as such, certain factories and warehouses have been designated for the processing in bond of imported materials and goods for ultimate re-export. These are of five types:

1 Designated bonded area owned or administered by the Japanese Government, local public bodies, or Japan National Railways.

2 Bonded sheds.
3 Bonded warehouses.
4 Bonded manufacturing warehouses.
5 Bonded exhibition sites.

Storage for imported goods is for up to twenty-four months but may be extended. The total number of bonded facilities in Japan is 3,300, located in nine areas – Tokyo, Yokohama, Kobe, Osaka, Nagoya, Moji, Nagasaki, Naha and Hakodate. Each contains all forms of bonded facilities.

Distribution in Japan

Japanese distribution is a particular problem for foreign companies seeking to enter Japan. Japanese trading companies have been accused (Foster, 1988) of taking on agencies for Western products in order to control their distribution while a decision is made about whether some associated manufacturing unit should bring out a duplicate. Other foreign companies, such as those in the automotive industry, are effectively trying to 'carry coal to Newcastle' in trying to penetrate the Japanese automotive market, as forty US auto parts manufacturers set out to do. Traditional market supply structures have to be taken into consideration. Also, pricing low will not secure a long-term advantage in Japan, whose buyer-seller relationships are traditionally close and secure. Nevertheless, TRW supply rack and pinion steering systems; Allied Signal supply turbo-chargers; Motorola supply car phones; Tenneco supply silencers (mufflers); and Champion supply spark plugs.

Often held to be a non-tariff barrier that blocks imports once they have been allowed into Japan, there are some significant changes taking place. First, the Japanese distribution system is very traditional, and it has the longest distribution channels in the world because of the system whereby manufacturers at the top, and all the intermediaries below, will have a cross-shareholding in each other. Inroads into this system have been made mainly by foreign companies creating new distribution systems as they enter Japan for the first time, such as Coca-Cola. Again, distribution systems in Japan have featured in the US trade talks with Japan under the banner of the Structural Impediments Initiative (SII). Yet, Japanese legislation, such as the Large Store Law, protects small retailers from predatory large stores.

Where bureaucracy gets in the way, there is usually also a way to circumvent it. For example, many companies have lured former civil servants as consultants, although this may often be seen to fall into a questionable 'grey area', as in the past with scandals over Lockheed payments to 'consultants'. Japanese former civil servants have to work one year then before joining the company as an adviser, then director, etc. Mitsubishi hired an adviser who is now Managing Director. At all times, creativity is required in dealing with the Japanese market. If, for example, it is not possible to get into the Defence Ministry, then perhaps contact Mitsubishi who is also a large defence supplier.

Perhaps another point to note also is that the Japanese distributor will look at annual sales, whereas a Western company may be more concerned with the immediate short-term results. Again, a Japanese importer may be more concerned with total sales volume than unit profitability, so here are some inherent differences in business approaches. While licensing has been popular in the past, and franchising is now very common, there is now the easing of restrictions on expanding large retail outlet chains in Japan, so there are increasing market opportunities and these could well be developed through joint ventures. In pharmaceuticals,

Table 15.10   The six big enterprise groups and their Shacho-kai (1 October 1983)

Group name / Shacho-kai name	Mitsubishi / Kinyō-kai	Mitsui / Nimoku-kai	Sumitomo / Hakusui-kai	Fuji / Fuyō-kai	Dai-Ichi / Sankin-kai	Sanwa / Sansui-kai
Main manufacturing corporations	Mitsubishi Chemical Industries Ltd Mitsubishi Rayon Co. Mitsubishi Steel Mfg Co. Mitsubishi Heavy Industries Mitsubishi Motor Industry Mitsubishi Electric Corporation Mitsubishi Oil Co.	Mitsui Toatsu Chemicals Inc. Tōray Industries Japan Steel Works Mitsui Engineering and Shipbuilding Co., Ltd. Toyota Motor Co. Toshiba Co.	Sumitomo Chemical Sumitomo Metal Industries Sumitomo Heavy Industries, Ltd. Nippon Electric Co.	Shōwa Denko K.K. Tōyō Rayon Co., Ltd Nippon Kōkan K.K. Kubola Ltd Nippon Seiko K.K. Nissan Motor Oki Electric Industry Co. Ltd. Hitachi Tōa Nenryō Kōgyō K.K.	Denki Kagaku Kogyo K.K. Asahi Chemical Industries Co. Kawasaki Steel Corporation Kawasaki Heavy Industries Ishikawajima-Harima Heavy Industries Isuzu Motors, Ltd. Fijitsu Hitachi Showa Oil Co. Asahi Optical Company Nippon Columbia Co.	Tokuyama Soga Co. Ltd Unitika Teijin Kobe Steel Hitachi Shipbuilding and Engineering Co. Daihatsu Motor Co. Sharp Corporation Hitachi Maruzen Oil Co.
Others	Nippon Kōgaku K.K.			Canon		
General trading company	Mitsubishi Corporation	Mitsui and Co.	Sumitomo Shōji Kaisha	Marubeni Corporation	C. Itoh and Co.	Nisshō-Iwai Co.

Source   Sumiya, T. (1984) *Kokka to kigyō*, pp. 82–83. Cited in: *Japanese Competition since 1945* (Morris-Suzuki, Tessa; Seiyama, Takuro, 1981), M. E. Sharpe Inc., Armonk, NY.

Table 15.12   Subcontractors, companies that subcontract, and subcontractors' output

Industry	Sub-contractors 1976	Sub-contractors 1981	Companies that subcontract 1976	Companies that subcontract 1981	Subcontractors' output 1976	Subcontractors' output 1981	Growth rate 1981/1976
Total manufacturing	60.7	65.5	32.5	37.0	140,898	265,489	88.4
Foodstuffs	14.5	17.5	4.9	5.5	13,497	15,790	17.0
Textiles	84.5	84.9	24.4	26.5	11,863	15,868	33.8
Clothing and other textile goods	83.9	86.5	39.1	40.9	6,197	11,445	84.7
Wood, woodwork	42.9	48.9	17.7	20.3	5,795	7,297	25.9
Furniture, furnishings	41.2	51.6	30.7	34.9	4,643	8,155	75.6
Pulp, paper and paper products	44.8	51.6	36.3	42.9	2,218	3,559	60.5
Publishing, printing and others	50.8	59.0	57.4	65.7	3,586	8,723	143.3
Chemicals	37.1	38.5	27.7	27.1	2,717	4,258	56.7
Oil and coal products	27.0	38.9	19.1	17.1	111	281	153.2
Rubber products	61.1	71.8	37.3	40.2	1,252	3,341	166.9
Leather, leather products, furs	62.5	68.8	32.0	31.4	834	1,409	68.9
Ceramics	29.4	36.6	21.0	24.5	1,942	4,206	116.6
Steel	70.4	72.0	44.6	41.6	5,370	8,050	49.9
Non-ferrous metals	68.7	73.6	46.1	47.4	3,174	6,093	92.0
Metal products	74.8	78.6	40.3	44.5	19,584	40,423	106.4
Machinery	82.7	84.2	54.9	55.7	17,560	34,755	97.9
Electric machinery	82.3	85.3	55.1	57.9	16,674	35,036	110.1
Transportation machinery	86.2	87.7	45.5	48.8	13,779	25,791	86.5
Precision machinery	72.4	80.9	54.8	54.4	2,782	6,764	143.1
Other manufacturing	56.5	62.2	31.9	37.7	9,294	20,817	124.0

Note
Percentage of contractors
$$= \frac{\text{No. of small and medium subcontractors}}{\text{No. of small and medium manufacturers}} \times 100$$
Source   MITI: Small and Medium Enterprise Agency. 'Basic Survey on Industry' cited in Sako, M. (1989) Partnership between small and large firms: the case of Japan. In *Partnership Between Small and Large Firms* (ed. DG XXIII – Directorate for Enterprise of the Commission of the European Communities), Brussels, Graham and Trotman Ltd., London.

foreign companies. Notice how, in Figure 15.14, the perception of the degree of adaptation to Japanese business produces changes between those actually doing business with foreign firms and those who are not. The same is equally true of other criteria which score a low evaluation, including delivery, after-sales service, product modification and development.

Taking this a stage further, Blenkhorn and Noori (1990) pinpointed nine criteria found to be crucial in the forming of relationships:

Exhibit 15.1

Beef producers try to whet Japan's appetite

MARKETING

OLIVER BERTIN

ALONG with a new-found taste for Scotch whisky, Pablo Picasso and other trappings of Western civilization, the Japanese have developed a liking for Western-style meat.

And that has opened a huge and lucrative market that Canadian meat exporters would dearly love to serve.

But the Japanese meat business is also one of the most difficult to enter, and that has forced Canada to employ a novel marketing approach that is slowly starting to pay off.

There is little doubt in Canadian minds that the market is worth the effort.

Andrew Raphael, executive-director of the Canada Beef Export Federation, reckons the Japanese will be consuming $3-billion worth of beef annually by the turn of the century. And, pork sales will be several times larger.

But Canada is only one of a host of countries that are trying to sell beef to Japan, and the competition is, to say the least, cut-throat.

At present, Australia has the bulk of Japan's beef import market with its specialty, tough, lean and cheap animals that have spent most of their lives running loose on the ranch.

The United States fattens its cattle for slaughter with corn, giving a melt-in-your-mouth steak that is also high in fat and tinged with an unappetizing shade of yellow.

Canada ranks No. 3 in the beef market and last year shipped 4,000 tonnes of beef, worth about $20-million.

Canada tends to the high-end market of the beef market. Cattle are usually fattened with western barley, giving a steak that is leaner than the American, but a little tougher and not as tasty. The fat is, however, gleaning white, a factor that appeals to the Japanese eye.

The beef business is expected to blossom in the next few years now that Japan has replaced its import quotas with a system of tariffs.

The quotas came off last April and were replaced with a 70-per cent import tariff that Mr. Raphael said was equivalent in its impact. The tariff drops to 60 per cent in 1992, 50 per cent in 1993 and, possibly, to 25 per cent after that.

That will allow Canadian exports to compete more effectively against Japan's high-cost, but highly subsidized domestic industry. By 2000, Mr. Raphael hopes to ship about 7,-500 tonnes of premium-quality Canadian beef to that country, worth about $250-million.

Canada is trying to get into that expanding market at the ground floor, a task that has been given to Mr. Raphael and his beef organization.

As with pork, which Canadian producers have been shipping to Japan for about 20 years, the beef people are trying a low-key, promotional campaign that is designed to open communications between buyers and sellers in the two countries.

This was necessary because Japanese buyers have little understanding of the peculiarities of Canadian beef, and Canadian packers are lost when confronted with the idiosyncratic and pernickety Japanese diet.

The vehicle for this campaign is the Canada Beef Export Federation, and industry-wide organization that was modelled on pork's equivalent, Canada Pork International.

To spread the word about Canada, the beef group has set up a trade office in Tokyo, and hired a Canadian and a Japanese food expert. They spend much of their time in restaurant kitchens and at trade shows and cooking demonstrations, introducing Japanese chefs to the Canadian product.

The process works in reverse when teaching Canadians about the Japanese. Mr. Raphael brings Japanese food buyers to Canada, and leads them on to the slaughterhouse floor with butcher's knife in hand, so they can give a lesson on cutting meat the Japanese way.

It's a difficult lesson for an industry that typically hacks off one-inch steaks with a band-saw and tosses them on to a styrofoam tray.

Instead, Canadian meat cutters are learning to shave wafer-thin slices, identical in size and shape, and lay them delicately in sophisticated, specially printed plastic boxes.

Mr. Raphael's group met considerable resistance when it first brought the Japanese to Canada. After all, meat packing is a conservative, hide-bound industry.

Packers insisted their product was good enough for the Japanese, and they came up with endless excuses to prove they couldn't adapt. But the Japanese market is so lucrative that packers are now prepared to listen.

More important, they are finding ways to out-compete the U.S. and Australian packers in the more profitable markets.

Canadians are trying to fill the niche markets that are too small for U.S. plans to bother with, and were promoting the best attributes of the Canadian meat – high quality and relatively low fat.

And they are learning, awkwardly at first the esoteric skills that are needed to cut obscure items in the Japanese beef diet, and to do it with the same aplomb as a Tokyo butcher.

Source *The Globe and Mail* (1991) Toronto, 2 July.

- *Well defined mandates, goals and objectives.* Teamwork and good communications evident.
- *Focussed customers.* Single sourcing with suppliers, close relations and close physical proximity.
- *Supplier aggressiveness.* Working on very low margins which creates the need for high productivity to maintain low cost structure.
- *User/producer interface* close in case of product development, general exchange of information.
- *Selection of suppliers based on equipment compatibility.* Equipment capability and compatibility rated more important than price.
- *Zero defect policy* found everywhere in Japan.
- *Just-in-time (JIT) delivery,* reducing inventory costs and lowering per unit costs.
- *Encouragement of innovative thinking* between the firm and its suppliers. Working on designs together.
- *Culture, people and attitude.* Japanese societal norms play a large role in the expectations of manufacturer/supplier relationship.

A comparison, then, between the Japanese and the North American supplier performance levels is outlined in Table 15.13. Yet, although this explains part, it does not explain all. The Zaibatsu organizational relationship, whose manufacturers have a financial equity stake in their suppliers, and perhaps all the way down the distribution channel, has also to be considered. Blenkhorn and Noori (1990) chart this organizationally and describe these

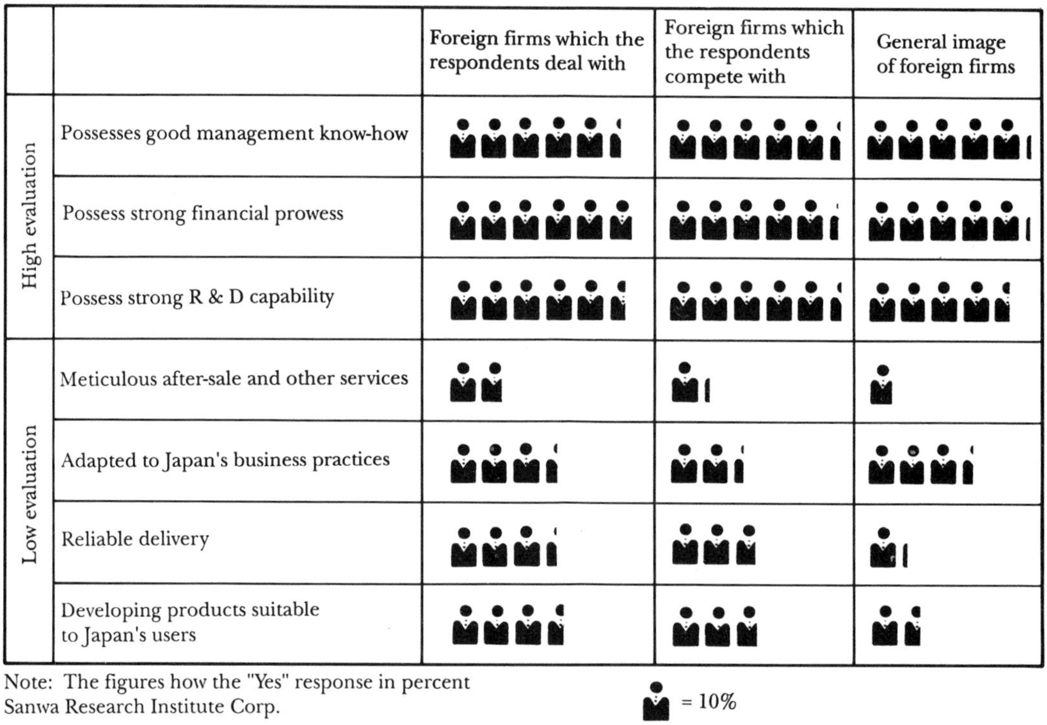

		Foreign firms which the respondents deal with	Foreign firms which the respondents compete with	General image of foreign firms
High evaluation	Possesses good management know-how	●●●●●●	●●●●●●	●●●●●
	Possess strong financial prowess	●●●●●●	●●●●●	●●●●●
	Possess strong R & D capability	●●●●●●	●●●●●●	●●●●●
Low evaluation	Meticulous after-sale and other services	●●	●	●
	Adapted to Japan's business practices	●●●	●●●	●●●●
	Reliable delivery	●●●	●●●	●●
	Developing products suitable to Japan's users	●●●●	●●●	●●

Note: The figures how the "Yes" response in percent
Sanwa Research Institute Corp.   ● = 10%

Figure 15.14   *How Japanese business people view foreign companies*
Source   Tokyo Business Today (1990) July, p. 27

Table 15.13　A comparison of Japanese and North American suppliers

Criterion	Attribute	
	Japan	North America
Quality	Part of the process	Monitored after production
JIT delivery	Not a new phenomenon: part of the total supply/delivery system	Imposed by external forces – customers or threat of competition from the Japanese
Process/equipment	Synchronized with their major customer(s) and suppliers	Firm specific centred rather entire system centered
Culture/people/attitude	Team playing, job enlargement, attempts to play down rank or hierarchy on job	Union centered them–us attitude
Innovative thinking	Mandatory to survive as auto assemblers demand innovative, cost saving solutions	Encouraged but historically not mandatory to survive as parts maker
Efficiency	Efficiency enhanced through manufacture of robots or modification of purchased equipment	Often look to external sources to increase efficiency
Competitiveness/price	Other Japanese firms seen as major competitors and in-house capability of auto assemblers	Offshore parts makers viewed as major competitors
User/producer interface	An ongoing R&D thrust with regular exchange of personnel	Often limited to the order at hand
Degree of computer linkage/ sophistication	The supplier/assembler interface perhaps is very similar in both Japan and North America	
	Extensive use of CAD/CAM in design engineering	Much less use of CAD/CAM
JIT necessity	Pressure to adopt came from the auto assemblers	
	Much more commonly utilized and understood	Being adopted by those suppliers that wish to remain suppliers
Design-to-cost criteria	Historically a common occurrence in the Japanese auto industry, but the rise in the yen has intensified its use	No data
Outsourcing	More outsourcing often offshore caused principally by increased value of the yen	More outsourcing precipitated by OEM's desire to reduce fixed costs
	More for both groups but for different reasons	

Source　Blenkhorn, D. L., and Noori, A. H. (1990) What it takes to supply Japanese OEM's. *Industrial Marketing Management*, **19**, 21–30.

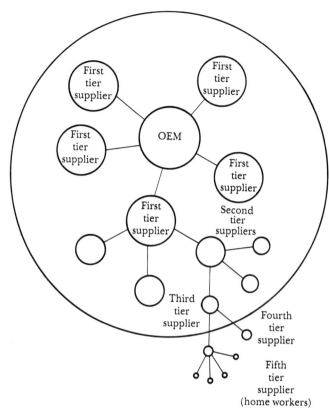

Figure 15.15   *The Zaibatsu approach to OEM/supplier relationships*
Source   Blenkhorn D. L., and Noori, A. H. (1990) What is takes to supply Japanese
OEMs. *Industrial Marketing Management*, **19**, 21–30

relationships as tiers in terms of closeness to the manufacturer. Tier 2 would be closest and
may be directly controlled by the manufacturer, but likely to be a single source supplier until
going through the tier. The organizational linkage with the manufacturer becomes weaker
and the supplier itself also becomes smaller in size (see Figure 15.15).

The importance of these relationships becomes clearer when one realizes that Hitachi, for
example, has 800 affiliated companies and only in August of 1990 did it drop the word
'keiretsu' from its organizational chart. This name change comes at a time when the
traditional 'keiretsu' system is coming under closer scrutiny as the USA argues that it lies at
the heart of Japanese protectionism, as keiretsu group members purchase as much as possible
from each other, thus limiting the potential for imports. Also, because of the recycled stock
holdings, it becomes more difficult for foreign firms to acquire Japanese companies. The
keiretsu have been traditionally strong in consumer electronics and in the automobile
industry in Japan, though there is some evidence that this is now changing (Fujigane and
Ennis, 1990).

There are three types of keiretsu:

1 Capital connected, including the former Zaibatsu, Mitsui, Mitsubishi, Simitomo, Fuji

Group including firms from prewar Yasuda Zanbateu; bank-centred groups led by Dai-Ichi Kangyo (successor to Furakawa Zaibatsu); and Sanwa Bank.

2 Production keiretsu, mainly in the automotive industry, characterized by the vertical integration of manufactures and their suppliers. Toyota has an auto parts association, called 'Kyohokai', grouping 178 companies, and another in plant and equipment 'Eihokai' with seventy-seven firms. Nissan has 'Takairakai' totalling 104 firms and participates in 'Shohokai', which has seventy companies, including Hitachi and Matsushita.

3 Sales distribution keiretsu, involving vertical integration of product distribution from factory to retail outlets, eg. Hitachi, Matsushita, but the number is declining. Matsushita has 25,000 retail shops; Toshiba, 12,500; Hitachi, 10,000; and Sanyo, 6,000. Product availability is limited to keiretsu stores which maintain prices at a high level.

The Japanese consumer

Japan's increasing affluence is also effecting societal change. Youth are now used to high technology products and express themselves through fashion rather than politics. More importantly, people are being freed from the old sex stereotyped roles. Traditionally, a housewife would be responsible for 80–90 per cent of the housework as well as for 80 per cent of the household's discretionary expenditure. As society changes and the individual's place within that society changes, it also has important implications for marketing because it means that the decision-making on products is shifting together perhaps with its usage. With increasing affluence, Japanese consumers are now developing expensive consumer tastes. Ohashi (1989) examined these changes from a marketing perspective and isolated seven

Table 15.14   The companies Toyota directly controls

	Shares owned by Toyota (%)
Toyota Automatic Loom Works, Ltd	23.1
Aichi Steel Works, Ltd.	21.2
Toyoda Machine Works, Ltd	21.0
Toyota Auto Body Co.	40.2
Toyota Tsusho Corp.	21.1
Aisin Seiki Co.	21.6
Nippondenso Co.	23.0
Toyota Boshoku Corp.	8.9
Kanto Auto Works, Ltd.	48.8
Toyota Gosei Co.	38.3
Hino Motors Ltd.	10.8
Daihatsu Motor Co.	14.1
Towa Real Estate Co.	49.0
Toyota Central Research and Development Laboratories Inc.	—

Source   Shimizu, Y., Tsutsui, M., Inaba, Y., and Umesawa, M. (1990) Production keiretsu: a new export from Japan. *Tokyo Business Today*, September, p. 30.

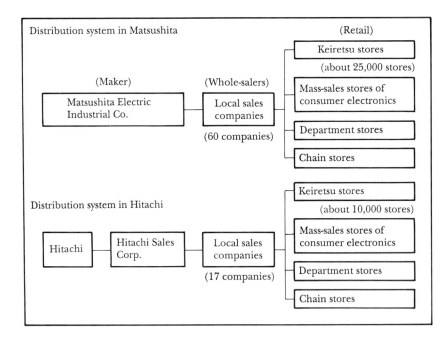

Figure 15.16
Source   Hara, E., Takito, H., and Umesawa, M. (1990) Distribution Keiretsu: Electronic stores rebel. *Tokyo Business Today*, September, p. 36

factors across four generations or cohorts within Japanese society. Of major importance are four particular trends which emerge from this study:

1 The growing influence of women and their ability to express themselves within society. This will cause a break with the old values which tied women to housework.
2 From self-orientation to individualization. Self-expression through consumption will spread to future generations as well.
3 A new family concept. Traditionally cohesive, there will be the advent of separate nuclear family units with children on an equal footing as individuals with their parents.
4 Importance of the living space. Younger generations will demand better quality and more spacious housing than presently exists, and will model themselves on Western-style living and leisure activities.

As regards the mobilization and institutionalization of the Japanese consumer, this is presently very low level. The consumer in Japan is poorly represented. Imports are expensive despite the yen being high, and Japanese consumer goods can often be bought more cheaply abroad than within Japan itself, but Japanese consumer groups appear to be protectionist by nature (Aishikawa, 1990). There are four main groups:

1 *Cooperative consumers' societies* which are tied to a political party. Out of power political parties have much to gain from being seen to be championing the consumer cause, as has been the case with the Japan Communist party.
2 *Housewives' organizations* which involved themselves in joint purchasing from farms, price

Table 15.15   A spate of recent recalls in Japan

Company/Product	Problem
Toyota Lexus Automobiles*	Cruise control, brake light
Mitsubishi Motors Pajero Wagon	Accelerator
Isuzu Trucks	Loose bolt
Fuji Heavy Rex Minicars	Clutch contact
Yamaha Virago Motorcycles	Transmission cog
Seiko Epson Laptop Computer	Circuit soldering
Toshiba TVs	High-voltage circuits
Pioneer Electric TVs	Circuit soldering
Matsushita TVs	Transformer insulation
Sony TVs	High-voltage circuits
*The only recall affecting the US market.	

Source   Neff, R. (1990) Now Japan is getting jumpy about quality. *Business Week*, (3148) 40–41.

surveys, recycling, studying consumer projections, testing products and organizing cookery classes.
3 *Advocacy groups*, e.g. Consumer Union of Japan (EUJ) founded in 1969 and heavily influenced by the US consumer advocate, Ralph Nader. Lawsuits and publicity for bad products, and championing of new legislation, are part of its repertoire. It is unconnected with any political party.
4 *Expert groups*, e.g. lifestyle consultants, lawyers, consumer affairs experts. They become involved in broadening the liability base for product defects and prevention of fraudulent contracts for example.

Consumer groups believe generally that Japan must be self-sufficient in food as in the highly political area of rice. The consumer groups have failed to find a united voice on many of the issues now confronting Japanese society. Japanese consumers are unaware of the power of consumer associations in other parts of the world. They seem to believe that free competition is not in the best interests of the consumer, and that government legislation is necessary to ensure adequate consumer protection from manufacturing firms. Meanwhile, while quality, reliability and after-sales service are held to be important, European firms emerged in a Japanese survey as being ill-prepared and failing to gather enough information about the market before actually entering it. The lack or inadequacy of instructions in Japanese was the leading reason to emerge after price for not buying European (*Marketing*, 1987).
Japan, home of the Deming Prize for quality, is not infallible, however, as recent reports show. The need to cut costs because of a high yen, and the introduction of parts and components now manufactured in the Pacific Basin, are contributory factors to what appears to be a slippage in quality. Higher automation and more imported components may be significant factors, but the Japanese Government has intervened to ensure that this deterioration does not become a slide. JD Power and Associates of California, who regularly evaluate cars, stated that defects per 100 Japanese cars sold in the USA dropped from 131 in

1987 to 121 in 1989, and that was better than any US car maker's record (Neff, 1990). Nevertheless, *Tokyo Business Today* (1990) stated that seven recalls were made in 1989 and ten in the first five months of 1990, and clearly showed concern. While it is heartening to see the urgent concern of the Japanese industry and of the Government, there is also a need to introduce a system to resolve and redress the consumer for damages as a result of product defects.

Product testing for imports

With motor vehicles, individual units may be tested on arrival or they may be subject to an exhaustive test when import is first undertaken, after which a model is given 'type approval' which then permits further imports of that model without testing. Testing can take several months and cost 20,000–200,000 yen. (The Japanese also politely point out that test cars are often not in a saleable condition afterwards.) There are a number of Japanese safety and environmental protection regulations for vehicles.

In the case of pharmaceuticals, all drugs or medical devices imported into, or manufactured in, Japan must be tested and then registered by the Ministry of Health and Welfare before being put on sale in Japan. The registration period is often lengthened to between six months and one year by regulations which require double blind testing of new products, ethical testing, and even supplying the authorities with vaccine serum in the case of new vaccines. These testing requirements also involve the exporter in costs which often reach several thousand pounds sterling. All importers of pharmaceuticals must be licensed by the Ministry of Health and Welfare to handle pharmaceuticals. This entails having at least one employee who is a registered pharmacist.

Electrical appliances have to be tested by the Japan Electrical Testing Laboratory and can take from one to three months. Gas appliances must be tested and approved by the Japan Gas Appliance Inspection Association before they can be sold in Japan.

Processed cheese is subject to an import quota and so the Japanese authorities may, in cases of doubt, test imports of natural cheeses in order to check that they are not processed ones, in spite of the fact that natural cheese is not on the import quota. In the case of natural cheeses, it is possible to avoid such testing provided the consignment is accompanied by an official public analyst's certificate to the effect that the import in question is a natural cheese.

Market prospects for exports to Japan

The prospects for exports to Japan are outwardly good but direct exports are difficult. In high value areas, such as cars or microelectronics, Japan exports at least four times as much as it imports.

1. Distance and resulting high costs where there is a ratio of high bulk to value on exports.
2. Tariffs and certain non-tariff barriers estimated to number 258 in all, including the designation of scheduled air traffic.
3. Distribution – in Japan this is said to be the major reason for the Western failure to infiltrate the Japanese market. This is often more difficult than entering Japan (Shimaguchi and Lazer, 1979; Czinkota, 1985). This is seen as a non-tariff barrier because of the high number of small firms, doubtless aided by the retention in Japan of retail price maintenance.

There are 300,000 wholesaling firms (Tonja) who keep on selling to each other and atomistic competition among its 1.6m retailers. A particular point to note is that retailers and wholesalers demand a lot from manufacturers. This has the following effects:

- Necessitating substantial capital investment by the manufacturer.
- Limited freedom on pricing, given that only wholesale selling prices can be determined by the manufacturer.
- Frequent price changes are best avoided, partly due to the depth of the distribution channel. A Japanese manufacturer summarized it thus: 'We cannot consider our growth without our dealers' growth, and our dealers' growth cannot be considered without ours.' This perspective engenders harmony but inhibits change taking place.
- Rebates (traditional in the Japanese food business) – the largest rebates may be higher than the normal margins allowed.
- Supply (prompt delivery is essential).
- Promotional assistance and budgeting are required.
- Sales – frequent personal visits to customers at all levels are most important.
- Training support for education, management, technical staff is required.

4 Royalties for manufacture under licence. Quick approval is usually granted. Previously licensing was the only method of entering Japan.
5 Capital investment in a joint venture manufacturing arrangement.

From the British perspective, Japan is the number one market for worsted cloth, number two for quality knitwear and number three for Scotch whisky, although this has been dropping from 3 million cases p.a. to 2.5 million. Parallel exporting has done some damage to established brand pricing and image. The overall picture which emerges, though, is of a commodity trade pattern with British exports to Japan being quite unlike Japanese imports into Britain, gauged either in overall value or unit value, as well as technological input.

Advertising in Japan

Advertising is seen to be creative rather than a sales tool. Bert Marsh of Young and Rubicam defined three main types of advertising in Japan: follow-the-leader, use of celebrities, and use of mood. The key to sales is distribution not advertising. Following the competition is not particularly frowned on. Celebrities are often used to position a product. Since Americans are considered to be great coffee drinkers, then it follows that US actors are in demand for coffee commercials. The actor's image is important to the positioning of the product. Direct confrontation or 'knocking copy' is not used. Mood is very extensively used, depicting perhaps the beauties of nature, and only at the very end of the commercial, introducing the product in question. To Westerners, this is not effective advertising, but to the Japanese, this form of advertising adds to the image of the company. Commercial films are left to the film producer rather than the agency and different agencies may be used for different media. Advertising is still secondary to good distribution in effecting sales in Japan.

Proctor and Gamble, despite being a very successful global company, foundered in Japan because of their inability to read the market. Price discounting alienated the wholesalers and retailers, and raised questions in the consumer's minds about the quality of the product. Advertising for brands, such as 'Cheers' and 'Camay', were of a hard sell with customer

Table 15.16   Ten golden rules for trading profitably with the Japanese

---

1   Do your homework first. Don't assume that the Japanese are just another customer – they're not.

2   Get your board's commitment. Selling to Japan isn't cheap, especially now.

3   Don't give up easily, even when all appears lost. If you persevere, and you have a reliable product and quality standard, you will sell eventually.

4   Behave in a low-key style. Stay unassuming, don't force your sales pitch. Aim to build bridges, not conquer them.

5   Keep your nerve. Don't take fright if the Japanese field a massive team against you. The more they bring to the meeting, the more you are probably respected.

6   Be patient but prepared. The Japanese take a long time to make a decision but, once it's made, seek action quickly. Use the long gestation time to prepare your ground, because that's what the Japanese are doing.

7   Beware of Japanese innocence. They may appear unworldly – they're not. Commercially they are both shrewd and clever, and you will need your wits about you. Once they have reached an agreement with you, they are loyal and honourable.

8   Relate your strengths to Japanese needs. Try to see your product from your Japanese customer's position. If you do, you will drive a better deal.

9   Protect your technology. Japanese companies work in closer harmony than British companies. Don't let your technology be ripped off.

10 Involve the whole company. Make sure your team know what is expected of them from Japanese buyers and inspectors. Good all-round performance means you are better placed for the next business, even though your price might not be the lowest.

Source: Dale, I. (1988). Cited in Hard sell in Japan. *Management Today*, (Foster, G.) September, 99.

testimonials and were soundly disliked. 'Cheers' advertisements were liked the least on Japanese television. Proctor and Gamble introduced disposable nappies (diapers) to the Japanese market, but fell from 90 per cent of the market to 15 per cent between 1981 and 1986 as a result of Japanese competition with an improved product. Proctor and Gamble lost, also, because they focused advertising on the brand and not the company. With Ariel they are preparing a formulation for the Japanese market to allow for short cycles, cold water and small machines, adapting to market needs at last (Trachtenberg, 1986).

Innovation and product development

As Figure 15.17 shows, Japan is a major global player in industrial innovation. The days when Japan simply absorbed technology from other countries and improved on it are long gone. Japan creates its own innovations and has all the resources needed to carry this through, including skills, engineering base and strong financial structure. New products, particularly in electronics, come from Japan and consumers in Britain or the USA now seek out Japanese products over domestic competitors. It raises again the question of whether a locally US or British made Japanese product can claim the country of origin of its host country, a very

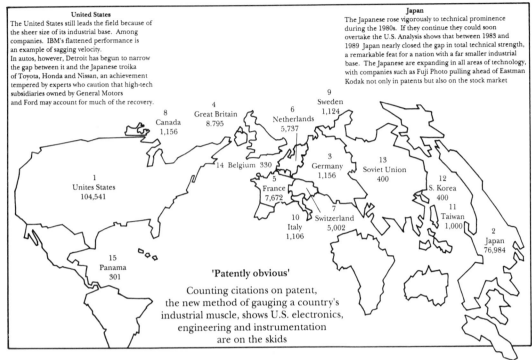

United States
The United States still leads the field because of
the sheer size of its industrial base. Among
companies, IBM's flattened performance is
an example of sagging velocity.
In autos, however, Detroit has begun to narrow
the gap between it and the Japanese troika
of Toyota, Honda and Nissan, an achievement
tempered by experts who caution that high-tech
subsidiaries owned by General Motors
and Ford may account for much of the recovery.

Japan
The Japanese rose vigorously to technical prominence
during the 1980s. If they continue they could soon
overtake the U.S. Analysis shows that between 1983 and
1989 Japan nearly closed the gap in total technical strength,
a remarkable feat for a nation with a far smaller industrial
base. The Japanese are expanding in all areas of technology,
with companies such as Fuji Photo pulling ahead of Eastman
Kodak not only in patents but also on the stock market

8
Canada
1,156

4
Great Britain
8.795

6
Netherlands
5,737

9
Sweden
1,124

14 Belgium 330

5
France
7,672

3
Germany
1,156

13
Soviet Union
400

12
S. Korea
400

1
Unites States
104,541

10
Italy
1,106

7
Switzerland
5,002

11
Taiwan
1,000

2
Japan
76,984

15
Panama
301

'Patently obvious'

Counting citations on patent,
the new method of gauging a country's
industrial muscle, shows U.S. electronics,
engineering and instrumentation
are on the skids

Figure 15.17
Source *The Globe and Mail* (1991) Toronto, 8 June, p. D5

complicated issue now before GATT's Uruguay round. In the USA, there is an Auto Parts Advisory Committee, an industry group which advises the US Department of Commerce. They estimated only 20 per cent and not 48 per cent of the Honda Accord was domestically produced (Holden, 1991). However, to take another source, Taylor (1991), writing in *Fortune*, states 75 per cent of the Honda Accord is US domestic content. Within this 75 per cent, however, most of the US parts come from Honda's own factories or other Japanese suppliers in the USA, leaving around one-quarter of the domestic parts to be sourced by traditional US producers.

Trademarks and industrial property rights

The Department of Trade recommends that the registration of trademarks be considered by any company seriously intending to do business in Japan, as it is relatively simple and inexpensive. Inventions should also be protected, although the processes are more complicated. For companies with a large range of designs, the protection of all of them could be very expensive and they might consider protecting only those designs which have greater potential in Japan. The Japanese classification is different from that in use in most European countries and makes no provision for service marks, but this is changing to conform with international classifications.

For application for registration to be successful, the inventions and designs must not have been known publicly or worked publicly in Japan; nor should they have been described in publications circulated in Japan or in any other country prior to the application. The first person to apply for registration of a patent or trademark obtains the right. Unlike the UK and some other countries, proof of prior use does not confer priority rights. The Japanese Unfair Competition Prevention has given some protection to unregistered designs and trademarks provided that they are 'well known' to Japanese consumers or dealers of the products concerned. However, under the Paris Convention for the Protection of Industrial Property to which both the UK and Japan are signatories, an application made in one of the signatory countries is treated as if it were made at the same time in other signatory countries, provided that the application claiming priority under the Convention is made in those other countries within twelve months of the first application in the case of inventions, and within six months in the case of designs and trademarks.

Doe (1988) cites a Nihon Keizai Shimbun report that two-thirds of major Japanese companies had been hurt by violations of their intellectual property rights, and that the pressure was now on to try to resolve a situation where patent violation cases in Japan were now steadily increasing. NEC Corporations sued Seiko for trying to sell an NEC compatible personal computer although Seiko eventually replaced the operating system software in question. Many other comparable products have since appeared. Doe (1988) cites also the case of two company employees who were convicted in criminal court of embezzlement for using a computer program from their old job in their new job. Yet, an important underlying assumption is that the Japanese tend to view improvements as new inventions in their patent laws and that may extend to software. If there is a 25 per cent improvement, then it is a new invention, and the same may happen in software. Doe (1988) points out also that Japanese law tends to be more concerned with the larger issues of user rights and the greater social good, than with simply the rights of the individual creator, believing that it is selfish and antisocial to keep to oneself that which everyone else needs.

Japan and the UK did not become parties to the Trademark Registration Treaty which was floated in August 1980 but failed. It would have meant that to register a trademark in the signatory nations designated by the application filing one application to the UN World Intellectual Property Organization (WIPO). Unless the government of a designated country refuses to register it within fifteen months of the publication by WIPO, it automatically becomes registered in that country. Applications are published by WIPO as soon as they are filed. It is not necessary to use the trademark in order to register it, but it will cease to be protected it if is not used within three years of registration.

Licensing

British companies have been slower than others to enter into licensing in Japan. Of 1,755 agreements (with a duration of more than one year) in 1978, the number of agreements entered into by UK companies was 135, compared with 870 for the USA, 186 for West Germany, and 206 for France. A study reported in the *Globe and Mail* (1991) showed that this situation has not materially changed.

Foreign investment in Japan

Tokyo Business Today (1990, July) produced a ranking of the top 300 foreign-owned companies and affiliated firms of which the first fifty are reproduced in Table 15.17. It may be

Table 15.17

Ranking 1989	1988	Names of company	Declared-income* 1989	1988	Growth (%)	Foreign cap-ital ratio (%)	Business lines
1	1	IBM Japan	1,319.75	1,443.05	−85	100.0	Computers
2	7	Matsushita Electronics	407.77	209.23	94.4	35.0	Electronics
3	3	Mitsubishi Petrochemical	*341.22	368.32	−7.4	21.0	Chemicals
4	2	Tonen Corp.	285.57	375.02	−23.9	50.0	Petroleum
5	6	Fuji Xeros	268.85	267.33	0.3	50.0	Electronics
6	12	Mazda Motor	*268.81	172.59	55.7	24.2	Automobiles
7	5	Coca-Cola Japan	256.99	280.31	−8.3	100.0	Beverages
8	4	Esso Sekiyu	181.85	321.10	−43.4	100.0	Petroleum
9	16	Banyu Pharmaceutical	171.83	119.60	43.7	50.0	Pharmaceuticals
10	10	Amway Japan	169.31	181.37	−6.4	100.0	Household goods
11	11	Nestle Japan	163.61	181.00	−9.5	100.0	Foodstuffs
12	30	Isuzu Motors	157.72	62.55	152.2	38.2	Automobiles
13	22	Nihon Unisys	143.41	92.79	54.5	33.3	Computer Sales
14	20	Nihon Digital Equipment	140.71	96.90	42.3	100.0	Computer Sales
15	19	Bayer Yakuhin	136.44	100.17	36.2	75.6	Pharmaceuticals
16	15	Yokogawa-Hewlett-Packard	134.56	120.82	11.4	75.0	Electronics
17	13	NCR Japan	133.90	148.81	−10.0	70.0	Electronics
18	14	Nippon Petroleum Refining	123.04	147.69	−13.3	50.0	Petroleum
19	25	General Sekiyu	119.96	79.54	50.3	49.0	Petroleum
20	23	BMW Japan	112.44	89.45	25.7	100.0	Automobiles
21	—	Salomon Brothers Asia	108.31	29.76	236.3	—	Securities
22	18	Sumitomo 3M	108.18	100.52	7.5	50.0	Chemicals
23	28	Yamatake-Honeywell	93.72	66.73	40.5	34.0	Electronics
24	27	Hennessy Japan	91.26	70.22	30.0	100.0	Beverages
25	21	Tonen Petrochemical	90.53	92.34	−2.5	50.0	Chemicals
26	24	McDonald's Japan	75.57	80.53	−6.2	50.0	Food services
27	35	Jardine Wines & Spirits	74.35	48.59	53.0	100.0	Food sales
28	33	Bridgestone Bekaert Steel	73.48	56.68	29.6	49.0	Steel products
29	32	Tappan Moore	67.41	60.19	12.0	45.0	Printing
30	26	Polyplastic	66.35	70.96	−5.3	45.0	Chemicals
31	8	Showa Shell Seklyu	53.35	202.80	−68.5	50.0	Petroleum
32	47	Pfizer Pharmaceuticals	62.88	35.62	76.5	100.0	Pharmaceuticals
33	40	Mercedes-Benz Japan	57.90	42.98	34.7	100.0	Automobiles
34	44	Louis Vuitton Japan	57.71	40.78	41.5	99.0	Accessories
35	41	AIU Insurance	57.71	42.96	34.3	—	Insurance
36	37	NOK Corp.	57.11	45.25	26.2	22.6	Auto parts
37	17	Nihon Oxirane	54.00	115.84	−53.4	50.0	Chemicals
38	34	Molex Japan	51.99	49.26	5.5	100.0	Electronics
39	—	Nippon Light Metal	51.05	—	—	46.5	Aluminum
40	67	Hoechst Japan	49.82	24.78	101.0	100.0	Chemicals
41	59	Shin Nikkei	49.27	28.12	75.2	46.5	Aluminum products
42	29	AMP Japan	*48.61	64.02	−24.1	100.0	Electronics
43	39	Koa Oil	47.63	43.69	9.0	50.0	Petroleum
44	31	Yokogawa Medical Systems	45.68	62.23	−26.5	75.0	Medical equipment
45	38	Dow Coming Toray Silicone	45.61	44.58	2.3	65.0	Chemicals
46	55	AIC	43.75	30.23	44.7	0.0	Financing
47	50	Du Pont-Toray	43.11	32.94	30.9	50.0	Chemicals
48	77	Nippon Glaxo	42.45	20.96	102.5	50.0	Pharmaceuticals
49	49	Printing Machine Trading	41.69	33.85	23.2	67.8	Machinery sales
50	43	Japan Upjohn	39.41	40.99	*3.3	55.0	Pharmaceuticals

Note   *denotes other irregular terms, with income annualized. *$ million at $1 = †144.55, average rate in December 1989.
Source   *Tokyo Business Today* (1990), July.

worth noting that the table includes companies in which there is a foreign equity, participation of more than 20 per cent, and so covers strategic investments made by foreign companies in Japanese companies, as well as joint equity ventures, such as the No. 2 listing of Matsushita and Philips, and the No. 1 listing of the wholly owned IBM subsidiary, IBM Japan. The report is based on information provided by the National Tax Administration Agency as corporate financial information was not freely available in all cases.

Foreign direct investment

Well over 1,000 foreign investors have already established a direct stake in Japanese industry. The MITI study of 1979 showed that half of these were US companies and there were only seventy-seven UK companies with a stake of less than 20 per cent in equity in Japanese companies. Other findings included:

- Fifty-two per cent of all foreign investors in Japanese firms were in manufacturing industry with a particularly heavy preponderance in the chemical and general machinery section.
- Of a total of 655 foreign-affiliated manufacturing corporations in Japan, 42 per cent (273 corporations) are 50 per cent foreign-owned; 26 per cent (172 corporations) are less than 50 per cent foreign-owned; and 32 per cent (210 corporations) are more than 50 per cent foreign-owned.
- Although foreign-affiliated Japanese firms were responsible for only 2.2 per cent of total sales of all Japanese enterprises in 1977, their share of certain business sectors has been increasing steadily and average profitability is consistently greater than domestic Japanese enterprises.

Joint ventures

Until the early 1970s wholly owned subsidiaries were discouraged. It was much easier to establish with 50 per cent or less of the equity. Measures in 1973 and 1975 allowed foreign investment of up to 100 per cent by new enterprises, but still controlled certain activities (e.g., nuclear energy, power, light and gas supply, manufacture of aircraft, arms and explosives), and restricted other activities (e.g., agriculture, forestry and fishing, petroleum and mining, leather and leather products manufacture). Even so, approval was automatic up to an ownership level of less than 10 per cent for a single foreign investor and less than 25 per cent for all foreign investors (15 per cent in the case of fisheries), provided that no one designated by the foreign investors was proposed as a director of the new company. Approval was also automatic for foreign ownership of 50 per cent in a new enterprise in the mining industry.

The amended law on foreign exchange and foreign trade control came into effect in 1980, introducing a prior reporting procedure, with in-depth examination of foreign investments confined to the restricted industries. Joint ventures still remain popular because they use the Japanese company's existing distribution network and leave personnel problems to the Japanese partner. However, the partners must agree on marketing methods, pricing policy, and definition of export areas. Joint ventures have tended to move away from distribution towards semi-processing to supply local manufacturing capacity. Provisions of the Anti-Monopoly Law and Fair Trade Commission should be given close examination in relation to

Table 15.18   Japanese mergers and acquisitions: number of transactions

	1985	1986	1987	1988	1989*
Japanese buyer/ Japanese seller	163 (56.4%)	226 (50.0%)	219 (46.7%)	233 (40.2%)	178 (36.9%)
Japanese buyer/ Japanese seller	10 (34.6%)	204 (45.2%)	228 (48.6%)	315 (56.8%)	294 (60.9%)
Overseas buyer/ Japanese seller	26 (9.0%)	21 (4.7%)	22 (4.7%)	17 (3.1%)	11 (2.3%)
Total	289	451	469	555	483

*January–September

Source   *Financial Times* Special survey: Japanese financial markets. (1990) 15 March.

each stage of an expanding joint venture. The majority of investments receive clearance from the Bank of Japan in two weeks. Remittance of profit or capital requires the permission of the Bank of Japan, but no difficulties should normally be encountered over this. Tax on the income of branches follows the same general lines as that on joint ventures or wholly owned subsidiaries.

Strategic business alliances: a better alternative to protectionism

Much of the response of the Western industrialized nations has been spent in terms of debating the merits and demerits of protectionism. The Japanese have been embarrassingly successful in their global trade of technologies which they have originally imported and developed themselves. One such example in machine tools is Fujitsu Fanuc, which controls half the world's market for numerically controlled machine tools, although they did not invent them. Another is the House of Fraser decision to open a Harrods shop within Tokyo's giant Mitsukoshi store. Marks and Spencer Plc faced initial success with their range of products in fifty Daiei stores, but then sales peaked and thought had to be given as to how to increase sales to the consumer. M & S have developed St. Michael boutiques in Japan with the Daiei chain and are now seeking to move up-market. Such cases of startling Japanese export success are found alongside domestic non-tariff barriers and a domestic currency which defies international pressure for revaluation. This has led to the creation of a trade ombudsman to handle complaints concerning imports. It remains to be seen whether this is simply a delaying tactic or a sincere response. As things stand, each and every official Japanese movement – whether Cabinet changes or an economic mission of the leading Japanese industrialists to Europe – is scrutinized for meaning, while in such areas as car exports, the Japanese are asked to exercise what is termed 'voluntary restraint'. By restricting the Japanese manufacturers to approximately eleven per cent of the British market, shiploads can be planned to the point where a Japanese car sold on the UK market is new – because of the voluntary quota – while a British car, because of having stockpiles of unsold inventory, will generally be at least fifteen months old at the time of sale. British protectionism in this case has turned to Japanese disadvantage.

Consider next the argument for co-operation, part of the official Japanese response to reduce the EC deficit with Japan of 10.7 billion dollars. Industrial co-operation is a phenomenon born of our times. Market development costs plus the size of market required to ensure a return on investment have led to the bringing together of industrial producers in a number of different areas, the most highly publicized of which has been the Honda Rover agreement.

Outlining the basis for an agreement – to ensure a community of interests and like benefits, and to define the respective duties of either party – is an essential prerequisite. A case study investigation of two Japanese factories matched with one British factory and one US, found that the implications for public policy were:

1 Direct investment of Japanese companies is not likely to have an immediate or substantial effect on local development.

2 Once Japanese multinationals establish their factories, they are less likely to shift their operations to some other region.

3 New investment in modernization and automation of production will not be able to make domestic companies competitive against Japanese.

4 A licensing agreement with, or takeover by, the Japanese would not be effective measures to revive competitiveness of the domestic industry.

In so far as Britain is concerned, the possible avenues for Japanese participation in British manufacturing industry have been reduced to joint venture or acquisition with public anxiety over the Japanese challenge to European industry, as in the case of Nissan, for example, in Britain.

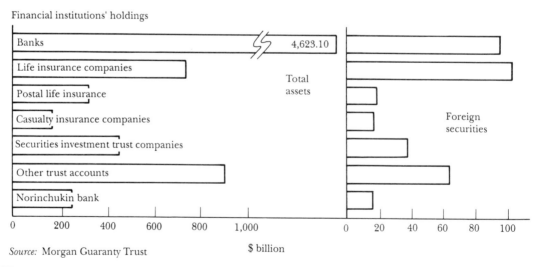

Source: Morgan Guaranty Trust

Figure 15.18
Source   *Financial Times* (1990) 15 March

Table 15.19   The world's ten largest banks, 1982, 1986

1982		1986	
1 Citicorp	USA	1 Dai-Ichi Kangyo Bank	Japan
2 Bankamerica Corp.	USA	2 Fuji Bank	Japan
3 Banque Nationale de Paris	France	3 Sumitomo Bank	Japan
4 Crédit Agricole	France	4 Mitsubishi Bank	Japan
5 Crédit Lyonnais	France	5 Sanwa Bank	Japan
6 Barclays Group	Britain	6 Citicorp	USA
7 National Westminster	Britain	7 Norinchukin Bank	Japan
8 Dai-Ichi Kangyo Bank	Japan	8 Industrial Bank of Japan	Japan
9 Société Générale	Japan	9 Crédit Agricole	France
10 Fuji Bank	Japan	10 Banque Nationale de Paris	France

Source   Burstein, D. (1990) *Yen! Japan's New Financial Empire and its Threat to America*, Fawcett Columbine, New York.

The car industry is such that negotiations are constantly taking place over possible joint ventures and industrial co-operation on the development of engines and gear-boxes. A close association with Honda may, therefore, blossom into a more permanent relationship, as has happened with industrial co-operation ventures elsewhere. Meanwhile, a test case in Italy has already established the Honda-Rover to be a British car, by virtue of the last substantial part of production, amounting in this case to 60 per cent by volume or 70 per cent by price.

Another example of co-operation is that between ICL with Fujitsu. This venture provided for co-operation in marketing, technology and semiconductor purchasing. ICL, in return for agreeing to market Fujitsu computers, received early access to the Japanese group's computer technology. Under this deal, ICL also purchased substantial quantities of microchips. For ICL, it presented an opportunity to restructure and complete its product range without over-reaching its already thin resources. For Fujitsu, there was the obvious advantage of market access, technology sharing and exports. This has since led to a majority Fujitsu stake in ICL.

In other industries, such as industrial robotics, petrochemicals, and telecommunications, agreements have been signed between Hitachi and GEC; ICI and Mitsui Petrochemical; Hitachi and Thomson; and Fujitsu and Siemens. TI and Fairchild are establishing semi-conductor plants in Japan.

The potential for industrial co-operation

Yet further possibilities present themselves if one considers the importance of the Japanese Sogo-Shoshas, the trading houses, with their worldwide network of offices and speciality in Eurodollar lending. Mr Ikeda of Marubeni Corporation, the fourth largest Japanese trading company, has gone on record (Keizam Koho Center, 1986) as having 17 per cent of his corporation's turnover in the form of 'third-country' trade.

While a recession lasts and while interest rates in the West are double those prevailing in Japan, reasons abound for inertia among Western nations. Interest rate differentials provoke

Table 15.20 The world's biggest commercial banks

Rank by assets 1989		Assets[1] $ Million	Percent change[2] in US dollars	Deposits[2] $ Million	Bank	Loans[3] $ Million	Net income[4] $ Million	Stock holders equity[5] $ Million	Employees Numbers
1 Dai-Ichi Kangyo Bank	Japan	413,214.4	6.9	313,457.2	1	219,890.0	1,531.2	20,988.7	18,411
2 Sumitomo Bank	Japan	407,227.3	12.1	296,940.0	2	205,524.4	1,619.5	10,497.3	18,038
3 Fuji Bank	Japan	397,629.5	10.3	284,485.1	3	207,099.7	1,419.9	10,767.5	15,032
4 Mitsubishi Bank	Japan	380,857.5	9.1	273,375.0	4	198,466.9	1,352.2	10,194.9	14,271
5 Sanwa Bank	Japan	373,404.5	12.9	269,885.9	5	210,025.8	1,264.3	9,341.0	13,946
6 Industrial Bank of Japan	Japan	292,154.9	7.0	124,326.6	26	156,758.6	652.1	9,261.6	5,253
7 Norinchukin Bank	Japan	244,902.7	3.8	211,436.6	6	102,481.6	318.1	1,389.2	3,130
8 Credit Agricole	France	242,578.3	15.2	211,173.7	7	213,913.6	709.2	10,055.1	73,714
9 Tokai Bank	Japan	238,783.4	4.9	176,158.1	11	130,628.9	498.2	6,179.2	11,865
10 Banque Nationale de Paris	France	232,024.2	17.8	162,556.0	15	166,857.7	535.6	4,651.5	60,333
11 Citicorp	US	230,643.0	11.1	137,922.0	22	135,383.0	498.0	10,076.0	92,000
12 Bank of Tokyo	Japan	222,382.7	19.9	150,781.1	18	110,779.7	473.1	4,823.2	17,040
13 Mitsubishi Trust & Banking	Japan	221,727.5	6.4	186,545.5	8	99,710.8	604.6	5,150.8	6,288
14 Mitsui Bank	Japan	220,363.2	4.3	159,544.2	17	130,045.3	607.9	5,785.3	10,256
15 Crédit Lyonnais	France	211,237.4	18.1	167,900.9	12	143,459.1	491.0	6,863.7	61,508
16 Sumitomo Trust & Banking	Japan	207,582.6	13.7	178,496.7	10	106,482.6	573.6	4,707.7	6,759
17 Barclays Bank	Britain	206,036.0	8.9	167,594.8	13	169,893.8	741.1	10,050.3	116,500
18 Deutsche Bank	Germany	203,601.1	18.3	183,676.3	9	159,783.6	699.2	8,776.2	56,580
19 Long-Term Credit Bank of Japan	Japan	196,628.1	6.4	149,730.8	19	126,131.7	412.1	5,503.9	3,488
20 Mitsui Trust & Banking	Japan	191,573.4	9.5	161,740.0	16	107,702.1	472.0	3,225.8	6,173
21 National Westminster Bank	Britain	187,587.1	5.2	163,469.7	14	161,643.7	326.3	9,603.0	113,000
22 Taiyo Kobe Bank	Japan	181,773.9	3.6	139,427.0	21	114,551.4	417.3	4,396.8	12,931
23 Bank of China	China	181,543.0	24.0	74,059.9	56	106,583.1	1,350.1	8,365.9	51,000
24 Société Générale	France	176,213.2	13.4	133,951.7	24	129,554.7	558.7	4,042.8	45,950
25 Daiwa Bank	Japan	162,031.9	7.5	84,805.0	39	87,400.7	304.7	3,070.4	8,688

26	Yasuda Trust & Banking	Japan	160,171.3	(4.6)	132,206.5	25	79,654.4	408.5	3,143.4	5,627
27	Groupe des Caisses D'Epargne	France	151,021.8	8.3	144,315.2	20	68,929.7	456.4	7,880.2	33,000
28	Dresdner Bank	Germany	147,723.5	13.4	134,995.9	23	120,232.3	334.6	5,516.1	36,898
29	Cie Financiére de Paribas	France	139,003.8	14.5	89,122.8	35	96,775.9	541.1	4,200.7	25,500
30	Hongkong & Shanghai Banking	Hong Kong	132,928.7	17.5	118,588.4	27	97,819.9	612.1	6,746.4	53,375
31	Tokyo Trust & Banking	Japan	124,616.5	3.1	105,717.9	29	97,416.9	319.8	2,170.2	5,078
32	Nippon Credit Bank	Japan	123,645.9	7.4	97,040.8	31	75,243.3	296.5	2,949.0	2,218
33	Union Bank of Switzerland	Switzerland	114,260.0	3.0	96,064.9	34	96,175.8	551.5	9,178.0	21,210
34	Commerzbank	Germany	113,379.2	11.5	104,343.8	28	92,679.6	298.7	4,064.8	27,631
35	Deutsche Genossenschaftsbank	Germany	110,639.1	48.0	102,701.5	30	87,383.3	118.4	1,806.6	9,597
36	Kyowa Bank	Japan	110,168.2	(0·4)	81,354.1	45	67,187.3	281.3	2,737.1	7,925
37	Istituto Bancario San Paolo Di Torino	Italy	107,700.0	31.9	79,641.6	47	51,939.3	477.6	3,706.0	20,407
38	Chase Manhattan Corp.	US	107,369.0	10.2	69,073.0	57	73,402.0	(665.0)	4,944.0	41,610
39	Swiss Bank Corp.	Switzerland	105,465.3	2.8	88,032.5	37	88,633.0	458.2	6,174.3	18,349
40	Westdeutsche Landesbank	Germany	105,021.6	12.9	96,842.3	32	82,721.1	182.8	3,106.6	9,652
41	Banca Nazionale Del Lavoro	Italy	104,524.9	14.9	83,692.7	41	76,706.4	(175.0)	5,054.8	26,238
42	Bayerische Vereinsbank	Germany	102,758.7	12.1	96,302.0	33	91,334.9	148.1	2,335.3	14,995
43	Saitama Bank	Japan	102,688.3	10.2	76,278.8	53	59,685.0	226.2	2,608.8	7,848
44	Midland Bank	Britain	100,872.3	0.1	88,280.9	36	85,541.1	(359.1)	4,334.9	60,237
45	Bankamerica Corp.	US	98,764.0	4.3	81,186.0	46	72,488.0	1,103.0	5,534.0	54,779
46	Royal Bank of Canada	Canada	97,657.4	8.2	75,961.4	54	70,895.8	444.0	4,924.6	47,989
47	Amsterdam-Rotterdam Bank	Netherlands	94,168.2	12.1	85,379.1	38	52,930.0	400.5	3,478.1	23,718
48	Lloyds Bank	Britain	92,901.6	(0.0)	84,591.7	40	77,865.7	(960.8)	3,818.3	84,679
49	Shoko Chukin Bank	Japan	91,776.8	(1.5)	82,229.0	44	73,649.3	73.4	2,238.6	6,118
50	Bayerische Landesbank	Germany	91,301.2	14.2	76,841.3	52	71,874.6	63.7	1,998.5	4,463

Source (1990) Fortune 500. *Fortune*, 30 July, p. 265

massive international monetary displacements. Japan, again peculiarly with a large amount of savings deposits, is relatively insulated from such shocks. By way of comparison, Britain, with its network of building societies, would appear to be investing its savings in unproductive investments.

The first advantage of the Japanese then is in capital and, secondly, in their dominance of the technologies which they have acquired and developed. For meaningful co-operation to develop, there has to be a mutually profitable exchange. At the moment, there is the universal impression of the Japanese being interested only in selling, not buying. Given a more outward-looking breadth of perspective, opportunities for Anglo–Japanese co-operation exist in the following areas.

Ongoing research and development and technology improvements

Already this is taking place as we have seen in computers, but scope exists to do likewise in other sectors of electronics or automotive engineering, an area in which the UK is particularly skilled.

Marketing and distribution in third markets

This is underway with Honda-Rover in continental Europe.

Joint entry into third markets

This was hinted at as a possible means of developing Anglo–Japanese trade and reducing a trade imbalance. Presently, this does not exist but could certainly do so.

Co-production and specialization of production

Co-operation is true of Honda-Rover. Specialization is also included but to a lesser degree as this particular agreement is of a shorter nature to that of the ICL-Fujitsu co-operation where there is clearer product line specialization taking place over time.

Financial services

Those on offer suggest a certain synergy with those of our own institutions. As yet this remains to be developed, although banking institutions are finding Japan to be an attractive site for location, given that Tokyo has emerged as a world financial centre, above London and New York.

The West have had their request sustained for an ombudsman for Japanese foreign trade in view of the complex Japanese administrative blocks, and major non-tariff barriers (fifty-seven non-tariff barriers, including import inspection, guarantees, testing, etc.). Tariffs were reduced on 323 items, including chocolate, biscuits, agricultural tractors and tobacco as of April 1983.

Simplification and improvement of import inspection procedures, and the strengthening of the Office of the Trade Ombudsman, are also being sought.

Pressures on the Japanese financial system

Pressures for change in the Japanese financial system arise due to the following.

Plentiful supply of capital. Japan is awash in capital and exports it. Japan was the largest single supplier of savings for the world in 1984, but since then OPEC is no longer a source of new cash. Japanese banks now dominate world banking.
2 *Domestic dissent.* Affluent savers want higher yields, corporate borrowers want more choice, and the strongest banks and brokerage houses are chafing under restrictions unlike those found in any other major market.
3 *Impatient foreigners.* The patience of foreign banks and businessmen with Japan's closed capital markets has run out. Unless some reciprocal privileges are offered soon, they are threatening to hold up the expansion of Japanese banks in their markets. 'Reciprocity' is now a key issue in all international trade talks.

Japan has been inching its way towards financial liberalization since it passed a major revision of its Foreign Exchange Law in 1980. The revision abolished formal controls that enabled the Government to regulate all foreign-currency transactions by Japanese residents. In theory, the new law allowed a free flow of funds in and out of Japan, but in practice the Government used administrative guidance with its banks to make sure they restricted flows.

If capital flows were free, a huge rush of money would quickly leave Japan at current interest rates. In the short term, the yen would weaken, but Japanese interest rates set by the market would then go up and capital would flow back into Japan. Unfortunately, the yen would be stronger than it is and Japanese companies would have to compete on the same basis with the same finance costs as Western companies.

The services sector

Growth of the service sector, together with the appearance of new electronics industries, has served to keep the Japanese economy moving during the past few years, while traditional pillars of the economic system have been crumbling (investment in services sector more than doubled that of either the auto or steel industries). However, the new 'soft' industries, as they have been called by Government ministers, have brought problems as well. According to the Finance Ministry, which created the term 'softnomics' (in a book on the Japanese economy issued in early 1983), the new trend means first and foremost that the Government has become seriously short of information about what is happening in the economy.

Service sector companies, as well as many of the small high-technology companies, as the major users of robots and numerically-controlled machines, tend to be small enough not to attract the attention of Japanese tax authorities and they are unlikely to be invited to become members of the various industry associations through which Japanese economic ministers keep in touch with different sectors of the economy.

A further problem posed by the growth of the new soft sectors is that of statistical definition. Japan's Industrial Taxation Index, which generally has been regarded as a key economic indicator, is based overwhelmingly on the product of the traditional 'hard' industries. A new industrial production index, which makes due allowances for soft sectors of the economy, is seen as an urgent necessity by the Ministry of Finance and is, in fact, in the process of preparation.

Services require less, but more frequent, investment than steel or shipyards. Thus, the questions arise as to whether they are more stable and whether it is possible to plan the necessary investment cycles more accurately than has been possible with other industries.

References

Alden, V. Z. (1987) Who says you can't crack Japanese markets? *Harvard Business Review*, **65,** (1), 52–56.

Anglo-Japanese Economic Institute (1991) *Japanese Addresses in the UK*, London.

Anglo-Japanese Economic Institute (1988) *Britain and Japan: Partners for Prosperity*, London.

Anglo-Japanese Economic Institute (1988) *Why Britain? Japanese Business Reasons for Investing in the UK*, London.

Berger, M. (1990) Japan report: breaking all the rules. *International Management*, **45,** (1), 58–59.

Berkwitt, G. J. (1986) Japan's three-tiered distribution. *Industrial Distribution*, **75,** (7), 53–57.

Blenkhorn, D. L., and Noori, A. H. (1990) What it takes to supply Japanese OEM's. *Industrial Marketing Management*, **19,** 21–30.

Broad, W. J. (1991) Japan breathes down America's technological neck. *Globe and Mail*, Toronto, 8 June.

Bruce, L. (1990) Special report: Japan, coming of age. *International Management*, February, 46–57.

Burstein, D. (1990) *Yen! Japan's New Financial Empire and its Threat to America*, Fawcett Columbine, New York.

Business Week (1984) A wary Japan starts to open up its financial markets. 5 March, pp. 30–33.

Campbell, N. C. G. (1987) Competitive advantage from relational marketing: the Japanese approach. Paper presented to the 1st Conference of the British Academy of Management, University of Warwick, 13–15 September.

Czinkota, M. R. (1985) Distribution in Japan: problems and changes. *Columbia Journal of World Trade*, **20,** (3), 65–71.

Czinkota, M. R. (1985) Distribution of consumer products in Japan: an overview. National Center for Export Import Studies, Georgetown University, Washington, DC, USA, *Staff Paper 17*, February.

de Mente, B. (1990) *The Japanese Influence in America*, Passport Books, A Division of NTC Publishing Group, Lincolnwood, ILL.

de Mente, B. (1990) *Japanese Etiquette and Ethics in Business*, 5th Edn, NTC Business Books, Lincolnwood, ILL.

de Mente, B. (1990) *How to do Business with the Japanese*, NTC Business Books, Lincolnwood, ILL.

Doe, P. (1988) Japan starts fighting for its own patent rights. *Electronic Business*, **14,** (17), 36–38.

Drifte, R. (1990) *Japan's Foreign Policy*, Routledge, London.

Economist (1991) Those perfidious Japanese, 20 April, p. 65.

Economist (1991) Japanese financial deregulation: are all banks equal? 23 March, p. 84.

Economist (1989) A yen for Bradizawa, 25 March.

Fields, G. (1989) The Japanese distribution system: myths and realities. *Tokyo Business Today*, **July**, 57–59.

Financial Times (1984) Japan survey, 23 July.

Financial Times (1983) Japanese industry survey, 12 December.

Fortune (1990) Fortune 500, 30 July, 265.

Foster, G. (1988) Hard sell in Japan. *Management Today*, September, 94–99.

Gregory, G. (1989) A stake in Japan. *Management Today*, November, 109–112.

Hara, E, Takito, H., and Umesawa, M. (1990) Keiretsu: what they are doing, where they are heading? *Tokyo Business Today*, September, 26–36.

Import Procedures and Industrial Property Rights in Japan (1979) BOTB, London.

Industrial Bank of Japan Review (1989) *EEC 1992 and Japanese Corporations*, 1-3-3 Marunouchi, Chiyoda-ku, Tokyo.

Ishikawa, K. (1990) *Japan and the Challenge of Europe 1992*, Pinter Publishing for Royal Institute of International Affairs, London.

Ishikawa, K. (1986) *Export to Japan: Guidebook for UK Exporters*, Jetro, London.

JMA Management News, Japan Management Association, Tokyo and Malibu, California quarterly.

Johansson, J. K. (1986) Japanese marketing failures. *International Marketing Review*, Autumn, 33–46.

Jones, N. *et al* (1986) The hollow corporation: the decline of manufacturing threatens the entire US economy. *Business Week*, 3 March, pp. 57–85.

Kang, T. W. (1990) *Gaishi: The Foreign Company in Japan*, Harper Collins, USA.

Keegan, W. J. (1984) International competition: the Japanese challenge. *Journal of International Business Studies*, **15** (Winter), 189–193.

Keizan Koho Center (Japan Institute for Social and Economic Affairs) (1984) KKC Brief No. 15, January, *Sogo Shoshas Spearhead a Growth Area - Third Country Trade.*

Kojima, K., and Ozawa, T. (1984) *Japan's General Trading Companies: Merchants of Economic Development*, OECD, Paris.

Kotler, P., Fahey, L., and Jatusripitak, S. (1985) *The New Competition – What Theory Z Didn't Tell You About - Marketing*, Prentice-Hall.

Fujigane, Y., and Ennis, P. (1990) Keiretsu – What they are doing: where they are heading? *Tokyo Business Today*, September, pp. 26–30.

Lazer, W., and Rynn, M. (1990) Japan. In *International Business Handbook*, V. H. (Manek) Kirpalani, Haworth Press, Binghampton, NY.

Lorenz, C. (1981) How Japan 'cascades' through Western markets. *Financial Times*, 9 November.

Marketing (1987) Institute of Marketing report: land of rising opportunities. **29**, (2), 48–49.

MITI (1983) *White Paper on International Trade*, November, Tokyo.

Nakamura, T.,and Grace, B. R. G. (1985) *Economic Development of Modern Japan*, Ministry of Foreign Affairs, Japan.

Neff, R. (1990) Now Japan is getting jumpy about quality. *Business Week*, 5 March, 40–44.

Nishikawa, K. (1990) Are Japanese products full of defects? *Tokyo Business Today*, August, 50–53.

Nishikawa, K. (1990) Why Japanese consumer groups oppose market opening measures. *Tokyo Business Today*, March, 40–43.

Noguchi, A. (1990) Pharmaceutical giants flex their muscle. *Tokyo Business Today*, March, 36–38.

Ohashi, T. (1989) Marketing in Japan in the 1990s: homing in on the holonic consumer. *Marketing and Research Today,* November, 220–229.

Ohta, H. (1988) A mixed blessing: Japan's perception of the unified EEC market. *The Anglo-Japanese Economic Journal,* **2,** (3), 4–6.

Porter, M. E. (1990) *The Comparative Advantage of Nations,* Macmillan, London.

Rapaport, C. (1991) 'The big split', Fortune, 6 May, pp. 38–50.

Rodger, I. (1989) Japan. *Financial Times, Special Survey,* 10 July, pp. I-XIV.

Ryans, A. B. (1988) Strategic market entry factors and market share achievement in Japan. *Journal of International Business Studies,* Fall, 389–409.

Sako, M. (1989) Partnership between small and large firms: the case of Japan. In *Partnership Between Small and Large Firms,* (ed. D.G. XXIII – Directorate for Enterprise of the Commission of the European Communities), Brussels, published by Graham and Trotman Ltd., London.

Sasseen, J. (1989) The rising sun over Europe: why Japan's latest thrusts into Britain and the Continent are causing alarm. *International Management,* July/August, 14.20.

Schlossberg, H. (1990) Japan market hardly closed to US firms. *Marketing News,* 9 July, pp. 1–2.

Shimaguchi, M., and Lazer, W. (1979) Japanese distributions channels, invisible barriers to market entry. *MSU Business Topics,* Winter.

Shimizu, Y., Tsutsui, M., Inaba, Y., and Umesawa, M. (1990) Production Keiretsu: a new export from Japan. *Tokyo Business Today,* September, 30

Shiotani, T. (1988) Outline of Japanese distribution system. *Business Japan,* August, 89–97.

Snoddy, R. (1990) Eastern promise for the FT. *Financial Times,* 5 June.

Taikeshi, H. (1990) *Japan's Economic Development,* International Society for Educational Information Inc., Tokyo.

Thornson, R. (1989) Japanese industry. *Financial Times, Special Supplement,* 4 December.

Tokyo Business Today (1990) A ranking of the most profitable foreign firms in Japan, July, 46–51.

Tokyo Business Today (1990) How to succeed in the Japan Market, July, 27–32.

Trachtenberg, J. A. (1986) They didn't listen to anybody. *Forbes,* 15 December, pp. 168, 169.

Turner, G. (1987) The future ambitions of Japan's financial grants. *Long Range Planning,* **205,** (105), 11–20.

Turpin, D. (1990) Persistence and the competitiveness of the Japanese firm. In *The World Competitiveness Report, 1990,* (IMD) Geneva.

Wagenaar, J. D. (1980) Advertising in Japan. *Marketing Trends,* (2) pp. 4–5.

Wagsty, S. (1990) Japanese financial markets. *Financial Times, Special Supplement,* 15 March.

Wilkinson, E. (1990) *Japan Versus the West,* Penguin Books, London.

World Opinion (1988) Japan greets the world. 22 February–13 March, pp. 5–8.

Wright, B. J., and Jenney, B. W. (1981) Secrets of Japanese success. *Management Today,* January, p. 64.

Yamamoto, S. (1986) *Japan's Culture and Economy,* Ministry of Foreign Affairs, Japan.

Key reading

Blenkhorn, D. L., and Noori, A. H. (1990) What it takes to supply Japanese OEM's. *Industrial Marketing Management,* **19,** 21–30.

Burstein, D. (1988) *Yen! Japan's New Financial Empire and its Threat to America,* Fawcett Columbine, NY.

Czinkota, M. R. (1985) Distribution in Japan: problems and changes. *Columbia Journal of World Trade*, **20**, (3), 65–71.

de Mente, B. (1990) *The Japanese Influence in America*, NTC Publishing Group, Lincolnwood, ILL, USA.

de Mente, B. (1990) *Japanese Etiquette and Ethics in Business*, 5th Edn, NTC Business Books, Lincolnwood, ILL, USA.

de Mente, B. (1990) *How to do Business with the Japanese*, NTC Business Books, Lincolnwood, ILL, USA.

Doe, P. (1988) Japan starts fighting for its own patent rights. *Electronic Business*, **14**, (17), 36–38.

Drifte, R. (1990) *Japan's Foreign Policy*, Routledge, London.

Financial Times (1986) Japanese ski makers freeze out the opposition, 11 August.

Fujigane, Y, and Ennis, P. (1990) Keiretsu — what they are doing: where they are heading. *Tokyo Business Today*, September, 26–30.

Kang, T. W. (1990) *Gaishi: The Foreign Company in Japan*, Harper Collins, USA.

Ohashi, T. (1989) Marketing in Japan in the 1990s: homing in on the holonic consumer. *Marketing and Research Today*, November, 220–229.

Smalley, M. (1986) Through Japan's half-open door. *Management Today*, October, 88–94.

Trachtenberg, J. A. (1986) They didn't listen to anybody. *Forbes*, 15 December, 168–.169.

Wilkinson, E. (1990) *Japan Versus the West*, Penguin Books, London.

16
Marketing to a less developed but mineral rich country: Nigeria

Economic and social background

Nigeria is essentially a raw-material supplying LDC since it is dependent on oil for 94 per cent of exports and on cocoa for 40 percent per cent of its non-oil exports. The cyclical effects of the oil industry have meant that since first adjusting to the wealth of oil during 1974–1975, Nigeria has had to readjust to financial stringency measures because of a $30 billion debt burden (which is still small by South American standards).

It has to be said that there is a scarcity of data on Nigeria. *The Economist*, in a special survey in 1982, commented that 'This is the first survey published by *The Economist* in which every single number is probably wrong, there is no accurate information about Nigeria', and then went on to say that nobody knows how many Nigerians there are and that according to cynical Government officials, nobody ever will! The population estimate of the World Bank is of 113.6 million. Needless to say, this lack of information makes life for the country's environmental planners virtually impossible, as no one can say with any certainty how many schools, hospitals or houses are needed, nor how much food or water or electricity is required. Nor can there be any agreement about what should be the appropriate political representation if there is no agreement as to the size of the constituencies.

A population census was held in 1973 but its findings (79.7 million) were annulled after allegations of rigging. There are plans for another official census in October 1992, but while problems of surmounting election malpractices remain, hopefully, the detailed preparations for this 1992 census will ensure its validity as an exercise and its acceptability to the population at large. This 1992 census has chosen to avoid questions on religion and tribe after a good deal of due consideration. The country has been divided into 200,000 enumeration areas of between 400 and 600 persons. Trials took place in December 1989, covering eighty-eight enumeration areas; in May 1990, covering 425 enumeration areas, and with the third and last covering 10,000 enumeration areas (Ayeni, 1991).

The official 1963 count, and still held to be the only credible census of the Nigerian population, was undertaken two years after independence, gave 55.7 million, averaging 2.5 per cent growth p.a., which would have yielded 88 million by the end of 1981; but since Nigerians have large families, a more feasible growth rate of 3.5 per cent would give 113 million, plus immigration from Chad (civil war), Niger (drought) and Ghana (poorer economy). A similar extrapolation of the 1973 figure would have given 106 million by 1985, while the Nigerian Census Board issued an official estimate of only 94 million in 1984. Nevertheless, by the year 2000 a population of 200 million is likely at current rates of growth, which will consume twice today's oil production plus twice the food currently produced. The future, therefore, is a bleak one unless foresighted political action is taken.

Nigeria is the most populous and economically powerful federation in Black Africa, but remains a developing country struggling to come to terms with its oil wealth. It is the giant of Africa, one of the world's ten most populous nations, strategically vital, and rich in natural resources, especially oil. Synge (1990) summed up Nigeria's plight as 'too poor to pay off what it owes at face value and too rich to earn itself the concessions available to most African countries.'

Nigerian society still shows strong tribal divisions, and population growth still continues to increase. The capital has been moved to Abuja, located more in the centre of the country. Most governmental ministries have already moved there, and by the end of 1992, all remaining ministries will have moved to Abuja, as well as taking with them all foreign embassies. The previous capital, Lagos, is hopelessly overcrowded with 5m population and an infrastructure that cannot support it. Yet, it says something for Nigerians that they can take a problem like commuting across Lagos and see an opportunity in it. The Eko Bridge has thus become a market for street traders to haggle with motorists in their cars, despite the fact that cars are only allowed on the roads one day in every two, depending on whether the car registration plate numbers are odd or even. Those commuting by bus have to confront salesmen with suitcases who also board the bus to do business. Despite the heat, the crowds,

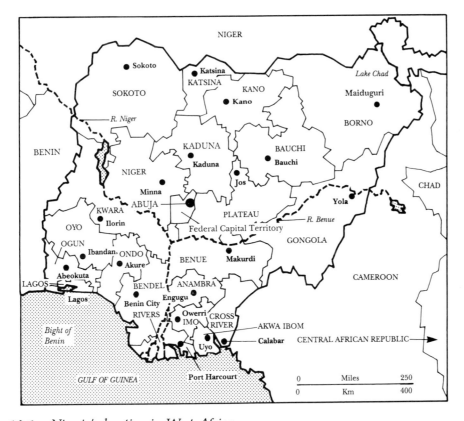

Figure 16.1   *Nigeria's location in West Africa*
Note   Two new states, Katsina in the North and Akwa Ibom in the South, were created in 1988
Source   *Financial Times* (1989) Special supplement: Nigeria, 6 March

the noise, the pickpockets, the sales pressure, and the often very poor quality of wares traded, Nigerians have a fondness for Lagos, which others may only see as a nightmare.

A point that has to be emphasized is that societal divisions continue and deaths, as well as substantial damage to property, have arisen frequently from rioting over religion. Northern Nigeria is Muslim and so quite different from the rest of the country. Muslims see the corruption in everyday society that everyone else does but see the solution in the creation of an Islamic state. Other Nigerians may see the Muslims as being troublesome, but in seeking to impose some control over them, only succeed in making matters worse. To a Muslim, the only authority that he recognizes is that of the Koran. Administrators who seek to intervene may well suffer the fate of being perceived as persecutors, coming between a man and his God, and if the administrator happens also to be a Christian, then this may be perceived as being the root cause of this action now seen as persecution and the worst possible conditions have arisen for another round of religious rioting. The Babangida Government has since taken Nigeria into full membership of the Islamic Conference. Approximately 50 per cent of the country is Muslim, mainly in the North, another 40 per cent is Christian, and of the remainder there is a large number who are believers in animism.

Like the rest of the world, Nigeria has been slow to react to environmental damage. In November 1989, the Federal Environmental Protection Agency (FEPA) and the National Council on the Environment were set up. Oil spillages have contributed to environmental ruin for fishermen as well as farmers. According to Ayeni (1991), despite the country's low level of industrialization, its environmental pollution rate is one of the worst in the world, especially in the areas of food, water, air, toxic waste and radiation. FEPA have since introduced guidelines on waste disposal and penalties so that manufacturing industries and private individuals will be liable to a fine of ₦100,000 for contravening environment laws while corporate bodies will be expected to pay ₦500,000.

Structural Adjustment Programme (SAP)

SAP was a necessary precondition to the restructuring of $26 bn of Nigerian debt in 1986. SAP set out to remove the heavy dependence of the non-oil productive base on imported

Table 16.1   Nigeria at a glance

GNP US $ million (1989)	28,314
Real growth rate (1980–1989)	−0.3
Population (1989)	113,665
Growth rate % (1980–)	3.3
GNP per capita (1989)	250
Real growth rate (1987–1989)	1.1
Agriculture's share in GDP	31
Daily calorie supply per capita (1988)	2,039
Life expectancy	51
Total fertility	6.5
Illiteracy % (1985)	58

Source   *The World Bank Atlas 1990*, World Bank, Washington, DC.

Table 16.2 Comparative risk assessments

		Turmoil	Financial transfer	Direct investment	Export market		Real GDP growth (%)	Inflation (%)	Current account $ billion	
El Salvador 1 Feb 1991	18 months	Very high	B−	B−	B	1986–90 avg	1.4	24.8	−0.25	Despite the lack of political liberalization, President Cristiani's liberalization of the economy and trade policy, together with somewhat firmer prices for El Salvador's agricultural products, has resulted in stronger economic growth. His government is actively seeking foreign investment, but security concerns will continue to hamper its efforts.
						1991	2.5	20.0	−0.20	
	Five years	Very high	D+	C+	C	1992–96	2.5	20.0	−0.05	
Malaysia 1 Feb 1991	18 months	Low	B+	A−	B+	1986–90 avg	6.6	2.4	+0.59	Tensions between the ethnic Chinese and the Malays will continue to be a potential source of violence and capital flight, but as long as the economy remains strong and Prime Minister Mahathir exercises some restraint in increasing the participation of the Malays in the economy, widespread violence is unlikely.
						1991	8.0	5.6	−0.85	
	Five years	Low	A	B+	B+	1992–96	7.0	6.0	−0.80	
Netherlands 1 Feb 1991	18 months	Low	A	A	A+	1986–90 avg	2.4	0.7	+5.64	The current government will continue to support most of the EC's goals for 1992. Its fiscal and monetary policy will be slightly more expansive than the predecessor government as it seeks to attend to the country's growing social and environmental concerns.
						1991	2.5	3.0	+8.50	
	Five years	Low	A	A	A	1992–96	3.0	5.0	+6.00	
Nigeria 1 Feb 1991	18 months	Moderate	D+	B	C	1986–90 avg	3.7	21.9	+0.59	There is a 50–50 chance that a moderate civilian government will emerge after elections in 1992 and will pursue policies somewhat less conducive to international business than the current government. However, a conservative group of military officers representing the interests of the north may stage a coup prior to or immediately following the elections.
						1991	5.0	30.0	+1.80	
	Five years	High	C−	C	D+	1992–96	4.0	40.0	+2.20	
Tunisia 1 Feb 1991	18 months	Moderate	B−	A−	B−	1986–90 avg	3.1	6.9	−0.20	Members of the government party, the RCD, have refused to allow an open election process, despite President Ben Ali's support for it. Their behavior will make it difficult for Ben Ali to give the opposition groups a political role that they would accept as legitimate. Serious long-term violence therefore appears likely.
						1991	6.0	8.0	−0.36	
	Five years	Very high	C	C−	C	1992–96	5.0	6.0	−0.10	
UAE 1 Feb 1991	18 months	Low	A	B	A+	1986–90 avg	−0.6	4.5	+1.92	The military buildup in the region and higher oil revenues resulting from the Iraqi crisis will boost economic growth, but the federation's increasing control over the business policies of its members is likely to lead to tighter restrictions on foreign investment. Violence from fundamentalists is not likely to increase over the five-year period.
						1991	4.5	10.0	+5.00	
	Five years	High	A	C+	B	1992–96	5.0	10.0	+5.00	
Venezuela 1 Feb 1991	18 months	Moderate	B	A−	A	1986–90 avg	1.7	40.7	−1.09	President Perez has continued to pursue the economic reform policies that would cut state control over the economy and diversify exports. Foreign investors have responded well to his moves, and economic growth has picked up. The biggest threat to economic progress is the massive public opposition to current economic reforms.
						1991	2.5	35.0	+1.50	
	Five years	Low	B−	B−	B−	1992–96	3.5	30.0	+1.00	

Source Compiled by Political Risk Services Inc. (1991), Syracuse, NY for *North American International Business*, April.

Table 16.3   Fuel types in use on a frequent basis for domestic purposes by households within rural and urban settings of Nigeria

Variable	Urban centres				Rural towns				Villagers			
	Cooking	Water heating	Home lighting	Food preservation	Cooking	Water heating	Home lighting	Food preservation	Cooking	Water heating	Home lighting	Food preservation
Firewood	50 31.3%	33 20.6%	—	79 58.1%	83 51.9%	62 38.3%	—	128 80.0%	159 99.4%	141 88.1%	—	160 100%
Electricity	—	49 30.6%	146 91.3%	57 41.9%	—	26 16.3%	144 90.0%	32 20.0%	—	—	—	—
Gas	36 22.5%	24 15.0%	—	—	16 10.0%	10 6.3%	—	—	—	—	—	—
Kerosene	74 46.3%	54 33.8%	14 8.8%	—	61 38.1%	62 38.8%	16 10.0%	—	1 0.6%	19 11.9%	160 100%	—
Total responses	160	160	160	136	160	169	160	160	160	160	160	160
Traditional fuels	50 31.3%	33 20.6%	—	79 58.1%	83 51.9%	62 38.8%	—	128 80.0%	159 99.4%	141 88.1%	—	160 100%
Non-traditional fuels	110 68.8%	127 79.4%	160 100%	57 41.9%	77 48.1%	98 61.3%	160 100%	32 20.0%	1 0.6%	19 11.9%	160 100%	—
Total responses	160	160	160	136	160	160	160	160	160	160	160	160

Source   Onyebuchi, E. I. (1989) Alternate energy strategies for the developing world's domestic use: a case study of Nigerian households' fuel use patterns and preferences. *Energy Journal*, **10**, (3), 121–138.

raw materials. Over 40 per cent of Nigeria's imports are capital goods, 20 per cent are manufactures, with food and chemicals also important imports. SAP abolished import licensing, reduced the list of prohibited imports, revised the tariff structure, and made moves towards a market-determined exchange rate.

The naira remains overvalued. It has already been devalued by 66 per cent, but even this was not enough to crowd out imports. To develop local industry will require:

- higher prices,
- changes in taxation, particularly capital allowances for new investments,
- trained middle management,
- adequate supplies of foreign exchange, and
- dependable national power supply.

SAP has sought to restore some direction to the Nigerian economy by means of:

1 stimulating growth in national output, including agriculture where the move has been to cut agricultural imports and move from food crops to cash crops;
2 promoting increased financial savings and efficient resource allocation;
3 generating employment (although overmanning is yet another problem);
4 moderating the rate of inflation; and
5 maintaining a healthy balance of payments.

SAP was a two-year programme (1986–1988), which extended into 1990, that was designed to alter Nigeria's patterns of production and consumption, and give a new emphasis to agriculture. The programme committed the Government to working toward fiscal and balance of payment equilibrium with nominal inflationary growth. Adopting a realistic exchange rate and devaluing the naira (e.g., in 1980, ₦1 = £1, but in 1988, ₦7 = £1, and in 1989, ₦7 = $1; and there is a black market rate, ₦10 = $1), liberalizing the external trade and payments system, and reducing the complicated price controls in force, have been strategies adopted towards these goals. These policies are now bearing fruit in projects coming on stream for ammonia and for LPG, to take but two examples.

Nigeria has been living under conditions of economic stringency since 1982. Although certain sectors, such as agriculture, have been identified as priority areas, they still need new foreign capital, but to achieve this will require restoring confidence in Nigeria itself, which can only be achieved through reform of the civil service and the creation of the Central Bank as an autonomous organization.

Nigerian economic potential

In developing a wide industrial base, Nigeria is looking toward turning itself into Africa's manufacturing giant. While the German-designed steel mill at Alaja is now producing long rods, and the rail link between Warri and Alaja is to be completed by the end of 1991, investment in the steel plant alone has been running at more than £1-1/2 billion at Ajaokuta, where a Russian-designed steel mill, based on outdated technology, below the Benue—Niger confluences, produces expensive poor quality steel from low-grade ore and coal. Only two mills are operating – the wire rod mill and the light section mill at 3.2 per cent and 5.6 per cent of their respective installed capacities. When the rivers have been dammed for year-round navigation and power, this may seem a good idea; but this complex, located 250 miles from the ports which handle the coke and iron ore, is supposed to include a raw material treatment plant, coke oven and by-products plant, sinter plant, blast furnace sheetworks, and four rolling mills. The river Niger needs dredging, and a new railway is needed to take the iron ore from Itakpe, 56 kms away. Consequently, costs are likely to exceed $6 billion before completion. Ajaokuta is seen by some Nigerians as an attempt to secure an industrial future. To others, Ajaokuta is unworkable and will never be more than a 'white elephant'. The planned capacity exceeds domestic demand envisaged up to the year 2010. Itakpe will have to build a benefication plant to enrich the iron-ore for use at Ajaokuta, but this is still to start. The river is not navigable without dredging and Ajaokuta is 150 kms from the nearest rail line. The blast furnaces need to be run continuously at a minimum 60 per cent capacity with coking coal that is imported. Production will have to wait then to see whether the World Bank gives the Nigerian Railway Corporation the $300 million financing necessary to rehabilitate the railways.

Other major infrastructure projects include ambitious programmes for power, telecommunications, roads, water supply, and oil-related plants producing such products as nitrogenous fertilizers. The natural gas reserves of Nigeria are considerable, estimated to be 85 trillion cubic feet of proven reserves in the oil rich Niger delta. Gas exploitation projects have made little progress to date, but a liquefied natural gas project is expected to come on stream in 1995 and earn the country $20 billion over its 20-year life.

In 1980, the UK share of the Nigeria market was worth about £1.2 billion of a total £7.5 billion import bill, with exports alone almost doubling compared to 1979; but with the decline in oil revenues, total Nigerian imports in 1989 were close to £3.5 billion of which the British share was just 360 million. Britain has maintained its market share, but the market is shrinking in size and most of the giant development projects are going to other European countries, the USA and Japan. Increasing pressures for countertrade have changed this situation over the years, jettisoning Brazil forward from a 1.5 per cent market share to being one of its main suppliers in 1985 as a result of a $1 billion countertrade oil deal which involves the use of an escrow account. The World Bank, IMF and the spirit of SAP are against countertrade. The French have been actively engaged in countertrade negotiations, and are the only Western nation to have experienced an upturn in sales to Nigeria in recent years. The UK share has been stagnating, but Nigerian revenues have also dwindled. Nigerian economic growth declined in the last half of the 1980s by 2–5 per cent annually, and per capita GNP in Nigeria was less in 1991 than it was four years before at $270, breaking the $300 threshold at which aid becomes available.

The problem Nigeria faces is that it is seen as potentially one of the strongest economies in Africa and so aid would be withheld. Nigeria does seem to be on the mend, however. Economic growth is 4 per cent although the debt burden will prevent Nigerians from seeing much of the benefits of this growth. Meanwhile, Britain's Export Credit Guarantee Department, which is undergoing the uncertainties of privatization after a long history as a governmental agency, has not provided medium-term or project cover for Nigeria since 1984. ECGD cover is only provided for British goods on the basis of cash against documents with an irrevocable letter of credit.

There is a danger, though, in just fixing on the short-term horizon. Natural gas is yet to play a significant role. The ultimate recoverable natural gas resources in the country may be as high as 95.0 trillion cubic feet from gas fields, both associated and non-associated with oil production. Of the 768.1 billion cubic feet of natural gas produced in 1980 only 8.6 per cent was consumed, while the rest was flared (Dayo, Adegbulugbe, 1988), and the main consumer was the Nigerian Electric Power Authority (NEPA). The electric power sector is likely to continue to dominate gas consumption, but electricity generation is also tabled for expansion, and as it is mainly gas that is used for electricity generation both should grow together. The increase foreseen for gas consumption then is quite dramatic from 2.75 million tons of oil equivalent in 1985 to 31.04 million tons of oil equivalent by 2010.

As regards oil, there is a reduction expected by the end of this century in global excess oil capacity. If this happens, then Nigeria's revenues from projected oil revenues will be formidable. (See Sohn, 1987, for alternative future oil scenarios.) Even if Nigeria does not diversify its source of hard currency away from oil, the projected tightening of the global oil market will require Nigeria to allocate only between 3 per cent and 14 per cent of its export receipts to meet interest payments on its external debt.

Market structure and international market conditions

The Nigerian infrastructure in many respects is weak. Transportation is a problem at several levels. Buses are old, crowded and infrequent. Airlines frequently fly old aircraft − often popularly compared to the buses − which further discourages passengers. Communications, such as telephones, are poor and among the most expensive in Africa. Vandalism, extreme climate, and connection of unauthorized telephones to the telephone system add further burdens on the system. The Nigerian Government announced a plan to introduce a national digital telephone service across the country by 1995.

In 1987, the Directorate of Foods, Roads and Rural Infrastructures (DFRRI) set out to address the problems of 80 per cent of the national population in rural communities with regard to water, roads, sanitation, and the provision of electricity. Fewer than 20 per cent of total households are connected to the national electric grid. The rest, in mainly rural areas have no electricity. The scale and the costs involved will mean that this will be an ongoing project for many years, but it is expected that 30–40 per cent of households will be electrified by the year 2000.

In so far as the Nigerian companies are concerned, a study by Fubara (1986) showed that the practice of long range planning in Nigeria is informal. Nigerian chief executives confuse annual and extended budgeting for corporate plans. Long range planning is futuristic, and the absence of that element in annual and extended budgeting inhibits corporate strategy and leaves the companies to muddle through and to succumb easily to the turbulence in the economy. In the opinion of Fubara (1986), in an environment with constant changes, like Nigeria, managers themselves should learn to become managers of change, and this would require formal long range planning with constant monitoring to redefine corporate objectives in order to replan situations that have become unplanned by the vagaries of the economy.

Adegbite (1986) undertook a survey of the ninety-three enterprises then listed in the Nigerian Stock Exchange so as to ascertain the special problems of planning in a less developed economic environment and how this affected the practice of corporate planning in such an economy. Most of the sample had significant equity held by multinational corporations who would then influence local practice, thus the sample could not be held to be the representative of wholly owned local enterprises and state-owned companies. Adegbite investigated four areas: corporate objectives, extent of formal planning systems, management and organization development, and investment criteria and procedures. Findings showed very well-developed practices in place, explicit statements of corporate objectives as to where the company should be heading and goals to be achieved. Most also had a keen sense of awareness of their social responsibilities. The planning horizon was found to be three to five years with revisions on an annual basis. All of the twenty respondents had well-developed procedures for major capital expenditure outlays. Many would not undertake projects with more than a two-year payback period because of political and economic uncertainties in Nigeria. The general conclusion was that modern management practices relating to corporate planning and allied areas had become institutionalized in the large scale industrial and commercial enterprises in Nigeria. Even though most of the multinational corporations had lost majority equity control following the indigenization decrees of the 1970s, they still retained effective management for most of the companies, all of which continued to benefit from the wealth of experience of their overseas partners.

As regards small Nigerian enterprises, Ogwo (1987) conducted a study which showed that small businesses in Nigeria do not make wide use of marketing in their business operations. It appears that they adhere more to a production philosophy. Factors identified included:

- The prevailing environment of scarcity and the consequent dominance of a seller's market.
- Government policies which protect emerging industry with the effect of stifling competition.
- A lack of understanding of what marketing can contribute to business and economic growth, compounded by inadequate dissemination of marketing information.
- Poor infrastructural facilities in Nigeria and other developing countries.
- A shortage of individuals trained in modern marketing management.

Exhibit 16.1

Nigeria's contraceptive market-traders

THE MARKET OF West Africa are centres of both commerce and social interaction. Because of their potential to reach thousands of people daily, markets provide a nearly ideal setting for a contraceptive distribution programme.

The Nigerian affiliate of Population Services International enrolled the market women of Nigeria's Ogun State in an experiment to sell condoms and spermicidal pessaries to their customers. Results after the first 10 weeks revealed that the women traders had sold more contraceptives than were distributed through the local family planning association in the entire previous year.

The project also aimed to determine the influence of different types of packing and promotion of sales. Half of the products were sold under brand names. 'Gold Circle' for the condoms and 'Confident' for the vaginal pessaries – in a researched package design. Half were unbranded and unpromoted. For the branded products, an advertising jingle, promoting the advantages of small families and the use of this particular brand, was recorded by a well-known Nigerian artist. The price of these products reflected the cost of the packaging and promotion.

As well as supplying the market women directly, the same products were also distributed through chemists and pharmacists so that a comparison of sales could be made. To ensure that the contraceptives were not hoarded to inflate the prices, both the market traders and shops were kept well-stocked. The market women were not offered any training other than the information provided by the sales force who toured around in a van using a megaphone to advertise their wares. Other than the recorded jingle, there was no major back-up or effort to use the media to create demand for the contraceptives.

Although more expensive, the branded products outsold the unbranded ones by 2.5 to one. The market traders' system of contraceptive distribution also proved to be more successful and cost-effective than a clinic-based delivery system or a community-based distribution effort which could have involved several weeks' training.

● From 'State of the World Population' (UNFPA) 1991

Source   West Africa (1991), 17–23 June, p. 982.

Nigerian Stock Exchange

The Lagos Stock Exchange was formed in 1960 and started trading in 1961. In 1977, it was reorganized and renamed the Nigerian Stock Exchange. It is owned by financial institutions, stockbroking firms, and a few individuals, and is self-regulatory. There are more than one hundred companies listed on the exchange. Tables 16.4 and 16.5 show the Nigerian Stock Exchange to be among the most active in the Third World.

The Stock Exchange has been less successful as an aid to companies seeking to raise equity finance; most of the quoted companies in the Exchange represent foreign companies that were forced to make flotations as a way of attracting Nigerian majority owners, and since the value of their shares is artificially depressed, these companies have no incentive to issue more shares while others have no interest in going public. There are also still some restrictions applying to what can and cannot be done on the Nigerian Stock Exchange, and this will also impede its progress.

Since SAP, the government has embarked on privatization, first selling Nigerian flour mills to be followed by sixty-seven fully privatized and twenty-five partly privatized ventures. Thirty-nine state-owned enterprises were sold off or liquidated in 1989. Nigeria also had a debt-equity swap programme to reduce foreign debt. The maximum private sector shareholding of the Nigerian National Oil Company to 40 per cent has also been raised. There are plans to privatize approximately ninety state-owned enterprises in all, including hotels, palm oil processors, telephone systems, breweries, development banks, and electricity generation and distribution. Foreign oil companies are now being actively sought after with offers of easier contract terms and exploration sites. Investment in electricity generation in the central and southern African states should give a boost to the gas industry, where gas-fired capacity is expected to rise from 9 per cent to 24 per cent by the end of the century, and hydro-electric power is expected to decline on a percentage of the total generated (Quinlan, 1990).

Dr Hamza Zayyad, Chairman of the Technical Committee on Privatization and Commercialization (TCPC) sees a difficulty in the ability of the capital market to raise ₦1 bn each year to make these privatizations happen. Dr. Zayyad sees four threats to commercialization (*Financial Times*, 1990):

1 Need to restructure the finances of the parastatals which may require $300 m so as to refinance and rehabilitate run-down and undercapitalized enterprises. The World Bank will support this move in principle but is unlikely to support it financially.
2 Second prerequisite is the recruitment and training of the skilled personnel needed to implement a programme of fundamental change throughout the parastatal sector.
3 Changing the enterprise culture, or in Dr Zayyed's words: 'Too many parasites who have turned these institutions into patronage centres.'
4 The question mark over the return to civilian rule in 1993, and the combination of inertia and vested interests that may follow, may make a commercialization policy unworkable.

Nicholas Woodworth, writing in the *Financial Times* (1990, 13 February), wrote that this rush to buy shares may have already peaked since bureaucracy in processing share applications has meant large amounts of money being tied up for six months without interest. Further disillusion set in among large-scale buyers when shares were eventually allotted subject to limitations on the numbers sold to individual buyers, many being disappointed to receive only a tiny fraction of the shares that they had expected. This has been borne out

Table 16.4 General trading environment of developing stock exchanges

Stock exchange	Date of foundation	Trading hours	Number of brokers	Type of market	Can foreigners invest?	Selling shares	Restrictions on: withdrawal of capital	dividend repatriation
Bangladesh (Dhaka SE)	1976	11.30–14.00	195	s	✓	✓	✓	✓
Barbados	June 1987	Tue/Fri 10.00 onwards	14	p/s/otc	✓	✗	✗	✓
Botswana (Stockbrokers Botswana)	19.6.89	9.00–12.00	1	p	✓	✗	✗	✗
Costa Rica	1976	10.00–11.30 Mon–Fri	117	p/s	✓	✗	✓	✓
Hungary (Budapest SE)	21.6.90	11.00–12.00	—	free auction	✓	✓	—	—
Jamaica	Jan 1969	Tue/Wed/Thu 10.00–11.00	9	p/s/otc	✓	✗	✓	✓
Kenya (Nairobi SE)	1954	89.00–17.00	6	p/s/usm	✓	✗	✗	✗
Mauritius	5.7.89	Wed/Thu 10.00–13.00	24	p/s/otc	✓	✗	✗	✗
Morocco (Casablanca SE)	1929	Mon–Fri 10.45–12.00	14	o/otc/usm	✓	✗	✗	✗
Nigeria	1977	11.00 onwards	76	p/s	✓	✓	✗	✗
Peru (Lima SE)	1970	11.00–13.00	41	p	✓	✗	✓	✓
Sri Lanka (Colombo SE)	1984	9.30–11.30	9	p/s	✓	✓	✗	✗
Trinidad & Tobago	26.10.81	9.30 onwards	9	p/s	✓	✗	✓	—
Uruguay	1864	14.00–15.00	76	p/s	✓	✗	✗	✗

Footnotes p = primary s = secondary otc = over-the-counter usm = unlisted securities market
Source Westlake, M. (1990) Emerging equity markets: who's next for the big league? Guide to developing markets. *Euromoney,* December, 42–57.

Table 16.5 Equity trading within developing stock exchanges

Stock exchange	Number of listings end '88	Number of listings end '89	Market cap ($m) end '88	Market cap ($m) end '89	Shares traded (av. daily no.) 1988	Shares traded (av. daily no.) 1989	Shares traded (av. daily val $) 1988	Shares traded (av. daily val $) 1989	total 1989	total 1990	New issues shares (m) 1989	New issues shares (m) 1990	val. ($m) 1989	val. ($m) 1990	Number of rights issues 1989	Number of rights issues 1990	Av. P/E ratio	Average price/book value ratio	Average yield (%)	Price index base value	Price index level 31.12.88	Price index level 31.12.89
Bangladesh	111	116	430	476	3,864	7,990	15,479	19,417	11	13	3.1	2.6	6.9	5.8	7	2	21.75	1.52	5.71	—	533.6060	467.7575
Barbados	13	14	244.2	290.3	14,800	21,187	41,479	63,930	1	—	3.0	na	3.0	na	0	0	9.5	—	6.3	1.1.88 = 100	na	1,268.75
Botswana	na	6	na	510	na	5,421	na	58,612	0	1	2.5	5.0	23.8	21.2	0	0	9.2	2.6	5.3	19.6.89 = 100	na	149.33
Cyprus	27	—	224.1	(1.9.90)	—	—	—	—	—	—	—	—	—	—	na	na	na	na	na	—	na	na
Jamaica	45	45	796	957	426,686	782,353	244,185	672,098	0	0	na	na	na	na	1	1	6		4	June 69 = 100	1,439.22	2,075.85
Kenya	55	57	747	449	—	—	—	—	4	1	38.8	9.0	15.6	13.1	2	0	5.77	2.95	0.32	1956 = 100	853.54	815.84
Mauritius	—	6	—	98	—	34,000	—	63,725	4	2	16.0	10.0	5.8	6.6	2	2	7	2.6	6.5	July 89 = 100	na	149.7
Morocco	71	71	446	621	4,154	1,970	132,654	58,293	—	—	—	—	—	—	—	—	na	na	6.88	1979 = 100	690.47	122.65
Nigeria	103	111	960	1,005	83,323	79,257	21,167	12,516	17	19	565.6	376.8	55.8	41.8	6	12	7	1.0	7.33	3.1.84 = 100	233.6	325.3
Peru	245	262	348	—	—	—	222,000	—	0	0	na	na	na	na	0	0	—	—	—	30.12.86 = 100	859.97	33,694.31
Sri Lanka	176	176	471	475	55,951	51,326	50,635	29,859	2	1	14.0	21.2	3.9	0.5	7	9	10.41	—	3.38	1.1.85 = 100 / 1.1.85 = 100	172.44	179.49
Trinidad & Tobago	34	31	268	411	423,616	944,117	203,039	457,150	2	1	23	21	4.7	4.2	1	0	10.8	0.81	3.48	1.1.83 = 100	32.41	48.68
Uruguay	40	39	24	—	—	—	4,518	2,752	—	—	—	—	—	—	—	—	na	na	na	na	na	na
Zimbabwe	—	54	774	1,067	—	—	0.1	—	—	—	—	—	—	—	—	—	7.0	1.3	9.8	—	—	—

Source Westlake, M. (1990) Emerging equity markets: who's next for the big league? Guide to developing markets. *Euromoney*, December, 42–57.

Exhibit 16.2

Sale of Cocoa Industries Limited (CIL)

Winners and losers

Paxton Idowu and Bola Olowo

IN EARLY 1989 the management of Odu'a Investment, which owns Cocoa Industries Limited (CIL), decided to sell 60 per cent of its 100 per cent shareholding in the company. CIL is a cocoa processing company in the Ikeja area of Lagos.

This disinvestment was considered a wise move. Not only was CIL losing money, but Oud'a was taking its cue from the federal government which had been unloading shares from its numerous companies. But the manner in which CIL shares were sold stirred up a hornet's nest. It made the governors of Ondo, Oyo and Ogun states livid with rage, not to mention traditional rulers and many others and brought accusations of tribalism.

The forerunner to the sale itself was a terse advertisement in the *Daily Times* of May 17 1989 inviting interested entrepreneurs and financiers to invest in a viable project. According to our sources 25 companies applied, amongst them Cadbury and Food Specialities. But only three companies were short-listed: Quantilex Nigeria Limited which had offices in Kaduna. Cafrina Agric Process Industries Limited at Apapa, and the Emerald Packaging Company Limited with offices in Lagos. All three were owned by a businessman named Alhaji Lawal Garba. Emerald's bid later proved successful.

Odu'a's first offer for the 18 million shares it wanted to unload (representing 60 per cent of its holdings) was based on a price of N4.03 per share. Surprisingly, the three shortlisted companies were those who said that this initial offer was unrealistic. All three sent letters criticising the offer, signed by different officials but with nearly identical wording. The letters said that they could only buy the shares for N9m, at 50k, per share.

When Odu'a decided to sell some of its CIL shares, it obtained advice from two consultants. These were Abacus Securities (a top Nigerian stockbroking firm) and Messrs Onakanmi and Partners (an estate survey and evaluation firm). Onakanmi valued CIL assets at N97.958m while Abacus valued CIL ordinary shares at N1.00 each. The initial N4.03 offer was determined by averaging these two valuations.

This initial offer would have allowed Odu'a to sell the 60 per cent shareholding for N72m. It would have been a good price for Odu'a shareholders who were ultimately the citizens of the three Odu'a states – Oyo, Ogun and Ondo, as the shares were held in trust by the state governments for all Oduduwa descendants.

In order to strengthen its bargaining power, Oud'a decided that before offering the 60 per cent shareholding it would recapitalise its six million CIL ordinary shares of N1 each to 12m. If Oud'a's had recapitalised, it would have gained N6.5m on the face value of the shares and N27.95m if the shares were then sold at the initial offer price of N4.03. But on March 22, 1990, after it had started to negotiate with Emerald, it decided not to recapitalise again without giving any reason. Instead, Oud'a raised N9m by transferring just the 6m offered shares to Emerald at the latter's initial price of N2.50 per share.

The one billion naira question is: why did Oud'a undervalue itself by not recapitalising? After all, Emerald had wanted to buy 18m shares, albeit at 50k, and while Oud'a's initial offer was N72m, that of Emerald was only N9m.

All three sent letters criticising the offer; signed by different officials but with nearly identical wording

---

The fact that CIL was eventually sold at N9m showed that not only did Oud'a swallow Emerald's offer hook, line and sinker, it also found a way to accommodate it.

The stage was all set for Emerald to obtain its shares, following all the initial negotiations, when Odu'a wrote a letter to Emerald on December 22, 1989 conveying the decision of the board to sell. But Emerald did not have N9m. Emerald went to Eko Bank Limited which approved a facility of N9m for it to purchase the shares. One of the conditions made by Eko was the completion of a blank share transfer form by CIL to the bank. This could not be immediately effected, and on March 28, 1990 a director of Odu'a Corporate Services, R. S. Aruna, wrote to CIL asking it to expedite action on the transfer of the blank share form of the previous day. The whole negotiation was concluded when Oud'a Investment delivered the blank share transfer form to Eko Bank, and Emerald became the proud owner of a 60 per cent shareholding in CIL.

The sale has opened a can of worms. The three governors who approved the sale (Col Oresanya from Oyo, Olabode George from Ondo and Lawal from Ogun states) left the scene after a cabinet reshuffle. The newly appointed governors took a close look at the sale and did not like what they saw. A royal father in Oyo state also expressed disapproval of it.

Odu'a Investment Company is a billion-naira octopus whose tentacles reach into all parts of the western state and especially Lagos. It was originally formed by Obafemi Awolowo's Action Group.

Observers say that the sale should not have been shrouded in so much mystery, and that Odu'a Investment should not have sold all the shares to just one individual but to a cross section of Nigerians. Questions have also been asked about why big companies such as Cadbury and Food Specialities, all with track records in food processing, should be turned down in favour of a commodity trader with no experience in the industry. A reliable source disclosed that one of the former governors who approved the sale was opposed to Cadbury because it was a rival to CIL.

The agreement between Oud'a and Emerald has been signed, sealed and delivered but the questions still remain. Inhabitants from the three states concerned are putting pressure on both the government and the management of Oud'a Investment to put matters to rights, and their efforts are yielding fruit. For example, group managing director Chief Olufemi Adewunmi has said the sale is yet to be settled, which contradicts the view he expressed after the scandal first erupted that the sale to Emerald was a 'normal business transaction'. There are strong indications that Adewunmi is responding to orders from the three new governors of the Ou-d'a's states. These governors not only expressed disapproval of the sale, but held an emergency meeting of the Odu'a board on January 17 to discuss it. Adewunmi has now assured those who are upset about the sale that every effort will be made to redress any wrongs caused by it.

Source   *West Africa* (1991), 11–17 February, p. 178.

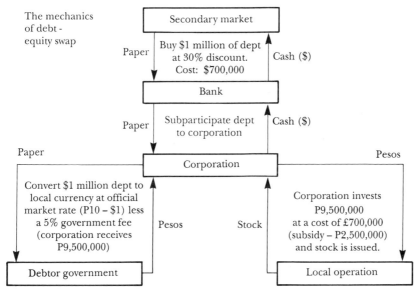

The mechanics of debt - equity swap

Secondary market

Paper | Buy $1 million of dept at 30% discount. Cost: $700,000 | Cash ($)

Bank

Paper | Subparticipate dept to corporation | Cash ($)

Paper | Corporation | Pesos

Convert $1 million dept to local currency at official market rate (P10 – $1) less a 5% government fee (corporation receives P9,500,000) | Pesos | Stock | Corporation invests P9,500,000 at a cost of £700,000 (subsidy – P2,500,000) and stock is issued.

Debtor government

Local operation

Source: Manufacturers Hanover Trust Company.

Figure 16.2
Source Wanamaker, M. (1988) No easy path for debt-equity swaps.
Euromoney, Debt Management Supplement, September, 2–14

with the offer of shares for the insurance company UNIC, one of Nigeria's most profitable insurance carriers, which was only slightly over-subscribed. Other factors likely to constrain future issues include the need first to restructure companies less viable than those already privatized; an ongoing Nigerian liquidity squeeze, and limits to the absorptive capacity of the stock market itself.

Debt conversion programme

Nigeria was the first African country to introduce a debt/equity programme, but the prime example (and perhaps only [?]) of a successful debt/equity programme is Chile, which since 1985 has reduced its commercial bank debt from $14 billion to $11.5 billion, mostly through the debt/equity programme. There are two sides to this issue. On the host country side, there is the desire to bring in new long-term investment capital flows in the form of equity investment. For the multinational corporations, who have undercapitalized their subsidiaries during the debt crisis, a debt/equity programme creates the opportunity to recapitalize at a discount on each dollar invested. An abuse, particularly prevalent in Nigeria, is 'round-tripping', where funds may be brought into Nigeria through a debt/equity programme and then the money is simply passed out via the black market at a higher rate of exchange.

An illustration of 'round-tripping' and of how the programme may lend itself to fraud is provided by Eric Hermann, Associate Director, Bear Stearns and a specialist in African corporate finance (Wanamaker, 1988):

Say you have a $5 million dollar invoice for the import of Mercedes Benz cars and you really imported rocks and not Mercedes — and the reason you did that is you're importing the rocks from yourself — and then you want to justify the payment at the official rate, not the parallel or black market rate, of $5 million dollars worth of cash. That's an enormous windfall profit when let's say the official rate is twice as good as a black market rate. If you're just going to take your $5 million and exchange it on the black market that's only worth $2–1/2 million. If you're going to make a phoney transaction, and get the $5 million paid out on the official rate that's worth $5 million. That's quite a windfall.

The issue of debt is now being tackled as an international problem (see separate reference to the Brady Plan). As time goes on and debt, therefore, diminishes, the debt stock will be quite different perhaps five years on. The factor that is perhaps most surprising in all this is the lack of response to these debt/equity programmes from outside. Chile conducted a $420 million debt/equity swap in 1988. However, there has been no other country as successful in this as Chile, there has been no international proliferation of debt/equity programmes, yet to increase investment and reduce debt are both laudable aims. In the end, investors look at the economy and the business culture before investing.

Nigeria's programme has been a qualified success, but after six auctions was able to redeem only $160.53 million dollars of promissory notes against an external debt totalling $30 billion. The problem in the case of Nigeria has been finding investors. The central bank has moved away from a stance that only promissory notes are eligible to include various other possibilities such as loan stock and most company debentures. However, the Enterprise Promotion Act says that before foreign investment can be made, the local shareholding has to be increased to keep the balance between foreign and local ownership. This is a serious constraint, as is the restriction on repatriation of funds. Nigeria insists on a time lag, where dividends and profits may not be remitted for five years and capital for ten years. On top of this, there is also a 2.5 per cent transaction commission on the face value of the promissory note, to be paid in foreign currency to the central bank's account at Morgan Guaranty in New York. Banks may not act on their own account but only as intermediaries.

In the first half of 1985, when $1 = ₦7.5, buying notes at 20¢ and offering them at a 50 per cent discount gave ₦12.5 for every dollar invested (Hawkins, 1990). Thus a $10 m. investment would bring 12.5 m naira — 66 per cent more naira than the 75 m naira obtained at the official rate of exchange. Since then, the naira has slipped while discounts have averaged 47 per cent, narrowing margins.

There are strict guidelines governing the eligibility of investments, with priority for new or expansionary projects that offer a high employment content in manufacturing, agribusiness, mining and forestry. Conversion can also be used by Nigerian nationals to acquire shareholdings in existing Nigerian companies, and also for financial restructuring.

Foreign trade

In the years immediately after the Second World War agricultural products provided 78.7 per cent of Nigeria's export earnings, while more than 60 per cent of its imports came from the UK. By 1980, oil accounted for 96.1 per cent of export earnings, with the UK providing 22 per cent of Nigeria's imports. Behind these figures are the fundamental shifts in Nigeria's trading. Its range of suppliers has widened largely to embrace more West European countries,

Table 16.6   Indicative prices for less developed country bank loans

Country	Indicative cash prices		Swap index	
	Bid	Offer	Sell	Buy
Algeria	92.50	93.50	6.65	7.67
Argentina	25.75	26.50	0.67	0.68
Bolivia	10.0	11.00	0.55	0.56
Brazil	50.25	51.00	1.01	1.02
Chile	60.75	61.50	1.27	1.30
Colombia	66.00	67.50	1.47	1.53
Costa Rica	13.50	14.50	0.58	0.58
Dominican Republic	19.00	21.00	0.62	0.63
Ecuador	25.50	26.50	0.67	0.68
Honduras	22.00	24.00	0.64	0.66
Ivory Coast	27.50	29.50	0.69	0.72
Jamaica	37.00	40.00	0.79	0.83
Mexico	49.50	50.25	0.99	1.01
Morocco	50.50	51.50	1.01	1.03
Nicaragua	2.00	4.00	0.51	0.52
Nigeria	27.00	29.00	0.68	0.70
Panama	25.25	26.25	0.67	0.68
Peru	6.00	7.00	0.53	0.54
Philippines	53.50	55.00	1.07	1.11
Poland	40.00	41.00	0.83	0.85
Romania	87.00	88.50	3.84	4.34
Senegal	48.00	50.00	0.96	1.00
Sudan	2.00	8.00	0.50	0.55
Turkey	98.50	99.50	82.25	99.75
Uruguay	60.50	61.50	1.26	1.30
Venezuela	54.50	55.25	1.10	1.11
Yugoslavia	47.75	49.00	0.95	0.98
Zaire	19.00	23.00	0.62	0.65

Source   Wanamaker, M. (1988) No easy path for debt-equity swaps. *Euromoney, Debt Management Supplement*, September, 2–14.

but the spread of its earnings has narrowed. It remains a mere exporter of raw materials and importer of manufactures. Various attempts have been made towards a national development policy but these have been at risk for the following reasons:
1 Smuggling.
2 Government has only limited control over the size of its export revenue and so responds to its rise and fall with import restrictions.
3 Government is committed to growth of manufactured exports and sees the somewhat stillborn Economic Community of West African States (ECOWAS) as the most accessible

Table 16.7   Nigeria: the debt conversion story

	30 Nov 88	29 Dec 88	3 Feb 88	31 Mar 89	28 Apr 89	23 Jan 89
Number of bidders	36	33	25	3	22	19
Number of fully successful bidders	7	17	5	3	10	7
Number of partially successful bidders	1	1	—	—	3	—
Unsuccessful bidders	28	15	20	—	9	12
Highest discount rate	58%	45.2%	50%	49.99%	53.81%	51.01%
Marginal discount	36%	37.2%	43.3%	45%	47.01%	43.0%
Exchange rate	5.3364	5.3530	7.2477	7.5875	7.5585	7.2741
Amount bid	$184.6m	$79.6m	$67.0m	—	—	—
Amount redeemed	$40m	$30m	$25m	$2.9m	$33.5m	$29.125m
Discount value of central bank promissory notes at the secondary market	21.22¢	20.5–21.5¢	19.5–20.5¢	20–20.5¢	20–21¢	21–22¢
Cumulative amount of naira redeemed	N127.6m	N95.3m	N94.6m	N11.9m	N128.4m	N111.04m
Cumulative amount of dollars redeemed	$40.0m	$30.0m	$25.0m	$2.9m	$33.5m	$29.125m

Source   *The Banker* (1989) October, VIII.

channel, but only limited tariff reductions have been agreed and deep-rooted problems like the convertibility of currencies remain. At the same time, Nigerian non-oil exports which constitute less than 5 per cent of exports have declined sharply.

Soviet aid packages to Africa have been cut in the past few years, with Soviets now looking to Africa to repay its debts rather than as before, hoping to extend political sway through financial help. However, as Adade (1990) has made clear, the cut should not cause alarm but instead, perhaps even be welcomed for the reasons that between 1980 and 1984, the USSR provided Sub-Saharan Africa with nearly $2.1 billion in economic assistance, while its arms deliveries accounted for more than $5.9 billion. For North Africa, the comparable figures are $650 million in economic aid and $7.9 billion in armaments supplies.

Export inspection agencies and PSI

The role of pre-shipment inspection (PSI) is seen as important for the developing countries as a means to contain corruption and capital flight. Before pre-shipment inspection, Nigeria was receiving fraudulent shipments labelled machinery that might only contain sand. Yet, the paperwork might be written in such a way as to require payment on sight of the consignment. PSI, which takes place in the country of the supplier, is one way to get around this, and involves a third party to arbitrate on the quality, price and legality of the goods to be sold. The initial effect is one of short-lived confusion, although it does lead to delays. For a country in a situation such as Nigeria, delays were welcome as it granted them a little while longer to find the hard currency necessary to pay for imports that were now worth exactly what they said they were on import licences. Import licences in the past had been subject to a great deal of abuse and there has been illegal trafficking in the sale of import licences. The abolition of import licences was, therefore, commonly welcomed.

For the exporter, delays cost money and often imperil the acceptability of letters of credit for payment. This then offers the importing country an opportunity to force down prices, and this pressure continues while the ship is on the open seas and still without a clean report of findings from the Inspection Agency for its cargo. Some exporting countries, such as those in Eastern Europe, will have nothing to do with price inspection.

The issue of export inspection has now passed to the GATT Uruguay round of negotiations, with many of the industrialized Western nations claiming export inspection to be a non-tariff barrier. Export inspection is to be found in approximately thirty LDCs, including Nigeria where despite coups and changes of government the basic system still remains in place.

All that has really changed is that the governmental contracts restrict the territorial franchise awarded to any one inspection company. Recent changes have instituted a larger number of smaller franchises for the inspection companies. There appears to be no motive other than the Nigerian Government would appear to be happier with several inspection agencies than just one alone, so avoiding any possible monopoly situation. North America, for example, has two, one inspection company for the US, another for Canada.

Regulations on exporting

The 'M' form and PSI are two facets of selling to Nigeria that deter exporters, in addition to the debt and general instability of the economy.

The licensing system (now abandoned) decided what the country should buy abroad and the 'M' form system, when first introduced in 1979 by the Central Bank, gave the Government for the first time some measure of what Nigeria spends in foreign currency, and their inspection agents then acted to check that the country was buying what it requires at reasonable prices. The inspection agency also requires verification that payment of the foreign exchange equivalent of import duties has been paid in Nigeria. That is the system, but there is no means of establishing exactly how successful this total approach has been.

Nigerian industry depends on raw materials and parts, and so, import restrictions have led to a cut-back in domestic production. The size of the population plus import dependency makes Nigeria still the most important export market in black Africa. The main benefit of the regulations for Nigeria is that export regulations act as a deterrent to those seeking to make overpriced sales into the Nigerian market or to make fraudulent sales. To this end, Lagos businessmen claim that it has had some success.

When PSI procedures were first introduced, they caused confusion among both importers and those selling to Nigeria, but the system has now bedded down and the sharp edge of the system has been blunted. The pre-shipment inspection scheme is just something else the trading community has to live with. It cuts out the worst abuses of Nigeria's insatiable desire for imports and can check that basic materials are not overpriced. For imports with a high technological content, and where there is a high level of added-value, the ability of this scheme to secure prices is much less effective. Nevertheless, without a correctly completed 'M' form (and the Central Bank maintains tight control), the exporter cannot be paid. Difficulties do often occur because exporters are unaware that the 'M' form has to be completed by the importers and requires comprehensive information on the goods. The onus, therefore, lies with the exporter to pass the correct information to his buyer. The information covers FOB price, freight, and ancillary charges. In addition, the importer is required to produce tax clearance and (in the case of raw materials) approved manufacturer certificates.

Once the 'M' form has been approved by the Central Bank, the importer can open a letter of credit and confirm the order. All orders over $5,000 in value are subject to PSI, but it is as well to check with the inspection agency beforehand. Exporters shipping prior to the 'M'

Table 16.8   Countries requiring pre-shipment inspection

	Year started	Agency
Angola	1980	SGS
Bolivia	1986	SGS
Burundi	1978	SGS
Congo	1987	Socotec
Ecuador	1985	SGS
Equatorial Guinea	1983	SGS
Ghana	1971	SGS
Guatemala*	1986	SGS
Guinea	1986	Bureau Veritas
Haiti	1983	SGS
Indonesia	1985	SGS
Iran	na	Cotecna
Ivory Coast	1975	SGS
Kenya	1986	SGS
Liberia	1972	SGS
Madagascar	1986	SGS
Mexico	1983	SGS
Nigeria	1985	SGS
Paraguay	1979	Cotecna/Bureau Veritas/Intertek
Peru	1983	SGS
Philippines	1987	SGS
Rwanda	1986	SGS
Surinam	1977	SGS
Tanzania	1982	SGS
Uganda	1972	SGS
Venezuela	1982	SGS
Zaire	1986	SGS/Bureau Veritas/Intertek
Zambia	1968	SGS
	1978	SGS

Source   Nisse, J. (1978) Trade finance: tiger by the tail. *The Banker*, October, 103–105.

form gaining Central Bank approval or without PSI are liable to forfeit payment or to have the goods confiscated. The inspection agents have to complete an import duty report, which they then send to the importer to enable him to clear customs. A clear report of findings will be issued after shipment, provided their inspections and price comparisons yield satisfactory results. Conversely, a non-negotiable report of findings will be issued should the consignment fail to meet all the requirements.

Despite the SAP, there are still limitations. Form 'M' is still in existence, but since 1986 there have been some significant changes. Banking has been deregulated and the foreign exchange market is now working relatively well. Foreign currency auctions are held every Wednesday and each bank bids to the Central Bank. In the past, these auctions have been erratic, from once a month to fortnightly, and now once a week. It means that banks are now usually able to get what they want, if not this week then the week following. It is proving to be the case that the wait is no longer than this for foreign funds. However, the larger Nigerian companies will have accounts with twenty to thirty banks and bid through these banks separately to get funds. This process may well be one way to get around the system, but it does mean that there are too many naira chasing too few dollars, and so, in turn creates and maintains an artificial rate of exchange.

Business ethics

Nothing so annoys and worries foreigners as the demand for 'exceptional' or unusual payments, often called 'dash' (see also Chapter 13 for a discussion on devising a corporate code of ethics). The people's deepest loyalty is to the home village and community from which most of them have very recently moved and with which even the most urban maintain strong personal links. The wants of families – infinitely extended through aunts, uncles, and cousins in a way incomprehensible to Europeans – are very real. The richest and best-educated Nigerians feel this pull of the home community at least as strongly as the poorest, perhaps because their fathers were village chiefs, with feudal obligations. There is a real and admirable collective solidarity, extending beyond the village to the tribe and the whole language group (of which Nigeria has approximately 200), but not to the nation and society as a whole. English, therefore, remains the national language, and Nigerian society has to be seen to contain many important undercurrents which could drag it under.

Getting power or money for yourself means sharing within the group. The poorest relation basks in the glory, and may even get some of the money, gained by the successful. Getting rich confers collective merit. Other loyalties – to the public service, the private firm, etc. – can never be as strong as that to the family and its tribal or ethnic extensions. To use a British parallel, the Nigerian who takes bribes sees himself as Robin Hood and not as the wicked Sheriff of Nottingham.

Applying the term bribery to 'dash' is applying a Western value judgement. No society anywhere approves or condones corruption, including Nigeria, although Nigeria itself has witnessed in the past some of the greatest excesses among its public figures. Michael Holman (1990), writing in the *Financial Times*, puts it quite bluntly: 'Corruption is endemic, vested interests continue to stand in the way of some reforms – management is weak, implementation slow.' Few Nigerians, according to Holman, believe that the days of vote buying and influence peddling are over, and the likelihood is that soldiers as well as ex-politicians will be active behind the scenes.

Exhibit 16.3

Death peddling

BETWEEN 40–50 per cent of fake drugs in Nigeria are domestically produced, the rest come from Europe, Thailand and the Far East. These drugs range from harmless chalk based products to lethal concoctions like paracetamol syrup containing ethylene glycol which recently killed 100 children.

Last year's paracetemol scandal led to the arrest of three people from an Onitsha pharmaceutical company and the initial banning of the drug.

The syrup had been mixed with ethylene glycol which was originally purchased for use in the oil industry. It was relabelled propylene glycol and resold to hospitals. When this deception was discovered the drug was initially banned. However, manufacturers, who had obtained public analysis certificates, were later allowed to resume production.

According to the World Health Organisation (WHO) director of drug policy, Dr John Dunne, the problem of fake drugs is endemic throughout Africa and the Third World. In Africa, 'Nigeria is the only country that has had the strength to be honest about this', Dr Dunne said.

Under health minister, Professor Olikoye Ransome-Kuti, the Federal Drug Administration has produced a booklet which catalogues the fake drugs on the market and their fraudulent packages. The sophisticated packaging of drugs like *Septrin*, a broad-based anti-biotic, produced in blister packs (requiring each tablet to be removed individually from its niche) has not deterred the fraudsters. Furthermore, the government recently announced that drug procurement would be centralised. Experts predict that this measure, together with Nigeria's Essential Drugs Act (which limits the type of drugs available for sale in public outlets) will greatly reduce the scope of the fake drug manufacturers.

But it's not only Third World fraudsters who are engaged in harmful pharmaceutical practices. British and American multinational companies have also been severely criticised by the WHO.

The WHO notes in a report that the Western pharmaceutical industry makes a huge $1bn profit from sales of positively harmful 'anti-diarrhoeal' drugs to poor countries. Through seductive advertising, these companies seduce poor parents into buying drugs which cause the deaths of 4m children a year.

'The production and sale of these "anti-diarrhoeals" cannot be justified', said the report.

Titled *The Rational Use of Drugs in the Management of Acute Diarrhoea in Children*, the report says that 'current patterns of diarrhoea treatment have shown that a large number of pharmaceutical agents of dubious efficacy and potential toxicity are widely used'.

Source Duodu, C. (1991) Menace of fake drugs. *West Africa*, 11–17. February, pp. 174–175.

Nigeria's banking sector

In 1989, there were fifty-four banks. Nine months later, the number had risen to sixty, and ten months after that there were eighty-four. Most of these new banks are termed 'merchant banks' but are just money changers set up to take advantage of the huge sums being made out of arbitrage between 'official' and 'parallel' rates of the naira. One high-ranking military officer commented in private that setting up so many so-called banks was effectively the 'privatization of corruption'. Banks can bid for foreign exchange at the currency auction, but as they have a set limit for how much foreign currency a company may get, the companies themselves will have multiple bank accounts or pay well over the going rate to acquire it, paying $1 = ₦14 as against the official rate of $1 = ₦7.9.

Most of the new banks are in Lagos and there is little to differentiate the merchant bank from the commercial bank in Nigeria, although merchant banks are not able to issue cheque books. In terms of lending, there is a difference in that 50 per cent of merchant bank lending is medium term rather than the short-term lending found among the commercial banks (*Banker*, October 1989). Another common point that is shared is that most are under-capitalized, over-extended and so lacking in liquidity. Banks are in a tough situation with collateral, such as property, now collapsing. Manufacturing is dependent on imported raw materials and that means foreign exchange. This forces small firms towards banks and large companies towards restructuring, but no bank can hold more than 10 per cent of a company's equity or invest more than 30 per cent of the shareholders' funds in any one company.

According to *The Banker* (October, 1989), the services seem to be in all in the wrong areas, and so the test is now to see how many of the banks will survive the testing times ahead. *The Banker* (September, 1990) also commented:

> Nigeria's banks should stand as a colossus over West and Central Africa if population and natural resources, notably oil, were a guide to economic strength. Yet no Nigerian bank, indeed no sub-Saharan bank – excluding four from South Africa – made it into The Banker's Top 1,000 Listing.

The Nigerian Government has a controlling stake in the banks, and so the Government in 1990 sacked the boards of the top twelve banks and has earmarked banks among its privatization plans. The banks had been given licences to operate by the Central Bank on the premise that Nigeria was underbanked, whereas, according to *The Banker* (August 1990), it is under-branched. Furthermore, newcomers brought no new services to the population and were all based in Lagos. In fact, *The Banker* refers to it as inviting a 'Trojan Horse' into the country.

Assembly unsuccessful

Volkswagen entered Nigeria in 1975 with an assembly operation, but of the six assembly plants in Nigeria, two are in receivership and the other four are marginal (Olowo, 1991). Under-utilization of capacity, and so low production quantities, high prices for their vehicles relative to imported cars, and low local content input are some of the problems. Certainly, successive governments have not adhered to their promises of protection, with import licences still being issued for imported finished models of some cars. The 10 per cent differential between assembled and imported cars is insufficient to give the assembled car any advantage, as necessary production parts and components when imported meet with a 40–45 per cent import duty, while if the Government had fulfilled its promises, new car component factories would have been established. As it is, high duties, a depreciating naira and high interest rates further exacerbate a difficult situation. The statistics, meanwhile, speak for themselves in that Peugeot Nigeria Ltd (PAN) has reduced production from 59,000 vehicles in 1981 to 5,900 in 1989, reducing its workforce accordingly; Volkswagen of Nigeria (VON), with a capacity for 25,000 vehicles, produces only 2,000; and Anambra Motor Manufacturing (ANAMCO), with a capacity of 1,000 trucks, produces only 200 per year. Local content in assembly is low, although it has increased from 1981 levels to 30 per cent for VON and 35 per cent for PAN, but it cannot go further. The survival of these plants is now very questionable without direct governmental aid so as to prevent the job losses that would result from closure.

Joint ventures and foreign direct investment

Since SAP, there has been a major overhaul of Nigerian joint ventures. The Government has retained for Nigerians exclusively only that small sector of business which is characterized as

Table 16.9 Nigeria's top ten banks

	Foreign participation	Year-end	Capital $m	Capital % change	$m	Assets Rank	Assets % change	Pre-tax profits $m	Pre-tax profits % change
1 Union Bank of Nigeria	—	30/09/89	75	35.1	1,080	3	26.0	21	35.7
2 First Bank of Nigeria	Standard Chartered Bank (38%)	31/12/89	70	22.8	1,102	2	19.2	21	31.5
3 United Bank for Africa	Banque Nationale de Paris (31%)	31/03/90	59	13.2	1,429	1	23.3	15	15.3
4 Federal Mortgage Bank of Nigeria (FMBN)	—	31/12/88	44	13.6	119	24	8.2	na	na
5 Afribank Nigeria	Banque Nationale de Paris/BIAO (40%)	31/12/89	38	37.6	329	5	−7.2	16	34.9
6 NAL Merchant Bank	American Express Bank (26%)	31/03/89	28	83.2	198	13	−7.3	6	54.2
7 Bank of the North	—	31/12/89	21	25.6	239	11	−20.6	5	2.5
8 Nigeria International Bank	Citicorp (40%)	31/12/88	18	127.9	300	7	59.4	21	27.9
9 International Merchant Bank (Nigeria)	First National Bank of Chicago (40%)	31/12/89	15	31.4	255	10	4.6	7	31.0
10 Nigeria Merchant Bank	United Bank for Africa (40%)	31/12/90	15	48.6	197	14	1.7	8	20.3

Source The Banker (1990) Africa: Top 50 Nigerian banks – no quick fixes, October, pp. 92, 94.

being small-scale. Foreign investors are able to invest but foreign participation is limited to not more than 20 million naira. In all other sectors, the Government has substantially overhauled existing legislation to allow foreign participation up to and including 100 per cent if that is the foreign investor's desire.

The IDCC

The IDCC was created as a one-stop agency to process foreign participation and to cut down red tape. Before the introduction of this agency, it could take a year or more to get approval for a joint venture as various ministries might be involved. These have all now been bypassed and the constitution of the IDCC requires it to provide a foreign investor with an answer within two months. The IDCC is also empowered to issue up to four visas for investment in the industrial sector, and has created means to facilitate remittances as well as institute tax breaks of five to seven years.

Factors for market success

1 Do not rush out to get yourself an agent. Nigeria has hundreds offering their services. Banks, as well as the Department of Trade, would be able to offer some qualitative evaluation of available agents, their financial standing and market performance. Think before you select.
2 Build relationships.
3 Practice marketing on the offensive, no one is waiting for you.
4 Nigeria has more to it than Lagos – so move around, listen and learn.
5 Bureaucracy abounds and Nigeria has its own particular style of bureaucracy.
6 Flexibility is important but if you have come out to do a deal, chances are that you will conclude a bad one.
7 Accentuate the positive, as the old saying goes. British companies follow in a long established tradition of being one of the top suppliers to Nigeria. Source of origin and home country base may be worth accentuating in any bidding situation.

References

Adada, C. Q. (1990) Soviets abandon Africa. *West Africa*, 8–14 October, pp. 2606–2607.
Adegbite, O. (1986) Planning in Nigerian business. *Long Range Planning*, **19**, (4), 98–103.
Akoch, I. P., and Riardon, E. A. (1988) 'Applicability of marketing knowhow in the Third World', *International Marketing Review*, **5**, (1), 41–55.
Central Bank of Nigeria (1984) *Circular Ref. ECD/AD/211/84*, 29 September.
Bartlett, B. R. (1990) Capitalism in Africa: a survey. *Journal of Developing Areas*, April, 327–350.
Dayo, F. B., and Adegbulugbe, A. O. (1988) Utilisation of Nigeria's natural gas resources. *Energy Policy*, **16**, (2), 122–130.

Dadzie, K. Q. (1989) Demarketing strategy in shortage marketing environment. *Journal of Academy of Marketing Science*, Spring, 157–165.

Duodu, C. (1991) Menace of fake drugs. *West Africa*, 11–17 February, pp. 174–175.

Economist (1982) Special survey: Nigeria. 23 January.

Emretane, M. O. (1986) Marketing in Nigeria: past, present and the year 2000. *Marketing News*, 29 August, p. 15.

Ethics, **5**, (4), 327–332.

Fubara, B. A. (1986) Corporate planning in Nigeria. *Long Range Planning*, **19**, (2), 125–132.

Financial Times (1989) Special Supplement: Nigeria, 6 March.

Green, R. T., and Larsen, T. L. (1986) Sudden wealth/sudden poverty: implications for export opportunities. *Columbia Journal of World Business*, **21**, (4), 7–12.

Hawkins, T. (1990) A cheap way in: debt-conversion programme gains popularity. *Financial Times, Special Supplement: Nigeria*, 19 March.

Holman, M. (1990) Nigeria. *Financial Times, Special Supplement*, 19 March, pp. I-XIV.

Holman, M. (1989) Nigeria. *Financial Times, Special Supplement*, 6 March, pp. 1–12.

Holstrom, L. (1990) Nigeria: Boom or bust? *Euromoney*, September, 95–98.

Nisse, J. (1987) Trade finance: tiger by the tail. *The Banker*, October, 103–105.

Olowo, B. (1991) Threat from imports. *West Africa*, 12–15 April, p. 556.

Onyebuchi, E. I. (1989) Alternate energy strategies for the developing world's domestic use: a case study of Nigerian households' fuel use patterns and preferences. *Energy Journal*, **10**, (3) 121–138.

Pirard, T. (1989) Developing the dark continent. *Satellite Communications*, **13**, (3), 68.

Quinlan, M. (1990) Energy finance: Africa woos the energy giants, *Euromoney*, June/July, 63–64.

Savage, P. (1987) Ammonia is a new key for Nigeria. *Chemical Week*, **141**, (10), 22–24.

SITPRO (1984) *Nigeria*, London.

Sohn, I. (1987) External debt and oil prices: some prospects for oil exporting developing countries. *Energy Policy*, **15**, (5), 408–420.

Synge, R. (1990) Searching for solutions. *West Africa*, 26 November–2 January, pp. 2898–2899.

The Banker (1990) 'Africa: top 50 Nigerian banks – no quick fixes, October, 92, 94.

The Banker (1990) Nigeria's Trojan Horse. August, pp. 4–6.

The World Bank Atlas 1990, World Bank, Washington, DC.

Wanamaker, M. (1988) No easy path for debt/equity swaps. *Euromoney*, September, 2–14.

Westlake, M. (1990) Emerging equity markets: who's next for the big league? *Euromoney*, December, 42–57.

Woodworth, N. (1990) Share-hungry Nigerians lose their appetite. *Financial Times*, 13 February.

Key reading

Akoch, I. P., and Riardon, E. A. (1988) Applicability of marketing knowhow in the Third World. *International Marketing Review*, **5**, (1), 41–55.

Dadzie, K. Q. (1989) Demarketing strategy in shortage marketing environment. *Journal of Academy of Marketing Science*, Spring, 157–165.

Duodu, C. (1991) Menace of fake drugs. *West Africa*, 11–17 February, pp. 174–175.

Quinlan, M. (1990) Energy finance: Africa woos the energy giants. *Euromoney*, June/July, 63–64.

Savage, P. (1987) Ammonia is a new key for Nigeria. *Chemical Week*, **141**, (10), 22–24.

Synge, R. (1990) Searching for solutions. *West Africa*, 26 November–2 January, pp. 2898–2899.

Wanamaker, M. (1988) No easy path for debt/equity swaps. *Euromoney*, September, 2–14.

17
Marketing to the Single European Market

To substitute for age-old rivalries the merging of essential interests; to create, by establishing an economic Community, the basis for broader and deeper community among people long divided by bloody conflict; and to lay the foundations for institutions which will give direction to a destiny henceforward shared

Preamble to the European Coal and Steel Community, Treaty of Paris, 1951.

Between 1957 and 1990 the European Community grew in size and changed in nature as its membership increased to twelve; and the Commission became more of a legal entity in its own right as individual member states including Britain edged closer towards the full economic integration of a free trade area without frontiers that was the overriding aim of its founding fathers.

The economic reality of a common market was given further impetus with the European Monetary System created in 1979 and the concerted effort by all member states to create by the end of 1992, a single unified market for goods and services. To this end, the Single European Act was agreed and signed by the governments of all member states in 1986 and became law on 1 July 1987. Europe after perhaps decades of economic sluggishness had once again become an exciting place to live. The political developments that shook Eastern Europe apart in 1989, created a unified Germany in 1990 and so the political and economic commentators look again at the prospects for a single Europe in 1993. As will be seen in the following statistics, the European Community on its own is a redoubtable force in world trade. We have then to consider the further enlargement of this market with the incorporation of the EFTA countries, creating a new European Economic Area (EEA) which we will discuss later.

The size of the market is large and without frontiers and with standardization of controls on patents, trademarks and general business practices, this economic bloc is now the largest single trading bloc in the world, accounting for approximately 40 per cent of global trade. With a total market size of more than 325 million people, it outnumbers the USA, but with nine official languages as opposed to one. With a total land area less than 2 per cent of the total world size, the EC accounts for 7 per cent of global population but this is expected to decline to 4 per cent by 2020. An unequal importance in global trade therefore relative to its land size or population. The potential cost savings through standardization are great and may soon show the EC's current 38 per cent of global trade to be an acute understatement of the position.

The Single European Act has been a major amendment to the Treaty of Rome. It has been ratified by all national parliaments and has not only given impetus to a 'Europeanization' which was dreamt of by the founding fathers of the Community, it has also changed the institutions of the Community. The European Parliamentary elections of June 1989 gave the electorate in each country the opportunity to vote on the movement towards ever closer union of the peoples of Europe. It also appointed 518 members of parliament of a higher calibre than before to a European Parliament that had been given new powers. To understand these changes, a study of the background is necessary.

Background to the Community size, structure and direction

Many attempts were made in the years immediately after the second world war to create alliances which would make war a thing of the past. However, the refusal by the USSR to remove itself from the lands which it had just liberated from Nazi Germany inevitably soured this atmosphere and created the two political blocs of Europe, East and West, which then led to the creation in 1948 of the Brussels Treaty Organization, which was the forerunner of the North Atlantic Treaty Organization (NATO), to meet an immediate need for the defence of democracy. Also in 1948, there was the creation of the Organization for European Economic Co-operation (OEEC), the immediate predecessor of the OECD and in 1949 the Council of Europe. However, by this time, the regional European-wide organization of the United Nations: the Economic Commission for Europe, established in 1947, for the purpose of economic reconstruction in Europe had already been rendered inoperable by the now very real division of two camps within Europe: East and West and the onset of a Cold War between them.

Economic integration began properly in 1951 with the establishment of the European Coal and Steel Community (ECSC). Initiated by the French, it sought to end the historic rivalry between France and Germany, who shared the coal of the Saar Valley and the steel of the Ruhr Valley; and to make war between the two nations not only 'unthinkable but materially impossible'. The plan was to create, by the removal of trade barriers, a common market in coal, iron and steel, with free access to all members: West Germany, France, Italy, Holland, Belgium and Luxembourg. This was, therefore, the creation of a grouping to be known for years thereafter as the Six. The EC came into being on 1 January 1958.

The Treaty of Rome established the EC. This called for:

- a free trade area eliminating internal trade barriers,
- a customs union creating a common external tariff,
- a common market with free movement of the factors of production, and
- an economic union aiming at a unification of monetary and fiscal policy.

Common policies were also to be established in agriculture and transport. It also established the European Social Fund (ESF) and the European Investment Bank (EIB). A common commercial policy was also a declared aim, to make special and separate trading arrangements for the former colonial territories which were still under-developed.

Assuming that there is a spectrum of international integration (Holland, 1980), at one end of the scale there is the independent national economy and at the other end is the economy which has become so completely integrated that it amounts in practice to a region in another wider economy. Between these extremes are five main stages of integration including:

1 A free trade area in which internal tariffs are abolished but countries' previous tariffs *vis-à-vis* other countries are maintained.

2 A customs union where a common external tariff on products is established, in addition to internal tariff abolition.

3 A common market in which restrictions to the movement of labour and capital between member states are abolished.

4 An economic union in which some national policies are harmonized in spheres other than tariffs, or labour and capital movements, but remain administered by the constituent member states.

5 Economic federalism in which certain key policies are administered by a central federal authority, rather than by the member states, and in which the previously independent national currencies are merged in a single common currency (or, on a weaker definition, bound in rigid and nominally invariable exchange ratios).

The period 1958–69 was a so-called transitional period but by this time, although the mechanism was still suffering from a number of imperfections it had also had its successes. Thus, in 1970 the members voted for the Community to have a source of income of its own. The first enlargement took place in 1973 with the UK, Ireland and Denmark. Greece then joined in 1981 and Portugal and Spain became members with effect from 1 January 1986. Each new member has, on accession, been given a number of years to make the transition to full membership of the EC; this transition meaning the dismantling of trade ties and tariff barriers.

The Community comprises of three separate legal entities:

● The European Coal and Steel Community (ECSC).
● The European Economic Community (EEC or Common Market).
● The European Atomic Energy Community (Euratom).

It is administered and controlled by institutions common to all three: Parliament, Council of Members; Commission; Court of Justice and Court of Auditors. An Economic and Social Committee acts in an advisory capacity.

Changes resulting from the Single European Act have given Parliament the power to review certain Council decisions. Yet the Parliament is still in Strasbourg, the Members with their offices and the Commission in Brussels and their constituencies back home in their member country. Parliament has been given new powers so as to give a second reading to all legislation. Instead of being simply a 'rubber stamp' for the Commission, Parliament has the right to amend or reject proposed legislation put before it. The Council of Members also works on a slightly different basis in that now a majority is necessary rather than unanimity. This serves to streamline the functioning of the EC as a whole.

Economic size and potential of the Community

The Community has conspicuously failed so far to reduce the inequalities among its present members. Unemployment remains unacceptably high in peripheral areas. The second expansion of the EC meant taking in countries where the average GDP per head is not much

Table 17.1 European Community in world trade (US dollars)

	Exports									Imports								
	1982	1983	1984	1985	1986	1987	1988	1989	1990	1982	1983	1984	1985	1986	1987	1988	1989	1990
IFS world total (billions)	1733.5	1681.9	1783.5	1808.1	1990.6	2342.1	2694.4	2906.6	3311.2	1803.0	1748.3	1862.8	1878.3	2056.1	2408.0	2873.5	3005.6	3448.8
DOTS world total (billions)	1720.5	1681.3	1786.6	1811.5	1978.8	2353.3	2707.5	2913.9	3334.6	1793.4	1738.5	1849.7	1890.3	2063.7	2933.0	2793.1	3000.3	3440.2
Belgium/Luxembourg	55,805	54,410	54,954	56,324	71,056	86,249	98,079	104.18	125.25	51,121	50,485	51,086	54,007	68,987	83,107	92,823	98.88	117.52
Denmark	15,490	15,265	16,070	17,501	21,791	24,408	25,680	25.97	30.79	15,418	15,928	16,173	16,981	20,901	25,233	27,736	28.24	34.63
France	113,173	103,393	103,400	106,657	123,877	152,744	172,701	189.06	228.25	97,889	95,642	96,017	100,797	122,459	146,476	167,079	179.49	218.45
Germany	135,814	136,357	137,858	143,252	175,846	209,418	233,754	246.31	317.20	173,252	165,691	167,492	181,992	237,561	287,745	318,123	330.47	399.76
Greece	11,519	10,523	10,822	10,845	11,044	12,677	14,715	16.11	19.04	5,609	5,777	5,969	5,905	6,414	7,654	8,302	8.98	9.48
Ireland	9,283	8,865	9,288	9,625	11,004	13,094	15,196	16.79	19.81	8,265	8,474	9,080	9,939	12,074	15,464	18,364	19.75	23.06
Italy	77,705	71,499	76,161	79,046	89,246	113,249	127,365	135.93	163.56	72,967	73,666	63,645	77,615	97,051	116,502	129,827	139.93	169.38
Netherlands	76,740	74,341	75,431	77,649	85,161	102,793	113,587	124.38	145.48	67,768	67,501	69,481	71,677	81,797	95,325	107,067	113.65	136.96
Portugal	8,682	7,720	7,218	7,056	8,943	12,952	16,186	18.26	22.91	4,286	4,662	5,437	6,009	7,829	9,850	11,238	13.28	17.24
Spain	28,688	27,516	26,588	28,255	33,754	47,265	57,176	66.06	79.99	21,358	21,467	23,757	25,503	28,562	34,789	40,740	43.17	53.87
UK	93,670	93,716	98,988	100,753	117,198	142,335	171,027	182.41	201.95	97,185	92,182	96,149	101,175	108,669	126,219	140,957	145.27	174.75
EC total (billions)	626.5	603.6	616.7	636.9	748.9	917.1	1045.4	1125.46	1354.23	615.1	600.4	614.2	651.5	792.3	947.7	1062.3	1121.11	1355.1
EC % IFS	36.1	35.8	34.5	35.2	37.6	39.1	38.7	38.7	40.8	34.1	34.3	32.9	34.6	38.5	39.3	36.9	37.3	39.3
% of DOTS world total	36.4	35.9	34.5	35.1	37.8	38.9	38.6	38.6	40.6	34.2	34.5	33.2	34.4	38.3	38.9	38.0	37.3	39.3

Source International Monetary Fund (1991) *Direction of Trade Statistics* (December), Washington, DC.

IFS – International Financial Statistics

DOTS – Direction of Trade Statistics

over half that in the Community in general, though at purchasing parities rather more. This means any serious policy commitment on equalization of incomes requires transfers from north to south.

In population, Greece, Spain and Portugal added 21 per cent to the population of the Nine while in 1973 the UK, Denmark and Ireland added 33 per cent to the then Community of Six. However, Greece, Spain and Portugal brought no Commonwealth and fewer cheap food complications. At the same time it has to be recognized that their accession into membership comes in time of recession rather than boom, and that these three countries are poorer and therefore likely to be more onerous partners than the UK, Denmark and Ireland. Greece, Spain and Portugal are highly competitive in traditional industries, extending in the case of Spain to steel and ships as well as textiles and leather goods. Spain and Greece are at an important stage in their industrial growth when they need to move from reliance on the traditional industries, such as textiles, to more advanced ones influenced by product innovation and specialization. Spain, which is in many ways comparable to Italy with a time-lag of a few years, is well advanced in this direction, but is still relatively weak in capital goods and more complex chemicals, let alone the high technology area. Greece has much further to go; and there is general agreement that for Portugal the distance may be too great to cover without substantial aid and time. Meanwhile, Hungary, Poland and Czechoslovakia (CSFR) signed a treaty with the EC in December 1991 making them associate members of the Community and creating the opportunity for full membership within ten years. Austria and Sweden are now keen to join the EC and have implemented national legislation to bring them into line with EC standards. Switzerland and Norway are also both contemplating membership and the Swiss have promised a national referendum on the subject. In any event, on 1 January 1993, two-thirds of the provisions of the Single Market will also apply to Switzerland, Austria, Sweden, Norway, Finland and Iceland.

Nevertheless, there are problems pending over:

- *Migrant labour,* given income differentials between the member states.
- *Agriculture* with the Mediterranean region including many underprivileged areas. There is the problem of a present wine surplus added to the fact that Spain is, too, a major wine producer. In fruit and vegetables, it is likely also that Spain and Greece will make inroads into this market which has been the preserve of Italy, France and Holland. There is, too, the question as to where Germany may buy its bananas.
- *Finance.* One could view the southern enlargement as a useful way of forcing a rich Europe to transfer large sums to the poorer states on its periphery but the unification of Germany has diverted attention away from these desirable objectives. Internally, the new Germany is trying to rebuild the economy of the newly acquired Six East German *lander* and without Germany's participation there is little likelihood of a redistribution of wealth within the Community. With regard to finance, there are a number of unknowns such as whether the problem of the Community Budget will resolve itself or whether there will be a radical re-alignment of the CAP but these problems have been swept aside for the moment as the pace quickens towards the unification of the Single European Market.
- *Foreign policy.* An EC policy requires uniformity and conformity. It will require all members to discipline themselves towards the aim of European unity. There will be little scope for opportunistic foreign policy on behalf of just one member state. The EC is a legal person able to conclude agreements with governments and international associations in its own right.

Basic statistics on the European Community and its twelve member states
comparison between the European Community (EUR 12), the USA and the Soviet Union

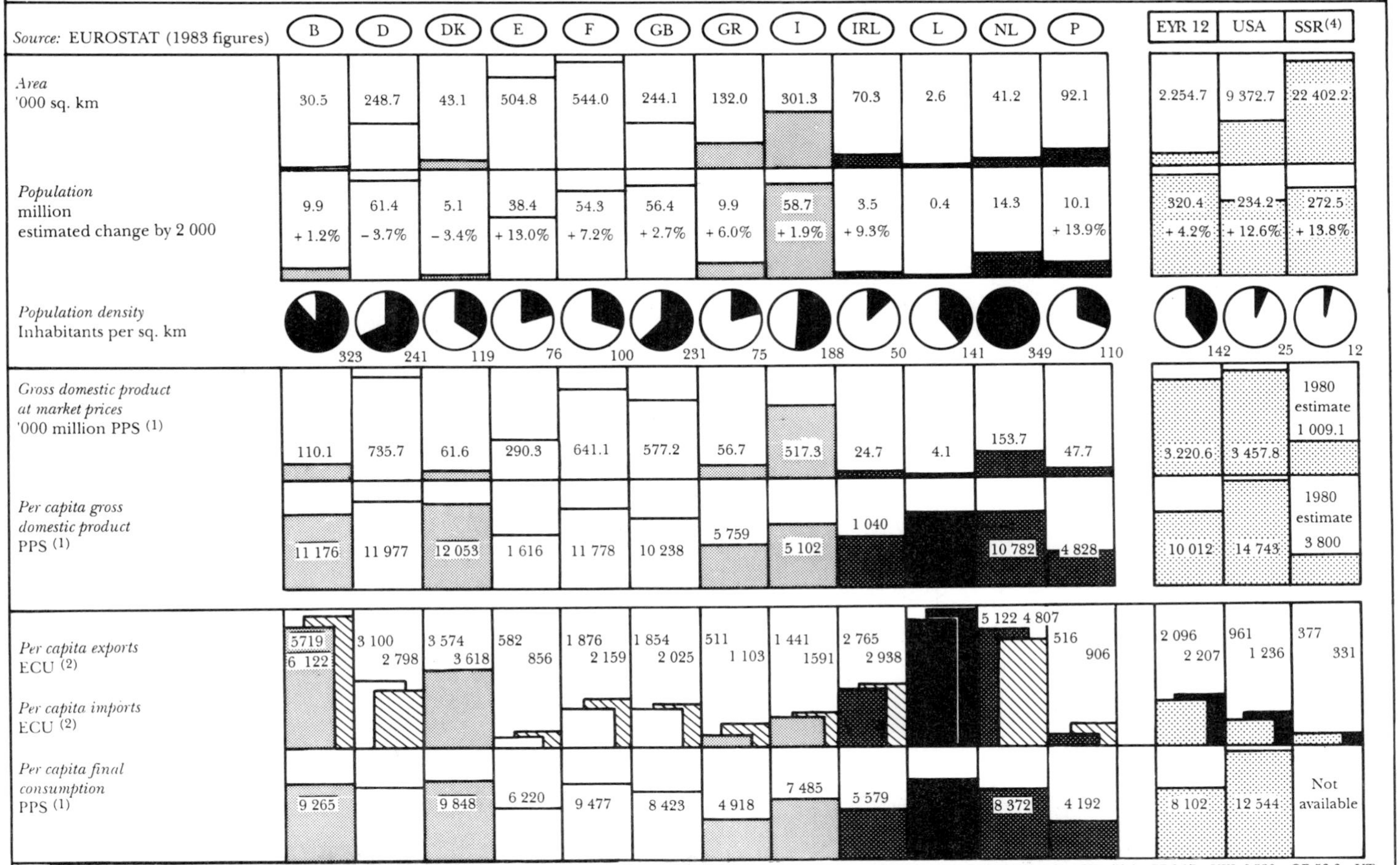

Source: EUROSTAT (1983 figures)	B	D	DK	E	F	GB	GR	I	IRL	L	NL	P	EUR 12	USA	SSR(4)
Area '000 sq. km	30.5	248.7	43.1	504.8	544.0	244.1	132.0	301.3	70.3	2.6	41.2	92.1	2 254.7	9 372.7	22 402.2
Population million	9.9	61.4	5.1	38.4	54.3	56.4	9.9	58.7	3.5	0.4	14.3	10.1	320.4	234.2	272.5
estimated change by 2 000	+ 1.2%	– 3.7%	– 3.4%	+ 13.0%	+ 7.2%	+ 2.7%	+ 6.0%	+ 1.9%	+ 9.3%		+ 13.9%		+ 4.2%	+ 12.6%	+ 13.8%
Population density Inhabitants per sq. km	323	241	119	76	100	231	75	188	50	141	349	110	142	25	12
Gross domestic product at market prices '000 million PPS (1)	110.1	735.7	61.6	290.3	641.1	577.2	56.7	517.3	24.7	4.1	153.7	47.7	3 220.6	3 457.8	1980 estimate 1 009.1
Per capita gross domestic product PPS (1)	11 176	11 977	12 053	1 616	11 778	10 238	5 759	5 102	1 040		10 782	4 828	10 012	14 743	1980 estimate 3 800
Per capita exports ECU (2)	5 719	3 100	3 574	582	1 876	1 854	511	1 441	2 765		5 122	516	2 096	961	377
Per capita imports ECU (2)	6 122	2 798	3 618	856	2 159	2 025	1 103	1 591	2 938		4 807	906	2 207	1 236	331
Per capita final consumption PPS (1)	9 265	9 848		6 220	9 477	8 423	4 918	7 485	5 579		8 372	4 192	8 102	12 544	Not available

(1) PPS = Purchasing power standard: a standard unit representing an identical volume of goods and services for each country. 1 PPS = BFR 37.2 – OM 2.27 – DKR 8.36 – PTA 78.1 – FF 6.17 – UKL 0.520 – OR 53.6 – UT 1036 – IRL 0.585 – UFR 37.7 – HFL 2.45 – ESC 48.0 – USO 0.947

(2) 1 ECU (3.2 1987) = BFR 42.67 – OM 2.06 – DKR 7.79 – PTA 145.81 – FF 6.87 – UKL 0.75 – OR 151.09 – LIT 1466.70 – IRL 0.78 – HFL 2.32 – ESC 160.43 – USO 1.15.

(3) Including Northern Ireland   (4) SSR = Union of Soviet Socialist Republics   (5) Belgium and Luxembourg

Figure 17.1

Marketing by population concentration: the 'Golden Triangle'

Over three-fifths of the Community population and of its GNP are found in a comparatively small area outlined in Figure 17.2, which is some five to six times better off than some outlying areas of the Community. This is obviously of interest to companies geared towards the mass market. Most important languages within the EC are English and French. Radio Luxembourg broadcasts in both of these languages plus others as well, to an audience which encompasses nearly all the inhabitants of the most populous and wealthy conurbations forming the 'Golden Triangle'. Most of this region is now also covered by satellite television increasing the possibilities for standardization of advertising even further, provided the member states and their peoples will accept it.

From a British perspective, this so-called Golden Triangle could well be challenged for including within it Leeds, Liverpool, Manchester and Birmingham, all of which are industrial cities which have 'peaked', most noticeably Liverpool. The most affluent areas are in London and the South of England. Hence the talk of a North/South divide within Britain. Liverpool has had very high levels of unemployment relative to any other city since the mid-1970s. Its industrial base has been much eroded as has its port which now only handles a fraction of the tonnage which it used to know. Leeds and Manchester are slightly different. Both have suffered from the slump in the world textile trade while Birmingham, being more dependent on the automobile industry, although also in recession, has perhaps suffered slightly less than the rest of this group, all of whom are struggling manfully to recover from a recession with declining industries.

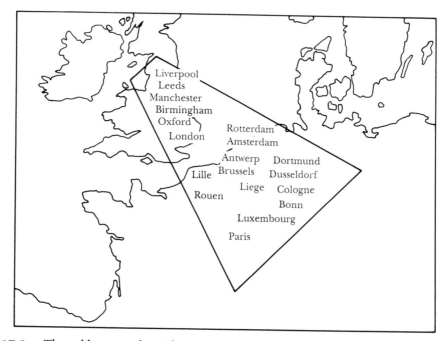

Figure 17.2   *The golden triangle of the EC*
Source   Drew, J. (1983) *Doing Business in the European Community*, 2nd edn, Butterworths, London, p. 83

Table 17.2

Cluster 1: UK and Ireland
- Northeastern Europe
- Average income ($11,450)
- Age profiles average of EC
- Common language (English)

Cluster 2: Central and Northern France, Southern Belgium, Central Germany, and Luxembourg
- Central Europe
- Average income ($15,470)
- Low proportion of middle-aged people and high proportion of older people
- French and German languages

Cluster 3: Spain and Portugal
- Southwestern Europe
- Young population
- Lower than average income ($6,530)
- Spanish and Portuguese languages

Cluster 4: Southern Germany, Northern Italy, Southeastern France (and Austria if it joins)
- Central Europe
- High proportion of middle-aged people
- Higher than average income ($16,740)
- German, French, and Italian languages

Cluster 5: Greece and Southern Italy
- Southeastern Europe
- Lower than average income ($7,610)
- Young population
- Greek and Italian languages

Cluster 6: Denmark, Northern Germany, The Netherlands, and Northern Belgium (and Switzerland, Iceland, Sweden, Norway, Finland if they join)
- Northern Europe and Switzerland
- Very high income ($19,420)
- High proportion of middle-aged people
- Multilingual: Scandinavian, French, Italian, and German languages

---

Source   Ryans, J. K., and Rau P. A. (1990) *Marketing Strategies for the New Europe: A North American Perspective on 1992.* American Marketing Association, Chicago.

Instead of viewing this as one market with a single area of affluence and relative degrees of poverty, Ryans and Rau (1990) identify six consumer clusters within this Community, each of which transcends national boundaries (see Table 17.2).

Regional variation within the Community

The free movement of capital, goods, services and individuals within the Community will have some regional implications. Doubtless there will be a reallocation of resources within the Community as a result, some resources being diverted from one region to another while still new ones are created. There are some important implications here.

The disparity between the regions is not only self-evident but has come to the attention of the EC. The Single European Act commits the Community to a policy of cohesion and convergence towards the regions. The European Regional Development Fund (ERDF) founded in 1975 received new powers towards that end on 1 January 1989. Previously, as much as two-thirds of the Community budget went on agricultural subsidies. The other area of EC funding is the Social Fund.

The problem is that 70 million people representing more than 20 per cent of the population of the EC live in areas where the per capita GDP is less than 75 per cent of the EC average. To correct this imbalance, funding for the ERDF has been stepped up from 4.8 per cent of the Community budget in 1975 to 6.1 per cent in 1979; 7.3 per cent in 1981; 8.6 per cent in 1986 and 9.7 per cent in 1989 amounting to 4.4 billion ECUs.

There are six types of regions recognized by the EC as outlined by Mellors and Copperthwaite (1990).

1 Regions lagging behind the rest of the Community. Low income, low productivity, high unemployment and dominant agricultural sector.
2 Declining industrial regions where aid is given to create new employment opportunities.
3 Agricultural regions. Only 9 per cent of the EC labour force works in agriculture but this is perhaps three times the UK figure which has a very high productivity rate in agriculture. These regions in question, however, exhibit the following characteristics:

- low productivity and small size of holdings
- low level of economic activity relative to other regions, and
- dependency on agriculture

4 Urban problem areas. Approximately 50 per cent of the EC population lives close to a town of 200,000 or more inhabitants. Problems arise from rapid population growth, high unemployment and low incomes relative to the EC average.
5 Peripheral regions. Relative isolation from the remainder of the Community creates small dispersed populations with higher costs because of transportation and small markets as in island communities. These account for 33 per cent of the EC population but more than 55 per cent of its area, 29 per cent of its employment and less than 25 per cent of its GDP.
6 Frontier regions as in two groups:

- those within the Community between members states.
- those between member states and countries outside the Community.

The Community produces a Synthetic Index that classifies regions by the intensity of their economic and social problems (see Table 17.3). The index is weighted by the following factors: GDP per head in PPS (25 per cent); GDP per person employed in ECU (25 per cent); unemployment adjusted for under-employment (40 per cent); prospective labour force change until 1990 (10 per cent). In Table 17.3 the lower the index number, the greater the intensity of regional problems (Mellors and Copperthwaite, 1990).

Table 17.3 Synthetic index of the intensity of regional problems in the European Community (1981–1985)

Rank	Region		Value	Rank	Region		Value
1	Basilicata	(I)	36.9	46	West Yorkshire	(UK)	84.0
2	Calabria	(I)	38.0	47	Corse	(F)	84.2
3	Andalucia	(ESP)	38.8	48	Heref. & Worcs., Warwicks	(UK)	85.7
4	Extremadura	(ESP)	39.2	49	Languedoc-Roussillon	(F)	87.2
5	Canarias	(ESP)	46.1	50	Cleveland, Durham	(UK)	88.1
6	Ireland	(I)	47.6	51	Namur prov.	(B)	89.2
7	Sardegna	(I)	49.4	52	Northumb., Tyne & Wear	(UK)	89.8
8	Castilla Mancha	(ESP)	50.0	53	Poitou-Charentes	(F)	90.7
9	Thrakis	(GR)	50.5	54	Limburg (N)	(NL)	91.4
10	Molise	(I)	50.6	55	Liège prov.	(B)	91.6
11	Murcia	(ESP)	51.3	56	Weser-Ems	(D)	92.2
12	Galicia	(ESP)	53.8	57	Friesland	(NL)	92.3
13	Ipirou	(GR)	54.4	58	Greater Manchester	(UK)	93.0
14	Comm. Valenciana	(ESP)	54.6	59	Bor. Cen. Fif. Lot. Tay.	(UK)	93.0
15	Sicilia	(I)	54.9	60	Lincolnshire	(UK)	95.0
16	Castilla Leon	(ESP)	55.0	61	Basse-Normandie	(F)	95.3
17	Campania	(I)	55.7	62	Lancashire	(UK)	95.8
18	Pelop. & Dit. Ster. Ell.	(GR)	56.9	63	Overijssel	(NL)	96.0
19	Puglia	(I)	57.2	64	Gwent, MSW, Glamorg.	(UK)	96.3
20	Thessalias	(GR)	57.2	65	Gelderland	(NL)	96.4
21	Catalunia	(ESP)	57.7	66	Kent	(UK)	96.5
22	Pais Vasco	(ESP)	58.3	67	Nord-Pas-de-Calais	(F)	96.6
23	Asturias	(ESP)	58.4	68	Noord-Brabant	(NL)	96.7
24	Portugal	(POR)	58.4	69	Cornwall, Devon	(UK)	96.8
25	Kritis	(GR)	58.4	70	Oberpfalz	(D)	96.9
26	Anatolikis Makedonias	(GR)	59.0	71	Bretagne	(F)	98.0
27	Aragon	(ESP)	59.5	72	Luxembourg (B)	(B)	98.5
28	Cantabria	(ESP)	59.7	73	Leics., Northants	(UK)	98.9
29	Madrid	(ESP)	59.8				
30	Navarra	(ESP)	59.9	74	Pays de la Loire	(F)	100.6
31	Anat. Stereas ke Nisun	(GR)	61.9	75	Derbys., Notts.	(UK)	100.7
32	Kent. ke Dit. Makedonias	(GR)	63.0	76	Highlands, Islands	(UK)	101.2
33	Northern Ireland	(UK)	64.4	77	Oost-Vlaanderen	(B)	101.3
34	Rioja	(ESP)	65.9	78	Vest for Storebaelt	(DK)	101.4
35	Baleares	(ESP)	66.8	79	Umbria	(I)	101.7
36	Nison Anatolikou Egeou	(GR)	67.1	80	Groningen	(NL)	102.0
				81	East Anglia	(UK)	102.2
37	West Midlands County	(UK)	67.8	82	Trentino-Alto Adige	(I)	102.4
38	Merseyside	(UK)	74.8	83	Ost for Storebaelt	(DK)	102.9
39	Abruzzi	(I)	75.7	84	Saarland	(D)	103.6
				85	Picardie	(F)	103.7
40	Dum. & Gal., Strathclyde	(UK)	76.2	86	Marche	(I)	104.1
41	Limburg (B)	(B)	78.1	87	Clwyd, Dyfed, Gwyn, Powys	(UK)	104.2
42	Hainaut	(B)	81.2	88	Niederbayern	(D)	104.3
43	Salop, Staffordshire	(UK)	82.1	89	Haute-Normandie	(F)	104.5
44	Humberside	(UK)	82.4	90	Trier	(D)	105.3
45	South Yorkshire	(UK)	83.2	91	West-Vlaanderen	(B)	106.1

Table 17.3   continued

Rank	Region		Value	Rank	Region		Value
92	Lazio	(I)	106.3	126	Oberfranken	(D)	117.5
93	Hants., Isle of Wight	(UK)	106.4	127	E. Suss., Surrey, W. Suss.	(UK)	117.6
94	Bremen	(D)	106.8	128	Zeeland	(NL)	118.5
95	Essex	(UK)	108.3	129	Cumbria	(UK)	118.7
96	Brabant	(B)	108.4	130	Antwerpen prov. (B)		119.8
97	Auvergne	(F)	108.5	131	Noord-Holland	(NL)	120.1
98	Aquitaine	(F)	109.0	132	Piemonte	(I)	120.1
99	Limousin	(F)	109.2	133	Schleswig-Holstein	(D)	120.4
100	North Yorkshire	(UK)	109.2	134	Hannover	(D)	120.8
101	Veneto	(I)	109.5	135	Giessen	(D)	120.9
102	Avon, Glos., Wilts.	(UK)	109.8	136	Zuid-Holland	(NL)	121.8
103	Midi-Pyrénées	(F)	109.8	137	Emilia-Romagna	(I)	128.1
104	Berks., Bucks., Oxon	(UK)	109.8	138	Koeln	(D)	129.8
105	Provence-Alpes-C.d'Azur	(F)	110.4	139	Rhone-Alpes	(F)	130.1
106	Lorraine	(F)	110.5	140	Schwaben	(D)	130.6
107	Lueneburg	(D)	110.5	141	Liguria	(I)	130.8
108	Bourgogne	(F)	110.9	142	Grampian	(UK)	132.6
109	Muenster	(D)	110.9	143	Lombardia	(I)	132.8
110	Champagne-Ardennes	(F)	112.2				
111	Utrecht	(NL)	112.4	144	Tuebingen	(D)	134.8
112	Arnsberg	(D)	113.0	145	Freiburg	(D)	134.9
113	Dorset, Somerset	(UK)	113.4	146	Greater London	(UK)	135.0
114	Friuli-Venezia Giulia	(I)	113.9	147	Dusseldorf	(D)	136.3
115	Beds., Herts	(UK)	114.0	148	Alsace	(F)	136.4
116	Franche-Comté	(F)	115.0	149	Mittelfranken	(D)	136.6
117	Braunschweig	(D)	115.4	150	Hovedstadsregionen	(DK)	141.4
118	Kassel	(D)	115.7	151	Berlin (West)	(D)	141.7
119	Koblenz	(D)	115.8	152	Valle d'Aosta	(I)	142.4
120	Drenthe	(NL)	115.9	153	Rheinhessen-Pfalz	(D)	143.4
121	Toscana	(I)	116.0	154	Luxembourg (GD)	(L)	144.2
122	Cheshire	(UK)	116.1	155	Karlsruhe	(D)	151.3
				156	Ile de France	(F)	151.5
123	Detmold	(D)	116.7	157	Hamburg	(D)	158.7
124	Centre	(F)	117.0	158	Stuttgart	(D)	160.5
125	Unterfranken	(D)	117.1	159	Oberbayern	(D)	165.7
				160	Darmstadt	(D)	171.8

*The lower the index value, the greater the intensity of regional problem. (EUR 12 = 100)
Source   *The Regions of the Enlarged Community: Third Periodic Report on the Social and Economic Situation and Development of the Regions of the Community* (CB-49-87-381-EN-C), Luxembourg, 1987.

Table 17.4 Priority sectors

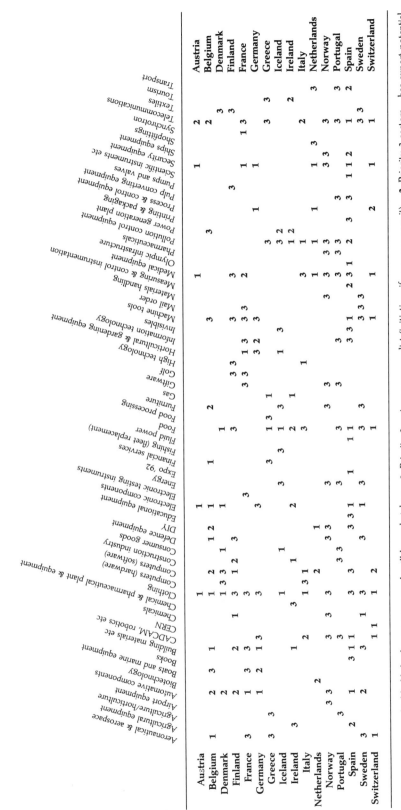

1 Priority 1 sectors – highly likely that initiative work will be undertaken.   2 Priority 2 sectors – reserve list (initiatives if resources permit).   3 Priority 3 sectors – has export potential, unlikely any initiative work

Note The priority sectors identified in this chart are regarded by the British Embassies as offering opportunities for UK business. All highlighted sectors have export potential, but the grading 1 (best) to 3 indicates an assessment of market scope for exporters. There are likely to be special initiatives in sectors given a category 1 assessment. For more information on these initiatives, contact: John Slate, DTI, Exports to Europe Branch, Room 374, 1-19 Victoria Street, London SW1H 0ET. Telephone: 071-215 5238.

Source Department of Trade and Industry (1990), *Single Market News*, (9), 20.

Decision-making bodies

These are the European Commission; European Parliament; Economic and Social Committee; Council of Members and European Court of Justice. The Commission is divided into twenty-three Directorate-Generals which are headed by seventeen Commissioners.

In addition, there are said to be 2,000 committees, sub-committees and working parties. In normal practice, the Commission would also consult where appropriate with COPA, the grouping of agricultural organizations and with UNICE, the industrial association.

Commissioners are appointed by the member governments for a once-renewable four-year renewable term, and are resident in Brussels. The main duty with which they are entrusted is to make proposals for Community action to the Council of Ministers. The President and

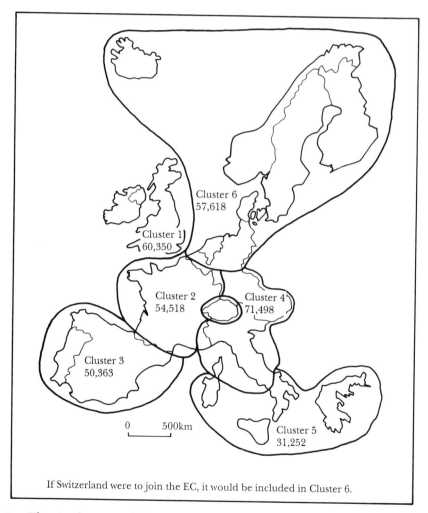

Figure 17.3   *The six clusters and their population*
Note   Figures are for 1990 and in 000's of people.
Source   Ryans, J.K., and Rau, P.A. (1990) *Marketing Strategies for New Europe: A North American Perspective on 1992*, American Marketing Association, Chicago

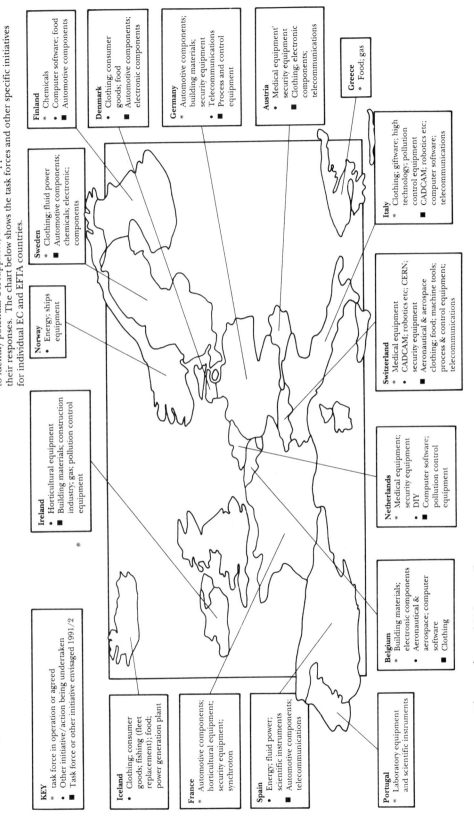

Figure 17.4 *The markets of Western Europe*
Source Department of Trade and Industry (1990) *Single Market News*, (9), 10

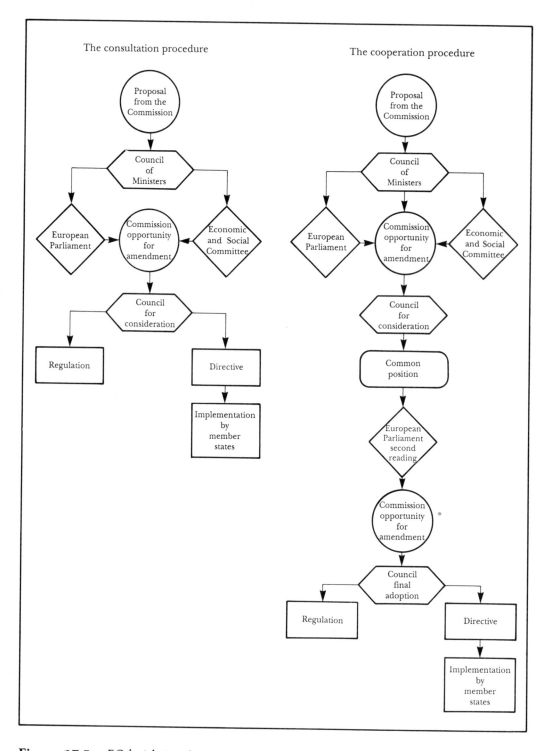

Figure 17.5   *EC legislation from start to finish (directives and regulations)*
Source   European Commission

Vice-President are chosen from among the seventeen and hold their offices for four-year renewable terms. The UK, Germany, France and Italy each nominate two Commissioners while the smaller states: Belgium, Holland, Ireland, Denmark and Luxembourg nominate one each. Spain has two, and Portugal and Greece one each.

Each Commissioner is responsible for a portfolio, although some will carry more than one portfolio. Each has a private office (cabinet) to which he makes the appointments. Invariably, the members appointed are of the same nationality as the Commissioner. His deputy is known as the *chef du cabinet*. Beneath the Commissioner, there will be one or more Director General – similar to the permanent head of a ministry – who is responsible for a broad policy area, and he will, in turn, have below him, Directors and Heads of Division. The need for Commissioners to be impartial at all times is enshrined in the Treaty of Rome, Article 157, which requires that Commissioners 'shall neither seek nor take instruction from any Government or from any other body.' However, as the Commission staff only employs 11,000 (including translators, interpreters and some 2,600 in the separate scientific and technological Joint Research Centre) as against perhaps 20,000 for a British Ministry it is not hard to see that the Commission can only hope to be effective if the governmental departments of its member states agree to administer its policies. If the Commissioners approve of the draft directive drawn up by a Directorate-General, after any necessary amendments, it is then proposed by the Commission as a draft directive to the Council of Ministers. This gives member states, through the Council of Ministers, the final say on whether the directive becomes law or not. It can, however, take years before legislation is accepted and becomes law. Curiously, the Single European Act gave an impetus to the Commission to resolve 286 obstacles to the proposed Single Market.

The Council of Ministers consists of a minister from each member-state government, and the ministers change according to the subjects on the agenda and the Council meeting taking place, e.g., Agricultural Council; Social Affairs Council where the appropriate number from each member state would be present. Ministers represent the interests of their own governments, but try to arrive at agreements which are in the Community interest. There is a system of qualified voting so that France, West Germany, Italy and the UK have ten votes each; Spain, eight; Holland, Belgium, Greece and Portugal five votes; Ireland and Denmark three; and Luxembourg two. For a qualified majority, fifty-four votes are required. The threat of being outvoted forces countries to make alliances and compromises that were not necessary when a simple veto was in place.

The Council of Ministers meets only for a certain number of days in a year, and are not resident in Brussels. Each member state takes a six-month turn to chair Council meetings, a national minister of foreign affairs being President of the Council during that period. There is a small permanent staff in Brussels but the main preparatory work is undertaken by the ambassadors and their embassy staff.

The ambassadors or representatives act as a link between the member countries and the Community. They meet in the Committee of Permanent Representatives known as COREPER. Over time, COREPER has become an important entity in its own right. The staff of COREPER are made up of civil servants seconded from their own government and experts. They service working parties, prepare agendas, and try to agree non-contentious proposals so that when the ministers attend much has already been agreed and only matters still in dispute need to be negotiated.

The European Council is a meeting of the heads of government and takes place three times per year. Contentious issues which have not been resolved at the Council of Ministers are discussed in the European Council. At the end of each Council, a communiqué is issued giving the broad outlines of what has been agreed. Scope for progress exists as the heads of governments are often also heads of state in certain cases. If the political will also exists for agreement to take place, then the Council is capable of meeting this challenge. Margaret Thatcher when in power tested the efficacy of this system on more than one occasion over the issue of British payments to the EC budget and the nature of European unity whether federal with sovereign governments or a full economic and monetary union with significant sovereign powers to be transferred to Brussels.

The Court of Justice is the ultimate interpreter of the treaties on which the EC is based and the final arbiter of disputes concerning secondary legislation whenever there is a query or disagreement about the meaning of a particular regulation, directive, or decision. Its rulings are binding and take precedence over the decisions of national courts. Each member state is represented by a judge. It is situated in Luxembourg with a staff of 460 and is totally different from the European Court of Human Rights in Strasbourg which is part of the Council of Europe. It arose out of the European Coal and Steel Community (ECSC) but now has a much wider brief. There are eleven judges, each appointed for six years. Hearings are in public but deliberations are in secret. A judge can only be removed by the unanimous vote of his colleagues to the effect that he is no longer capable of carrying out his duties. A quorum consists of seven judges; there must be an odd number sitting and decisions are reached by simple majority. The Court produces its own reports containing the basic facts of the case, the summing up by the Advocate-General, and the judgement. Companies on whom the Commission has imposed fines may appeal to the Court. The Court also gives preliminary rulings for the benefit of national courts. It may proceed against member states if a member state is not fulfilling its legal obligations. It reviews the legality of Community acts, and it settles disputes.

The European Court set a precedent in May 1985 when it gave a ruling against the Council of Ministers, finding them guilty of breaching the Treaty of Rome by failing to ensure freedom to provide transport services across the Community. The complaint has been made by the European Parliament supported by the Commission and it establishes for the first time that the Parliament can take the Council to court. It will be seen by parliamentarians as opening a new door to extending their influence over Community politics and policies. It was not an unqualified success, however. The Court did not support the contention of the European Parliament that the Council was at fault for failing to agree a common transport policy. The Court said that the Council had failed to take measures to comply with the Treaty of Rome which stipulated that freedom of services should be established within the twelve-year transitional period after the Treaty signature in 1957. It is a moral victory for the Parliament although impossible to enforce. The Council has been told that it is its duty to agree, but it can hardly be forced to do so. The Council therefore remains free to deal with most of the Commission's fourteen pending specific training proposals as it pleases. The Court did not accept the view of Advocate-General Lenz that the Council had a duty to reach a decision on such proposals as the weights and measurements of heavy goods vehicles, co-ordination of taxation of such vehicles, and harmonization of social measures in inland shipping. Nor did the Court accept the Dutch Government's proposal that it should transform freedom of transport services from a Treaty objective into directly applicable law, enforceable in national courts.

The European Parliament was greatly strengthened by the Single Act which previously only voted on money. It now had power to initiate legislation: amend or reject legislation rather than just give opinions as before. It still does not have an executive dependent on it and its power applies to the Commission not the Council.

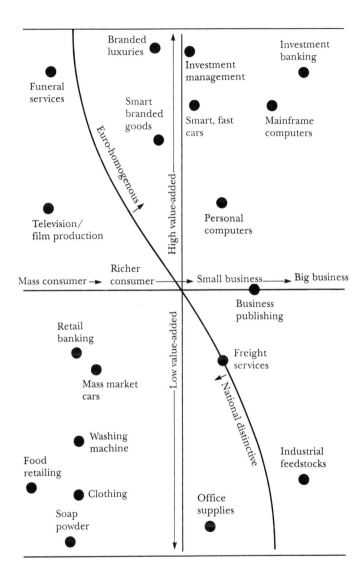

Figure 17.6   *The Colchester–Buchan diagram*
Source   Colchester, N., and Buchan, D. (1990), *Europower*, Economist Books and Random House, New York

Until 1981 the European Parliament held one-third of its sessions in Luxembourg and two-thirds in Strasbourg, in Eastern France. In 1981, it decided to hold no more sessions in Luxembourg, and this was upheld by the Court of Justice. However, more than three-quarters of the Parliamentary secretariat of approximately 2,600 are based in Luxembourg which means that they have to travel between Luxembourg and Strasbourg regularly but in the longer term it is most likely that the European Parliament will be based in Brussels. The first direct elections to the European Parliament were held in June 1979 and every five years thereafter. It is the only directly elected institution of the Community. There are now 518 members of the European Parliament who control eighteen important permanent committees which scrutinize Commission proposals and prepare reports. They have a consultative role in proposals emanating from the Commission and ultimately have the right to dismiss the government, i.e., the Commissioners, provided over half the members vote. They also have the right to request changes within the European Community budget allocation, and may even reject the budget as a whole. They vote on European laws sent from the Commission to the Council of Ministers and have the right to approve new members of the Community or new association agreements with outsiders.

The Economic and Social Committee is purely consultative. Its membership is appointed

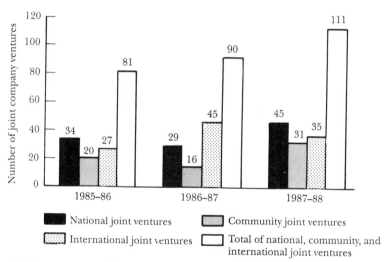

Figure 17.7   *Joint ventures in the European Community, 1985–88*
Source   Hufbauer, G.C. (1990) *Europe 1992: An American Perspective*, Brookings Institute, Washington, DC

Table 17.5   Significance of 1992

- Creation of European industrial standards
- Opening of public procurement markets
- Harmonization of company law
- Liberalization of services sector
- Freeing of capital movement
- Intellectual property law
- Approximation of indirect taxes
- Abolition of borders

for four years and currently numbers 156: twenty-four from France, West Germany, Italy and the UK; twelve from Belgium and Holland; nine from Denmark and Ireland; and six from Luxembourg. Its membership is wide: producers; workers; farmers; merchants; the professions; universities; consumer organizations; transport operators; or any appropriate interest group. Its members are selected by the Council from lists submitted by member states. No particular importance is assigned to its role. Its functions are more like an in-house opinion poll for the Council and Commission. Its decisions are reached in open debate in full sessions rather than by lobbying.

A market without frontiers

Colchester and Buchan (1990) have illustrated from their research which businesses are likely to be 'Euro-homogeneous' and which are likely to be 'national-distributive'. They differentiate first in terms of value-added. High value-added with either a company or a rich individual as customer means a product area can be branded and distributed across Europe without, as they say, an urgent need for local skills, local investment and local adaptation of the product. On the other hand, the cheaper the product, the closer to the customer, the more investment is required in local understanding, local product variation and local distribution. (See Figure 17.6.)

Yet frontiers also provide obstacles to trafficking in drugs; they prevent undesirable aliens and others including rabid dogs from entering the country; they help to counter terrorism and collect taxes. National police forces do not have powers as yet to cross frontiers traditionally regarded as inviolate.

The frontiers will be down for those within the Community. The question then arises of treatment of those without. Fears have been expressed of a Fortress Europe if protectionism were to hold sway in the event of a recession. These fears are discussed later in considering the views of those entering the EC from outside.

Harmonization measures for internal trade

The significance of 1992 is seen in Table 17.5, creating a new market greater than the USA or Japan which would streamline the efficiency of what is already the world's single largest trading bloc.

The White Paper of June 1985 spelled out 286 actions required to complete the internal market. The White Paper then is like an eight year plan which was the intention of President Jacques Delors, that it would take the time of two full Commissions to complete the internal market i.e. eight years. Delors was reappointed for a second term of office and has been the only President as yet to receive that distinction. Proposals had to be drafted in legal form to become Community law but had also to be ratified by the individual member states. Table 17.6 illustrates the three broad headings under which the changes were required:

- physical barriers,
- technical barriers, and
- fiscal barriers.

The main incentive was not only standardization and simplification of trade procedures but to certain politicians the inherent appeal of free market forces to work within Europe. This had

Table 17.6   The EC white paper June 1985 286 actions required in three areas

---

1 *Physical barriers*
   ● Control of goods: introduction of Single Administrative Document pending abolition of controls of internal frontiers in 1992.
   ● Control of individuals. Removal of immigration and passport controls.

2 *Technical barriers*
   ● Removal of all barriers of trade between member states.
   ● Dismantling of barriers to the free movement of goods, capital, services and workers.
   ● Mutual recognition of industrial standards creation of conditions for industrial cooperation.
   ● Common protection for intellectual and industrial property.
   ● Opening of public procurement

3 *Fiscal barriers*
   ● Approximation of indirect taxation – VAT rates and excise duties.
   ● Consequent removal of fiscal checks at frontiers.

Table 17.7   EC border administration costs (ECU millions)

Administration	7500
Delays	415–830
Business foregone	4500–1500
Government spending on intra-EC customs controls*	500–1000

---

*On 6-country basis: Belgium, France, Germany, Italy, Netherlands and the UK.
Source   Cecchini, P. (1988) *The European Challenge: 1992 – The Benefits of a Single Market*, Wildwood House, Aldershot, Hants, p. 9.

tangible benefits as Cecchini was to point to the actual costs of maintaining present systems with overladen bureaucracy. Cecchini pointed to the costs of administration as being 7.5 billion ECUs (approximately = US $1). Freeing these markets of burdensome administration would mean savings for business and greater competition as well. Member governments were therefore given carte blanche to wield the axe at any expenditure of this kind and at the same time receive widespread public acclaim for so doing. Another area was the potential price savings if price differentials were to be smoothed over the Community. Pharmaceuticals, telephones and motor vehicles were a few of the items selected for scrutiny as in Table 17.7.

Yet another but more contentious area is that of public procurement which Cecchini

Table 17.8 A typology of costs — resulting from divergent standards and regulations

For companies
- duplication of product development
- loss of potential economies of manufacturing scale
- competitive weakness on world markets and vulnerability on European markets as companies operate from a narrow national base

For public authorities
- duplication of certification and testing costs
- not getting value for money in public purchasing, whose non-competitive nature is often reinforced by national standards and certification

For consumers
- direct costs borne by companies and governments means higher prices
- direct and larger losses due to industry's competitive weakness and inefficient structure

Source Cecchini, P. (1988) *The European Challenge: 1992 — The Benefits of a Single Market,* Wildwood House, Aldershot, Hants.

estimated as being worth 15 per cent of Community GDP in 1986. Discounting that portion which falls outside contracted procedures, Cecchini pointed to a sizeable market of 240–340 billion ECUs, equivalent to 7–10 per cent of Community GDP. Cost savings of 8–19 billion ECUs for the five countries surveyed in 1984: Belgium, France, Germany, Italy and the UK would arise from:

1 The static trade effect meaning public authorities buying from the cheaper (i.e., foreign) suppliers (3–8 billion ECUs)
2 The competition effect creating a downward pressure on prices charged by domestic firms in previously closed sectors to strive to compete with foreign companies entering the market (1–3 billion ECU).
3 The restructuring effect. The longer run effect of economies of scale as industry reorganizes under the pressure of new competitive conditions (4–8 billion ECU). This saving is concentrated in certain high tech sectors such as computers, telecoms, and aerospace.

However, it would create a new European-wide competitive environment and Cecchini looked at the way in which this would affect key sectors in the short and longer term, as shown in Table 17.10.

Harmonization: the common commercial policy

In the period up to 1980 the Council of Ministers had adopted about 136 directives relating to industrial products and over fifty concerned with foodstuffs. The industrial products

Table 17.9 Potential price savings (%)

Pharmaceuticals	52 (FRG), 40 (UK)
Office equipment	12 (Fr), 27 (Italy)
Telephone switching	60 (Belg), 40 (Fr), 70 (FRG), 50 (Italy, UK)
Telephones	20 (Belg), 43 (Fr), 39 (FRG)
Electrical equipment	47 (Belg), 14 (Fr), 15 (FRG), 14 (Italy), 7 (UK)
Motor Vehicles*	13 (Fr), 4 (FRG), 10 (Italy), 9 (UK)
Coal	50 (FRG), 25 (UK)

*weighted averages

Source   Cecchini, P. (1988) *The European Challenge: 1992 − The Benefits of a Single Market,* Wildwood House, Aldershot, Hants.

include motor vehicles (approx. forty); metrology, i.e. measuring equipment; cosmetics; solvents and other dangerous substances; and electrical equipment. In the case of foodstuffs, directives govern their labelling, durability, additives as well as packaging (restriction on the use of PVC), presentation, advertising and composition. Additives have been subject to provisions specifying maximum levels. Much had therefore been done but there was still a long way to go since the Commission had given this figure. It was already a very time-consuming process. Also, technological progress renders existing standards obsolescent and therefore renewed effort has to be diverted into constantly bringing them up to date. The Community was therefore forced to adopt a speedier process in respect of agreeing common standards.

The new policy introduced was that of 'mutual recognition'. In other words, if a product was safe for use or consumption in one member state it was held then to be safe for use or consumption in all other member states of the Community. At a stroke, this abolished the long administrative delays and long complicated quarrels over the agreement of community standards. Community standards were now the standards agreed nationally. This proved to be a popular move in that it expedited the transition towards the Single Market. Politically it was astute as it was expedient and it gave decision making to member states.

Table 17.10 Main characteristics of some key markets

Product	Approx. EC market m ECUs	Estimated capacity utilization (%)	Significance of intra-EC trade
Boilers	2,000	20	negl
Turbine generators	2,000	60	negl
Locomotives	100	50–80	negl
Mainframe computers	10,000	80	medium to great
Public switching	7,000	approx. 70	medium
Telephones	5,000	90	negl

Source   Cecchini, (1988) *The European Challenge: 1992 − The Benefits of a Single Market,* Wildwood House, Aldershot, Hants.

However, although this meant that goods lawfully produced or marketed in one state should have access to all member states, there were still:

- health, safety and environmental protection barriers,
- CoCom barriers to intra-EC trade, and
- limits to the portability of social security benefits, pensions, etc.

Controversies raged over the export of British lamb and beef to France arising from the incidence of BSE or 'mad cow disease' in Britain. Similarly German 'purity' laws on beer were undermined when it became clear that British beer could now be sold in Germany. Each viewed the other as lax in a certain dimension but now each member states' standards had to be respected and in all Community markets.

Certification procedures also created problems. The definition of what is a British, French or German car becomes more obscure once one takes note of the multinational sourcing that takes place in the automobile industry for example. The British Association of Chambers of Commerce allows for 'the last substantial stage of manufacture taking place in Britain' as sufficient to warrant the product in question being labelled of British origin. This created real practical difficulties as well as legal difficulties. Taking the example of Nissan cars manufactured in Sunderland, Britain - at what stage, if any, may these cars be termed 'of British origin'? Measures such as percentage of value-added; and percentage of volume of components sourced locally both give different figures. At stake for Japanese manufacturers like Nissan is entry to the Community-wide market. If the car is Japanese it may be subject to voluntary restraint agreements as well as Community external tariffs. If, on the other hand, a Japanese car made in Britain is British then exports to say France are of British cars and quotas on voluntary restraint agreements between France and Japan are unaffected. In view of the importance of the economic stakes involved, both France and Italy have fought vociferously to block Japanese imports into the Community.

Single Administrative Document

Introduced into the UK on 1 January 1988, the Single Administrative Document (SAD) replaced literally hundreds of separate export, transit and import forms which could now be computerized and even carry an electronic signature.

In practice, whenever goods moved between EC member states three separate declarations were needed and these varied between states. SAD is a very necessary step towards substantial reform in intra-Community trade prior to 1992. SAD can be used as an export, transit and import declaration for any consignment moving within the Community. At the same time, a number of options for clearance were introduced which include the creation of Inland Clearance Depots (ICDs), facilities to clear goods at traders' own premises and simplified procedures for exports whereby goods may be cleared on the basis of minimum data with full declarations being provided subsequently. One innovation was the introduction of Customs Procedure Codes to identify the customs regime to and from which the goods are moving, e.g., warehousing, freeport, etc. SAD required seventeen acceptances to come into force. Now in force it will enable greater and better information than ever before to be placed before GATT negotiations, for example. It is important to emphasize that the SAD was not a relaxation in controls but a change in paperwork. However, this very necessary change in administrative procedures will lead to greater efficiency in trade with and within the Community.

TARIC customs tariff

This new tariff came in alongside the SAD on 1 January 1988. Previously, the EC used a common customs tariff (CCT) to specify rates of customs duty and a separate but related system (NIMEXE) to collect trade statistics. Both are based on the Customs Cooperation Council Nomenclature (CCCN) which had become outdated.

A single goods description system has to satisfy the requirements of international trade. This means transport operators, governments and manufacturers. Inevitably, there will be pressures also for the ability of this system to accept computerization. A system has to meet a variety of different needs: to determine freight charges; collect customs duties; compute national production and international trade statistics and within industry, identify products. Technological development led to an ever increasing number of products being bundled into the 'other' category, as there was no specific category for them. As a result of these divergent pressures, the Customs Co-operation Council finally introduced after lengthy consultation with many international bodies, a Harmonized Commodity Description and Coding System. This system which came to be known as the Harmonized System was adopted on 14 June 1983.

The HS incorporates products which had not been invented when the CCCN had been developed. It also offered more detail than other systems. Nine thousand eight-digit headings of the CCCN are replaced by 14,000 eleven-digit headings. As a result of this new system, it is held to be easier to see whether goods are subject to quotas, tariff preferences; surveillance; countervailing duties; or anti-dumping duties to name but a few of the possible uses. It also introduced problems of reclassifying goods and products which may now with reclassification become liable for duty.

Patents, trademarks and standards

A European Patent Office was established in Munich in 1978. It is anticipated that a Community-wide patent will replace national patents before too long. Meanwhile, it should be noted that the Commission opposes the use of trademarks, patent licences and know-how agreements as a means of market protection. European standards are being established by the European Standards Organization CEN (European Committee for Standardization) and CENELEC (European Committee for Electro-Technical Standardization). These consist of over 160 committees presently dominated by French and German representatives. These standards are incorporated into national standards rather than being replaced by them. The German DIN organization (Deutsches Institut für Normung) is already the European leader. CEN and CENELEC are disappearing meanwhile under the weight of their own bureaucracy.

Competition policy within the EC

The foundation stone of the EC being free trade, it is not surprising then to find the Commission implacably opposed to all forms of cartel and collusion which 'have as their object or effect, the prevention, restriction or distortion of competition within the common market.'

Community competition rules are enshrined in Articles 85 and 86 of the Treaty of Rome which proscribe certain agreements, concerted practices and abuses of dominant positions which distort free trade in the Community. This applies to agreements which have as their object the restriction of competition as well as agreements which result in the restriction of competition. The removal of internal governmental restrictions that impede the free flow of goods, persons, services and capital is central to the Treaty of Rome which was to some extent superseded by the Single European Act.

In 1962, there were eighteen national trading monopolies in the Community covering goods ranging from potassium, gunpowder and explosives to alcohol and tobacco. Partly by negotiation and partly by taking recalcitrant offenders to the European Court, the Commission has frequently achieved the objective laid down by the European Treaties, namely the abolition of discrimination between nationals of the member states in the procurement and marketing of goods. Despite recent advances, minor problems still exist, notably in the marketing of tobacco in Italy and France. In Greece, which joined the EC in 1981 the dismantling of state monopolies has been slow.

Yet for outsiders, it is different again. They fear that as these internal blockages disappear, the Community will reinstate them as a Community-wide move against foreign entrants. Internally, the only loophole is Article 36 which justifies restraints on trade provided it does not constitute a means of arbitrary discrimination or a disguised trade restriction where there are issues of public morality, public security, protection of health and life of humans, animals or plants; protection of national treasures possessing artistic, historical or archaeological value or the protection of industrial and commercial property. In a competition context the following are scrutinized very thoroughly:

1 *Market sharing agreements* which create protected markets, often in one member state. The Commission in 1969 banned a quinine cartel and imposed a fine, and in 1973 acted against a sugar cartel. At the beginning of 1989 there were 3,457 cases pending and they lack the resources to deal with them all.
2 *Price fixing agreements* such as the dyestuffs cartel which controlled 80 percent of the European market. Producers had agreed to raise their prices by the same amount and at virtually the same time. This was the first occasion when companies headquartered outside the EC were fined for their actions within its territories. In 1988, in the Wood Pulp Cases, the EC held that anticompetitive agreements by US firms operating in the USA to restrict direct sales into and within the Community will be subject to EC jurisdiction. In 1989 the EC imposed a total of ECU 60 million against cartels including twenty-three companies manufacturing thermoplastic products.
3 *Exclusive purchase agreements* to buy from specified manufacturers or importers, or exclusive supply agreements to sell to certain buyers. Such agreements, which have arisen in areas as diverse as records and heating equipment, are usually proscribed by the Commission as they create unfair advantage and act to distort free trade.
4 *Agreements on industrial and commercial property rights.* The exclusive use of patents, trademarks and works of art is not necessarily excluded from competition rules.
5 *Exclusive or selective distribution agreements.* Selective distribution arrangements are some-times permitted if they improve the quality of the service provided. Discrimination against retailers for their pricing policies can be severely punished. However, it also encourages

positive developments particularly with regard to co-operation between small and medium-sized firms. Escaping the general ban are the following types of agreement:

- Exclusive representation contracts with trade representatives.
- Small-scale agreements, taking account of turnover and market share (which must not exceed 5 per cent of the total market in a substantial part of the Community or where the aggregate annual turnover of the companies in question amounts to less than 50 million ECUs. In these instances, the Commission will not intervene.
- Subcontracting agreements.
- Information exchanges between companies, joint studies and joint use of equipment.

Finally with regard to mergers, the position is less clear. The Commission is able to act only with respect to mergers which arise under the European Coal and Steel Treaty. The Commission did seek extra powers in this regard in 1973 and again in 1981, asking that the largest mergers be subjected to its scrutiny. The Commission also asked for the power to ban mergers which, in its view, pose a threat to effective competition in the Community. Yet cross European merger activity, like GEC-Siemens, could restructure many of the present European industries including retailing where Casino of France; Argyll of the UK; and Royal Ahold of Holland are to form a joint arrangement.

EC merger regulations seek surveillance over major mergers with a Community diversion, but provided the continued market share does not exceed 25 per cent, mergers will be allowed. The Community is more concerned with mergers in areas where the market share exceeds 30 per cent; the industry is already highly concentrated with significant entry barriers and price leadership is in the hands of a few powerful firms. An illustration is provided by the Commission's intervention in the British Airways' takeover of British Caledonian Airways even after the UK Monopolies and Mergers' Commission had given their approval. British Airways then had to expand opportunities for new competing carriers to obtain operating licences and at the same time hand over Heathrow slots for previous British Caledonian routes in Europe so as to limit to some extent its market dominance.

Strategic alliances are likely to prove more important than mergers and hostile takeovers where Britain has accounted for more than 70 per cent of those to date, but are just as likely to be the focus of EC intervention as any of the other more traditional forms of market cooperation. Strategic alliances are discussed more fully in Chapter 7.

Common Agricultural Policy (CAP)

The objectives of the CAP, as detailed in Article 39 of the Treaty of Rome are:
- To increase agricultural productivity.
- To ensure a fair standard of living for the agricultural community.
- To stabilize markets
- To provide certainty of suppliers
- To ensure supplies to consumers at reasonable prices.

Approximately 70 per cent of the Community's total budget is accounted for by the CAP which did not come into operation until the 1960s. The most important prices fixed at Community level are:

1 Indicative or guide prices which are the expected prices for the producer.
2 Intervention price which is a lower price at which the Community is obliged to buy products from farmers, traders and co-operatives if they cannot be sold in the Community markets or be exported. When production exceeds demand there are surpluses, and in agricultural production, there are many such surpluses within the EC.

CAP also benefits the larger farmers since the more a farmer has to sell, the more he benefits from the revenue-enhancing effect of the policy. This created incentives for farmers to force up yields, expand consumption of inputs and develop intensive methods of farming, displacing labour. To reduce milk production, slaughter premiums were granted but this did not meet with success as the farmers collected the premiums and invested them in ever more productive dairy cattle.

Over the years, the Community has been trying to change towards a more viable farm size to improve the economics of its agricultural production and support schemes. The Mansholt Plan which was not adopted, was for a farm of 200–300 acres for wheat production, forty to sixty cows for milk, 15–200 head of cattle for beef and veal production. Its aim was not to coerce but to create financial inducements to speed the adoption of the desired changes, particularly in regions with the worst structural problems.

Thanks to subsidies, the Community farm prices remain high by world market price levels, and guaranteed prices only stimulate further supplies thus exacerbating the situation further. The problem lies with CAP itself. Its objectives, as outlined above include terms which are outwardly agreeable but practically expensive to maintain. For example, providing certainty of supplies is usually a feature only of the public utilities: gas, water and electricity. To offer a 100 per cent level of service means inevitably that you have excess stocks by up to 10 per cent higher than anticipated demand. This obviously carries extra costs with it. As for the rest of its aims, it is open to question whether they are mutually exclusive, whether indeed it is possible to provide a fair standard of living, stabilize markets, ensure supplies at reasonable prices, all at the same time.

As previously noted, this accounted for two-thirds of the Community budget in the mid-1980s. Yet, in the move towards a Single European Market, no mention is being made of the CAP as the Community as a whole races to eliminate obstacles to trade according to the timetable it has set for itself.

A report by the National Consumer Council (NCC, 1988) found the CAP to be seriously deficient when measured against the following criteria:

- price which affects standard of living as well,
- quality and safety,
- access and choice,
- information and redress,
- efficiency and cost,
- equity, in the sense of resource allocation,
- transparency and accountability,
- representation.

The damning report by the NCC is worth citing

Prices are kept artificially high inside the EEC, and destabilised outside the EEC by the dumping of surpluses onto world markets. Despite claims to the contrary, the quality of food is

Table 17.11 Merger activity by EEC industrial corporations 1984–88

Sector	National				Community				International				Total			
	1984–1985	1985–1986	1986–1987	1987–1988	1984–1985	1985–1986	1986–1987	1987–1988	1984–1985	1985–1986	1986–1987	1987–1988	1984–1985	1985–1986	1986–1987	1987–1988
Food and drink	20	25	39	25	1	7	11	18	1	2	2	8	22	34	52	51
Chemicals, fibres, glass, ceramic wares, rubber	25	23	38	32	23	28	27	38	5	6	6	15	53	57	71	85
Electrical and electronic engineering, office machinery	13	10	33	25	5	0	6	4	4	3	2	7	22	13	41	36
Mechanical and instrument engineering, machine tools	24	19	21	24	4	3	8	5	3	7	2	9	31	29	31	38
Computers and data-processing equipment	2	1	2	2	0	0	0	1	1	0	0	0	3	1	2	3
Production and preliminary processing of metals, metal goods	13	14	15	28	3	1	4	9	1	2	0	3	17	17	19	40
Vehicles and transport equipment	8	6	15	3	2	0	6	9	0	4	0	3	10	10	21	15
Wood, furniture, and paper	10	18	17	24	5	4	7	6	3	5	1	4	18	27	25	34
Extractive industries	7	7	8	9	0	3	1	2	0	0	0	1	7	10	9	12
Textiles, clothing, leather, footwear	7	7	4	11	0	1	2	2	0	1	0	1	7	9	6	14
Construction	14	12	13	21	1	2	3	12	0	0	3	0	15	14	19	33
Other manufacturing industry	3	3	6	10	0	3	0	5	0	0	1	7	3	6	7	22
Total	146	145	211	214	44	52	75	111	18	30	17	58	208	227	303	383

Source Hufbauer, G. C. (1990) Europe 1992: An American Perspective, Brookings Institute, Washington DC.

Table 17.12

Recommendation 1
The Council should agree to transfer more of the resources currently devoted to price policy to the Community's three structural funds to provide integrated programmes to support rural development and structural adjustment in the areas of the Community which are particularly dependent on agriculture.

Recommendation 2
The Council should adopt a Community scheme for direct income aids for a limited period to assist producers during the transition to a more market-orientated price policy. Given the diversity of agriculture and attitudes to agriculture in members states, Community schemes are unlikely to meet all member states' aspirations and needs, or reach all producers adversely affected by a more market-oriented price policy.

Recommendation 3
The Council should adopt a scheme allowing member states to operate direct income support policies designed to meet their own policy objectives, subject to Community guidelines to ensure the free movement of goods, fair competition and that there are no conflicts with Community agriculture policy objectives.

Recommendation 4
The Commission should ensure that the environmental consequences of all new agricultural policy proposals are properly evaluated and that no new measures are adopted which are inconsistent with environmental policy objectives. Environmental impact assessments should be required for all major new investments, such as large drainage and irrigation schemes.

Recommendation 5
The Commission should draw up a set of Community rules to ensure that national policies for preventing environmental damage are consistent with the free movement of goods and fair competition. The 'polluter pays' principle should be applied.

Recommendation 6
The Council should agree to the speedy introduction of Community schemes to encourage environmentally friendly agriculture. These should be co-financed from the CAP structural policy budget in the same manner as other structural policy measures.

Recommendation 7
The Council should agree to adopt a programme of sustained cuts in support prices until demand and supply are brought into balance and, at the same time, phase out quotas, co-responsibility levies and other indirect attempts to reduce the level of production. If the Council find it necessary to have some kind of quantity restraints as an intermediate step then guarantee thresholds should be used which trigger cuts in support prices when they are exceeded.

Recommendation 8
The Council should agree to reduce the role of intervention buying to its originally intended role of short-term market stabilisation when there are excessive fluctuations in a particular market; cease the destruction and denaturing of food; impose limits on the amount of produce which can be held in store; only maintain stocks of essential foods

Table 17.12   continued

such as wheat on a regular basis. In the short term, consumers, particularly low-income consumers, should benefit from the disposal of surpluses as long as they exist.

Recommendation 9
The Council and the Commission should agree to phase out all measures aimed at restricting the consumption of products which compete with CAP products and not to introduce any new measures of this nature (for example, a tax on oils and fats or cereal substitutes).

Recommendation 10
The Council should take a much more positive position in the current negotiations in the general agreement on tariffs and trade and agree to reduce the level of protection it provides for agricultural products as well as the trade distortions caused by its export policy. Restrictions on imports of food should be reduced. In particular, restrictions on imports of products which are not adequately supplied by Community producers should be removed. Export refunds should be phased out. The Community's food aid programme should be separated from the CAP so that it can concentrate on meeting the development needs of developing countries rather than the need to dispose of Community surpluses.

Recommendation 11
The Council should agree to phase out the special green ECU used for the CAP, and the system of border taxes and subsidies, known as monetary compensation amounts (MCAs) should also be phased out so that a genuine common price policy and a genuine common market for food can be established. This should be phased in with the completion of the internal market scheduled for 1992. This reform would also have the advantage of reducing the opportunities for fraud.

Recommendation 12
The Council of Ministers should adopt a longer-term planning process for agricultural policy. The Commission should draw up such a plan for say, five years, which should set out a clear programme for reform. This would help the Community to move away from the short-term crisis management of agricultural policy.

Recommendation 13
The Commission should ensure that all its proposals for agriculture contain an assessment of all the consequences and not just concentrate on the budgetary effects. These assessments should include quantitative estimates of their effects on producers and consumers, and the distribution of these effects within these groups.

Recommendation 14
The agriculture directorate general (DGVI) should consult more widely both within and outside the Commission in the preparation of its proposals so that there is an opportunity for wider interests to be taken into account at an early stage. Proposals to Council and the European Parliament should include an annex listing all those who have been consulted.

Recommendation 15
The agriculture directorate general should ensure that there are greater opportunities for non-agricultural interests' views to be presented to the management committees. DGVI should ensure that other DGs and European lobby groups whose interests are likely to be affected are made aware of the issues being discussed by management committees in time for them to comment. Commission officials and national civil servants from other DGs/ national ministries should be able to attend meetings to represent these views.

Recommendation 16
The agriculture directorate general should reform the agricultural advisory committees along new lines. As currently organised they merely act to legitimise a thoroughly undemocratic process. The balance of membership should be altered so that all interests are equally represented. Environmental interests should be included in the membership. Balance generally should be achieved by reducing the number of members. The committees should always be consulted at the initial stage of policy formation. They should be efficiently administered, so that meetings are not cancelled or rescheduled at short notice, papers are available in adequate time and expenses are paid promptly. In addition the Commission should prepare an annual report to the European Parliament on the operation of the committees and how it has taken their views into account.

Recommendation 17
The consumer protection directorate (DGXI) should reform the consumers' consultative committee along the lines proposed by the House of Lords select committee on the European communities in their 1986 report on EEC consumer protection policy. It cannot work effectively as currently organised. It should have its own independent secretariat funded by the Commission and be able to appoint specialist advisers. Its opinions should be published.

Recommendation 18
The consumer protection directorate (DGXI) should actively seek to improve consumer representation and integration of consumer and agricultural policy at EEC level. While we welcome DGXI's proposal to seek to assist member states to achieve better consumer representation and integration of consumer policy and other common policies at national level, this action should go hand in hand with improvements at Community level.

Recommendation 19
The Council of Ministers should ensure that there is greater involvement in decisions on the CAP of ministers who are not primarily concerned with agriculture but whose areas of responsibility are affected by agricultural policy. The Council should also ensure that there are greater opportunities for non-agricultural interests to be represented on the various committees which prepare proposals on agricultural policy for the Council, in particular the special committee on agriculture.

Recommendation 20
At the national level, member governments should actively seek to involve all interests likely to be affected by agricultural policy in decision-making. This should include those involved in the food chain and environmental protection as well as consumers. Ministries of agriculture should ensure that their procedures for consultation allow for a balanced representation of all views.

Recommendation 21
In particular, member state governments should ensure that consumer organizations are able to become more involved in agricultural policy issues, as recommended by the Commission in the first report on the integration of consumer policy into the other consumer policies of the Community. Member governments should provide better information about the impact of the CAP on consumers. This should assist in raising awareness about the consumer costs and in enabling consumer groups to participate in the debate on the future development of food and agricultural policy.

not particularly enhanced by the policy and modern farming methods introduce health risks, are damaging to the environment, and reduce access to the countryside. While access to food supplies in toto have been guaranteed by the policy, the range of foods to which access is guaranteed has been unnecessarily restricted by EEC regulations.

The policy does not measure up well on either efficiency or cost criteria: it is extremely expensive, highly bureaucratic and prone to fraud. In terms of equity it is a highly regressive policy for both consumers and producers - that is, it artificially inflates prices in a commodity which takes up a particularly high proportion of the budget of low-income families and regions, while giving most help to the larger, richer producers. The system completely lacks transparency: it is largely incomprehensible to all but a select few, and strategic moves involving large sums of money are often made behind closed doors, with consumers being scarcely represented at the vital moments of decision.

Bankruptcy has threatened the future of the Community on several occasions, always as a result of the CAP policy of supporting agricultural prices at too high a level rather than stimulating structural reform. Several 'crisis' summit meetings of heads of state have taken place to try to control a runaway budget. On 2 February 1988 for the first time a legally binding ceiling was introduced for CAP price policy spending. Compensation was introduced for farmers who set aside arable land for at least five years. Longer term reform beyond budgeting stabilizers is required.

Questions as to representation of consumer interests were clearly raised by the NCC Report but not answered. To cite their report again:

> We have concluded that consumers' interests are paid scant regard at all levels and stages of the decision-making process. At the national level, policy formation is dominated by the agricultural lobby and its sponsoring ministries. Where formal consultative committees exist, consumer representatives always form a small minority. At Community level, consumer interests have virtually no influence on policy formation. Agricultural policy proposals are formulated in the agriculture directorate (DGVI) – the sponsoring directorate of farmers – which works in virtual isolation from other directorates. It has established agricultural advisory committees but, again, consumer interests are in a small minority and, in any case, these committees are often not consulted early enough in the decision-making process to affect policy.

The NCC had 21 recommendations to make as regards reform of the CAP as detailed in Table 17.12.

Entering the EC from the outside

The Associate Members of the Community: The Lomé Convention

The aid agreements currently in force between the Community and the sixty-six African, Caribbean and Pacific (ACP) countries are of a commercial and financial nature, granting the advantage of preferential access to Community markets. The Convention covers the following:

Trade co-operation

Practically all products from the ACP countries may be imported freely into the EC, but the arrangement is not reciprocal. ACP countries may charge import duties provided that they do not discriminate between member states.

Financial and technical co-operation

The common unit of currency for conversion purposes is the ECU (European Currency Unit). Funds of nearly 6,000 million ECU were set aside for use up to 1985. (The financial details of Lomé 4 are discussed later in this chapter.) These funds were to finance investment projects by the ACP countries and will be managed jointly. Four major sectors share most of the aid: rural development, industrialization, economic infrastructure and social development. There is also provision for regional co-operation of two or more ACP countries and support for small and medium-sized firms.

Stabilization of export earnings

The STABEX system compensates ACP states for losses if the volume of exports in their most important products falls below a certain level. The poorest countries do not have to repay the compensatory amounts, but other countries do if the situation improves. The scheme is intended to even out large deficit and surplus positions which have caused such wide price fluctuation that, in some instances, the rational planning of a developing economy has become almost impossible.

Industrial and agricultural co-operation

The intention is to grant aid to help ACP countries to develop and diversify their industrial production, in particular through the transfer of technology. This policy will raise the important question of the Community's obligation to buy the goods which the industries of the Third World produce. This will put pressure on Community industries, in particular very heavy pressure on labour-intensive, low-technology industries. It will accelerate their decline and push industry within the Community into higher technologies and more sophisticated service. Co-operation will be stepped up in areas such as new energy sources. Private investment will also be encouraged.

Institutions

The Lomé Agreement is implemented by a Council of Ministers aided by a Consultative Assembly of representatives of the ACP countries and the European Parliament. In each of the countries – totalling over sixty – there is a representative of the Community, whose task is to manage the operation of the Convention. Although at present only trade relations are involved, there is clearly present the germ of the idea of Community representatives acting more as ambassadors to the ACP countries. It could make individual embassies largely redundant in time.

The principal agreements between the Community and the Mediterranean countries are:

1 With Maghreb countries – Algeria, Morocco and Tunisia.
2 With the Mashreq countries – Egypt, Jordan, Syria and Lebanon.

3 The agreements with Israel, Cyprus, Malta and Yugoslavia.

The commercial aspects of the agreements involve free access for industrial goods to the Community and concessions covering some agricultural products. The agreements are not reciprocal, although in the case of Israel there will be a free trade area for industrial products by 1989.

Arrangements have been made in the agreements to ensure that the nearly one million Maghreb workers in the Community benefit from the same pay and conditions of work as Community nationals. A Council of Ministers determines the policies behind the various treaties, but the negotiation and renegotiation of the treaties is the responsibility of the Commission.

There have been three Lomé agreements since 1975. The third Lomé agreement came into force 1 May 1986 for a five-year period. However, despite the elaborate structure created to encourage trade with the Community, Lomé has not been a success. Between 1975 and 1990 ACP exports to the EC have declined from taking first 8 per cent of EC imports to 3.8 per cent of EC imports and within that, 90 per cent of these exports are represented by bulk commodities. Lomé is nevertheless important, it provided $9.4 billion in aid between 1985 and 1990. Measures exist for ACP exports to enter the EC quota and duty-free and there is a mechanism to stabilize the earnings of the ACP commodity exporters. Lomé 4 was signed in December 1989 for a ten year period with a total package valued at ECU 10.7 billion.

However, despite these clear advantages, the Lomé conventions have not been successful and the ACP countries have perhaps even been less successful at penetrating the Community markets than any other group worldwide. Certainly, aid has not been co-ordinated and the ACP wished to be treated as a group rather than have differential rates of preferential treatment. During the period 1975–1990 liberalization of trade has meant also that perhaps even if the Lomé Convention did not exist, that 70 per cent of ACP exports would still enter duty-free (Laurie, 1990). This indicates competition and the lack of protection from third party suppliers as perhaps before. Over the years, too, the EC has expanded and its newer members including Spain and Greece have a significant financial interest in fruit and vegetables. Bananas and rum are two items produced by the ACP countries and subject to national quantitative restrictions. A longer term plan with certain guarantees and offering the opportunities for economic diversification through an aid package may prove to be highly beneficial.

Lomé 4 proposes some changes to previous arrangements. Firstly with regard to the rules of origin, the ACP share in value-added has been reduced to 45 per cent instead of 60 per cent. Next and most importantly, there have been changes to the Stabex system which started in 1985. Stabex accounts for 12 per cent of the European Development Fund. The conditions have changed in that payments made under Stabex do not now need to be repaid although in practice this was already the case. The Lomé 4 fund has been increased to ECU 1.5 billion to allow for bad years such as 1988 when the coffee and cocoa market prices experienced a severe downturn.

Longer term, marketing is the only way in which the ACP countries can hope to survive. Aid has not worked except to partially cushion some of the worst effects of commodity price crises. Focusing on developing new markets, improving production, improving general competitiveness and creating more awareness and efficiency through marketing systems is the only alternative to the bottomless purse expected of the Lomé Conventions.

Japan's view of the Community

Japan ... has been the object of sustained discrimination at the hands of the Community since its establishment.

(Ishikawa, 1990)

Japan looks at the Community as a community of member states and sees quite different levels of treatment emanating from its member states. Its worst scenario would be for the EC to turn inward into Europe. EC-EFTA trade in 1987 was almost equal to EC-US and EC-Japanese trade taken together. An introspective Community may well lead to further protectionism and fears then of a Fortress Europe. Britain which has attracted more direct investment from Japan than any other country within the EC, does not have any of the 131 indirectly imposed restrictions on 107 products to be found elsewhere in the Community in 1988 (Ishikawa, 1990, 7). Although forty-two of these restrictions were lifted by the EC in March 1989, these did not relate to major Japanese export items and are thus unlikely to have any effect on total Japanese exports to the Community. While the Community strives for the removal of national restrictions presently permissible under Article 115 of the Treaty of Rome, it does not rule out Community-wide restrictions in areas considered to be sensitive and here it is worth noting that the Community's external tariff ranges between 4 and 22 per cent.

In total Japanese trade with the world as a whole, more than 1,000 products are subjected to national quantitative restrictions. To emphasize that Japanese restrictions belong more to the past than the present, see Table 17.15. Within the automobile industry, national restrictions are plentiful. Fiat has 60 per cent of the Italian market whereas the Japanese have only 1 per cent. In France, Japan is limited to 3 per cent of the market; in Britain 11 per cent

Table 17.13 Discriminatory quantitative protections on imports from Japan 1 December 1988

Country	Agricultural	Industrial	Total	Applied only to Japan
Benelux	0	7	7	7
West Germany	0	2	2	2
Denmark	0	2	2	2
France	4	13	17	5
UK	0	0	0	0
Greece	0	2	2	0
Italy	3	33	36	33
Ireland	0	1	1	0
Spain	1	40	41	41
Portugal	0	23	23	23
Total Community	8	123	131	113

Source Official Journal C37, 16 February 1987; Official Journal C57, 5 March 1987; and Japanese Ministry of Foreign Affairs. *Cited in* Ishikawa, K. (1990), *Japan and the Challenge of 1992*, Royal Institute of International Affairs, London.

Table 17.14   Community anti-dumping duties against Japan

Year and month		Product	Type of measure	Duty (%)
1983	10	Outboard motors	DD	22
1984	7	Miniature ball-bearings	DD	4–15
1985	6	Ball-bearings	DD	1–22
		Tapered roller bearings	DD	2–45
	6	Hydraulic excavators	DD	3–22
	6	Electronic typewriters	DD	21–35
	8	Glycine	DD	15
1986	4	Electronic scales	DD	1–27
1987	2	Housed bearing units	DD	2.24–13.39
	2	Plain paper photocopiers	DD	7.2–20
	5	Outboard motors	DD-Conf.	22
1988	4	*Electronic scales & parts	DD-Ext.	†65.63
	4	*Electronic typewriters & parts	DD-Est.	†21.83–65.14
	5	Electronic typewriters & parts (Kyushu Matsushita)	UT (DD-1988.4)	
	7	Electronic typewriters & parts	UT	
	8	Video taperecorders (Funai & Orion)	PD	18
	9	Electronic scales & parts	C (DD-1988.10.)	
	10	*Plain paperphotocopiers (Matsushita, Toshiba & Konica)	DD	†28–225
	11	Dot matrix computer printers (15 firms)	DD	4.8–47.0
	12	Photocopiers (Matsushita & Toshiba)	UT (DD-1988.10.)	
1989	1	Serial impact fully formed character	DD	23.5
	1	Audio-cassettes & audio-cassette tapes	II	
	2	Photocopiers (Konica)	UT (DD-1988.10.)	

Source   The European Communities, *Official Journals.* Cited in, Ishikawa, K. (1990) *Japan and the Challenge of Europe 1992*, Royal Institute of International Affairs, London.
Key   DD = definitive duties, PD = provisional duties, UT = undertakings, C = cancellation, II = Initiation of investigations, Conf = confirmation, Ext = extention.
*Against 'screwdriver' assembly plants.   †Ecus per unit.

under a voluntary export restraint agreement and so only in Germany is there free trade. The Japanese cite figures to show that they have 40 per cent market share in Ireland, Finland, Greece and Norway; and 30 per cent in Austria, Denmark and Switzerland. However, none of these countries has an automobile manufacturer.

The EC is worried that Japanese foreign direct investment within the Community will only aggravate existing excess capacity. The issue of origin applicable to Japanese cars made within the Community is another thorny problem. Britain was happy to certify that Nissan cars made in Britain with a 60 per cent local content were British. However, applying the label 'made in Britain' would allow these cars entry into other member states of the Community bypassing national quantitative restrictions presently in force. The issue of how to measure local content and the level which may be required for certification purposes is difficult. Derek Barron, Chairman of Ford UK, recommended that the level should be fixed at 80 per cent and that this should not be measured as at present by ex-factory value which can introduce marketing costs and even profit. Only the actual cost of the product should be taken as a base. At first, France and Italy resisted but climbed down in April 1989; they establish 80 per cent local content as being a minimum requirement for acceptance of these Japanese cars as British. Japan's fears extend then into anti-dumping measures against what the Community has called 'screwdriver' assembly plants; fears of new rules of origin; and of the Community applying what it terms reciprocity in trade as viewed by the Community alone. The issue of EC rules of origin regulation 802/68 and the Kyoto convention are discussed in Chapter 7.

US view of the Community

In 1988 US exporters sold and shipped $75 billion worth of goods to the EC but affiliates of US multinational firms sold a further $620 billion worth of goods, approximately equal to the sales of European affiliates in the USA that year (Hufbauer, 1990).

From a US viewpoint, the single market will have a bearing on:

1 US exports to the EC and indirectly to the third markets.
2 A unified Europe may turn protective towards high technology industries and grant them preference over foreign competitors including the USA.
3 The issue of 'reciprocity' which has been raised many times, that in return for US companies being allowed to operate freely in the Community, the same might be given to European companies in the USA. This could lead to problems in protected areas such as US banking.
4 Quantitative restrictions are currently national in character. If applied in a unified manner across Europe, the EC could be seen to be championing trade protectionism.

Table 17.15   Comparison of residual quantitative restrictions

Country	Agricultural and fisheries products		Manufacturers and minerals		Total	
	(1)	*(2)*	*(1)*	*(2)*	*(1)*	*(2)*
Japan	55	22	35	1	90	23
USA	1	1	4	6	5	7
West Germany	19	3	20	1	39	4
UK	19	1	6	2	25	3
France	39	19	35	27	74	46
Italy	12	3	8	5	20	8
Benelux	10	2	4	3	14	5
Denmark	62	5	2	0	64	5

Source   GATT. Cited in Ishikawa, K. (1990) *Japan and the Challenge of Europe 1992*, Royal Institute of International Affairs, London.
Notes (1) At the end of December 1979, (2) At the end of April 1987.

Table 17.16   Japanese direct investment in the community (Cumulative total 1951–86, $m)

	Manufacturing		Non-manufacturing		Others	Total	
	No./cases	Amounts	No./cases	Amounts	Amounts	No./cases	Amounts
UK	287	484	725	3585	561	190	4125
Germany	149	277	620	1026	249	817	1552
France	309	317	379	536	117	742	970
Italy	51	100	87	70	33	156	203
Belgium	52	240	180	468	84	249	793
Netherlands	47	199	294	2134	4	354	2337
Luxembourg	1	4	98	2304	—	99	2308
Ireland	44	160	16	170	2	62	332
Denmark	5	2	32	15	0	39	17
Greece	8	94	8	1	—	16	96
Spain	87	462	58	63	76	163	601
Portugal	17	22	9	5	0	28	27
EC-12 total	1057	2361	2506	10,377	621	3915	13,363
USA	2610	9267	8886	25,080	1107	13,757	35,455
World total	11,847	28,206	24,580	74,285	3479	40,123	105,970

Source   Japanese Ministry of Finance. Cited in, Ishikawa, K. (1990) *Japan and the Challenge of Europe 1992*, Royal Institute of International Affairs, London.

5 Technical standards. The concept of 'mutual recognition' applies between member states except where there are issues of health, safety or the environment. The degree to which the EC will accept US certification and product testing is not clear.
6 Government procurement procedures are to be opened up as one of the main measures of the 1992 programme. This raises some fears of favouritism for European companies and specific fears for the continuation of US exports of telecommunications equipment, for example.
7 Competition policy. The pursuit of an antitrust policy when vetting mergers and acquisitions by non-European companies is awaited with some trepidation.

The EC is the USA's largest export market and in 1988 accounted for 24 per cent of US exports more than the 22 per cent going to Canada, or the 12 per cent going to Japan. In terms of value, 45 per cent of US exports to the EC were in the high technology area whereas only 29 per cent of US exports to Japan could be so classified (Hufbauer, 1990). However, the US Administration are likely to concern themselves more with operating conditions within Europe rather than export opportunities to Europe which can fluctuate more wildly. Overall the US is favourable towards the changes taking place. Most of the disputes (80 per cent) as in US complaints to GATT about EC treatment have concerned agriculture and fisheries and were caused by what were seen to be EC nontariff barriers and subsidies.

A survey of US multinational executives by Ryans and Rau (1990) showed more than 70 per cent believed that 1992 will benefit US producers (see Table 17.18).

There was agreement that 1992 would result in the consolidation of present European production sites; the establishment of European regional headquarters; a faster learning curve

Table 17.17 JETRO's survey 1988. What are your motivations and reasons for starting to produce in Europe?

	(a)	(b)	(c)	(d)	(e)	(f)	(g)	(h)	(i)	(j)	(k)	(l)
Food	10	4	5	—	3	1	4	—	—	—	4	2
Textiles	4	4	1	—	—	—	3	—	1	1	1	1
Pulp & paper	1	1	—	—	—	—	—	—	—	1	—	1
Chemicals	29	20	8	2	4	6	4	2	1	9	7	1
Pharmaceuticals	5	4	1	1	—	—	1	1	—	—	1	1
Rubber products	8	1	—	1	—	3	2	—	4	1	2	3
Ceramics	4	4	1	—	—	1	1	1	—	1	—	—
Non-ferrous metals	2	2	—	—	—	—	—	—	—	—	—	—
Metal products	9	5	1	1	—	3	1	—	—	1	5	2
General machinery	25	9	3	13	1	5	2	2	5	3	7	6
Electronics*	71	29	8	37	—	9	12	11	19	14	19	9
Transport†	17	7	—	6	—	3	—	5	2	—	—	6
Precision‡	5	3	1	2	—	2	1	1	—	—	3	—
Other	26	20	2	4	2	2	8	2	—	4	15	1
Total	216	113	31	67	10	35	39	25	32	34	64	33

Key (a) Total; (b) Developing new markets; (c) Reducing production costs; (d) Avoiding market integration; (e) Acquiring cheap raw materials; (f) Avoiding the risk of exchange-rate fluctuations; (g) Building up overseas market information capabilities; (h) Preparing for the 1992 market integration; (i) Maintaining orders from sales subsidiaries or the parent company; (j) Preferential tax treatment; (k) Meeting the diversified needs of consumers; (l) Other.
* Electronics and electrical equipment.   † Transport machinery.   ‡ Precision machinery.

Source JETRO, The Current Management Situation of Japanese Manufacturing Enterprises in Europe, Tokyo, March 1989, p. 36. Cited in, Ishikawa, K. (1990) Japan and the Challenge of Europe 1992, Royal Institute of International Affairs, London.

Table 17.18   US executives' view on general EC-92 issues

Issue	Agree/ disagree	Degree of agreement
I feel that EC-92 will result in:		
(1) increased market opportunities for US firms.	Agree	3.982
(2) access to additional markets.	Agree	3.667
(3) more interest in the EC market by the US exporters.	Agree	4.203
(4) an increase in EC membership.	Agree	4.203
(5) overall, an improvement in US Balance of Trade.	Disagree	3.316
(6) an increase in corporate mergers among EC firms.	Agree	4.644
(7) increased tariffs for exporters from outside European Community.	Agree	3.831
(8) more competition in Europe from EC based firms.	Agree	4.672
(9) increased non-tariff barriers for US exporters.	Agree	3.879
(10) increased European nationalism.	Agree	3.828
(11) loss of key developing country markets due to their special trading status with the European Community.	Disagree	3.298
(12) a necessity to establish EC production.	Agree	4.386

Note   (scores below 3.5 indicate disagreement and scores above 3.5 agreement).
Source   Ryans, J. K., and Rau, P. A. (1990) *Marketing Strategies for the New Europe – A North American Perspective on 1992*, American Marketing Association, Chicago.

for managers about intra-European differences; greater flexibility in moving managers from one country to another; more US firms establishing in an EC subsidiary; and greater parity in wages across countries.

In terms of marketing-related issues, they strongly support the greater use of global and regional marketing strategies while at the same time there may be some stricter regulations then in force. Some greater difficulty is foreseen in finding EC-wide distributors though it is not identified as a major problem. It may well, however, prove to be a problem for those particularly small and medium size companies entering the market late (see Table 17.19). A physical presence was seen to be necessary although it is expected that the competitive environment will intensify after 1992. A single European location for distribution to all twelve European member states will then become feasible and will encourage development of Eurobrands; and mergers and acquisitions leading to further industry concentration. A 'Fortress Europe' scenario is quite likely resulting from the increased internal competition. Finding good European wide distribution may become a problem although standardization of market conditions will lessen the effect of cultural differences and limit the need for a 'nation-by-nation' approach to marketing across Western Europe. Finally, US companies will be able to exploit labour mobility, management transfer flexibility and an overall 'intra-European' managerial learning curve (Ryans and Rau, 1990).

Postscript

The year '1992' has become a milestone for the Community in that by the end of that year, significant measures will have been taken to unify the internal markets of the Community and

Table 17.19   US executives' view on marketing-related EC-92 issues

Issue	Agree/ disagree	Degree of agreement
I feel that EC-92 will result in:		
(1) fewer cultural differences over time between EC countries.	Agree	3.780
(2) reduced need for a nation-by-nation approach to European Community.	Agree	3.983
(3) the use of a global/regional marketing strategy including advertising.	Agree	4.254
(4) the possibility of developing Eurobrands.	Agree	4.089
(5) stricter regulations.	Disagree	3.458
(6) greater difficulty in finding EC distributors.	Disagree	2.932

Note   (scores below 3.5 indicate disagreement and scores above 3.5 agreement).
Source   Ryans, J. K., and Rau, P. A. (1990) *Marketing Strategies for the New Europe – A North American Perspective on 1992*, American Marketing Association, Chicago.

create common market conditions. Harmonization of taxation rates will have to take place or member states will face huge diversions of revenues and a good deal of tax-dodging besides. *The Economist,* for example, pointed to the anomalies of taxation and indicated how mail order by Mothercare of the UK of children's wear into France could be expected to be very successful if tax rates remain the same and Britain's remains at zero.

The year in which we begin then to see changes will be 1993 not 1992 as the schedule allows for harmonization measures to be effected up to the end of 1992. By 1993 there will still be no common currency unit or ECU although the European Monetary System or EMS is bringing the implementation of the ECU much closer. Britain will still stay with imperial measures until the end of the decade. Alcoholic beverages will continue to use gills, and pints and petrol (gasoline) will continue to be priced per gallon. Even if current practice in filling stations (gas bars) is for prices to be displayed per gallon and per litre, pumps have been recording this in litres not gallons. In pubs and restaurants, it is quite different. Beer is dispensed in automatically controlled quantities of half and one pint and glasses by law must be stamped as accurately containing a half or one pint. To allow for beer froth, fill lines are indicated often on the outside of these glasses. In this area, metrication will be costly in the conversion. In other areas, such as confectionery and biscuits, the conversion is piecemeal and packages will be found currently on supermarket shelves stating either metric or imperial weights.

Many steps have already been taken e.g., EC passports and driving licences. 1993 will see harmonization of the majority of existing anomalies but not all – Britain will still continue to drive on the left, but for the first time will be connected to the rest of Europe as a result of the Channel Tunnel. In 1990, the two ends of the tunnel being bored forty metres under the English Channel actually met. This will carry two rail tunnels and one service tunnel for security/safety, each 35 km long crossing the Channel between Calais and Folkestone. Rail services through the tunnel are scheduled to start 15 May 1993. 30 million passengers and 15 million tons of freight should use the tunnel in its first year of operation which with the French high speed train, the TGV, should see the distance between London and Paris reduced to three hours. This will lead both to creation and diversion of investment and resources to the new European gateways. The Channel Tunnel will put places like Dunkirk within easy reach of London, Paris, Brussels, Bonn, Luxembourg and the Hague and within easy reach of 80 million consumers: one-third of the population of the entire Community. A free warehousing system together with an Enterprise Zone 25 kms from the cross-channel tunnel will give Dunkirk a head start in the industrial relocation that is likely to take place before 1992 and after the rail tunnel is opened in 1993.

European Economic Area (EEA)

The EEA would be the new name for an economic bloc created from a merger of the EC and EFTA. This would create on 1 January 1993, a new market with a single set of rules and a total population of 380 million. As this merger would stop short of actually joining the EC there are some legal obstacles still to be resolved before this association becomes a reality. It has become an important issue for non-EC courntries as how best to ensure continued access to EC markets as of 1992. Neutrality is not an obstacle to membership as Ireland's continued membership of the EC will testify. Among the EFTA membership, it is not an issue for Austria or for Sweden who have applied separately for membership of the EC, and even Finland which is rumoured to be about to apply for EC membership. Therefore although one can see some difficulties ahead the fact that the individual member states of the EC and EFTA want this association to happen will bring it about.

References

Blackwell, N. (1990), Way around Europe. *Management Today*, August, 86–87.

Caulkin, S. (1988), Ford tunes up Europe. *Management Today*, July, 38–44.

Cecchini, P. (1988) *The European Challenge: 1992 – The Benefits of a Single Market*, Wildwood House, Aldershot, Hants.

Colchester, N., and Buchan, D. (1990), *Europower*, Economist Books and Random House, New York.

Department of Trade and Industry (1990), *The Single Market: A Guide to Public Purchasing*, Victoria Street, London.

Department of Trade and Industry (1990), *Single Market News*, (9), Winter.

Drew, J. (1983) *Doing Business in the European Community*, 2nd edn, Butterworths, London.

'Eurotunnel: it's off!' (1988) *L'Usine Nouvelle*, (22), 2 juin.

Hufbauer, G. C. (1990) *Europe 1992 – An American Perspective*, Brookings Institution, Washington DC.

Ishikawa, K. (1990) *Japan and the Challenge of 1992*, Pinter Publishers for Royal Institute of International Affairs, London.

Laurie, S. (1990), Unequal partnership. *Banker*, January, 40–41.

Mellors, C., and Copperthwaite, N. (1990) *Regional Policy*, University of Bradford and Spicers European Policy Reports, Routledge, London.

National Consumer Council (1988) *Consumers and the Common Agricultural Policy*, HMSO, London.

Ryans Jr., J. K., and Rau, P. A. (1990) *Marketing Strategies for the New Europe: A North American Perspective on 1992*, American Marketing Association, Chicago.

Vermulst, E., and Waer, P. (1990) European Community rules of origin as commercial policy instruments? *Journal of World Trade,* **24,** (3), 55–99.

Key reading

Budd, S. A. (1987), *The EEC – A Guide to the Maze,* 2nd edn, Kogan Page, London.

Burton, F. N. (1989) *Trade Friction between Europe and Japan: The Need for a European Consensus,* Manchester School of Management report, available from the author at Manchester School of Management, UMIST, PO Box 89, Manchester, M60 1QD

Cecchini, P. (1988), *The European Challenge: 1992 – The Benefits of a Single Market,* Wildwood House Ltd. Aldershot, Hants.

Colchester, N. (1989), *Survey of Europe's Internal Market 1988 and 1989,* Economist Publications, London.

Colchester, N. and Buchan, D. (1990), *Europower,* Economist Books and Random House, New York.

Commission of the European Communities (1988), *Europe 1992: Developing an Active Company Approach to the European Market,* Whurr Publications Ltd., London.

Dahrendorf, R., Hoskyns, J., Curzon Price, V., Roberts, B., Wood, G. E., Davis, E., and Sealy, L. S. (1989), *Whose Europe? Competing Visions for 1992,* Institute of Economic Affairs, London.

Richard, D. (1990), 1992–2002: the future evolution of financial markets in Europe. *Royal Bank of Scotland Review,* (165), March, 3–16.

Dudley, J. W. (1989), *1992 – Strategies for the Single Market,* Kogan-Page, London.

Europe 1992 (1988) *Economic Policy - A European Forum (1988),* (9), October.

H M Customs and Excise (1987), Notice 484: *Single Administrative Document,* Customs Freight procedures for 1 January 1988, London.

Hufbauer, G. C. (1990), *Europe 1992 – An American Perspective,* Brookings Institution, Washington, DC.

Inglis, A., and Hoskyns, C. (1989), The Europe 1992 Directory - A Research and Information Guide, ITCU/Coventry Polytechnic, Coventry.

Ishikawa, K. (1990), *Japan and the Challenge of 1992,* Pinter Publishers for Royal Institute of International Affairs, London.

Keynote Guides (1989), *1992: The Single European Market,* Keynote Publications Ltd., Hampton, Middlesex.

Mellors, C., and Copperthwaite, N. (1990), *Regional Policy,* University of Bradford and Spicers European Policy Reports, Routledge, London.

Mendes, A., and Marques, J. (1987), *Economic Integration and Growth in Europe,* Croom-Helm, London.

National Consumer Council (1988), *Consumers and the Common Agricultural Policy,* HMSO , London.

Palmer, J. (1988), *Trading Places: The Future of the European Community,* Radius, London.

Partnership Between Small and Large Firms (1989). Proceedings of the Conference held in Brussels, 13 and 14 June 1988, (ed. D. G. XXIII – Directorate for Enterprise of the Commission of the European Communities and T.I.I. European Association for the Transfer of Technologies, Innovation and Industrial Information), Graham and Trotman, London.

Perry, K. (1987), *Business in Europe: Opportunities for British Companies in the EEC,* Heinemann, Oxford.

Pitts, G. (1990), *Storming the Fortress: How Canadian Business Can Conquer Europe in 1992*, Harper Collins, Toronto.

Quelch, J. A., Buzzell, R. D., and Salama, E. R. (1990), *The Marketing Challenge of 1992*, Addison-Wesley, Reading, MA.

Ryans Jr., J. K., and Rau, P. A. (1990), *Marketing Strategies for the New Europe: A North American Perspective on 1992*, American Marketing Association, Chicago.

Silva, M., and Sjögren. B. (1990), *Europe 1992 and the New World Power Game*, John Wiley & Sons, New York.

Taylor, C., and Press, A. (1988), *1992: The Facts and Challenges*, Ernst and Whinney for the Industrial Society, London.

Thurley, K., and Wirdenius, H. (1989), *Towards European Management*, Pitman, London.

Ugeux, G. (1989), Europe sans frontières: the integration of financial markets. *Royal Bank of Scotland Review*, (162), June, 9–25.

van Ypersele, J., and Koeune, J.-C. (1985), *The European Monetary System*, Commission of the European Countries: European Perspectives' Series, Luxembourg, Office for Official Publications of the European Communities.

18
Marketing to the industrialized countries of Eastern Europe

The Soviet Union did not last through the last days of 1991 but as 1992 approached was replaced by a Commonwealth of Independent States (CIS) sharing a mutual distrust of central control, eager to maintain their new found freedom and sovereignty. Previously, Westerners regarded all of the Soviet bloc countries under the Soviet sphere of influence as similar to their own domestic economy. This is not to equate levels of personal disposable income but to emphasize that significant economic differences existed within this bloc requiring more than one marketing strategy. What has happened since, has only reinforced this point.

To begin with, in this new Commonwealth of Independent States, we have to acknowledge the existence of a number of separate republics, the largest of which is the Russian Federation accounting for the bulk of the population of the former Soviet Union and most of its mineral wealth and natural resources. The Russian Federation includes a number of autonomous republics including: Kabardino – Balkaria; North Ossetia; Checheno – Ingushetia; Dagestan; Kalmykia; Mordovia; Chuvashia; and Mari-El.

Some of these regions have a population which is predominantly Muslim and therefore may ally themselves more with neighbouring Muslim countries than with central government.

The Independent Republics

These now include the Russian Federation; Latvia; Estonia; Lithuania; Byeorussia; Ukraine; Georgia; Moldavia; Armenia; Kazakhstan; Azerbaijan; Turkmenistan; Kirghiz, Uzbekistan; and Tadzhikistan. The bulk of the population lives within the Russian Federation leaving twenty-six million (the population of Canada) dispersed among the remaining republics.

The East European economies

The fall of the Berlin Wall led to the fall of the Soviet empire. East Germany became part of the new unified Germany and the newly liberated Poland, Czechoslovakia and Hungary sought and gained associate membership of the European Community further distancing themselves from their previous colonial masters and at the same time taking steps to ensure their continued independence. Eastern Europe was never one homogeneous region and the drive towards marketization of these previously centrally planned economies has created further marked differences. Again, one needs to think of segmentation. There is an array of different opportunities to be found within these economies but one strategy will not work for all. For one thing, these countries are now all truly independent, and for another they know it and want to be courted as independent states and not as colonies. We shall deal with segmentation strategies later. (See Figure 18.1.)

The meaning of 'Perestroika'

As much of what has happened throughout Eastern Europe and the CIS owes its existence to *perestroika*, it is worth reflecting on the very essence of what *perestroika* or 'restructuring' is

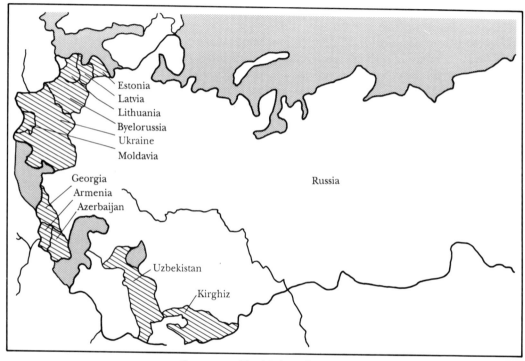

Commonwealth of Independent States

Area: 22,402,200 sq. km.
Republics
The Russian Federated Republic – 76.22%
Kazakhstan – 12.1%
The Ukraine – 2.7%
Turkmenia – 2.17%
Uzbekistan – 2%
Byelorussia – 0.93%
Kirghiz – 0.9%
Tadzhikistan – 0.64%
Azerbaijan – 0.4%
Georgia – 0.31%
Lithuania – 0.29%
Latvia – 0.28%
Estonia – 0.21%

Moldavia - 0.15%
Armenia – 0.13%
(The White Sea 0.4% and the Sea of Azov 0.17% are not formally included in any republic).
Population – 290 million
Nationalities – 120
Languages 130 (70 literary languages)
Religious communities – 1070
Largest nationalities
Russians – 145 million
Ukrainians – 53 million
Uzbeks – 13 million
Byelorussians – 9.7 million
Kazakhs – 7 million

Tatars – 6.5 million
Azerbaijanis – 6 million
Armenians – 4.5 million
Georgians – 3 million
Lithuanians – 3 million
Moldavians – 3.2 million
Tadzhiks – 3.2 million
Germans – 2 million
Kirghiz – 2 million
Jews – 1.8 million
Chuvashes – 1.8 million
Latvians – 1.5 million
Bashkirs – 1.5 million
Mordovians − 1.3 million
Poles – 1.3 million
Estonians – 1.1 million

Figure 18.1   Who wants out?, *Economist* (1991)

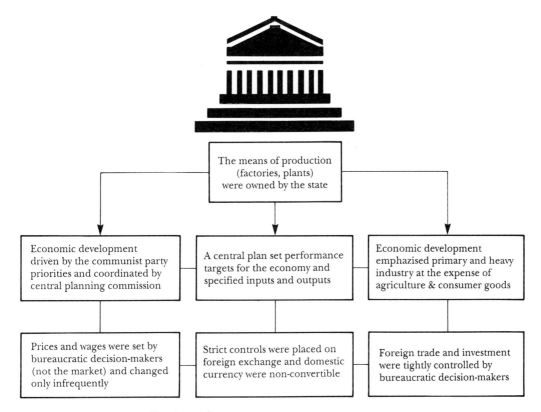

Figure 18.2   *The centrally planned economy*
Source   *Poland: A Guide to Business Opportunities* (1990), Prospectus Publishing, New York

really about. Some insights into the mission confronting Gorbachev can be found in his book entitled *Perestroika*.

> ... The essence of what we plan to do throughout the country is to replace predominantly administrative methods by predominantly economic methods. That we must have full cost accounting is quite clear to the Soviet leadership.

This would appear then to be clearly at odds with the policies of previous Soviet leaders and so to legitimise this policy change, reference has to be made to the founding fathers of the Russian Revolution, preferably Lenin, to make the ensuing policy palatable to the party:

> In my report of 22 April 1983 at a gala session dedicated to the 113rd anniversary of Lenin's birth, I referred to Lenin's tenets on the need for taking into account the requirements of objective economic laws, or planning and cost accounting, and intelligent use of commodity-money relations and material and moral incentives. The audience supported this reference to Lenin's ideas ...

Endorsement from Lenin is what is needed to ensure party support. Grave weaknesses continue to exist in the economy as are clearly pinpointed in this book which the official censor would not have allowed to be published, had it been anyone other than the Soviet

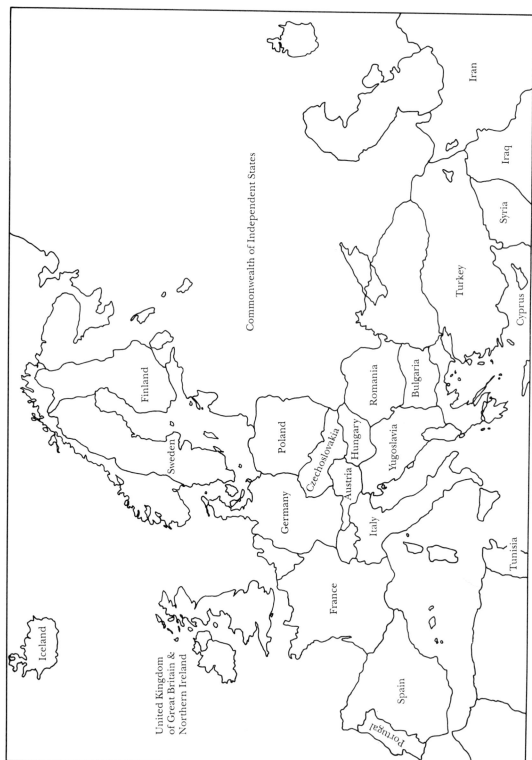

Figure 18.3 *Map of Eastern Europe*

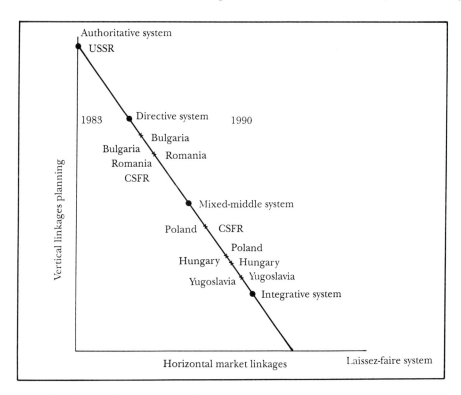

Figure 18.4 *Spectrum of macroeconomic systems*
Source Adapted from Samli, A.C., and Jermakowicz (1983) The stages of marketing evolution in East European countries. *European Journal of Marketing*, **17**, (2), 29

leader himself who had written it. The analysis is sharp and the style quite open, frank and totally uncharacteristic of any book which had come out of the Soviet Union before. Some of the weaknesses pinpointed for action include:

Industrial stagnation

The gap in the efficiency of production, quality of products, scientific and technological development. The production of advanced technology and the use of advanced technology and of advanced techniques began to widen and not to our advantage.

Lack of product development

On this issue, Gorbachev singles out the Zil car factory for particular criticism as the manufacturer of cars for party officials at high cost and without any product development.

Low productivity

The country is still spending far more on raw materials, energy and other resources per unit of output than other developed nations.

Resistance to change

Management unwilling to part with its rights and prerogatives.

Failure of government

Political flirtation and mass distribution of awards, titles and bonuses often replaced genuine concern for the people, for their living and working conditions, for a favourable social atmosphere.

Reduction of the public sector

The composition and volume of state orders will gradually be reduced with the saturation of the market in favour of the growing direct ties between manufacturers and consumers.

   This last direct quotation suggests the introduction of privatization and of marketing instead of central planning. Control over the restructuring process, 'perestroika', comes through 'glasnost' which means 'openness', and this has been guaranteed by legislation. It

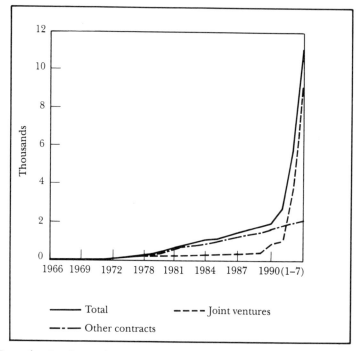

Figure 18.5   *Growth of industrial co-operation contract registrations by CMEA countries, 1966-mid 1990*
Source   UNECE (1990) Promotion of trade through industrial co-operation, Trade/R564, 17 September

means in effect a freer press than before, able to criticize shortcomings in the economy and through this open glare of publicity, to force change. A revolution from the top, it is hoped that this reform movement will permeate all levels of the Soviet economy.

The political changes of 1989

The Eastern European states had individually undergone many series of economic reforms before 1989: Hungary in 1956; Poland under Gomulka also in the 1950s; Czechoslovakia in 1968. These dates included economic reforms which were politically unacceptable and so military intervention ensued. What was different then in 1989 was that the political will for change had arrived. Both economic and political reform took place simultaneously as a grass-roots revolution got under way. A decisive factor was the attitude of the USSR under Gorbachev but this was to present no stumbling block. Besieged by troubles within the Soviet Union and recognizing the validity of the complaints of the East European peoples, Gorbachev could only be sympathetic to these cries for reform. The great irony is that the democratization of Eastern Europe could only have been possible with the acquiescence of the leader of a totalitarian state.

The differences still exist between Eastern Europe and the CIS in the way in which the reform movement got under way. In Eastern Europe, it has been a grass-roots bottom-up revolution whereas in the CIS the reform movement has been led from the top down. This is significant particularly when assessing the present state of the region. The power base in Eastern Europe is now with the people; in the CIS, it is with a President who is taking forever more and more power into the post of presidency. In the period immediately following the December 1991 events, Yeltsin as President of the Russian Federation has taken on many of the powers which were controlled by Gorbachev as Soviet President. It is similar to the cry 'The King is Dead! Long live the King!' It is important to point out though that the Soviets have lived with Communism longer than the rest of Eastern Europe and perhaps are more used to being directed, and like their East European compatriots, have seen many attempts at economic reform before. The secret to political life in the CIS is now once again in gauging the degree to which the leader is serious about reform. Timing is of the essence and without commitment, these reforms will fail and yet it is the entire period since 1918 that has created this situation. Generations have been brought up to believe that they were taking part in a struggle that simply had class divisions between capitalist and worker. The CIS have less now to struggle for than their East European counterparts for while the East Europeans have realized their dreams of independence and are now cultivating a pride in themselves once again, the CIS have had this struggle which was their *raison d'être* and the excuse for generations of shortages, explained to them as being a vain pursuit. Heavy defence spending finally made the Soviet Union crumble, the substitutions demanded to allow continued defence spending finally became unbearable even for the Soviet Union.

In the aftermath of 1989 the path towards reconstruction is taking place with closer ties between East and West than for many generations. The East European states are now much changed. Their leaders are national leaders of resistance and reform who are wary of communism. Changes taking place in Eastern Europe are to marketization and privatization of the state monolith. East Germany merged with West Germany as of October 1990, Poland abolished all central planning on the 1 January 1990 and Czechoslovakia has changed its name to the CSFR: the Czech and Slovak Federal Republic. Only Bulgaria voted for the continuation of communism. Overall, these changes have been both sweeping and fundamental and must be seen as permanent.

Structural economic changes

The path towards a free market economy is slow and painful. Despite its economic and production potential, the share of Eastern Europe and the Soviet Union in global trade is low. It is a stark case of underachievement encouraged only by the desires of successive politicians to maintain a steady status quo relative to the Soviet Union and so to trade internally within Comecon.

The Eastern bloc has traditionally manifested common characteristics in terms of foreign trade, where, in each member state, foreign trade has been a state monopoly. There has always been, though, a latitude of freedom in the degree of centralization/decentralization applied to the management and control of the foreign trade system. Between the two extremes of centralization and decentralization there are a number of mixed systems. Figure 18.4 explained further in Table 18.1 shows that the position on this gradient or stage in the centralization/decentralization spectrum does have significant meaning for the marketing function: authoritative; directive; mixed-middle system; and integrative. A laissez-faire system may be incompatible with the very nature of socialism but it has been the path chosen by Poland in following the IMF route to a free market.

What Table 18.2 does not show is that the East European economies have been living with shortages for generations. All have been hard pushed to find the convertible currency to repay outstanding borrowings. This influenced Hungary and Poland, the two most indebted nations, to follow the lead of Romania in joining the IMF. The policy everywhere had been the same: anything that could be sold on Western markets was sold there. It is also worth noting that all of the East European nations reduced their imbalance in trade with the West either by selling more on Western markets and/or reducing Western imports. Table 18.3 shows the two most indebted East European nations on a comparative basis with other severely indebted nations.

Market entry methods

In the past, licensing was the most appropriate alternative to direct exports. Not without dangers of creating a potential competitor, licensing remained the most popular because of the inability until the 1970s of engaging in more complex longer lasting ventures. According to Marxist ideology, ownership of the means of production could not be in the hands of foreigners but remain in the hands of the people, so direct investment was curtailed and there was little enthusiasm on either side for joint ventures. However, since the 1970s, there have been many changes. The 1970s saw a short-lived period of détente which gave birth to more than 1,200 contractual joint ventures termed officially 'industrial cooperation'. The 1980s gave few indications of the changes that might take place in 1989. The motivating force was the accession of Gorbachev to the Soviet leadership and a new regime started which Margaret Thatcher signalled in her comment on being one of the first Western leaders to meet Gorbachev: 'This is a man I can do business with'. The changes which he has instituted directly or indirectly since are legend. A new definition had then to be created of what was possible in terms of trading or investment in the Soviet Union. Yet even Gorbachev did not go as far or as quickly as many economic and political commentators have pointed out was necessary. What held Gorbachev back was that he was still a communist and still tied in important ways to the system in which he grew up. (See Table 18.5.)

Nevertheless, against this background, joint ventures are now once again being examined.

Table 18.1   Four stages of marketing evolution in East European countries

---

Stage 1   Totally planned and controlled distribution systems (authoritative economic system)
- National economy is treated as a big nationwide enterprise.
- All decisions about structure of production and directions of investment are made at the central governmental level in the planning council.
- Directive form of management.
- Ration-card type distribution system.
- Nationalised retailing structure with virtual monopoly of sales in urban areas.
- Nationwide seller's market.

Stage 2   Directly planned and controlled distribution systems (directive economic system)
- An enterprise is regarded as a ministry association.
- Some competition among ministries.
- Some pressure on the producers to attract customers.
- Introducing of input-output analysis at the governmental level.
- Large-scale advertising of an ideological character is utilised.
- Better method of estimating, thanks to input-output analysis where, when and what the consumers will buy.
- Increased choice for the ultimate consumer.

Stage 3   Partially planned and more indirectly controlled distribution systems (mixed-middle system)
- An enterprise is regarded as an industrial association.
- Some competition among the industrial associations.
- Moderate degree of decentralisation.
- Planning of market consumption goods and services is decentralised.
- Some product differentiation – particularly free market mechanism for individual consumption products.
- Increased availability of consumer credit.

Stage 4   Indirectly planned and controlled distribution systems (integrative economic system)
- The focal point in the economy is the enterprise.
- Competition among the enterprises.
- Government influences the behaviour of enterprises indirectly only by the use of economic parameters.
- Free market mechanism for all goods and services.
- High autonomy for enterprises to improve their marketing efforts.
- High product differentiation and market segmentation.
- Ability to fluctuate prices.
- Increased discretionary income and luxury items.

Source   Samli, A. C. and Jermakowicz, W. (1983) The stages of marketing evolution in East European countries. *European Journal of Marketing*, **17**, (2), 29.

Table 18.2   CIS and Central Europe: a quick profile

- Population 403m.
- Not one market but several.
- Pragmatism replacing ideology.
- In CIS *perestroika* revolution has been 'top-down'. In Eastern Europe it has been 'bottom-up'.
- Differences emerging as East European nations move towards free market economies.
- German unification: October 1990.
- Central planning being dismantled (Poland broke away 1 January 1990).
- CoCom listing reviewed 1 July 1990.
- End of monopoly control by a FTE over an industrial sector.
- Awarding of foreign trade rights to major producers.
- Hard currency shops to close under Shatalin Plan.
- Privatization and dismantling of state ownership.
- Convertibility being introduced.
- Decrease in countertrade envisaged.
- Direct investment possible but no infrastructure to permit private capital investment.
- Debt-equity swaps now being discussed (Polish debt trading at 7c = 1$).

Table 18.3   Overview of East European economies

	Bulgaria	CSFR	Hungary	Poland	Romania	USSR	Yugoslavia
Population	9	15.6	10.6	37.8	22.9	284.0	23.4
% age profile under 15	22	24	22	25	25	26	25
Currency uinit	Lev	Koruna	forint	zloty	lei	rouble	dinar
Capital city	Sofia	Prague	Budapest	Warsaw	Bucharest	Moscow	Belgrade
% age work-force agriculture	22.0	14.0	20.0	30.0	30.0	20.4	30.0
Passenger cars per 1,000	122	173	145	105	12	42	126
Hard currency exports	3.2[1]	5.8	5.9	7.7	7.7	56.38	n.a.
Hard currency imports	4.5[1]	5.9	5.2	6.7	3.9	49.3	n.a.
Gross external debts	10.1[1]	6.9	20.1	39.9	1.2	43.33	22.25
Per capita income	2,806[2]	8,300	4,180	2,000	2,020	5,500	3,109

[1] billion US$.   [2] US $. The EC average is $9155.
Sources   UN World Trade Organization (1988) *Yearbook of Tourism Statistics*, 2 vols, Madrid; *Eurobusiness, Eastern Europe: Facts and Figures*, March 1990.

Previously, issues of control were paramount. This has changed to a realization that networking to ensure effective market penetration is what determines commercial success. Decades of self-imposed isolationism from global markets, poor management, poor coordina-

Table 18.4 Debt, debt service, and growth indexes for SIMICs*

Country	Debt outstanding, 1989[a]		Debt service, 1989–90[b]		Debt ratios (per cent)		Average annual growth rates, 1982–88 (per cent)				
	Total (US$ billions)	From private sources (per cent)	Total (US$ billions)	Interest (US$ billions)	Debt-GNP. 1988	Interest-exports. 1988	GNP	Exports	Imports	Invest-ment	Per capita consump-tion
Argentina	61.9	74.3	14.7	9.0	60.5	27.5	0.9	2.3	0.6	−2.7	−0.1
Bolivia	5.8	12.2	1.0	0.4	135.5	17.2	−1.0	1.5	4.6	−5.0	−2.7
Brazil	112.7	75.2	30.4	17.4	30.7	36.1	4.7	5.6	−1.4	2.6	2.4
Chile	18.5	68.8	4.5	3.1	96.6	15.1	4.6	7.0	4.6	15.4	0.4
Congo	4.2	53.4	1.7	0.5	238.3	13.3	−0.7	3.3	−10.2	−15.2	−2.8
Costa Rica	4.6	47.4	1.4	0.4	100.0	13.4	3.8	1.9	9.3	9.1	3.5
Cote d'Ivoire	14.0	61.6	4.2	1.8	161.8	15.7	0.5	−3.0	−7.0	−7.6	−3.4
Ecuador	11.5	51.5	3.9	1.6	113.3	12.7	2.2	6.6	−1.0	−20.0	−1.5
Honduras	3.4	22.3	0.7	0.3	81.9	15.6	2.8	2.9	4.6	7.7	−1.0
Hungary	17.9	87.4	4.9	2.2	65.2	10.1	1.4	3.9	3.0	0.4	1.4
Mexico	102.6	76.0	28.4	16.3	58.0	27.3	0.2	4.7	1.6	−5.0	−1.5
Morocco	20.8	26.2	5.6	2.4	105.9	15.3	4.1	6.1	1.1	0.1	0.9
Nicaragua	8.6	19.6	1.5	0.6	0.0	25.0	−0.7	−12.9	0.8	2.0	−1.5
Peru	19.9	43.0	4.4	1.1	47.3	5.6	2.1	−1.8	−4.5	−2.4	0.6
Philippines	28.5	56.1	7.3	4.1	72.9	18.6	−0.2	6.3	2.5	−10.7	−0.2
Poland	40.1	31.2	12.5	4.5	63.9	5.6	4.5	5.5	6.3	3.5	3.8
Senegal	3.6	15.5	0.8	0.3	76.6	12.1	2.5	−1.3	−3.5	1.7	−1.5
Uruguay	4.5	79.1	1.1	0.6	50.1	18.3	1.8	4.6	1.5	−4.0	1.3
Venezuela	34.1	94.7	11.9	5.8	57.7	24.1	2.1	6.0	1.2	2.1	−2.1
Total[c]	517.5	65.4	142.0	72.3	53.6	22.3	2.5	4.8	1.3	−0.7	0.4

[a] Estimated total external liabilities, including the use of IMF credit.
[b] Debt service is based on all external debt at end 1988. It does not take into account new loans contracted or debt reschedulings signed after that date.
[c] Based on recent data Egypt would be classified as severely indebted instead of moderately indebted. For purposes of this report, Egypt is classified as moderately indebted.

* Severely Indebted Middle-Income Countries.
Source World Debt Tables 1989–90, p. 30.

Table 18.5 East European net debt/export ratios*

Country	1986	1987	1988	1989p
Bulgaria	143	175	196	263
CSFR	66	78	78	95
East Germany**	89	107	106	118
Hungary	312	324	290	326
Poland	570	556	504	532
Romania	98	76	32	−1
Soviet Union	79	82	90	113

p = Preliminary.
*(Debt-reserves)/exports (goods only) in convertible currencies. The net debt/export ratio is regarded as the single best indicator of a country's relative indebtedness because exports provide the hard currency to service debt.
** Includes transactions with West Germany.
Source *Financial Times*, 1 March 1990.

tion and low competitive quality ensured that the USSR and Eastern Europe had only a very small share of global trade relative to its potential. The CIS has 3.7 per cent of global trade as against 11.3 per cent for the USA; 11.4 per cent for Germany; and 9.3 per cent for Japan, because internationalization was given only a low priority and the focus of attention was the undemanding regional CMEA market. All leaders agree that this has to change and to do so in the short term requires the use of a joint venture. This has not prevented the *Financial Times* from commenting: 'Many joint ventures formed in the past two years are more like entrepreneurial fairy tales than industrial realities'.

Geographical changes

The major change has been the unification of the two Germanys in October 1990. However, the force which was unleashed by *'perestroika'* has led to demands for self-determination in various parts of what was previously known as the 'Soviet bloc'. Hungary and Romania are at odds with each other over Transylvania which is inhabited mainly by Hungarians although postwar it has been part of Romania. Romania's answer to this question under the Ceaucescu leadership was to erase these Hungarian settlements with bulldozers. Ceaucescu is no longer leader or even alive but the ethnic question remains. The Soviet Union is now no longer but the CIS faces the greatest challenge to its continued ability to retain power and yet continue to hold together in a union a number of disparate states with fiercely independent aspirations. The USSR accounted for one-sixth of the Earth's land mass; a population of 284 million people in fifteen republics speaking 114 languages. How much of this will survive into the year 2000AD is open to question. Even a CIS with such bitter internal dissension continuing will be greatly weakened. Poland has been reassured of its right to maintain its postwar boundaries by the newly unified Germany but internally the Czech and Slovak Federal Republic (CSFR) and Yugoslavia are now fighting internal divisions within their own boundaries. As one Polish Foreign Ministry official put it:

Table 18.6

	East–West industrial co-operation in 1970s	*East–West joint ventures of 1990s*
Areas for possible collaboration	Decided by Planning Commission, Industrial Ministries and Associations	Few restrictions:; outside of military/defence nuclear industry and public utilities
Possible partners	Decided by industrial ministry, FT Ministry and Industrial Association	No restrictions
Acceptability of project	Integration with central plant for five year period	Central planning abolished in 1990
Project size	Decided by Industrial Ministry, Foreign Ministry and Foreign Trade Bank	Decided by enterprise and/or Western company with approval of IMF
Project duration	Decided by Industrial Ministry, Foreign Ministry and Foreign Trade Bank	Decided by enterprise and Western company
Risk sharing	Limited contractual liability	Open-ended
Repatriation of capital	Very limited. Payment terms usually included a form of countertrade	Hard currency settlement. No restriction on repatriation of profits earned on exports. Within next four years, no restrictions on profits made from internal sales within Poland
Market expansion	Hard currency markets sought outside CMEA	CMEA markets now become markets for hard currency exports
Pricing	Wages and prices politically set	Enterprises now use full-cost accounting. Require to be self-sustaining
Quality	Variable, lack of intensitive to do otherwise	Ability to retain profits from exports creates incentive to improve product quality
Management	Poor quality. Included safe party political faithfuls promoted to positions of power on basis of party loyalty rather than individual competence: the 'nomenclatura'	Need for structured management training, recognition of management competence and ousting of the ''nomenclatura', the Communist party faithful from management levels.

The vision of Europe is very badly needed in Poland. We need European standards, European respect for human rights, European technical and environmental standards. To make long term and deep changes at home, we need a model.

That model is to be the free-market economic model which will in turn mean that we can expect the Eastern Europeans to become more important trading partners.

CoCom embargo list

CoCom is the Co-ordinating Committee for Multilateral Export Control. It is an informal non-treaty organization of sixteen member countries of NATO less Iceland plus Japan. It was a postwar organization which imposes export controls on goods to: Afghanistan; Albania; Bulgaria; People's Republic of China; CSFR; Hungary; Mongolia; North Korea; Poland; Romania; USSR and Vietnam. There is an agreed list of goods which are prohibited for export to these countries and some countries in addition may add certain further items to their particular list. This may be seen to create a loophole, i.e. exporting from a Western country where the restrictions are not so rigorously applied. The USA however, claims control over many exports from other countries including the UK where the goods are of US origin, include components of US origin or were produced using US-origin technology. In such cases, under US export regulations, a US re-export licence is required whether or not a UK export licence is needed or has been granted.

The CoCom list of Security Export Control comprises of three lists: the industrial list; the munitions list; and the atomic energy list. Applications for export licences are detailed particularly in the so-called area of sensitive technologies and so full supporting documentation is required including a precise description of the goods to be exported, complete technical specifications, and if the goods contain any computer or digital processing element, a completed computer questionnaire.

Some nations' lists are shorter than others, allowing for 'leakage' of technology if shipped via a subsidiary abroad in a more lax CoCom-member country or a neutral one such as Austria, Sweden, or Switzerland which account for a considerable amount of East–West trade. In addition, there are now a multitude of developing countries in the Far East producing sophisticated electronic equipment such as Taiwan, Hong Kong and Singapore. These currently escape the controls. However, Singapore has become the first country outside NATO, France and Japan to say publicly that it is ready to co-operate to prevent the diversion of sensitive high-technology products to Soviet-bloc countries. The CoCom list as such is also open to political manoeuvring in that what is considered to be a 'strategic', and hence a prohibited export is seldom either constant or consistent, but varies with the prevailing diplomatic climate which moves between *détente* and 'Cold War'. New CoCom procedures provide for revision of 25 per cent of the CoCom list of all items every four years.

The CoCom list has been one of the main reasons for the antiquated telephone systems and low computer power of the East European nations relative to their West European counterparts. Automatic switchboards are in effect like computers and as long as the thought still prevailed that we were dealing with the enemy in embarking on East–West trade, it did not make any sense therefore to improve East European communications systems as these may clearly have a military use.

In the light of the political changes taking place, Western nations reviewed the CoCom list in July 1990 and rolled back many of the existing restrictions on the export of telecommunications equipment and computer hardware such as personal computers.

It is now possible to sell many items that were previously prohibited but the problem of indebtedness remains and so the ability to pay without countertrade may be called into question.

CMEA and Warsaw Pact

CMEA or Council for Mutual Economic Assistance was larger than just Eastern Europe which was often referred to as the Soviet bloc. In addition to the East European countries: Cuba, Mongolia, Albania and Vietnam were also members. Yugoslavia has only ever had observer status being seen by the West as part of the Eastern bloc but within Eastern Europe as part of the West.

As a region which was controlled by the Soviet Union, the two organizations which all member states belonged to were the CMEA and the Warsaw Pact which was a military alliance. The political changes have been so sweeping that the new incumbents in power have chosen to withdraw from both. CMEA was founded on the principle of central planning priorities for the entire region. Now, with its member states moving away from central planning to marketization there is no role to be played by the CMEA which is now down to its last faithful communist, Cuba's Fidel Castro. Similarly, the military alliance that was the Warsaw Pact was dismantled in 1991. It lost credibility as a counterweight to NATO with the events of 1989 when the new leaders of Poland, CSFR and Hungary quickly committed themselves towards the abolition of the Pact's joint military command and staff. Eastern Europe now sees itself wanting to play a greater role within Europe.

The problems of trading within the old CMEA, or (Comecon) area, are that one is dealing with undemanding markets and payment is made only in soft, unconvertible currencies which cannot be exchanged on world markets. Trading with soft markets is easy and undemanding but it is the demanding customer who will get the best out of a company, forcing the level of service ever higher thus creating a competitive edge for the company and barriers to entry for rivals. Within the old Comecon area, these concepts are new particularly to management who have traditionally had to answer only to political chiefs. However, on 1 January 1990, the CMEA moved to convertible currency payments as a result of pressure from member countries with valuable things to sell – notably the Soviet Union with its oil and natural gas. The CMEA in February 1990 was replaced by a new body – the Organization for International Economic Cooperation (OIEC) which has since failed and many of its members have already applied for membership of the EC and other international organizations including the IMF. Over the next few years as privatization measures continue to take force, state enterprises will have to be window-dressed before a suspicious national populace to entice them to invest in their own state industries. Management is perhaps one of the weakest areas in these economies where entrepreneurs have been compared to black-marketeers, discouraged and disliked by the public at large. To develop management skills within this framework where perhaps only grandparents may remember a free market, will require time, a lot of patience and a lot of money. To this end, Britain has created a Knowhow Fund for Poland of £75m and for Hungary of £50m, and similar sums for Czechoslovakia and the former Soviet Union. The EC and OECD are working together on the reconstruction plans for Eastern Europe as the Group of 24, so as to consolidate and co-ordinate their aid inputs most effectively as in the newly constituted European Bank for Reconstruction and Development (EBRD).

Business climate

Traditionally, East–West trade has been generally low profile, highly dependent on the political winds of change. As such, investment has been limited despite the potential which they present as these nations are industrialized and have an educated trained workforce. Nevertheless, a short term view of East–West opportunities has prevailed to date. As a result, its share of foreign trade of any of the major Western nations with the exception of Germany, has been low and because trade between the two blocs has been at a low level, there is a low level of knowledge, much less open distrust than before but still the same unwillingness to invest. Communications have been poor because the main language would be German rather than English and telephone systems are totally inadequate to handle international calls; fax machines are rare and still need a telephone socket connection, and culturally, there has been a psychological block as regards sending business letters. Sending a letter under the communist regime was equivalent to being named as the person responsible for whatever action was detailed. Everyone shirked that responsibility so letters were not sent. This was a psychological rather than language problem which will need to be dealt with and soon by the new regimes in power.

What has emerged now is a new trading atmosphere in which the limits to what is possible are bounded only by the ability to create the financial innovations to facilitate and develop this new era of opportunity for trade and investment. The goodwill exists in abundance and has now to be consolidated into some tangible force that can be harnessed to facilitate the new era of East–West trade.

Doing business with Eastern Europe

Eastern Europe is a region composed of several states each with its own unique character and set of features. The great mistake that many marketers make is to think of it as one market which it is not. Segmentation can be practised here as elsewhere, and targeting is as important here as elsewhere, so:

1 There is not one Eastern European market but several. Within each market the degree of movement away from direct central planning is quite distinct. Poland abolished central planning totally, the Russian Federation appears to be still living with it to some degree, and functioning with a hybrid system.
2 Buying points. Previously, in the traditional socialist model, foreign trade was a state monopoly and there was a Foreign Trade Enterprise for each industrial sector. All importing and exporting for production enterprises in that industrial sector were channelled through a foreign trade enterprise or FTE. The FTE then generally used its monopsony purchasing power to play off potential suppliers against each other to gain maximum price advantage. This lies at the heart of the 'whipsawing' accusations levelled against the FTEs. The FTE suffered communications problems with the enterprises it was

established to service and in the Soviet Union there were many cases where one FTE may be responsible for fifty or more production enterprises. The FTE had poor communications internally, but externally, as the FTE had a different name from the many enterprises it serviced or even the association or corporate group of enterprises, it created further confusion among Western companies unsure exactly of who they were dealing with. Buying points have now changed in that foreign trade rights have been awarded to all major producers in the CIS and in Poland for example, while new private companies and privatized state companies start to emerge. The production enterprise now has its own export/import office on site to handle all these matters and is able also to retain a proportion of its profits from foreign trade, so a new incentive has been created to produce saleable goods for export. Ironically, it is the concept of profitability that is now being instituted in the former socialist countries.

3 Time consuming. Doing business in Eastern Europe has always been slow to reap rewards, is company executive intensive, and so expensive. It is not so difficult to identify potential buyers as to identify decision makers and assess their credit worthiness.

4 Many centres within Eastern Europe are still struggling with hybrid systems which are still primarily conceived within the central planning framework. Psychologically it is difficult for managers now to break free of these fetters or rather to realize that these fetters are no longer there. This is a major problem for management which has never had an explicit role in the socialist model. Even in Poland when Solidarity came to power it created for itself a structure that was based on central planning systems. This was not by design but because the generations born in Poland during and after the war years knew no alternative to central planning. Their feelings were for democratic systems but their thinking was automatically of central command systems. It will take a few generations to undo this style of thinking totally.

5 Requests for countertrade will continue as indebtedness continues to exist. It is important to check whether countertrade obligations can be reassigned to a third party or not.

6 Opportunities now exist that were inconceivable only a few years ago for direct investment and joint equity ventures.

7 There is now an embryonic market mechanism at present to allow for the pricing, purchase and sale of shares in East European enterprises but the public at large need to be educated in this regard.

8 Market and product supply information is particularly hard to find as a result of years of statistical distortion under communist regimes to make bad situations appear better than they were. Figures of total industrial consumption and unit prices are difficult to estimate and different statistical bases are used, which reduces the scope for comparability of country data. On a positive note, many new market research agencies and consultancies are now springing up all across Eastern Europe and this will fill a need but at a price.

9 Identification of decision makers is still difficult but because the productive enterprises now have their own retained earnings for exports, they are able to work more independently than before. This means then working directly with an enterprise rather than before when negotiations also included the Industrial Ministry, Foreign Ministry, Planning and Design Institutes as well.

10 While enabling legislation has been passed to change the business environment and encourage active Western participation in new growth ventures, the bureaucracy still continues to move like molasses. It is like comparing theory with practice so do not build up expectations of anything happening quickly. Expect protracted frustrating negotiations. Poland has moved further along the road towards privatization than any of its

neighbours but the parliamentary record in speedily enacting the necessary legislation is sadly deficient rather like the French Parlement immediately before the Revolution. Yet is is no wonder that this socialist system created so many chess masters. Undertaking any shopping in the Eastern bloc has always required a game plan complete with contingencies to deal with the daily unexpected. This mentality of expecting a negative response all of the time is endemic to the Eastern bloc and is unlikely to change other than in the long term. It has, however, some positive problem-solving aspects if harnessed properly by joint venture partners, for example.

11 Permanent company representation is no longer a problem. Instead it is openly welcomed. For those not wishing to invest it is still possible to use one of the many Western agents, or state agencies based in Eastern Europe to represent you.

12 Designation of sales territories were always a problem in negotiations with East Europeans who wanted to earn hard currency from exports to the West while Western companies could only see the potential of the East, not fully realizing this was only a soft, inconvertible currency market. With the move towards free market exchange rates, this now becomes possible at last, although these countries still remain poor, traditional sellers' markets where there has been poor phasing of production to meet even seasonal needs.

13 Propaganda is as important today as ever before. To entice Western companies in a recession at home to invest in a foreign environment is a very difficult task not made easier either by differences in culture and language. Even a measured success will therefore perhaps be paraded over-enthusiastically to entice other Western companies to invest.

14 Personal contacts are more important than ever before because of the organizational and structural changes throughout these economies and so contacts must be developed and maintained. Communication and co-ordination are generally poor and this together with the speed with which things are changing makes it highly advantageous to be able to turn to someone and simply ask: 'What is going on? Who should I speak to?' In the USSR it was always possible for example, to coordinate counter purchases across several FTEs but not for example in Poland where there has been little understanding of this concept of project or venture management which as practised in the West requires the co-ordination of all interested parties in the commissioning and establishment of a new industrial undertaking. Again, where there is no organization, being able to liaise with the individuals most closely involved is the next best thing. Personal contacts will remain very important irrespective of what future scenarios we may describe for the East European nations.

15 Advertising has now been freed of restrictions and television advertising is possible although the level of advertising quality is poor and the role of advertising in a modern economy is little understood in a bloc where traditionally it held no value. The problem now is of a different nature from before. Now the goods are available on Eastern shelves but they are priced at Western market levels and these consumers are earning only East European wages, which means that in the Soviet Union the monthly salary would be only £5 sterling equivalent. Much attention has been focused on the establishment of a McDonald's restaurant in Moscow as though this were a sudden response to the changes now taking place whereas in fact it took fourteen years of negotiations and planning to establish a vertically integrated food chain supplying only into McDonalds.

16 Distribution systems are poor. There is a shortage of warehousing space, retail outlets too few in number and too small in size to properly serve the communities in which they are

located. Compounded with a cultural tradition of panic buying, shortages are inevitable. Once sold out, bare shop shelves cannot easily be refilled because of the shortage of distribution vehicles to service these tiny retail outlets. The reason people queue for hours outside McDonald's in Moscow is because they know that they have food there. The McDonald's restaurant queue has replaced the queue for Lenin's Mausoleum in terms of importance, while elsewhere officials wonder what to do with the yellowing cadavre of a politician who has fallen from grace.

17 East European branding is almost non-existent and there appears to be no coherent policy here, apart from apathy which does not equate with a policy. The Eastern Europeans prefer instead to waste money in exchanging what are often good quality highly saleable products in low-return countertrade while the same goods could be sold directly in Western markets although with some degree of investment but at a much higher return. There seems little interest on their part in so doing, preferring instead simply to take whatever money goods will realise in a strategy dubbed as 'disaster pricing'. The pattern has been to ask Western partners to undertake on their behalf, marketing and promotion on Western markets. Slowly, the situation is changing: Polish foods in Britain are now branded 'Pek' or 'Krakus'; there is the Polski-Fiat car now renamed the FSO and another more recent one, the Polonez; and the Soviet Lada car which in late-1984 introduced a number of 'add-ons' to create a customized finish, e.g., front spoilers, aerodynamic sills, etc. – a most unusual step for a central planned economy to take towards satisfaction of a consumer in the West, particularly as Western manufacturers would not normally undertake this themselves but leave such car customization to specialist suppliers instead.

18 The rouble overhang. It is said that there are rouble millionaires. 'The USSR has between 15,000 and 30,000 millionaires, mostly from dealing in the thriving black market,' said a member of the Government commission on economic reform. Estimates vary in terms of number because of the exchange rate assumed for the dollar against the rouble. This reflects clearly the level of pent-up consumer demand. Similar estimates have indicated perhaps \$3 billion lying under Polish mattresses as a result of distrust towards Government agencies and State banks. The shortages have always been compensated to a degree by the availability of goods for hard convertible currency either in the official hard currency shops or on the black market which also sold hard currency. The noble duty of saving *per se* does not enter into it, as the low market supply of consumer goods lends little alternative but to stockpile currency which cannot be used to purchase goods or services. At present a 'Big Mac' can be bought for roubles in Moscow but the rouble price is likely to increase also with the general rise in food prices and move towards convertibility and full market prices.

19 'Pay before you own' has been the system operating in all areas of consumer durables. Cars had to be paid for perhaps six years before taking possession but any subsequent price increases during this period were passed on to the consumer and paid in full up to the point of actually taking delivery. Positions in the waiting list were sold but the details of the car, colour, etc. could not be chosen. Party privileges included jumping the queue which created further social friction where the alternative to waiting was to buy a car outright for hard currency from one of the hard currency shops or else import one from abroad.

20 Service as a concept is foreign and so is the idea of the consumer having a choice or having any form of power, which again is totally alien to the socialist system. Management thinking will have to be changed from thinking of a production economy to a market driven economy.

As old problems disappear, new problems emerge

Commercial risk is greater than before

Previously it only took time to do business and the waiting paid off in a large contract guaranteed by the FTE and by the State Bank. The risk is now of trading with an independent enterprise with a new or changed name and not knowing whether it will be able to repay. The FTE had its own funds agreed by a Ministry of Foreign Trade whereas enterprises now have retained earnings but who will back them financially in the new system? Private enterprises which are likely to take over from state enterprises also pose another risk because they are unknown and have no trade record. For Western companies especially those who have been dealing with the soon to be disbanded hard currency shops, there was the certain knowledge that the buyer would be able to repay, because he was earning hard currency. In the moves towards a free market all goods are available for local currency which is in turn convertible against all other currencies. Here there is both risk from domestic influence and foreign currency exchange risk exposure.

Weak infrastructure for local investors

The ability to raise capital has been greatly curtailed by the non-existence of a stock exchange, and consequent ability to raise capital for industry from within the public at large. The same is true of employee share ownership schemes which have been successful in Britain as with the privatization of the National Freight Corporation. Pension funds in Eastern

Table 18.1   Western auto industry plans for Eastern Europe

CSFR	Renault & British consortium competing for van project in Bratislava
	Skoda – taken over by Volkswagen AG of Germany
	Fiat – tendering for Skoda engine part.
Poland	Fiat: letter of intent with FSO, Warsaw, to product Tipo
	FSM in Bielsko-Biala to begin licensed production in 1991 of Fiat Micro (replacement for 126) 300,000 per year by 1995
Hungary	Opel to produce 200,000 engines per year and assemble 30,000 Kadetts per year
	Szentgotthard
	Suzuki to produce 100,000 small cars per year in Esztergom by late 15,000 per year in 1992
CIS	Fiat-joint venture to produce 300,000 Panda-sized small cars at new plant in Yelabuga from 1992
	Fiat-tendering for production of Soviet Oka small car
Bulgaria	Rover Group in talks with VAMO about possible production of Maestro

Source   *Financial Times*, 13 March 1990 and subsequently updated.

Europe are holding onto money that they do not know what to do with but are reluctant about investing in their own enterprises.

Creation of a professional management cadre

Previously many of those top management posts went to party 'hacks' the so-called feared 'nomenclatura' because of their dogmatic party allegiance rather than their entrepreneurial vision or management skills. Polish people are only too well aware of the inadequacies of their management as a result of which the management would not get the workers' vote if it meant investing workers' cash in the enterprise. Yet whether the enterprise is privately owned, foreign owned or state owned, management is a problem that has to be addressed if improved economic results are ever to emerge.

It may be argued that the problem will be eased in Poland to a degree by the provision of four MBA programmes now under way but in talking to some of the students on these programmes, their desire was to obtain an MBA so as to have portable qualifications that held currency in the West. Others spoke of their wish to look for large Western multinationals. None of these Polish MBA students volunteered a personal desire to revitalize state industry or create a new enterprise in Poland. Without an infrastructure in which Polish MBAs can usefully employ their training there is little point in having MBA programmes. First, then the infrastructure needs to be developed. Second, the importance of management in the economy needs to be heightened. Thirdly, suitable rewards and incentives need to be introduced to create a pool of middle and junior managers who see the MBA route as prestigious and worthwhile and so in turn create a demand for such programmes.

A similar difficult situation exists with management development programmes. ICL Ltd., a British computer company taken over by Fujitsu in 1990 has operated the largest jointventure in Eastern Europe, employing 7,200 in Poland. In 1989 they created a management training centre, appointing as director an academic from the University of Warsaw who was now to organize three-day courses for more than 6,000 from supervisory to senior management levels. In this particular case, the British Knowhow Fund for Poland lent support for visits to create the network of personnel needed to operate the seminars.

Lack of patent protection and general interest

There is a lack of protection for intellectual property including copyright and computer software as compared to the West. Despite all that is happening in Eastern Europe the potential of the total market may still amount to significantly less than what is occurring in Western Europe as it approaches the Single Market and so many companies will not consider Eastern Europe at this time.

Potential for East–West trade

The potential is for the long term rather than the short term because:

1 Financial infrastructure has to be created which will facilitate equity investment.

2 Removal of CoCom restrictions are necessary for growth in high technology areas of trade.
3 Multilateral payments systems have to replace bilateral payments.
4 As political risk diminishes the commercial risks increase with the appearance of new and hitherto unknown prospective clients in Eastern Europe.

However, there are opportunities particularly in the following areas:

- Environmental control, where Warsaw for example has only 30 per cent of the city on a town sewage system.
- Food production and distribution as witnessed in all media reports coming out of the area.
- Healthcare, not in terms of doctors but in terms of health education and resources.
- Transportation. Public transport has been ridiculously cheap because of subsidies which have not encouraged investment to speed communication between cities.
- Pulp and paper and packaging generally is in a very bad way.
- Consumer goods, poor quality, indifferent service and low availability.
- Communications, as discussed above, due mainly to the CoCom strategic embargoes.
- Tourism, but at the moment, only Hungary is able to entice Western tourists to stay for more than three days. Lack of hotels, restaurants and infrastructure such as shopping means that only a few centres such as Budapest will be able to compete for Western tourists in the short term (Paliwoda, 1991).

References

Dept of Trade and Industry, (1989) Security export control, a guide to the Export of Goods (Control) Order 1989, March and August.
Eurobusiness (1990) Eastern Europe: facts and figures, March,
Federerowicz, J. (1990) *Poland a guide to business opportunities* (1990), Prospectus Publications, Toronto.
Financial Times, 12 March 1990, Special Supplement: USSR.
Gorbachev, M. S. (1989) *Perestroika*, Ethics and Public Policy Centre, Wokingham.
Paliwoda, S. J. (1991) Changing East-West trade patterns: implications for global tourism. *World Travel and Tourism Review*, **1**, CAB International, Wallingford, Oxon.
Samli, A. C., and Jermakowicz, W. (1983) The stages of marketing evolution in East European countries. *European Journal of Marketing*, **17**, (2) 29.
UN World Trade Organization (1988) *Yearbook of Tourism Statistics*, 2 vols, Madrid.
UNECE (1990) Promotion of trade through industrial cooperation: statistical survey of recent trends in East-West industrial cooperation, Trade/R564, September.
International Bank for Reconstruction and Development (IBRD)/World Bank Group (1990), *World Debt Tables 1989–90*, Economic Analysis and Projections Department, External Debt Division, NY.

Key reading

Aganbegyan, A., and Brown, M. B. (1988) *The Economic Challenge of Perestroika*, Indiana University Press, Bloomington, Indiana.

Business International Ltd. (Weekly), *Business Eastern Europe*, London.

East European Trade Council (EETC), London, monthly bulletin.

IMD World Economic Forum, *The World Competitiveness Report 1990*, Geneva, Switzerland (includes survey of Hungary).

Knight, M. G. (1987) *How to do Business with Russians: A Handbook and Guide for Western World Business People*, Quorum Books, New York and London.

Liebrenz, M. L. (1984) *Transfer of Technology: US Multinationals and Production Ventures*, Praeger, New York..

Lindsay, M. (1989) *International Business in Gorbachev's Soviet Union*, St. Martin's Press, London.

London Chamber of Commerce and Industry (1990), *Winning Business in Eastern Europe: A Guide to European Community Funding and Opportunities*, June.

Mandel, E. (1989) *Beyond Perestroika: The Future of Gorbachev's USSR*, Verso, London.

Moscow Narodny Bank Ltd. (bi-monthly) *Press Bulletin*, London.

Paliwoda, S. J., (1985) Marketing in Eastern Europe. In *International Marketing Management* (Kaynak, E.) Praeger, New York, pp. 286–304.

Paliwoda, S. J., and Liebrenz, M. L. (1984) Expectations and outcomes of multinational joint ventures in Eastern Europe. *European Journal of Marketing*. **18**, (3).

Paliwoda, S. J., and Liebrenz, M. L. (1985) Transfer of technology to Eastern Europe and Transfer of technology within Eastern Europe. In Samli, A. C., *Technology Transfer*, Praeger, New York.

Poland: A Guide to Business Opportunities (1990) Prospectus Publications, Toronto.

19
Marketing in China

Economic background to the world's most populous nation

China is the world's most populous nation, and the third largest country in the world by size of landmass. Eighty per cent of this is uninhabitable mountainous and desert regions, so the population live in an area that measures 740,000 square miles which is approximately the size of Mexico. With 7 per cent of the world's cultivated land, China feeds 22 per cent of its population (De Mente, 1990). Population estimates by *Business China* forecast an annual average rate of 14–15 million persons over the next ten years while per capita grain output is expected to stay at 370–380 kg per year. The Eighth Five-Year Plan (1991–1995), and the Ten-Year Economic Program to the year 2000, call for 6 per cent per annum GNP growth.

The People's Republic of China (PRC) was established in 1949, but it chose to maintain an isolationist policy with the rest of the world until the early 1970s when it joined the United Nations and began to involve itself in world affairs. Since 1949, the important events have been the 'Great Leap Forward' in 1958, an early attempt to modernize China, but the border conflict with the USSR soured Sino—Soviet relations and led to them questioning the wholesale implementation of the Soviet Communist model. The Cultural Revolution, which isolated China from foreign influence, lasted from 1966 to the death of Mao in 1976. Since then, the Chinese Communist model has moved even further from the Soviet model. Canada and China established diplomatic relations in 1970. In 1972 China signed a treaty with Japan, in 1975 with the EC, and in 1980 joined the IMF and the World Bank.

In 1978, economic reform started in China, well ahead of the USSR. This was designed to transform the country into a powerful modern socialist state, by means of the 'Four Modernizations' viz. industry, agriculture, national defence, and science and technology, to quadruple its 1980 GNP by the year 2000. The 'Four Modernisations' are attributed to Deng Xiaoping, but had been advocated earlier, in 1975, by the late Premier Zhouen Lai, who lived in the shadow of Chairman Mao. The 'Open Door' resulted from the Sixth Five-Year Plan (1981–1985). It was the first published plan since the First Five-Year Plan (1953–1957). In 1984, there began the sale of stock in state-run companies. In 1985 the first Trademark Protection law and, in 1988 the Copyright Agency of China was established in Beijing, at the same time as the Shanghai Municipal Copyright Office. Also in 1988, the state monopoly on banking was broken with the first independent development bank.

Countertrade is likely to play a large role in this modernization programme, for China is an underdeveloped country and a market unlike other communist countries, partly due to its size, housing one-quarter of the world's population (which means more than one billion inhabitants, of whom 800 million are peasants), and partly to its politics which ensured its isolation from the rest of the world.

Arriving now with the intention to spend on industrial investments, China is being well received by world trading, banking and financial communities, yet per capita income in 1989 was $360. The Bank of China signed numerous agreements with leading banking institutions in the West and Japan for both private commercial credits and government backed export credits, although its foreign trade represents a very small share of its national income. China needs both to encourage exports and lower tariffs.

Foreign investment is being successfully drawn into the Special Economic Zones, such as Shenzen and the fourteen coastal cities (or ETDZs) of which more later. China's trade with the West has been small but of growing importance. China's exports to NATO countries accounted for more than 40 per cent of China's total 1989 exports of $52.5 billion, while China's imports from NATO countries accounted for more than 20 per cent of China's total 1989 imports of $59.1 billion.

With the rise to power of Deng Xiaoping in December 1978, China underwent a series of changes. Firstly, in the political arena, many Chinese citizens who were alienated under former regimes have been rehabilitated. Moves are taking place which, taken together, are very significant, for example: direct election of representatives at the county level; and a

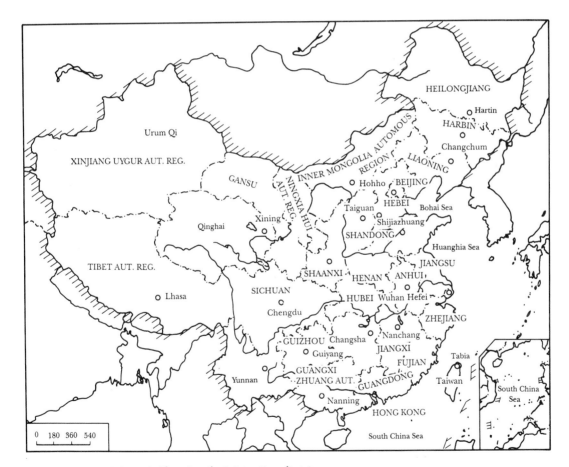

Figure 19.1 *Map of China's administrative divisions*
Note This map gives approximate geographical coverage. It does not, however, imply any position, on the part of the UN regarding territorial disputes.
Source UN Economic and Social Commission for Asia and the Pacific (1985) *Guidebook on Trading with the People's Republic of China*, 3rd edn, Bangkok, Thailand

greater role for legislation, developing a basic criminal and civil code as well as laws relating to the operations of foreign firms in China. In the absence of commercial law, trade took place on trust. Secondly, intellectual liberalization is greater than before but not yet complete. The Communist Party adheres rigidly still to four basic tenets: the leadership of the party; the guiding role of Marxism, Leninism and Maoism; the maintenance of the 'people's democratic dictatorship' as China's form of government; and the pursuit of a socialist road to economic development. Thirdly, since 1958 there has been 're-adjustment' of the Soviet model of development, which was transplanted wholesale into China in 1953. This rift widened with the border conflict with the USSR in 1960, but continued during the decade of the Cultural Revolution in the late 1960s, when a Chinese model of communism was being searched for, and on into the 1970s. Chinese communism has placed the political focus on the economy and not on the 'class' struggle.

Trading with a centrally planned economy

Since 1982, the pattern has been one of decentralization. The Ministry of Foreign Economic Relations and Trade (MOFERT) has had to share its authority with other ministries and provincial governments. This was designed to stimulate local involvement in foreign trade but has also created confusion over authority for necessary approvals. There is flexibility in the Chinese form of central planning which allows for the special treatment of the Special Economic Zones. Provided a proposed foreign investment is able to comply with the Five-Year Plan, the Open Door Policy encourages that investment. Whereas in the Soviet model of central planning only state enterprises have the right to undertake foreign trade. In China there have been cases of joint ventures and, even wholly foreign-owned subsidiaries being

Table 19.1   China at a glance

GNP US$ Million (1989)	393,006
Real growth rate, 1980–1989 (%)	9.6
Population (1989)	1,105,067
Growth rate, 1980–1989 (%)	1.3
GNP per capita (1989) US$	360
Real growth rate, 1987–1989 (%)	4.8
Agriculture's share in GDP (%)	32
Daily calorie supply per capita (1988)	2,632
Life expectancy (1989)	70
Total fertility (1989, per woman)	2.4
School enrolment (1987, % of schoolage)	82
Illiteracy (1985, %)	31

Source   *The World Bank Atlas 1990*, World Bank, Washington, DC.

Table 19.2   Capital goods output, 1990

	1990	1989	% Change 1990/89
Cotton yarn (million tons)	4.5	4.8	−5.6
Paper and paper board, machine made (million tons)	13.3	13.3	−0.2
Synthetic detergents (million tons)	1.5	1.5	1.2
Aluminum wares (million tons)	72.7	82.2	−11.6
Energy production, i.e., standard fuel (billion tons)	1.0	1.0	2.4
Crude coal (billion tons)	1.1	1.1	2.5
Crude oil (million tons)	138.0	134.6	2.5
Electricity (billion kwh) of	618.0	584.7	5.7
which hydro-electricity	126.0	118.3	6.5
Steel (million tons)	66.0	61.6	7.2
Rolled steel (million tons)	51.2	48.6	5.4
Cement (million tons)	203.0	209.9	−3.3
Timber (million cubic metres)	54.0	58.0	−6.9
Sulphuric acid (million tons)	11.7	11.5	1.4
Soda ash (million tons)	3.8	3.0	23.3
Chemical fertilizers (million tons)	19.1	18.0	6.1
Chemical insecticides (thousand tons)	229.3	207.9	10.5
Power-generating equipment capacity (million kw)	11.4	11.7	−2.7
Machine tools (thousands)	117.8	178.8	−34.1
Motor vehicles (thousands)	509.1	583.8	−12.8
Tractors (thousands)	39.0	39.6	−1.5
Locomotives	655.0	680.2	−3.7
Steel ships, civilian use (million tons)	1.2	1.4	−13.4

Source   *Business China*, Business International Asia/Pacific Ltd., Hong Kong.

allowed to undertake foreign trade. China, therefore, describes itself as a planned economy with market regulations. Soviet delegations were visiting the PRC to see how to create flexibility within central planning to allow this 'open door' to foreign investors. China seeks to maintain strong control only over those commodities which are essential to people's lives.

China needs an infusion of capital, technology and Western management expertise as it has a technology gap in most of its basic industries of up to ten years. To eliminate the black market in bonds, fully computerized stock exchanges were set up in Beijing, Shanghai, Shenyang, Wuhan, Guangzhou and Haikou. Originally this was to be a national stock and bond market. Shenzhen, which is a semi-official stock exchange, trades in stocks and bonds. The Shanghai exchange has the potential to become the most important for the international business and banking community, but the only joint venture to be listed there is Shanghai Volkswagen (Business China).

China does have some industrially advanced regions but reforms are needed to increase the productivity of investments, meet the multiple objectives of a modernizing economy and the diversified needs of the people. The Chinese are still, though, a long way from a fully-fledged stock exchange. The number of companies trading on the stock exchange is very low:

eight in Shanghai and thirteen in Shenzhen. There are restrictions on foreign companies operating in China which would hinder the development of the stock exchange, but there are deficiencies also in legislation and general regulations relating to securities, as well as in accounting practices. Furthermore, the volatility which can make a lucky speculator rich does not exist in the Chinese model. Beijing has ruled that the limit of fluctuation cannot exceed 0.5 per cent either way in any one business day. Still, there exists the problem of how to absorb the latent purchasing power that exists in China for which estimates vary as to how much is in free circulation among this population of approximately 1.2 billion people. The desire is to mop up this excess spending power and to divert this to some of the enterprises that urgently require funds. The problem, however, is still the state control planning system. When faced with rising levels of unemployment in 1989, Chinese leaders turned to one of the companies on the Shanghai exchange and ordered it to hire 2,400 employees from other failing enterprises. This kind of situation is not encountered in Western markets and would generally not be regarded as an 'off-the-balance-sheet' risk that may be encountered. The Chinese infrastructure is young and weak, and the integration of capitalism and communism is poorly defined, and so what emerges is a weak hybrid of a system unable to please anyone.

This new China has set lower industrial targets but higher targets for light industry which produces consumer goods. This is intended to absorb greater purchasing power and meet new consumer demands, as seen in declining sales of plain clothing, characteristic of the

Table 19.3   Agricultural Output, 1990

	1990	1989	% Change 1990/89
Grain	435.0	407.7	6.7
Cotton	4.5	3.8	18.1
Oil-bearing crops	16.2	13.0	24.7
Rapeseed	6.9	5.4	27.5
Sugarcane	57.3	48.8	17.4
Beetroot	14.5	9.2	7.2
Jute, ambary hemp	0.7	0.7	9.5
Cured tobacco	2.3	2.4	−6.2
Silkworm cocoons	0.5	0.5	0.4
Tea	0.5	0.5	−0.3
Fruit	18.8	18.3	2.4
Port, beer and mutton	25.0	23.2	7.7
Milk	4.1	3.8	8.2
Wool	0.2	0.2	1.8
Pigs, slaughtered (million head)	310.0	291.9	6.2
Large animals in stock (million head, year-end)	130.0	126.6	2.'7
Hogs in stock (million head, year-end)	360.0	349.5	3.0
Sheep in stock (million head, year-end)	210.0	211.7	−0.8

Note   Figures in million metric tons, unless otherwise specified.
Source   *Business China*, Business International Asia/Pacific Ltd., Hong Kong.

Table 19.4   Consumer products output, 1990

	1990	1989	% Change 1990/89
Cloth (billion metres)	18.0	18.9	−4.9
Woollen fabric (million metres)	280.0	280.0	0.0
	5.7	5.0	14.0
Sugar (million tons)	19.8	5.0	−29.9
Crude salt (million crates)	32.9	31.9	3.0
Cigarettes (million crates)	31.4	36.8	−14.6
Bicycles (millions)	26.6	27.7	−3.8
TV sets (millions)	10.2	9.4	8.8
Colour TV sets (millions)	29.7	23.5	26.4
Tape recorders (millions)	1.9	2.5	−22.6
Washing machines, household (millions)	6.5	8.3	−20.9
Refrigerators, household (millions)	4.8	6.7	−29.2

Source   *Business China*, Business International Asia/Pacific Ltd., Hong Kong.

Table 19.5   Foreign income statistics, 1990

	1990	1989	% Change 1990/89
Merchandise exports	62.1	52.5	18.1
Merchandise imports	53.4	59.1	−9.8
Balance	8.7	−6.6	
Foreign capital			
contracted	12.3	11.5	7.4
utilized	10.1	10.1	0.4
Direct foreign investment	3.4	3.4	0.0
Overseas construction and labour service projects			
income	1.7	1.4	23.0
contract amount	2.5	2.2	13.0
Tourism income	2.2	1.9	19.2
Foreign visitors (millions)	27.5	24.5	12.1

Note   Current US$ billions unless otherwise specified.
Source   *Business China*, Business International Asia/Pacific Ltd., Hong Kong.

Maoist period, and the desire for more fashion. However, although productivity changes have been taking place, the share of old people in the population is rising alongside these other social trends. Whereas, previously, bicycles, sewing machines and watches have been most important, this has now changed to colour televisions, refrigerators, tape recorders, washing machines and cameras, in that order. Politically, there is no longer the need for China to be internally so self-reliant, and so, China's new leaders have greatly expanded trade with the West. Guangdong Province, close to Hong Kong, is now rivalling the performance of the 'Four Dragons': Singapore, Hong Kong, Taiwan and South Korea.

Table 19.6   Trade of NATO with China, 1986–89

	1986			1987		
Country/area	Total from (or to) entire world	From (or to) China	Trade with China as % of world trade	Total from (or to) entire world	From (or to) China	Trade with China as % of world trade
Imports (CIF)						
European NATO	802,736.9	4,221.8	0.5	979,317.9	6,161.7	0.6
Canada (FOB)	81,313.7	407.8	0.5	87,583.2	582.0	0.7
USA (FOB)	369,961.2	4,771.2	1.3	405,900.0	6,294.0	0.9
Total NATO	1,254,011.8	9,400.8	0.7	1,472,801.1	13,037.7	0.9
Exports (FOB)						
European NATO	806,813.7	6,576.0	0.8	971,213.7	6,545.0	0.7
Canada	86,663.2	795.6	0.9	94,394.4	1,086.0	1.2
USA	217,304.4	3,106.8	1.4	252,866.4	3,496.8	1.4
Total NATO	1,110,871.3	10,478.4	0.9	1,318,474.5	11,127.8	0.8

	1988			1989		
Country/area	Total from (or to) entire world	From (or to) China	Trade with China as % of world trade	Total from (or to) entire world	From (or to) China	Trade with China as % of world trade
Imports (CIF)						
European NATO	1,105,464.4	7,903.9	0.7	1,199,952.9	9,456.5	0.8
Canada (FOB)	106,819.2	776.4	0.7	114,140.4	999.6	0.9
USA (FOB)	441,282.0	8,512.8	1.9	473,396.4	11,988.0	2.5
Total NATO	1,653,565.6	17,193.1	1.0	1,787,489.7	22,444.1	1.3
Exports (FOB)						
European NATO	1,077,262.7	7,057.2	0.7	1,160,232.0	7,149.1	0.6
Canada	111,942.0	2,115.6	1.9	116,200.8	964.8	0.8
USA	320,385.6	5,038.8	1.6	363,765.6	5,806.8	1.6
Total NATO	1,509,590.3	14,211.6	0.9	1,640,198.4	13,920.7	0.8

Note   Figures in millions of dollars.
Source   United States Department of State Bureau of Intelligence and Research (1990) Trade of NATO Countries with China 1986–9, Intelligence Research Report IRR-9, Unclassified, 20 November.

Table 19.7 Trade of NATO countries with China, 1986–89

Country/area	1986	1987	1988	1989	1986	1987	1988	1989
Imports								
Belgium-Luxembourg	211.0	206.4	240.0	256.8	0.3	0.2	0.3	0.3
Denmark	194.3	244.8	318.0	321.1	0.9	1.0	1.2	1.2
France	708.0	1,096.8	1,441.2	1,726.8	0.5	0.7	0.8	0.1
FRG	1,250.4	1,924.8	2,462.4	3,087.6	0.6	0.8	1.0	1.1
Greece	26.9	38.9	70.0	77.0	0.2	0.3	0.6	0.5
Iceland	2.1	2.7	4.0	4.6	0.2	0.2	0.2	0.3
Italy	681.6	1,021.2	1,438.8	1,790.4	0.7	0.8	1.0	1.1
Netherlands	267.8	350.4	466.8	502.8	0.4	0.4	0.5	0.5
Norway	52.9	171.8	109.1	165.8	0.3	0.8	0.5	0.7
Portugal	15.0	41.6	64.1	49.0	0.2	0.3	0.4	0.3
Spain	232.2	248.9	385.1	529.1	0.7	0.5	0.6	0.7
Turkey	93.8	172.6	114.8	76.7	0.8	1.2	0.8	0.5
UK	478.8	640.8	789.6	868.8	0.4	0.4	0.4	0.4
Total European NATO	4,221.8	6,161.7	7,903.9	9,456.5	0.5	0.6	0.7	0.8
Canada (FOB)	407.8	582.0	776.4	999.6	0.5	0.7	0.7	0.9
USA (FOB)	4,771.2	6,294.0	8,512.8	11,988.0	1.3	1.6	1.9	2.5
Total NATO	9,400.8	13,037.7	17,193.1	22,444.1	0.7	0.9	1.0	1.3

Note Figures in millions of dollars CIF.
Source United States Department of State Bureau of Intelligence and Research (1990). Trade of NATO Countries with China, 1986–89, Intelligence Research Report IRR-9, Unclassified, 20 November.

Table 19.8 Trade of NATO countries with China, 1986–89

Country/area	1986	1987	1988	1989	1986	1987	1988	1989
Exports								
Belgium-Luxembourg	359.8	271.2	348.0	355.2	0.5	0.3	0.4	0.4
Denmark	129.7	184.8	129.5	96.8	0.6	0.7	0.5	0.3
France	667.2	849.6	925.2	1,549.2	0.6	0.6	0.6	0.9
FRG	2,863.2	2,796.0	2,786.4	2,457.6	1.2	0.9	0.9	0.7
Greece	29.0	21.1	20.8	28.0	0.5	0.3	0.3	0.4
Iceland	insig.	0.2	0.2	1.2	insig.	insig.	insig.	insig.
Italy	1,002.0	1,086.0	1,315.2	1,312.8	1.0	0.9	1.0	0.9
Netherlands	209.0	181.2	266.4	244.8	0.3	0.2	0.3	0.2
Norway	66.6	81.5	67.3	102.8	0.4	0.4	0.3	0.4
Portugal	23.2	21.8	31.8	21.5	0.3	0.2	0.3	0.2
Spain	319.7	267.5	218.8	226.8	1.2	0.8	0.5	0.5
Turkey	120.6	103.7	215.6	68.4	1.6	1.0	1.8	0.6
UK	786.0	680.4	732.0	684.0	0.7	0.5	0.5	0.4
Total European NATO	6,576.0	6,545.0	7,057.2	7,149.1	0.8	0.7	0.7	0.6
Canada (FOB)	795.6	1,086.0	2,115.6	964.8	0.9	1.2	1.9	0.8
USA (FOB)	3,106.9	3,496.8	5,038.8	5,806.8	1.4	1.4	1.6	1.6
Total NATO	10,478.4	11,127.8	14,211.6	13,920.7	0.9	0.8	0.9	0.8

Note Figures in millions of dollars, FOB.
Source United States Department of State Bureau of Intelligence and Research (1990) Trade of NATO Countries with China, 1986–89, Intelligence Research Report IRR-9, Unclassified, 20 November.

Table 19.9 Selected countries' and regions' foreign trade with China, 1984–88

(million $)	1984	1985	1986	1987	1988	% Change 1988/87
Hong Kong/Macao						
Imports (CIF)	2,987	4,851	5,690	8,546	12,131	+41.90
Exports (FOB)	7,232	7,455	10,100	14,204	17,501	+23.20
Total	10,219	12,306	15,790	22,751	29,632	+30.20
% of total China trade	19.7	17.7	31.9	24.4	28.8	
Japan						
Imports (CIF)	5,957	6,482	5,670	7,478	7,928	+6.12
Exports (FOB)	7,216	12,477	9,850	8,337	11,058	+32.64
Total	13,173	18,959	15,520	15,815	18.986	+20.20
% of total China trade	25.4	17.2	19.1	21.0	18.4	
USA						
Imports (CIF)	3,381	4,224	5,241	4,831	6,629	+37.20
Exports (FOB)	3,004	3,856	3,105	3,037	3,377	+11.20
Total	6,385	8,080	8,346	7,868	10,006	+27.20
% of total China trade	12.3	11.6	12.6	11.3	9.7	
West Germany						
Imports (DIF)	1,331	2,407	3,556	3,131	3,434	+9.66
Exports (FOB)	811	734	1,004	1,224	1,485	+21.27
Total	2,142	3,141	4,560	4,355	4,919	+13.00
% of total China trade	4.1	4.5	6.2	5.2	4.8	
USSR						
Imports (CIF)	711	982	1,440	1,272	1,782	+40.17
Exports (FOB)	616	996	1,200	1,247	1,476	+18.35
Total	1,327	1,979	2,640	2,519	3,258	+29.30
% of total China trade	2.6	2.8	3.6	3.0	3.1	
Canada						
Imports (CIF)	1,127	1,159	1,022	1,398	1,860	+33.04
Exports (FOB)	270	235	307	409	387	−4.70
Total	1,397	1,394	1,318	1,807	2,249	+24.50
% of total China trade						
Italy						
Imports (CIF)	464	910	1,138	1,238	1,547	+24.98
Exports (FOB)	320	294	363	556	746	+34.19
Total	784	1,204	1,501	1,795	2,293	+27.70
% of total China trade	1.5	1.7	2.0	2.1	2.1	
UK						
Imports (CIF)	533	746	1,011	900	898	−0.17
Exports (FOB)	349	354	1,433	532	659	+23.90
Total	1,082	1,100	2,444	1,432	1,557	+8.70
% of total China trade	2.1	1.6	1.7	1.7	1.5	

Source *China Business Review* (1990), May–June, pp. 44–45.

Market information

There is more readily available market information than ever which, while significant progress, is still scant by Western standards.

Livingstone (1987) summed up the problems of conducting market research in China quite neatly, in saying:

> Not least, it is a closed society in the information sense, with advertising by poster or television relying on a blunderbuss effect rather than targeting; and where, as one student suggested, the only realistic manner of acquiring a sampling frame for local consumer market research would be to enlist the cooperation of the local police station, as the only source of information.

Westerners who wish to learn more of the opportunities available may contact:

- Foreign Trading Corporations (FTC)
- CITIC: China International Trust and Investment Corporation
- Leadership in specially designated areas: the SEZs and ETDZs.

As credit is presently squeezed, the means to attract foreign trade and investment will comprise chiefly of variants of joint ventures and countertrade. Access to the internal domestic Chinese market is still limited. Chinese consumers are generally more confident of the quality of imported goods, so the challenge is that of giving an imported-look to joint-venture products. As 99 per cent of the population speak only Chinese, but while the Chinese characters will remain the same, this entails a number of different dialects. Mandarin, based in the North, is the most common. To Westerners it creates confusion as to whether we use the term Beijing or Peking to refer to the same place. Ogilvy and Mather opened in Beijing in 1986 and have developed Chinese packaging for Maxwell House, Pond's, Seagrams, and Johnson and Johnson, among others (Fyock, 1990).

The workings of the domestic Chinese market

Before 1978, private enterprise was not allowed. For Chinese nationals, there are three types of economic enterprise permitted in China – individual, collective and state. Economic reform allows farmers as well as industrial enterprises to sell their surplus or to swap their produce for other products. Industrial enterprises are being made responsible for their own profits and losses under the Assets Management Responsibility System. Unprofitable enterprises have been closed, or threatened with closure, (small iron plants run by prefectures and counties have been reduced in number) while profitable ones have been allowed to retain a greater part of their net income to use for bonuses, benefits and new investments. Enterprises have also been leased to individuals or groups under contracts.

Chinese society remains rooted around the concept of the commune which consists of a cluster of villages around a traditional market town with a population which varies between 15,000 and 50,000. These resemble large villages. Next down the scale is the co-operative and there may be eight or ten of these per brigade. However, even here change is taking place as responsibility shifts to smaller units and the family groups, the households classed as self-employed, which are so important for China's agricultural output. In total, six kinds of businesses are permitted under the individual enterprise form (Reader, 1984):

- Commercial – retailing items purchased wholesale from collective and state enterprises.
- Handicrafts – making and selling simple items such as toys or baskets or art works; some forms of art work, such as paintings, can only be sold to the state for resale by the state.
- Transportation – primarily 'pedicabs' or three-wheeled bicycles with a seat for one or two passengers.
- Repairing – shoe repair, bicycle repair, etc.
- Services – barbering, hairdressing, tailoring, etc.
- Food preparation – from street stands to small restaurants.

With the permission of the local AIC (Administration of Industry and Commerce), and through contracts approved by them, individual enterprises may hire up to five apprentices and up to two assistants. The reasons offered for this are to better serve the needs of consumers and to help alleviate the pressing problem of unemployment.

Keith and Kimberley (1983) interpret these changes in the Chinese system as follows.

1 The commune system should be seen in a historical perspective as a product of evolutionary adaptation and not as an immutable institution created during a heroic period of socialist construction.
2 Experimentation with alternative institutional arrangements has always been part of the Chinese style of rural development and thus, the recent innovations and experiments are consistent with past approaches to development problems.
3 There is an economic logic to the commune system that can best be understood when the household economy is regarded as the base of the system and the fourth tier of a four-tiered institutional hierarchy.
4 The essence of the new reforms is a shift of responsibility for crop cultivation from the production team to the household economy, but not to the private sector. This shift does not imply the imminent disbandment of the commune system, although in some circumstances the commune system could be severely weakened and even destroyed.
5 Some aspects of the new reforms, if not corrected, could lead to greater inequality, lower levels of capital accumulation and slower long run rates of growth of output, but these consequences are not inherent in the reforms.
6 Such evidence as exists indicates that the distribution of collective income in rural areas, including collective income originating in the household economy, continues to be relatively egalitarian.
7 Moreover, in the few cases where comparisons over time are possible, there is no evidence that the reforms have been associated with an increase in the degree of inequality at the local level.

China's party and state bureaucracies are in need of reform. Bureaucracy is being reduced with planned decentralization and the average age of officials to be reduced while their expected level of education is increased. The present economic system is highly centralized with:

- decision-making confined to the leading central economic organs,
- highly centralized planning precludes the functioning of markets, and
- functioning of the economy depends mainly on administrative measures with little impetus from economic interests.

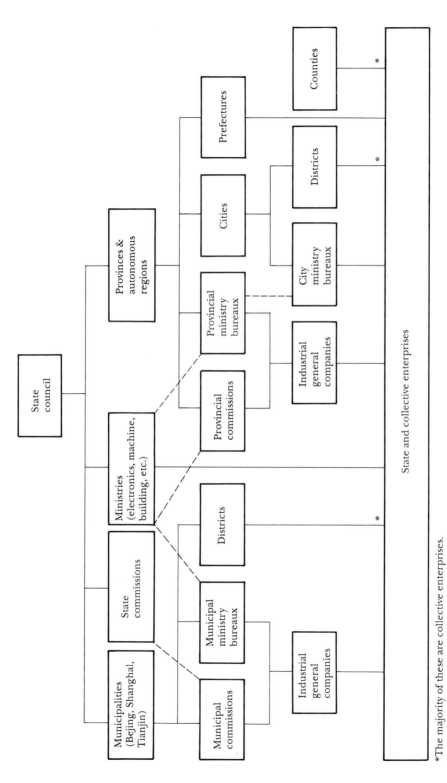

*The majority of these are collective enterprises.

Figure 19.2 *China's state planning system*
Source Campbell, N. (1987) Enterprise autonomy in the Beijing municipality. In *Management Reforms in China* (Warner, M.), Frances Pinter, London

Much has to be done in the range, quality and design of these manufactured products. While in energy, China is beginning to experience shortages, although petroleum exported was only 12 per cent of output and coal exported was only 1 per cent of output, it does mean that there is little scope here for export expansion as things exist. Longer term, China's economic development will depend on export earnings from coal, steel, oil and petroleum-related commodities, but in the short term, will have to focus on tourism and consumer goods. Meanwhile, transportation remains a problem and harbour facilities are not sufficiently developed to serve an expansion of foreign trade.

Special Economic Zones (SEZ)

The first was Shenzhen in the province of Guangdong (or Canton) in 1979. Since then, three further SEZs have been established in South China: Shenzhen and Zhuhai, also in Guangdong, and at Huli in the City of Xiamen in the province of Fujian. Further decentralization came about in 1984, making the conditions more favourable to foreign investment, and in 1988, Hainan Island acquired SEZ status at the same time as being promoted to being an autonomous province. The SEZ are able to accept foreign investment in virtually any area of economic activity of interest to China, including services as well as production. Since May 1990, foreigners are now able to engage in land development, and to install electric power and telephone services, and to operate these utilities in one of the designated investment zones. Technologically advanced investments benefit from a reduced level of taxation.

Economic and Technical Development Zones (ETDZ)

Economic and Technical Development Zones were created in 1984. These comprise of the fourteen coastal cities and are now being termed China's new Gold Coast:

Dalian	Qinhungdao
Tianjin	Yantai
Qingdao	Lianyunggang
Nantong	Shanghai
Ningbo	Wenzhou
Fuzhou	Guangzhou
Zhangjiang	Beihai

Preferential administrative procedures and tax incentives would be made available to foreign investors within ETDZ boundaries provided that the economic activities, which they financed, qualified as high technology by Chinese standards or as production enterprises for export. For production enterprises, or scientific and technological research institutions, the ETDZ has much to commend it, but these are the limits within which the ETDZ is allowed to operate. Yet, there is the advantage here of location, unlike the four SEZs which are all located in South China. Regulation is on two levels, national and local, and applicable to the ETDZs themselves, but there is overlap and lack of definition of terms and direction.

Each ETDZ has a sino-foreign joint venture management company managing it, which acts as the regulatory authority, but the question of jurisdiction enters into financing, for example.

Investments in Shanghai of thirty million dollars require central Government authorization, but elsewhere the quota limit will be lower.

The ETDZ is able to levy a local income tax, usually around 10 per cent, but this is decided locally and so the coastal cities of China have to be compared with each other. Legislation changes in 1986 offered particular tax incentives to exporting companies and technologically advanced foreign companies. The services sector was, therefore, excluded. This may be because of Chinese disappointment with both the levels and the nature of foreign investments in the period 1979–1985, which was centred mainly on hotels and tourism with some Hong Kong investment in relatively unsophisticated technology (Larson, 1988). Yet, prior to 1985, China had no legislation in force relating to contracts with foreign parties. Two principles are important to note here. The first is that of 'equality and mutual benefit.' The other is of 'achieving unanimity through consultations.' These two principles are embedded in Chinese legislation.

ETDZs offer:

- preferential treatment,
- infrastructure and services,
- experienced management pro-sino-foreign joint ventures, and
- proximity to other foreign investing companies.

Investing in a joint-venture project

China openly welcomes both equity and contractual forms of joint venture with its 'open door' policy on foreign investment. In 1979, the Government established the Foreign Investment Control Commission to scrutinize and approve all joint-venture agreements. The law on joint ventures requires foreign investors to abide by Chinese laws and decrees; second, it protects the rights and interests of foreign investors; and third, it emphasizes the need to accelerate the pace of China's 'Four Modernizations', which include the comprehensive modernization of industry, agriculture, national defence, and science and technology. Enterprises which are export-oriented receive a special priority. The foreign investor is expected to provide the advanced technology and equipment, while China contributes the necessary land and workforce. This means that ventures which are labour intensive are best suited to these conditions.

Arising from this law, the China International Trust and Investment Corporation was established. Known as CITIC, it operates under the control of the Chinese State Council, and can assist to contact various ministries, provincial and local administrations. CITIC is a holding company with its own bank and trading company, and is able to invest in a joint venture with a Western partner and to even issue its own bonds abroad.

China's Ministry of Foreign Economic Relations and Trade (MOFERT) issued new rules on 22 October 1990 which state that joint ventures, other than in the following restricted categories, can now run indefinitely:

- service trades including hotels, apartments and offices, entertainment, restaurants, taxi services, photo development, mechanical maintenance, and consultancy,
- land development and real estate,
- resource exploration and extraction, and
- projects restricted by the state and projects for which state laws require a time limit.

The Eighth Five-Year Plan, while emphasizing agriculture, transportation, raw materials and energy as priority sectors, has lowered the growth rates that were written into the Seventh Plan (1986–90).

Establishing a joint venture in China is not particularly easy. Whereas in the past, foreign

Table 19.10   An investor's lexicon

Approval authority
Shenpi jiguan

The organization that has the legal authorization to approve an activity involving a foreign investment enterprise. For example, the Ministry of Foreign Economic Relations and Trade or their local-level counterpart is the approval authority for foreign investment contracts.

Contractual joint venture (CJV)
Hezuo jingying qiye

Contractual joint ventures can take two forms: 1) a limited liability entity with legal person status that closely resembles an equity joint venture; 2) a business partnership in which the parties cooperate as separate legal entities and carry out their respective contractual obligations without establishing a joint management entity. In either case, contractual joint ventures differ from equity joint ventures in two important respects: the forms of investment contributed by each party need not be in cash or in kind (e.g., labour and utilities have in some cases been allowed as contributions); and profits are shared based on a ratio specified in the contract, not necessarily according to investment contributions. Contractual joint ventures are also often called cooperative ventures or coproduction agreements.

Department in charge
Zhuguan bumen

The department in charge of a joint venture is generally the Chine partner's supervisory organization. For example, in a light industrial joint venture with a factory as the Chinese partner, the local light industrial bureau will usually be the department in charge of the joint venture. The department in charge has primarily administrative functions and acts as a channel for the joint venture's business with China's bureaucracy. For example, project proposals, joint venture contracts and feasibility studies, and advanced technology applications are first submitted to the department in charge, which then forwards them to the appropriate approval authorities.

Equity joint venture (EJV)
Hezi jingying qiye

A limited liability corporation in which the Chinese and foreign partners jointly invest in and operate the corporation. Profits and risk are shared according to the percentage of equity held by each partner. Investment contributions may be in cash or in kind.

Foreign investment enterprise (FIE)
Waishang touzi qiye

Term used to collectively refer to equity joint ventures, contractual joint ventures, and wholly foreign-owned enterprises. Does not include offshore oil investment contracts. Much of China's new investment legislation is being written to apply to these three types of projects.

Wholly foreign-owned enterprise (WFOE)
Waishang duzi qiye

A limited liability entity solely owned and operated by a foreign investor. The foreign investor receives all profits and bears all risks.

Source   Zhang, S. X., and Snyder, J. L. (1988) The Five Ps. *China Business Review*, March–April.

investors did put up with inefficient work practices, exorbitant overheads and cumbersome bureaucracy just to get established, there is now a different attitude among Western investors who see less appeal in China, and consequently, are taking a more pragmatic and tightly focused approach to Chinese market entry. Selwyn (1990) points to three trends taking place:

1 foreign companies are driving harder bargains,
2 they are choosing their joint venture partners carefully, and
3 they are seeking longer joint venture contracts to give them time to amortize start-up costs.

Issues over CoCom strategic export controls have yet to be lifted. This means that some technologies and some exports will not be allowed by the NATO-member countries, even if these same technologies may be available within the Pacific Basin itself.

There were 100 companies which had established trade relations with China by 1976, rising to 174 in 1980, and 182 in 1981. In terms of the often very necessary international trade agreements and protocols which facilitate international trade, China had concluded eighty-eight of these in 1980 alone, and by the end of 1980 had signed foreign credit agreements totalling $20 billion, and more than 360 joint venture projects were set up with foreign funds amounting to $1.5 billion.

By 1991, China had established 29,000 joint ventures. Ownership is determined by the proportionate percentage of capital committed. Management is by a board of directors appointed in proportion to the equity ownership of the participants. Joint ventures are expected to generate foreign exchange. Gross profits are taxed under the Joint Venture Income Tax Law at a rate of 30 per cent, plus a tax surcharge of 10 per cent, unless the entity is located in a designated economic zone in which case special tax incentives are granted (Larson, 1988).

Political interference in joint ventures increased following the Tiananmen events, and this was reflected in Chinese representation on mixed boards of control and also demands for paid political study for the workforce. Approvals were held up and bureaucratic delays worsened, not only between ministries but between the provinces and MOFERT. Accounts receivable were extended beyond 100 days and were dubbed 'unreceivables' by one Western general manager (*China Business Review*, 1990). Credit squeeze and inability to access investment

Table 19.11   Foreign investment enterprise (FIE) headaches

> - Too many people involved in negotiations
> - Unfamiliarity with international practice
> - Aversion to risk
> - Impractical goals
> - Secrecy
> - Diverse objectives
> - High housing costs
> - Labour issues
> - Procurement problems

Source   Givant, N. (1990) Investing in Shanghai.
China Business Review, March–April, 28–30.

Table 19.12   Disincentives to invest

1   Historically inefficient allocation and use of natural human resources. 2   Inadequate infrastructure for absorbing and disseminating technology rapidly. 3   Inability to translate experiential laboratory or small-scale production successes into broader gains. 4   Inadequate management skills, training, discipline and problem-solving expertise. 5   Labour costs that have not been competitive with other Asian countries. 6   Lack of qualified scientific, engineering and technical personnel. 7   Absence of standardisation in instrumentation and scientific manufacturing equipment. 8   Shortage of hard foreign currency and inability to generate foreign exchange through exports of high technology products due to substandard products. 9   Lack of uniform dissemination and enforcement of laws, rules and regulations.

Source   Chwang and Thurston (1987) Technology takes command: the policy of the People's Republic of China with respect to technology transfer and protection of intellectual property. *The International Lawyer*, **21**, (Winter), 132. Cited in Larson, M. R. (1988) Exporting private enterprise to developing communist countries: a case study on China. *Columbia Journal of World Business*, **23**, (Spring), 85.

capital posed another major obstacle. The retrenchment following the Tiananmen events also dated the very interesting study by Frankenstein and Chao (1988) of decision-making in the Chinese Foreign Trade Administration.

The negative impact of the events of Tiananmen in June 1989 are seen also in the levels of incoming foreign investment to China, although the time lag involved in these contracts from signature to official ratification made the situation look better than it in fact was, and so, although the investment conditions had not changed, the will of foreign investors had suddenly dissipated. That will has since revived, but China is showing itself to be more selective about the kinds of investment that it wants to bring in, emphasizing technology and export-intensity, and dragging its feet on investment proposals related to luxury goods.

Zhang and Snyder (1988), in a study of foreign investment projects in China, came up with a checklist that amounts to Five Ps: project, partner, pattern, profitability,and protection, each of which includes a number of variables.

Wholly Foreign-Owned Enterprises (WFOE)

Since 1 April 1986, it is possible for a wholly foreign-owned enterprise (WFOE) to be established outside, as well as within, a SEZ or ETDZ provided that it 'utilises advanced technology and equipment, or exports all or a major portion of its products' (Larson, 1988). The ground rules are still to be defined, however, and so the SEZ or ETDZ seems safer against an assurance that the Government will not nationalize an enterprise 'except under special circumstances' as yet to be defined.

WFOEs have been the most controversial forms of foreign investment and their terms of incorporation remain unclear (Barale, 1990). Nevertheless, the number of WFOEs is increasing, some 423 such contracts were signed in the first six months of 1989. WFOEs are expected to show that they are self-sufficient, that their foreign exchange income meets their needs and exceeds their renminbi income. Where a WFOE involves $10 million or less, then

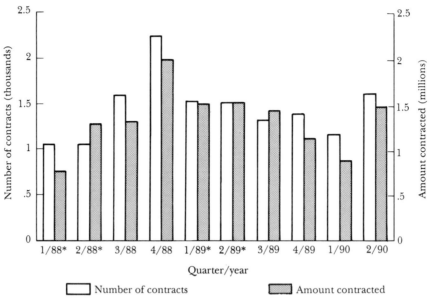

*Figures were derived by dividing Jan.–June totals in half

Figure 19.3   *Foreign investment in China 1988–90*
Source   *China Business Review* (1990) Two years of troubles, November-December, p. 33

the authority for approval lies with the provinces. A WFOE may not produce items for local sale that are restricted by the State, or manufacture export items that require export licences from MOFERT. The provinces and local authorities still report approvals to MOFERT. The five stages are:

1 A company interested in establishing a WFOE prepares a proposal stating the general purpose of the project, its products, planned production, registered capital and loans, intended market, and estimated size of facilities and number of employees.
2 If there is support from the department in charge of the industry, the foreign company is asked to prepare a feasibility study which will be examined alongside the project proposal by the State Planning Commission.
3 MOFERT approval, which is more legalistic in nature assessing the good financial standing of the company and power of attorney of the local representative.
4 Application to the local Administration of Industry and Commerce (AIC) for a business licence. This is then the completion of the formal legal establishment. AIC may seek changes, particularly where there may be domestic sales of the WFOE's products.
5 Tax registration must follow within twenty days. WFOEs are taxed at the rate of the Foreign Enterprise Income Tax Law rather than those of the Joint Venture Law.

The largest WFOE in China to date is that of Panda Motors, with a proposed investment of up to $1 billion. The company has been linked with the Rev. Sun Myung Moon's Unification Church, popularly known as the 'Moonies' (Harwit, 1990). The proposal to build 300,000 small cars in 1995 is exceedingly ambitious and will require higher levels of local content than Volkswagen's current production of 15,700 Santanas; Chrysler's 6,630 Cherokee vehicles, and Peugeot's 5,000 cars. It will also require a large absorptive market, but as a WFOE, will face some obstacles in trying to penetrate the domestic Chinese market from existing state-owned producers.

Joint-venture dissolution

These is a lack of clarity in the existing Chinese legislation, but Article 102 of the Implementing Regulations to the 1979 Equity Joint Venture Law states six permissible bases for terminating an equity joint venture (Frisbie and Kay, 1990):

- termination of contract duration,
- inability to continue operations due to heavy losses,
- inability to continue operations due to the failure of one of the parties to carry out its contractual obligations,
- inability to continue operations due to heavy losses caused by force majeure,
- inability to obtain the desired objectives of the operation and at the same time to see a future for development, and

Table 19.13   Potential investor checklist

Project
- Is the proposed investment project compatible with Chinese planning goals?
- Does it fall into a priority sector of China's economy?

Partner
- Is the potential Chinese partner authorized to participate in foreign investment projects?
- Do other parties need to be involved in the transaction?
- What are the advantages and drawbacks to your potential partner?

Pattern
- What type of investment structure is best for the project?

Profitability
- What is the project's market and anticipated market share?
- What form will profits take?
- What are the restrictions on using and repatriating foreign exchange?

Protection
- What kind of protection does Chinese law provide this type of investment?
- How will disputes be resolved?

Source   Zhang, S. X., and Snyder, J. L. (1988) The Five Ps. *China Business Review*, March–April.

- occurrence of other reasons for dissolution prescribed by the contract and articles of association.

Very few joint ventures have been terminated relative to the number in operation. Aside from the expiry of contracts, where it may be noted that the average duration of joint ventures is between eleven to fifteen years, a unanimous vote of the board of directors and approval of the government department that originally approved the joint venture contract – usually MOFERT – is also required. The decision has to be publicized in local newspapers to give creditors notice of intention to cease operations. The quite different philosophical approach of Chinese Government officials to Western accounting conventions will undoubtedly present problems in the evaluation of assets and liabilities, including obligations to the redundant workforce.

The future

In foreign policy, China has maintained its own independence, totally separate from, and often conflicting with, the Soviet Union. Yet, politics are drawing China closer to full membership in the Pacific Basin. China will have responsibility for Hong Kong after 1997 and Macao after 1999, and Taiwan has now dropped its vehement opposition to the PRC which will increase the potential for trade. Enlargement of ASEAN to include Japan, China and Taiwan would create a redoubtable force for trade.

Ironically, the USA was the prime mover in this region of the world before the economic rise of Japan, and had done much to foster economic integration within the region. Singapore, South Korea, Taiwan and Hong Kong are good success stories, referred to as either Newly Industrialized Countries (NIC) or, more popularly, as the Four Dragons. Their success in forging a place for themselves in the World League of Industrial Nations was to have their GSP (Generalized System of Preferences) tariff rates removed by the USA in 1988.

References

Barale, L. A. (1990) Wholly foreign owned enterprises: changing policy, changing attitudes. *China Business Review*, January-February, 30–35.
Baldinger, P. (1990) Grinning and bearing it: developers of the huge Shanghai Centre are determined to conquer political, financial and structural obstacles. *China Business Review*, March-April, 40–43.
Brecher, R. (1990) The end of investment's wonder years. *China Business Review*, January-February, 27–29.
Business International Asia/Pacific Ltd., *Business China*, twice monthly report on China, Hong Kong.
China Business Review (1990) Two years of troubles, November–December, 32–37.
Dennis, R. D. (1982) The countertrade factor in China's modernisation plan. *Columbia Journal of World Business*, Spring, 67–75.
Denny, D. C. (1989) Can you do market research in China? *China Business Review*, May-June, 36–46.
Frankenstein, J., and Chao, C.N. (1988) Decision-making in the Chinese Foreign Trade Administration: a preliminary survey. *Columbia Journal of World Business*, Fall, 35–40.

Frisbie, J., and Kay, D. B. (1990) Joint venture dissolution: few legal guidelines make contract language the key. *China Business Review*, November-December, 42–45.

Fureng, D. (1983) Some problems concerning China's strategy in foreign economic relations. *International Social; Science Journal*, (97), 455–566.

Fyock, D. A. (1990) Packaging an image: China's enterprises are struggling to adapt public relations to a socialist society. *China Business Review*, September-October, 20–22.

Gillespie, R. E., and Ruwart, S. E. (1989) Hainan: facts, figures and fantasies. *China Business Review*, January-February, 20–30.

Givant, N. (1990) Investing in Shanghai: since Tiananmen, city officials have taken a more intrinsic approach to foreign projects. *China Business Review*, March-April, 28–39.

Griffin, Keith, and Griffin, Kimberley (1983) Institutional change and income distribution in the Chinese countryside. *Oxford Bulletin of Economics and Statistics*, **45**,(3), 223–248.

Harding, H. (1984) The transformation of China. *Brookings Review*, Spring, 3–7.

Harwit, E. (1990) China's elusive panda: the controversial new auto manufacturer looks to succeed where others have stalled. *China Business Review*, July-August, 47–47.

Horsley, J. P. (1989) Foreign investment incentives in Hainan. *China Business Review*, January-February, 31.34.

Larson, M. R. (1988) Exporting private enterprise to developing communist countries: A case study on China. *Columbia Journal of World Business*, Spring, 79–89.

Lieberthal,K., and Prahalad, C. K. (1989) Maintaining a consistent China strategy. *China Business Review*, March-April, 47–49.

Lim, L. Y. C., and Stoltenberg, C. D. (1990) Becoming a region: Southeast Asia's economic integration presents opportunities for U.S. companies active in China. *China Business Review*, May-June, 24–32.

Lim, W.-S. (1990) Pragmatic partners: Stable trade and expanding investments link China and Singapore. *China Business Review*, July-August, 22–29.

Livingstone, J. M. (1987) The marketing concept in China – a qualified acceptance. In *Management Reforms in China* (Warner, M.), Frances Pinter, London.

Macleod, R. (1988) *China: How to do Business with the Chinese*, Bantam Books, Toronto and New York.

de Mente, B. (1990) *Chinese Etiquette and Ethics in Business: A Penetrating Analysis of the Morals and Values that Shape the Chinese Business Personality*, NTC Publishing Group, Lincolnwood, Chicago.

Pearson, M. (1990) Party and politics in joint ventures. *China Business Review*, November–December, 38–40.

Pye, L. (1982) *Chinese Commercial Negotiating Style*, Oelgeschlager, Gunn & Hain Publishers Inc., Cambridge, MS.

Reader, J. A. (1984) Entrepreneurship in the People's Republic of China. *Columbia Journal of World Business*, Fall, 43–51.

Seligman, S. D. (1989) *Dealing with the Chinese: A Practical Guide to Business Etiquette in the People's Republic Today*, Warner Books, New York.

Selwyn, M. (1990) China: where the tough get going. *Asian Business*, **26**,(11), 54–57.

Simon, D. F. (1990) Shanghai's lure for high-tech investors. *China Business Review*, March-April, 44–49.

The World Bank Atlas 1990, World Bank, Washington, DC.

Warner, M. (1987) *Management Reforms in China*.

Weil, M. (1990) China's exports: on the edge. *China Business Review*, January-February, 36–43.

Woodward, K. (1991) Tianjin comes of age. *China Business Review*, January-February, 20–25.

Yi, X. B. (1990) *Marketing to China: One Billion New Customers*, NTC Publishing Group, Lincolnwood, Chicago.

Zhang, S. X., and Snyder, J. L. (1988) The Five Ps. *China Business Review*, March-April, 14–18.

Key reading

Barale, L. A. (1990) Wholly foreign owned enterprises: changing policy, changing attitudes. *China Business Review*, January-February, 30–35.

Business International Asia/Pacific Ltd., *Business China*, twice monthly report on China, Hong Kong.

Frankenstein, J., and Chao, C. N. (1988) Decision-making in the Chinese Foreign Trade Administration: a preliminary survey. *Columbia Journal of World Business*, Fall, 35–40.

Frisbie, J., and Kay, D. B. (1990) Joint venture dissolution: few legal guidelines make contract language the key. *China Business Review*, November-December, 42–45.

Fyock, D. A. (1990) Packaging an image: China's enterprises are struggling to adapt public relations to a socialist society. *China Business Review*, September-October, 20–22.

Harwit, E. (1990) China's elusive panda: the controversial new auto manufacturer looks to succeed where others have stalled. *China Business Review*, July-August, 47–47.

de Mente, B. (1990) *Chinese Etiquette and Ethics in Business: A Penetrating Analysis of the Morals and Values that Shape the Chinese Business Personality*, NTC Publishing Group, Lincolnwood, Chicago.

Pye, L. (1982) *Chinese Commercial Negotiating Style*, Oelgeschlager, Gunn & Hain Publishers Inc., Cambridge, MS.

Seligman, S. D. (1989) *Dealing with the Chinese: A Practical Guide to Business Etiquette in the People's Republic Today*, Warner Books, New York.

Yi, X. B. (1990) *Marketing to China: One Billion New Customers*, NTC Publishing Group, Lincolnwood, Chicago.

20
Trade, aid and development

Trade between developed and developing nations

Trade, whereby a nation pays for its imports by means of its exports, does not take place according to these rules as far as the developing countries are concerned. The less developed countries range from the newly industrializing, but still agricultural, to the raw-material supplying (and usually single commodity dependent), to those without tangible exports but with great import needs. Apart from the size of the capital injection required, the other problem which these countries face is that they lack qualified people in sufficient numbers to allocate and direct inward capital flows. This is the 'absorptive capacity' which is sometimes referred to, which is necessary for development and usually found to be lacking (Behrmann, 1984).

The discussion and debate which has taken place on the question of development aid from the richer countries of the Northern hemisphere to the poorer countries of the Southern hemisphere, has led to this question being referred to as the 'North–South debate'. However, the continued discussion over this question has also produced many reports such as the Brandt Commission Report (1980) which we shall discuss later. Although piecemeal, an evolution has been taking place with regard to thinking on development aid. In the past, development aid was administered by the former colonial powers to their newly independent states more in the form of enlightened charity. The colonial power usually continued also to claim credit for the infrastructure that was left behind as the state became independent. Colonial charity or self-interested subsidy behind exports continues to be an issue. So called 'mixed credits' which contain an aid element in the package, can in the longer term work out more expensive than international tendering for the developing country. This mixing of aid with commercial export lending is an issue which has troubled the OECD for many years.

The OECD has formed the Development Assistance Committee (DAC) to handle this very problem. According to the rules, which are not strictly observed, the aid element cannot be less than 20 per cent. If under 25 per cent, other countries must be notified promptly to the OECD. The USA has referred to this as predatory financing.

In the past, to aid the newly independent state, financial help would have been offered, but these 'soft' credits offered at preferential rates of interest were 'tied' in that they were available only for the purchase of certain items.

The figures for foreign aid in 1989, taken from *The Economist*, are shown in Figure 20.1, which lists fifteen countries which account in themselves for two-fifths of aid from Western governments and multinational agencies. Note that the proportion of developing country GNP accounted for by aid varies, but in the case of Mozambique, it is 64 per cent.

In a shrinking world market situation, rivalry among the leading industrialized nations has helped to curb this particular practice of trade related aid, although other malpractices continue unabated, as we shall see. In addition, there has also been the development of external sources of financing, e.g., World Bank, IMF, Bank for International Settlements, Bank for European Reconstruction and Development, and Eurodollar market. The Eurodollar market, based on London, created an opportunity for less developed countries to borrow for any particular purpose that they considered to be necessary. Development has also progressed through the active agencies of the United Nations, e.g., UNCTAD, UNIDO, GATT, UNICEF, and the International Labour Organization (ILO) which has been responsible for establishing management development centres and programmes in many parts of the developing world. However, to help shape some perspective on this problem, it is worth remembering that world military expenditure greatly exceeds spending on development aid. The two great colonial powers, the USA and USSR, accounted for half of annual global military expenditure of approximately 450 million dollars, with annual spending on official development aid only 20 billion dollars (note that both sets of figures are old estimates). To

Table 20.1   Reasons for suspecting a consistent trade bias against the LDCs

1   The high cost of capital due to market imperfections and direct transfer costs.
2   The consistent underestimation of returns.
3   A growth threatened by the political situation.
4   The discount rate includes a higher rate factor for LDCs.
5   The longer gestation period for LDCs due to lower levels of motivation, skills, governmental efficiency and infrastructure.
6   A typical Western firm would cut off any projections within a LDC at five years.

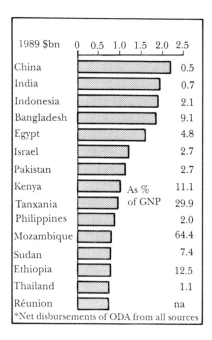

Figure 20.1   *Aid: top ten recipients*
Source   *The Economist* (1991) 13–19 April

Table 20.2   Trade in major weapons

| | Ranking | | Trade |
	Third World	World	1985–89, $bn*
Importers			
India	1	1	17.35
Iraq	2	2	12.00
Saudi Arabia	3	4	8.76
Syria	4	5	5.88
Egypt	5	6	5.80
North Korea	6	8	5.28
Exporters			
China	1	5	6.86
Brazil	2	11	1.39
Israel	3	12	1.18
Egypt	4	15	0.77

* 1985 constant prices
Source   *The Economist* (1991), 23 March, p. 50.

take another perspective on this, the World Health Organization estimated that it would cost about 450 million dollars to eradicate malaria forever as a disease in the same way as they have done successfully with smallpox, which now no longer exists. Regrettably, the WHO is short of funds and is unable, therefore, to undertake this programme, which requires funding of the level of only one-thousandth of world annual military spending.

Aid may be channelled on a bilateral basis between the respective governments, or through official world aid agencies such as the World Health Organization, or through recognized international charities such as Oxfam or War on Want or Save the Children. However, awareness of British exporters to the potential offered by foreign development was very low in a 1983 survey of 1,000 British exporters, which revealed that 85 per cent were virtually ignorant of the world aid agencies as a source of overseas contracts, although the provision of low technology for poorer countries earned British exporters 166 million dollars in 1982. A spokesman for the UK Department of Trade World Aid Sector, Peter Morris, emphasized this importance of foreign development aid in soliciting trade when he stated: 'We are doing well in some areas and not so well in others, but for every pound Britain invests in the World Bank, we are winning work valued at £1.60.'

As development advances though, there would be fewer contracts available for infrastructural development, such as highways for example, and more for higher technology and manufacturing production knowhow – a product life cycle in action.

Trade between developed and developing countries is only a small percentage of total world trade. The bulk of world trade takes place within the developed industrialized nations who tend to trade among themselves. If we take the USA, Canada and Germany, their combined exports are higher than the total for all developing countries taken together. In each year, imports were higher than exports so the corresponding share of world trade is,

Table 20.3   Exports and imports of all developing countries

	1982	1983	1984	1985	1986	1987	1988
Exports	31.8	30.4	28.9	28.1	25.8	25.6	26.5
Imports	32.7	31.9	31.8	30.9	26.8	27.5	27.4

Source   IMF (1989) *Direction of Trade Statistics Yearbook*, Washington DC.

Table 20.4   UNCTAD: integrated programme for commodities (IPC) commodity list

Bananas	*Cocoa
*Coffee	*Cotton and cotton yarn
*Hard fibres and products	*Jute and jute manufactures
Bovine meat	*Rubber
*Sugar	*Tea
Tropical timber	Vegetable oils and oilseeds
Bauxite	*Copper
Iron ore	Manganese
Phosphates	*Tin

* Core Commodities
Source   *UNCTAD Commodity Yearbook 1990*, New York.

therefore, reflected in higher percentages for imports over exports. Too many unfulfilled needs still exist to be able to curtail imports even in times of economic necessity. These countries are mainly dependent on their commodities to buy them the imports that they need, but commodities are highly volatile. UNCTAD recognizes eighteen commodities covered by the Integrated Programme for Commodities (IPC). The ten core commodities are indicated by an asterisk in Table 20.4.

Another UN initiative was the Generalized System of Preferences set up in 1977 to allow developing countries certain benefits from trade preferences, enabling them, hopefully, to attain economic self-sufficiency by means of trade liberalization. However, these preference systems involve large restrictions (Schultz and Schumacher, 1984):

- not all industrial products subject to tariffs are included (the list of exceptions is particularly long in the USA),
- not all developing countries receive preferential treatment (the number of countries excluded by the USA is particularly large),
- with many products, individual developing countries may be excluded (United States) or the supply which is tariff free may be limited (EC, Japan).

A proof of these restrictive practices is seen in Table 20.8.

Table 20.5   The characteristics of developing countries

1   Economic characteristics
     low output per worker
     low income per capita
2   Conditions of production
     small industrial sector
     few economies of scale
     primitive and crude techniques
     lack of specialization
     low capital per worker
     small savings per head for the bulk of the population
     lack of enterprise
     inadequate physical and social infrastructure
     low agricultural output per acre
     concentration of exports on a few primary products
     low volume of international trade per head
3   Living conditions
     large proportion of expenditure on food and necessities
     under-nutrition
     malnutrition
     high mortality rates
     bad housing and overcrowding
     bad hygiene, public health and sanitation
     inadequate cultural facilities
4   Aptitudes
     absence of training facilities
     inadequate education
     illiteracy
     ignorance, false beliefs and useless or harmful knowledge
5   Attitudes to work and life
     poor discipline and punctuality
     caste, religious or racial prejudice
     superstition
     lack of foresight
     lack of ambition
     apathy
     lack of adaptability
     unwillingness to bear risks, venture, innovate
     inability to cooperate outside the family or tribe
     contempt for manual work
     submissiveness
     low standards of hygiene
     work-spreading attitudes
     absence of birth control and high fertility rates
6   Institutions
     land tenure hostile to improvements
     uneconomic division of plots
     poor markets for labour, credit, capital

Table 20.5 continued

> poor marketing facilities for products
> poor information
> weak government (national and local)
> political uncertainty
> corrupt, inefficient and inadequate administration
> rigid class, caste system
> inequality
> absence of opportunities
> arbitrary legal administration
> non-enforcement of contracts
> prevalence of child labour
> inferiority of women's status
> weak or absent middle class

Source   Kinsey, J. (1988) *Marketing in Developing Countries*, Macmillan, London.

UN price stabilization agreements to aid single-commodity exporters

There are still many countries today whose economy is dependent on a single commodity or crop. These include Nigeria (90 per cent oil), Zambia (94 per cent copper), Mauritius (90 per cent sugar), Cuba (84 per cent sugar) and The Gambia (85 per cent ground nuts and ground-nut oil). For these countries, sudden movement in the trading price of their particular commodity or harvest conditions can bring success or ruin. To mitigate this, UNCTAD has been instrumental in recent years in arranging price stabilization agreements for sugar, tea, coffee, cocoa and rubber, while OPEC, as a producer's cartel, has sought to maintain control over the price and volume production of crude oil. More is said of commodity specific stabilization schemes and Stabex, the European Community's scheme for the stabilization of export earnings of individual countries in Asia, Caribbean and Pacific (ACP) regions, in Chapter 17.

Meanwhile, certain of these supplier countries have been actively developing their infrastructure so as to diversify their economy more in future years. Saudi Arabia has moved into steel and is to use the gas presently flared from its oil wells for production in its own plants. Oil remains the leading commodity in world trade, accounting for one-eighth of it. There are great disparities, however, in its worldwide consumption. While this creates more business for the oil states and more revenue, their problem is in finding a way out of dependency on oil. Without an infrastructure of any kind, many states, such as Oman, hire expatriates to work for them as consultants, advisers, university lecturers, language specialists, doctors, nurses, etc.

In the least developed nations, the populations are rural and illiterate, and these countries have little exporting. An example is Somalia which is dependent on the export of animals. Others have no exports. There are many countries in this category with severe long-term constraints on development, and they have been identified by means of the criteria devised by the World Bank and discussed further in the following pages:

1 per capita GDP less than $580,
2 share of manufacturing of 10 per cent or less of GDP,
3 20 per cent or less of the population are literate.

The United Nations has singled out twenty-three of these least developed countries for special attention. They are located in two main areas. The first extends across the middle of Africa from the Sahara in the north to Lake Nyasa in the south. The other begins with Afghanistan, stretching eastward across South Asia and some East Asian countries. These belts extend also into other areas, e.g., in Africa, it extends into Kenya; in Asia, it extends into Burma, Cambodia, Vietnam and parts of India. The question then arises whether parts of countries which have the same characteristics and handicaps as the least developed countries should not be treated on a par with them, e.g., India.

The Food and Agriculture Organization (FAO) published a report in 1974 which tried to work out how many could be fed by the soils of the Third World. Beginning with maps of soils and climates, it then superimposed to create cells with distinctive combinations of soil, slope, rainfall, etc. Each cell was then checked by a computer against fifteen major food crops to select the crop that would produce the highest yield of calories. From there it was a simple step to calculate the potential caloric output, work out how many this would feed, and compare the results with actual populations. As the level of farming has a great impact on yields, the sums were done for a low level of inputs roughly equivalent to subsistence farming. On these projections, the Third World would be able to feed just over one and half times their expected population of 3,600 million in the year 2000. All major regions would be capable of self-sufficiency in food. However, assumptions included felling two-thirds of the world's tropical forests, cultivating all available land, and not feeding any grain to livestock. By making adjustments for other land use and land coming into cultivation, by the year 2025 only Asia should be self-supporting.

In 1975, there were fifty-four countries that could not feed their existing populations from their entire land base using low inputs. The number will rise to sixty-four by the end of the century. Twenty-nine of the fifty-seven such countries in Africa, with two-thirds of the continent's population, would be critical in the year 2000.

Segmenting LDC markets

The term 'LDC' is disliked by the developing nations, but rather than use this blanket term for all, it is much better to look closer and start to question whether this is either appropriate or desirable. There are several means by which one could evaluate the LDC economy, but it reveals the fact that there are clusters or groupings on which we should focus, rather than staying with the single term 'LDC' which has the added disadvantage of implying that there is only one model when there are several. To emphasize the point, one could take oil-rich Saudi Arabia, booming South Korea, (a recent host of the Olympic Games), and the Soviet Union as examples of LDCs, but also of the need to define exactly what we mean by LDC and what it is exactly that this disparate trio have in common. The classification used here will be that of the UN, viz:

1 High-volume, low-value raw material exporters, but with infrastructural base (HVLVRME + I).

Table 20.6 Commodity prices, 1979–1989 (US Dollars)

Region country or area	1979	1980	1981	1982	1983	1984	1985	1986	1987	1988	1989	1990 7 months
Price (US dollar per metric ton)												
1 Wheat	156.8	205.8	190.9	167.1	139.5	136.2	109.3	88.5	87.3	133.0	151.6	125.9
2 Wheat	163.3	176.0	177.7	161.5	158.1	153.3	137.8	114.9	114.5	146.4	170.1	151.7
3 Maize	154.8	210.3	181.0	137.4	161.7	167.1	135.3	112.9	109.4	135.7	140.8	133.2
4 Maize	134.5	150.4	151.9	123.5	149.3	152.3	126.6	101.9	91.8	126.2	133.5	131.8
5 Rice	334.4	433.7	482.8	293.6	276.8	252.3	217.3	210.2	229.8	301.6	320.3	296.0
6 Sugar	212.9	631.8	372.4	185.3	186.6	114.7	89.5	133.4	149.0	224.7	282.0	311.9
7 Beef	2,886.7	2,775.0	2,472.3	2,389.6	2,440.8	2,261.2	2,153.1	2,094.0	2,384.8	2,517.8	2,569.1	2,534.8
8 Bananas	325.7	373.8	401.4	374.7	437.1	369.5	380.3	400.7	373.5	449.1	488.5	540.8
9 Bananas	346.1	415.9	424.0	405.1	448.8	418.2	405.1	486.9	584.6	541.4	449.5	679.0
10 Pepper	2,374.1	2,073.3	1,732.2	1,474.0	1,794.6	3,009.8	4,036.6	4,898.9	5,775.6	4,601.9	2,851.3	1,817.1
11 Soybean meal	242.9	258.6	252.7	218.4	237.8	197.2	157.2	284.8	203.3	267.5	247.0	214.1
12 Fishmeal	394.9	504.4	467.5	352.9	452.6	373.3	280.1	320.6	383.4	544.4	408.4	390.4
13 Coffee	4,043.4	3,942.2	3,204.0	3,275.7	3,121.9	3,248.1	3,436.3	4,851.0	2,721.6	2,717.1	2,362.0	2,098.3
14 Coffee	3,825.5	3,399.4	2,823.9	3,083.5	2,901.4	3,180.1	3,209.1	4,249.1	2,475.6	2,977.3	2,358.1	1,934.7
15 Coffee	3,647.9	3,244.0	2,267.9	2,448.2	2,736.3	3,045.8	2,675.6	3,259.0	2,256.1	2,096.7	1,668.8	1,183.5
16 Coffee	3,737.5	3,354.8	2,554.9	2,755.6	2,821.5	3,112.7	2,934.2	3,768.3	2,376.7	2,556.5	2,021.0	1,549.3
17 Cocoa	3,291.9	2,602.7	2,076.5	1,749.8	2,118.7	2,395.7	2,254.5	2,068.1	1,996.2	1,589.3	1,246.1	1,234.5
18 Tea	2,157.6	2,227.9	2,019.1	1,931.7	2,324.6	3,456.8	1,983.6	1,930.2	1,705.2	1,764.4	2,010.6	2,024.5
19 Soybeans	297.8	296.3	288.4	244.5	281.7	282.1	225.3	208.4	215.8	303.5	275.0	247.3
20 Soybean oil	662.2	598.3	506.9	447.3	527.2	724.0	572.0	342.8	334.3	463.4	431.5	435.4
21 Sunflower oil	761.6	632.6	639.0	528.6	558.1	766.5	602.3	365.6	360.3	476.3	481.8	485.9
22 Ground nuts	564.5	498.5	635.6	385.0	392.2	438.2	360.8	323.3	288.5	292.2	294.9	287.6
23 Ground nut oil	888.7	858.5	1,042.8	585.4	710.9	1,016.7	904.9	569.4	499.8	509.3	774.8	931.4
24 Copra	672.7	453.0	378.8	314.0	495.8	709.3	386.0	197.6	309.2	397.7	347.9	243.3
25 Coconut oil	984.5	674.3	570.0	464.4	729.8	1,154.6	590.2	296.5	442.3	564.8	516.8	358.3
26 Palm kernels	499.5	345.1	317.3	265.0	365.6	528.7	291.2	141.5	181.4	263.8	253.3	206.1
27 Palm kernel oil	1,049.3	725.5	588.3	458.2	709.0	1,037.2	551.2	288.2	426.1	538.8	472.2	349.4
28 Palm oil	653.8	583.9	570.7	445.1	501.5	728.8	500.6	257.0	342.6	437.2	350.1	276.4
30 Linseed oil	344.0	397.1	359.9	519.1	484.6	571.5	627.5	419.2	314.3	521.5	756.7	753.9
31 Cotton	3,426.0	3,432.3	3,424.6	2,866.7	3,178.5	3,674.0	3,593.8	3,466.3	3,591.5	5,495.4	6,379.1	6,603.0
32 Cotton	1,707.1	2,076.3	1,879.4	1,604.9	1,869.3	1,770.4	1,361.2	1,165.0	1,678.3	1,398.5	1,673.4	1,780.7
33 Cotton	1,494.7	1,871.0	1,744.4	1,454.2	2,593.4	1,652.8	1,413.1	1,093.3	1,541.9	1,356.9	1,588.6	1,766.6
34 Cotton	1,700.8	2,065.3	1,853.5	1,599.5	1,853.8	1,783.6	1,319.3	1,057.0	1,647.7	1,399.4	1,672.5	1,829.7
35 Wool	5,249.9	5,974.1	6,125.1	5,725.0	5,397.1	5,575.9	4,952.9	4,656.0	7,135.9	11,647.6	9,259.4	8,453.8

36 Wool	4,199.6	4,288.7	3,601.4	3,124.1	2,646.2	2,081.4	1,809.4	1,627.9	4,032.0	4,565.0	4,213.1	3,734.8
37 Jute	383.6	313.7	304.0	283.3	298.3	558.0	569.3	225.9	296.6	308.9	344.4	434.4
38 Sisal	737.3	786.7	687.4	621.9	637.8	651.5	619.0	613.3	612.1	639.2	709.8	741.4
39 Sisal	712.9	764.8	645.3	593.2	570.8	583.8	525.7	514.2	512.1	550.6	653.1	710.7
40 Hides and skins	366.1	230.3	170.6	179.8	189.7	234.5	202.1	173.9	191.7	259.6	260.8	256.4
42 Tropical logs	211.5	251.6	214.8	175.9	160.8	175.1	173.9	221.6	258.9	270.9	273.7	327.9
43 Tropical sawnwood	339.1	367.6	314.2	302.0	304.3	306.8	275.9	266.9	276.1	306.6	421.9	532.8
44 Plywood	259.7	273.8	244.5	234.1	229.9	227.0	210.9	273.7	399.4	358.7	350.3	337.2
45 Rubber	1,283.1	1,422.7	1,085.1	844.4	1,054.1	936.9	754.9	797.9	993.3	1,159.2	949.0	839.5
46 Phosphate rock	34.0	43.0	52.5	40.0	31.5	33.3	33.5	34.8	31.0	36.0	40.5	40.5
47 Manganese ore	135.0	163.5	171.5	164.3	136.9	136.9	138.5	137.5	127.5	165.0	285.2	393.7
48 Iron ore	23.0	26.8	23.2	24.2	23.7	22.4	22.0	21.6	22.1	22.3	24.3	25.9
49 Iron ore	—	28.1	28.1	32.5	29.0	26.1	26.6	26.3	24.5	23.5	26.6	30.8
50 Aluminium	1,541.1	1,728.3	1,277.6	1,006.9	1,473.9	1,332.7	1,081.0	1,198.0	1,565.6	2,586.8	1,951.3	1,534.0
51 Copper	2,035.6	2,235.5	1,846.4	1,607.4	1,706.9	1,471.9	1,445.5	1,425.5	1,789.4	2,627.6	2,855.1	2,604.2
52 Copper	1,984.4	2,173.4	1,742.1	1,480.3	1,592.1	1,377.9	1,417.5	1,373.8	1,781.4	2,600.0	2,846.7	2,589.9
53 Lead	1,160.7	936.2	805.4	563.3	478.2	563.1	420.5	486.2	792.3	824.5	883.8	1,017.9
54 Lead	1,203.4	906.6	727.1	545.8	425.6	443.0	391.1	406.2	596.9	656.3	673.4	486.6
55 Zinc	822.1	825.1	982.5	848.2	912.4	1,071.5	889.8	837.9	937.1	1,326.6	1,808.0	1,717.1
56 Zinc	741.4	761.6	846.5	744.7	764.7	895.7	755.6	712.2	798.9	1,241.5	1,713.5	1,596.3
57 Nickel	5,705.3	6,785.8	6,317.8	5,132.1	4,806.8	4,896.8	4,988.5	4,089.9	5,023.7	13,479.3	13,207.2	8,313.5
58 Nickel	—	6,520.0	5,952.4	4,837.0	4,671.4	4,753.4	4,901.2	3,886.3	4,872.7	13,777.9	13,308.2	8,382.5
59 Tin	15,446.6	16,785.1	14,155.3	12,823.3	12,990.5	12,238.9	9,956.1	4,302.6	6,874.7	7,182.5	8,688.1	6,413.2
60 Tin	14,807.4	16,402.7	14,044.3	12,929.4	13,018.7	12,450.43	9,935.9	5,495.2	6,689.5	7,046.2	8,492.3	6,249.7
61 Tungsten	138.8	144.4	143.5	106.3	80.9	81.2	67.7	47.6	49.1	55.9	56.6	48.6
62 Tungsten	—	—	—	—	—	92.1	74.2	55.2	57.3	60.6	65.1	63.1
63 Gold	306.7	612.6	459.7	390.0	424.2	360.4	317.3	367.5	446.5	437.0	381.4	382.6
64 Silver	1,109.4	2,057.8	1,046.4	786.7	1,143.9	814.1	614.2	547.0	700.9	645.1	549.9	506.7
65 Crude petroleum	29.2	35.5	34.1	31.4	28.4	28.3	27.0	13.8	17.8	14.2	17.2	16.7
Indices (1985 = 100)												
All food	139	191	155	115	123	118	100	107	101	126	137	122
Food and tropical beverage	139	202	162	119	125	114	100	114	106	130	133	129
Tropical beverages	126	118	97	92	96	110	100	124	81	82	70	60
Food	145	240	192	131	138	116	100	110	117	152	161	160
Vegetable oilseeds and oil	135	117	112	90	107	144	100	62	73	96	85	73
Agricultural raw materials	123	136	119	103	110	111	100	102	119	129	129	134
Minerals, ores and metals	129	144	121	105	113	105	100	96	113	164	164	145
Total	134	171	142	111	118	114	100	104	107	135	135	129
Total in SDRs	105	134	122	102	112	112	100	90	84	102	107	99

Source UNCTAD, *Monthly Commodity Price Bulletin.*

Table 20.7   Share of three leading commodities in total exports by developing country

Country	(A) Export dependence on three leading commodities[a]		(B) Export dependence on three leading non-oil commodities[a]	
	Average 1975–77	Average 1985–87	Average 1975–77	Average 1985–87
USA				
St Vincent and the Grenadines	97.1	99.0	97.1	99.0
Saint Pierre and Miquelon	25.0	99.0	20.0	99.0
Netherlands Antilles	97.0	94.2	1.0	0.3
Venezuela	96.5	94.1	2.9	6.2
Cuba	91.6	87.0	91.6	79.5
Greenland	60.4	85.4	60.4	84.3
Guyana	77.8	84.9	77.8	84.8
Suriname	73.8	82.2	73.8	82.2
Ecuador	80.4	77.7	34.4	36.8
Guatemala	60.6	77.5	60.6	77.5
Trinidad and Tobago	93.5	75.7	3.1	1.8
Paraguay	46.6	74.3	46.6	74.3
Colombia	65.0	73.9	64.6	53.7
Saint Lucia	58.0	73.0	58.0	73.0
El Salvador	68.8	72.0	68.8	72.0
French Guiana	81.4	70.0	81.4	70.0
Honduras	57.2	68.5	57.2	68.5
Bolivia	68.4	68.5	45.8	19.3
Nicaragua	55.8	67.5	55.8	67.5
Guadeloupe	82.0	67.3	82.0	67.3
Panama	71.6	65.5	50.6	65.5
Dominica	63.7	65.2	63.7	65.2
Martinique	79.4	65.0	60.3	50.2
Grenada	94.6	60.4	94.6	60.4
Jamaica	70.1	59.6	70.1	59.6
Costa Rica	61.1	58.7	61.1	58.7
Dominican Republic	69.2	58.6	69.2	58.6
Mexico	35.2	55.1	21.3	7.2
Chile	62.2	54.9	62.2	54.9
Belize	56.5	53.5	56.5	53.5
Saint Christopher	57.5	47.0	57.5	39.3
Falkland Islands	99.0	43.9	99.0	43.0
Bermuda	59.5	40.0	23.1	—
Peru	41.8	39.6	41.8	32.3
Haiti	52.4	32.5	52.4	32.5
Argentina	34.8	28.9	34.8	28.9
Uruguay	35.3	27.5	35.3	27.5
Brazil	34.5	20.5	34.5	20.5
Bahamas	43.2	14.1	0.2	0.7
Barbados	39.1	11.6	39.1	1.6
Antigua and Barbuda	18.2	—	1.1	—
Montserrat	33.3	—	33.3	—
Africa				
Zambia	93.2	99.0	93.2	99.0
Uganda	97.9	99.0	97.0	99.0
Angola	99.0	99.0	28.0	3.1

Guinea	99.0	99.0	99.0	99.0
Somalia	80.3	99.0	80.3	99.0
Nigeria	97.5	99.0	4.9	3.1
Algeria	89.3	97.8	1.0	0.3
Chad	96.9	94.5	92.8	94.5
Libyan Arab Jamahiriya	99.9	93.3	0.0	0.0
Cameroon	69.1	92.1	69.1	70.3
Zaire	83.5	91.8	81.6	77.5
Comoros	64.5	91.2	64.5	91.2
Liberia	88.4	90.6	88.4	90.6
Congo	86.3	90.1	21.8	8.3
Equatorial Guinea	94.6	89.8	94.6	89.8
Seychelles	99.0	89.0	43.4	17.2
Burundi	99.0	88.6	99.0	88.6
Cape Verde	34.8	88.4	34.8	88.4
Gabon	91.0	87.6	15.3	16.4
Mauritania	99.0	86.6	99.0	86.6
Niger	94.8	85.9	94.8	85.9
Ethiopia	70.5	85.7	70.5	81.8
Ghana	83.1	78.8	83.1	78.8
Malawi	78.2	78.2	78.2	78.2
Rwanda	91.9	77.7	91.9	77.7
Mali	99.0	76.6	99.0	76.6
Reunion	84.5	76.4	84.3	76.4
Mozambique	46.3	73.0	46.3	70.2
Togo	87.5	70.4	87.5	70.4
Kenya	60.5	67.8	44.9	57.7
Senegal	59.5	67.7	59.5	54.6
Dijibouti	1.4	66.7	—	24.4
Madagascar	59.5	65.6	59.5	65.6
Egypt[b]	60.1	74.5	44.5	27.8
Benin	36.9	64.6	36.9	62.1
Côte d'Ivoire	75.7	63.6	75.7	62.1
Sao Tome and Principe	86.6	63.5	86.6	63.5
Guinea-Bissau	89.0	63.5	89.0	58.6
Central African Republic	69.9	58.2	69.9	58.2
Sudan	77.1	58.1	77.1	58.1
Sierra Leone	29.2	52.9	29.2	51.9
Burkina Faso	69.2	51.9	69.2	51.9
Swaziland	47.2	46.6	47.2	46.6
Mauritius	79.6	41.9	95.4	41.9
Gambia	95.4	36.6	95.4	36.6
Tunisia	60.2	35.9	19.8	8.6
Morocco	57.4	34.7	57.4	34.7
Zimbabwe	25.1	29.8	25.1	29.8
Botswana	61.9	12.8	61.9	12.8
Lesotho	48.3	12.5	48.3	12.5

Asia

West Asia

Iran (Islamic Republic of)	99.1	99.0	0.8	2.2
Iraq	95.4	99.0	0.6	0.8
Yemen	92.1	94.2	16.3	3.8
Saudi Arabia	99.6	93.1	0.0	0.6
Oman	100.0	92.1	0.2	1.4
Bahrain	91.1	90.6	7.2	6.4

Table 20.7 continued

Kuwait	89.9	87.1	0.2	0.3
Qatar	100.0	85.9	0.0	—
United Arab Emirates	95.0	77.3	0.3	1.6
Syrian Arab Republic	82.3	67.1	18.8	11.7
Jordan	42.9	26.2	42.9	26.2
Cyprus	24.9	17.1	24.9	13.2
Turkey	41.5	11.0	41.5	10.5
Lebanon	5.1	8.3	5.1	8.3

South and South-East Asia

Brunei	99.3	91.1	0.0	0.2
Cambodia	45.3	82.4	45.3	82.4
Myanmar	82.3	77.3	82.3	77.3
Indonesia	84.5	74.0	17.,4	19.1
Afghanistan	51.7	68.7	47.6	31.1
Maldives	62.8	60.8	62.8	60.8
Sri Lanka	70.6	46.6	70.6	43.7
Malaysia	52.8	46.0	51.3	29.7
Nepal	55.4	27.8	55.4	27.8
Thailand	37.6	27.2	37.6	27.2
Bangladesh[c]	76.2	50.0	76.2	50.0
Lao People's Dem. Republic	60.0	25.5	60.0	25.5
Pakistan[b]	41.0	32.8	41.0	32.8
Singapore	35.2	23.6	5.2	3.8
Philippines	39.9	15.8	39.9	15.8
India	18.1	14.9	18.1	13.5
Taiwan	8.7	5.3	8.7	4.9
Republic of Korea	12.2	5.3	11.7	3.5
Hong Kong	2.1	2.1	2.1	2.1
Macau	4.1	1.1	4.1	1.1

Europe

Yugoslavia	7.3	6.7	7.3	5.9
Malta	12.8	4.3	6.3	2.8

Oceania

New Caledonia	90.4	79.8	90.4	79.8
Solomon Islands	81.5	77.6	81.5	77.6
Fiji	79.6	66.0	69.2	53.8
Samoa	89.7	65.4	89.7	65.4
Vanuatu	72.4	61.4	72.4	61.4
Papua New Guinea	65.2	52.7	65.2	52.7
Tonga	80.7	51.7	80.7	51.7
Kiribati	87.3	48.0	87.3	48.0
Nauru	100.0	39.7	100.0	39.7
Pacific Islands	38.1	20.3	38.1	20.3
Cook Islands	60.0	12.0	60.0	12.0
American Samoa	4.1	7.3	4.1	7.3
French Polynesia	22.9	6.9	22.9	6.9
Guam	24.7	4.7	0.9	2.4
Niue	50.0	—	50.0	—

[a] Excluding gem diamonds
[b] The three leading commodities include cotton yarn
[c] The three leading commodities include jute goods

Note   Figures in percentages, ranked by 1985–1987, average A.
Source   *UNCTAD Commodity Yearbook 1990*, New York.

2 High-volume, low-value raw material exporters, but with little infrastructural base (HVLVRME-I).
3 Low-volume, low-value traditional exporters, but with infrastructural base (LVLVTE + I).
4 Least developed nations.

The dangers of applying criteria such as GNP per capita have already been highlighted in Chapter 4. Here, it is important to focus on segments within countries and to see whether these same market segments may be found also in neighbouring countries, whether in fact there is in effect a cluster of similar segments within the region in question. To take these in turn:

1 There are those countries which are high-volume, low-value raw material exporters, but have an infrastructural base. Many of the countries in this group have sizeable populations and hence domestic markets; geographic size; agricultural bases, industrial nucleus; relatively sophisticated transportation and communications infrastructures; relatively large numbers of skilled labourers and competent technocratic and managerial elites. These countries have a fairly good chance of being self-sustaining after the oil or phosphates run out. Algeria, Iraq, Iran (all oil-producing) and Morocco (phosphates) are in this category.
2 There are the high-volume, low-value raw material exporting countries with little infrastructure. These countries are characterized by small populations, small internal markets, little agriculture, and lack of industrial bases. They have little infrastructure where needed, no skilled workforce, only a smattering of technocrats and managers, but possess

Table 20.8   Affirmative countervailing actions* as a proportion of initiations; 1 July 1980– 30 June 1985 (per cent)

| | | | Initiating country | | |
Target group[1]	USA	EEC	Canada	Australia	Total
Industrial countries	33.0;	50.0	37.5	5.9	31.7
Developing countries	64.0	40.0	—	—	63.1
Eastern trading area	—	—	—	—	—
Total	46.4	42.9	33.3	5.9	43.1

* Actions terminating with the application of duties or suspended through agreement.
[1] Groups defined as follows: (i) Industrial countries: Australia, Belgium, Canada, Switzerland, Federal Republic of Germany, Spain, Finland, France, UK, Ireland, Italy, Japan, Luxembourg, the Netherlands, New Zealand, Norway, Portugal, Sweden, South Africa, USA, Yugoslavia; (ii) Developing Countries: Argentina, Brazil, Chile, Colombia, Dominican Republic, Hong Kong, Israel, India, Indonesia, Korea, Malaysia, Mexico, Philippines, Singapore, Thailand, Trinidad and Tobago, Taiwan, Turkey, Uruguay, Venezuela, Pakistan, Panama; (iii) Eastern Trading Area: China, Czechoslovakia, Democratic Republic of Germany, Hungary, Poland, Romania, USSR.

Source   Marcelo de Paiva Abreu and Winston Fritsch, 'Market access for manufactured exports from developing countries: Trends and prospects' in John Whalley (1989) *Developing Countries and the Global Trading System*, Vol. 1: Thematic Studies from a Ford Foundation Project, University of Michigan Press, Ann Arbor.

the capital to attract the people they need from other countries. Libya, Kuwait, Qatar, UAR and Oman are examples of this group.

3 There are the low-volume, low-value traditional exporters with infrastructural bases. These countries are reasonably well endowed with roads, railways, ports, skilled labour, educational centres, and relatively extensive domestic markets. They do not have the credit worthiness of the earlier two groups or the ability to influence their growth. Here, the examples offered may include India and Egypt, both endowed with a university system and service and management elite superior to many of its neighbours. In the Middle East, many of the oil states have chosen to invest in universities when a generation ago there was no proper schooling.

Countries such as Egypt and India have long had this established infrastructure. Their economies remain poor though because of overpopulation and lack of arable land, and their agricultural output and export earnings are, therefore, low in relation to import demands. Egypt benefits from its OPEC neighbours while India, although still enjoying good links with Britain, exhibits the characteristics of an independent country which seeks to remain non-aligned to any particular economic bloc.

The main point about this latter cluster of countries is that in the transfer of technology it is easier and much less costly to transfer know-how that is firm-specific rather than industry-specific. A certain level of knowledge may be assumed beyond which training is required. Transferring technology to countries other than these would require perhaps a greater grounding in the basic fundamentals of the technology before the specifics of the actual technology were due to be transferred.

Egyptian and Sudanese cotton, Tunisian olive oil, Turkish labour do not earn as much foreign exchange as oil and gas. Egypt uses approximately 40 per cent of its export earnings to service its public external debt. Egypt, Sudan, Syria, Tunisia and Turkey are countries which belong to this group.

4 The least developed nations include those dependent on occasional exports of such things as live animals and hides. Yemen, previously split into two separate entities, North and South, each following a different ideological direction, united when oil reserves were found and it could not be established beyond reasonable doubt in whose legal jurisdiction these oil reserves actually lay. With this discovery, Yemen has the potential now to move out of this group, but countries such as Somalia and Ethiopia still remain in this group, and also have to contend with civil unrest and frequent droughts, making the task of feeding the people even more difficult.

Kinsey (1988) has pointed out how 'less developed' is less objectionable than 'Third World' or 'undeveloped', but still implies that such countries should model themselves on those which are developed. 'Developing', as Kinsey emphasizes, no matter what terms one chooses to use, means, basically, 'poverty'. World population projections point to a global population explosion over the next sixty years, from a present five billion to somewhere between eleven and fourteen billion, and 90 per cent of this growth will occur in poor countries.

Analysis of marketing opportunities

The marketing infrastructure is underdeveloped in most LDCs including media, communications and traditional channels of distribution, which also has to take note of what is often an

Table 20.9 World Bank classification of economies

		1. By income	
Low income countries		*Middle income countries*	
Bangladesh	Madagascar	Algeria	Malaysia
Benin	Malawi	Argentina	Malta
Bhutan	Maldives	Belize	Mauritius
Burkina Faso	Mali	Bolivia	Mexico
Burundi	Mauritania	Botswana	Morocco
Central African Republic	Mozambique	Brazil	Nicaragua
Chad	Myanmar	Cameroon	Oman
China	Nepal	Cape Verde	Panama
Comoros	Niger	Chile	Papua New Guinea
Equatorial Guinea	Nigeria	Colombia	Paraguay
Ethiopia	Pakistan	Congo, People's Republic of the	Peru
Gambia, The	Rwanda	Costa Rica	Philippines
Ghana	Sao Tome and Principe	Cote d'Ivoire	Poland
Guinea	Sierra Leone	Djibouti	Portugal
Guinea-Bissau	Solomon Islands	Dominican Republic	Romania
Guyana	Somalia	Ecuador	St. Vincent
Haiti	Sri Lanka	Egypt, Arab Republic of	Senegal
India	Sudan	El Salvador	Seychelles
Indonesia	Tanzania	Fiji	Syrian Arab Republic
Kenya	Togo	Gabon	Swaziland
Lao People's Democratic Republic	Uganda	Grenada	Thailand
Lesotho	Yemen, Republic of (PDR)	Guatemala	Tonga
Liberia	Zaire	Honduras	Trinidad and Tobago
	Zambia	Hungary	Tunisia
		Jamaica	Turkey
		Jordan	Uruguay
		Korea, Republic of	Vanuatu
		Lebanon	Venezuela
			Western Samoa
			Yemen, Republic of (YAR)
			Yugoslavia
			Zimbabwe

Note Low-income countries are those in which 1989 GNP per capita was no more than $580, and middle-income countries are those in which GNP per capita was more than $580 and less than $6,000.

Source World Bank (1990) *World Debt Tables 1990–91*, 2 Vols., Washington, DC.

important and thriving black market for goods either in scarcity or being rationed. It is interesting to note how there is hardly a country in the world which does not spend on advertising, even the poorest among nations, from private companies to state-owned enterprises, include a budgetary allocation irrespective of the efficacy of such likely expenditures. The marketing mix for LDCs has, therefore, to be tailored to the quite different needs of the environment, relative to Western markets. The role of the state, the level of development of the supporting infrastructure from education to highways and railroads are all important factors in this equation. Yet, the ability to provide this infrastructure is often lacking, without either consistently favourable commodity price markets or the provision of

Table 20.10   World Bank classification of economies

1. By debt and by income

Severely indebted low-income countries (SILICs)[1]	Severely indebted middle-income countries (SIMICs)[1]	Moderately indebted low-income countries (MILICs)[2]	Moderately indebted middle-income countries (MIMICs)[2]
Benin	Argentina	Bangladesh	Algeria
Burundi	Bolivia	Central African Republic	Cameroon
Comoros	Brazil	Ethiopia	Cape Verde
Equatorial Guinea	Chile	Gambia, The	Colombia
Ghana	Congo, People's Republic of	Indonesia	Dominican Republic
Guinea	Costa Rica	Pakistan	Gabon
Guinea-Bissau	Cote d'Ivoire	Sri Lanka	Guatemala
Guyana	Ecquador	Uganda	Jamaica
Kenya	Egypt, Arab Republic of	Yemen, Republic of (PDCR)	Paraguay
Liberia	Honduras		Syrian Arab Republic
Madagascar	Hungary		Turkey
Malawi	Mexico		Yugoslovia
Mali	Morocco		Zimbabwe
Mauritania	Nicaragua		
Mozambique	Peru		
Myanmar	Philippines		
Niger	Poland		
Nigeria	Senegal		
Sao Tome and Principe	Uruguay		
Sierra Leone	Venezuela		
Somalia			
Sudan			
Tanzania			
Togo			
Zaire			
Zambia			

Notes

[1] Defined as countries in which three of the four key ratios are above critical levels. These ratios and their critical levels are debt to GNP (50 per cent), debt to exports of goods and all services (275 per cent), accrued debt service to exports (30 per cent), and accrued interest to exports (20 per cent).

[2] Defined as countries in which three of the four key rations fall in the following ranges: debt to GNP (30–50 per cent), debt to exports of goods and all services (165–275 per cent), accrued debt service to exports (18–30 per cent), and accrued interest to exports (12–20 per cent).

Source   World Bank (1990) *World Debt Tables 1990–91*, 2 vols, Washington, DC.

Western development funding. Kinsey (1988) noted that subversive measures to stop or render ineffective the adoption of marketing may be expected from the civil servants of many of these developing countries for mainly personal reasons in that they may feel either their supremacy or their authority being challenged, e.g.

1 Lack of marketing qualifications and ability of government officials to use marketing.
2 'Official omnipotence' and centralized power structures often characterized by corruption.
3 Resistance by government officials to marketing being used for fear that their inadequacies are revealed.

Table 20.11 World Bank classification of economies

1. By debt

All severely indebted countries	All moderately indebted countries	Other developing countries
Argentina	Algeria	Belize
Benin	Bangladesh	Bhutan
Bolivia	Cameroon	Botswana
Brazil	Cape Verde	Burkina Faso
Burundi	Central African Republic	Chad
Chile	Colombia	China
Comoros	Dominican Republic	Djibouti
Congo, People's Republic of	Ethiopia	El Salvador
Costa Rica	Gabon	Fiji
Cote d'Ivoire	Gambia, The	Grenada
Ecuador	Guatemala	Haiti
Egypt, Arab Republic of	Indonesia	India
Equatorial Guinea	Jamaica	Jordan
Chana	Pakistan	Korea, Republic of
Guinea	Paraguay	Lao People's Democratic Republic
Guinea-Bissau	Sri Lanka	Lebanon
Guyana	Syrian Arab Republic	Lesotho
Honduras	Turkey	Malaysia
Hungary	Uganda	Maldives
Kenya	Yemen, Republic of (PDR)	Malta
Liberia	Yugoslavia	Mauritius
Madagascar	Zimbabwe	Nepal
Malawi		Oman
Mali		Panama
Mauritania		Papua New Guinea
Mexico		Portugal
Morocco		Romania
Mozambique		Rwanda
Myanmar		St. Vincent
Nicaragua		Seychelles
Niger		Solomon Islands
Nigeria		Swaziland
Peru		Thailand
Philippines		Tonga
Poland		Trinidad and Tobago
Senegal		Tunisia
Sao Tome and Principe		Vanuatu
Sierra Leone		Western Samoa
Somalia		Yemen, Republic of (YAR)
Sudan		
Tanzania		
Togo		
Uruguay		
Venezuela		
Zaire		
Zambia		

Source World Bank (1990) *World Debt Tables 1990–91*, 2 Vols., Washington, DC.

Table 20.12   The alternative Livingstone classification of developing countries

These may be subdivided according to:

Size: A country may be considered to be *large* if its population is 30m or over. This is simply an empirical cut-off point, blurred in the Third World by a rapidly rising population. But given a domestic population of 30m and with adequate and equitable per capita income, a country could sustain modern industry for its domestic market alone.

A country is considered to be *small* if its population is under 30m.

Wealth: A country is considered to be *rich* (or potentially rich) if its earnings from the production and sale of raw materials are comparable (or, in prospect, comparable) with the income per head of an industrially developed country. It is often the internal political and cultural situation rather than the lack of exploitable resources which has thus far prevented many countries from achieving a standard of living comparable with industrial nations.

A country is considered to be *poor* if its earnings from the production and sale of proved raw materials are well below, and not likely to achieve, the per capita income of an advanced country.

This gives a classification as follows:

Large (potentially) rich countries, e.g., Nigeria
Large poor countries, e.g., Bangladesh
Small rich countries, e.g., Saudi Arabia
Small poor countries, e.g., Malawi

A subset drawn from large (potentially) rich, large poor and small poor countries constitutes the *newly industrialised* category. These countries are said to have broken out of the trap of underdevelopment and have achieved technological bases which enable them to produce a wide range of products. However, some are very much more successful than others. Indeed some, such as Singapore, Hong Kong and Taiwan, have moved into a situation broadly comparable with industrialised countries, which they are rapidly joining. Others are much further behind in their development.

Source   Kinsey, J. (1988) *Marketing in Developing Countries*, Macmillan, London.

4 An extremely complex marketing environment within developing countries and conditions which intervene in the easy implementation of marketing.

Western multinationals are often resented, if not distrusted, for three main reasons (Medawar and Freese, 1981):

1 The corporation's business objectives, and often the major policies behind them, are determined at a corporate headquarters abroad.
2 Wherever the real sources of wealth, or real savings on costs, the lion's share of an MNC's profits inexorably finds its way back home.
3 Being a global machine, the MNC can be independent of any one country. Indeed, there is

remarkably little that can be done to call a multinational to account for what it does around the world, for there is no single instrument with the power or authority to do this.

In addition to the characteristics of developing countries outlined in Table 20.5, also expect the following:

- Shortage of market information and unreliability of what is available. Commercial marketing research is only available for about one third of the developing countries, and the Third World is not homogeneous. For countries that are covered, interviewers are not trained as fully as in developed countries, and there is little understanding of the complex techniques used in the advanced countries. In some countries, it is a case of not only getting permission to interview but also submitting questionnaires for approval.
- National statistics and, particularly, estimates have to be treated with caution. In some countries, a census can create social unrest, and even revolution, when one part of the population finds itself politically underprivileged relative to the rest of the country. Aside from political representation, there is also the resource allocation issue, and this has created conflict (even in the USA) after a national census has been conducted and certain cities feel aggrieved at either underrepresentation or a low allocation of the national income.
- English is the language which is shared among others by Nigerians and Indians, who each have hundreds of languages in their own country. Using the local language will have limited effect even in the small region served as it may cause the product to be identified as a local product and local products are usually treated with contempt over imported products.
- Scanning for profitable market segments means making at best estimates of personal disposable income and so individual buying power, shopping patterns and distribution channels used. Pring (1987) has suggested seven key variables, which are not mutually exclusive, to help better understand Third World markets:

  1 prosperity and the mix between rich and poor,
  2 ethnicity which is about races, tribes, nationals, and immigrants,
  3 urbanity which has to do with lifestyles and standards of living relative to rural areas,
  4 politics which condition the way people live,
  5 religion meaning observances, laws and lifestyles,
  6 culture, including issues of age, sex, lifestyles and authority, and
  7 language meaning literacy, dialects and nuances.

- Governmental attitudes towards business are important, and these will help determine whether a new venture is successful or not. Iancu Spigler coined the term 'compulsory disbursement taxes', or 'CDTs', for those taxes invented by governments to tax incoming multinationals where no tax regime had existed before.
- Where the government engages in national planning, this will reveal national priorities for the next few years ahead, and so perhaps opportunities for foreign firms to invest or else supply imports.
- When the decision to proceed with investment is made, it should also be recognized that this will usually entail a vertically integrated operation to ensure continuity of supplies. Companies investing in Nigeria have built into their plants both water treatment and electricity generators. Similarly, when McDonalds opened in Moscow, it meant that to assure supplies of all the raw materials, from quality beef to packaging, that McDonalds had to take these tasks in-house, even importing beef cattle and growing potatoes.

Table 20.13   Education at the third level: number of students per 100,000 inhabitants

Country	Sex	Number of students per 100,000 inhabitants				
		1975	1980	1985	1987	1988
Africa						
Algeria	MF	261	533	804	881	860
	M	—	792	1,105	—	1,201
	F	—	277	505	—	519
Argentina	MF	2,291	1,741	2,790	3,079	—
	M	2,406	1,736	2,669	2,894	—
	F	2,175	1,745	2,909	3,262	—
Bahrain	MF	259	551	973	1,079	1,176
	M	223	559	667	762	918
	F	301	541	1,412	1,530	1544
Bangladesh	MF	207	272	453	385	413
	M	351	455	710	612	648
	F	54	78	179	145	164
Bhutan	MF	—	26	17	—	—
	M	—	39	27	—	—
	F	—	12	7	—	—
Bolivia	MF	971	1,093	1,492	1,440	1,540
	M	—	—	—	—	—
	F	—	—	—	—	—
Canada	MF	3,600	4,057	5,100	4,950	5,024
	M	3,980	4,026	4,843	4,643	4,693
	FD	3,222	4,088	5,351	5,251	5,350
China	MF	54	117	168	190	187
	M	71	174	230	249	242
	F	36	56	102	127	129
Costa Rica	MF	1,689	2,435	2,414	2,568	2,477
	M	—	—	—	—	—
	F	—	—	—	—	—
Cyprus	MF	153	254	579	630	748
	M	168	329	604	579	632
	F	138	180	555	681	862
Cuba	MF	886	1,559	2,365	2,589	2,456
	M	—	1,578	2,135	2,255	2,071
	F	—	1,539	2,603	2,937	2,855
Dominican Republic	MF	882	—	1,929	—	—
	M	975	—	—	—	—
	F	785	—	—	—	—
Egypt	MF	1,323	1,724	1,796	1,749	—
	M	1,821	2,327	2,485	2,.319	—
	F	808	1,103	1,086	1,161	—
Ethiopia	MF	20	37	65	66	69
	M	—	—	107	110	114
	F	—	—	23	23	25
El Salvador	MF	692	—	1,479	1,511	1,519
	M	919	—	1,686	1,741	—
	F	465	—	1,277	1,288	—
France	MF	1,971	1,998	2,318	2,395	2,655
	M	2,102	—	2,361	2,394	2,574
	F	1,845	—	2,276	2,395	2,732

German Democratic Republic	MF	2,291	2,395	2,600	2,640	2,645
	M	2,160	2,147	2,502	2,649	2,649
	F	2,404	2,613	2,687	2,633	2,641
Germany, Federal Republic of	MF	1,684	1,987	2,540	2,675	2,779
	M	2,170	2,447	3,098	3,273	3,409
	F	1,240	1,566	2,030	2,123	2,196
Iran, Islamic Republic of	MF	456	—	411	511	599
	M	647	—	590	719	825
	F	260	—	228	296	365
Iraq	MF	781	803	1,067	1,076	1,188
	M	1,033	1,077	1,333	1,277	1,446
	F	522	519	791	868	920
Ireland	MF	1,440	1,610	1,979	2,047	—
	M	1,889	1,901	2,238	2,293	—
	F	990	1,315	1,718	1,800	—
Israel	MF	2,462	2,504	2,742	2,752	2,753
	M	2,641	2,438	2,915	2,963	2,960
	F	2,283	2,570	2,570	2,541	2,547
Japan	MF	2,017	2,065	1,944	2,063	2,117
	M	2,773	2,.280	2,575	2,636	2,678
	F	1,284	1,333	1,334	1,507	1,575
Netherlands	MF	2,108	2,544	2,795	2,833	—
	M	2,851	3,090	3,335	3,273	—
	F	1,370	2,007	2,267	2,403	—
New Zealand	MF	2,143	2,463	2,950	3,197	3,217
	M	2,718	2,942	3,232	3,353	3,369
	F	1,566	1,989	2,673	3,043	3,068
Philippines	MF	1,808	2,641	3,580	4,399	2,659
	M	—	2,455	—	—	—
	F	—	2,828	—	—	—
Poland	MF	1,692	1,656	1,221	1,221	1,306
	M	1,593	1,504	1,109	1,098	1,177
	F	1,785	1,800	1,327	1,339	1,429
Saudi Arabia	MF	364	662	979	1,091	—
	M	555	882	1,090	1,237	—
	F	154	403	847	916	—
Sweden	MF	1,985	2,062	2,200	2,209	2,242
	M	2,281	—	—	2,122	2,127
	F	1,594	—	—	2,294	2,355
Tunisia	MF	365	499	573	575	699
	M	536	693	728	714	859
	F	191	300	413	434	535
Turkey	MF	817	554	934	1,020	1,112
	M	1,348	819	1,228	1,322	1,437
	F	269	281	622	700	769
Uganda	MF	49	45	65	75	—
	M	81	70	101	111	—
	F	17	20	30	40	—
UK	MF	1,304	1,468	1,824	1,913	—
	M	1,710	1,911	2,040	2,099	—
	F	917	1,049	1,618	1,735	—
USA	MF	5,179	5,311	5,118	5,270	5,438
	M	5,836	5,298	4,988	—	—
	F	4,553	5,324	5,242	—	—
USSR	MF	1,905	1,971	1,859	1,827	1,804
	M	2,034	—	—	1,772	1,780
	F	1,793	—	—	1,876	1,825

Source   *Unesco Statistical Yearbook 1990*, Paris.

- The permanency of the investment or new venture will depend on a number of things, such as the political complexion of the government in power and its attitudes towards business and foreign investment, also the available infrastructure, for to expand will require skills and knowhow as well as perhaps local finances. These will then be severely tested. If found to be inadequate, the LDC will be relegated to a small assembly operation within highly protective tariff walls. An international comparison of the number of students in higher education is seen in Table 20.13.
- As Pal and Bowander (1979) point out, in the case of exports, the main problem is that the successful firms sell mainly the products of tomorrow. The sale of yesterday's products usually show very sharp declines, and today's products will also decrease gradually in sales turnover. These changes in demand, coupled with the expense of new and advanced products in foreign markets by other countries, make export marketing very difficult.

Wortzel and Wortzel (1981) identified five stages of exporting through which a firm from an NIC or LDC could pass. The firm moves from Stage I to Stage II, from passive dependence or 'importer pull', to active pursuit of an 'exporter push' strategy. Beyond Stage II, each successive stage is marked by the exporting firm's increasing control over product design, the marketing and physical distribution efforts required to get its product from the plant to the consumer's household. As of Stage III, the marketing organization is becoming more elaborate, and so it will increase its external marketing activities in the domestic economy as well as abroad, where it may open small offices in one or more of the markets to which it exports. Stage IV introduces a further significant step away from contract manufacture to producing and marketing its own products. At Stage IV, it is the producer rather than the importer who decides what the firm will produce. Price is still the most important competitive weapon. Finally, in Stage V the local firms become almost indistinguishable from their counterparts in the advanced industrial nations. The metamorphosis at this stage is completed from price-based to product feature-based offerings. At this Stage V, the firm will have a marketing and sales organization similar to that of the indigenous firms with which it competes. (See Table 20.14.)

Wortzel and Wortzel maintain that Stages IV and V will not be appropriate for all firms, that extensive capital investment is usually required for a move from Stage I to Stage II, but not for the move from Stage II to Stage III which offers several strategic options in diversifying product lines: trading up to a higher priced quality good within its present product line; or concentrate on long runs of standardized products. Kaynak and Gurol (1987) developed an export marketing model for Turkey which could be used by other LDCs. It has five stages (see Figure 20.3.).

Basically, if Turkey can plan their export marketing scientifically in light of the latest developments in international trade theory and the Japanese experience, it could use cheap labour as a competitive advantage, slide down the experience curve fast, and become the dominant producer of many of the mature products in the European Community. If able to plan and implement quickly, Turkey can move completely away from the agrarian economy.

The stages in more detail are as follows:

Stage I

Product selection — selection of those products that are exportable from the LDCs that are mature or moving into maturity, and have the following characteristics:

Table 20.14 Wortzel and Wortzel: stages of export marketing development

	Product					Price			Promotion				Physical distribution at destination	
	Internal design	External design	Package design	Quality control	Branding	First cost	Price to retailer	Price to consumer	To importer – Locally	To importer – Destination	To retailer	To consumers	To distributors	To retailer
I Importer pull / *export push*	1	1				X								
II Basic production capacity marketing	X	1	1			X			X					
III Advanced production capacity marketing	X	X	X	1		X				X				
IV Product marketing channel push	X	X	X	X	1	X	1			X	1		X	1
V Product marketing consumer pull	X	X	X	X	X	X	X	1		X	X	X	X	X

Notes
1 = Partial responsibility
X = Pull responsibility

Source Wortzel, L. M., and Wortzel, H. V. (1981) Export marketing strategies for NIC and LDC based firms. *Columbia Journal of World Business*, **16**, (Spring), 51–60.

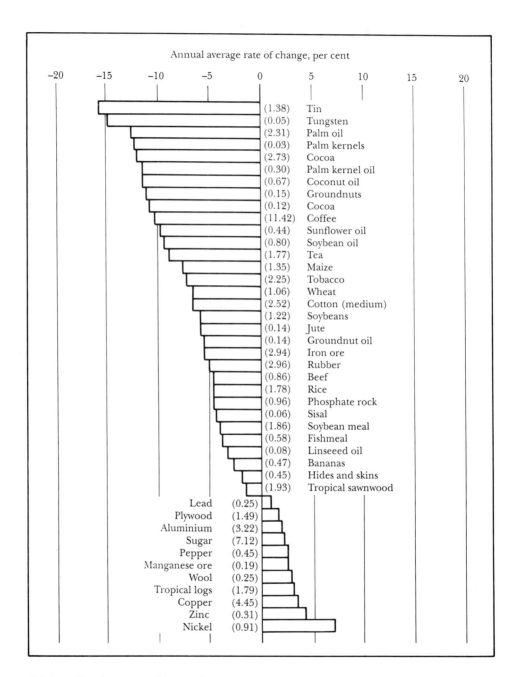

Figure 20.2 *Trends in monthly market prices for principal non-fuel primary commodities, 1982–1990*
Note   Figures in constant dollars
Source   *UNCTAD Commodity Yearbook* 1990, New York

Figure 20.3
Source   Kaynak E., and Gurol, M.N. (1987) Export marketing management in less developed countries: a case study of Turkey in light of the Japanese experience. *Management International Review*, **27**, (3), 54–66

- high domestic raw material content
- a labour intensive technology to benefit from low labour costs
- standardized, with long production runs that will allow functioning of the experience curves
- highly price elastic demand
- initially high domestic demand and later high international demand for the product

Stage II

Domestic sales – investing to build production. Economies of scale are important but domestic capacity limited. Necessary technology imported quite cheaply relative to the original R & D costs, which have since been covered. Starting from a low base, experience is quickly gained, which in turn lowers costs and prices.

Stage III

Export to the Middle East. As experience is gained and costs start to fall, larger and relatively more capital-intensive production facilities are built, and exporting to Middle Eastern and North African countries starts. International marketing experience is gained, and moving further along the experience curve reduces costs and prices, further stimulating additional domestic as well as international demand.

Stage IV

Export to the EC. Before exporting to the EC, quality preferences and standards of the EC member states should be investigated, and necessary product improvements made to satisfy the quality-conscious European customer. Larger capital investments are then made to cater for the substantial demand of the Community. As the technology is standard and economies of scale are being fully exploited, Turkey is able to use its lower labour costs to capture a substantial share of the EC market for highly price-sensitive products.

Stage V

Export to the USA – The products that are successful in the EC could be exported to the USA, because mass production with lower labour rates, cheaper raw materials and perhaps

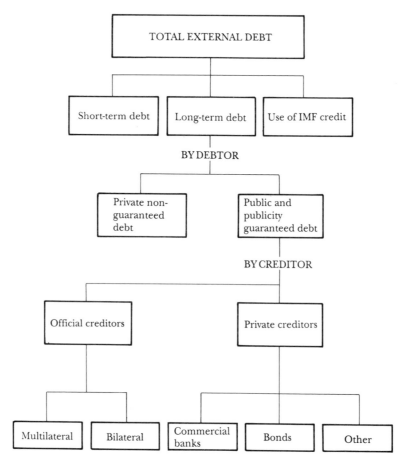

Figure 20.4   *Debt stock and its components*
Source   World Bank (1990) *World Debt Tables 1990–91*, 2 vols, Washington, DC

newer plants will enable Turkey to produce at a lower cost than the USA. Ocean freight and US duties have to be considered as additional costs before exporting to the USA. US producers pricing at full cost might only be undercut if marginal costs are used for export pricing to gain entrance to this competitive market. (Note though that this would leave the exporter open to accusations of dumping.)

Debt and the newly industrializing countries

Given the economic handicap which many of these developing countries face, it is no surprise, therefore, to have to consider the debt burden which they have to contend with. The structure and meaning of debt is explained in Figure 20.4 which details the sources as well as the labels frequently used for different types of borrowing whether sovereign or private.

Mexico, Brazil and Poland are all examples of newly industrializing countries. They are

Table 20.15 Indicators of structural differences between the SILICs and the SIMICs

Indicator	SILICs	SIMICs
Annual population growth (1988)	3.2	2
GNP per capita (*World Bank Atlas*) (US$, 1988)	288	1,632
Gross domestic investment/GCP (current prices, 1987–88)	14	22
Exports as a share of GDP (1987–88)	18	16
Share of manufacturing in exports (1987–88)	8	43
Infant mortality (death per 1,000 live births, 1987)	109.8	55[a]
Primary school enrolment (1986, percentage of age group)	67.3	103[b]
Official development assistance as a share of GDP (1987)	8.2	0.6[a]
Long-term official debt as a percentage of total debt	67	35

Note Figures in per cent unless otherwise indicated.
[a] 1988 figures
[b] 1987 figures

Source World Bank (1990) *World Debt Tables 1990–91*, 2 vols, Washington, DC.

also the countries most frequently spoken about with regard to the international debt crisis. Each of these invested heavily in the 1970s. In some instances, there was over-investment; in others, an impossibly short time horizon scheduled either for production resulting from imported technology or for the repayment of these loans on a medium-term basis rather than a long-term basis. Elsewhere, the money was channelled into consumer imports and illegal capita flight which could do nothing to support the domestic economy. The crash of these, the largest of the newly industrializing countries, makes the more moderate industrialization policies adopted by such countries as Malaysia or Thailand appear more prudent, but there still remains a massive bunching of debt maturities from the mid 1980s.

The appearance of these newly industrialized countries on the world product market has been evident for many years. Their industrialization policy, eagerness for exports, and generally low factor costs have enticed many multinationals to set up subsidiaries or engage in joint ventures and fully exploit the freeports where they exist. Sports goods, watches and electronic goods including domestic electrical equipment and home computers, are now all to be seen emanating from these centres. Average growth rates for these newly industrialized countries have been consistently higher than world averages. By this standard, it means that Brazil's economy may soon equal that of Germany.

It is important to recognize the difference between those countries termed SILICs (severely indebted low-income countries) and the SIMICs (severely indebted middle-income countries). It is more than a question of degree. The essential difference between the two groups is one of economic structure. These structural differences are deep as may be seen in Table 20.15.

The indebtedness of the twenty-six SILICs is made much worse by the fact that they have a low share of exports in manufacturing, high population growth with high infant mortality and low primary school enrolment. Official development assistance accounts also for a sizeable per centage of their GDP which is low relative to any other grouping.

The total outstanding debt of the SILICs at the end of 1989 was approximately equal to the GNP of these countries. Another characteristic which differentiates the SILICs from the

Table 20.16 Debt indicators for selected years, 1980–89

County group	Share of 1989 total debt	Debt-export ratio						Debt service ratio					
		1980	1982	1985	1987	1988	1989	1980	1982	1985	1987	1988	1989
All developing countries	100	134	182	214	232	201	187	22	28	28	28	27	22
Without debt-servicing difficulties	18	78	96	121	107	91	86	11	15	20	22	17	14
With debt-servicing difficulties	82	159	232	268	332	295	272	27	36	33	34	35	29
Severely indebted	58	174	285	315	391	341	315	30	44	36	34	35	28
Middle-income	49	196	297	318	375	320	294	36	49	37	36	36	29
Low-income	9	96	214	296	513	524	493	10	20	30	22	27	23
Moderately indebted	24	128	141	179	227	211	194	19	22	28	32	35	31
By region													
Sub-Saharan Africa	13	97	185	244	366	381	371	11	20	28	23	26	22
East Asia and the Pacific	18	90	114	137	122	100	90	14	18	24	24	18	16
South Asia	9	161	210	265	297	279	273	12	15	23	28	27	25
Europe and the Mediterranean	11	104	142	153	159	135	131	18	24	24	25	25	19
Middle East and North Africa	11	136	145	194	274	263	250	20	21	24	28	31	31
Latin America and the Caribbean	37	197	272	315	369	315	284	37	48	39	38	40	31

Note Figures in per cent.
[a]Debt indicators are based on total external debt (long-term debt, short-term debt, and use of IMF credit), and associated payments of debt service.
Source World Bank (1990) *World Debt Tables 1990–91*, 2 vols, Washington, DC.

SIMICs is that of official debt, which in most SILICs accounts for more than 70 per cent of total debt, but only 35 per cent in the SIMICs. Lower average dollar interest rates in 1990, continued extensions of maturities under the Brady Initiative, and the Paris Club rescheduling have brought some relief.

Within these aggregate figures a few interesting trends appear. Commercial loans from banks are only a very small fraction of what they were in 1980 to 1982, and even to 1984. Bonds have also declined, but official development finance has increased and so, too, has foreign direct investment which shows a strong sustained increase over the same periods. The figures are contained in Table 20.17.

The case for aid

The umbrella term 'aid' is often held to encompass military aid, commercial transactions, development assistance, and food aid. It is generally thought that aid serves five main objectives (Bandow, 1988):

1 Humanitarian – relieving human suffering.
2 Development – promoting economic growth.
3 Security – stabilizing potentially unsteady societies.
4 Military – improving the defence capabilities of allied governments.
5 Political – buying influence for the donor government.

The real world is complex and so are the motivations for granting or withholding aid to the Third World, including national self-interest, commercial considerations, historical links, political goals and the straightforward desire to accelerate economic growth in less developed countries.

Riddell (1987) points to three reasons behind the moral case for aid:

1 the needs of extremely poor people in extremely poor countries,
2 large and growing inequalities between those with excess resources and those with insufficient resources, and
3 historical relationships evaluated as unjust and requiring restitution and/or compensation.

Yet the complex relationship between morality and national interest produces five different views, as follows:

1 National interest considerations are important in deciding whether aid should be given, to whom, in what quantities, and in what form, but so, too, are moral considerations, and both should be referred to in assessing the basis for providing aid.
2 National interest considerations are important in aid decisions, but the needs of the Third World create such an overriding moral imperative to assist that prior consideration should be given to helping to solve these problems, even if this results in conflicts with the broad national interest of the donor.
3 National interest considerations are fundamental in decisions on aid, but the needs of the Third World provide an important moral perspective, and to the extent that the provision of aid on the basis of this moral perspective is in harmony with pursuing the national

Table 20.17 Aggregate net resource flows (long-term) to developing countries, 1980–90

	1980	1981	1982	1983	1984	1985	1986	1987	1988	1989	1990
Aggregate net resource flows (long term)	82.8	99.9	88.4	68.2	61.9	56.6	51.2	46.1	60.9	63.3	71.0
Official development finance	32.6	33.7	33.8	31.6	34.0	31.8	33.6	32.2	36.3	36.6	46.9
Official grants	12.5	11.4	10.4	9.9	11.4	13.2	14.0	14.9	18.0	18.6	19.5
Official loans (net)	20.1	22.3	23.4	21.7	22.6	18.6	19.6	17.3	18.3	18.0	27.4
Bilateral	12.2	12.9	11.9	10.6	10.3	6.4	6.3	4.9	6.8	6.1	10.4
Multilateral	7.8	9.4	11.5	11.0	12.4	12.2	13.3	12.4	11.5	11.9	16.9
Private loans (net)	41.1	53.3	43.6	28.1	19.6	14.3	8.1	0.7	5.5	4.3	2.3
Commercial banks	30.8	44.0	30.9	19.8	14.6	4.7	2.4	−1.1	0.7	3.0	
Bonds	1.1	1.3	4.8	1.0	0.3	5.0	1.3	0.2	2.2	0.3	
Other	9.2	8.0	7.8	7.4	4.7	4.5	4.4	1.6	2.6	1.0	
Foreign direct investment (FDI)	9.1	12.9	11.1	8.5	8.3	10.5	9.5	13.2	19.1	22.4	21.8
Aggregate net transfers (long term)	37.0	45.7	27.4	10.5	−0.9	−7.4	−10.0	−16.8	−9.5	−1.0	9.3
Memorandum items:											
Private grants	2.3	2.0	2.3	2.3	2.6	2.9	3.3	4.0	4.3	4.2	4.3
Net Use of IMF Credit	3.9	6.9	6.6	11.1	4.4	−0.2	−2.5	−5.8	−5.5	−2.3	2.1
Real aggregate net resource flows (long-term) (OECD deflator)	109.3	137.0	124.4	96.2	89.2	80.6	58.9	46.1	56.8	56.9	61.4
Real aggregate net resource flows (long-term) (import unit value index)	72.0	85.2	79.2	62.9	59.2	56.7	53.7	46.1	59.6	60.3	63.8
OECD deflator	75.7	72.9	71.1	70.9	69.4	70.2	87.0	100.0	107.1	111.3	115.7
Import unit value index	114.9	117.2	111.7	108.6	104.6	99.7	95.3	100.0	102.2	105.0	111.4

Note Figures in US$ billions.

Source World Bank (1990) *World Debt Tables 1990–91*, 2 vols, Washington, DC.

interest, then aid should be granted; to the extent that it is not, then aid should be withheld.
4 National interest considerations are fundamental in decisions on aid and all other criteria are quite irrelevant.
5 National interest considerations are fundamental in foreign policy decision issues, and the national interest is best served by providing no aid to the Third World.

Riddell (1987) cites the Conservative Party policy statement in 1980 as saying: 'It is arguable that the greatest contribution which Britain could make to the problems of many Third World countries would be to maintain a prosperous and open market here at home.'
Under British aid statistics, credits provided to private companies under the ATP (Aid and Trade Provision) to enable them to sell to aid-recipient countries are counted as part of the aid receipts of those countries. In 1982, these amounted to 10 per cent of bilateral aid flows.
There are many critics of aid, and Riddell sees them as falling into three groups:

1 Those who question the very objectives for which government aid is, or could be, given as they believe that there is no moral obligation for governments to provide, or even to assist in, the process of development. Some argue, in fact, that there is a moral obligation not to help.
2 Those, while accepting that there is some obligation to help solve the problems of the Third World, reject the notion that government aid can, and does, help the objectives of development, either for a prior reason or because of their analysis of the evidence.
3 Those for whom moral questions – of alleviating poverty, redistributing income, reducing development gaps or whatever – are irrelevant because other principles are claimed as the only legitimate ones on which governments should base their aid programme.

Admittedly, there have been many studies on aid but very few evaluations of aid programmes. For the development process to be self-sustaining, Rostow required three conditions:

1 A significant increase in the rate of net investments in the economies of poor countries.
2 One or more of the manufacturing sectors of the economy tries to exhibit a high rate of growth.
3 An institutionally favourable environment to ensure that the impulses derived from growth are transmitted throughout the economy.

Yet, despite its critics, aid can assist in the alleviation of poverty, both directly and indirectly.

Intermediate technology and the LDCs

The case is made that Western products are often too sophisticated and overpriced to meet only the very basic needs of the LDCs. In the case of hospital beds, there are those which are electrically controlled for operating theatres and will lift and raise the patient to the desired position, but they cost more than $20,000 each, and in the developing countries a simple operating table would be sufficient. In other areas, though, such as aircraft, the developing countries may well find it difficult to find the $75 million required to buy a Boeing 747, and so resort to second-hand machines that are less fuel-efficient and have higher recurrent ongoing costs of fuel and maintenance. National sovereignty, competition and political suspicion will often also prevent developing countries from collaborating with neighbouring countries and developing an effective marketing alliance.

The Intermediate Technology Development Group, based in Rugby, England, sprang from Fritz Schumacher's vision of economic freedom for people based on simple productive technologies. They now employ 180 staff, 34 per cent overseas, mostly local nationals in nine countries, with full-time representatives and officers in Peru, Sri Lanka, Bangladesh and Zimbabwe. The focus is on development. Taking the example of Bangladesh, one of the poorest countries in the world, where 83 per cent of the population is rural but 80 per cent do not own enough land to support a family, Intermediate Technology is playing a pivotal role identifying the most suitable equipment, providing training in products and processes, and helping to ensure that economic activities are as profitable as they can be, with maximum benefits going to the producers themselves. Intermediate Technology is providing the key technical support and advice to community-based organizations working with the rural poor. In Zimbabwe, Intermediate Technology is promoting the development of sustainable small-scale enterprises. In Sri Lanka, Intermediate Technology is involved with three main technical areas: the Fuel for Food Stove programme; the Micro Hydro programme, working with two Tea Plantation Boards as an alternative to grid electricity; and the Food Processing programme, providing assistance to small-scale rural food processing initiatives through extension services and training in product development. In Peru, Intermediate Technology is engaged in food processing, hydro energy, irrigation and housing. These are but brief illustrations as Intermediate Technology has representatives in nine countries, but they are indicative of their work to improve the quality of life. A further seven case studies of sustainable industrial development is to be found in Carr, 1988.

Proposals for change

Brandt Report (1980)

The Brandt report was an independent investigation into the urgent problems of inequality in the world, and the failure of its economic systems, by a group of international statesmen and leaders from many spheres. *North-South: A programme for survival* emphasizes the belief that major international initiatives are needed if mankind is to survive. The tone, however, is not negative nor filled with projections of doom because, although recognizing present problems, it also pinpoints areas of mutual interest between North and South, and how in future years imaginative responses will be required to avert an imminent global economic crisis. This concept of mutuality is an important one. The 'dialogue of the deaf' between the rich countries of the North and the poor countries of the South must end. Instead of a dialogue of Southern 'demands' and Northern 'concessions', there must be a symbolic relationship based on mutual benefits.

The report makes a number of recommendations, such as seeking an action programme comprising emergency and longer term measures to assist the poverty belts of Africa and Asia, and particularly the least developed countries. Measures would include large regional projects of water and soil management; the provision of health care and the eradication of such diseases as river blindness, malaria, sleeping sickness and bilharzia; afforestation projects; solar energy development; mineral and petroleum exploration; and support for industrialization, transport and other infrastructural investment. Such a programme would require additional financial assistance of at least four billion dollars per year over twenty years or special concessional terms that were assured over long periods to be flexible and available.

Other recommendations included:

1 Creation of an International Grains Agreement, larger international emergency reserves, and the establishment of a food-financing facility which would help assure food security internationally.
2 New trading rules recognizing that the GSP Generalized System of Preferences (GSP) negotiated in UNCTAD in 1968 for the developing countries is in need of revision. It also recommends that GATT and UNCTAD should merge into one body.
3 A new international framework to allow developing countries and multinational corporations to benefit from direct investment.
4 Legislation to regularize the activities of multinational co-operators with regard to ethical behaviour, business practices, cartels, etc. An international code would be a useful step in that direction.
5 Co-operation by governments in their tax policies to monitor transfer pricing and to eliminate the resort to tax lowness.
6 Harmonization of fiscal and other measures and policies towards foreign investment among host governments.
7 International discussion and consultation on measures affecting direct investment and the education of multinational corporations.
8 Greater information flow both between and within nations improving the speed, relevance, and current standing of existing systems.
9 Greater support for technical assistance and transmission of technology. More support to be given to provide the local basis for research and evaluation of needs.
10 Research into more efficient production, development, and marketing to defend and improve the market competitiveness of those raw materials mainly produced in developing countries.
11 A study of the implications of technological breakthroughs in the North which may lead to automation, and deprive the South of its comparative advantage in low wage costs.
12 Research and development aid studies. Only 1 per cent of research and development in the North is concerned with the problems of the South; whereas 57 per cent is devoted to defence, atomic and space research.
13 Aid agencies should use more local skilled people to avoid perpetrating dependency on individual countries.
14 Freedom to choose within a 'tied' aid package.
15 Greater international coordination of research affecting the South.
16 A substantial increase in the transfer of resources to developing countries so as to finance:

- projects and programmes to alleviate poverty,
- exploration and development of energy and mineral resources, and
- stabilization of the prices and earnings of commodity exports.

17 Enlarging official development finance by:

- a sliding scale of contributions related to national income,

- an increase of official development assistance to 0.7 per cent of GNP by 1985, and to 1 per cent by the end of the century, and
- levies on international deals on arms production; and international levies on the global commons, especially sea-bed minerals.

18 Improved lending facilities through:

- Increased monetary capability of the World Bank.
- Doubling the borrowing to capital ratio of the World Bank from its present gearing of 1:1 to 2:1, and similar action by Regional Development Banks.
- Abstaining from the incorporation of political conditions and the operations of unilateral institutions.
- Channelling an increased share of development finance through regional institutions.
- A substantial increase in programme lending.
- The use of IMF gold reserves, either for further sales — whose profits would subsidize interest on development lending — or as collateral to borrow for on-lending to developing countries.
- Giving borrowing countries a greater role in decision making and management.

19 A new approach to development finance:

- Funds for development must be recognized as a responsibility of the whole world community, and placed on a predictable and long-term basis. All countries — West and East and South, excepting the poorer countries — should contribute. Their contributions should be on a sliding scale relating to national income.
- More funds to be raised from levies related to international trade, military expenditures or arms exports.
- World Bank and Regional Development Banks should take new steps to increase their lendings.
- Borrowing for on-lending to developing countries should take place against the collateral of the retained portion of the gold reserves of the IMF.
- The serious gaps found in the present range of financing, particularly the lack of programmed lending, must be filled.
- Major additional multilateral finance is required to support mineral and energy exploration and development in developing countries.
- The commercial banking system should continue to lend to the developing world and on an adequate scale. The World Bank and other financial institutions should provide guarantees and play their part in ensuring a continued flow of commercial funds.

20 Finally, an Emergency Programme, 1980–85, whose principal elements included:

- a large scale transfer of resources to developing countries,
- an international energy strategy,
- a global food programme, and
- a start on some major reforms in the international economic system.

The Brady Plan

In 1989, US Treasury Secretary Nicholas Brady introduced a political initiative to deal with the debt problems of the severely indebted middle-income countries (SIMICs), involving a $25 billion write-down of debt. The Brady Plan deals with commercial debt, not official debts, so for seven of the SIMICs, who owe more than half of their debt to official creditors, it will do little to alleviate their arrears problems. Countries which adopted adjustment programmes were to obtain access to debt and debt reduction facilities supported by international financial institutions including the World Bank, IMF, and official creditors. Although there are thirty-nine debtor nations on the list, 75 per cent of this debt is concentrated in Brazil, Mexico, Argentina, Venezuela, and Chile. Adjustment programmes under the Brady initiative were concluded in 1990 with Costa Rica, Mexico, the Philippines, Venezuela, Morocco and Uruguay. These agreements are complex and have been time consuming. Basically they allow LDC governments to negotiate purchase of their debt to foreign commercial banks at deep discounts. Agreements with Costa Rica, Mexico and the Philippines have reduced debt outstanding to foreign commercial banks by $9.5 billion. These adjustment programmes have involved swaps of debt for private equity sometimes linked to government privatization schemes, as with Argentina. SIMICs require as a precondition for renewed development to undertake structural adjustment to their economies.

For the banks, favourable tax and accounting treatment has eased the position on their perceived reserves after writing-off much of their developing country debt portfolio. Third World debt has since moved into bonds and equity. It has allowed banks to make new credit available to these countries, as with Citicorp in Mexico extending its existing credit there by 25 per cent or $400–500 million. However, as with all forms of aid, the Brady Plan has its critics who maintain that the Brady Plan will retard, rather than accelerate, growth among the LDCs as it diverts resources still to the payment of debts which could otherwise be seen as new money for investment. Critics argue that the only way to solve the crisis is for the poor countries to grow out of it by undertaking deep structural reforms to move their economies from highly controlled to more market-oriented. What is required is a move away from inward-oriented import-substituting policies to export-promoting outward-oriented policies.

UNCTAD

The UN Conference on Trade and Development has taken, since its inception, a pro-LDC stance. In 1982, UNCTAD opposed the patent system, arguing that developing countries would then be able to produce their own pharmaceutical products or buy from the cheaper source, but that is also to ignore the potentially significant public health problems due to manufacture that is not linked to quality and stability.

In 1985, UNCTAD examined the options for debt-laden LDCs and concluded that debt relief was the only viable way to revive growth and reduce debt, recommending that commercial banks write off 30 per cent of their Third World loans, which would ease debt servicing and release foreign exchange for investment. Banks would also benefit because their remaining debt would be worth more on the secondary markets (see section above on the Brady Plan).

In 1987, UNCTAD formulated the UN Convention on Conditions for Registration of Ships, an attempt by a number of LDCs to develop flags of convenience as they argued that these hindered the development of merchant fleets in countries which did not offer a flag of

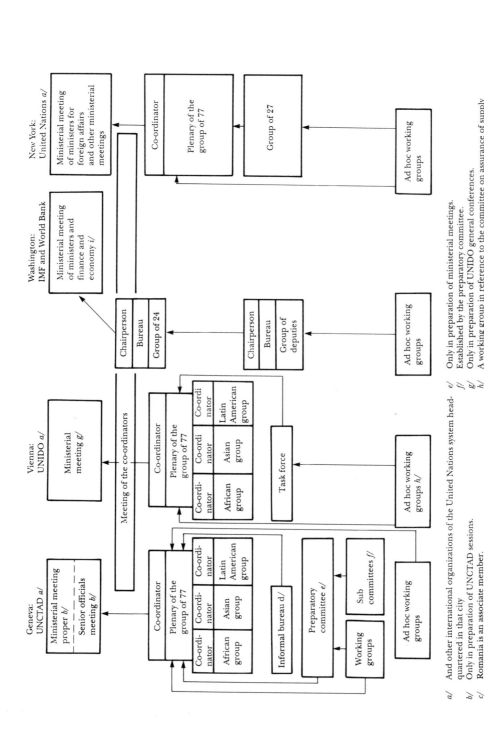

Figure 20.5 *The multi-central structure of the Group of 77*

Source Sauvant, K. P. (1981) *The Group of 77: Evolution, Structure, Organisation,* Oceania Publications, New York

a/ And other international organizations of the United Nations system headquartered in that city
b/ Only in preparation of UNCTAD sessions.
c/ Romania is an associate member.
d/ Consisting of the co-ordinator of the group of 77 and the co-ordinators
   of the regional groups.

e/ Only in preparation of ministerial meetings.
f/ Established by the preparatory committee.
g/ Only in preparation of UNIDO general conferences.
h/ A working group in reference to the committee on assurance of supply
   of the international atomic energy agency has a somewhat more
   permanent character.
i/ So far, only one such meeting, on 29 September 1979, took place.

convenience, and secondly, served only to facilitate ship safety hazards. While the agreement covers ship management, ownership and staffing, its provisions are unfortunately unenforceable.

In 1988, UNCTAD produced a report on the impact of captive insurance companies on the insurance markets of developing countries. Its conclusions have been endorsed by all the LDCs. Basically, it says that captive insurers can benefit the insurance markets and economies of the LDCs by forcing insurers to alter their pricing systems and provide broader increased coverage with more liberal policy conditions. Whereas their negative aspects focused on technical competence and the diversion of insurance and foreign exchange for developing countries in which captives operate, UNCTAD had previously campaigned for the creation of a system of international cooperation for the supervision and regulation of reinsurers, pointing to the fact that 75 per cent of the world's reinsurance firms have been formed in the past 25 years and thus lack experience. UNCTAD could, therefore, provide an international regulation standard. However, the International Insurance Advisory Council (IIAC) and the European Insurance Committee, meeting to discuss these issues, shared a consensual view that developing countries have been following unsound advice from UNCTAD which supports state reinsurance monopolies. UNCTAD has also presided over negotiations for an international sugar agreement since 1983.

When established in 1964 UNCTAD's role was the resolution, negotiation and adoption of multilateral legal instruments for international trade. UNCTAD has consistently taken a pro-LDC stance, much to the annoyance of the USA and other Western nations. In 1981, for example, UNCTAD proposed creating a buffer stock, buying up surplus supplies as an alternative to export quotas. A listing of UNCTAD core commodities for support is to be found in Table 20.5.

Group of 77

The Group of 77 came into being at the first session of UNCTAD in 1964. Its name is a misnomer as it currently encompasses 122 developing countries in all. It is a radical ginger group acting on behalf of the developing countries which felt frustrated at their lack of progress within UNCTAD, an irony in that most Western nations have come to view UNCTAD almost as a left-wing anarchist organization. UNCTAD, when first formed, had regional membership rather than individual country membership. Region B was synonymous with OECD membership while Region D included the CMEA member states which left the developing countries in Regions A and C. The developing countries then grouped together and, since then, new members to either the A or C region of UNCTAD have automatically also become members of the Group of 77.

The Group of 77 launched the idea of the New International Economic Order in the 1970s. It was an innovative approach to a new world order. Since then, the initiative has been allowed to lapse for lack of support from the industrialized Western nations, but the Group of 77 continues to play an important role within the framework of the United Nations, as representatives of the collective economic interest of the Third World in all global negotiations with the developed countries. It has no constitution, and what organizational structure it has, has evolved from the informal nature of its early origins. Julius Nyerere summed it up in his address to the Group of 77 in February 1979 (Sauvant, 1981):

> What we have in common is that we are all, in relation to the developed world, dependent – not interdependent – nations. Each of our economies has developed as a by-product and a subsidiary of development in the industrialised North, and it is externally oriented. We are not the prime movers of our own destiny. We are ashamed to admit it, but economically we are dependencies – semi-colonies at best – not sovereign states.

The non-aligned countries considered themselves to be playing a catalytic role within the Group of 77. Yet cohesiveness is not natural to this organization which is not homogeneous in membership, nor has it any strong unifying force. The Group of 77 has since spread away from its central focus on UNCTAD to a multi-centre organization focusing on UNIDO in Vienna, IMF in Washington, World Bank in Washington and the UN, itself, in New York, as well as UNCTAD in Geneva, and, virtually all UN Conferences.

References

Baker, S. (1988) Will the planet pay the price for Third World Debt? *Business Week*, (3076), 24 October, 88 L-T.

Bandow, D. (1988) Foreign aid: the oxymoron of the 1980s. *Business and Society Review*, (67), Fall, 35–39.

Behrmann, J. N. (1984) *Industrial Policies: International Restructuring and Transnationals*, Lexington Books.

Carr, M. (1988) *Sustainable Industrial Development: Seven Case Studies*, Intermediate Technology Publications, London.

Chileshe, J. H. (1986) *Third World Countries and Development Options: Zambia*, Vikas Publishing House PVT Ltd., New Delhi, India.

Cline, W. R. (1984) *Exports of Manufacturers from Developing Countries: Performance and Prospects for Market Access*, Brookings Institution, Washington, DC.

Economist (1990) A taxing burden of debt, **316,** (7671), 87.

Economist (1990) Brady's bazaar, **315,** (7654), 77.

Financial Times (1990) Survey: Nigeria, 19 March.

Halper, D. G., and Moon, M. C. (1990) Striving for first-rate markets in Third World Nations. *Management Review*, May, 20–22.

Intermediate Technology Annual Report, 1989–90, Myson House, Rugby.

Kaynak, E., and Gurol, M. N. (1987) Export marketing management in less-developed countries: A case study of Turkey in light of the Japanese experience. *Management International Review*, **27,** (3), 54–66.

Kinsey, J. (1988) *Marketing in Developing Countries*, Macmillan, London.

Krueger,A. O., Harberger, A. C., Edwards, S., and McKinnon, R. I. (1990) Developing countries' debt problems and efforts at policy reform. *Contemporary Policy Issues*, **VIII,** (1), 1–38.

Lipson, H. A., and Lamont, D. F. (1969) Marketing policy decisions facing international marketers in the less-developed countries. *Journal of Marketing*, **33,** (October) 24–31.

McNamee, M. (1989) Fed lifts the Brady Plan out of its sickbed. *Business Week*, (3127), 9 October, p. 43.

Medawar, C., and Freese, B. (1981) Drug multinationals in the Third World. *Business and Society Review*, Summer, 22–24.

North:South: A Programme for Survival (1980) The Report of the Independent Commission on

International development issues under the chairmanship of Willy Brandt, Pan Books, London.

Page, S. (1990) *Trade, Finance and Developing Countries: Strategies and Constraints in the 1990s*, Overseas Development Institute, London, and Barnes and Noble Books, Savage, Maryland, USA.

Pal, S. K., and Bowander, B. (1979) Marketing challenges of technical industries in developing countries. *Industrial Marketing Management*, **8**, 69–74.

Pring, D. C. (1987) Third World research is difficult, but it's possible. *Marketing News*, 28 August, 50–51.

Riddell, R. C. (1987) *Foreign Aid Reconsidered*, Johns Hopkins University Press, Baltimore: James Currey, London in Association with the Overseas Development Institute, London.

Sauvant, K. P. (1981) *The Group of 77: Evolution, Structure, Organization*, Oceania Publications Inc., New York.

Schultz, S., and Schumacher, D. (1984) The reliberalisation of world trade. *Journal of World Trade Law*, **18**, (13), 206–223.

The Banker (1990) Casualties of slow growth, September, 27–28.

The Banker (1989) Give Brady a chance, **139**, (764), 120.

UN Centre on Transnational Corporations (1985) *Transnational Corporations in World Development*, 3rd survey, New York.

Whalley, J. (1989) *Developing Countries and the Global Trading System*, 2 vols, University of Michigan Press, Ann Arbor, Michigan.

Wortzel, L. H., and Wortzel, M. V. (1981) Export marketing strategies for NIC and LDC-based firms. *Columbia Journal of World Business*, Spring, 51–59.

Key reading

Bandow, D. (1988) Foreign aid: The oxymoron of the 1980s. *Business and Society Review*, (67), Fall, 35–39.

Carr, M. (1988) *Sustainable Industrial Development: Seven Case Studies*, Intermediate Technology Publications, London.

Cline, W. R. (1984) *Exports of Manufacturers from Developing Countries: Performance and Prospects for Market Access*, Brookings Institution, Washington, DC.

Kaynak, E., and Gurol, M. N. (1987) Export marketing management in less-developed countries: A case study of Turkey in light of the Japanese experience. *Management International Review*, **27**, (3), 54–66.

Kinsey, J. (1988) *Marketing in Developing Countries*, Macmillan, London.

Krueger, A. O., Harberger, A. C., Edwards, S., and McKinnon, R. I. (1990) Developing countries' debt problems and efforts at policy reform. *Contemporary Policy Issues*, **VIII**, (1), 1–38.

Riddell, R. C. (1987) *Foreign Aid Reconsidered*, Johns Hopkins University Press, Baltimore: James Currey, London in Association with the Overseas Development Institute, London.

Page, S. (1990) *Trade, Finance and Developing Countries: Strategies and Constraints in the 1990s*, Overseas Development Institute, London, and Barnes and Noble Books, Savage, Maryland, USA.

Sauvant, K. P. (1981) *The Group of 77: Evolution, Structure, Organization*, Oceania Publications Inc., New York.

Whalley, J. (1989) *Developing Countries and the Global Trading System*, 2 vols, University of Michigan Press, Ann Arbor, Michigan..

Whalley, J. (1989) *The Uruguay Record and Beyond*, University of Michigan Press, Ann Arbor, Michigan.

Wortzel, L. H., and Wortzel, H. V. (1981) Export marketing strategies for NIC and LDC-based firms. *Columbia Journal of World Business*, Spring, 51–59.

21 Case studies

Case Study 1: Producton Torolandia, S.A.* case study

This case study was prepared by Gustavo Lopetegui, MED-86, under the direction of Francisco Parés, Lecturer and Professor Lluís G. Renart. It is intended to be used as a basis for class discussion rather than to illustrate either effective or ineffective handling of an administrative situation.

The General Manager of Producton Torolandia, S.A. had to take a decision in March 1985 with regard to an order that had arrived from Cleopatria through the 'parallel' channel. He had been carrying out this type of transaction for about three years and he constantly wondered whether he should continue them or not, as they placed him at great risk of discovery by the parent company, located in the country of Hollywood. The General Manager of the parent company, Ronald Dollar, had laid down very clearly which countries Producton Torolandia, S.A. could sell to and, were these 'parallel transactions' to be discovered, Dollar would not only bring them to an immediate stop but there was also a strong likelihood that he would dismiss him.

However, on the other hand, the profitability of this 'channel' was very high and enabled Producton Torolandia, S.A. to attain its sales targets. Up until now everything had been done with extreme caution and no major mishaps had occurred. At most, Hollywood Inc.'s auditors had made some inquiries as to certain sales but the incident had gone no further. Nevertheless, this order from Cleopatria was the largest that had been received until now through the parallel channel, amounting to approximately 160 million reals (reals are the legal tender in Torolandia). The order could be divided into several part deliveries but in any case, the jump in the Turislandian distributor's sales from one year to the next would be very noticeable. Turisland belonged politically to Torolandia but was considered a free trade zone. Hence, this distributor was used as a 'cover' for the parallel transactions. In any case, the order was tempting, especially considering the crisis that was affecting the domestic sales of Producton Torolandia, S.A.

The company

Producton Torolandia, S.A., founded in 1975, is a wholly owned subsidiary of Producton Hollywood Inc. Both firms manufacture a wide range of consumer goods whose factory sales price varies between 2,000 and 12,000 reals. (In 1985, the official rate of exchange was about 200 reals for one US dollar.) The 'Producton' brand was recognized worldwide, and while some products were produced in both countries, others were only produced by one of the firms. Since its foundation, Producton Torolandia, S.A. had achieved steady sales growth,

* Producton Torolandia, S. A. is a fictitious name. Other data, names and circumstances are also fictional. However, any similarity to reality is not pure coincidence. No part of this case study may be reproduced without the permission of IESE.

doubling them year after year. However, as the recession deepened, the growth rate had atarted to slow down after 1980.

Exports

Right from the start, the parent company had divided up the world market so that neither company would compete with the other in the same market. Thus, Producton Torolandia, S.A. had exclusive distributorship for the Indebted Continent while Hollywood had the rest of the world. This division was due to the language and cultural links existing between the inhabitants of Torolandia and those of the Indebted Continent, who spoke very similar languages.

In the case of goods that were manufactured by only one of the two companies, these were invoiced at cost price by the manufacturing company to the other company so that it could sell them on its domestic market or re-export them to the countries within its own export area. Officially no shipments were made from the parent company in Hollywood to a country in the Indebted Continient of countries was observed without exceptions. The parent company regularly sent auditors to Producton Torolandia, S.A. in order to verify, among other things, the fulfilment of this very point. Any breach would cost more than one Producton Torolandia, S.A. manager his job, especially knowing Ronald Dollar's reputation for toughness.

The sales policy followed by both companies was to appoint an exclusive distributor in each country who was required to satisfy a certain number of conditions, such as holding certain stock levels or ongoing brand advertising.

In the first years of trading (1975–1981), exports by PRODUCTION Torolandia, S.A. to the Indebted continent grew rapidly due to the quality and novelty of the whole range and the sales efforts made.

The crisis

Around 1982, most countries in the Indebted Continent were suffering from an economic crisis due to a large extent to heavy borrowing overseas, which upset their balance of payments. Consequently, in many of these countries, it was prohibited to import goods of

Table 21.1

Year	Sales to Turisland	Parallel exports	Total apparent purchases by Turisland
1982	430	20	450
1983	220	230	450
1984	150	300	450

Note   Figures in million reals.

the type sold by Producton Torolandia, S.A. as they were considered superfluous or 'luxury'. This prohibition could be direct or by the central banks of each country not giving foreign exchange to the importers. Thus, the export figures progressively decreased while domestic sales levelled out due to the weakening of the Torolandia economy.

In view of this drop in sales, authorization was requested from Producton Hollywood, Inc. to allow Producton Torolandia, S.A. to sell to those countries where, in spite of belonging to Hollywood's export areas, this company had not yet appointed any distributor or the distributor appointed was not operating satisfactorily. The answer was a categorical no. There was no chance that such a request would be accepted.

The 'parallel customers'

Meanwhile, people from countries in the parent company's export area often visited Producton Torolandia, S.A.'s offices, expressing interest in buying its products. They were generally from countries in the Reconstructed Continent or the Dark Continent.

These potential customers were motivated to come to Producton Torolandia, S.A. for various reasons.

1 The official channel through which Producton brand goods came to their country was

$$\boxed{\text{Producton Hollywood, Inc.}} \rightarrow \boxed{\text{Official distributor}} \rightarrow \boxed{\text{Retail store}} \rightarrow \boxed{\text{Final consumer}}$$

Obviously, considering that these products enjoyed a certain demand, buying them from Producton Torolandia, S.A. meant that they could skip the official distributor or simply replace it. The aspirant pirate 'importer', even though he had to sell at the same prices as the official distributors, was able to take advantage of the distributor's advertising and as his overhead expenses were perhaps more streamlined, his operating expenses would be lower. Another argument was that the demand for some products within the range was greater than for others. However, the official distributor was required to buy and stock the whole range. Naturally, the pirate 'importer' did not have to fulfill this requirement.

2 In some countries, the official distributor appointed by Producton Hollywood, Inc. had difficulty in getting the foreign exchange or the government authorizations required for importing. On the other hand, a third company who had 'contacts' or 'acquaintances' in government departments was able to succeed where the distributor had failed. This third company then came to Producton Torolandia, S.A. as the parent company, respecting the exclusive distributorship awarded, would obviously not sell to anybody else.

3 Finally, in neighbouring countries where imports were strictly prohibited, Producton's goods were smuggled in in 'ant fashion'. This meant that people crossed the frontier daily carrying two or three items hidden. The person who sold to these 'ant' customers found it better to import directly than to supply himself from the local official distributor.

Possible outlets

When a potential customer from the export area allocated to Producton Hollywood, Inc., contacted Producton Torolandia, S.A. because he wished to buy, the only 'legal' (here the word legal refers to the Company's own internal rules and not to national laws) alternative for Producton Torolandia, S.A. was to divert these orders to one of his wholesalers in Torolandia so that he could carry out the export operation to the customer in the 'prohibited' country. However, were this method to be used:

- The price advantage would disappear as the buyer paid Producton's price plus the local wholesaler's margin.
- If Producton Hollywood found out about this operation, it would order Producton Torolandia, S.A. to reprimand the local wholesaler as well as ordering it not to allow this type of sale to occur again.

As has been said, the parent company kept a very strict control which meant that if it was decided to parallel export to companies in Hollywood's area, the process used would have to be such that, even if the 'parallel' operations were to be discovered, it had to be impossible to trace them back to Producton Torolandia, S.A. or any of its customers, so that it would be possible to continue them. The General Manager of PTSA, in view of the steady drop in sales on the domestic market and the impossibility of exporting to the Indebted Continent, asked his export manager to think up some system which would enable him to export to customers in the 'prohibited' countries behind Producton Hollywood, Inc.'s back.

The path chosen

First of all, the matter was discussed with PTSA's distributor in Turisland, with whom the business relationship was very close. Although Turisland is part of Torolandia from the political point of view, it is considered under Torolandia's legislation as a free trade zone. Thus, legally speaking, all goods to be sent to Turisland had to be exported from Torolandian wholesalers.

One advantage of using this wholesaler as a 'bridge' or 'cover' through which the 'parallel' orders were channelled was that his buying volume was very high. It would thus be easy to hide these new orders. Any increase in sales to a normal wholesaler would have immediately attracted the parent company's attention. Thus, when a potential customer from a country not allocated to it came to Producton Torolandia, interested in buying, he was either told that it was not possible to sell to him, or if it was found that the customer was trustworthy, it was hinted to him that somebody would contact him indirectly. If the Turislandian distributor was used as a 'cover', the next problem was how to cover *him*. For this, the following system was devised.

a The parallel customer visits Producton Torolandia, S.A. expressing interest. He is officially told that it is not possible to sell to him, but a record is made of his name and address. A confidential note is then passed on to Empresapuente, S.A.
b Empresapuente, S.A. (a firm specializing in international trade whose owners and managers have nothing to do with Producton Torolandia, S.A., but which is located in the same city) makes contact, establishes a business relationship and finally makes the 'parallel' customer an offer for the products he wishes to buy.
c The 'parallel' customer accepts the offer, places a firm order and opens an irrevocable letter of credit in favour of Empresapuente, S.A. for the total value of the goods it wishes to buy.

d When the letter of credit is opened, Empresapuente, S.A. informs PTSA. PTSA sells and invoices the goods to the Turislandian distributor as if it was a normal order.

e The goods are cleared through customs and leave Torolandia customs jurisdiction. In all the documentation, it is stated that they are being sent to Turisland but, once cleared through customs, instead of being physically sent to Turisland, they are diverted and stored in a free warehouse in Flamenquilla (PTSA was located near Flamenquilla) under the Turislandian distributor's name, who is now its legal owner.

f The Turislandian then transfers ownership of the products to Empresapuente, S.A. by means of a simple letter addressed to the free warehouse.

g Finally, Empresapuente, S.A. orders that the goods be shipped from the free warehouse in Flamenquilla and invoices the parallel customer. All the shipping, invoicing and payment documents state that the vendor is Empresapuente, S.A.

For this service, Empresapuente, S.A. and the Turislandian distributor received a 10 per cent commission. Three per cent of this was used to cover administrative expenses and the remaining 7 per cent was divided equally between the two.

In order to help understand this circuit, Exhibit 21.1 shows the physical and documentary routes followed by the exported goods.

PTSA's export manager commented:

We normally only do this type of operation when we receive a specific order from a certain customer and country. Thus we always know the goods' final destination. We do not authorize operations with countries where we know that the official representative is operating satisfactorily and buys large quantities from Producton Hollywood, Inc. We have sales statistics for all the countries which are sent to us by the parent company so that it is easy to know in which countries there would be problems if we sold in parallel and in which countries there would be no problems. In actual fact, we could quadruple our present parallel sales figures if we accepted all the orders we receive, but we are limited by having to pass all transactions through just one distributor. If Torolandia had more free trade zones, we could channel them through other distributors but, at present, we can only do it with the Turislandian distributor.

At the same time, an effort was made for the Turislandian distributor's sales to increase progressively, breaking up certain orders. All this was done so that the parent company would not notice anything unusual. The fall in this representative's internal sales in Turisland helped to hide these extra sales. The customers were required to open a letter of credit four or five months in advance and no guarantee was made as to delivery. The large margin obtained on resale softened the harshness of these conditions, which in other circumstances would have been unacceptable.

PTSA's export manager commented:

Once the official distributor of the Kingdom of Blackgold, which is a country in Hollywood's export area, noticed that goods manufactured by PTSA were being sold in his country that had not been marketed by him and at lower prices, he immediately complained to Producton Hollywood, Inc. which, in turn, asked PTSA who had sold the goods. Of course, PTSA's reply was to say that it knew nothing about the matter, stating that it could have been any Torolandian wholesaler or retailer or even a third party. Producton Hollywood, Inc. managed to ascertain that the vendor was a company called Empresapuente, S.A. PTSA answered that it had never sold to this company and that it did not know who could have made the sale. The incident went no further but in any case, to avoid any future complications, sales to the parallel customer in the Kingdom of Blackgold were discontinued.

Thus, Producton Torolandia, S.A.'s management had definite proof that, even if the presence of parallely imported products was detected, it was impossible to trace them to PTSA. The only hypothetically traceable clue was the letter filed in the Flamenquilla free warehouse transferring the legal ownership of the goods from the Turislandian distributor to Empresapuente, S.A. In other words, it was virtually impossible that any auditor could gain access to these files which were totally unrelated to PTSA and of course private (not public). Generally, two types of customers were received:

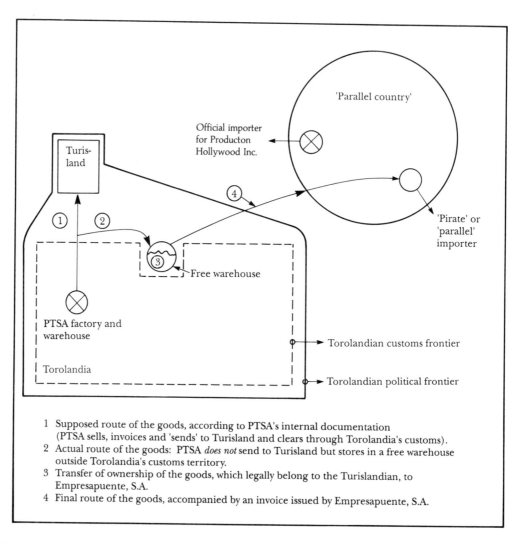

1 Supposed route of the goods, according to PTSA's internal documentation (PTSA sells, invoices and 'sends' to Turisland and clears through Torolandia's customs).
2 Actual route of the goods: PTSA *does not* send to Turisland but stores in a free warehouse outside Torolandia's customs territory.
3 Transfer of ownership of the goods, which legally belong to the Turislandian, to Empresapuente, S.A.
4 Final route of the goods, accompanied by an invoice issued by Empresapuente, S.A.

Exhibit 21.1   *Producton Torolandia, S.A. – physical and documentary routes of the goods exported*

- Those with whom there already existed an ongoing relationship (these were attended to directly in PTSA and the operation was finalized there).
- Unknown customers (they were informed that PTSA could not sell to them and they were discretely passed on to the Turislandian or Empresapuente who made an offer to them).

The collection and payment circuit

A major problem was posed when it came to justifying to the banks the transfers of foreign exchange. Not because of their illegality, as everything was done legally, but because of the lack of provision of Torolandian legislation for these special cases. The critical point of the operation was converting into reals the foreign currency received by Empresapuente, S.A., as this company officially had not exported anything. As the General Manager of PTSA commented:

> When we began all this, the banks did not readily understand the operation. They offered us all types of alternatives except the one needed, which was something legal and logical. They told us that if we had not been the exporters, they did not know what logical reasons they could give to the Central Bank of Torolandia that would justify receiving remittances of large

> The parallel customer opened a line of credit for Empresapuente, S.A. for the amount of the operation in foreign convertible currency. In order to enable this foreign currency to be converted into reals, the Bank of Torolandia required that Empresapuente, S.A. produce its 'export license'. Naturally, Empresapuente, S.A. did not have this license as it had not made the export. Instead, a note of exception is presented with which Torolandian customs issues a 'special case exports' form, called B3. The normal certificate issued by customs in current cases is B1 and this is what most of the banks know.
>
> As form B3 was not regulated, no bank accepted it for carrying out the conversion and consequently each time a note explaining the operation had to be presented. By this means, authorization to convert the foreign currency in reals was finally obtained. After obtaining the reals, Empresapuente, S.A. paid the Turislandian distributor and the latter paid Producton Torolandia, S.A. in reals, as in all its operations. Remittance of reals between Torolandia and Turislandia (which is still within its political territory) are free and do not require any kind of special permit or authorization.
>
> In June 1984, and perhaps due to the frequency of the operations, the Bank of Torolandia formalized the form B3 as sufficient justification for convertibility. At the same time, it required that the use of this type of form be recorded in a special register in which a 'financial activities number' (FAN) is given, which must be presented to the bank. This put the whole affair on a normal footing. Expressed in graphic form, the payment circuit is as follows:

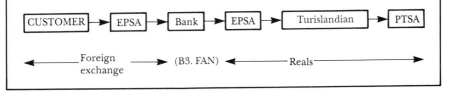

Exhibit 21.2 *Producton Torolandia, S.A. – the collection and payments circuit*

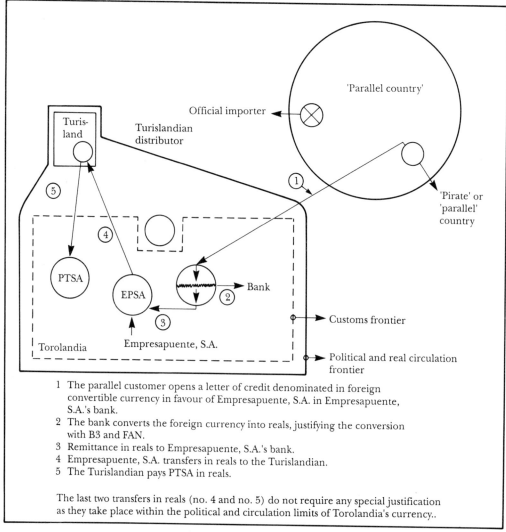

1   The parallel customer opens a letter of credit denominated in foreign
    convertible currency in favour of Empresapuente, S.A. in Empresapuente,
    S.A.'s bank.
2   The bank converts the foreign currency into reals, justifying the conversion
    with B3 and FAN.
3   Remittance in reals to Empresapuente, S.A.'s bank.
4   Empresapuente, S.A. transfers in reals to the Turislandian.
5   The Turislandian pays PTSA in reals.

The last two transfers in reals (no. 4 and no. 5) do not require any special justification
as they take place within the political and circulation limits of Torolandia's currency..

Exhibit 21.2   *(continued)*

quantities of foreign exchange from abroad. They didn't know how to 'dress' the operation.
They asked us whether we wanted them to transfer the foreign currency into a numbered
account in Alpland or something similar. Of course we needed the money in Torolandia to pay
the Turislandian and for him to pay in turn Producton and thereby bring the operation to a
close.

This was finally solved according to the system shown in Exhibit 21.2.

When this type of operation started to function regularly, the Turislandian distributor
learned the lesson and started to carry out similar parallel operations with other products'
brands for which he also acted a representative. This brought about further bureaucratic
difficulties which were finally solved, as shown in Exhibit 21.3.

Exhibit 21.3 *Producton Torolandia, S.A. – other parallel operations by the Turislandian distributor and Empresapuente, S.A.*

Parallel operations in international trade come about for several reasons and may be carried out in several ways. The way chosen by PTSA is only one of them and, by way of example of other methods, there follows an explanation of other parallel operations carried out by the Turislandian distributor and Empresapuente, S.A.

The Turislandian distributor of PTSA also acts as distributor for other international brands. In some cases he has been appointed by the Torolandian subsidiary of the parent company (as in the case of PTSA), and in other cases it is the direct representative of the parent company, especially in the case of those companies that do not have a subsidiary in Torolandia.

With regards to the products of one brand in particular, the use of the parallel channel had an additional attraction. One company from Ario that did not have a subsidiary in Torolandia sold to its Torolandian and Turislandian distributors at dumping prices in order to introduce its products on the Torolandian and Turislandian markets. This dumping was only done in these two areas. As a result, this increased the prices advantage when reselling to other countries from Torolandia as it was possible to re-sell at even better prices than the parent company. It could even reach the paradoxical situation where any Torolandian distributor of this company could resell the products to customers in Ario for less than the manufacturer itself, although this had not yet happened. The Turislandian distributor, who was formally prohibited to re-export, sold these products through the parallel channel to other countries in which the Aryan parent company had official representatives. The mechanism used was similar to that for Producton, i.e., the goods were transferred to EPSA who officially re-exported them from Turisland to the parallel importer in the other country.

It is interesting to note that the most serious problem from implementing the system has been the 'red tape' or the 'specific forms' available which do not provide for special, albeit completely legal cases.

The disadvantage here was the currency exchange risk run when collecting payment in foreign exchange (from the parallel customer) which had to be changed into reals (as in any export) to be then rechanged into foreign exchange (to pay the Aryan company) as in any import. Obviously it was possible to lose large amounts of money due to differences in the exchange rates.

Torolandian legislation provides for the case whereby a local company acts as an intermediary between two foreign companies, in an operation known as 'triangular operation'. This operation means that a Torolandian company who buys from a foreign company to resell to another foreign company can use this system and legally be allowed to open an account in foreign currency, thus avoiding the risks and the commission of the two changes of foreign currency into reals and vice-versa.

This operation is formalized by means of a form called 'TE-25' (see reproduction following). This form gives the details of the three companies taking part in the operation, i.e. the Torolandian company, the selling company and the buying company, as well as the details of the operation (amount, dates of collection and payment).

However, in the particular case of the Torolandian distributor and EPSA, two Torolandian companies act as intermediaries, as a result of which the banks did not accept the 'TE-25' presented. A Torolandian company must have this TE-25 form in order to be able to hold a bank account in foreign currency.

Finally, this problem was got round by having the bank 'consolidate' two TE-25s into a third TE-25 presented by the same bank. The Turislandian distributor filled in one TE-25 with its details and those of the supplying company, i.e. it filled in only 'half' of the form. Empresapuente, S.A. also filled in another TE-25 with its details and those of the buying company. Finally, the bank filled in a third TE-25 with its details and those of the foreign buying and selling companies. These three forms were presented to the DTOFT (Department of Torolandian Overseas Financial Transactions) who authorized Empresapuente, S.A. to hold a bank account in foreign exchange.

Normal operation: communication of triangular operation

1. Applicant's name and address: ☐☐☐☐☐ Intermediary company in Torolandia	2. Number of triangular operation: ☐☐☐☐☐☐☐
	3. Accepting bank: ☐☐☐
4. Goods (description and number of units): ☐☐☐☐☐☐	
Details of purchase	Details of sale
5. Vendor:	6. Buyer:
7. Country of vendor: ☐☐☐☐	8. Country of buyer: ☐☐☐☐
9. Class of currency of purchase: ☐☐☐	10. Class of currency of sale:: ☐☐☐
11. Amount of purchase in foreign currency	12. Amount of sale in foreign currency

13.   Date of payment of purchase:
   Day Month Year
   ☐☐☐☐☐☐
	14. Date of collection of sale:
	   Day Month Year
	   ☐☐☐☐☐☐

15. Conditions of delivery of purchase:	16. Conditions of delivery of sale:
17. Currency class of expenses: ☐☐☐	18. Operation's expenses in foreign currency:
19. Profit of operation after expenses (in currency of sale):	20. Profit of operation after expenses (in reals):
21. Signature and stamp of applicant:	22. Verification by accepting bank:

23. Signature and stamp of accepting bank:	24. Verification ⎫
	            ⎬ by DTOFT
	   Authorization ⎭

'Parallel' triangular operation: normal operation communication of triangular operation

1. Applicant's name and address: `[ ][ ][ ][ ]` 'EMPRESAPUENTE, S.A.' Av. Desconocida, 12 Flamenquilla TOROLANDIA	2. Number of triangular operation: `[ ][ ][ ][ ][ ][ ][ ]` 3. Accepting bank: `[ ][ ][ ]`
4. Goods (description and number of units): `[ ][ ][ ][ ][ ][ ]`	
Details of purchase	Details of sale
5. Vendor:	6. Buyer: 'IMPORTADOR PARALELO, S.A.'
7. Country of vendor: `[ ][ ][ ][ ]`	8. Country of buyer: `[ ][ ][ ][ ]` CLEOPATRIA
9. Class of currency of purchase: `[ ][ ][ ]`	10. Class of currency of sale: `[ ][ ][ ]` ARYAN MARKS
11. Amount of purchase in foreign currency	12. Amount of sale in foreign currency
13. Date of payment of purchase: Day Month Year `[ ][ ][ ][ ][ ][ ]`	14. Date of collection of sale: Day Month Year `[ ][ ][ ][ ][ ][ ]`
15. Conditions of delivery of purchase:	16. Conditions of delivery of sale:
17. Currency class of expenses: `[ ][ ][ ]`	18. Operation's expenses in foreign currency:
19. Profit of operation after expenses (in currency of sale):	20. Profit of operation after expenses (in reals):
21. Signature and stamp of applicant:	22. Verification by accepting bank:
23. Signature and stamp of accepting bank:	24. Verification } Authorization } by DTOFT

Instructions for completing the form TE-25

Box 1. Name and address of applicant: State the name, address and city of the resident natural person or body corporate performing the operation. State in the inset in the upper right-hand corner the fiscal identification number or national identity document number, as appropriate.

Box 2. Number of triangular operation: This number will be assigned to the operation by the accepting bank. It consists of nine digits. The first three on the left correspond to the number assigned to the accepting bank and are stated in attachment E of circular number 248. The following six digits will be the operation number, starting from 1, assigned to it by the accepting bank, writing leading zeros if the number is less than six digits.

Box 3. Accepting Bank: Specify the name of the Accepting Bank (Bank, Savings Bank, etc.) for the operation and in the inset, state the number assigned to the Bank by circular number 248, attachment E (this will be the same number stated in the first three positions of the inset in box 2).

Box 4. Goods (description of units): State in detail the goods and number of units, weight, volume, etc. State in the inset the statistical position of the goods, in accordance with customs nomenclature.

Box 5. Seller: State the name, address and city of the seller.

Box 6. Buyer: Same as above for the buyer.

Box 7. Country of the seller: State the country of residence of the seller and the number assigned to this country by circular 248, attachment C.

Box 8. Country of the buyer: Same as above referred to the buyer.

Box 9. Class of currency for the purchase: State the class of currency in which the purchase is performed and the number assigned to it in circular 248, attachment D.

Box 10. Class of currency for the sale: Same as above but referred to the currency for the sale.

Box 11. Amount in foreign exchange of the purchase: State the total amount of the purchase in the foreign currency stated in box 9; this amount will include the total sum for all related expenses.

Box 12. Amount in foreign exchange of the sale: State the total amount of the same in the foreign currency stated in box 10.

Box 13. Date of payment of the purchase: State in number form the day of the month in the first two positions; in the next two positions the number of the month (from 1 to 12) and in the last two positions the number corresponding to the last two figures of the year in which the purchase has to be paid.

Box 14. Date of collection on the sale: Same as above referred to the sale.

Box 15. Condition of delivery of the purchase: State this condition, in accordance with the INCOTERMS currently in force.

Box 16. Condition of delivery of the sale: Same as above referred to the sale.

Box 17. Class of currency of the expenses: State, where appropriate, the class of currency of these expenses and the code assigned in circular 248, attachment D.

Box 18. Cost of the operation in foreign currency: State the total amount of these expenses if, in accordance with the condition of delivery of the purchase, sale or both, they must be paid by the person or corporation carrying out the operation.

Box 19. Profit of the operation after expenses in foreign currency: State the net profit, after deducting expenses in the currency of sale.

Box 20. Profit of the operation after expenses: State the value in reals, at the official buying rate of exchange on the date of presenting the form, of the profit specified in box 19.

Box 21. Signature and stamp of the applicant: This box must contain the signature of a sufficiently authorized person and the stamp, if it is a company. If the applicant is a natural person, he/she should only sign.

Box 22. Verification by the accepting bank: This box will contain the signature of a sufficiently authorized person and the stamp of the bank in the event that, in accordance with the provisions of the order of 10 December 1980, and circular 17/80, the operation does not require verification by the DTOFT.

Box 23. Signature and stamp of the accepting bank: This box will contain the signature of a sufficiently authorized person and the stamp of the bank. This box must be filled in in all cases, even if box 22 has also been filled in.

'Parallel' triangular operation: normal operation communication of triangular operation

1. Applicant's name and address: ☐☐☐☐☐ 'DISTRIBUIDOR TORISLANDES, S.A.' Calle de las tiendas, 89 Turisland TOROLANDIA	2. Number of triangular ☐☐☐☐☐☐☐ operation:
	3. Accepting bank: ☐☐☐
4. Goods (description and number of units): ☐☐☐☐☐	
Details of purchase	Details of sale
5. Vendor: 'CASA CENTRAL ARIA, S.A.'	6. Buyer:
7. Country of vendor: ☐☐☐	8. Country of buyer: ☐☐☐
9. Class of currency of purchase: ☐☐ ARYAN MARKS	10. Class of currency of sale:: ☐☐
11. Amount of purchase in foreign currency	12. Amount of sale in foreign currency
13. Date of payment of purchase: Day Month Year ☐☐☐☐☐☐	14. Date of collection of sale: Day Month Year ☐☐☐☐☐☐
15. Conditions of delivery of purchase:	16. Conditions of delivery of sale:
17. Currency class of expenses: ☐☐☐	18. Operation's expenses in foreign currency:
19. Profit of operation after expenses (in currency of sale):	20. Profit of operation after expenses (in reals):
21. Signature and stamp of applicant:	22. Verification by accepting bank:
23. Signature and stamp of accepting bank:	24. Verification ⎱ ⎰ by DTOFT Authorization ⎱

'Parallel' triangular operation: normal operation communication of triangular operation

1. Applicant's name and address: ☐☐☐☐☐ 'BANCO PREDUSPUESTO TOROLANDES' Av. Financiera, 22 Flamenquilla TOROLANDIA	2. Number of triangular operation: ☐☐☐☐☐☐☐
	3. Accepting bank: ☐☐☐

4. Goods (description and number of units):
☐☐☐☐☐☐

Details of purchase	Details of sale
5. Vendor: 'CASA CENTRAL ARIA, S.A.'	6. Buyer: 'IMPORTADOR PARALELO, S.A.'
7. Country of vendor: ☐☐☐☐ ARIO	8. Country of buyer: ☐☐☐☐ CLEOPATRIA
9. Class of currency of purchase: ☐☐☐ ARYAN MARKS	10. Class of currency of sale: ☐☐☐ ARYAN MARKS
11. Amount of purchase in foreign currency	12. Amount of sale in foreign currency
13. Date of payment of purchase: Day Month Year ☐☐☐☐☐☐	14. Date of collection of sale: Day Month Year ☐☐☐☐☐☐
15. Conditions of delivery of purchase:	16. Conditions of delivery of sale:
17. Currency class of expenses: ☐☐☐	18. Operation's expenses in foreign currency:
19. Profit of operation after expenses (in currency of sale):	20. Profit of operation after expenses (in reals):
21. Signature and stamp of applicant:	22. Verification by accepting bank:
23. Signature and stamp of accepting bank:	24. Verification ⎫ ⎬ by DTOFT Authorization ⎭

The order from Cleopatria

During 1984, parallel exports of this type had amounted to 300 million reals, while total exports had been almost 3,000 millions. Domestic sales by PTSA amounted to 10,000 million reals. For the last three years, the Turislandian distributor's purchases from PTSA had amounted to 450 million reals, which had been composed as shown in Table 21.1

The Turislandian expected his sales within Turisland to stabilize at 150 million and in March he had already made parallel sales abroad worth about 100 million; orders already agreed on for the rest of the year amounted to over 300 million more. This new order from Cleopatria, worth 160 million, would increase his total sales to a suspiciously high level.

The General Manager of PTSA had to decide whether to authorize the order to Cleopatria to be served or not. The export manager always required the signature of the General Manager as he wished to cover himself with respect to future problems with the parent company. The order would be just one more of those that were apparently sent to Turisland to be sold locally. The major doubt was whether current volumes would attract the attention of Producton Hollywood, Inc. or not. The Turislandian distributor's annual sales figures this year would be considerably higher than those of any of the other Torolandian distributors. This was what worried the General Manager of PTSA.

Case Study 2: Mazola*

> This case study was prepared by Ramón Ceravalls and Professor José Lluis Nueno, June 1986. It was prepared as the basis for class discussion rather than to illustrate either effective or ineffective handling of an administrative situation.

On 12 November 1980, the New Products Department of the Consumer Division of CPC España S.A. (Corn Products Corporation) met to review the MAZOLA corn oil launch plan. This launch plan was to follow the test area model and would be carried out in the Madrid and Barcelona areas. The commission was composed of the Managing Director, the New Products Director, the Sales Director and the New Products Product Manager.

Exhibit 21.4 contains a summarized description of CPC's organization chart in 1981.

The Spanish edible oil market

Present technology enables fats and oils to be extracted from a wide variety of animals and plants. In general terms, a distinction can be made between animal fats or oils and vegetable fats or oils.

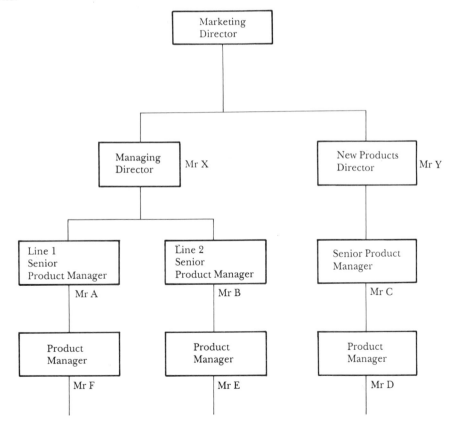

Exhibit 21.4 *Summarized sales organization chart of CPC (1981)*

* No part of this case study may be reproduced without the permission of IESE.

Without entering into exhaustive detail, our main interest lies in the vegetable oils. These can be further divided into those that are extracted by pressing the fruit of a plant and those that are extracted from the seed of that plant. Thus, all plants bear fruit and from the seeds of those fruits can be obtained various types of oil.

In Spain, the most widely known vegetable oils are, on the one hand, olive oil, derived from the fruit of the olive tree, and, on the other hand, sunflower, soya, corn, marc, grape pip, etc. oil, better known as seed oils.

The seed oil segment is a growth segment in Spain (see Exhibit 21.5). This case will centre on corn oil.

Corn is highly nutritious. Thus, CPC extracts from the corn grain cornflour which it markets under the MAIZENA brand or glucose which it markets as an industrial additive for candies or cookies.

The corn grain has a small core called the germ. This germ is pressed to give corn germ oil, an oil which is highly prized as a food product.

In Spain, the situation of the vegetable oil market has been traditionally weighted in favour of olive oil. However, a series of changes over the past twenty years have led to a gradual replacement of olive oil by sunflower oil, which is much cheaper. Paradoxically, this has not meant the abandonment of the use of olive oil but rather a coexistence with other oils. Thus, olive oil is used to dress salads while sunflower oil is used to fry and cook foods.

In 1979, olive oil consumption was 330 million litres while seed oil consumption was 400 million litres. This difference is expected to widen in the future in favour of seed oils.

The changes that have occurred in Spanish dietary habits must also be taken into account. Especially in the more developed areas, the consumption of corn oil, which is much more expensive than soya oil or sunflower oil, had increased by 30 per cent in 1979. This undoubtedly reflects a greater awareness by Spanish people of those foods that are better for the health. In 1979, 6.4 million litres of corn oil were consumed in Spain and consumption was expected to increase by 12 per cent in 1980.

The Spanish corn oil market

Corn oil is a byproduct of the grinding of corn grain, from which the main products extracted are cornflour, glucose and other vegetable sugars. The latter are used both by the soft drink industry and by the sweets and biscuits manufacturing industry.

In Spain, corn oil is a State-controlled market (i.e., oil imports are not allowed to satisfy

Exhibit 21.5   *Vegetable oil market*

		1979	1980
Olive		331	339
Sunflower		224	246
Corn		6,4	7,6
Others		170	159
	Total	732	751

temporary increases in demand). Thus, the supply of corn oil, extracted from the corn germ, depends on the demand from the sweets, soft drink and flour manufacturers.

Three firms in Spain specialize in corn grinding. One of them is CPC, the sector leader. The other two are Campo Ebro and Levantina Agrícola Industrial (LAISA). When the demand for glucose or flour is high, the supply of germ increases and therefore, if the demand for corn oil remains unchanged, oil prices fall. These situations are especially favourable for the local and regional oil brands: being able to purchase the oil at a good price, they can then market it at competitive prices.

The companies dominating the sector are vegetable oil refining companies. In other words, they are not multi-product firms but rather firms with three or five brands of different types of oil. The usual mix is one or two brands of olive oil, one or two brands of sunflower oil and one brand of corn oil. These companies usually depend on one brand for most of their income and use the others as a promotional tool or to support their introduction through pressure on the channel. Thus, if KOIPE is market leader in a certain area with its olive oil, it can use the leading oil as a pretext for introducing corn oil or else it can encourage its introduction by promoting sunflower oil. In the same way, what for Santiveri would be a large order (twenty boxes) would be an order remnant for KOIPE.

Another concept that interested the new products group was the notion of cash generator versus profit generator, which can be assigned a grosso modo to the oil and non-oil companies, respectively. The oil companies operate with huge volumes at minute margins while the multiproduct companies aim to introduce small volumes of oil at large margins.

The market that CPC planned to enter was segmented as follows:

- Leader: Artua
- Major brands: Mazurka, Maizuca
- Others: Superior quality. Targeted at the health food and selective distribution segments: Santiveri, Vigor
- Regional and local. Low-priced, locally-distributed oils, no advertising or significant sales activity performed. Continually appear and disappear from the market.

There follows a more detailed discussion of the various brands. At national level, there were three main brands in 1980: ARTUA, MAZURKA and MAIZUCA.

ARTUA

The market leader. It was the first to appear on the market and the only one that was advertised in previous years. It belonged to the KOIPE group which marketed other olive and sunflower oils. Its market share in 1979 was 53 per cent, although in 1978 this had been 73 per cent.

MAZURKA

Belonging to the ELOSUA group, this brand held 19 per cent of the market in 1979, having increased from 9 per cent in 1978. Both ARTUA and MAZURKA had launched the one-litre cylindrical can, although MAZURKA had originally been bottled in plastic bottles and cardboard packs very similar to the can had been detected in the market.

MAIZUCA

In October 1980, it launched the one-litre cylindrical can. It belonged to the UCA-Salgado group, which also marketed other oils; its market share was 7 per cent.

Alongside the national brands, there were a variety of regionally distributed brands such as Vigor, Santiveri, Pujol, Cesar, Altivo, etc., which held between them 21 per cent of the market in 1979, having grown from 13 per cent the previous year. Most of these brands are sold on the basis of their price. Their growth coincides with supply surpluses, being sold at low price to regional bottlers who only buy when they see an opportunity for quickly selling the product at low prices.

According to studies held by the new products team, 82 per cent of the corn sales were made in the following regions: Catalonia-Balearic Islands, Valencia-Alicante-Murcia, North and Madrid Metropolitan Area, the first two accounting for 55 per cent of total consumption in Spain.

Eighty-five per cent of sales were made in large surface area retail outlets. (Hypermarkets, self-service stores and large traditional stores − this type of retail outlet accounted for 37 per cent of all food retail outlets in Spain in 1980 and, geographically, 70 per cent of them were located in the above-mentioned regions.)

Prices

In 1980, three price levels exist in this market:

1 Corn oils targeted as a health food or quasi-health food with a price bordering on 200 pesetas/litre (Santiveri, Vigor).
2 Corn oils whose price ranges between 140–150 pesetas/litre (Artua, Mazurka).
3 Regional brands, priced around 125–130 pesetas/litre; their quality is inferior to group 2.

The market price is set by the leader: this is 142 pesetas to the retailer and 150 pesetas to the consumer. This is the only oil whose price is not regulated by the Government, which set prices and markups per litre for olive, soya and sunflower oils.

Exhibit 21.6 shows the latest prices available in 1980 for Artua. It was a customary practice in the vegetable oil market not to offer per cent discounts but rather in pesetas per litre.

Exhibit 21.6   *ARTUA prices (14 October 1980)*

Box of 10 cans					
				Discount scaling (boxes)	
RRP	*List price*	*0 to 7*	*8 to 29*	*30 to 149*	*150 plus*
150	142	−	2,5 ptas/1.	3,25 ptas/1.	4 ptas/1.

2 per cent discount on cash payments.
Normal terms of payment: 30 days.

Advertising

As opposed to what was happening with other consumer products, no major investments were made in advertising in the corn oil market in 1980. Only ARTUA had advertised in recent years, which had enabled it to establish itself as the market leader and the most well known brand nationwide.

In the past seven years, it was estimated that investment by ARTUA in advertising had totalled 12 million pesetas, with a special effort being made in 1976 which enabled it to take 73 per cent of the market in 1977 and 1978.

Consumers

On the basis of the qualitative information available, it was estimated that there were two types of target consumer:

a Main consumers. Those who seek a diet that is more healthy, natural and balanced in fat intake. They are aged between twenty-five and forty-five, middle or upper-middle class, with a fairly high purchasing power and understand the advantages provided by a diet that includes products good for one's health and which enhance the natural tastes of foods. They are mainly town-dwelling and pay careful attention to all diet-related matters.

They consume not only corn oil but also other types of oils, such as olive oil, used unfried to dress salads, etc.
b Secondary consumers. Those who, by medical prescription, must consume this type of oil. According to statistical data, in three of every ten homes in Spain, there is one or more persons who in 1980 needed to follow a special diet, and for which corn oil is highly indicated.

The decision to launch the oil

MAZOLA, the best-selling corn oil in the world, was launched in Spain for several reasons. First, the seed oil market (and the corn oil market, in particular), was increasing in importance and major growths in consumption were expected in the next few years. On the other hand, there was a real opportunity for introducing on the market a superior quality brand, backed by good advertising and nationwide distribtuion. A present, this could only be offered by three of the brands currently marketed.

There were also major distributional synergies as the areas that had the most sales and, above all, the type of retail outlet coincided with those areas and outlets where CPC's distribution and sales pressure was the strongest.

Trends in consumption habits were changing and it seemed to be the right time to make the launch, in a growth market where the market trends themselves would help to boost sales.

Finally, MAZOLA was one of CPC's internationally known brands and there was a body of experience, lessons and technology available which, with the passing of many years, had built up a far from negligible asset.

The meeting's main goal was, having set the overall goals, to decide what information the new products department would want to obtain from the test area as regards product, price,

Exhibit 21.7   *MAZOLA*

	Goal	*Recommended*
Marketing and channel actions budget	7.5	8.5
Contribution	(1,871)	(2,816)
Gross profit	5,684	5,684
Volume	150,000	150,000
Market share, Nielsen	—	—
Distribution	—	—

distribution, consumer and advertising in order to design the launch in the test area and, on the basis of this information, the final launch nationwide. It was therefore necessary to set these goals in detail before deciding on the resources to be used.

Based on previous experience in product launching, it had been agreed that a sample of 100 retail outlets in Barcelona and 150 in Madrid would be sufficient. These were self-service stores and supermarkets with a floor area of over 100 square metres which had been selected beforehand by the Barcelona and Madrid regional managers.

The other aspects, such as pack design, prices, discounts, possible promotions and advertising would also be decided on in the meeting, after which MAZOLA corn oil would be launched in the test area, according to the plan, on 17 November 1980.

A major limitation for CPC in 1980 was the non-existence of local TV channels, which hindered sufficient coverage during the trial launch and generated resource wastage and confusion in the channel and final consumers. A special concern for the new products group was whether the action should be directed at established corn oil consumers or whether it should be indiscriminately directed at all vegetable oil consumers. Some members of the team defended much more aggressive positions, such as targeting MAZOLA in the test area at the segment of sunflower oil consumers. As general qualitative aims, it was sought to position MAZOLA as a healthy oil, attain a high level of brand recognition and obtain the trial of the product, the first purchase and the repeat purchase. The budget available and the goals set are shown in Exhibit 21.7

Case Study 3: Flamagas, S.A*

This case study was prepared by Gustavo Lopetegui, MBA-86, under the direction of Francisco Parés, Lecturer and Professor Lluís G. Renart, February 1986. It was prepared as the basis for class discussion rather than to illustrate either effective or ineffective handling of an administrative situation.

On 23 March 1984, Jordi Planas, General Manager of Flamagas, S.A., was reading again his own report of his recent trip to Japan. In January of the same year he had been visiting for the first time with the aim of finding an importer-distributor for the marketing in Japan of the 'Clipper' lighter, which was FSA's main product.

The world market for lighters may be divided in three substantially different segments:

a Expensive jewel type lighters (trade marks Dupont, Cartier or Dunhill).
b Medium (Ronson, Silver-Match or Flaminaire).
c Inexpensive lighters (could be associated with disposable lighters as those from Gillette (Cricket), Bic or Tokai Seiki).

See picture of the Clipper lighter, in Exhibit 21.8

During 1983 he had obtained the names of some possible distributors he had visited personally during his fifteen days in Japan. After visiting four possible importers/distributors, only one of them had shown a real interest. This was a smoking pipe manufacturer who supplied around 4,500 customers which were mostly retail stores selling tobacco and smoking goods, department stores and smoking goods wholesalers.

While the distribution of lighters in Spain was mainly carried out through three channels (bars and cafeterias 40 per cent, tobacco and smoking goods outlets 40 per cent, and food products 20 per cent) Planas knew that in Japan one channel prevailed (smoking goods outlets) with about 80 per cent of the sales, surpassing food products outlets (around 15 per cent). This product was totally absent in bars and cafeterias.

The 4,500 customers of the pipe manufacturer, Mr Hirata, accounted for over 80 per cent of the total market in this channel. Planas assumed that in the event of his accepting Hirata's offer, the negotiations to commence business relations would take about one year.

Planas had one doubt: would the Japanese market be profitable for Flamagas? Would the travel and communication expenses be recovered?

One alternative in order to obtain a wider distribution than that offered by Hirata was to look for a dealer to cover outlets in food products as well. However, due to the relative unimportance of these outlets with regards to total sales, Planas rejected this course of action from the start as he thought that it would not be worth the effort and additional costs, nor did he have the necessary time to find this dealer and to work out an agreement with him.

What market share would make it profitable to go into Japan? The decision to try to enter this country had been taken for various reasons:

● The size of the Japanese market.
● The showcase effect to be obtained from selling in Japan as this could be used as an argument when entering other countries.

* No part of this case study may be reproduced without the permission of IESE.

● The idle capacity of the manufacturing plant that had to be filled up in some way or another.

However, Planas was not yet convinced about the validity of these reasons. There were a number of countries to which no exports had been made, which were probably easier to negotiate with which required lower expenditure on travel and which had stronger affinities. Japan was quite far away, its managers were very meticulous and the market was very competitive. All of this was in Planas' mind while the automatic manufacturing machines in Barcelona kept making Clippers at high speed. Something, optimal or not, had to be done soon.

The history of Flamagas, S.A.

FSA has been active in Barcelona since 1959. The firm 'Industrias Metálicas Castelló' (IMC), forming part of the PUIG group manufactured metal castings for a number of industries. (The

Exhibit 21.8   *Clipper refillable*

Puig group is an important conglomerate of companies of Catalan origin mainly devoted to the perfume and cosmetics industry. Their interests are diversified having a number of firms in different industries such as FSA, for instance.) In the mid fifties a French citizen from the Flaminaire company, placed an order for metal covers for the lighters manufactured by that firm in France. This supplier's relation between IMC and Flaminaire went on for a number of years, transforming IMC, S.A. after a certain time into a lighter manufacturer in Spain, under the Flaminaire licence. The Puig group founded Flamagas, S.A. in 1959 for the manufacturing of lighters, separating this operation from IMC, S.A.

During the 1960s their own technology was developed, and finally in 1972 FSA obtained the most successful product in the history of the company: the Clipper. This was the first inexpensive lighter manufactured and sold in Spain. The inexpensive lighter was being developed and marketed at the same time by big multinational companies which became leaders in the world market.

From 1973 onwards, national and international sales of the Clipper grew rapidly (see Exhibit 21.9) but in 1975 the problems started for FSA. The company was affected by the change in world demand from middle priced to inexpensive lighters. Thus the sales of the whole medium lighter range, which accounted for a big share of the total sales of FSA, progressively collapsed.

On the other hand, the Clipper itself had its own set of problems. In 1975, two of the multinational companies in the field entered Spain: Bic and Gillette (with trademark Cricket). Both these brands were very well known for the manufacture and marketing of disposable products and they launched their lighters aggressively in the Spanish market, capturing a big share.

Both companies offered good quality products and lower prices than Clipper, backed by an intensive mass advertising campaign. In 1975 Bic offered its lighters at a price of 45 pesetas, while Clipper was sold at 75 pesetas (in 1984, one US dollar was worth 150 Spanish pesetas, after several years of continuous increase in value, up from some 75 pesetas per US dollar in 1979).

The competitive situation of FSA got worse with the passing of time. Their 'star' product, the Clipper lighter, became obsolete both in quality and price. Its manufacturing process was 90 per cent manual as opposed to the almost full automatization of its competitors. In addition to distributing lighters manufactured by FSA, the company acted as importer distributor of foreign-made products, thus adding to, and completing, its own range of products.

At the end of the 1970s, the management of the company put more emphasis on the import of goods, increasing the number of imported items with the aim of making up for the loss of Clipper sales as well as that of other lighters. The selection of the imported items was not successful judging by the decrease in sales of imported products after that process. An even less careful selection of customers (obviously taking into account a sales slump) led to a financial crisis in 1982 due to several problems:

- High inventories of hard-to-sell imported products.
- The Clipper lighter could not compete in the national or international markets.
- About 50 per cent of bills were unpaid.

The company was in serious danger of going bankrupt, but the Puig group decided to rescue and relaunch it after an unsuccessful attempt to sell Flamagas, S.A. to a foreign multinational company.

Exhibit 21.9 *Clipper sales evolution (in thousands of units)*

Concept	1972	1973	1974	1975	1976	1977	1978	1979	1980	1981	1982	1983	P.1984	P.1985	P.1986
Export	1562	2862	4676	5595	6600	6344	8500	7887	11029	9496	7632	15426	15100	24400	30000
Foreign factories*						1700	2700	3700	6300	2613	2328	1754	1600	2000	3000
TOTAL EXPORT	1562	2862	4676	5595	6600	8044	11200	11587	17329	12109	9960	17180	16700	26400	33000
Traditional Market	1800	2500	2600	4096	4240	4667	3627	4004	5292	6642	6582	7943	12000	15000	17000
As advertising support	300	500	758	692	460	483	1132	1031	848	1064	1312	850	1600	1700	1800
Canaries	100	300	342	236	300	470	341	511	719	769	471	824	1200	1200	1200
DOMESTIC TOTAL	2200	3300	3700	5024	5000	5620	5100	5546	6859	8475	8365	9617	14800	17900	20000
TOTAL OF TOTALS	3762	6162	8376	10619	11600	13664	16300	17133	24188	20584	18325	26797	31500	44300	53000
Percentage of increase over previous year:															
Export sales		83	63	20	18	22	39	3	50	(30)	(18)	72	(3)	58	25
Domestic sales		50	12	36		12	(9)	9	24	24	(1)	15	54	20	12
Total sales		64	36	27	9	18	19	5	41	(15)	(11)	46	15	40	20

P = Provision = Forecast.
* Produced under licence in Morocco, Portugal and Turkey.

Source Flamagas, S.A.

The recovery

Jordi Planas was then appointed as new General Manager to rescue the company. At the same time, the Puig group contributed several hundred million pesetas in new capital. Planas carried out a number of changes with the aim of refloating Flamagas, S.A.

Production

The Clipper lighter had a complicated manufacturing process. The lighter is composed of twenty parts among which the following are of importance:

- The plastic body.
- Flintstone support and the flintstone itself.
- The wheel to act on the flintstone.
- A pipe for the conduction of the gas.
- The metallic upper cover.
- A valve for opening/closing the flow of gas.

Planas stated:

Ninety per cent of the Clipper manufacturing process was manual. Apart from increasing direct cost, this fact was the cause of the quality not being uniform in the end-product. In other words, the flame that came out of the Clipper was not always of the same size. For this reason, a flame regulator was incorporated enabling the amount of gas to be regulated. This extra feature (the regulation of the flame) was to conceal the technical inability to produce a lighter with a flame of a standard size. The decision to automate production was taken. A strong investment in R&D was necessary, as the technology for the production process was created by ourselves. All in all, 350 million pesetas were invested in two production lines, including R&D expenditures. Two lines were installed to make the most of the R&D costs. To set up a third line would now cost less than 100 million.

The two new lines started working in January 1983, allowing for a direct cost of 18 pesetas per unit against 36 pesetas which was the former direct cost. The new Clipper did not have a flame regulator although it continued to be refillable. The design was more stylish, giving it a better appearance. The new theoretical capacity of the plant went up to 60 million units per year (6,000 units for each line per hour per 8 hours per 3 shifts per 208 days per 2 lines).

Personnel matters

As a result of production, automation, and administrative rationalization, the total staff of 415 persons in May 1982 had been reduced to 240 in April 1983. These changes caused labour unrest and absorbed part of the refloating funds as redundancy payments. Some changes were also made at the management team level. These were completed one year later at the beginning of 1984 when nineteen executives were made redundant, although eleven new ones were taken on. The majority of these new executives came from other companies of the Puig group.

Financing

Some of the refloating funds were used to rebuild the current assets and the period for bill collection was reduced from 130 to 80 days. This enabled expenditure to be reduced. Bill collection efficiency was also improved by means of a specific team devoted to this task.

Marketing

The range of products on sale before 1982 was very wide. The marketing was carried out by two separate sales teams, one for Clipper and the other for the 'writing items and medium type lighters' range.

With the management team, the range of products was reduced with the elimination of about 2,500 items out of a total of 5,500. The two sales teams were unified. When commenting on these decisions Planas stated:

> We changed the criteria by which the product range was selected. Up to that moment, the product selection had been made mostly on criteria of novelty. From then on, we first defined the kinds of retail stores that we were going to cover with our sales force. No new products would be included in our product range which did not fit with the existing channel of distribution. The only possible exception to this rule would be if we decided to open up a new sales division.

> At the same time we implemented a number of marketing changes with our Clipper lighter, such as engraving them with the customer's trade mark or logo for advertising purposes, or giving the body a wider range of colours.

Present situation

The simplified structure of the firm in March 1984 is shown in Exhibit 21.10. In that year the company expected to sell some 5,000 million pesetas of which 60 per cent correspond to imported products and 40 per cent to own manufactured products. Of the latter, 40 per cent are exported, the other 60 per cent would be sold locally. The overall results were highly positive and substantial profits were expected in 1984.

Exports

The Clipper lighter was well accepted in international markets from the beginning. But due to the problems described above, the export sales volume was stagnant in 1979/80, and started to dwindle abruptly during 81/82. The recuperation of foreign markets after the refloating process was not only necessary but a definite must.

The production capacity of the plant was of about 60 million units a year and little more than 8 million had been sold in the Spanish domestic market in 1982. The modification of the production facilities had been effected in a few months (from June 82 to January 83) but the reshaping of the management team took more time. By March 84 it had been almost fully completed. Therefore it was in 1983 that the need to export coincided with the lack of sufficient adequate management time available.

At the end of 1982 Rensenmik (this is not a real name) comes into the scene. This was a Dutch company which proposed an exclusive distribution for the new Clipper lighter for Europe and the USA. The proposal was accepted by FSA, except for Italy and the UK. In these two countries FSA already had important dealers. Planas commented on this decision:

> Rensenmik was fully introduced within our company. They were a supplier to FSA of imported medium type lighters and they had close relations with the old management team. In any case, in spite of these relations we were free to give them our distribution or not. They were already agents for the inexpensive Tokai-Seiki lighters, that is, the second world manufacturers after Bic. Finally we accepted their proposal. This was mainly justified by the fact that the management team could not devote more time to this task.

During 1983 only one member of the management team looked after the relations with Rensenmik, among other duties. During that year exports increased but not those carried out through this distributor. Of the total export for that year, 90 per cent was effected to the UK, Italy, Lebanon, Israel and other countries, through direct action, and only 10 per cent through Rensenmik. This made us suspicious that they were not really interested in selling our Clipper

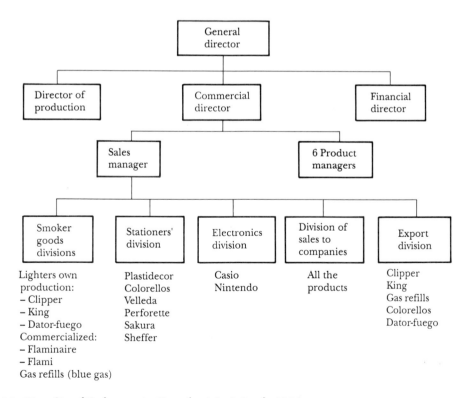

Exhibit 21.10 *Simplified organization chart in March 1984*

lighters, but quite on the contrary, they were using our agreement almost to keep us out of the market in favour of the Japanese make. In February 1984 the agreement with Rensenmik was cancelled.

By that time, and as the management team had been consolidated, the export policy was changed. A specific team was set up to boost exports. The team consisted of the following three persons:

- **José Blanco.** Former member of the management team who left his other duties to devote himself full-time to exporting.
- **Jordi Planas.** General Manager, would devote a substantial part of his time to exports.
- **Luis Argüelles.** He joined the company in 1984. He had been working before in the mother company of the group, having some experience in the export of perfumes and cosmetics.

The strategy to be followed by this team was to try to penetrate as many countries as possible, teaming up with a sole importer-distributor in each country. This strategy was based on the assumption that a diffusion strategy is the key to the penetration of markets and fast increasing sales volume. Later on, a further penetration strategy would be developed and implemented.

The world market for inexpensive lighters

By the mid-seventies the first inexpensive lighters appeared on the world markets. These were products clearly aimed at substituting matches and they were sold in the retail stores. The inexpensive lighter is clearly associated with a concept of 'disposable' because of its low price. It is bought on impulse, without any brand loyalty. The product was readily accepted by the consumers and the demand grew rapidly. From 1975 to 1981 the world demand grew at a 10 per cent yearly rate. From that year the annual growth rate has been lower (1982: 6 per cent, 1983: 4 per cent) and the expectancy for 1984 is a growth of 2 per cent, with stationary demand for 1985. In 1984 the world demand is expected to reach 1,400 million units/year. Average unit selling prices have been reduced every year up to 1980. From 1980 onwards, unit selling prices have been quite stable.

The combination of these two facts has made the 'demand' (total sales in monetary units) constant, making up for the lower prices with bigger unit sales volume (see Exhibit 21.11). Three large companies supply about 80 per cent of the world's needs: Bic (about 40 per cent world share), Tokai-Seiki (slightly more than 30 per cent) and Feudor-Gillette (10 per cent). (Probably the fourth company in the world is Swedish Match through its Match division which is said to be trying to purchase the Cricket division of Gillette. Match has already some inexpensive lighter manufacturing facilities in France, Holland, Switzerland, Phillippines and Argentina, selling a total of around 100 million lighters in 1983.) Five to ten small and medium companies such as Flamagas make up the rest.

Currently the fight to increase the market share is very bitter as world demand has no growth. Competition is mostly based on price. Planas commented: 'The time is over for big TV advertising campaigns. Nowadays there are no big advertising budgets. The best way to sell is to secure a place in the distribution channels. The retail price, in real terms, is nowadays half of what it was ten years ago and the price war is not coming to an end.'

The most important countries, as far as consumption is concerned, are the USA and Japan which account for 36 per cent and 25 per cent of the world market respectively. Exhibit 21.12 shows the geographic distribution of the world's demand.

The 'Clipper' in the world wide environment

In 1983 almost 27 million Clippers were sold worldwide, which accounted for almost 2 per cent of the world market. In Spain the market share was of 20 per cent with around 10 million units sold. Exports were made to a number of countries (see Exhibit 21.13).

Clipper lighters have an unique feature: they are refillable. Planas said:

For us as manufacturers, the fact that the Clipper lighters are refillable does not just mean

Exhibit 21.11   *Prices and world volume*

Year/country	1975	1976	1977	1978	1979	1980	1984
US dollar	1.49/100	1.49/100	1.–/67	0.90/61	0.75/50	0.60/40	
Canada dollar	1.75/100	1.49/ 85	1.30/74	1.30/74	1.–/57	1.–/57	
Germany DM	2.50/100	2.–/ 80	1.30/52	1.10/44	0.98/39	0.90/36	
Switzerland Sfr.	2.50/100	2.–/ 80	1.60/64	1.20/48	1.–/40	1.–/40	
France Ffr.	5.–/100	5.–/100	4.90/98	4.50/90	3.75/75	3.–/60	
Belgium Bfr.	40.–/1–	35.–/ 88	35.–/88	30.–/75	25.–/63	25.–/63	
Arithmetical mean	100	88	74	65	54	49	49
World production thousands million of units	0.70/100	0.80/114	0.90/129	-	-	-	1.40/200

Note   Read, for example: in 1975, in the USA a disposable lighter was sold at 1.49 dollars per unit. In 1980 that sale price had fallen to 0.60 dollars per unit, that is, it was 40 per cent of the price in 1975, taken as basis.
Source   FSA estimation.

injecting new gas from the bottom. It also means that a number of improvements have to be built into the lighter, because it will last longer. For instance, it must have a support for the flintstone, allowing for its substitution, or we must mount a stronger 'wheel'. If it did not incorporate all of these extra features, the lighter would not have a longer life, even if it was possible to refill it with gas. This means that our inexpensive lighters are stronger built than those of the competitors. At the same time these characteristics make the direct cost of our product around 50 per cent higher.

The fact that our 'Clipper' is refillable gives us some competitive advantages in comparison with the disposable lighters from other brands, which cannot be refilled. These competitive advantages may be segment-specific. We feel we have some advantages:

a **In countries with low 'per capita' income.** In these countries people have lower buying power and some consumers welcome the possibility of refilling the lighter because refilling costs about 10 per cent of the cost of purchasing a new lighter.
b **In countries with flat taxation referred to unitary lighters.** Italy has a tax of 1,800 lire for each lighter and in the United Kingdom the tax is of 0.5 pounds. This stimulates the refill. These are not import duties, but taxes levied on all lighters, whatever their origin (domestic made or imported).
c **As an advertising – public relations item for companies.** The message to be transmitted, engraved in the lighter, will certainly have a longer life on a Clipper than on a disposable lighter.

In the past, the biggest problem encountered by FSA in trying to increase its export sales was production problems. These have already been solved through the expansion of the production facilities.

Present situation of exports

Since January 1983 FSA badly needs international markets to increase sales volume to make the production facilities profitable as a consquence of the restructuring of the company. As a

Exhibit 21.12   *Geographical distribution of the world demand for inexpensive lighters*

	Annual millions of units	%
USA	500	36.3
Japan	350	25.4
German Federal Republic	65	4.7
Spain	60	4.3
France	50	3.6
Rest of Europe	60	4.3
Rest of Asia	120	8.7
Rest of USA	100	7.3
Africa	75	5.4
World total	1,380	100.0

Source FSA estimation.

Exhibit 21.13   *Destination of the FSA's exports*

	1982 *million pesetas*	%	1983 *million pesetas*	%
UK	49	18	102	24
Switzerland	91	33	94	22
Israel	11	4	63	15
Low countries			42	10
Lebanon	41	15		
Other countries	85	31	123	29
	277		426	

Exports increase 1983–1982 = 54 per cent

Source Official Census of Exporters. Edited by the National Institute of Exporting (INFE), Madrid, Spain.

consequence the decision was taken to try to boost export sales to as many countries as possible.

The product does not need after sales service, nor can FSA become a leader in the market because we are confronted with the largest multinational companies who are our competitors. This has led us to choose a 'diffusion' strategy. The General Manager commented: 'Nowhere are people waiting with open arms to buy our lighters. Therefore, wherever we can sell 'something' we will do so although the market share we may obtain may be minimum. This will be the key to increasing our sales volume later. We have to act in this way, humbly, little by little.'

Only those countries with serious currency problems have been discarded off-hand. For instance, the majority of Latin American countries are burdened by enormous external debts. In these countries the governments restrict the availability of foreign currency to importers even if they may have local currency readily available for their purchase, if the products are not essential for the country. In these countries FSA would have great difficulties in collecting the money, although the market is potentially very important.

Since at least 1982, Flamagas, S.A. had been exporting to four countries where it had continued to export:

United Kingdom. Since 1977 the export activities are carried out with only one importer. This company is the largest match distributor in the country. They are marketing other lighters as well and all the advertising is carried out by the importer. Two regular visits are paid to their offices each year and the importer also comes to Barcelona on two further visits. Our market share is 23 per cent.

Italy. There are no direct exports to this country but the management of FSA suspects that the lighters sold to Switzerland somehow end up being sold in Italy mainly by street vendors to passers-by, for instance at traffic lights.

Lebanon. The export activity has been carried out by one importer for many years. The final destination of the exports to this country is not well known. However, it is assumed that many of them are re-exported.

Israel. Only one distributor who markets razor blades and small batteries as well.

In search of new markets

Once a country has been selected, the first step is the search for an importer/distributor with good connections preferably without inexpensive lighters in his range of products. 'Good connections' mean that the importer must be using the marketing channels through which inexpensive lighters are sold. These are mainly:

● Tobacco and smokers' items shops.
● Bars and food product outlets.

In each country the importance of these channels varies and other different channels eventually appear or may exist. Planas described the process:

> For instance we'll look for toothpaste, chewing gum or cigarette distributors. Some of the members of our management team travel to the selected country, we choose the importer and arrange with him a FOB price to start our commercial relations. Once he is ready to start selling, FSA adapts itself to the requirements of the customer with regard to packing, displays, colours and printed patterns. All of our products are marketed under the registered trade marks Clipper or King. (King is the trade mark of another of FSA's lighters, with a price which is three times that of the Clipper. Its manufacturing process is still manual and the quantities manufactured are much lower than that of the Clipper. It could be said that this lighter 'completes' the range.)

Following this strategy, approaches had been made to the USA, France, Japan and Middle East countries. But up till now, no distributor had been appointed in these countries.

Japan's dilemma

To start approaching the Japanese market from Barcelona, the company contacted JETRO (Japan External Trade Organization) in Madrid, requesting a list of companies dealing with smoking articles. Planas explained his decision: 'We discarded from the beginning the possibility of reaching the food products outlets through the usual distributors for these shops. We know that no Japanese food product distributor would accept the marketing of lighters. On the other hand this channel accounted only for 15 per cent of lighter sales in Japan.'

JETRO sent a list of 30 companies: 'You could find everything on the list: makers of expensive (jewel-like) lighters and medium-type lighters, other distributors who were already marketing inexpensive lighters, manufacturers of pipes and tobacco merchants. We sent leaflets and samples to all of them. We only received responses from four of them.' The four which responded were the following:

● One manufacturer of expensive jewel-like lighters.
● Two manufacturers of medium range lighters.
● One manufacturer of smoking pipes.

Due to the importance of the Japanese market (see Exhibit 21.12) Planas went personally to Tokyo in January 1984, staying fifteen days in that country. He visited the four interested companies. He made the following comments:

The manufacturers of expensive lighters were not interested in the long run, and the marketing mentalities of their management teams did not fit with our product. The two manufacturers of medium range lighters had already contacted FSA as we had purchased from them some of their products for distribution in Spain. They showed interest, but they were 'very oriental'. The Japanese are very meticulous, perfectionists and conservative. The negotiations of distribution contracts with these companies could have necessitated more than one year in spite of the fact that they were interested in the product and they knew our company. Finally, the manufacturer of pipes was a family company with about 40 years of activity in the market. The company was headed by a 'westernized Japanese'. He had studied in the USA and this was of great help in the negotiations. The others were too complicated, too difficult for a Spaniard.

Hirata's company had a substantial prestige in the market and its sales were of 18 million dollars a year to its almost 4,500 clients. These customers included smoking items outlets and large department stores. Hirata was enthusiastic about the Clipper lighter as it would be a new addition to this present range of products and he assumed that after carrying out the adequate marketing action, the sales of the Clipper lighter could account in five years for 20 per cent of his turnover.

After a number of interviews with Hirata, Planas came back to Barcelona with the agreement to continue negotiations with this possible distributor. In March 1984, Planas thought that a second visit to Japan was needed and possibly a third one before beginning commercial dealings. This would mean months before the first shipment could be carried out.

Japan, with its 120 million inhabitants and almost 8,000 US$ per capita income, was the second world market for inexpensive lighters. The Japanese purchase 350 million lighters a year and Tokai-Seiki is a Japanese company selling more than 400 million lighters a year to 63 countries.

The decision

Japan was important for FSA not only because of its potential sales volume. The 'showcase' effect obtained by a successful entry into that market would then make the introduction of the Clipper easier in other markets.

But these markets were closer than Japan. Would FSA be able to generate enough sales at least to cover the high travel expenses? (In 1984 the cost of a return ticket to Japan in tourist class and 'group tariff' was about 150,000 pesetas. In the case of an individual passenger, some travel agencies would 'group together' a number of passengers in order to obtain lower priced group tickets. In addition to the air ticket, other costs of around 50,000 pesetas a day such as hotel, meals, taxis, etc. had to be taken into consideration. Therefore, a one week trip could cost a minimum of 500,000 pesetas.) Japan was far away, not only geographically but also 'culturally', both by the negotiation habits of its managers as well as the purchasing habits of its inhabitants. Planas knew that there was some written matter on marketing channels in Japan. He would have to locate it (see Appendix A). Could this introduction be made aggressively? What would be the cost of this kind of marketing? And if negotiations were continued with Hirata, what would be the steps to best take next?

Appendix A Distribution of consumer products in Japan (1)

Introduction

Japanese distribution system is vast, with an enormous quantity of wholesalers and retailers per head, in any case much higher than that of any other developed country.

This distribution system, still effective nowadays, is the result of various forces which have been influential in giving it this unusual pattern. Among these geography, the Japanese character, and Japanese history have to be taken into account.

Some history

The country consists of four large islands. Historically, commerce and transfer of goods were restricted among the islands. As a consequence many small manufacturers existed in each of them.

Due to its small size these companies needed assistance. This was carried out with regard to payment terms, marketing actions or stock carrying and it was supported by the wholesalers.

With a stratified channel system the products could reach the user at lower prices.

Another important reason has obviously been the Japanese manufacturers insistance on operations rather than in marketing.

There are many small-sized individual retailers. They are active in small geographic areas (many of them with poor communications) and they depend also on the wholesalers with regards to financing and stocks.

Many of the retailing outlets belong to pensioners who, due to their reduced pensions, are forced to establish small businesses to aid their living.

The results of these facts is the 'KEIRETSU-SYSTEM':

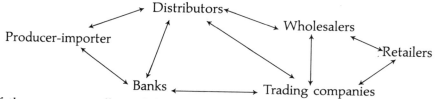

All of them commercially and financially interlinked even by means of high level management.

Main reasons:

- Financial needs
- Reduction of collection risks
- Importance of discounts and transfer of goods
- Stocks
- Fast deliveries
- Long term expectations
- Retailer limitations as to space and resources

Wholesalers

Mainly defined by:

- Functional areas

- Geographic considerations
- Product

They usually furnish marketing material and commercialization know-how at the same time as financial assistance given the fact that *immediate delivery* is required at all stages, and must be very close to the retailers.

It is to be observed that 'space' is vital for retailers. This is the reason why all of them keep minimum stocks.

There were 368,000 wholesalers in 1979 of which 18 per cent were in Tokyo and 11 per cent in Osaka, the two most important towns.

The following differences may be noted as compared to USA

	USA (1977)	Japan (1979)
Annual sales per wholesaler (in million dollars)	3.3	3.4
Population per wholesaler	643.0	351.0
Employees per wholesaler	11.4	10.0
Retailers per each wholesaler	4.8	4.5
Number of wholesalers	383,000.0	368,000.0

From the above it is noticeable that in Japan the population per wholesaler is half as large as compared with the USA. Many sales do not go through this channel in the USA.

As far as size is concerned, 47 per cent of wholesalers have one to four employees, 48 per cent from five to twenty-nine and only 5 per cent employ more than thirty persons. This will give an idea of the small size of the majority of Japanese wholesalers.

The relations they hold with retailers are very 'tied'. In general, close and long lasting.

They are characterized by the number of visits, courtesy and personal contacts. The biggest problem is the 'shelf space' which is very scarce. The introduction of new products requires, apart from much patience, a higher investment than in other countries.

The marketing efforts must be continued even after a successful introduction.

Apart from offering a minimum delivery period, wholesalers must accept the return of goods not only in the event of faults but also in case of lack of sales ... or simply because the retailer wishes to send it back.

In many cases the delivery of the product is made directly from the manufacturer to the sales outlet but the operation is covered by the wholesaler or wholesalers (they support the payment terms of the sales outlet and guarantee the money collection to the manufacturer).

Retailers

These are divided by sales outlet type and/or by type of product. There is a tradition in specialized medium sized shops. Overall there are 1.7 million sales outlets of which 9.5 per cent are in Tokyo and 7.3 per cent in Osaka, the two largest towns. The rest is dispersed throughout the whole country.

The following is a comparison between retailers in Japan and in the USA.

	USA (1977	Japan (1979)
Number of retailers	1,855,000	1,673,000
Number of employees	12,740,000	5,960,000
Yearly turnover of all retailers together (millions of dollars)	725,000	330,000
Yearly turnover per retailer (dollars)	381,000	197,300
Inhabitants per retailer	122	69

Eighty-five per cent of the retailers have less than four employees; 14 per cent from five to twenty-nine and only 1 per cent more than thirty employees. These figures give us an idea of the small size of Japanese retailers.

As to specialization, only 8 per cent are department stores and 15 per cent self services. Imported products are mainly marketed through department stores.

The retailer demands a lot from the manufacturers and/or wholesalers because the end users also make demands from them. Change of goods for any reason, financing and fast delivery are usual requirements.

They offer many services to their customers: purchase clubs, bonuses, prices and advice.

In most cases they are located in small streets which are impossible to go to by car.

Although the relation with the end user is long lasting and stable, the competition between retailers is very great in quality as well as prices and packing.

All these requirements are to be fulfilled by the manufacturers as well as by the importers. The products *must* adapt to the market.

Summary

As a conclusion, an exporter must take into account the following suggestions while contemplating sales to Japan:

- High quality and originality.
- Adaptation to culture, tastes and habits.
- Careful investigation of the market.
- Continuous commercial action.
- After sales service.
- Careful choice of – type of distribution, and
                         – location.
- Put a focus on good will to try to win the co-operation of importers, wholesalers and retailers.
- Strong will to obtain success, and patience to obtain it in the medium term.

Summarized from Czinkota, M. R. (1985) *Distribution of Consumer Products in Japan: An Overview.* National Center for Import-Export Studies, Georgetown University, Washington, DC.

Case Study 4: Cavas Masachs*

This case was prepared by Pere Gil, MED-87, on the basis of a first draft by Melissa Martincich, MED-86, supervised by Francisco Parés, Lecturer, and Professor Lluís G. Renart. It is intended to be used as a basis for class discussion rather than to illustrate either effective or ineffective handling of an administrative situation.

Holidays? What holidays?

This was the typical answer that you would hear in Cavas Masachs in August 1985 when anyone asked about holidays. It seemed as if nobody in Cavas Masachs took any, which was not normal in Spain where, in August, activity is reduced to the indispensable minimum. But in Cavas Masachs things were happening too fast to put them off for a month, or even a week. Since Josep Masachs, 31, had taken over as General Manager of the company in 1978, sales figures had soared (Exhibit 21.14) and the current growth plan foresaw sales of 500,000 cases in 1992 (Exhibit 21.15). The construction of a new wine cellar was on the point of

Exhibit 21.14 *Sales by Cavas Masachs in cases*

Year	Home	Abroad
1978	160	0
1979	1,700	0
1980	5,000	0
1981	10,000	800
1982	30,000	2,000
1983	50,000	3,200
1984	75,000	4,500
One case contains 12×750 ml bottles or a total of 9 litres.		

Source Company data.

Exhibit 21.15 *Forecast sales by Cavas Masachs*

Year	Home	Abroad
1985	100,000	20,000
1986	128,000	40,000
1987	160,000	60,000
1988	200,000	80,000
1989	250,000	100,000
1990	310,000	115,000
1991	335,000	125,000
1992	360,000	140,000

Source Company data.

* No part of this case study may be reproduced without the permission of IESE.

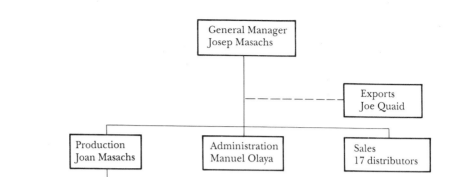

Exhibit 21.16   *Cavas Masachs organization chart*

starting and, once completed in August or September 1986, it would double the present capacity of 125,000 cases a year. And since agreement had been reached in 1983 with Joe Quaid, exports had begun to take on a significant role in the growth of sales and it was hoped that they would account for 30 per cent of sales by 1992. The rapid growth of Cavas Masachs seemed to fully occupy its key men and Joe Quaid (Exhibit 21.16) and everybody radiated enthusiasm. Although nobody wished to predict exactly how far they could go, it was felt that Cavas Masachs was surging upwards like a bubble rising up from the bottom of a chilled glass of their sparkling wine.

Cavas Masachs

The Masachs family had been grape growers for generations, supplying various of the local sparkling wine producers until José Masachs — the grandfather of the present General Manager — decided to experiment with his own sparkling wine in 1940. (Throughout the case, unless otherwise indicated, 'sparkling wines' means 'sparkling wines fermented in the bottle using the traditional "methode champenoise" production process'. Appendix B contains a brief description of the product and its history in Catalonia). In that year he produced a cava with the name Masachs in a small cellar in the back of the basements where Masachs operations are still carried out today. He produced a limited number of bottles, in a spartan cellar, for the family and some friends until 1977, when his two nephews Josep and Joan (Joan is the Catalan form of the masculine name John) took over the running of the business. Josep, as General Manager, decided to test Masachs on the Spanish market and, in 1980, he introduced it successfully at the Incavi Catalonia Wine Fair in Barcelona where the company took a stand. (The Catalunya Institute for Vineyards and Wines (Incavi) was a body created by the Generalitat de Catalunya (the Autonomous Government) to promote and strengthen the grape and wine sector. Among other things, it sponsored and co-ordinated the concession of denominations of origin in order to help the wines of Catalonia to compete in international markets. It also provided business information to the producers and organized a yearly wine show in Barcelona's Rambla de Catalunya. In spite of the fact that the co-ordination of the sparkling wine sector is controlled by the central government, Incavi had developed its own complementary initiatives to strengthen the sector in Catalonia.) The next year, Joan Masachs, who was in charge of production, used grapes from, as Josep Masachs used to say, 'the other side of the hill' to produce a new sparkling wine which had a flavour slightly different from that marketed under the Masachs label. As the grapes from the other side of the hill had a higher yield than those used in the making of Masachs, the new sparkling wine, called 'Louis de Vernier' was sold at a slightly lower price. Louis de Vernier, which is described as less robust than Masachs, also achieved considerable success at the annual Incavi Trade Fair and Cavas Masachs slowly established distributors first in Catalunya and, later, throughout the north of Spain, Madrid, Valencia and the Balearic Islands. Although a great part of the Spanish market was still not covered, Cavas Masachs underwent a spectacular increase in national sales turnover and continued to work ambitiously on developing its future.

Although their products had only recently been offered on the Spanish market, Mr Masachs had, since 1980, been interested in developing exports for various reasons. In the first place, taxes on national sales were so high that it was often more advantageous for producers of sparkling wine to export. (The fiscal treatment of the sparkling wine sector in Spain was determined by whether the product was destined for the home or the export market and this was the spur that opened the minds of the producers towards the possibilities of the overseas market. Speaking very generally, sparkling wine produced in Spain and marketed there was subject to the payment of levies in respect of Agrarian Social Security (14 per cent) Turnover Tax (5 per cent) and Luxury Tax (24.3 per cent), which came to a total surcharge of 43.3 per cent payable by the distributor on the producer's price. On the other hand, Spanish sparkling wine destined for export was not only exempt from the foregoing levies, but was also eligible for an export rebate (called desgravacion fiscal) of 10.4 per cent. In any case, there are two matters to be borne in mind when considering these figures. In the first place, that the governments of the importing countries could raise tariff and other barriers against the importing of Spanish cava. In the second place, the imminence of Spain's entry in the EEC set for January 1986, and the progressive internationalization of the Spanish market was giving rise to a progressive phasing-out of favourable tax treatment for exports. As a result, in the sparkling wine sector, this export rebate fell from 14.5 per cent in 1980 to 10.4 per cent in 1985.) On the other hand, Mr Masachs had seen his neighbours, Freixenet and Codorniu became two of the best known producers of sparkling wine in the world as a result of the almost instantaneous success of their exports to the USA. Finally, the fact that the domestic market had accepted their sparkling wine so rapidly, acted as a spur to go into the foreign markets which, though much bigger, were more difficult to conquer. In the words of Manuel Olaya, the Administrative Director of Cavas Masachs:

> When we started to talk about exports in 1981 or thereabouts, we knew that it was going to be more difficult to sell our products abroad than it had been in the domestic market but, to us, it seemed to be virgin territory, waiting to be discovered. It was so big that we felt that there must be a place for us. At that time, Spain's entry into the EEC was imminent and we thought 'why not get ready now instead of waiting until Spain was a fully-fledged member?' Certainly any planning of an increase in production must be done well in advance as the sparkling wine must stay in the cellar for at least nine months. We knew that we had to have a plan to increase our production capacity in the near future if we wished to push exports. On the other hand, there

was a risk that we might find ourselves left with a great deal of unsold stock. However, we were of the opinion that if exports failed we always had the cushion of the unexploited part of the domestic market to fall back on.

Mr Masachs exported his first cases of sparkling wine, in 1981, thanks to a family contact in Mexico and, in 1982, he sent a consignment of 2000 cases to a potential distributor in New York, whom he knew through friends in a local business. The response to these first two consignments was not very encouraging. In fact, there was no response worth talking about and Mr Masachs was wondering what he might do next.

It was at this point when Joe Quaid, an independent wine dealer, began to take an interest in the products of Cavas Masachs. Quaid was a fifty-five year old American who had been living in Spain since the early 70s. He had worked in sales and marketing for almost thirty years, first as sales director of Honda in the USA, then as Vice President of Sales at Lotus Cars and, from 1965 to 1968, as Sales Director of Bultaco Motorcycles in the USA (the Bultaco motorcycles were manufactured in Barcelona, Spain). His connection with the Bultó family, the owners of Bultaco, brought him to Spain in 1970. This was a time of increasing interest abroad in Spanish wines and some friends in the USA and Europe had asked him to be on the lookout for Spanish wines and olive oil with export potential. Indeed, what started as a favour to his friends took on proportions of its own and, in 1977, Mr Quaid found himself working full-time representing Spanish wine in order to keep up with the export demand.

Quaid and Masachs first met at the 'Confraria de Vins de Cava de Sant Sadurní, and the 'Acadèmia de Tastavins Sant Humbert', two local wine associations formed to generally promote this sector. (The Confraria de Vins de Cava de Sant Sadurní, located in Sant Sadurní d'Anoia, was a society formed to promote Catalan sparkling wines. Its members were either individuals or companies whose interest was not of necessity commercial. They paid a yearly subscription, published bookets, organized discussion groups as well as talks, dinners and entertainment for its members. The Academia de Tastavins de Sant Humbert, in Vilafranca del Penedés, was formed to promote the district's non-sparkling (or still) wines and its structure and way of operating was rather similar to that of the Confraria.) Quaid had been suitably impressed by the Masachs products and had begun to include Masachs and Louis de Vernier in the samples of local sparkling wine which he sent to interested clients. He soon discovered that Louis de Vernier was preferred to the other sparkling wines because of its splendid price-quality relationship and he felt increasingly attracted by the sales potential of the product. He and Masachs began to talk quite informally about what they would need in order to seriously develop the export market. Cavas Masachs lacked both the capital and the personnel for a large-scale marketing operation and neither did they have sufficient capacity to immediately boost sales. Due to this lack of resources, Quaid and Masachs agreed that the most logical way to make Cavas Masachs' products known to potential buyers and importers was through international trade fairs, given its relatively low cost. Both men had had success at trade fairs in the past. Masachs had used national trade fairs to launch his sparkling wines on the domestic market and Quaid had attended many of them in his capacity as Sales Director of Honda. In April 1983, as a result of these conversations, Joe Quaid accepted an offer to work with Masachs in exporting his sparkling wines. Quaid agreed to deal only in sparkling wines produced by Cavas Masachs, although he continued to represent a variety of still table wines. In return, Masachs offered Quaid the exclusive rights to sell his products for export. Even though a formal contract was not signed, it was understood that Cavas Masachs would pay Quaid's travelling expenses connected with the sale of sparkling wine and a 5 per cent commission on sales made. If Quaid should visit an importer or distributor who was interested in buying any of the other wines which Quaid represented, the wine cellar and Cavas Masachs would share Quaid's expenses. The relationship between Quaid and Masachs continued to develop on a personal basis until each got to know what the other one expected from him. Finally in December 1983, Quaid rented some office space in the Masachs building in Vilafranca del Penedés, which had been offered to him at a reasonable rent, and, in spite of being an independent wine-dealer representing various products, he soon found himself dedicating the greater part of his time to Cavas Masachs. 'Many people thought I was crazy for having agreed to such an arrangement', said Joe Quaid referring to his connection with Cavas Masachs. 'Even Josep realizes he's getting a good deal. However, I was happy. It was something personal which had to do with my freedom and the fact that I didn't want to get involved in any corporate structure. It is the price I'm prepared to pay for my freedom and not having to be bound by anyone's regulations but my own.'

In 1983, Quaid and Masachs attended jointly their first trade fair, the San Francisco Wine Expo. Trade fairs, which may last two days or two weeks, are organized all over the world by governments interested in promoting trade or by industrial associations who wish to provide a forum where their members might get to know interested buyers. At the trade fairs, exhibitors rent a space in which they can show off their products to their best advantage. In his stand, the exhibitor is in complete control and may concentrate on his customers without being distracted by telephone calls or interruptions. He knows that his visitors have been selected for their genuine interest in the goods on display in the trade fair and that it is very worthwhile to regard many of those who visit his stand as potential clients. Thus, trade fairs provide an excellent opportunity for meeting people and even making sales.

However, sales are not the only reason for taking part in trade fairs. Even the largest and most renowned manufacturers keep on coming to the most important trade fairs in order to keep in contact with the industry, keep in touch with the market, deal with important clients, see the latest developments of their competitors and to maintain their own image. For many exhibitors, the main reasons for attending include the contacts they may make and the knowledge obtained of the latest trends in the industry, among their competitors and in the market. For Cavas Masachs, the trade fairs were, principally, a cheap way of physically placing their products in front of many potential importers and distributors. Cavas Masachs' strategy was to use those contacts made at the fairs to build the foundations for solid export growth. In the opinion of Manuel Olaya, 'One must participate for at least three or four years consecutively before any benefits are really seen. The fairs are where one starts, where the contacts are made.'

Joe Quaid insisted that most importers were not likely to take much interest in a product unless they had seen it repeatedly at the major fairs because, to a certain extent, this amounted to a statement of a serious wish to export and to continue exporting.

'The importers want to be sure that your enthusiasm for exporting is no passing fancy. An importer who establishes relations with a newcomer at a trade fair is running the risk of losing whatever he may invest to promote the product if the manufacturer then realises that he is not in a condition to export, that his capacity is insufficient or simply that the time and energy needed are beyond him.'

Given that it was unusual to establish working relations after taking part in just one trade fair, Cavas Masachs were pleasantly surprised when, during their first trade fair – the San Francisco Wine Expo – they were visited by Robert Desommes, a Vice President of Joseph Garneau Co., one of the biggest distributors of alcoholic beverages in the USA. Desommes asked them to send samples of Cavas Masachs' products to Joseph Garneau Co.'s head office in Kentucky. Cavas Masachs were even more surprised when, after getting the samples,

Exhibit 21.17   *List of international trade fairs attended by Cavas Masachs*

Date	Fair	Place
5/1983	San Francisco Wine Expo	USA
3/1984	Spectrum – Warrington/Manchester	UK
5/1984	Washington D.C. Fancy Food Fair	USA
6/1984	London Olympia Fair	UK
6/1984	SIAL – Paris	France
1/1985	Berlin's Green Week	FRG
2/1985	London International Food Exhibition	UK
5/1985	Wine and Spirits Wholesalers of America (WSWA)	USA
6/1985	VinExpo – Bordeaux	France
10/1985*	Anuga	FRG

*Forecast.

Joseph Garneau Co. indicated their interest in distributing Louis de Vernier in the USA. Unfortunately, at that moment, Cavas Masachs could not guarantee the minimum production of 100,000 cases a year which Joseph Garneau Co. requested! Even though Quaid and Masachs were disappointed that they had not been able to reach an agreement with Joseph Garneau, the interest shown by the Brown-Forman Corporation in Louis de Vernier seemed to confirm that there were possibilities for selling it in the USA. (The Brown-Forman Corporation of Louisville, Kentucky is a company specializing in distilling, importing and distributing wines and alcoholic beverages. It has as subsidiaries the following companies: Canadian Mist Distillers Ltd. (Canada), B-F Spirits Ltd., Brown-Forman International Ltd., California Cooler Inc., Jack Daniel Distillery, Early Times Distillers Co., Joseph Garneau Co., Southern Comfort Corp. of the USA while it is in turn a subsidiary of Brown-Forman Inc.) Thus, and in view of the apparent openings available for the product, they agreed to continue working together and to attend nine more international trade fairs in 1984 and 1985, two of which were in the USA (see Exhibit 21.17).

After ten international trade fairs, the importers were beginning to show some interest in Cavas Masachs and, by the middle of 1985, they had received orders for almost 18,000 cases and were awaiting three additional orders due at the end of the year (see Exhibit 21.18). However, as many of these importers were placing first orders, it was not yet possible to say what the final outcome would be. In general, Cavas Masachs had tried to avoid granting exclusive rights for its products and these first orders were not based on a written contract but on a mutual promise about the amount of sparkling wine to be sold during the year after the first order. This amount was based both on the amount which Cavas Masachs hoped to be able to supply and the volume which every importer-distributor thought he would be able to sell and in no case did it constitute an absolute guarantee. When deciding whether or not to work with a particular distributor, the most important consideration for Joe Quaid was flexibility. As it was, the majority of the importers with whom they had made agreements were relatively small. Quaid felt that this sharing of sales between various importers reduced the risk to the company of depending on one client. However, it was also true that in most cases, Quaid was not given the opportunity of deciding between various importers, which would have been better for a strategic plan. Quaid explained it this way: 'It is often difficult for a manufacturer, who has begun to export, to come to an agreement with the major distributors in any given country. Normally he has to be content with a distributor who is, himself, setting up in business because the larger and more solvent prefer to sign distribution contracts with the more established manufacturers.'

Cavas Masachs fixed FOB prices for the cases of sparkling wine they exported, although they were prepared to quote CIF prices if they were asked to. The importers in the USA were advised that by ordering in container loads of 850 cases they could effect substantial transport cost savings (up to $510 per order in 1984). 'In 1984', said Masachs, 'the average retail price of Masachs sparkling wine was between $7 and $8, which made it roughly $1.00 more expensive, per bottle, than that of their Spanish competitors, Freixenet and Codorniu (see Exhibit 21.19). Cavas Masachs could normally ship an order three weeks after receipt.' (The fair trading laws which permitted the manufacturer or the distributor of a registered product to fix his retail prices were abolished in the USA with the introduction by President Ford, in December 1975, of the Consumer Goods Pricing Act. However, it is obvious that the granting of exclusive dealership or the fact of enjoying a small outlet, as was the case with Cavas Masachs, are factors which tend to make retail prices more uniform. In any event, one should not forget the notable tax differences in the various states, which led to a certain imbalance in the prices paid by the end consumer, from state to state.)

Spanish wines on the US market

Where wine was concerned, the USA was considered to be a sleeping giant; the huge potential of its market for wines, both in relation to its overall size and the low per capita consumption, had barely been exploited (see Exhibit 21.20). In fact, both wine sales and per

Exhibit 21.18 List of exports by Cavas Masachs in 1985

Destination	Distributor	Cases
Blaunelt, NJ	BNC Distributing	1,700*
Chicago, IL	Direct Import Wine Company	1,890†
Los Angeles, CA	Transcontinental Trade Corporation	3,460*
Monterey, CA	Monteroy Wine Imports	500*
New York, NY	International Imports	620†
Copenhagen	DBS Imports	133‡
Copenhagen	Molwengels Vinimport	1,026†
London	Caravelle Wine Shippers	1,155†
Frankfurt	Spengler Imports	1,412*
Hamburg	Max Piehl	1,350†
Verl, FRG	Beza Import	340†
The Hague	Warmond	380†
Caracas, Venezuela	Exclusivas Ibéricas	2,605†
Andorra	Codipa	196*
Milan	La Mercantile	1,140†

*No longer distributes Cavas Masachs.
‡Contacted by means other than trade fairs.
†New distributors – first order.

Exhibit 21.19   *Price list for Barcelona, Spanish pesetas*

MASACHS CAVA (méthode Champenoise)

Brut Gran Reserva	: 4,850,- per 12 × 750 ml Export Case
Nature	: 3,750,- per 12 × 750 ml Export Case
Brut	: 3,379,- per 12 × 750 ml Export Case
Seco or Semi Seco	: 2,437,- per 12 × 750 ml Export Case
Brut Rosé	: 2,823,- per 12 × 750 ml Export Case
Magnum, Brut	: 3,916,- per 12 × 750 ml Export Case

LOUIS DE VERNIER CAVA (Methode Champenoise)

Brut Nature Reserva	: 3,516,- per 12 × 750 ml Export Case
Brut	: 2,823,- per 12 × 750 ml Export Case
Seco or Semi Seco	: 2,325,- per 12 × 750 ml Export Case
Brut Rosé	: 2,823,- per 12 × 750 ml Export Case
Magnum, Brut	: 3,510,- per 6 × 1.5 l Export Case

Note

1 MASACHS and LOUIS DE VERNIER Magnums are packed and delivered standard in individual gift cartons.
2 With a minimum of forty-five days prior notice, all MASACHS and LOUIS DE VERNIER CAVAS in 750 ml bottles can be packed and delivered in rustic wood gift boxes with imprinted logos. Prices of boxes are as follows:
Single Bottles: 175,- Ptas. ea. Two Bottles: 225,- Ptas. ea.
Three Bottles: 252,- Ptas. ea. Six Bottles: 415,- Ptas. ea.
3 All prices quoted above are subject to final confirmation.

Exhibit 21.20   *Wine consumption in the USA*

Year	Cases (000's)	Per capita
1973–1977 mean	126,140	0.571
1978	146,500	0.655
1979	154,400	0.686
1980	165,600	0.731
1981	174,300	0.765
1982	178,100	0.777
1983	182,600	0.792
1984		
1990*	459,244	1.913

*Forecast.

Source   *Wine Marketing Handbook*, 1984.
Includes both national production and imports, and both sparkling and non-sparkling wines.

capita consumption were increasing consistently and it was hoped that this trend would be maintained long enough to allow the Americans, whose knowlege of wines was not very great, to become increasingly more sophisticated drinkers. At that time, 33 per cent of the wine consumed in the USA was sold in the following areas: California, which had the largest wine-producing industry in the USA, Florida, Illinois, Texas and the New York area.

Imports had been taking an increasingly large share of the growing consumption of wine in the USA, rising from 13 per cent of sales in 1975 to 25 per cent in 1984. It was thought that imports would continue to play an important part in the future sale of wine in the USA, for two reasons: in the first place because domestic production was limited by the lack of suitable land for grapevine growing and, in the second place, because it was expected that the dollar would remain strong, thereby helping to make the prices of imported products more competitive (in August 1985 the dollar was quoted at about 168 pesetas, after peaking to about 190 in March of the same year). At the same time, Europe had a great glut of wine, which made the young North American market an important goal.

The Spanish wine-producers lost the battle for the US market, fought out between the European producers. Its share of imports fell from 18.8 per cent in 1974 to 6.2 per cent in 1985, its lowest in fifteen years. According to an article in *Expansión*, the official Spanish export magazine, this slump was the fault in many respects of the Spanish wine producers who believed that their work was done once they had signed a contract with an importer, frequently not bothering to make any further marketing efforts. This article was published in the June 1985 issue of *Expansión* and was entitled 'Spanish wines in the USA: a diagnosis'. The article attributed the problem to a general ignorance of the North American market on the part of the Spanish producers, who tended to underestimate its size, its complexity and the fickleness of the US consumer. A study of the North American market sponsored by 'Wines of Spain' in New York ('Wines of Spain' with offices in London, New York, Toronto and Dusseldorf, is a division of the Spanish Trade Office, whose function is to promote knowledge about and consumption of Spanish wines on foreign markets) disclosed a series of obstacles encountered by Spanish producers when they attempted to market their products there.

The first and most important was a general indecision on the part of the Spanish producers when it came to backing their wines with advertising or promotions. As a result, there was no generic familiarity with Spanish wines, to say nothing of brand awareness. Lacking a generic identity, the product did not 'pull' at the points of sale, which is something almost indispensable in order to achieve an efficient distribution and minimum guaranteed sales.

Spanish wines suffered, at the same time, from a persistent image of low quality, the result of certain mishaps suffered by North American importers who imported Spanish wines during the fifties and sixties. The Spanish producers had not successfully explained the metamorphosis taking place in Spanish wine cellars where the degree of modernization was nearly as good as that taking place in California. In addition, they were slow to learn the US custom of equating price with quality, consequently damaging the image of their products when they sold them at low prices.

Finally, the Spanish producers had not been able to improve the level of service to their distributors. What they wanted were wines of high turnover and strong sales back-up, all of which demanded that the producers invest in production capacity, specially for export. The Spanish producers traditionally saw exports as a way of getting rid of gluts. Thus, they did not want to invest in export capacity, adapt their products, bottle or label them to suit the demands of the US consumer. This meant that the distributors were often obliged to sell a product which was not really suited to the market and, even if they managed to drum up demand, they ran the risk of bad service by some Spanish producers, only interested in their domestic market.

In general terms, the market study concluded that the Spanish producers' conceit concerning their product was, in the case of the North American market, more of a disadvantage than an advantage. Their belief that the product would sell itself misled them into ignoring various sales requirements. This fatal attitude, in the highly competitive wine market, contrasted sharply, for example, with the Italian wine producers who had had a spectacular success thanks to their sales programmes (see Exhibit 21.21).

The North American sparkling wine market

Compared to the still wine market, sales of sparkling wines and champagne had rocketed in the last four years in the USA and the forecasts for the future were optimistic (see Exhibit 21.22). At a time when the Americans were becoming more health conscious, light white wines of low alcohol content were replacing spirits and other stronger alcoholic beverages. The Americans included sparkling wine in the range of light refreshing alcoholic drinks which they had started to sell in the seventies. And, while previously sparkling wine and champagne has been mainly drunk as aperitifs at cocktail parties and parties, they were, by then, considered acceptable drinks at any time of the day, and even at dinner.

Quaid explained as follows the competitive situation of Spanish industry in the North American sparkling wine market:

Spain, in fact, has been one of the major beneficiaries of the explosive growth in the consumption of sparkling wines, with three Spanish companies among the top 10 suppliers of foreign sparkling wines to the United States. Freixenet was the leading exporter of 'Cava' Spanish sparkling wine, with exports to the US which were calculated at 7.2 million bottles

Exhibit 21.21   *Comparison between exporters of Spanish and Italian wines*

Spain	Italy
● Wine producers —'I produce, you sell'	● Wine dealers
● Small companies	● Large companies
● Mostly export production surpluses	● Prepare special export product
● Unfamiliar with US market	● Very familiar with US distribution channels and consumers
● Traditional product made to local taste	● Product designed for American taste, with special attention to grape varieties and fermentation methods
● Believe in quality	● Believe in image
● Short-term profit mentality, thinking in terms of cases and wanting instant success	● Long-term profit mentality, creating brand recognition and achieving high margins from high sales volumes
● Low level of advertising	● Aggressive advertising campaigns

Source Spanish wines in USA: a diagnosis (1985) *Expansion Journal*, (16).

Exhibit 21.22   *Sparkling wine consumption in the USA*

Year	Million bottles
1979	122.4
1980	133.2
1981	150
1982	164.4
1983	182.4
1984	

Source Impact Data Bank.

(600,000 cases) in 1983, which is more than the main suppliers of Italian sparkling wine and French champagne. The second biggest is Codorniu who exported 5.1 million bottles to the United States in 1983. Together, Freixenet and Codorniu sell about 80 per cent of all the Spanish sparkling wine exported to the United States. Both have experienced a spectacular increase in sales during the last three years, partly as a result of the strength of the dollar. An efficient sales programme has, however, been an essential element in their success (Freixenet's success was attributed, in good measure, to its appearance. It used a curious black bottle for its Cordón Negro, a clear gold bottle for its Carta Nevada. They had established a subsidiary – Freixenet USA – to take charge of the marketing and distribution of its products in the USA).

Although the growth of Spanish sparkling wine exports to the United States has been phenomenal, it is certain that there has been a drop in their share of the market. Compared to France and Italy, who have maintained their respective market positions, Spain has been losing ground. Spanish sparkling wine is holding its position between the low-quality American gassified wines and the more appreciated French champagnes. Its strong point is its very good value-for-money. It is considered a good quality product that sells for an average of $2.00 cheaper than the American brand Korbel and from $10 to $15 cheaper than the majority of French champagnes.

All the import duties, taxes and tariffs were paid by the American importer (see Exhibit 21.23). Federal taxes and customs duties were the same no matter where the wine was sent to in the United States but the State import taxes varied from 1 cent per gallon in California to $1.75 in Florida. Sales taxes also varied from State to State and affected retail prices considerably in the case of imported wines, the same as transport costs and the various retail and wholesale mark-ups. As a general rule, profit margins were about 50 per cent for the importer, 50 per cent for the wholesaler and 33 per cent for the retailer. (This refers to mark-ups charged at every stage of the products' progression, over its purchase price as opposed to 'discount margins', which represents the percentage over the sales figures. In our case, the ratio 50-50-53 shows that the consumer is paying 2.99 times the 'landed cost' (CIF plus tax). These percentage margins are quite theoretical and vary widely from case to case. The course of events was more or less determined by the supplier's sales position, the turnover of his sparkling wines at the retail outlet and the quality of the wines themselves. A ratio of 50-30-30 was considered to be competitive.)

The European market

The European market differed from that of the USA for various reasons. First, consumption per capita of wine was greater than that of the USA in almost all European countries (see

Exhibit 21.24) Second, Europe was, generally speaking, a mature market, with a zero or minimal growth in demand. However, a closer look at the market revealed significant differences in market trends in different countries. In general, there had been a drop in

Exhibit 21.23   *Import duties, levies and tariffs imposed in the USA*

	Internal Revenue Service (alcohol tax)	Customs duties	Total
Sparkling wines Price below $6.00/gallon			
1 litre	10.78	3.71	14.49
750cc	8.08	2.78	10.86
Price above $6.00/gallon			
1 litre	10.78	3.71	14.49
750cc	8.08	2.78	10.86
Non-sparkling wines No more than 14° of alcohol in containers less than 1 gallon			
1.5 litres	0.89	0.54	1.43
750cc	0.89	0.40	1.29
375cc	0.89	0.40	1.29

Note   Values in dollars per case of twelve bottles.

Exhibit 21.24   *Wine consumption per capita in Europe in litres*

Country	1980	1981	1982
France	95	90	89
Portugal	91	85	88
Italy	93	74	80
Spain	65	60	62
Greece	45	46	48
FRG	26	25	25
Belgium	20	20	20
Denmark	14	16	18
Holland	13	13	13
UK	9	10	10
Europe	50	51	45

Source Market Research Europe. June 1983.

consumption in the countries with a higher per capita consumption, like Italy, France, Spain and Portugal, also the biggest producers, while consumption had been growing in Northern Europe. In Europe, the UK is considered a prime target for wine exports because of its very low per capita consumption and the lack of a domestic wine industry. Forecasts for the period 1984–90 predicted a 50 per cent increase in the consumption of wine in the UK, with the greatest increase in consumption in white wines. However, in both the UK and the USA, Spanish wines had suffered from an image of cheapness and poor quality, which had resulted in a drop in the market share (the market share of Spanish sparkling wine imports in the UK fell from 19 per cent in 1977 to 10 per cent in 1983). Thus, with the exception of the sparkling wines, Spain had not been able to benefit from the growth of the British market. In the words of Josep Masachs:

> In spite of the differences in the habits of wine consumption in the United States and Europe, sparkling wines have been enjoying a similar success on both sides of the Atlantic. Once again, in Europe just as in the United States, Freixenet and Codorniu have benefited tremendously from this growth and are regular suppliers of sparkling wine to Great Britain, Germany, Sweden and Denmark. (In Appendix C there is an article taken from the Barcelona newspaper *Avui* of 19 July 1986, concerning the export of Catalan 'cava' (sparkling wine) in recent years.)

INFE

Cavas Masachs was able to pay some of the expenses of attending trade fairs abroad by using the services provided by the INFE (the National Institute for the Promotion of Exports, created by the Spanish government on 2 April 1982 to develop and protect the export of Spanish goods and services). One division of the INFE was solely concerned with helping businesses trying to generate exports by attending international fairs. This division sponsored official National Pavilions in several major trade fairs throughout the world implementing a system for reducing expenses for interested Spanish companies. Exhibit 21.25 contains a brief list of the fairs which the INFE attended in 1985 with an official National Pavilion. The National Pavilion only exhibited Spanish products, which, in the opinion of Quaid, made it more attractive to visitors, since Spanish products were relative novelties on the world market. By taking part in the Official National Pavilion, Cavas Masachs was able to save a large part of the cost of attending a trade fair (Joe Quaid estimated that Cavas Masachs spent on average 430,000 pesetas to attend a trade fair under the ONP) since the INFE not only took care of a great part of the administrative work of registering for the fair, the design and construction of the stands but, moreover, they also paid part of the travel expenses of one of the managers who would attend the fair, in order to encourage the exhibiting companies' active participation in the fair. There was a further saving as the exhibitors in the National Pavilion shared the cost of jointly shipping their samples and materials for the fair. As well as all these savings, the exhibitors benefitted from the preferential location, from the point of view of the circulation of visitors, given in general to national pavilions. As a result, during their first two years attending trade fairs, Cavas Masachs decided that they would only go to those where the INFE sponsored a National Pavilion. However, in their plans for 1986, Cavas Masachs had included various major fairs at which INFE was not going to be present. This meant that Cavas Masachs would be responsible for registering and designing and mounting its own stand, as well as the expenses of the round trip to the trade fair, all of which meant greater costs, not only in money but in time (see Exhibit 21.26 for a list of the trade fairs scheduled for 1986). In addition, Cavas Masachs could not hope to be allocated such a preferential location as it would have got through the National Pavilion, if it attended on its own account. However the INFE offered subsidies to companies that desired to attend

Exhibit 21.25   *Official calendar of foreign fairs (January–June 1985)*

por sector

AGROALIMENTACION
- Semana Verde. Berlín. 25 de enero al 3 de febrero.
  Ponente: Mª Luz Moya.
- Saudi Food. Riyadh. 10 al 14 de febrero.
  Ponente: Vicente Rovira.
- Food and Drink. Londres. 25 de febrero al 1 de marzo.
  Ponente: Vicente Rovira.
- VINEXPO. Burdeos. 17 al 21 de junio.
  Ponente: Mª Luz Moya.

MAQUINARIA Y BIENES DE EQUIPO
- FOODPACK CHINA 85. Tianjin. 23 al 28 de abril.
  Ponente: Mª Cruz Moreno.

MODA
Ponente: Sidonia Ignatowicz.
- SEHM. París. 2 al 5 de febrero.
- Moda infantil. París. 2 al 5 de febrero.
- INTERFEX. Tokio. 26 al 28 de febrero.
- NAMSB. Nueva York. 24 al 27 de mayo.
  marzo.

MULTISECTORIAL
- Feria Internacional de Casablanca. 25 de abril al 5 de mayo.
  Ponente: Elvira Cánovas.
- Feria Internacional de Burdeos. 11 al 20 de mayo.
  Ponente: Mª Luz Moya.

NAUTICA
- Boot. Düsseldorf (R.F.A.). 19 al 27 de enero.
  Ponente: Brita Seligmann.

cronológico

ENERO
- Boot. Düsseldorf. 19 al 27 de enero.
- Semana Verde. Berlín. 25 de enero al 3 de febrero.

FEBRERO
- SEHM. París. 2 al 5 de febrero.
- Moda infantil. París. 2 al 5 de febrero.
- Saudi Food. Riyadh. 10 al 14 de febrero.
- Food and Drink. Londres. 25 de febrero al 1 de marzo.
- INTERFEX. Tokio. 26 al 28 de febrero.

MARZO
- NAMSB. Nueva York. 24 al 27 de marzo.

ABRIL
- Feria Internacional de Casablanca. Casablanca, del 25 de abril al 5 de mayo
- FOODPACK CHINA 85. Tianjin. 23 al 28 de abril.

MAYO
- Feria Internacional de Burdeos. Purdeos, del 11 al 20 de mayo.

JUNIO
- VINEXPO. Burdeos. 17 al 21 de junio.

Source Expansion, (10), December 1984.

Exhibit 21.26   *Calendar of international trade fairs which Cavas Masachs intended to attend in 1986*

Fair	Place	NP*
Green Week – Berlin	FRG	Yes
Foodex	Tokyo	Yes
Wine and Spirits Buyers of America	Cannes, France	No
Wine and Spirits Wholesalers of America	Reno, NV	Yes
SIAL	Paris	Yes
Tax Free World Exhibition	Nice	No
Hotelympia	London	No

* Indicates whether Cavas Masachs had applied or was going to attend the trade fair under the National Pavilion.

trade fairs alone and Cavas Masachs tried to get the maximum subsidy possible. The aid offered by the INFE reached a maximum of 3,000,000 pesetas per company per annum out of a budget in 1984 for this type of aid amounting to 650,000,000 pesetas. In 1984, INFE had spent its budget by October and that made people fear that, in 1986, it would probably not be possible to give subsidies to all of the applying companies. Appendix D shows an application form to attend a trade fair on the Official National Pavilion sponsored by INFE.

Going to trade fairs under the banner of the Official National Pavilion carried its own risks because it appeared that, in the event that demand for space would exceed supply, preference would be given to those firms applying to INFE for the first time. The result could be that more experienced firms, like Cavas Masachs, might have to choose between attending the trade fair privately or accepting less preferential space in the National Pavilion. As Cavas Masachs had attended eight trade fairs in the last two years under the sponsorship of the National Pavilion, INFE could have felt less inclined to subsidize it, in line with INFE's policy to not try to replace private attendance, but to help those companies who, given the cost and the novelty of attending trade fairs, had decided not to do so on previous occasions. Eventually Cavas Masachs would be considered capable of going on its own.

'Louis de Vernier' in the USA

When negotiating with US distributors, Quaid had found himself constrained by an agreement Masachs had signed with Dave Wilson at the beginning of 1984. Quaid had learned, to his surprise, that while he was at the Fancy Food Fair in Washington DC, Masachs had granted the exclusive rights of sales and distribution of Louis de Vernier throughout the USA to Wilson. In return, Wilson had agreed to sell a minimum of 5000 cases a year. In short, in Quaid's words, 'Mr Masachs had sold the United States for 5000 cases.' Louis de Vernier was Cavas Masachs' best-seller and, although Quaid would continue to be paid his commission for every sale of Louis de Vernier to Wilson, he was limited to offering the Masachs brand to whatever interested importer he could get to do business with him. Even if Quaid understood that Masachs had believed, in good faith, that the contract with Wilson was good for both parties, he was convinced that the North American market was too big for a sole distributor, unless it was a very large company like Seagrams or Joseph Garneau Co., with an already established extensive sales network throughout the country. Neither was he pleased to have to depend on somebody he did not know for that task and he felt hampered in his efforts to interest good distributors when all that he could offer them was the Masachs brand. Because of this, Quaid had insisted that the agreement with Wilson be cancelled and he finally convinced Masachs not to renew Wilson's exclusive rights when they were due to expire in September 1985. Masachs' decision not to renew was strengthened by the fact that Wilson was in breach, not having sold the minimum quantities contracted. It was only when Masachs decided on the cancellation that Quaid could offer Louis de Vernier to potential North American distributors, for delivery at the end of 1985. Nevertheless, Quaid was of the opinion that the Wilson contract could have cost Masachs up to 15,000 cases, in sales in the USA between 1984 and 1985.

Cavas Masachs in Japan

Masachs was keen to export to Japan, as well as to the USA and Europe. Through an INFE newsletter called BISE (*The Bulletin of Selected Export Information*), Cavas Masachs had made contact with a potential Japanese importer who at that time was trying to get an import licence. Masachs was hoping to travel to Japan under the auspices of INFE, which had a programme to subsidize companies who were trying to export to a given country for the first time. If a company met INFE's standards in relation to its capacity and will to export, INFE was prepared to give up to 10 million pesetas ($62,500) over a period of two years in order to help firms protect their export contracts, even to the point of helping them to seek market information, obtain patents and register trade marks, send samples, advertise and promote products and cover travel expenses for exporter and importer alike if it were necessary in order to tip the balance in favour of a contract. Masachs was very enthusiastic about the idea of exporting to Japan because its market for sparkling wines was very young and in a phase of rapid growth and, as far as he knew, Codorniu was about the only — and the biggest — Spanish producer of sparkling wine who was exporting to Japan.

August 1985

'Joe' — it was Quaid's secretary calling at his door, 'Mr Masachs has just arrived. Do you want him to ring you?' 'No, I'm coming immediately, thanks!'

This was his first working day after his return from Denmark. The trip had been a success and he felt pleased by the way things had gone. In general, Quaid was confident that Cavas Masachs had all the right qualities to turn it into a leading company: a good product, a young and enthusiastic team and a management which was open-minded and did not shy away from taking necessary risks. However, at times, it annoyed him to see Masachs fall a victim to the same doubts that prevented many small Catalan wine producers from expanding. People tended to be conformist, which caused them to adopt what Quaid considered to be an excessively conservative sales strategy. At times it appeared that these sparkling wine producers thought that their product could disappear from the retail shelves as if by magic! Without any promotion or advertising or investment or risk, of course! At times Quaid felt as if he had to be pushing Masachs constantly to make that extra move or to take that additional undertaking, in spite of the fact that Masachs was enthusiastic about the idea of exporting.

'Well', thought Quaid, 'everyone has their reasons. It's only my opinion that Cavas Masachs could be doing better. Simply, I would not like to see it all slip through their fingers.'

He knocked loudly on Masachs' door before entering. Manuel Olaya was inside talking to Masachs who was standing behind his desk rummaging around in its drawers. He wore blue jeans and a check shirt, which contrasted with his cold, neat and functionally designed office. Bottles of Cavas Masachs filled the glass show-cases alongside the various prizes and certificates won during the past few years. There was a map of the world, printed by Maersk Line, a large international container shipping company, on one of the walls, ... 'the cosmopolitan spirit', thought Quaid.

'Hola, Joe', said Masachs, in Spanish, as Quaid came in. (Neither Masachs or Olaya spoke English or any other foreign language.) 'How's it going? Let's sit down for a minute so that you can fill us in on Denmark.'

The three men sat down to talk around the table in the corner of the office. 'Well, I'm glad to say that the trip turned out better than any of us had imagined', began Quaid, 'I had hardly to say a word. Over there, Louis de Vernier has practically sold itself unaided. All that I had to do was to agree with their opinions about the product, and they were always laudatory.' He related how Magasin, one of the biggest stores in Denmark, had decided to stock Louis de Vernier as their only Catalan sparkling wine (cava), ousting none other than Freixenet from their shelves and how SAS (Scandinavian Air System, a state-owned airline jointly operated by Norway, Denmark and Sweden) had decided to stock Louis de Vernier and include it in the next tasting to decide the wines served on their flights. Both Masachs and Olaya greeted this news with enthusiasm and satisfaction.

'It would appear that our distributor there is doing a great job', said Quaid, 'but he is going to ask us to offer him some promotional assistance in the near future. I also wanted to show you this . . .' Quaid took out a large envelope. 'I got this from our distributor in England while I was away. They are the drafts of possible brochures to promote our product among the retailers. They are informative, with some gaudy padding. I guess that the retailers have asked for some literature on the product.' (See Exhibit 21.27 for a copy of one of these drafts.)

Manuel Olaya glanced at the accompanying letter. 'Five thousand pounds sterling for five thousand brochures?', he asked.

'Yes', answered Quaid, 'and, as yet, we haven't really analysed their polo proposal; would we sponsor a Louis de Vernier trophy for ten thousand pounds? They say it's cheap considering the publicity and brand-image we could achieve.'

'Fifteen thousand pounds, and only in this and in England', thought Olaya. He was aware that Quaid wanted to spend 15 per cent of export sales on advertising in 1986. Quaid wanted to provide the distributors with funds for co-operative advertising, for T-shirts, posters advertising Cavas Masachs, as well as advertisements in leading trade magazines specializing in the sector, such as *Decanter* and *Impact*. Olaya thought that 10 per cent of the sales figures would be sufficient for advertising during 1986. In the matter of exports, he wished to proceed step by step. The greater part of the distributors had ordered their product for the first time that year and Olaya thought that, before giving them the initiative in sales, Cavas Masachs would have to know what they were thinking and what they needed. He felt that it was only when it was known what could be expected of them, that they could be given greater responsibility and scope for initiative in marketing. It had also to be borne in mind that the expansion plan had been calculated according to what Cavas Masachs could do on its own, without outside financing, although, were it necessary, there did not appear to be any reason why they could not seek loans. But, thought Olaya, we were still really in phase one of our export plan, which was to see how far we could go using the trade fairs. Olaya had always shared the enthusiasm and drive that characterized the people at Cavas Masachs. Not without reason, because he had quit an important job in a solid company some years before to join the firm. However, he was asking himself if Cavas Masachs could jump to the second phase, which demanded promotions, advertising, publicity and much more money. But, once again, if they wanted to reach the target sales figures for 1992 . . .

Quaid was still determined to improve the product's image. He wished to consolidate the Cavas Masachs image and give the company its own characteristic seal – a cachet, which would benefit all its products. Joe was aware of the effort and resources that would require, but he was convinced that they could not wait any more. It had to be done before Cavas Masachs grew any more. Quaid was also worried about the channel: he was aware that they had a good product, a competitive price and an ambitious management team but still they had a lot to do. Cavas Masachs' negotiating ability was still weak and they lacked a solid list of customers to put on the table when they were talking to an importer/distributor. On the other hand, their financial resources were limited and, at the moment, they could not plan an aggressive sales policy to promote their product at final consumer level.

Factors conditioning the sales strategy

Josep Masachs was reading the letter that came with the brochures, 'It would appear now to be a good idea to include some literature about our product, as we are constantly receiving requests for information. This is important . . .' Masachs was thinking that, perhaps, he should take charge of advertising himself but there were still many things to decide about what

Exhibit 21.27   *Draft brochure to be distributed among the UK retailers (1985)*

money should be invested, and how. He was conscious of the fact that, on the basis of the sales mix, Cavas Masachs could achieve margins of between 20 per cent and 40 per cent for their exports. These percentages on export sales turnover indicated the maximum amount that might be used for promotional purposes, without having to look for outside money (the Brut sparkling wines sold less but were gaining in popularity; their margins were greater than those of sweet or semi-dry sparkling wines). However, having reached this point, he thought that INFE's potential had only started to be exploited and he hoped to continue taking advantage of its programme of subsidies and trade fairs for as long as he could.

At the same time, he respected both Quaid's and Olaya's opinions. He felt satisfied with the results of their work together and, even though he knew that Quaid had no desire to become a salaried member of staff, Masachs hoped that he would continue to play an important role in the development of Cavas Masachs export strategy. A great deal was owed to Quaid that exports should have so quickly become the key to Cavas Masachs' growth, but he did not know how he could keep Joe and his distributors happy without entering into undertakings which were considered to place excessive demands, both in terms of time and of money. But, when all was said and done, his was a business venture of intuition, decision and risk.

Josep Masachs felt the need to plan his international expansion in certain detail. He knew that the fulfilment of the sales forecasts for 1992 was a major business challenge. However, the fact of having a table of figures, like that of Exhibit 21.14, was of little help to him if it was not viewed within the context of a more precise plan of action. He recalled, with certain bitterness, the impotence he felt when he was unable to meet the large order placed by Desommes after the San Francisco Wine Expo of 1983. But neither did he wish to rush into decisions, which perhaps had happened when he had granted the exclusive US distribution rights to Wilson in 1984.

Josep Masachs realized, however, that there were many parameters difficult to assess. Basically, he would have liked to determine, with precision, the right moment to advance from the present sales policy of 'push' to one of 'pull', more aggressive and firmer with respect to the channel. But what he was prepared to analyse to the limit was the suitability or not of his present channel policy, the money it was appropriate to invest in its support, the prices to suggest and the margins to give, the distribution of his sales budget between trade promotions and publicity and, above all, the adequacy of his policy of not granting exclusive dealerships in every national market.

'One of the aspects which appears to me to be more interesting to analyse', commented Masachs, in relation to the distribution channels, 'is the turnover which the retailers and distributors manage to generate from sparkling wines in general to the 'cavas' in particular, in the North American market. Perhaps it is somewhat premature to pose this type of question because I believe that we are still in a phase of sounding out and priming the market but, without doubt, one of the aspects which will make our Louis de Vernier more or less attractive to the trade is turnover in the retail shelves and, above all, compared with other competitive products.'

Finally, Masachs was deeply concerned about the generic image of Spanish 'cavas' at that time in the USA. He was aware that Cavas Masachs was still too small a company to decisively influence this and he was interested in adequately positioning his product, in relation to the other Spanish 'cavas' and sparkling wines in general.

Appendix B

Cava

No matter how carefully they follow the methods used by the producers of the famous French champagnes, producers of sparkling wines the world over cannot use the name 'Champagne' when referring to their products. This name has been reserved exclusively for the sparkling wines made according to the 'méthode champenoise' in the region of Champagne, in Northeast France, which is the historic seat of champagne making. However, the history of sparkling wine in Spain is almost as long as the history of champagne in France. It was only after travelling to Catalonia (an autonomous region in Northeast Spain) in search of the cork that would effectively hold in the characteristic gas found in sparkling wines, that Dom Pérignon, the Benedictine monk who devoted his life to the development of champagne in the seventeenth century, was able to perfect his 'méthode champenoise'. His short stay in Spain, when he was working on cork processing, was enough to sow the seeds of the Spanish sparkling wine industry, which began to flourish in the area of Penedés in the mid-nineteenth century. Nowadays, the name 'Cava' is officially used to refer to sparkling wine made in Spain in accordance with Dom Pérignon's procedures.

The Spanish sparkling wine industry is regulated by the Regulatory Council of Sparkling Wines (CRVE), which has laid down strict rules for the production of four classes of sparkling wines. 'Fizzy' wine, which is the lowest quality, has carbon dioxide injected into it to produce the bubbles characteristic of sparkling wine and it is the only sparkling wine that does not undergo a second fermentation. The other three acquire their characteristic sparkle during the second fermentation, which is produced by the addition of sugar and a fermenting agent, usually yeast, to a wine which has gone through the normal first fermentation. The sparkling wine called 'Granvas' undergoes its second fermentation in great stainless steel vats while the wine known as 'Fermented in bottle' goes through the second fermentation in a bottle, but is re-bottled before sale. 'Cava', the only sparkling wine made in Catalonia using the 'méthode champenoise', must be sold to the public in the same bottle in which it underwent its second fermentation. Once the second fermentation has started, the cava must stay at least nine months in the bottle before it is finally corked. During these nine months the cava is traditionally stored in great cool underground galleries called 'cavas' or wine cellars, from which it takes its name. Since cava is sold in the same bottle as it is made in, a vital part of the process consists of removing the natural sediments which remain in the bottle after fermentation. First, the sediment is made to settle in the neck of the bottle through a delicate process of daily rotation of the bottle, known as *remoción* and still done by hand in many wine cellars. Then the sediment is quick frozen to solidify it, before being removed by means of a process called *deguelle*. Before being finally corked, a certain amount of concentrated sweet wine is added, called the *dosaje*, which determines the cava's degree of sweetness. In accordance with the CRVE, the driest cavas are classified as Brut, folowed by Sec, Semi-sec and Dulce, or sweet cava. Cava may also be bottled without the *dosaje*, in which case it is called *Brut Nature*.

Once the cava has been corked and labelled, it is ready for sale. In general sparkling wines cannot be kept for as long as table wines and are almost drunk soon after sale. The sweetest cavas, however, may be improved by ageing in the bottle for three or more years.

The Spanish sparkling wine industry is the third largest in the world, after Italy and France. There are also major sparkling wine industries in Germany and California, in the USA. In Spain, as in most wine producing countries, the grape is classified not only by variety but also according to where it has been grown. This enables wines that are made from grapes from certain regions to be awarded a 'denomination of origin', considered to be indicative of a certain quality or style. About 95 per cent of Spanish cava is made in the regions of Penedés and Anoia in Catalonia. Consequently, Vilafranca del Penedés, the principal town of the Penedés region, a small country town surrounded by vineyards, has, together with Sant Sadurní d'Anoia, become the centre of the Spanish cava industry.

The Spanish cava industry is dominated by two producers competing for world leadership of sparkling wine production according to the 'méthode champenoise', Codorniu and Freixenet, both from Sant Sadurní d'Anoia, located a few kilometres from Vilafranca. Together, both hold over 75 per cent of the domestic market. While Codorniu is the oldest cava in Spain, Freixenet owes its position to its almost instantaneous success in the North American market, in 1979, and it continues to export a large part of its production.

The remainder of cava production in Spain is divided between some one hundred lesser producers. In spite of Freixenet's success, the small producers have, in general, been loath to take risks with promotions and extra capacity to increase sales. Few cava producers have tried to market their products aggressively, most of them concentrating their production and marketing efforts on highly 'craftmanship' quality levels, selling their cavas in small quantities at high prices.

Exhibit 21.28   *Louis de Vernier labels approved for importing into the USA*

	1984		1985		Percentage comparison %	
	Litres	Pesetas	Litres	Pesetas	Litres	Pesetas
Vino a granel	10,978,705	344,797,218	9,174,083	310,611,550	−16.51	−9.91
Vino evasado	10,043,202	1,517,118,921	10,331,094	1,873,034,647	+2.86	+23.45
Espumosos	20,024,225	6,040,282,523	21,455,512	6,821,934,838	+7.14	+12.94
Licores	1,390,579	434,015,766	1,114,308	402,772,126	−19.86	−7.19
Total	42,446,71	8,336,214,428	42,074,997	9,408,353,161	−0.68	+12.86

The growth of cavas since 1984

Year	Litres (00s)	Bottles (750 cc.)	% difference over the previous year	Pesetas (000s)	Average price (750 cc. bottle)	% difference over the previous year
1974	2.657	3,542,662	—	171,087	48.29	—
1975	2.284	3,045,333	−14.04	154,614	50.77	−9,63
1976	3.337	4,449,333	46.10	244,923	55.04	58,41
1977	4.151	5,534,666	24.39	335,200	60.56	26,86
1978	4.416	5,888,000	6.39	437,964	74.39	30,65
1979	6.732	9,976,000	52.44	710,633	79.17	62,20
1980	7.536	10,048,000	11.94	1.097,975	109.27	54,50
1981	10.442	13,896,000	38.29	1.845,737	132.82	68,10
1982	13.646	17,952,580	29.19	2.961,232	164.94	60,43
1983	17.287	23,049,921	28.39	4.650,334	207.75	57,04
1984	20.585	27,447,060	19.07	6.148,208	224.00	32,21
1985	23.073	30,769,357	12.10	7.089,537	230.40	15,31

Note These tables, prepared by the Consejo Regulador de Vinos Espumosos (Regulatory Council of Sparkling Wines) show that wine exports from Catalonia are making steady progress and that there is a move towards the quality products and away from wines in bulk, as well as a drop in liquors, generalized in Spain and even in other European countries. In the cava subsector, exports continue to increase, although at a progressively slower rate because large volumes have already been reached. In just ten years, exports have increased from 3,000,000 to almost 31,000,000 bottles in 1985.

Major customers of cava in 1985

		Litres	Pesetas
1	USA	12.978.697	4.477.073.810
2	Canada	1.660.548	421.895.755
3	West Germany	1.526.671	437.835.220
4	United Kingdom	815.719	193.246.816
5	Sweden	450.022	106.140.665
6	Switzerland	424.773	129.498.116
7	Italy	338.351	143.384.369
8	Japan	254.494	81.661.488
9	Venezuela	226.440	77.099.691
10	Holland	160.370	43.160.513

Note The USA have been the main customer for Catalan cava for many years. During the past year alone, 12.9 million litres were purchased, equivalent to 4,477 million pesetas. Canada is in second place with 1.6 million litres, followed very closely by Western Germany with 1.5 million litres, the UK with 815,719 litres and Sweden with 450,022 litres. Also worth mentioning are the 254,494 litres exported to Japan, until now a fairly difficult market for this product.

In spite of the reluctance of many cava producers, Spain has had considerable success in exporting its cava, principally through Freixenet and Codorniu. Since, in the past, Spanish wines were not quality controlled, every export shipment of cava is now subject to government inspection in order to check that it fulfills the necessary production and classification specifications. The greater part of exports are also subjected to controls at their respective destinations where inspection agencies, such as the Food and Drug Administration, in the case of the USA, watch over the interests of the consumers to protect them from adulterated or falsified products. All bottles for export must be properly filled and labelled before they can be sold on foreign markets and each country has its own laws which must be obeyed (see Exhibit 21.28 for an example of the Louis de Vernier label, approved for import into the USA).

Appendix C

Good progress in 'cava' exports

Barcelona – the export figures for cava for the year 1985 are sufficiently eloquent to permit confidence in the future of this product, so much our very own and which is earning so much prestige for Catalonia all around the world.

It is clear, however, that this prestige and these results did not come about by chance. Since the first pioneers started to work with wine in order to produce what, in those days, we were allowed to call 'champagne', to the present day, many generations of farmers, enologists and businessmen have worked resolutely and skilfully to achieve a quality product, esteemed and sought after both by domestic and foreign consumers alike.

A necessary task, carried out by the marketing people with their customary professionalism, has been to create an atmosphere that would propitiate consumption and enhance the social prestige of the discerning who knew what to drink with each dish as well as the best time for each drink and who progressivly developed a palate able to appreciate the strength, the flavour and the quality of what they were offered.

Years ago, when the majority of the people from Catalonia only drank champagne, sorry 'cava', to celebrate Midsummer's Eve and Christmas, nobody bothered how fizzy it was, or if it was sweet, semi-sweet or dry. I suppose that only the few people rich enough to drink cava regularly knew of the existence of brut.

Today, it is completely normal to sit down at a table where everyone has sufficient knowledge to give their opinion about the cava, in the beginning through pure snobbery but which with time has consolidated. The interest that started to be felt some years ago for cava has grown such that now there are many who know this beverage thoroughly and which flavours and brands are better quality.

The same producers and above all, the Confraria dels Vins de Cava and the Institut Català del Vi have fostered this movement in favour of domestic consumption and have brought on to the market small and, not so very long ago, unknown productions which have proved to be of excellent quality.

This has clearly shown that generic advertising of a product can be just as efficient as the exclusive advertising of a particular brand.

It has been this constantly increasing domestic consumption which has allowed the producers, without losing any of their craftsmanship, to modernize their work and production systems and reach high production levels. And this has allowed them to export cava at a range of competitive prices, without sacrificing quality.

The tables which have been included and which were prepared by the Consejo Regulador de Vinos Espumosos (Regulatory Council for Sparkling Wines) show clearly how our exports to various countries of the world have increased. The fact is that our raw material is high quality and varies little from year to year, which cannot be said of other producing regions which lack the light and the sun necesary for a good product.

All of that has enabled us to penetrate the US and European markets. If we do things as they should be done and, if they let us, membership of the EEC should not raise any difficulties for increasing the market penetration of Catalan cava in Europe.

There are companies which are taking major steps in this direction. They are, naturally, the bigger producers which, on the other hand, can also be those that, in some way, can feel the effect of the preferences of some minorities for the products of smaller producers, more craft products which give to the person who asks for them a name for being a connoisseur of cava among his fellow diners.

Some great Catalan firms have not limited themselves to selling outside Catalonia and Spain. They have, also, established themselves in producing areas, from where they hope to work with greater efficiency.

We can be highly competitive in offering value for money to the European market. The quality of our grapes, our prices, the sector's technological and production capacity enable us to view the future with a certain amount of optimism.

However, it is necessary to continue working seriously to improve our brand image and overcome the inertia of the consumers and their routine preference for French products which, if they hold the market, it is not for their quality alone. It will be difficult to undermine the virtual monopoly they have enjoyed for many years. We are fairly well placed in this battle in the USA. It is going to be a lot more difficult in Europe, but not impossible. We have the foundations, the knowledge and the tools to turn cava into a source of wealth and prestige for Catalonia.

Note
This Appendix is a translation from Catalan of the text and tables in the article published in the Barcelona newspaper *Avui*, 19 June 1986, entitled 'Bona Marxa de les Exportacions de Cava'.

Appendix D   Application for Attendance

TRADE FAIR ....

COUNTRY............................ DATE ....

COMPANY

NAME OF COMPANY ....FISCAL Nº ....

ADDRESS ....TELEGRAPHIC ADDRESS ....

CITY ....ZIP CODE .... PROVINCE ....

TELEPHONE............................... TELEX ....

PERSON IN CHARGE AT FAIR ....POSITION ....

Nº OF EMPLOYEES .... SHARE CAPITAL .... % FOREIGN CAPITAL ....

NATURE

MANUFACTURER: YES ☐ NO ☐ IF IT IS A DISTRIBUTING COMPANY; THE NAME OF THE
MANUFACTURER OF THE GOODS: ....
....

HAS IT AN EXPORT LICENCE?   SI ☐ NO ☐ (INDICATE YEAR GRANTED: 19...) ....

In the last four years (in millions)		19...	19...	19...	19....
	YOUR COMPANY'S SALES VOLUME ...	....	....	....	......
	YOUR COMPANY'S TOTAL EXPORTS .	....	....		
	EXPORTS TO THE COUNTRY HOSTING THE FAIR				
COUNTRIES TO WHICH YOU EXPORT (State the 1st four)		....	....	....	......
		....	....	....	......
		....	....	....	......

**DATA CONCERNING YOUR REPRESENTATIVE IN THE COUNTRY
HOSTING THE FAIR**

NAME................................ ADDRESS.................................

CITY .... POST BOX ....

TELEPHONE .... TELEX ....

GOODS

LIST OF GOODS TO BE EXHIBITED	CUSTOMS CATEGORY
....	....
....	....
....	....
....	....
....	....

BRAND NAMES ....
....

SPACE

INDICATE SPACE REQUESTED: M^2 INSIDE .... M^2 OUTSIDE ....

IN CASE OF SPECIAL GOODS SIZES, INDICATE THE MAXIMUM:

LENGTH .... HEIGHT .... WEIGHT ....

VOLUME .... AND WEIGHT .... OF ALL GOODS TO BE EXHIBITED

IN THE FAIR.

PREFERRED LOCATION ....

HOW MANY TIMES HAVE YOU ATTENDED .... OR EXHIBITED IN THIS FAIR ......

....

EXPERIENCE	STATE IN THE SPACE PROVIDED THE NUMBER OF TIMES, DURING THE LAST THREE YEARS, YOU HAVE CARRIED OUT THE FOLLOWING PROMOTIONAL ACTIVITIES IN THE HOST COUNTRY: (state the most recent) ☐ VIAPRO (19 ...) ☐ F.A.O.T. (19 ...) ☐ MARKET OPENING PROGRAM (19 ...) ☐ SALES MISSIONS (19 ...) ☐ EXHIBITOR IN OTHER FAIRS (19 ...) ☐ PRIVATE TRIPS BY YOUR COMPANY (19 ...)
GOALS	WHY SPECIFICALLY DOES YOUR COMPANY WANT TO EXHIBIT AT THIS FAIR? ☐ ATTACK THIS MARKET FOR THE FIRST TIME ☐ FIND NEW CUSTOMERS ☐ APPOINT A REPRESENTATIVE ☐ INTRODUCE A NEW PRODUCT ☐ FIND A DISTRIBUTOR ☐ FIND A PARTNER TO MANUFACTURE LOCALLY ☐ OTHER REASONS (explain) ....

CONDITIONS FOR ATTENDANCE

1 This form must be returned within the time stipulated to the National Institute for the Promotion of Exports (INFE), P.O. Box 14,710 Madrid or to the regional office of the Ministry of Economy and Commerce.
2 Send the aforementioned correspondence relating to this Fair to INFE, P.O. Box 14,710, Madrid.
3 Keep the stand manned by authorized personnel during the whole of the fair, even though INFE does not subsidise every day of the fair.
4 Accept the rules and decisions of the Pavilion management and of the INFE's representatives.
5 Fill in all sections the Data Card which you will receive if your application is accepted, within the time specified by INFE, and enclosing payment for the space allocated.
6 Send on the necessary staff for setup so that the stand will be completely set up 24 hours before the fair is opened.
7 If a company states that it will not attend, without claiming an Act of God, at least one month prior to the date of shipping of goods to the fair, 50% of the amount paid will be returned. If cancellation is received after that date, you will not be entitled to any repayments.

I ....(State position)..................................... certify the authenticity of the data herein and I agree to the terms of attendence. At the same time I promise to inform INFE, through the Pavilion Manager, and again 6 months after the end of the fair, of the results obtained, the general impression gained and about any other aspect concerning our attendance.

....19..........
(Signature and Company stamp)

Important
Please give all the information requested.

Case Study 5: Chemical Labour Grouping, European Economic Interest Grouping (CLG, EEIG)*

> This case study was prepared by Professor Lluís G. Renart and Francisco Parés, lecturer. It was prepared with the help of a grant by the European Foundation for Entrepreneurship Research. The names of the main participants, their companies, and the Grouping itself have been changed.

It was early April 1990, and Joseba Garmendia was looking forward to Easter to be able to at least take a few hours off to rest and reflect. In addition to being general manager and co-owner of Química del Atlántico, S.A., Joseba Garmendia had taken on the additional responsibility of being co-ordinator of Chemical Labour Grouping, European Economic Interest Grouping (CLG, EEIG). This Grouping had been registered in the Bilbao Company Registry on 13 March 1990, and had been set up by four paint manufacturers from different countries: LACKE UND FARBE GmbH (LF), from Germany; MARCEAU ET FILS, S.A. (Ma), from France; UNITED COLOURS, LTD. (UC), from the UK; and QUIMICA DEL ATLANTICO, S.A. (QA), from Spain.

The agreement had taken almost two years to negotiate. Joseba Garmendia and the managers of the other three companies were very pleased about the way things had progressed up until the legalization of their Grouping. Not only had new and exciting competitive prospects opened up for them on an European scale but even during the agreement planning process, they had started to put into practice certain co-operation mechanisms, specifically the joint purchase of certain raw materials, which had already begun to produce very tangible results in their respective income statements.

However, Joseba Garmendia was also aware that his Grouping was one of the first EEIG's formed in Europe and definitely the first that had been formally registered in Spain. None of its four partners had any experience in this type of alliance. The planning had been relatively smooth but they were now venturing into virgin territory, mapping the route as they walked.

Joseba Garmendia had written down a list of issues that had presented themselves during the process. Some of them seemed to suggest new opportunities of vast potential, while others could harbour dangers, or at least doubts.

He was looking forward to the Easter holidays to be able to reflect on each of these issues.

Química del Atlántico, S.A. (QA)

Química del Atlántico, S.A. was founded in 1932. At about that time, it started to manufacture air-drying, nitrocellulose paints for automobile body repairs and was the first company to supply these products on the Spanish market.

In 1955, the company opened its plant in Baracaldo, a few kilometres from Bilbao; in 1990, this plant was still the corporate headquarters.

Over the years, the company had steadily grown up and had opened two more factories: Portugalete and Santurce, both near the corporate headquarters. In 1990, QA's facilities occupied a surface area exceeding 60,000 square metres.

---

* No part of this case study may be reproduced without the permission of IESE. In July 1991 this case received first prize in the EFMD/COS case writing awards.

The company had consistently allocated significant effort and resources to research and development, as a result of which it had been able to launch products, systems and processes such as:

- polyester finishes for wood products,
- baked enamels for refrigerators,
- implementation of water soluble baths by immersion, used mainly in automobile factories,
- paint application systems using electrodeposition,
- powdered paints, and
- the Kolormatik system, able to select from among more than 5,000 hot or cold colours; basic or complementary colours; absolute or relative colours; monochromatic, polychromatic or achromatic colours; and obtain any range of tints or hues.

This desire to be always on the leading edge of technology had led the company to sign technology transfer agreements with companies such as Dai Nippon (Japan), Fuller O'Brian (USA), I.C.I. (United Kingdom), Lacke und Farbe GmbH (Germany), etc.

Química del Atlántico, S.A.'s sales turnover in 1985 amounted to about 8 billion pesetas (The rate of exchange of the US Dollar against the Spanish Peseta reached an all time high of 190 pesetas for one dollar in early 1985. From there, the US dollar stumbled to below 100 ptas. per dollar in 1990). Home decorating paints accounted for about 20 per cent of this figure and automobile body repair paints (refinishing) accounted for 30 per cent. Thus, these two types of paint represented 50 per cent of QA's sales, that is, approximately half of the company's production consisted of standard paints manufactured for stock and subsequently sold through decorating shops and other retail outlets. The company estimated that its products were sold in 75 per cent of the approximately 12,000 retail outlets existing in Spain in 1985.

The other 50 per cent of QA's sales were paints manufactured to order for industrial customers. The most important industrial sector for QA were the automobile OEM's, which accounted for about 30 per cent of the company's total sales, with a volume of about 6,000 tonnes of paint. (The design process, manufacture and application of industrial paints in the automobile industry is explained in Exhibit 21.29, while Exhibit 21.30 provides a description of the paint sale process to automobile OEMs.)

The remaining 20 per cent was sold to other industrial sectors, such as domestic appliance manufacturers, automobile components and spare parts, toys, metallographic industry (printing on tinplate or aluminium used in the manufacture of cans for food products or soft drinks), furniture, electrical material, railroad rolling stock, etc.

In 1986, QA's total workforce amounted to about 575 employees and this figure would remain virtually unchanged until 1990.

Química del Atlántico, S.A. had been leader in the refinishing segment in Spain since the end of the Spanish Civil War with exactly three products: two black paints and one white paint.

When SEAT started manufacturing cars in Spain towards the end of the 50's, QA was able to position itself well, sharing the client with Lory.

Subsequently, other automobile OEMs and other paint manufacturers established manufacturing facilities in Spain. QA's management estimated that in 1985, the last year before Spain joined the EC, its company's market share in the specific segment of paint supply to Spanish automobile OEMs was about 15 per cent. The classification of paint suppliers for that year in Spain would probably be the following:

Exhibit 21.29   *Design, manufacture and application of industrial paints in the automobile industry*

Although paint companies are usually included in the 'chemical sector' of a country's economic activity, its manufacturing process is basically a *physical* process, consisting of mixing together a number of ingredients that do not chemically react with each other.

The total process of creating, manufacturing and applying a paint usually comprises four main phases or stages, which may coincide with the company's various technical-production departments.

Design or formulation

This department is set in motion by the task of solving a certain painting problem, which may be completely new for the company, or simply the need to improve a certain aspect or attribute of one of the formulae already existing in the company.

Its mission consists of developing a paint formula able to solve the particular problem or need, and manufacturing a small sample of the formula in question. In other words, it carries out the 'product engineering'.

Five possible types of ingredient can be used:

1 *Resins*

These give flexibility, adherence and protection (for example, against rusting). They go from a liquid state to a polymerized state after application.

2 *Pigments*

These give colour.

3 *Fillers*

Such as barite or calcium carbonate. They give consistency.

4 *Solvent*

This is the vehicle that facilitates or enables application. After application, the solvent evaporates and disappears.

5 *Additives*

They give the paints certain properties. They are usually added in relatively small quantities.

Determination of the process

The following step, often carried out in another department, consists of determining the exact process to be carried out on an industrial scale to be able to manufacture the paint in question effectively and efficiently. Manufacture is by batches.

The basic task is to determine the machines (and their accessories) to be used, also stating how long each part of the process will last.

In other words, it is not enough to carry out the 'product engineering' but it is also necessary to carry out the 'process engineering'.

The manufacturing process as such

The Manufacturing or Production Department implements the prescriptions given by the Design and Process Departments in order to obtain the paint in question in industrial quantities.

The manufacturing process as such usually consists of several stages or phases:

1 *Dispersion/homogenization*
This state, also called sometimes 'first mixture' consist of mixing in a tank part of the ingredients in order to break up the lumps and disperse the pigment, which is the most expensive ingredient per kilogramme of component.
   In this first mixture, it is customary to add 100 per cent of the total pigment that the finished product will have, 100 per cent of the fillers, about 60 per cent of the resin and 20 per cent of the solvent. The rest of these ingredients and the additives will be added towards the end of the process (stage 3, further on).
2 *Grinding or disintegration*
The pigment's molecular dispersion is intensified in suitable machines, although *not* to the point of breaking its molecular structure.
3 *Transformation/dilution tank*
In this stage, the rest of the solvent and resin is added, in addition to the additives required to give the paint being manufactured the required specific properties.
   At this point, the actual characteristics of the paint manufactured are checked out in order to verify that it meets the prescribed specifications. It is at this point also that the colour can be controlled, in order to ensure that the specific batch has the exact hue prescribed.
4 *Packaging*
After verifying the characteristics of the batch that has been manufactured, it is then packaged.
   In the case of industrial paints, including the paint supplied to the automobile manufacturers, the product is usually packaged in 200-litre drums, 1,000-litre containers or tank wagons.

The application process

If the paint has been manufactured for use in home decorating, it is packaged in smaller containers which will be sold through decoration shops and it will be applied by a professional painter or by the user himself.
   However, in the case of industrial paints, and particularly in the case of the supply of paints to automobile manufacturers, the process is only completed when the paint is applied. In other words, after the manufacturing process as such, carried out in the paint manufacturer's plant, there is another application process ('painting') which is carried out in the automobile manufacturer's plant.
   Over the years, the paint manufacturers' responsibilities within the automobile production plant have steadily increased.
   Specifically, at the beginning of 1990, the paint application process in an automobile production plant usually consisted of five stages.

1 *Degreasing, phosphating, washing and drying of bodywork*
2 *Application of the primer* by means of a cataphoresis process, consisting of immersing the bodywork in a large tank (up to 500m³) to apply a first coat of a neutral-coloured paint which gives it rust-resistant properties. The immersion is electrophoretical, in other words, an electric field is applied so that the paint adheres better to all parts of the bodywork.

3 *Application of the primer*
This second coat of paint, also of a neutral colour (i.e., it is usually the same colour, regardless of the colour of the top coat that will be applied in the following stage). It gives body and elasticity to the paint, smoothing over rough spots and improving the adhesiveness of the to coat that will be applied next.

4 *Application of the top coat*
This is the coat that gives the colour that the buyer of the vehicle sees and appreciates. It may be an opaque or metalized coat.

5 Final bake, in which the polymerization takes place. (As a matter of fact, bake takes place after each step 1, 3 and 4).

It should be emphasized that the application process of the various coats of paint is a very important process for the automobile manufacturer, both as regards the maintenance of a certain production rate on the assembly line and as regards the quality of the final product.

Thus, if at one time the paint manufacturer could have thought that his mission ended when he delivered the 200-litre drums of paint at the automobile manufacturer's goods inwards warehouse, over the years there has been a growing 'co-involvement' process of the paint manufacturer in the final result obtained in the application of his products.

Therefore, the paint manufacturers usually have a technical representative, helped by one or two assistants, also employed by the paint manufacturer, in each of the automobile production plants supplied by them. The mission of these people is to work closely with the automobile manufacturer's personnel in order to ensure that the application process takes place smoothly.

The technical representative usually has a physical space where he can 'correct the barrels' in at least two ways:

- Because the paint in the barrels supplied by the paint manufacturer usually has a higher viscosity or less liquid consistency than the viscosity for application. This means that solvents must be added to the barrels' contents to give them the optimal viscosity for application.
- Because the particular circumstances under which the paint is applied (relative humidity, air temperature, etc.) may vary from one day to the next, as a result of which the paint must be adapted to the circumstances prevailing at any one time.

The managers of paint manufacturing companies admit that although they try to bring to bear all their 'scientific' abilities, the application of paint continues to have something of 'alchemy', sometimes bordering on 'magic', about it.

It is therefore obvious that the paint manufacturer's technical representative in the automobile production plant plays a key role in two areas:

- In the technical area as such, due to his ability to solve or help to solve any problem that might crop up.
- In the human area, by maintaining an ongoing and close relationship with the automobile manufacturer's personnel, in particular with the supervisors and managers responsible for the smooth operation of the painting line.
  It is in the second area that the technical representative's people skills, the languages he may speak and a facility for cultural empathy may be decisive for the continued presence of a certain paint brand as supplier to an automobile manufacturer.

Exhibit 21.30   *The process of selling paints to automobile manufacturers*

The automobile manufacturers as a market segment of the paint manufacturers is characterized by:

- being composed of a *few customers,*
- being present in a *number of countries,* i.e., being globalized,
- able to buy paints in *large volumes,* and
- but *very demanding,* both from the financial viewpoint (mainly sales prices and conditions of payment) and from the technical viewpoint. Within the technical requirements, one should be able to differentiate between those referring to the paint itself, those referring to the supply system (Just-In-Time, etc.) and those referring to paint application.

Using automobile manufacturer terminology, the paints are 'material production', that is, a supply provided by a supplier which is added to the final product (as opposed to the 'non-production material', which are the ancillary materials required to carry out the automobile manufacturing process but which are not included in the final product, that is, they are eliminated before the car is sold to the final consumer).

Stages in the buying process

Approval of the paint manufacturer as possible supplier

Sometimes this approval process is defined as 'vendor qualification'. The automobile manufacturer starts by carrying out an *in depth* analysis of the potential supplier as regards its technical capacity, economic capacity, organization level, quality assurance system, etc.

Nowadays, it is almost impossible to obtain new homologations in Europe. However, paint manufacturers, particularly the small and medium-sized manufacturers, feel a growing threat of losing their homologation, due to the strong tendency of automobile manufacturers to *reduce* the number of suppliers in general, including paint suppliers.

With the forthcoming Single European Market, which will come into force on 1 January 1993, this pressure has been stepped up considerably and the European manufacturers wish to only deal with suppliers able to serve them at a pan-European level.

By way of final point, we will emphasize that both the company itself and its products must be approved.

High level political decision
In a second phase, the automobile manufacturers take an initial decision as to rough percentages into which they wish to divide their paint purchases among the homologated manufacturers.

One could perhaps make a distinction here between two major types of decisions or influences: those coming from the most senior levels of the company and those that come from the Purchasing Department. Consequently, in this second level, factors such as the relationships between the respective plants parent companies (in Germany or in France ...), the relationships established at local level, internal policies as regards the allocation of purchasing quota among the suppliers, and, of course, the prices and conditions the paint manufacturer is able to offer come into play.

Decision with respect to a specific product

Finally, the automobile manufacturer will allocate the purchase of a particular colour for a particular car model. Of course, the 'neutral' colour paints to be used in the cataphoresis (first coat) or the sealant (second coat) or the waxes, etc. are also allocated.

At this level, the process is usually the following. At any time, which may be just before launching a new car model or before a restyling or at any time in which the automobile manufacturer wishes to launch on the market a new palette of colours for a particular model, the manufacturer will issue a set of specifications detailing the characteristics of the paint to be purchased.

In some cases, the paint manufacturer, working closely with the automobile manufacturer's design team, may manage to tip the balance in its favour by arranging that the specifications prescribed match better the characteristics of the paint that he is able to manufacture, although this may only occur when the supplier is able to offer some kind of innovation.

The usual procedure is that all the homologated suppliers have access to the set of specifications issued.

The suppliers send back an offer, which obviously must fulfill the prescribed specifications.

From the technical and specifications viewpoint, what the customer usually asks for could be defined as 'an unstable balance of characteristics', such as:

- gloss, colour and persistence over time,
- ease of industrial-scale application,
- hardness,
- anti-rust or anti-acid protection,
- no cratering,
- no dripping of the paint (i.e., no tear or sheet formation),
- no bubbling due to gas being given off during the curing stage,
- impact flexibility,
- etc. . . .

Together with its offer, the supplier also has to send a sample which will be analysed by the customer's laboratory to verify that the paint offered really has the characteristics and features asked for. This is normally checked out using standard and ad hoc testing procedures (STM standard, stability tests in special cubicles with saline mist or CO_2, Florida Test, etc.) (In fact, the continuous increase in the standards demanded by automobile manufacturers is one of the paint manufacturers' most powerful incentives to innovate. After achieving an innovation, the supplier may then apply it to other customer segments that are less demanding technologically.)

The next step is to perform a test run on the production line (the major automobile manufacturers (more than 3 million vehicles/year) usually have a special testing line).

If the paint passes the test, the Purchasing Department is authorized to send orders to the paint suppliers. This is usually done on the basis of allocating a certain paint hue for a certain model to a specific supplier. As the final consumers' preferences vary (for example, normally more white or red cars are sold than blue or green cars), the allocation of a particular colour implies the allocation of a certain purchasing volume. (An average car's 'skin' usually requires purchasing and applying about 6.6lbs of primer (cataphoresis), about 8.8lbs of filler-sealant and a further 8.8lbs of top coat. These figures do not include the paint used for other components and miscellaneous vehicle parts.)

Normally, the Purchasing Department sends an order for three months, of which the first month is 'firm' and the other two months are 'orientative'. The scheduling is reviewed monthly, except in the case of the cataphoresis primer, in which, due to the tank's large capacity, the contracts are medium and long-term, with annual price reviews.

As the Industrial Paints Sales Manager (including automobile) of Química del Atlántico, S.A. said:

> This process is neither rigid nor excessively formalistic but is constantly evolving in a constant search for improvement. Thanks to a constant and close contact between supplier and customer, the former must strive to find out what concerns the latter, that is, what types of improvements in the characteristics of the paints used at any particular time may sufficiently interest the buyer to spark off a new buying process which, with luck, may culminate in the replacement of another supplier's paints by his paints.
>
> Of course, all the suppliers are trying to do the same!

In addition to influencing purchasing volume through technical characteristics, the supplier may also influence it through aesthetic features, that is, through colour hues:

> The subject of hues is very complex and also absolutely vital. Some pigment compositions may be difficult to obtain or imitate because the number of base pigments is limited for technical reasons (a new pigment requires lengthy and detailed tests to determine its durability, persistence of gloss, . . .). Therefore, the paint manufacturer usually takes the initiative to propose particular hues to the manufacturer's design department. If they are accepted, the paint manufacturer may have a certain advantage as he already knows the specific pigment composition that gives that exact hue.

Finally, the paint manufacturer can influence the volumes purchased by the automobile manufacturer through his technical representative, who is in daily contact with the plant's painting team.

> Situations may arise in either direction: the workers and supervisors on a line may work more or less openly against a supplier and find all sorts of minor defects and failures. Or, vice versa, even though Purchasing has established that the purchases of a certain paint be divided between two suppliers according to a certain percentage (e.g., 50/50), in the end, one of them sells 60 per cent and the other 40 per cent because the painting line personnel prefers to use the former's paints.

Of course, the variations in the quantities sold by each supplier may also be due to errors or mistakes by the paint manufacturer.

Química del Atlántico, S.A.'s industrial director classified the possible errors or mistakes as follows:

- *Venial sin* When the automobile manufacturer's laboratory detects some variation or analytic difference in the paint that the supplier has been selling him month after month without this difference being detected in the painting line.
- *Mortal sin* When incidents occur in the painting line which require the painted products to be reworked or which cause complaints on the quality of the work done (for example, the appearance of craters or other failures).
- *Excommunication* When incidents occur that cause a decrease in the line speed or which even make it necessary to stop the line.

Exhibit 21.31   *Exports by Química del Atlántico, S.A. (million pesetas)*

Exports during ...	1984	1985	1986	1987
Saudi Arabia	51.4	7.6	*	8.1
Egypt	18.4	13.2	*	162
Libya	13.6	7.6	2.3	*
Ecuador	3.9	*	*	*
France	*	19.5	*	*
Portugal	*	*	10.5	9.9
Andorrra	*	*	5.0	*
Nicaragua	*	*	3.5	*
USA	*	*	*	13.5
Other countires	9.7	15.1	3.7	42.3
Total exports	97	63	25	90
Total QA sales†	7,179	8,000	8,630	9,400

Source   *Censo Oficial de Exportadores Españoles* published annually by the INFE/ICEX (Spanish Institute for Foreign Trade).
‡*Fomento*, bussiness magazine.
Note   *Censo Oficial de Exportadores*, only provides information on the four main countries that a particularly company exports to in any one year. Therefore, the indication of an asterisk (*) in the table should be interpreted as meaning that the *Censo* does not provide separate information on the country in question for that year and if exports had been made to that country, they have been included in the item 'other countries'. Thus, for example, we do not know if the company exported or not to Saudi Arabia in 1986. If it had exported to this country, the quantity would be included under 'other countries' and in any case would be less than the 2.3 million pesetas exported by QA to Libya in 1986.

- Glasurit (Basf)
- Química del Atlántico
- Ivanow (Akzo)
- Herberts (Hoescht, A.G.)
- PPG
- Du Pont/Lory (International Paints)

As yet, QA had had little export activity. As can be seen in Exhibit 21.31, in recent years exports had accounted for less than 1.5 per cent of the company's total sales.

At last we're in the EC!

After several years of contacts and hard negotiating, the treaty by which Spain became member of the European Communities was signed in Madrid on 12 June 1985. This treaty specified that Spain, together with Portugal, would be fully-fledged members of the EC on 1 January 1986. The treaty provided for a seven-year transition period during which tariffs would be progressively reduced.

Joseba Garmendia remembered that in those early days in 1986 he had felt distinctly optimistic. QA had a strong competitive position in Spain, it had proprietary technology, and it hoped that during the transition period the cost of imported raw materials would steadily fall as a result of the tariff reductions. 'Everything will go better', he had thought.

And to a large extent, he was right. Also, after several years of economic recession, the Spanish market was starting to pick up speed. QA closed 1986 with total sales amounting to 8.63 billion pesetas (*Fomento de la Producción*, special issue 'Las 2.500 mayores empresas españolas', September 1987). The budget for 1987 forecast a further substantial increase to 9.4 billion pesetas.

However, halfway through 1987, Joseba Garmendia started to become aware of certain changes that were taking place in the paint industry as a result of the 'importation' from Japan of certain operating procedures that until then were little known in Spain:

- The 'kanban' or Just-in-Time system, which demanded a greater degree of commitment and involvement from suppliers to their customers. (The 'kanban' or Just-in-Time system basically consists of an assembly line operating on the basis of a 'pull' organization system. Thus, each subsequent phase or stage in the process indicates to the previous phase the quantities and exact time when it needs the items required for the following process. For further information, see Monden, Y. (1987) *El sistema de producción de Toyota*, Price Waterhouse-IESE, 1987).
- The tendency to reduce the number of suppliers. It was mentioned that the Japanese automobile manufacturers had four times less suppliers than their Western counterparts.
- Stricter quality requirements, both in the products delivered and in the service provided: everything had to work properly the first time round, with no failures or delays or rejects...
- A tendency to extend these quality requirements to the supplier's own factory to increase its efficiency and thereby lower costs.

From 1988 onwards, Joseba Garmendia started to notice that the Spanish automobile OEMs were starting to put into practice these operating procedures:

- The number of suppliers was starting to be reduced, although this was offset by the fact that the 'survivors' received larger orders. However, in exchange, the manufacturers demanded better sales prices.
- People were starting to talk about ODETTE, a telematic interface network that would link automobile production plants with their suppliers in real time, with the possibility of modifying almost instantly supplies, parts and component vendors' delivery schedules in response to changing needs.
- Total quality requirements were starting to be implemented.
- And, finally, the Spanish automobile OEMs, all of them belonging to large multinational groups, were asking QA's a key question, 'This paint your're supplying me in Spain, can you supply it to me just the same in the UK, or in Germany, or in France?'

At that time, approximately 30 per cent of QA's sales were to automobile manufacturers. The storm clouds that were gathering over such a large part of its billing seemed to be becoming increasingly more threatening. In his gloomiest moments, Joseba Garmendia saw himself shut out from the OEM automobile market in the very near future. What could he do to prevent this from happening? In fact, although his sales turnover to the automobile OEM industry in Spain had remained constant in volume terms, his market share had probably fallen to about 10 per cent. (Perhaps the most dramatic situation had happened in 1982 when General Motors opened its new factory in Figueruelas (Zaragoza): all the decisions were taken by GM-Opel in Germany so that QA was not even able to get itself homologated as a supplier.)

An unexpected telephone call

It was Lothar Steinhübel, Lacke und Farbe GmbH's (LF) Managing Director and an old acquaintance of his. This German company had sold technology to Química del Atlántico, S.A. although the products manufactured using technology purchased from LF had never exceeded 1 per cent of QA's total sales.

Lothar Steinhübel asked him three questions regarding the OEM automobile industry.

1 Do you want to co-operate on more general business issues, beyond the field of technology transfer?
2 Are you prepared to operate at a pan-European level?
3 Are you prepared to include other partners in this co-operation system?

After answering 'Yes' to all three questions, Joseba Garmendia was invited to a meeting that would be held in Cologne (FRG) in September, 1988. Also answering Steinhübel's invitation, in addition to Garmendia and Steinhübel, the meeting was also attended by John Brown from United Colours, Ltd.

The sole subject discussed at this meeting was the supply of paints to automobile manufacturers. The three men soon realized that their respective companies were all facing the same problem: 'The automobile industry demands that we be able to supply them any product to any of their European plants at any time.'

All three stated that they were prepared to face the challenge and to fight to keep their sales to the automobile industry. They felt that the solution lay in mutual co-operation and said that they were willing to get to work on the matter although they were not yet sure what form this co-operation would take.

One thing they were clear about was that they needed a fourth partner who, due to the European automobile manufacturers' production structure, should be French (see Exhibit 21.32). One of them suggested the name of Marceau and the others agreed. They did not consider it necessary to include an Italian partner, at least not for the moment, as the only automobile manufacturer in Italy was the Fiat Group, which had its own domestic suppliers and inhouse production of paints.

Each of the partner companies ratified their desire to preserve their independence and freedom.

The 'territorial' aspect or functions of each partner within the alliance were established as follows. A complete paint supply transaction to an automobile manufacturer involves certain actions (mainly production) which are performed on site in the paint supplier's factory. However, such transactions also include a series of actions, mainly service, that must be performed off-site away from the paint factory, and sometimes even in the customer's

Exhibit 21.32   *Automobile OEMs in Europe at the end of 1988, and location of main production plants*

	West Germany	UK	France	Spain	Other countries
General Motors	X	X		X	Belgium
Ford	X	X		X	Belgium
Renault			X	X	Portugal
Peugeot-Citroën		X	X	X	
Volkswagen-Audi-Seat	X			X	Belgium
Rover		X			
Nissan		X		X	
Mercedes	X			X[1]	
BMW	X				
Volvo/Saab					Sweden
Fiat/Alfa Romeo/Lancia					Italy

[1] Only commercial vehicles.

factory. Consequently, it was agreed that each partner would obviously carry out all the production operations in its own factory. However, all the off-site operations would be performed by the partner in each country, regardless of who manufactured the paints being applied. This off-site operations included the operation of the 'mixing room' in each customer factory, logistics, implementation of Just-In-Time, etc.

In the course of the conversations they also ascertained that each of the three manufacturers only supplied the automobile factories in their own country, with the sole exception of substantial quantities supplied by Steinhübel to a French plant operated by the Peugeot Group.

The return flight ... and some reflections

At the end of the meeting, Joseba Garmendia caught the train back to Düsseldorf. When he arrived at the airport to catch his direct flight back to Bilbao, he found that all flights had considerable delays due to a strike. With the memories of the meeting still fresh in his mind, he went to one of the lounges and sat down to patiently wait for his flight to be called while he continued to think about what had been discussed in the meeting.

It was quite clear to him that all paint manufacturers were facing more or less the same problems. However, in spite of having common interests, there were clear cultural differences, different ways of thinking. 'I'll have to learn to put myself in their shoes', thought Garmendia.

While he sat waiting in the airport, another thought suddenly came to him: they had only been talking about the automobile industry, but it seemed very likely that other industries that were also customers of the same paint manufacturers would sooner or later make the same demands as the automobile industry. For example, the first could be the automobile component industry, followed shortly after by the domestic appliance manufacturers, which were concentrated in a few groups operating on a pan-European scale. Or the metallographic industry, which printed the metal sheets that were then turned into cans for use by a small number of soft drink brands...

Skipping from one idea to another, Joseba Garmendia realized that if Química del Atlántico, S.A. wanted to give on its own a commercially suitable response throughout Europe to the various industries currently supplied in Spain, it would come up against at least two problems. First, a serious financial problem caused by the large investments required to adequately serve so many manufacturers in so many industries and in so many different countries. In fact, to sell paints to a large industrial customer, it is normally necessary to have at least two people per plant (point of supply) able to make *in situ* the necessary corrections to the formulation and to supervise the paint application systems. It would also be necessary to have sufficient physical space to work, a buffer stock and office space to carry out invoicing and control tasks.

Second, undoubtedly there would be control and communication problems caused by the need to operate in different cultures and using different languages. Garmendia reached the conclusion that the only apparently viable option lay in co-operation.

But all these reflections raised one question that at that time he was unable to answer: 'If at the Cologne meeting we have only agreed to co-operate in supplying the OEM automobile industry, what will Química del Atlántico, S.A. have to do to continue supplying customers in other industries? Will we have to form other alliances specialized in serving different industries?'

In any case, Garmendia realized that although perhaps this alliance could co-ordinate their paint sales to other industries, that is, the entire range of paints manufactured 'to order', under no circumstances would it extend to home decorating paint sales or sales to the car refinishing market segment. (Garmendia knew that the percentage of sales to the automobile OEM industry varied for each one of the four allied manufacturers. However, the volume of paint in tonnes sold by each of them to the automobile manufacturers was fairly similar. (See Exhibit 21.33).)

A few days later, he received in Baracaldo the minutes of the Cologne meeting written by Steinhübel. In synthesis, it was the expression of a 'summary of wills that pointed to something that could become a letter of intent.'

Shortly before Christmas 1988, Garmendia and Steinhübel went to Paris to meet Pierre Marceau, Managing Director of Marceau et Fils, S.A. They did not carry with them any pre-prepared documents and their intention was just to ask him the same questions they had analysed in Cologne.

Pierre Marceau had agreed to see them and after they had been talking with him for a short while, it soon became apparent to the visitors that he was concerned about the same problems. However, although courteous, the meeting was cold; Garmendia thought that it was because Marceau was aware that he was talking with competitors.

Garmendia had never been in Marceau et Fils, S.A. before. Later he would remember that the offices seemed to have an air of Spartan austerity. He liked this and he felt that it went well with the idea of a company and management that seemed to have an 'industrial mentality' like Química del Atlántico, S.A., i.e., a sober style with few people in the offices.

Marceau listened to them, seemed to understand their reasoning and asked them to provide him with some documentation on the project. It therefore seemed clear that he was interested in going forward together with them although, at the end of the meeting, he

Exhibit 21.33 *Sales by main sectors*

	% sold to industrial customers out of each company's total sales	% sold to automobile OEMs out of each company's total sales	Volume represented by the latter % in tonnes
Química del Atlántico, S.A.(1)	50%	30%	= 6,000 tonnes
Marceau et Fils, S.A.	100%	30%	= 5,600 tonnes
Lacke und Farbe GmbH	100%	60%	= 7,000 tonnes
United Colours, Ltd.(1)	90%	60%	= 6,000 tonnes

Source Personal estimates by Joseba Garmendia.
(1) The rest, both in the case of Química del Atlántico, S.A. and United Colours, Ltd. are sales of paint for home decorating and automobile refinishing.

explicitly told Steinhübel that this would mean finding some type of solution to the fact that they competed as suppliers to Peugeot in France.

Garmendia left the meeting very pleased, not only by the apparently positive results achieved but also by the favourable impression he had received of the French manager's personality. In some way, he could relate better to him than to Brown or Steinhübel, not only because he found it easier to talk in French but also because they seemed to have similar ways of thinking. In short, there seemed to be a greater cultural affinity between Garmendia and Marceau that between Garmendia and Brown or Steinhübel. It seemed to Garmendia that this foursome relationship would be 'more balanced'.

1989: the torch changes hands

The beginning of 1989 was marked by two events: on the one hand, Marceau and Steinhübel had to solve the problem of their competing for Peugeot and Brown, on the other, seemed to be adopting a rather passive attitude.

For his part, taking as his basis the minutes of the Cologne meeting, Joseba Garmendia asked a Bilbao law firm to study the best way to give a legal framework to the project. It just so happened that Miguel Torres, one of the lawyers working in the firm, had prepared a study on Regulation 2137/85, which had been approved by the EEC Council of Ministers in 1985 and was to come into force on 1 July 1989. Consequently, the lawyer proceeded to write a new document on which to base the co-operation between the four paint manufacturers, adapting it to the legal framework of the European Economic Interest Groupings (EEIG). (See Exhibit 21.34.)

It seemed to Joseba Garmendia that the legal form of the EEIG's was 'just what the doctor ordered' for the type of co-operation they wanted to implement. He quickly summoned another plenary meeting, which took place in Paris in March 1989, that is, three months before the EEIG Regulation was to come into force.

Exhibit 21.34 *Summary of the main requirements and characteristics of an European Economic Interest Group (EEIG)*

- It is governed by Regulation (EEC) No. 2137/85 of the European Council, 25 July, 1985, applicable as from 1 July, 1989.
- The EEIG's are a Community legal instrument whose purpose is to facilitate economic activity between its members, particularly at pan-European level.
- It is formed by means of the legalization of a 'grouping contract', which should then be registered in one of the EC member States (the country in which the Grouping's official address is situated).
- It shall be governed by the law of State in which the official address is situated.
- Its activity may only be ancillary to its members' economic activity.
- Companies or natural persons carrying out an economic acitivity may be members of an EEIG. Other legal bodies governed by private or public law may also be members. The members must have their official address and central administration in the Community. An EEIG may not have non-Community members.
- Its organs are the members acting collectively and the manager or managers. Other bodies may be provided for.
- Its purpose is not to make profits for the Grouping itself. If profits or losses are obtained, these will be considered as belonging to the members and will be distributed among them (i.e., it is fiscally transparent).
- It may not invite investment by the public.
- The members are joint and severally liable for the Grouping's debts.
- New members will be admitted by unanimous decision.
- A member may be excluded if he causes or threatens to cause serious disruption or if he seriously fails in his obligations. Unless provided for otherwise, if one member withdraws, the Grouping will continue for the other members.
- It may be wound up by unanimous decision of its members, unless the formation contract provides otherwise. It may also be wound up for other reasons, including by court order. If it is wound up, it must be liquidated.
- The EEIG's are subject to national laws governing insolvency and cessation of payments.
- The Grouping is not a holding company and the members continue to be economically, legally and financially independent. The Grouping may not have share capital.
- At present, the EEIG is the only supranational legal instrument available to carry out co-operation activities between partners from two or more European countries.

Source Regulation (EEC) No. 2137/85, summarized by the casewriter.

When Garmendia presented in Paris the proposal to create the alliance by giving it the legal form of the EEIGs, the news of this new legal possibility came as a complete surprise to the other three manufacturers and it seemed to them to be exactly what they needed.

This caused a wave of enthusiasm in the meeting. However, John Brown, being more prudent and cautious, pointed out to his colleagues, that they would have more than enough time to do things together and that they should not forget that it was very likely that their needs, interests and priorities were divergent. Therefore, Brown proposed that they start little by little and choose as their first area of joint action a subject that seemed to be clearly to the best interests of all four: co-ordination of raw material purchasing policies and the consequent negotiation with suppliers. The aim was to show that co-operation could be undeniably *profitable* for all four.

Joseba Garmendia, for his part, realized that if his purchasing volume was about 5 billion pesetas, among the four of them, they would have a purchasing power of about 20 billion pesetas! They all agreed to immediately start co-operating in this area.

On returning to their respective factories, each of the four partners appointed one of their purchasing managers to sit on the Raw Material Joint Purchasing Committee. This Committee started to act in a very flexible and informal manner. The suppliers' reaction was highly positive from the point of view of the newly grouped buyers. The Committee found that by buying together in a co-ordinated fashion, they could obtain substantial discounts, averaging about 30 per cent, on the prices each one had been able to buy at individually. If we consider that the cost of raw materials accounted for about 70 per cent of a paint's sale price, it was clear that the discounts that were being obtained would have a direct and immediate effect on each of the four manufacturers' profit and loss statement.

This excellent and very tangible result of their initial co-operation efforts encouraged them to continue and added more fuel to the co-operation process. As Joseba Garmendia said 'We were like Saint Thomas: seeing is believing. I think that that also marked the point of no return. As soon as it was seen that joint purchasing gave tangible financial benefits, I don't think that any of us had any doubts any more as to the desirability of co-operating. It was clear that co-operating was useful and beneficial and that we should take it further.'

More or less at the same time and without there being any specific declaration being made to such effect, Joseba Garmendia took on the responsibility for leading and co-ordinating the group.

As has already been said, the EC Regulation provided that EEIGs could be formed and formally registered after 1 July 1989 in the member States that had passed suitable legislation. The corresponding Spanish legislation had been passed in the Congress but was stopped in its passage through the Senate by president Felipe Gonzalez's decision to dissolve Parliament and hold early elections. Consequently, the corresponding Spanish Act had not been enacted. However, on 1 January 1990, the Company Registry Regulation came into force, allowing EEIGs to be registered in Spain even in the absence of the above-stated legislation.

All four partners agreed that Joseba Garmendia should be responsible for forming the EEIG in Spain, no doubt because he and his lawyer had given legal form to the agreement and also because he was a 'neutral' partner between France and Germany, the English partner being the most passive and also the smallest of the four.

Thus, culminating the formation process, the Grouping was formally and officially registered in the Bilbao Company Registry on 13 March 1990.

Reflections in early April 1990

Joseba Garmendia made an effort to put his ideas in order. When he thought about everything that was happening in the EEIG, the first thing that came to his mind was that overall the following changes had occurred:

- Before 1986, Química del Atlántico, S.A. was one of the companies that 'called the shots' in the Spanish paint market: it was a company with a good brand image, three factories, a competent workforce and, above all, a high share of the Spanish paint market. In a Spanish ranking of paint manufacturers, QA held one of the top three places.
- However, with Spain joining the EC, and even though the total sales forecast for 1990 would amount to about 12 billion pesetas, on looking at Química del Atlántico, S.A.'s position within the entire EC, even though its image and strengths remained intact, its market share was virtually negligible. In an EC wide ranking, it would have come in at about 50th. As has already been indicated, its strategic position with respect to 'globalized' customer segments would probably have become increasingly untenable. In a medium term difficult to determine exactly, it would perhaps be ruled out as a supplier to the major pan-European manufacturers of automobiles, domestic appliances, metallographic printing, etc.
- However, the formation of the EEIG repositioned the four manufacturers together as the *fourth* European supplier of paints sold to automobile manufacturers, only behind the big multinationals PPG, Hoescht and BASF and ahead of AKZO, Du Pont and ICI. (See Exhibit 21.35.) As PPG was a North American company, CLG, EEIG would be the third 'pure European' supplier.

As Joseba Garmendia put it: 'The alliance put us back among the EC big shots in automobile paints.'

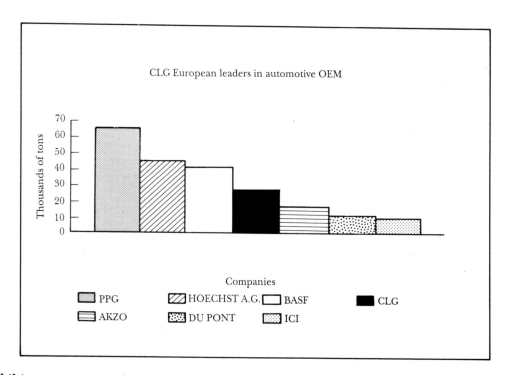

Exhibit 21.35   *Ranking of EC suppliers of automobile paints, and position of CLG, EEIF within it*
Source   CLG, EEIG.

This not only seemed to be very important from a strategic viewpoint but it would also perhaps be vital within the framework of the Single Market that would come into force as from 1 January 1993.

Also, the mere announcement of the formation of the alliance to the main pan-European automobile OEMs had managed to get the four partners off the 'list of small suppliers to be phased out.' It seemed that they had managed to turn the tide in their favour. However, there was still a very important question to be settled: Would the four partners be able to successfully compete together against the big paint multinationals established in Europe? In other words, what could be their specific competitive advantages against suppliers as important as those that have been mentioned in the previous paragraphs?

The four partners had accepted that, in a particular country, all operations to be carried out in the car manufacturer's plants would be carried out by the partner located in the country concerned. In other words, none of the four were prepared to start up or supervise logistics operations (storage and unloading paint at destination), dilute 'concentrated' paint manufactured in the home country, make final adjustments, etc. in any country that was not their own. (The final adjustments consisted of adding pine oils, silicones or other ingredients which favoured good application of the paint, in accordance with the temperature, humidity, air cleanness, etc. conditions in force at that time in the factory where cars or other objects were being painted.)

Only if one of the partners should refuse to supervise such operations for another partner could the said partner seek help from a third party.

Finally, the subject of what to do in the markets of other EC member countries seemed to remain open to future analysis and decision.

Thinking about the 'globalized customers' such as the automobile industry, Garmendia wondered what would happen in a case such as the following:

An automobile brand decides to buy a certain type of paint for all or several of its European factories. A co-ordinated tender is sent by the EEIG and the manufacturer agrees to buy at a certain price. As all four companies are independent, it could happen that the sale price is attractive for some of the four but not for some other(s). Does the company that decides 'not to serve' have the right not to be involved in the operation? If this were to be so, it could harm those who have decided to serve as the automobile manufacturer may demand or buy for all its plants or not buy for any . . .

Another subject open to discussion was that of technology transfer. For example, Marceau et Fils, S.A. had developed and sold paints for the French high-speed train (TGV). Spain had just decided in 1989 to build and run the high-speed train between Madrid and Seville. This would probably be followed by the Madrid-Barcelona line, linking up with the French frontier. According to the agreements, Química del Atlántico, S.A. should supply the special paint for the Spanish high-speed train. How much should it pay Marceau et Fils, S.A. for the formula? Or, in other words, if the sale of high-speed paint to the Spanish railway company (RENFE) produced a certain gross profit, how should this gross profit be distributed between Química del Atlántico, S.A. and Marceau et Fils, S.A.?

Up to now, it had not been planned to designate any 'General manager' or 'Executive secretary' at the head of the EEIG. For the moment, Joseba Garmendia was carrying out these functions but . . . could he or did he want to carry on performing them?

If a manager was recruited for the EEIG, what should be his/her personal profile? How should he/she be paid? What would be his/her duties? How should his/her performance be monitored?

As yet, it had not been decided whether any type of 'membership fee' or economic 'contribution' should be paid up, whether fixed or variable, one-off or regular, by the Grouping's partners. So far, each company had paid for its own travel expenses, management time, etc. Should this system continue? Was it fair? Was it practical?

Who should be responsible for getting potential customers to homologate the paints that the Grouping's partners could supply?

The EC had implemented a research aid programme called BRITE-EURAM (see Exhibit 21.36). Only alliances of companies from several EC member countries could apply for these earmarked funds. CLG, EEIG had applied for 1 million ECUs in aid for a programme at the beginning of 1990. This programme would be implemented by the Grouping members in co-operation with the Peugeot Group.

Joseba Garmendia was also reflecting on the following situation. In 1988, a Turkish trade mission visited Spain. A Turkish trade agent contacted QA and asked whether it would be prepared to supply powdered paint to Turkish companies to paint domestic appliances and automobile parts and components. (Powdered paint was a new, technically advanced and complex system of paint application. Apparently, the Turkish companies had made a 'qualitative technical jump' by going directly from relatively antiquated paint systems to high-tech system). The agent would provide the customers and would take care of the physical distribution. QA would invoice directly to the customers provided by the agent.

An agreement was reached and supply was started in 1988. However, Garmendia was aware that by working in this fashion, 'in remote mode' as it were, without giving a good service to the customer *in situ* adapted to each application's specific circumstances, neither was he providing the excellent level of service that QA usually provided to its customers in Spain nor was he obtaining full benefit of the possible additional market opportunities that could arise in Turkey.

As QA was sure that it did not want to become a multinational company in the normal meaning of the word, that is, by establishing a local subsidiary in Turkey, the idea solution would probably be to find a Turkish partner willing to manufacture and serve the Turkish customers.

Garmendia wondered whether he did or did not have some kind of moral obligation to offer the other EEIG partners part of this business opportunity.

Not only had they started joint purchasing but at some moment of particular optimism they had talked of investing together in building a new resin factory which would be a captive supplier of this important raw material to the four grouped manufacturers. The investment would amount to about 400 million pesetas. Was it a good idea?

European legislation on the EEIGs stated very explicitly that the Grouping's activities should confine themselves to areas that were ancillary to each of the member company's economic activities. However, could one expect that the Grouping would become increasingly necessary for all four companies? And if this were so, would it lead to a merger between the companies?

While he reflected on all these issues and perhaps on a few more that possibly had remained unmentioned or had not had time to come to the surface due to the short time the Grouping had been operating, Joseba Garmendia wondered whether the EEIG that had been created could be considered as something solid or not. What difficulties or disagreements could arise between the partners? If disagreements should arise, how should they be settled?

At one point, the thought occurred to him that perhaps the four partners were going

Exhibit 21.36   *Description of the Brite/Euram Programme*

BRITE/EURAM: a Community programme for saving traditional industry
BRITE/EURAM is an association of programmes aimed at supporting co-operation in industrial research. This project, implemented by the EEC Commission, will be in force for four years after 1989 and will have a budget of almost 500 million ECUs (about 70 billion pesetas) to subsidize à fonds perdu R&D projects that meet the requirements detailed below.

The programme's main goals are to encourage technological research at industry level and to help to help achieve a greater competitiveness of manufacturing industries on the world markets. It also seeks to promote technology transfer between industrial sectors and particularly between sectors with a high proportion of SMEs who need to have access to new technologies to improve their performance.

The BRITE/EURAM programme seeks to provide, through investigation and technological development (IDT) the technical resources required to improve products and processes.

The general areas in which BRITE/EURAM projects may be submitted are listed below.

Participation in the programme is open to all industrial companies, research centres, and other interested institutions from EEC and EFTA countries.

The general conditions for inclusion are the following:

- The projects should be carried out co-operatively.
- At least two legally independent industrial companies should be involved and they must come from at least two member States.
- The co-operating companies should be independent. Co-operation between a parent company and its subsidiary in another country will not be accepted.
- The projects should be innovative and not redundant with other R&D projects being performed in other EEC locations. If this is not the case, the proposers should prove that their project concerns an innovative application of a known technique for a product, in the development of a process or a new material.
- The project should last from two to four years.
- The project should have a clear industrial impact and be supported by a financial contribution from the participating companies.
- A research institution receiving in the form of direct payments an industrial financing amounting to 50 per cent from named industrial sponsors involved in the conceptual management of the project, may qualify as an independent industrial company.
- The projects should be large scale and cover a minimum of ten man-years and have a total cost ranging from one to five million ECUs.
- The consortium should accept joint responsibility for a substantial part of the costs: 50 per cent of the costs will normally be financed by the Community.

Proposal design and presentation
The proposals should be presented in three physically separate parts, as follows:

First part: administrative and financial data. These will refer to the project proposed, cost breakdowns and an abstract or synopsis of the proposal or technical project.

Second part: description of the proposal. This should include the applicants' purpose in presenting the proposal and their knowledge of the current situation worldwide in the field of research proposed. This part should provide evidence for the economic and technical benefits that the project's application will provide for the Community, and establish detailed technical and management plans to ensure success of the project.

Third part: details on the association. The purpose of this part is to define the functions of the partners involved in the project and describe the industrial partners' intentions as regards the utilization of the results. In this section, the merits of the institutions that will carry out the work and of the personnel that will supervise the research should be described. All the factors that may limit practical utilization of the results should also be pointed out.

After the proposals have been evaluated by a group of qualified experts appointed by the Commission, the Commission will publish a list giving the proposals selected and the names of the participants.

The CDTI (Centre for Technological and Industrial Research) is the (Spanish) body selected by the EEC to present the Spanish projects to the Commission.

TECHNOLOGY IN ADVANCED MATERIALS
- Metal materials and metal matrix compounds
- Materials for magnetic, optical, electrical and superconductivity applications
- Non-metallic materials for high temperatures
- Polymers and organic matrix compounds
- Materials for specialized applications

PRODUCT AND PROCESS DESIGN AND QUALITY METHODOLOGY
- Quality, reliability and maintainability in industry
- Process and product assurance

APPLICATION OF MANUFACTURING TECHNOLOGIES
- Advanced manufacturing practices for specialized industries, many of which are SMEs
- Flexible material manufacturing processes, particularly manufacturing of clothing and footwear, but also other materials including those used in the preparation of composite materials and in the food and packaging industries

MANUFACTURING PROCESS TECHNOLOGIES
- Surface treatment techniques
- Moulding, assembly and joining
- Chemical processes
- Particle and powder processes

Source Información Económica, Boletiín de la Cámara de Comercio, Industria y Navegación de Barcelona, (200), April 1990, p.10.

through a 'honeymoon' period and that it would not be long before disagreements and disputes started to crop up. What could be done to avoid them and to achieve the consolidation of the EEIG which, in turn, would enable ambitious strategic goals to be achieved?

Perhaps one of the possible solutions would be to consider the EEIG as 'a catalytically elastic solution.' With this rather cryptic phrase, Garmendia meant that CLG, EEIG would be 'like a forum for business opportunities, these being not only opportunities for new projects but also the opportunity to obtain profits by rationalizing production costs, technical homologations by customers, etc. and that it be the companies themselves which, after stating their desire to share in a particular business opportunity, would establish bilaterally, trilaterally or multilaterally relationships with the partner that has presented the project, in accordance with each company's needs'. However, if this were to be the case, should all the relationships and actions be 'optional'? Or should there be certain actions that are 'obligatory by the mere fact of being member of CLG, EEIG'?

Whatever the case, Garmendia was convinced that if the Grouping had been formed and started up, it had been 'to win the war' and not to just win 'battles', no matter how important these might be.

Case Study 6: Minitel*

This case has been prepared by Professor Elisabeth Rossen as a teaching device. Certain information has been altered. © Group ESC Lyon and Professor Elisabeth Rossen, 1991.

13 May 1991, 7.30 p.m.

Henri Legrand, Director of International Business Development for Intelmatique† worked late at his office located in Paris near the heart of Chinatown. It was one of the few full work weeks in France in May without official state holidays (last week there were three days off during the week for state holidays) and he felt pressured to finish redefining his international strategy before Paris business activity diminished for the summer, around Bastille Day, 14 July. This is always a difficult time of year in France, either matters get resolved almost immediately or postponed until September.

He discussed the situation with his staff including a young woman in her mid-20s with a French business school degree and a doctorate in telecommunications, Dominique Duval, Project Manager at Intelmatique. Another new project manager was present, Oliver Marceau, who primarily listened. The President of Minitel USA, Hilary Thomas who was in Paris at that moment, joined the meeting from time to time. Ms Thomas is a British citizen who has lived in the USA for over ten years. She is one of the early pioneers of the USA videotext‡ industry.

In France, we continue to be the worldwide leader in videotext: both in the range of our services as well as the degree of our global scope. We have over 15,000 services and operate practically around the globe. Four key factors have contributed to the success of Minitel in France:

- The highly developed national network linked to the interactive electronic telephone book.
- Free nationwide distribution of Minitel terminals.
- 'Pay as you use' charge system with same charge for telephone and Minitel services and no subscription necessary.
- Easy to access, like a telephone, user remains anonymous.

Minitel-Teletel has been a major success in Italy, thanks to the brilliant efforts of our friend and colleague there, Vito Stampanoni Bassi, who was the innovator of the Italian videotext system. Italy has seen their national videotext traffic grow from 30,000 hours/month to more than 500,000 hours/month in a very short period of time. Videotext terminals are now

* No part of this case study may be reproduced without the permission of the author, Professor Elisabeth Rossen.
† Subsidiary of France Telecom; primary mission is the internationalization of Minitel (see organizational chart in Appendix E).
‡ Videotext has been defined by the ITU (International Telecommunications Union) as: '...an interactive service which through appropriate access by standardized procedures allows users of videotext terminals to communicate with databases via telecommunication networks.'

coming on the Italian market at the rate of 10,000 units a month. Furthermore, the Italian telephone company, SIP, has recently allocated 1 billion dollars over the next three years to develop the videotext system in Italy. There is a subscription fee for videotext in Italy. Since the end of 1991 consumers in Italy have had the option of choosing between a subscription fee or a 'pay as you use' charging system.

Two years ago, the predominant standard in Italy was the British one, Prestel (80 per cent) with only 20 per cent of the traffic on the French standard, Teletel. That has been reversed and Teletel practically dominates the Italian videotext market now. Through having a multi-standard terminal the consumer has been responsible for choosing Teletel. The Italians seem to be following almost completely the French experience.

Their main problem at present is in accessing the system. The Italian method of using a password has created security problems. People tend to carry their cards around with the access code and these cards then get into the hands of too many people. Consequently, SIP will be replacing it with the French 'pay as you use', charging system in the near future. The 'pay as you use' system indirectly generated increased usage of the Minitel. As there is only one bill for both phone and Minitel usage, the customer is less conscious as to how he is being billed for videotext services.

The Italian mentality is not too different from the French mentality. Latins are more like one another than the Anglosaxons. Even though the 'messagerie rose' (personal services on videotext) is not advertised in Italy, those guys like to use it. Like the early success of Minitel in France, the personal services of the 'messagerie rose' in Italy have helped boost videotext adoption there. Furthermore, France can share common services with its neighbours. Lamy, co-ordinated trucking-transport service, and the airlines with their international reservation systems are examples of this.

In the USA, puritanical attitudes reinforced by tight US regulations keep videotext personal services off the market. Americans don't seem to like to enjoy themselves and anything that could be wrong with their videotext market is. They don't even seem to understand what videotext is. They think it is quite different from what is actually offered by Minitel-Teletel services. They confuse it with other services called videotext, like IBM's Prodigy.

Why can't the videotext terminal be like a pay television offering the consumer many channels in foreign markets? Why can't the individual choose what he or she likes and be billed for it by a system like 'pay as you use'? (This is the case in Italy.) The consumer is not concerned about what standard of videotext he is using. He wants reasonably priced services, quick and easy to use that satisfy his needs.

It is the service company that chooses the standard in a multi-standard environment like Italy or the Netherlands.

The service provider is in business for that purpose as well as to reap a profit from his activities. Therefore, he wants a standard that will enable him to fulfil those objectives. The customer then indirectly exercises his preference for a standard through using specific services.

Hilary Thomas reiterates what she said in her speech at the Infodial 1990 Conference last October, in Paris, 'what must emerge in North America is a truly multi-standard environment in which the choice is driven by the market ... The first thing that has become clear is there is not one mass market (in the US) but many; and that that is resulting in increasing awareness that there is not one videotext solution, as we see in France, but many. The market is divided in many ways − regionally, technically and demographically.'

Most of the factors which contributed to the success of Minitel in France, are not to be found in the United States, partly because of American regulations, partly because the market is different: personal computers are much more common than in France and there are more services available over the telephone, like 24-hour banking.

Regulations and industry structure have required an approach completely different from that in France. Penetration strategy has consisted of trying to piece together different parts of a broken puzzle with vendors, RBOC's (Regional Bell Operating Companies) and marketers. Remember this has been in the context of the quick-searching-bottom-line-oriented Business America.

In 1983, AT&T started implementing a nationwide videotext system, not dissimilar to Minitel in France. Then everything changed. The infrastructure that was in place to enhance its development (the RBOC's) was chopped into pieces, and the project was shelved. The high projected costs of implementation led many to be critical about its likelihood of survival even before AT&T was broken up.

The most significant change in the relevant US regulations over the last few years has been the ruling by Judge Green, on 7 March 1988, that the Regional Bell Operating Companies would be permitted to operate videotext gateways. Nonetheless, the RBOC's are still not allowed to generate information with videotext, thus all interactive systems are illegal.

However, since 1988, the RBOC's have experimented with various plans to implement videotext systems.

Hilary Thomas, President of Minitel USA, says, 'The RBOC's have lost interest in videotext as their formal plans have failed to reap rewards as quickly as expected by Corporate America.'

The typical American clearly sees the relationship between videotext and the personal computer but sees no relationship whatsoever between videotext and the telephone. Not that it is his fault. US regulations prevent the existence of a nationally networked electronic phone book, free nationwide distribution of Minitel terminals, and simply adding Minitel services to phone bills. It is ironic that from France we can access NYNEX and obtain the telephone number of someone living in New York City whereas someone based over there with a Minitel terminal cannot even obtain his own phone number! What a difficult and complicated market the US is; yet it is important to our global strategy. We cannot continue to be a world leader in videotext by limiting our geographic scope in the critical Europe – United States – Japan triad.

We feel confident in our ability to identify the factors which have led to Minitel's success in France, but we are much less confident and knowledgeable about the key success factors necessary in foreign markets. Apart from following the basic French system as much as possible, other elements also seem to play a significant role.

Contradictory though it may appear to be, the foreign markets where there has been competition for Teletel (i.e. other standards) have proved to be the most successful markets. This has particularly been the case where multiple standards have been accompanied by heavy investment. This has been true of Italy and to a lesser, but significant, degree the Netherlands and Ireland. Denmark and Portugal also have multiple standards but limited investment. Outside of France, Italy, the Netherlands and Ireland have mass markets but other markets still remain undeveloped.

Japan proves to be a hard nut to crack. The market is very closed there; many technical and legal problems need still to be addressed in order to establish a significant videotext system there based on Teletel. We opened Minitel-Net there almost two years ago but it has gone nowhere. It's not the fault of the company which sells it for us in Japan. There are not that many customers in Japan looking for a French database; just some French expatriates and

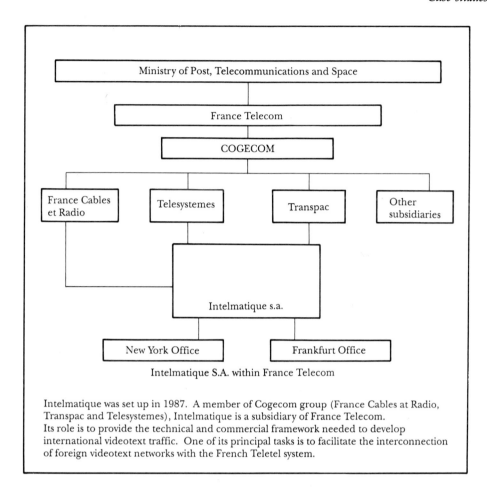

Ministry of Post, Telecommunications and Space

France Telecom

COGECOM

France Cables et Radio — Telesystemes — Transpac — Other subsidiaries

Intelmatique s.a.

New York Office — Frankfurt Office

Intelmatique S.A. within France Telecom

Intelmatique was set up in 1987. A member of Cogecom group (France Cables at Radio, Transpac and Telesystemes), Intelmatique is a subsidiary of France Telecom.
Its role is to provide the technical and commercial framework needed to develop international videotext traffic. One of its principal tasks is to facilitate the interconnection of foreign videotext networks with the French Teletel system.

Exhibit 21.37

other people dealing with France. It seems in some ways as though Japan is ready for a significant videotext system. All the companies which we called on in Japan seem to be ready and waiting for it. Furthermore, the Japanese are willing to invest in the information sector.

In addition, Japan has significant problems that could be resolved to some degree by a major videotext system; there are not enough workers in Japan to undertake all the necessary services. A highly developed videotext network could help alleviate this situation with mass-market interactive terminal services such as an electronic telephone directory, travel services, home shopping and also corporate applications.

Several versions of videotext have been tried in Japan, none have grown very far. The best known, CAPTAIN, is very expensive ($300–$400 for the cost of the terminal) and so has never had many services or customers. Nintendo, the games company, has also given the videotext industry a try in Japan; but it too has not got very far. Their system is unable to process information about stocks efficiently and this is a major shortcoming for the Tokyo business market.

Japan has been successful in developing a videotext terminal with screen. We at France

Telecom see this telephone with screen as the videotext terminal of the future; we are still trying to develop it. AT&T is also working on this; however, their 'Smart Phone' appears potentially to create many problems in a market already full of them.

The Smart Phone is compatible with only one standard, a new American one, thus closing that system to other videotext services or to customers without the Smart Phone. What a contrast to Italy where the terminal is compatible with four standards.

Japan has other problems too. The Teletel system would have to be adapted drastically there. That would be very expensive and complicated both technically and legally. Japan's distribution system has the deserved reputation of being a maze; and this applies to their telecommunications industry.

Yet for all its complexity, Japan is a less closed market than the USA as a result of Judge Greene's legal decision. Almost 95 per cent of Japan is served by just one telecommunications company, NTT. Almost no one speaks French in Japan. Everything must be translated; we must have full-time interpreters and much more support staff than we require in other countries. Furthermore, the difference in the Japanese alphabet requires a major revamping of Teletel as regards both hardware and software. Three to four million francs have been committed to a market study; is it worthwhile to continue?

I don't know what is worse; the Americans and all their regulations, or the Japanese and their invisible fortress. No matter how aggravating they are to deal with, I am not sure we can live without them.

However, we are in Europe and the potential for developing market share in neighbouring countries is perhaps more appealing.

13 May 1991, 9.30 p.m.

Henri Legrand, tired, looks at his travel schedule and asks Dominique Duval to help him redefine Minitel's international business expansion/strategy objectives and asks:

● What should the major priorities of Intelmatique be in developing an international business strategy?

1. Focus mainly on promoting and penetrating into the European market?
2. Delve deeper into the United States?
3. 'Go' or 'no-go' as regards Japan?

● What measures need to be taken to implement these objectives?

Sifting through her endless stacks of documents, Dominique starts to compose a response to Legrand. She makes note of what information is necessary to reach conclusive answers to these questions. It is unlikely Dominique will be able to obtain any financial data before formulating her recommendations. However, she is aware that Legrand will be able to adapt his strategy to budgetary forecasting information that is unavailable to her as a junior manager.

Duval feels that a lot of attention during that meeting was devoted to the United States, Japan and Italy. She searches for other significant information about Europe and finds an article in the European Journal of Communication, Summer 1991 on 'The Dynamics of Videotext Development in Britain, France and Germany' by V. Schneider, J. M. Charon, I. Miller, D. Thomas and T. Vedel.

Dominique Duval must prepare her response to Legrand by 1 July concerning the issues raised in the 13 May meeting.

Minitel screen selection

Main menu

1 Services by category
2 Alphabetic directory
3 French connection
4 Minitel news

(Selection 1)

Service Categories MINITEL
1 Chat, forums and messaging
2 Sports and games
3 World news, travel and events
4 Business and investing
5 The trading place
6 Health and fitness
7 Learning and reference centre
8 Selected French services
9 Lifestyles and Potpourri

For a list of services,
enter category #'...   [SEND]
For main menu, press   [INDEX]
For Help, press   [GUIDE]

(Selection 3)

World news, travel and events MINITEL

Code	*	Service names	$/min
AFPRO	M	AFP-PRO	1.83
ALINE	E	ALINE	0.20
BWENT	A	ENTERTAINMENT WIRE	0.20
B WIRE	A	BUSINESS WIRE	0.20
CTL	M	CTL CITY	0.17
EVENT	M	FRENCH COMMUNITY EVENTS	0.17
FLIKS	M	FLIKS	0.20
HORAV	M	AIRPORT/AIRLINES FRANCE	0.43
SABRE	M	EAASY SABRE	0.17
USAT	M	USA TODAY	0.17

*: M = MINITEL, A = ASCII, E = EITHER

Enter code to connect:......   [SEND]
Enter code? for description.

For prior page, press   [INDEX]
For next page, press   [SEND]
For Help, press   [GUIDE]

Bibliography

Marchand, M., and Ancklin, C. (1984) *Telematique: Promanade Dans les Usages*, La Documentation Française, Paris.

Marchand, M. (1988) *The Minitel Saga: A French Success Story*, Librairie Larousse, Paris.

Muet, S., and Hintzy, J. (1986) *Nouvelles Numerotation, Nouvelle Communication: Le Succès sur Toute la Ligne*, La Documentation Française, Paris.

OECD (1988) *New Telecommunication Services: Videotext Development Strategies*, Paris.

Schneider, Charon, Miles, Thomas and Vedel (1991) The dynamics of Videotext (SIC) development in Britain, France and Germany. *The European Journal of Communication.* **6**, (2).

AT&T's Smart Phone to utilize existing network. *Consumer Information Appliance*, July 1990, **1**, (2).

Interviews with: Jean Pierre Gouzil, Director of International Business Development, Intelmatique − Paris, Cecile Richir, Project Manager, Intelmatique − Paris, Jean Michel Souleur, Project Manager, Intelmatique − Paris, Hilary Thomas President, Minitel − New York, and Vito Stampanoni Bassi formerly Director of Italian Videotext for SIP in Rome.

'Personal Computers go on the Blink'. *Financial Times*, 20 May 1991, p. 17.

Speech of Hilary Thomas, President, Minitel USA, Inc. − Presentation at 'Infodial 90' Conference, 3 October 1990 − Paris, *The Videotext Market in the United States*.

Videotext International: Fortnightly International Newsletter on the Videotext Industry, No. 95 special report, *the Videotext Market in the US.*, January 1989.

Index

THIRD EDITION

Marketing PLANS

HOW TO PREPARE THEM: HOW TO USE THEM

MALCOLM McDONALD

- The UK's top marketing bestseller

- Ideal for marketing managers and business executives

- Written by the UK's top marketing guru

- Recommended reading for the CIM examinations

- Greatly expanded to include recent developments in marketing techniques

- Resource pack available for tutors

- Combines theory with practice

- Practical step-by-step guide

> To Order:
> Phone: 01933 414000

March 1995 • 246 x 189mm • 360pp
Paperback • 0 7506 2213 X